lonely planet

Melbourne & Victoria

Kate Morgan, Kate Armstrong, Cristian Bonetto,
Peter Dragicevich, Trent Holden

PLAN YOUR TRIP

JURGAR / GETTY IMAGES ©

KOALA IN GREAT OTWAY NATIONAL PARK P184

NICOLE PATON / GETTY IMAGES ©

MORNINGTON PENINSULA P235

ON THE ROAD

Contents

JOHN SONES / GETTY IMAGES ©

WILLIAM RICKETTS SANCTUARY P140

Welcome to Melbourne & Victoria

Melbourne is food-obsessed, marvellously multicultural and a showpiece for Australian culture. Beyond the city limits, Victoria offers rich history, stunning wilderness and culinary excellence.

Food & Wine

Melbourne loves its food. A passion for street food and experimental fine dining has been grafted onto a long-standing multicultural culinary scene that has few peers. Regional Victoria does not play second fiddle to this – its epicurean credentials continue to skyrocket in small country towns such as Kyneton, Beechworth, Birregurra and Red Hill. It also comes with loads of respected wine regions, from the Yarra Valley to the King Valley, Mornington Peninsula to the Bellarine Peninsula and Rutherglen. There's also a catalogue of boutique breweries and coffee roasters to round it out.

Great Outdoors

Victorians are spoiled for wilderness. Southwest, the Great Ocean Road follows one of the world's most spectacular coastlines, while the further east you go the wilder it gets, from wildlife-rich Wilsons Promontory to Gippsland's aptly named Wilderness Coast. The rivers and epic forests of Errinundra and Snowy River yield to the picturesque mountains of the High Country, where year-round activities make it a perfect adventure destination. Northwest, almost in the outback, desertlike national parks occupy vast swathes of the state. Opportunities to explore are endless.

Great Indoors

In the 19th century, gold-rich Melbourne and small towns in Victoria were stamped with architectural wonders. These days many of those grand buildings survive as luxury hotels, theatres, top-notch restaurants or state-of-the-art galleries. Seek out the cultural goldfields area, in particular, with towns such as Ballarat, Bendigo and Castlemaine, or the preserved sandstone buildings crammed with history in Beechworth. Melbourne is an art lover's smorgasbord, with signature art-strewn laneways, but regional Victoria holds its own when it comes to reasons to pray for a rainy day.

History's Canvas

Victoria's history is epic, but couldn't be more accessible. The state's Indigenous story serves as a subtext throughout, but it takes centre stage with rock art and creation stories at Gariwerd (the Grampians). Fast forward a few millennia, and Victoria's 19th-century gold rush left behind some of Australia's most atmospheric old towns, among them Ballarat, Castlemaine, Maldon and Beechworth. And the old Murray riverboat culture of Australia's pioneering days lives on in Mildura, Swan Hill and Echuca.

Why I Love Melbourne & Victoria

By Kate Morgan, Writer

A Melburnian and Victorian at heart, I grew up near the Mornington Peninsula, lived in inner-city Melbourne and now call the Bellarine Peninsula area home while I dream about my next move...perhaps to a charming town in the High Country. The calm bay beaches of my childhood, crashing surf pounding the red cliffs as I drive the Great Ocean Road, a kangaroo hopping along a country road at dusk, glasses of wine in the sun overlooking vineyards or pots of beer at a gig in a divey Melbourne pub – nowhere else inspires wanderlust in me quite like Victoria.

For more about our writers, see p384

Above: Coastline views along the Great Ocean Road (p173)

Melbourne & Victoria

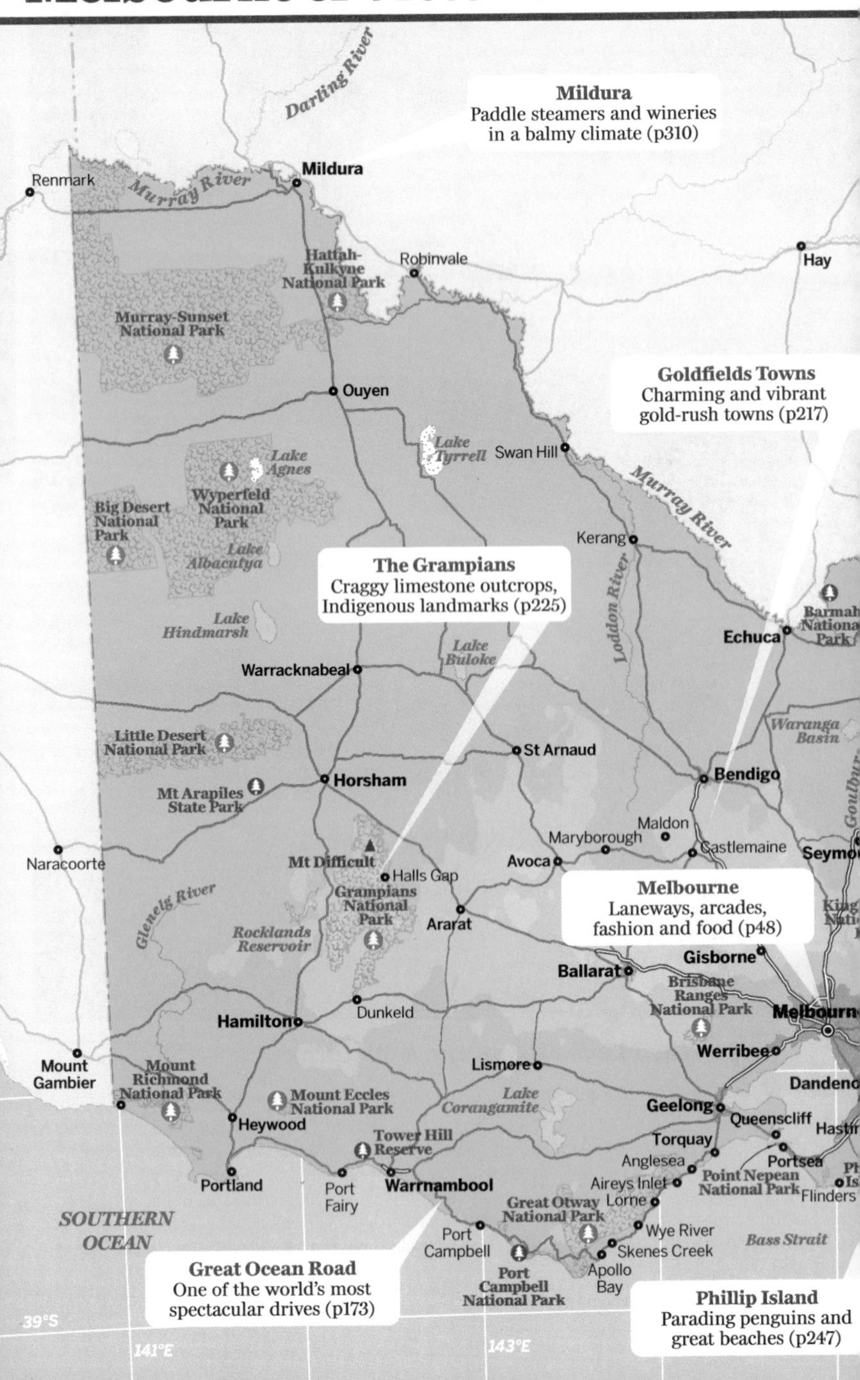

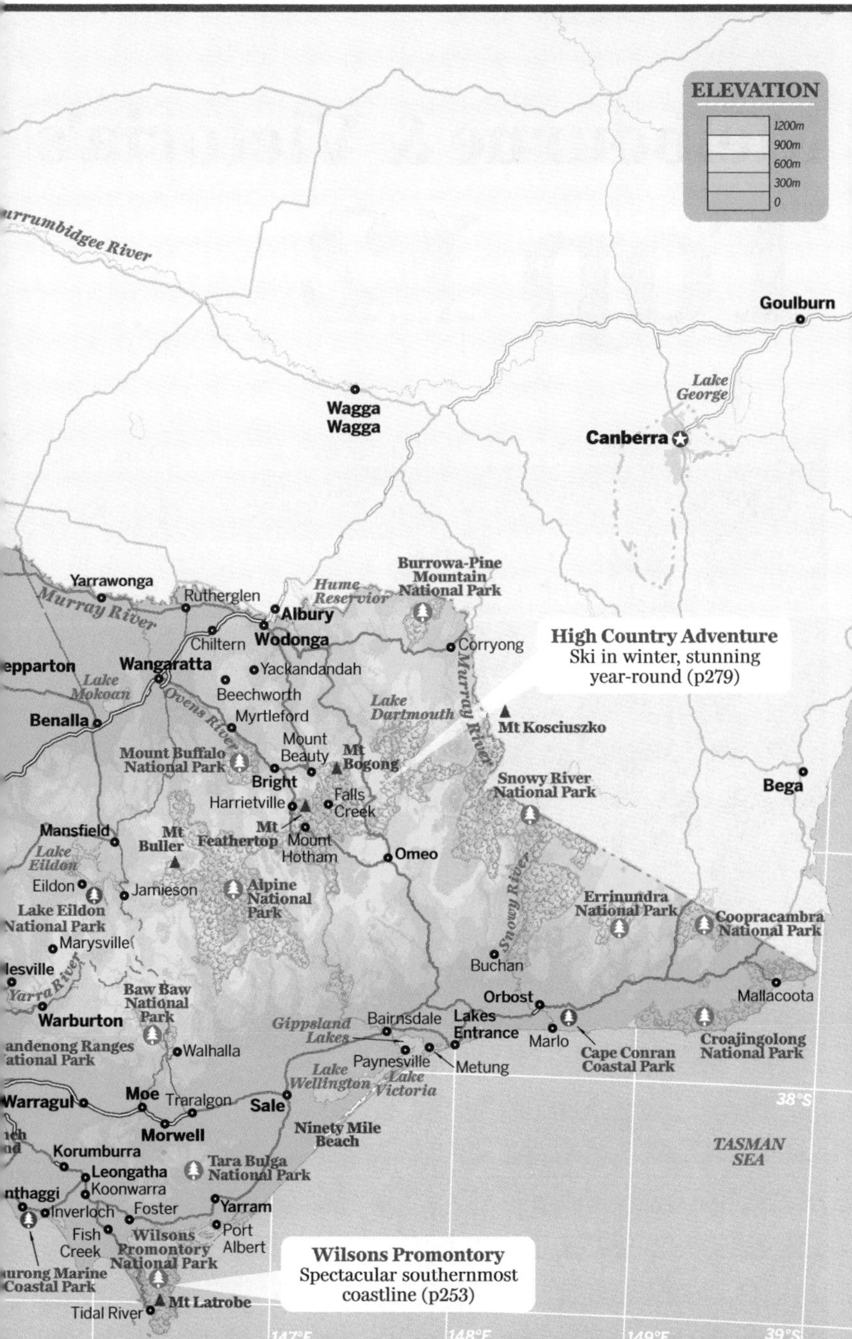

0 100 km
0 60 miles
ELEVATION
1200m
900m
600m
300m
0
Goulburn
Lake George
Canberra
Wagga Wagga
Burrowa-Pine Mountain National Park
Hume Reservior
Yarrawonga
Murray River
Rutherglen
Albury
Chiltern
Wodonga
Corryong
High Country Adventure
Ski in winter, stunning year-round (p279)
Wangaratta
Yackandandah
Lake Mokoan
Beechworth
Lake Dartmouth
Murray River
Mt Kosciuszko
Benalla
Ovens River
Myrtleford
Mount Beauty
Mt Bogong
Mount Buffalo National Park
Bright
Snowy River National Park
Bega
Harrietville
Falls Creek
Mansfield
Mt Feathertop
Mount Hotham
Mt Buller
Omeo
Lake Eildon
Eildon
Jamieson
Alpine National Park
Snowy River
Errinundra National Park
Lake Eildon National Park
Coopracambra National Park
Marysville
Buchan
Yarra River
Baw Baw National Park
Orbost
Mallacoota
Warburton
Gippsland Lakes
Bairnsdale
Lakes Entrance
Marlo
Croajingolong National Park
Walhalla
Paynesville
Metung
Cape Conran Coastal Park
Lake Wellington
Lake Victoria
Warragul
Moe
Traralgon
Sale
38°S
Morwell
Ninety Mile Beach
TASMAN SEA
Korumburra
Leongatha
Tara Bulga National Park
Koonwarra
Yarram
Inverloch
Foster
Port Albert
Fish Creek
Wilsons Promontory National Park
Wilsons Promontory
Spectacular southernmost coastline (p253)
Mt Latrobe
Tidal River
147°E
148°E
149°E
39°S

Melbourne & Victoria's Top 12

Great Ocean Road

1 Take it slow driving on a road (p173) that curls beside spectacular beaches then whips inland through rainforests. Check out Bells Beach's legendary surf, see kangaroos in Anglesea, swim at Lorne and go koala spotting at Cape Otway. Then stand in awe at the Twelve Apostles, one of Victoria's most vivid sights. Head inland for gourmet treasures in Timboon and Forrest, watch whales in Warrnambool and discover the maritime treasures of Port Fairy. For the ultimate in slow travel, hike the Great Ocean Walk.

Drinking & Dining Around Melbourne

2 Head down the many street-art-strewn laneways and hip streets in Melbourne's (p48) CBD and inner-city 'hoods to seek out cool cafes, hidden bars and the hottest restaurants. Have baristas play mad scientists as they brew you a siphon, pourover or cold-drip single-origin coffee then take your pick of food-driven cafes or gastropubs for lunch before planning your dinner at the latest degustation darling to top the city's best-restaurant list. Let the evening steer you upstairs to a rooftop bar serving inventive cocktails and craft beer with city views. Below right: Restaurants & bars along Centre Place.

AUSTRALIAN SCENICS / GETTY IMAGES ©

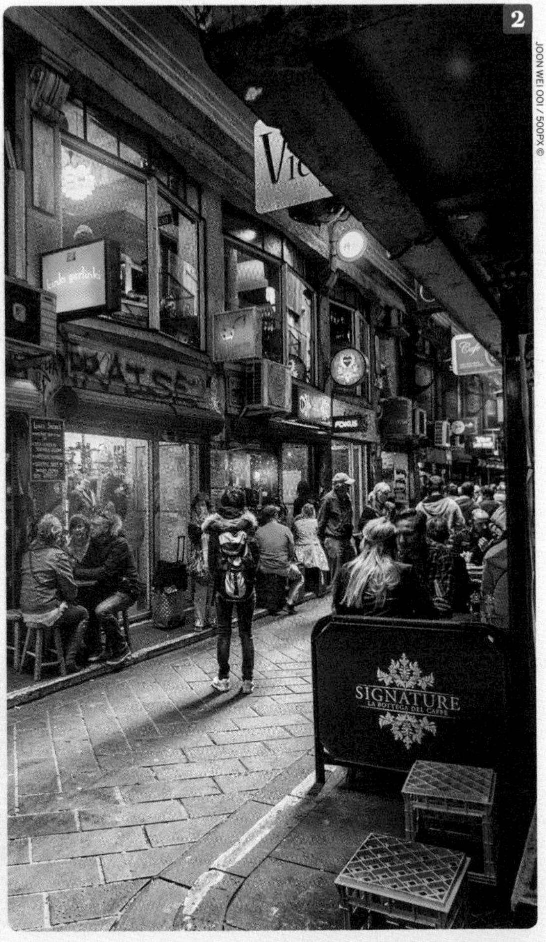

2

JOON WEI OOI / 500PX ©

Bellarine to Mornington Peninsula

3 The Bellarine (p168)and Mornington (p236) peninsulas are roughly equidistant from Melbourne and boast a bounty of top wineries, breweries and beaches as well as local-produce-driven eateries tucked away in bush, on farms or attached to scenic vineyards. While Melburnians tend to have a fondness for one coast or the other, visitors can ignore the divide and explore one peninsula before a short sail on the Queenscliff–Sorrento ferry to discover the riches of the other. Top: Point Lonsdale lighthouse, Bellarine Peninsula (p168)

The Grampians

4 Rising up from otherwise pancake-flat countryside, the landscape of the Grampians (p225) is as timeless as it is tempting. The sandstone and granite outcrops here are custom-made for rock climbing, abseiling and bushwalking. Not that adventurous? You can drive to waterfalls, stunning lookouts and bush camps carpeted in wildflowers, sample local wines, and learn stories of how Indigenous Australians lived in a place called *Gariwerd*. Families or romantic couples will find just as much to do here as adventurers.

3

4

TRAVELGAME / GETTY IMAGES ©

NEALE COUSLAND / SHUTTERSTOCK ©

Gippsland Lakes

5 Water, water, everywhere. Aside from the famous Ninety Mile Beach, East Gippsland's lakes district (p265) is a glistening patchwork of waterways and inlets where boating and fishing are a way of life. Experience the coastal charm of villages such as Paynesville, Metung and gorgeous Mallacoota, cruise the lakes to wineries and waterside pubs, and gorge on the state's freshest seafood. Throw in some of Victoria's wildest coastal parks, among them World Biosphere Reserve Croajingolong, and you've a trip to remember.

Country Charm

6 There's a lot to like about Victoria's country towns, and many are only a short drive from Melbourne. Head to the historic goldfields towns (p217) of Kyneton, Castlemaine and Maldon, with grand 19th-century buildings, galleries, markets and eateries to explore. Day trip to Hepburn Springs for relaxing spa treatments, or leafy Trentham for long cafe sessions. In the northeast, the gorgeous towns of Beechworth, Chiltern, Yackandandah and Bright are a year-round delight with pretty streetscapes, dining options, classic pubs and a friendly welcome. Top right: Chiltern (p292)

Sporting & Cultural Melbourne

7 If it's footy season in Melbourne (p48), you'll know about it. But it's not just winter that sees absolute sporting dedication from Melburnians: come spring it's the horse racing; summer it's cricket and tennis – and everyone's invited to join the conversation and watch the action. The arts scene is also strong: explore Melbourne's art galleries and wear your best dark clothes to one of the many literary, theatrical, comedic and musical events that pack the diaries of Melburnians. Above left: Footy fans watching AFL.

BETHUNE CARMICHAEL / GETTY IMAGES ©

Wilsons Prom Wilderness

8 For sheer natural beauty, Wilsons Promontory (p258) has it all. Extending out into Bass Strait, it's isolated but accessible, boasting sublime beaches and some of the best wilderness hiking in the state. There's a well-maintained network of trails and camping areas – just grab a map, strap on a pack and disappear into the wilds. The overnight walk across the Prom from Tidal River to Sealers Cove and back is a great way to get started, but serious hikers can tackle the 3-day Great Prom Walk, staying a night in gloriously isolated lighthouse keepers' cottages.

Phillip Island & the Penguin Parade

9 Who can resist the nightly parade of cute little penguins waddling out of the ocean and into their sandy burrows? Clearly not the three-million-plus tourists who visit Phillip Island (p247) annually. Luckily there's plenty more to this little island: fabulous surf beaches, wildlife parks, a MotoGP circuit that will satisfy revheads, and loads of things to keep kids busy. For something different, jump on the ferry for the short trip to French Island, where there are no sealed roads or mains power.

Seaside Charm in St Kilda

10 It's not just the palm trees, bay vistas, briny breezes and pink-stained sunsets that give St Kilda (p75) its appeal. An eclectic cast of characters call this place home, so it caters to everyone. Dine at an assortment of chic eateries, or indulge in one of Acland St's historic European cake stores. Up the road you can ride a rickety 1920s roller coaster at Luna Park while taking in the bay views, then hit the cocktail list in a zhooshed-up bar or knock back beers in an old divey pub. Bottom right: Luna Park (p79)

High Country Adventure

11 The mountains and valleys of the High Country (p279) are Victoria's year-round adventure playground. In the 'white season', some of the best skiing, snowboarding and après-ski in the country can be found on the slopes of Mt Hotham, Mt Buller and Falls Creek. In the 'green season', you can make like the *Man from Snowy River* riding horses on the high plains, or dive into high-adrenaline pursuits such as mountain biking and paragliding. If all that gets too much, hit the wine-and-cheese trail in northeastern Victoria's gourmet region. Top: Cyclists near Falls Creek (p300)

Cruising the Murray to Gourmet Mildura

12 Riverside towns on the Murray (p307) take you back to paddle steamer days then fast-forward to houseboats, water sports and wineries. Mildura is an oasis town with a glorious climate, relaxed attitude, art-deco architecture and some of regional Victoria's best gourmet dining. Spend the morning cruising to a winery, lunch on a restored paddle steamer, the afternoon swimming, kayaking or golfing, and the evening choosing from the restaurants on the Grand Hotel's 'Feast Street' – get a table at Stefano's if you can!

11

12

Need to Know

For more information, see Survival Guide (p363)

Currency
Australian dollar ($)

Language
English

Visas
All visitors, aside from New Zealanders, need a visa to visit Australia. Visas can be applied for online at www.border.gov.au; each allow a three-month stay.

Money
ATMs can be found in most towns, and credit cards are widely accepted.

Mobile Phones
All Australian mobile-phone numbers have four-digit prefixes beginning with 04. Australia's digital network is compatible with GSM 900 and 1800 handsets. Quad-based US phones will also work. Local SIM cards are readily available.

Time
Australian Eastern Standard Time (GMT plus 10 hours; plus 11 hours during daylight saving)

When to Go

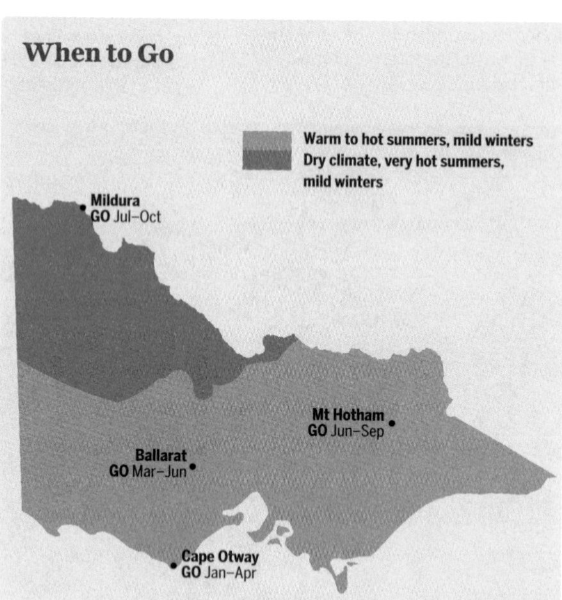

High Season (Dec & Jan)

➡ Beaches full of local holidaymakers enjoying school holidays; book months ahead for coastal accommodation, including camping.

➡ Easter and June/July school holidays are also busy times.

➡ Loads of festivals and summer events.

Shoulder (Feb & Mar)

➡ Quieter time with many more accommodation vacancies.

➡ Late summer weather can be particularly hot.

Low Season (Apr–Nov)

➡ Milder weather; often decent rainfall from September to November.

➡ July to September is peak whale-watching season at Warrnambool.

➡ Ski-resort high season from June to August.

Websites

Lonely Planet (www.lonelyplanet.com/australia/victoria) Destination information, hotel bookings, traveller forum and more.

Visit Victoria (www.visitvictoria.com) Official state tourism site.

Parks Victoria (www.parkweb.vic.gov.au) Profiles Victoria's national parks with details on accommodation.

Broadsheet (www.broadsheet.com.au) Finger-on-the-pulse site devoted to getting the best out of Melbourne and Victoria.

The Age (www.theage.com.au) Local news.

Bureau of Meteorology (www.bom.gov.au/weather/vic) Guidance for the weather, which can change at a moment's notice.

Important Numbers

Callers from outside of Australia need to drop the first '0' in a mobile-phone number and the '0' of Victoria's 03 area code.

Country code	61
International access code	00
Police, fire & ambulance	000
Parks Victoria	13 19 63
Vic Emergency	1800 226 226

Exchange Rates

Canada	C$1	A$0.98
Europe	€1	A$1.38
Japan	¥100	A$1.15
New Zealand	NZ$1	A$0.93
UK	£1	A$1.61
US	US$1	A$1.30

For current exchange rates, see www.xe.com.

Daily Costs

Budget: Less than $130

- Dorm beds or camping: $20–40
- Cheap meals: $15–20
- Local live music: $10–20
- DIY walking tour: free

Midrange: $130–300

- Hotel room: $130–250
- Breakfast at a quality cafe: $20–30
- Tapas and a couple of cocktails: $80–120
- A live major gig: $70–120

Top End: More than $300

- Hotel room or luxury guesthouse: $250–400
- The top restaurant in town: $150–250
- Tickets to an event or theatre show: $120–250

Opening Hours

Banks 9.30am-4pm Mon-Thu, to 5pm Fri

Bars & Clubs 5pm-late

Cafes 8.30am-4pm

Post Offices 9am-5pm Mon-Fri 9am-noon Sat

Pubs noon–1am

Restaurants lunch noon–3pm, dinner 6–10pm

Shopping Centres 9am-5.30pm, often to 9pm Thur&Fri

Tourist Offices 9am–5pm daily

Arriving in Melbourne

Melbourne Airport (Tullamarine) (p371) SkyBus (p135) runs express services every 10 to 30 minutes to/from Southern Cross Station ($18), taking approximately 25 minutes. Taxis cost around $50 to $60 to the city and take around 25 minutes.

Avalon Airport (p371) The Avalon Airport Shuttle (p135) meets every flight and takes passengers to Geelong ($22), Bellarine Peninsula ($35), Torquay ($50) and along the Great Ocean Road. SkyBus operates the Avalon City Express and meets all major flights with services to Melbourne's Southern Cross train station ($22).

Getting Around

Melbourne's public transport system has great coverage, but the same can't be said for public transport around the rest of the state. Buses are infrequent and the rail network is excellent but limited in reach. Hiring a car is the ideal way to explore the state and make the most of your time here. Alternatively, consider hiring a bike or bring your own bike on the train.

Private bus tours cover many of Victoria's main sights, although they allow limited time at most stops. One way to get around this is to arrange to stay overnight near the sight and then return on the next day's tour.

Long walks are gaining in popularity and shuttle-bus services are starting up to connect walkers with accommodation and public transport.

For much more on **getting around**, see p371

What's New

QT Melbourne

The uberhip QT chain has finally brought its kooky sensibility to Melbourne in the form of this chic boutique hotel. Even if you're not staying here, make your way up to the terrific rooftop garden bar. (p86)

Great Ocean Road Breweries

You can now add 'sampling craft beer' to your long list of reasons to tour this scenic stretch. Drop in at a new crop of breweries, including Great Ocean Road Brewhouse at Apollo Bay, Rogue Wave at Aireys Pub and Blackman's in Torquay. (p184) (p178) (p174)

Bullawah Cultural Trail

Gain an insight into local Indigenous Australians on this 2km cultural trail in Wangaratta. It features sculptures and explanation panels, and crosses two suspension bridges. (p329)

Lee Ho Fook

Blanketed in colourful street art, the narrow Duckboard Place laneway in Melbourne's city centre has seen a couple of brilliant new restaurants open, including cutting-edge Chinese Lee Ho Fook. (p95)

Striking Gold in Old Gaols

Goldfields towns Castlemaine (p218) and Bendigo (p211) have taken their historic gaols and breathed new life into them – the only crime patrons can now be accused of is having too much of a good time listening to live music and catching some theatre.

Loch Brewery & Distillery

A bit of Old Blighty tucked away in south Gippsland, this excellent brewery in a 19th-century bank pours pints of traditional UK cask ale from a wooden hand pump. If beer's not your thing, go the London dry gin or the Australian variation using native botanicals, all distilled on-site. Keep an eye out for its single malt, due for release in 2018. (p256)

IGNI

Cementing Geelong's reputation as a culinary star on the rise, IGNI's well-lauded chef, Aaron Turner, dishes up tasting menus featuring surprising ingredients cooked over a wood-fire grill fuelled by ironbark and red gum. (p164)

Winton Wetlands

The southern hemisphere's largest wetlands restoration project is a twitcher's paradise. The 32 wetlands are spread over 8750 hectares in Benalla, attracting more than 180 species of bird. (p329)

Four Pillars

Taste-test inventive gins or grab a paddle of G&Ts in this slick new gin distillery off Healesville's main drag. (p145)

Spanish Grill

Renowned Mildura chef Stefano de Pieri has turned his attention to the Grand Hotel for his latest venture. Spanish Grill cooks up locally sourced meat over gum and mallee-root coals, and is a fabulous addition to this foodie hot spot. (p314)

For more recommendations and reviews, see **lonelyplanet.com/australia/victoria**

If You Like...

Beaches

Victoria's beaches are spectacular, from wild coastlines with world-renowned surf where the winds whip in from Antarctica, to gentle bay beaches ideal for family holidays.

Ninety Mile Beach One of the longest stretches of sand on the planet. (p266)

Squeaky Beach Wilsons Prom's celebrated beach comes with its own sound effects. (p260)

Cape Bridgewater A near-perfect arc of white sand in the state's far west. (p199)

Bells Beach Natural amphitheatre where the surf is the stuff of legend. (p173)

Croajingolong National Park Remote and pristine beaches in the state's far east. (p277)

Cape Conran Coastal Park They don't call this the Wilderness Coast for nothing. (p274)

Port Phillip Bay Barely a ripple disturbs beaches at Mornington, Mt Martha and Sorrento, which combine proximity to Melbourne with a family vibe. (p240)

Bellarine & Great Ocean Road Spoiled for choice, from family-friendly Point Lonsdale to the long stroll-worthy stretches at Ocean Grove and Fairhaven, and holidaymaker favourites Apollo Bay and Lorne. (p158)

Country Towns

Victoria's historic settlements brim with beautiful period architecture. Most owe their existence to the state's glittering gold-mining heritage, while signposts to bushranger exploits also survive.

Maldon Quintessential goldfields town where the past comes alive in architecture and antiques. (p223)

Kyneton Nineteenth-century bluestone buildings carry echoes of prosperous gold-mining days and now house excellent eateries. (p217)

Castlemaine Boom-era architecture provides a backdrop for a new boom in artistic endeavour. (p218)

Beechworth Almost uniform sandstone architecture dominates this historic settlement, which has a growing reputation for culinary excellence. (p289)

Yackandandah Its historic main street is the ideal setting for a slew of antique shops and associated paraphernalia. (p291)

Chiltern A main street that looks like it was built for a film set, surrounded by box-ironbark forests. (p292)

Echuca Wonderfully preserved old port that still sends paddle steamers out onto the Murray River. (p317)

Ballarat There's no finer evocation of the gold-rush days than at Sovereign Hill and the stunning grand architecture lining Ballarat's main streets. (p203)

Queenscliff Nineteenth-century buildings and maritime history combine in this quaint seaside town. (p168)

Walhalla Despite most of the sepia-toned period buildings being reconstructions, Walhalla resembles a living museum to the gold-rush heyday. (p263)

Live Music

Pubs and band venues around the state play host to a range of musical talents. Open spaces – including wineries, country paddocks and spots by the beach – also get musical, particularly in summer.

Melbourne Pubs Melbourne loves its rock and roll in divey pubs and bars. From the Tote and Cherry to the Gasometer and the Espy, music is in the blood. (p122)

Melbourne International Jazz Festival Melbourne's premier jazz festival attracts international and local artists at venues across the city. (p21)

Port Fairy Folk Festival Catch international and local folk musicians at the renowned folk festival in Port Fairy. For other coastal tunes, check out the massive Falls Festival in Lorne or the Queenscliff Music Festival; look forward to sea breezes and happy festival vibes. (p195)

Barwon Club Many seminal Victorian punk, rock and indie bands got their start at Geelong's long-standing Barwon Club. Other great regional live-music pubs to look out for include the Bridge Hotel (Castlemaine) and the Karova Lounge (Ballarat). (p165)

Meredith Held in the outdoor amphitheatre outside the small town of Meredith, the sister Golden Plains and Meredith Music Festivals are wildly popular long weekends of camping and great live music attracting big-name international and homegrown acts. (p21)

Markets

Weekend markets are regular features across Victoria, from monthly food-rich farmers' markets to craft markets in the small towns of Melbourne's hinterland.

Queen Victoria Market From tacky souvenirs to delightful deli produce, it's all here. (p60)

Rose Street Artists' Market Clever and crafty artists gather each weekend to sell their wares and talk shop. (p130)

Camberwell Sunday Market Where Melburnians purge their belongings, and bargain and fashion hunters have a field day. (p130)

St Andrews Community Market Saturday market known for food in all its forms and its slightly alternative feel. (p148)

Red Hill Market Monthly craft, food and tasteful bric-a-brac market that's the best of its kind around Melbourne. (p244)

Top: Queen Victoria Market (p60), Melbourne

Bottom: Kangaroo in Wilsons Promontory National Park (p258)

Gippsland Farmers Markets Check the calendar to see what markets are on as you pass through the quiet towns of southern Gippsland. (p258)

Mill Markets Former factories and mills in towns such as Ballarat and Daylesford have morphed into a chain of retro-goods markets. (p155)

Abbotsford Convent Monthly slow-food and clothing markets, and a summertime Supper Market featuring live music. (p66)

Museums & Galleries

Melbourne is home to a number of excellent galleries showcasing an impressive range of homegrown talent as well as international heavyweights. Not all art is locked up indoors, either – the city's laneways serve as urban galleries. Regional Victoria has its share of top-class museums and galleries, too, with beautiful pieces of national importance.

Melbourne Major galleries such as Ian Potter Centre, NGV International and ACCA, and smaller, impressive, contemporary spaces such as Tolarno and West Space. (p50)

TarraWarra Museum of Art Spot some of Australia's best contemporary art in an impressive gallery in the rolling hills of the Yarra Valley. (p141)

Horsham Regional Art Gallery Check out cutting-edge photography, plus paintings by Brett Whiteley and Fred Williams, in an art-deco building. (p231)

Geelong Art Gallery Nineteenth- and 20th-century Australian and European paintings in a historic building in the heart of town. (p159)

Art Gallery of Ballarat This must-see gallery is the oldest and largest in regional Victoria, exhibiting the likes of Howard Arkley, Sidney Nolan and Tom Roberts. (p203)

Warrnambool Art Gallery One of the oldest galleries in Victoria; don't miss Eugene von Guérard's famous oil landscape *Tower Hill*. (p190)

Bendigo Art Gallery One of the best art galleries in regional Victoria with an impressive collection of colonial and contemporary Australian paintings. (p212)

Wildlife

A fabulous destination for nature lovers, Victoria has some of eastern Australia's prime tracts of wilderness and most accessible native wildlife.

Cape Otway One of the best places on earth to see wild koalas, just off the Great Ocean Road. (p184)

Phillip Island The Penguin Parade gets all the headlines, and rightly so, but don't forget the fur seals at Seal Rocks. (p247)

Warrnambool Watch southern right whales frolic with their young off Logan's Beach from May to September. (p192)

Anglesea Kangaroos dodge golf balls on the fairways of the town's golf course along the Great Ocean Road. (p175)

Wilsons Promontory National Park Glorious wild-coast scenery combined with bird and animal life in its natural setting; do the Prom Wildlife Walk. (p258)

Otway Eco Tours Paddle around on a guided canoe trip at dawn or dusk to try your luck at spotting the elusive platypus. (p183)

Healesville Sanctuary If you're not lucky enough to spot native animals in the wild, check them out here – from koalas and Tassie devils to kangaroos and platypuses. (p141)

Cape Bridgewater Take a boat cruise or swim in a cage to get up close and personal with seals at the colony here. (p200)

Sorrento Swim with the dolphins in Port Phillip Bay. (p240)

Month by Month

TOP EVENTS

Australian Open, January

Port Fairy Folk Festival, March

Tastes of Rutherglen, March

AFL Grand Final, Late September or early October

Melbourne Cup, November

January

It can get asphalt-melting hot, with the only respite to be found in cool-water beaches or in the High Country. Beach towns are packed with local holidaymakers and their families.

Australian Open

The world's top tennis players and huge crowds descend on Melbourne Park for Australia's Grand Slam championship. Grab a ground pass or book ahead to see a top seed from the arena seats.

Chinese New Year

Melbourne has celebrated the Chinese lunar new year since Little Bourke St became Chinatown in the 1860s. The time to touch the dragon in the Dragon Parade happens either towards the end of January or early February. (p55)

Midsumma Festival

Melbourne's premier gay and lesbian arts festival has been going strong for 30 years and features more than 130 events with a Pride March. Expect everything from film screenings to same-sex dance sports and massive dance parties. (p366)

February

Heat waves are likely, but since school holidays have ended, accommodation is plentiful by the beach. City folk are still in summer mode, filling the long evenings and weekends outside.

St Jerome's Laneway Festival

Pretty young things pack into the riverside area in Footscray for this one-day festival to check out the latest breaking bands.

St Kilda Festival

The St Kilda Festival is a suburb-wide street party held on a Sunday with massive crowds that come for both the live music and atmosphere.

White Night Melbourne

Melbourne stays up all night for free art, light shows and street performances. Expect throngs of people after dark.

March

Possibly the most festival-packed month of the year, March has fine weather, but can also dish out the odd sweltering day, though everyone starts to notice the turning leaves.

Melbourne Food & Wine Festival

Market tours, wine tastings, cooking classes and presentations by celeb chefs take place at venues across the state for this festival. Wineries and restaurants across Victoria hold events profiling local produce.

Australian Formula One Grand Prix

Normally tranquil Albert Park Lake becomes a Formula One racetrack and the buzz, both on the streets and in your ears, takes over Melbourne for four days of revhead action. (p73)

Tastes of Rutherglen

Food and wine lovers take over the usually quiet town of Rutherglen for this two-day festival showcasing the best local produce and wines. (p293)

Moomba

The action at Moomba is focused around the Yarra River, where waterskiing and the wacky Birdman Rally (watch competitors launch themselves into the water in homemade flying machines) take place.

Port Fairy Folk Festival

Historic Port Fairy is charming at any time of year, but it fills with music fans every Labour Day long weekend for this folk festival. Join them for an impressive line-up of roots acts from around the world. (p195)

Stawell Gift

The central-west town of Stawell has held a race meet (www.stawellgift.com) on Easter Monday since 1878. The main event is the prestigious 120m dash. It's the richest foot race in the country, attracting up to 20,000 visitors.

White Night, Ballarat

In March it's Ballarat's turn to stay up all night checking out free art installations, performances and light shows. (p208)

Golden Plains

Held over the Labour Day long weekend at the Meredith amphitheatre, this three-day outdoor festival attracts big-name international and local acts.

April

Mild weather and the promise of a few laughs and blooms give Melbourne an April glow.

Melbourne International Comedy Festival

Local and international comedians entertain Melbourne with four weeks of mostly stand-up comedy. After the laughfest, comedians hit the road to spread the love around the state. Often begins in March.

Melbourne International Flower & Garden Show

The Royal Exhibition Building and the surrounding Carlton Gardens are taken over by backyard blitzers, DIYers and award-winning landscape designers for this show (www.melbflowershow.com.au). Sometimes held in March.

May

It's time to breathe in the last of the summer fragrances before shrugging on a jacket. It's still warm in the northwest, but nights are getting chilly.

Next Wave Festival

Biennial festival (www.nextwave.org.au) that encourages young artists to do their thing. There's a small international contingent, and work includes performance, hybrid and new media and visual arts. The next festivals are scheduled for 2018 and 2020.

St Kilda Film Festival

Australia's premier short-film festival (www.stkildafilmfestival.com.au) has a grab bag of genres and talents on show.

Clunes Booktown Festival

Thousands of bookworms make the annual pilgrimage to tiny Clunes for two days of author readings, performances and workshops at this standout literary festival. (p224)

June

It's getting darker earlier and people are rugging up and polishing their skis for a trip to snow-covered alpine regions.

Melbourne International Jazz Festival

International jazz cats head to Melbourne and join l ocals for festival gigs at venues around town.

July

Though it's cold in Melbourne and icy in the alpine regions, coastal towns such as Lorne are cosy for weekenders.

Skiing & Snowboarding

It does snow in Australia! The snow zones of Mt Buller, Mt Hotham and Falls Creek are perfect for skiing and snowboarding. Baw Baw suits families (and won't burn a hole in skiers' pockets).

August

The region is cold and darkness continues to fall early, so it's truly time to head inside for some art- and literature-inspired enlightenment.

Melbourne International Film Festival

Midwinter movie love-in brings out Melbourne's black-skivvy-wearing cinephiles in droves. The film festival is held over two weeks at various cinemas across the city.

Melbourne Writers Festival

Beginning in the last week of August, the Writers Festival features forums and events celebrating reading, writing, books and ideas.

September

The end of September (and the AFL grand final) signals the end of rugging up on weekends and the start of sunny days.

AFL Grand Final

It's not easy to get a ticket to the AFL grand final, but it's not hard to get your share of finals fever any-

Top: Australian Open grand slam tennis tournament (p361)

Bottom: Chinese New Year parade, Chinatown (p55), Melbourne

where in Melbourne. Pubs put on big screens and barbecues (often accompanied by a spot of street kick-to-kick at half-time).

Melbourne Fringe

The Fringe has gone from alternative to relatively mainstream without losing its edge. It showcases experimental theatre, music and visual arts.

Royal Melbourne Show

The country comes to town for this school-holiday fair (www.royalshow.com.au), where carnival rides and junk-filled show bags face off against traditional farming exhibits.

October

Spring has sprung, and the fillies are out as Melbourne glams up for the races. The weather should be warming up with summer just around the corner, although cold snaps are common.

Australian Motorcycle Grand Prix

Phillip Island's grand prix circuit attracts the world's best motorbike riders for this three-day event. (p250)

Mildura Country Music Festival

It may not be Tamworth, but Mildura's annual knees-up is a fabulous celebration of all things country. (p312)

Melbourne Festival

Held at various venues around the city, this arts festival features an always-thought-provoking program of Australian and international theatre, opera, dance, visual art and music.

Spring Racing Carnival

Culminating in the prestigious Melbourne Cup in November, these race meets (www.springracingcarnival.com.au) are as much social events as sporting ones.

Wangaratta Festival of Jazz

Wangaratta plays hosts to Australia's most important jazz and blues festival. The line-up is often stellar; New York greats make regular appearances. (p330)

November

Just when you think it's going to be hot, it's usually not. Like most of the year, pack for four seasons in one day. The pace in the city heats up as holiday preparations begin.

Melbourne Cup

The Cup, held on the first Tuesday in November, is the horse race that 'stops the nation' and is a public holiday in Victoria. It's all part of the fashion-conscious Spring Racing Carnival.

Queenscliff Music Festival

This long-running music festival in the seaside town of Queenscliff on the Bellarine Peninsula has a down-to-earth folksy/blues feel and makes for a great weekend. (p170)

December

It's peak holiday time as school takes a break and offices close down until mid-January. Cricket is on the screens and streets.

Boxing Day Test

Day one of the Boxing Day Test draws out the cricket fans on 26 December. Crowds are huge and excitable – expect some shenanigans from 'Bay 13', the infamous section of the MCG.

Falls Festival

The lively, traffic-jam-inducing Falls music festival is held in rainforest surrounds near Lorne. (p178)

Meredith Music Festival

Three-day music festival held in a natural amphitheatre just outside the town of Meredith.

PETER HARRISON / GETTY IMAGES ©

Plan Your Trip
Itineraries

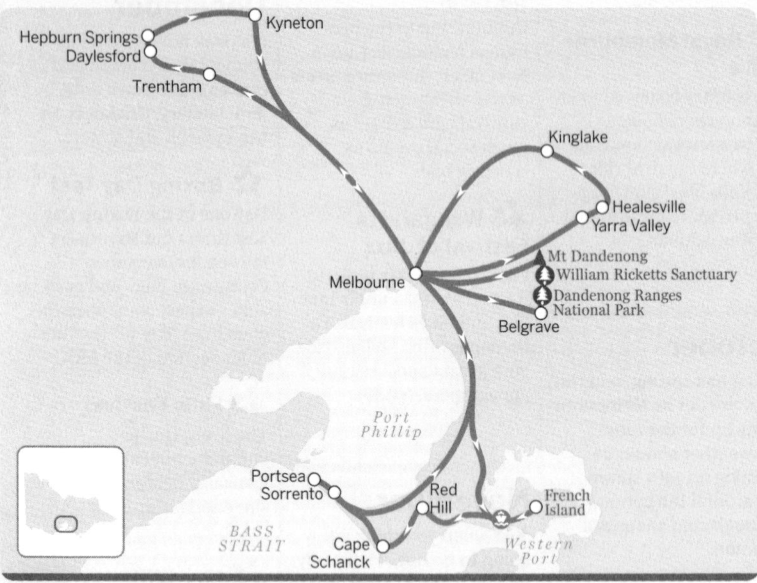

1 WEEK Melbourne & Around

Melbourne is the centrepiece of this itinerary, which combines day trips with some overnight stays. Dedicate at least two full days to Melbourne and then hit the road around the region, returning to Melbourne for the night between excursions.

After a couple of days in Melbourne, begin day three by heading southeast across the Mornington Peninsula and make for Stony Point, from where the ferry leaves for **French Island**. Stay overnight to really appreciate this special place where koalas abound and the clamour of modernity seems a world away. The next morning, return to the mainland and journey inland to check out a couple of **Red Hill** wineries. Turn back to the coast and continue to the **Cape Schanck** lighthouse. Next stop is the seaside playgrounds of the wealthy, **Sorrento** and **Portsea**, on your way back to Melbourne.

Early next morning, head to the Dandenongs, which offer a cool and leafy respite from the noise of the city. From the Burwood Hwy, drive east to Belgrave and climb aboard Puffing Billy for a steam-train journey through the mountains to

View of Sorrento (p240), Mornington Peninsula

Gembrook. Back at Belgrave, take Monbulk Rd through **Dandenong Ranges National Park** and head to Sassafras for its village atmosphere, then grab something to eat at Piggery Cafe in Olinda and continue on to explore **William Ricketts Sanctuary**. Round off the day by taking in the view from nearby **Mt Dandenong**, before returning to Melbourne for the night.

Start day six by heading from Melbourne along the Maroondah Hwy to indulge in some wine tasting in the **Yarra Valley** before reaching **Healesville**, a lovely town with a fine animal sanctuary on the edge of the Yarra Ranges National Park. Enjoy a pub lunch at the Healsville hotel and and drop into the gin distillery. In the afternoon, head directly west via Yarra Glen and Dixons Creek to the Melba Hwy. Return to Melbourne via St Andrews.

With one day left, spend it touring the charming towns of **Daylesford, Trentham** and **Kyneton** via Woodend. Favourite weekend escapes for Melburnians, they are full of fine restaurants, cafes and shops to browse. Make time for a spa and massage at the bathhouse and spa at Hepburn Springs, and head back to Melbourne in a state of bliss.

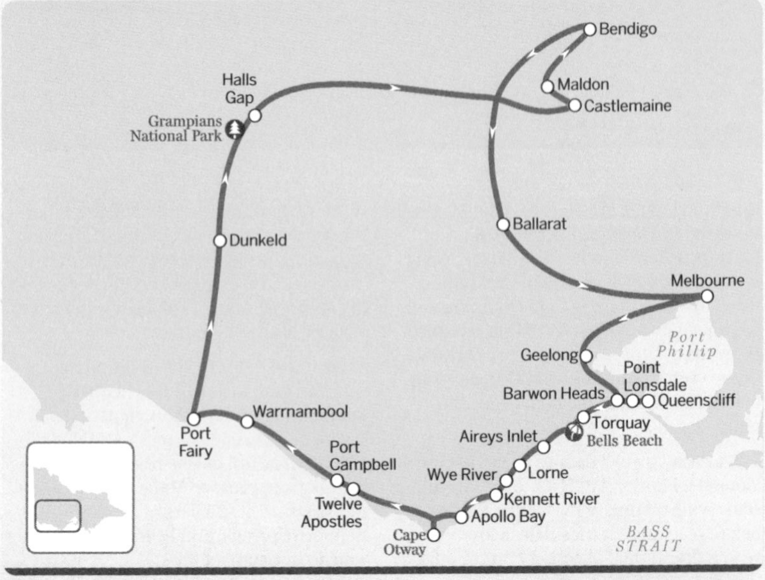
Bendigo
Maldon
Castlemaine
Halls Gap
Grampians National Park
Ballarat
Dunkeld
Melbourne
Port Phillip
Geelong
Point Lonsdale
Barwon Heads
Queenscliff
Warrnambool
Port Fairy
Torquay
Bells Beach
Aireys Inlet
Port Campbell
Wye River
Lorne
Kennett River
Twelve Apostles
Apollo Bay
Cape Otway
BASS STRAIT

AUSTRALIAN SCENICS / GETTY IMAGES ©

RODNEY HYETT / GETTY IMAGES ©

Top: The Twelve Apostles (p187)Port Campbell National Park
Bottom: Waterfall, Great Otway National Park (p184)

Great Ocean Road, Grampians & Goldfields

The Great Ocean Road is one of the most popular touring routes in the country. Take around 10 days to get the best from this region, starting in the Bellarine Peninsula. Then spend the second half of your trip winding down through the Grampians and Goldfields.

From Melbourne, take the Princes Hwy southwest to **Geelong** to stroll the waterfront and spend the evening at breweries and the latest restaurant. The next day, drop by the Bellarine Peninsula's excellent wineries before visiting the coastal towns of **Barwon Heads** and **Point Lonsdale**, then on to **Queenscliff**, one of the state's most appealing seaside towns. The Great Ocean Road begins in earnest at **Torquay**, one of the surf capitals of the world, and gateway to the legendary swells of **Bells Beach**. Further down the coast, drop in to Anglesea then tour the lighthouse at **Aireys Inlet** before stopping for a night or two in **Lorne**, with its fine beach, stunning waterfalls and tasty eating options. Head further down the coast to **Wye River** for a beer at the pub, with spectacular ocean views, then to **Kennett River** for koala spotting. Chances are that it's close to sunset by the time you return to the coast and **Apollo Bay** for a night or two. Next up, explore **Cape Otway**, then it's on to Port Campbell National Park and its famed **Twelve Apostles** before spending the night in nearby **Port Campbell**. Look for whales off the coast of **Warrnambool** then continue west to quaint **Port Fairy**.

On the way to the otherworldly Grampians, stop for a meal at Dunkeld's acclaimed **R**oyal Mail. Make **Halls Gap** your three-night base for your time among the sandstone and granite rock formations in the **Grampians National Park**. A loop through the gold-mining towns of **Castlemaine** and **Maldon** is a rewarding journey through the terrain that formed the basis for Victoria's prosperity – evident in the grand old buildings that dominate streetscapes across the region. Count on at least a night or two in Castlemaine. Detour north to overnight in **Bendigo**, one of Victoria's rural towns to watch, before sweeping back down through **Ballarat**, with its art gallery, stunning streetscapes and world-class Sovereign Hill historic park, for the final night of your tour.

The East

Eastern Victoria combines the state's thrilling coast with a mountainous and deeply forested interior – the unifying theme wherever you go is wilderness.

From Melbourne, it's a two-hour drive down to **Phillip Island** to check out the cute little penguins, seals and surf beaches. On your way southeast, sleepy seaside **Inverloch** and foodie-heaven **Koonwarra** warrant a visit before spending the night in the art-deco pub in bohemian **Fish Creek**. Next stop is the breathtaking **Wilsons Promontory National Park**. The Prom is utterly spectacular, as good for pristine beaches and wandering wildlife as for the remote lighthouse and fine walking trails. A couple of nights in the area is essential.

If you can tear yourself away, follow the coast to the quiet fishing village of **Port Albert** for the freshest seafood, then rush for the north, passing through Traralgon en route to the timeworn gold-mining town of **Walhalla**. If you're after some time out, this is the place to do it thanks to there being no TV reception, or mobile phone or internet coverage. On your way back to the coast, pass through Sale on your way to stunning **Ninety Mile Beach**, either at Golden Beach or Seaspray. Further east, **Paynesville** (reached via Bairnsdale) is a fine little detour, as well as a gateway for the koala colonies of Raymond Island. Overnight in **Metung**, another lovely little seaside town then head on to **Lakes Entrance** for boat tours, long walks and fine seafood at day's end.

The next morning, head north to the caves at **Buchan**, then loop up through the gravel tracks of **Snowy River National Park** via McKillops Bridge, before detouring into the exceptional forests of **Errinundra National Park**. Camp overnight in one of the parks, then pass through Orbost on your way to **Cape Conran Coastal Park**, where the Wilderness Coast really earns its name – soak it up over a couple of days. As far east as you can go in Victoria, **Mallacoota** has a wonderful end-of-the-road feel to it, which is true up to a point – if you travel from here out into **Croajingolong National Park**, you'll really feel like you've fallen off the map. Stay three days; you'll never want to leave this wildly beautiful place.

Top: Wilsons Promontory National Park (p258)
Bottom: Koala on Phillip Island (p247)

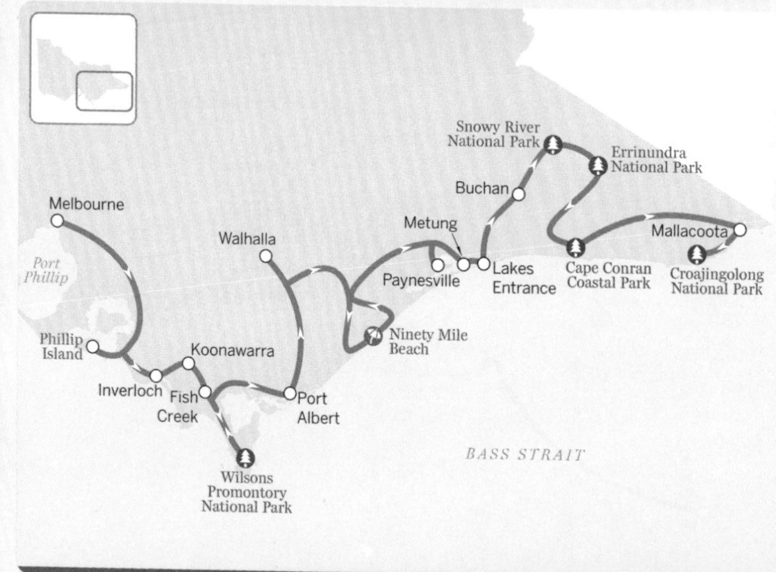
Melbourne
Port Phillip
Phillip Island
Inverloch
Koonawarra
Fish Creek
Wilsons Promontory National Park
Port Albert
Walhalla
Ninety Mile Beach
Paynesville
Metung
Lakes Entrance
Buchan
Snowy River National Park
Errinundra National Park
Cape Conran Coastal Park
Mallacoota
Croajingolong National Park
BASS STRAIT

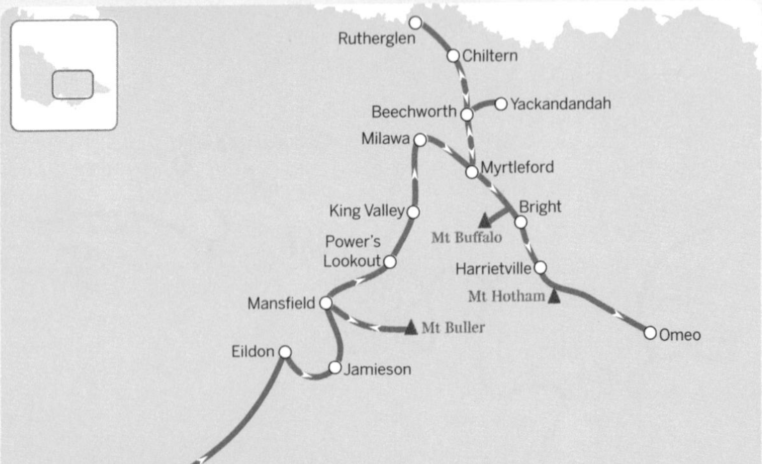

Rutherglen
Chiltern
Yackandandah
Beechworth
Milawa
Myrtleford
Bright
Mt Buffalo
King Valley
Power's Lookout
Harrietville
Mt Hotham
Mansfield
Mt Buller
Omeo
Eildon
Jamieson
Melbourne
Port Phillip

AUSTRALIAN SCENICS / GETTY IMAGES ©

High Country

Victoria's High Country is a fabulous place for car and motorcycle touring, especially outside the winter months, when even the highest roads are clear of snow. With historic towns, stirring mountain scenery and renowned gourmet regions to serve as focal points for your explorations, even 10 days may not prove sufficient.

Start your journey from Melbourne by heading up through the Yarra Valley, over the scenic Black Spur and up to **Eildon**, the base for fishing and houseboat holidays on Lake Eildon. From here, take the southern road around the lake to **Jamieson**, a quaint little former gold-mining town with an excellent brewery. Then it's on to the all-seasons adventure town of **Mansfield**, gateway to **Mt Buller** and a base for horse riding and mountain biking; stay a couple of nights. The utterly scenic Mansfield–Whitfield Rd winds up and over the ranges before plunging down to the King Valley – don't miss **Power's Lookout** about halfway along. Spend a few hours in the **King Valley** – an increasingly important wine region – before hitting the gourmet trail in earnest at **Milawa**, where wines, cheeses and mustards are all on offer.

As the sun nears the horizon on day five, head for gorgeous **Beechworth**, a stone-built village that glows golden close to sunset and which has wonderful restaurants, local honey and a brewery. Three nights is ideal here, with visits to the postcard-perfect town of **Chiltern**, and on to **Rutherglen** for a night or two to tour the historic wineries renowned for fortified wines and big brash reds. Next up, make your way back through Chiltern to **Yackandandah**, a great place to nurture your love of antiques. Returning down the Great Alpine Road, detour up spectacular **Mt Buffalo** and drop your bags off for a couple of nights in **Bright**, famous for its autumn colours and spring blossoms. From here, branch out to **Harrietville** and the hairpin ascent of **Mt Hotham**. Enjoy the expansive alpine views from the summit before continuing through alpine meadows to the historic town of **Omeo**.

GRAHAM DAY / GETTY IMAGES ©

Top: View of Mt Buller (286) near Mansfield (p284)
Bottom: Rutherglen winery (p294)

1 WEEK Murray River

Victoria's Murray River is utterly unlike anywhere else in the state, with soulful riverbank towns, drowned forests of eucalypts and the semidesert Mallee region not far away. It's hard to lose your way on this route – although roads in these parts don't always follow the river, it's never far away, and sticking close to it means you can't go wrong.

Begin by flying from **Melbourne** to **Mildura**, a lovely town to get acquainted with – we recommend at least two nights; its food and wine are worth the trip alone. Out here, you feel like you're on the cusp of the outback. To get a taste of what we mean, pick up a rental car and head out for an overnight camping trip at **Hattah-Kulkyne National Park**, where you can pitch alongside one of the Murray River's beaches. Or you could take to the water by renting a houseboat for a few nights.

Follow the river's path through the landscape southeast to overnight in **Swan Hill**, another important provincial centre by the river. There's an attractive riverside park and other important landmarks; Swan Hill's Pioneer Settlement is a wonderfully evocative place to learn about the town's past. On your way to Echuca, **Gunbower National Park** boasts some of the most beautiful river-red-gum forests in the state and is well worth a detour.

Echuca is arguably the pick of the Murray River towns and deserves at least two nights. Apart from being a picturesque town in its own right – its main street is quintessential rural Australia – its paddle steamers and historic port are where the Murray's historic role as lifeblood of Victoria's north really comes alive. Consider sleeping on a houseboat.

Sticking to the river, check out the drowned river red gums of **Barmah National Park** and continue on to **Yarrawonga**. Check out Lake Mulwala and hop on a lunch cruise around this dammed section of the river to get among the sculpturelike remains of long-dead trees.

Top: Paddle steamers on the Murray, Echuca (p3
Bottom: Swan Hill Pioneer Settlement (p315), Swan

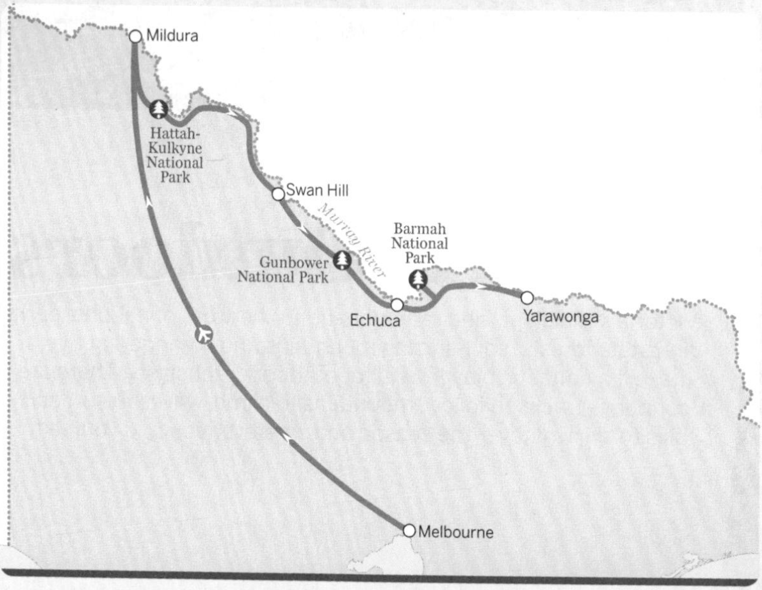

Mildura
Hattah-Kulkyne National Park
Swan Hill
Murray River
Barmah National Park
Gunbower National Park
Echuca
Yarawonga
Melbourne

Hiking up Mt Arapiles in the Grampians (p2

Plan Your Trip

Victoria Outdoors

Victoria's excellent (and rather beautiful) network of national parks and state forests, soul-stirring mountains and meandering rivers make it a fantastic playground for outdoor enthusiasts. There are countless tracks to follow, mountains to climb, waves to surf and hills to ski, whatever the season and wherever you find yourself.

Best of the Outdoors

Best Walks

Great Ocean Walk Walk from Apollo Bay to Port Campbell National Park and the Twelve Apostles.

Great Prom Walk A 45km loop through spectacular Wilsons Promontory, southeast of Melbourne.

Best Bike Trails

High Country Mountain bike or take the rail trails through the alpine region when the snow melts.

Great Ocean Road Enjoy mountain-biking tracks inland from the stunning Great Ocean Road.

Best Adventure Activities

Snowboarding Hurtle down the slopes on a snowboard at Falls Creek and Mt Hotham.

Rock Climbing Climb Mt Arapiles, Victoria's premier rock-climbing destination.

Best Surf Breaks

Ocean Grove Gentle, consistent wave well suited to beginners and intermediate surfers.

Bells Beach Excite your inner surfer at this world-famous wave.

Mornington Peninsula & Phillip Island Experienced surfers can brave the breaks at Gunnamatta and Woolamai.

Boating

You can explore Victoria's seemingly endless combination of waterways – oceans, rivers, bays and lakes – in a seemingly endless number of ways. Sailing clubs and their yachts surround Port Phillip Bay, while pleasure craft abound in the Gippsland Lakes (around Metung, for example) and low-key Mallacoota Inlet. Water sports that tend towards an adrenaline rush are particularly prevalent on Lake Eildon and in Yarrawonga. Travelling on ancient paddle steamers is a possibility in Echuca, while cruising off into the sunset on the Murray River in Mildura and Swan Hill is a classic way to spend a holiday in Victoria.

Houseboat Hijinks

Plan on spending at least $1500 to get yourself and a bunch of friends on a houseboat for a few days. Houseboat life on the Murray (especially in holiday periods) can be raucous and fun, and the houseboats themselves – some with palm trees, kitchen-sized BBQs and spas – match luxury homes for facilities (there can be a whiff of overindulgence).

Walking

Victoria is classic bushwalking country, with countless trails leading out into the wilderness. Most trails can be found in the eastern half of the state, especially in Gippsland and the High Country, but there are some fine hikes elsewhere as well. For a serious, long-distance undertaking, the 655km Australian Alps Walking Track is world-class, beginning in Walhalla, crossing the roof of Australia and finishing close to Canberra. Some of our favourite Victorian hiking areas:

➡ **Great Ocean Road** Several wonderfully long walks that can be done as an entire leg or in separate sections.

➡ **High Country** Try Baw Baw National Park, Mt Hotham, Mt Beauty and Mt Buffalo.

➡ **Wilsons Promontory National Park** A wonderful interweaving of marked trails, stunning scenery and lovely camping spots.

➡ **Grampians National Park** More than 150km of well-marked walking tracks that pass towering waterfalls and sacred Aboriginal rock-art sites.

➡ **Croajingolong National Park** Near Mallacoota in East Gippsland, this national park offers rugged inland treks and easier coastal walks.

Canoeing & Kayaking

Victoria's waterways offer ample opportunities for paddling in a canoe or kayak. Melbourne's Yarra River is a great place to start, whether around Docklands and

Melbourne's city centre or along the river's gentle lower reaches, accompanied by a bird soundtrack.

The Glenelg River (p200), in western Victoria on the South Australian border, is a great place for multiday trips. The river works its way through deep gorges with stunning riverside wildflowers and birdlife. Best of all, it has special riverside campsites en route, many of which are only accessible by canoe.

Apollo Bay, along the Great Ocean Road, is a popular spot for short sea-kayaking trips.

Out in the east, kayaking and/or canoeing is possible around Wilsons Promontory, Port Albert, Lakes Entrance and Croajingolong National Park. Also in the east, white-water rafting down the river in Snowy River National Park could just be the most fun you can have on water.

Canoe hire costs from $35 to $75 per day, depending on the operator. Extra expenses may include equipment delivery and pickup.

Kayaking (p80) on the Yarra River, Melbourne

RESPONSIBLE BUSHWALKING

- Stay on established trails, avoid cutting corners and stay on hard ground where possible.
- Before tackling a long or remote walk, tell someone responsible about your plans and contact them when you return. Consider carrying a personal locator beacon (PLB).
- Use designated campsites where provided. When bush camping, look for a natural clearing and avoid camping under river red gums, which have a tendency to drop their branches.
- Don't feed native animals.
- Take all your rubbish out with you – don't burn or bury it.
- Avoid polluting lakes and streams – don't wash yourself or your dishes in them, and keep soap and detergent at least 50m away from waterways.
- Use toilets where provided – otherwise, bury human waste at least 100m away from waterways (consider taking a hand trowel).
- Boil water from waterways for 10 minutes (or purify with a filter or tablets) before drinking it.
- Dogs and other pets are not allowed in national parks.
- Use a gas or fuel stove for cooking.
- Don't light fires unless necessary – if you do need a fire, keep it small and use only dead, fallen wood in an existing fireplace. Make sure the fire is completely extinguished before moving on. On total-fire-ban days, don't under any circumstances light a fire – that includes fuel stoves.

Cycling around Mt Hotham (p304) in Victoria's High Country

Cycling

Just about anywhere in Victoria can be good for cycling, whether you prefer long, flat tracks or winding mountain trails. The network of rail trails (www.railtrails.org.au) is brilliant, ranging from 134km from Tallarook to Mansfield or 116km from the Murray to the mountains, down to single-kilometre trundles around Melbourne.

Melbourne has an excellent network of long urban bike trails, and scant hills. City riders take advantage of this to commute during the week, or relax on weekends – it's hard to miss the Lycra-clad cafe breakfasts of the bike club scene. The city's Melbourne Bike Share (p372) system has just the blue beast for you to get around town on. You'll also find a huge number of shops selling bikes and accessories, as well as volunteer repair workshops at city parks such as Carlton Gardens and Ceres Community Environment Park (p70).

Disused railway lines and riverside industrial sites have been gradually turned over to cyclists, with a number of bike paths in greater Melbourne providing excellent touring.

Out in the country the state's spectacular landscapes are the perfect backdrop for mountain bikers and road riders alike. Check Mountain Bike Victoria (www.mountainbikevictoria.com) for a list of trails and events. You'll find thousands of kilometres of diverse cycling terrain, much of it readily accessible by public transport.

The Great Ocean Road has mighty fine mountain tracks hidden in the hinterlands, while during the 'green' season there are exhilarating climbs and descents for mountain bikers in the various ski resorts and the mountains around Bright.

Events

Great Victorian Bike Ride (www.bv.com.au; adult $895, child 13-17yr/6-12yr/under 5yr $655/330/free; ⏲Nov) A nine-day annual ride attracting thousands of cyclists of all ages and fitness levels. Payment for this fully supported ride includes meals, mechanical support and access to camping grounds. Hosted in different parts of the state each year – the 2017 event is in Gippsland.

Around the Bay in a Day (www.bicyclenetwork.com.au/around-the-bay; entry fee $40-235;

Fishing on the pier at Cowes, Phillip Island (p247)

Oct) This 250km single-day ride attracts around 20,000 keen cyclists each year. It covers the length of Port Phillip Bay from Melbourne to Sorrento, crosses on the ferry to Queenscliff and heads back to Melbourne (or vice versa). There are options for shorter routes, also.

Need to Know

- Keep an eye on surrounding cars, of course, but also on magpies: beware of the occasional dive-bombing attack by these black-and-white birds in spring.
- Wearing an approved bicycle helmet is compulsory in Victoria.

Cycling Maps

Bicycle Victoria (www.bv.com.au) and VicRoads (www.vicroads.vic.gov.au) have printable, online maps of the state's cycle paths and other resources.

Fishing

Victoria has some world-class fishing, whether you want to fly-fish for rainbow trout in a mountain stream, lure a yabbie out of a dam, catch a deep-river redfin or hook a yellowtail kingfish from a surf beach.

In the east, the vast Gippsland Lakes is popular for large snapper and bream, especially around Bairnsdale, Paynesville, Metung and Lakes Entrance. Further east, Mallacoota is another favourite family fishing spot, with excellent estuary, river and ocean fishing yielding catches of bream, flathead, whiting and mulloway.

In the state's west, there are top fishing sites all along the Great Ocean Road. Apollo Bay and Port Campbell make good bases, while Warrnambool offers the chance to hook mullet, bream or garfish in the Merri and Hopkins Rivers, or whiting, Australian salmon and trevally off the wild ocean beaches.

Marine Parks

Around 5% of Victoria's coastline is protected by marine national parks and smaller marine sanctuaries, and all fishing is banned in these protected areas. For a full list of no-go zones, see the Parks Victoria website (www.parkweb.vic.gov.au).

Licence to Fish

To fish in Victoria's marine, estuarine or fresh waters that are nonprotected areas, anglers between the ages of 18 and 70 must purchase a Recreational Fishing Licence (RFL), which costs $10 for three days, $20 for 28 days or $35 for a year. Licences are available online at http://agriculture.vic.gov.au.

Horse Riding

It's impossible to watch *The Man from Snowy River*, the film about 19th-century cattlemen in Victoria's High Country, without getting the itch to saddle up and go trailblazing through this stunning terrain. Some of the state's best riding is found in these mountains: Lake Eildon and Mansfield are top horse-riding centres. A swag of companies offer tours in the High Country, with a choice of one-hour rides to multiday pack trips (some as long as 12 days).

For those who have dreams of cantering along a lonely windswept beach as the sun

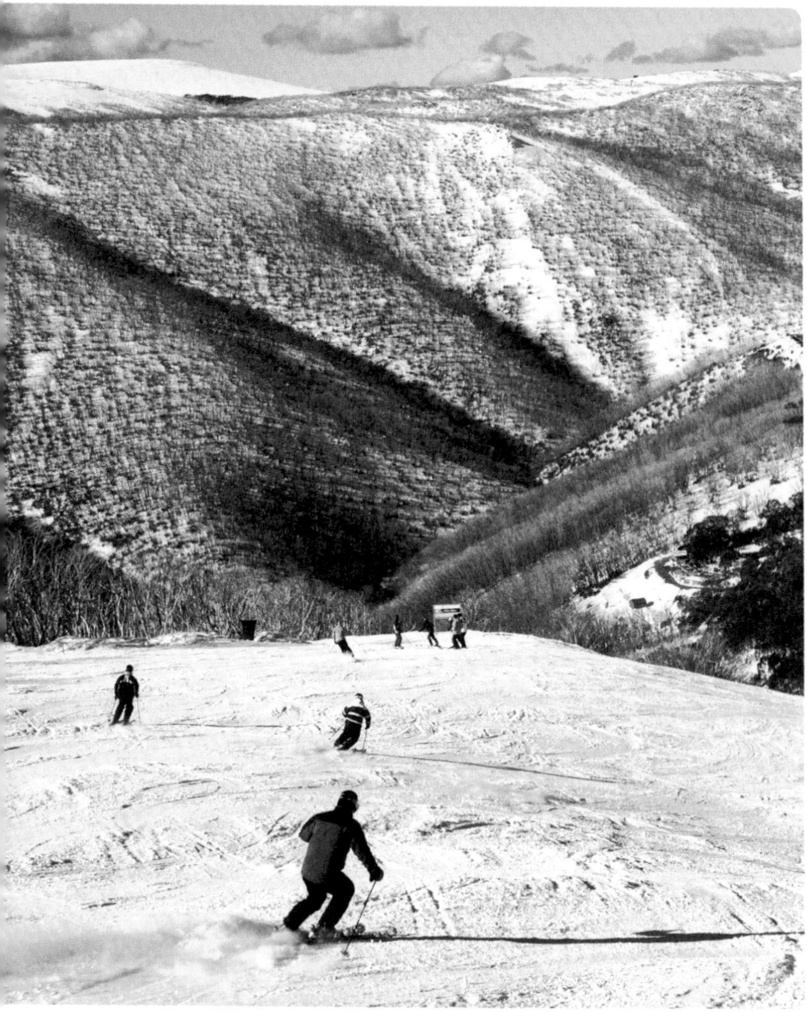

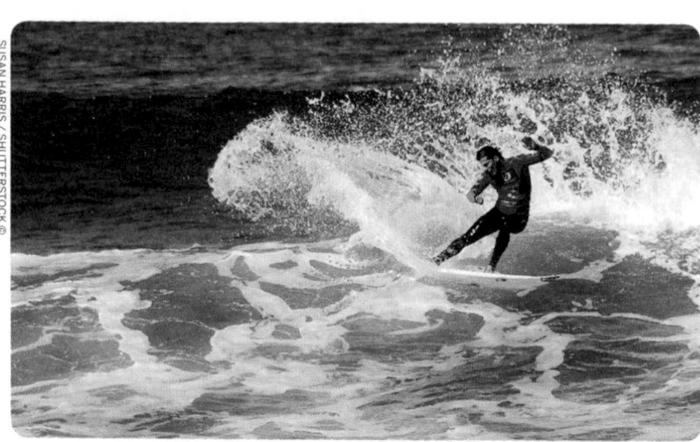

Top: Skiing at Falls Creek (p300)

Bottom: Surfing at Bells Beach near Torquay (p173)

SUSAN HARRIS / SHUTTERSTOCK ©

sets on the horizon, Victoria's coastline is an enticing option. Close to Melbourne it's possible to ride through bush and beach on the Mornington Peninsula, and on Fairhaven beach on the Great Ocean Road.

Skiing & Snowboarding

Victoria has seven alpine ski resorts scattered around the high country of the Great Dividing Range. The two largest ski resorts are Mt Buller and Falls Creek. Mt Hotham is smaller, but has equally good skiing and is the highest ski resort. Mt Baw Baw and Mt Buffalo are also smaller resorts, popular with families and less-experienced skiers. For day trips from Melbourne, Mt Buller and Mt Baw Baw are the closest options for downhill skiers, while cross-country skiers can choose between Lake Mountain and Mt Stirling.

The ski season officially commences on the first weekend of June. 'Skiable' snow usually arrives later in the month, and there's often enough snow until the end of September. See the Snow Victoria Report (http://snowvicreport.com) for the latest on snow, weather and road conditions, and check the Parks Victoria website (www.parkweb.vic.gov.au) for more info on snow sports in national parks.

Note that rates are cheaper if you hire gear for longer periods. For a package deal (which can include meals and/or lessons, lift tickets, ski hire and transport), you can book directly with lodges, through travel agents or through accommodation booking services located at the major ski resorts.

Surfing

With its exposure to the relentless Southern Ocean swell, Victoria's rugged coastline provides plenty of quality surf. But the chilly water (even in summer) has even the hardiest surfer reaching for a wetsuit. A full-length 3mm- to 4mm-thick wetsuit is the standard for winter, and booties and even wetsuit gloves might make that extra-long session a bit easier.

Great Ocean Road

The best waves (and best variety of surfing experiences) are to be found along the Great Ocean Road. No other surf beach in Australia is more celebrated than Bells Beach. It plays host to the Rip Curl Pro (p175) every Easter, bringing with it an international entourage of pro surfers, sponsors and spectators. Just up the road, local and international surfers gravitate to Thirteenth Beach near Torquay. The town is home to legendary brands Quiksilver and Rip Curl with their surf shops, as well as plenty of surf schools and the Australian National Surfing Museum (p173).

Further along the Great Ocean Road, Johanna Beach is part of the Shipwreck Coast (west of Cape Otway) and offers possibly the most powerful waves in Victoria. It faces southwest and is open to the sweeping swells of the Southern Ocean, making it the place to go if you're after big waves. Extreme care must be taken, however, as some breaks are isolated, subject to strong rips and undertows, and are generally only for the experienced surfer. It's probably best to surf with someone who knows the area.

For the less experienced, popular places with surf schools include Anglesea and Lorne.

South & East of Melbourne

The back beaches of Portsea, Sorrento, Blairgowrie, Rye, St Andrews, Gunnamatta, Cape Schanck and Flinders on the Mornington Peninsula are among the most popular spots, but they can be fairly wild, so check with locals before heading in. The same applies to the legendary Quarantine break at Point Nepean National Park. Down on Phillip Island, Cape Woolamai is also a popular spot for experienced surfers.

Smiths Beach (Phillip Island), Inverloch and Lakes Entrance are good for beginners.

How's the Swell?

Surf reports for Lorne, Torquay, the east coast, Queenscliff, Phillip Island and the Mornington Peninsula are available on Coastal Watch (www.coastalwatch.com). Try Swell Net (www.swellnet.com) for reports, 'surfcam' images and forecasts.

Beach huts, Brighton, Melbourne (p50).

Plan Your Trip

Travel with Children

With its manageable distances, abundant wildlife, child-centric attractions and activities, and a tradition of family-friendly holidays, Victoria is an ideal destination for families. Melbourne is a fine place to spend time with kids, thanks to its interactive museums, sweeping parklands and innovative playgrounds.

Best Regions for Kids

Mornington Peninsula & Phillip Island

Smooth bay swimming and strawberry-picking in summer, mazes, wildlife parks, a puzzle world, a chocolate factory and those mighty cute penguins.

Great Ocean Road

Warrnambool has childhood covered with its annual winter kids festival, Fun4Kids, and there are few better spots to view whales. Stop by the Great Ocean Road Chocolaterie en route to Anglesea or the Otway Fly treetop walk.

The Murray

Echuca has paddle steamers chugging up the Murray and kids will enjoy watching waterskiers carving up the river; book them in for a lesson.

High Country

Head here during the ski season; Mt Baw Baw and Mt Buffalo are particularly well suited for families.

Melbourne

Plenty on offer for kids in the city from Scienceworks, the aquarium and the Melbourne Museum to the Royal Melbourne Zoo and Luna Park. Add to that loads of parks, gardens and playgrounds.

Geelong & the Bellarine Peninsula

Geelong's waterfront is a great spot for families with a kids' pool, Play Zone and a merry-go-round, while a short drive away is Victoria's biggest theme park, Adventure Park.

Eating Out

Families dining out together are a pretty common sight these days in Victoria, especially in Melbourne. Cafes not serving 'babycinos' (small cup of steamed milk) are few and far between, and a number of restaurants provide papers and pencils for colouring in. Many restaurants have a children's menu, and even upscale restaurants can often provide an option for children, if asked.

Children's Highlights

Train Journeys

Puffing Billy (p140) Steam train that chugs along the Belgrave–Gembrook line in the Dandenongs, and has long been a family favourite.

Bellarine Peninsula Railway (p170) The Queenscliff–Drysdale line regularly sees special visits by Thomas the Tank Engine (and friends).

Mornington Railway (Map p238; ☎1300 767 274; www.morningtonrailway.org.au; Mornington Train Station; return adult/child $20/10) Steam train runs most Sundays.

Wahalla Goldfields Railway (p264) Passing over scenic gorges and a number of bridges on its 20-minute journey.

Historic Villages

Pioneer Settlement, Swan Hill (p315) Has everything from horse-and-carriage rides to a sound-and-light show.

Flagstaff Hill, Warrnambool (p190) A maritime delight with shipwrecks and lighthouses, and its sound-and-light show is fun for older kids.

Sovereign Hill, Ballarat (p203) Has an exhilarating evening light show and, by day, sports an authentic gold-rush feel.

Wildlife

Cape Otway (p184) Koalas are bountiful in this region of the Great Ocean Road, and also at Kennett River and at Tower Hill near Warrnambool.

Anglesea Golf Club (p175) Kangaroos can be easily spotted.

Phillip Island (p248) Penguins are plentiful here; St Kilda's colony shouldn't be missed either.

Healesville Sanctuary (p141) A host of native animals that the kids might have missed seeing in the wild can be found here.

Warrnambool (p192) Southern right whales play offshore from May to September.

Ballarat Wildlife Park (p207) The Tassie devils, komodo dragons and native animals will thrill and delight kids.

Family-Friendly Beaches

Fisherman's Beach, Torquay (p173) Well protected and a family favourite.

Point Roadknight, Anglesea (p175) A lovely, somewhat hidden beach perfect for kids.

Lorne (p178) Not only offers a great stretch of beach but plenty of activities on the beachfront, too.

Planning

When to Go

Victoria's beach towns are hot, packed and brimful of other families during the summer school holidays. Provided you're OK with cooler and unpredictable weather, travelling in low season (out of school-holiday periods) means life is calmer, accommodation providers and restaurant staff are happy to see you and prices are rock bottom.

Accommodation

If you're travelling with infants, port-a-cots are often available at an additional cost of $20 to $30. Most hotels, however, only have a limited supply, so get in early to reserve one.

In summer, caravan parks are often filled with other families, which is great for kids to socialise.

If you're on a tight budget, YHA hostels have family rooms that sleep three to four, though motels with a double and single bed are usually cheaper. Whatever your budget, 'family room' usually means that you'll all be in the same room – if you'd prefer more space (which may be a mutual feeling if your kids are older), you can often find well-priced apartments with two bedrooms.

Although it's rare, a few regional boutique hotels have a strict no-children policy, which is usually made clear at the time of booking. When booking rooms through discount websites, make sure you check the 'maximum occupancy'; often the cheapest rooms are for two adults only.

JAVEN / SHUTTERSTOCK ©

Luna Park (p79), St Kilda

What to Pack

➡ Pretty much everything is available on the road in Victoria, although pharmacies may close early, so pack basic medications.

➡ Basic bedding (sheets and a pillow slip) can be useful if you need to turn the couch into a bed.

RAINY-DAY ACTIVITIES

Australian Centre for the Moving Image (ACMI), Melbourne (p50) Has age-appropriate video games and movies 'on demand'.

Melbourne Museum (p69) and **Scienceworks, Melbourne** (p72) Both have fantastic zones for younger kids and great exhibits for older ones.

State Library of Victoria, Melbourne (p60) Has a terrific Play Pod, and you can also show the kids Ned Kelly's armour.

City Circle tram, Melbourne (p85) Free tram, or you can circle Melbourne on the Visitor Shuttle.

Regions at a Glance

Melbourne

Food
Sights
Activities

Gourmet Dining

Dining out is an obsession in Melbourne. It means restaurants bursting with experimental fervour, serving up intriguing Asian-inspired dishes, Mod Oz creations and everything in between. Coffee, cocktails and even beer get the same top-class treatment.

Architecture

Federation Sq may be the contemporary showpiece, but central Melbourne's architecture spans the centuries, from Docklands' growing community of city dwellers to Melbourne's gold-rush-era buildings and arcades.

Kayaking the Yarra

Drifting down the winding Yarra River under your own (paddling) steam, you'll take in the best of the Melbourne skyline, including the 88-storey Eureka Tower, without the crowds jostling around you.

p48

Around Melbourne

Relaxation
Food & Wine
Landscapes

Spa Towns

The delightful town of Daylesford and its spa-town sister Hepburn Springs lie just a short trip from Melbourne. Their easy-to-access lakes, creeks and natural mineral springs inspire indulgence and relaxation.

Local Produce

Just an hour or so from Melbourne lie two excellent wine and food regions: the Yarra Valley, famed for its hills, vineyards and microbreweries; and the Macedon Ranges, where you can enjoy excellent local produce at charming country eateries.

Mountains

Rise above Melbourne's eastern urban sprawl and drive through the soaring forests of the Dandenong Ranges. Here, impossibly tall trees tower over quaint little settlements where garden walks and Devonshire teas draw in-the-know Melburnians.

p138

Great Ocean Road

Activities
Beaches
Sights

Coastal Walks

Known as Victoria's premier drive, the Great Ocean Road also offers incredible walks. Long strolls along the sand between dramatic headlands are the way to start – or you could try walking the length of the Great Ocean Walk from Apollo Bay.

Bells Beach

Enclosed by steep cliffs, this world-famous surf beach is an intensely beautiful natural amphitheatre, and the scene of swells that draw the world's best for surf competitions and pilgrimages alike.

Twelve Apostles

The splendour of the iconic, rocky Twelve Apostles jutting out from the ocean is undeniable. The journey here, along the winding Great Ocean Road, is one of the most rewarding trips in the country.

p158

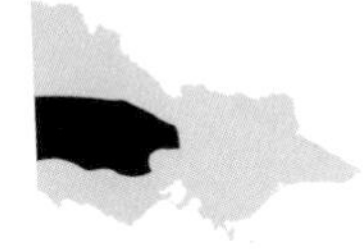

Goldfields & Grampians

Activities
Food & Wine
Historic Sights

Hiking the Grampians

The Grampians is one of Victoria's most dramatic natural landscapes. Get up close and personal while bushwalking the endless trails that lead through fire-scarred forests and beneath (or up to the summits of) stirring rocky outcrops.

Wine Tasting

Less well known than other Victorian wine regions, the Grampians has numerous vineyards that are quietly gathering plaudits from critics and travelling punters. Olive farms and renowned eateries in the surrounding area round out the taste experience.

Goldfields Towns

Victoria's 19th-century gold-rush past lives on in the glorious streetscapes of Castlemaine, Kyneton, Ballarat and Bendigo. Visiting Maldon and Sovereign Hill is like travelling back to the state's storied past.

p202

Mornington Peninsula & Phillip Island

Activities
Wildlife
Wine

Bay & Back Beaches

Quiet bay beaches line up along the eastern shore of Port Phillip Bay like a roll call of family-friendly summer playgrounds. The peninsula's back beaches are wild and waiting for experienced surfers and lovers of a good stroll along unspoiled stretches of sand.

Penguins & Koalas

The nightly parade of little penguins along the southern shore of Phillip Island is one of Australia's greatest wildlife spectacles, while French Island is home to some of the tamest wild koalas in the country.

Red Hill Wineries

The Mornington Peninsula's premier wine region centres on Red Hill with its winning combination of picturesque countryside, cellar-door sales and restaurants. It's great for day trips, or for longer stays that delve into the local pinot noir in a more lingering way.

p235

Gippsland & Wilsons Promontory

Landscapes
Water Activities
Hiking

National Parks

From the forests of Snowy River and Errinundra, where you'll be serenaded by birdsong, to the deserted beaches of Croajingolong, Victoria's far east is wild, rugged and pristine in equal measure. It's all about wilderness in its purest form.

Lakes

There's no shortage of opportunities to get out on the water with the network of waterways in the Gippsland Lakes district. Take a wine cruise at Lakes Entrance, throw a line in and chance your luck in Paynesville, or boat around the bay in pretty Metung.

Wilsons Prom Walks

With more than 80km of walking trails, mainland Australia's southernmost point has something for everyone. Either a short day walk or tackling the three-day Great Prom Walk immerses you in fine beaches, abundant wildlife and stunning scenery.

p253

High Country

Activities
Food & Wine
Village Life

Skiing & Snowboarding

Mt Buller, Mt Hotham and Falls Creek promise the full downhill adrenaline rush on the snow and a heady mix of aprés-piste hedonism. Mts Baw Baw and Buffalo are perfect for more family-focused fun.

Gourmet Towns

One of Victoria's best regions for artisanal food experiences, Milawa and its surrounds – such as the King Valley and Myrtleford – take in world-class wineries, cheese and butter factories, and a whole range of gourmet goodies.

Beautiful Beechworth

Beechworth's golden sandstone architecture ranks among the best-preserved period architecture in the state, and provides the backdrop to a buzzing culinary and cultural life that captures the essence of regional Victoria's appeal.

p279

The Murray

Activities
Food & Wine
Nature & Wildlife

River Fun

You could view the Murray River from the riverbank, but kayaking in Mildura or revisiting the river's history by boarding one of its grand old paddle steamers in Echuca gets you up close and personal.

Renowned Dining

Mildura has a strong dining scene that attracts food lovers from far and wide. Italian restaurateur Stefano de Pieri put the town on the culinary map in the 1980s with his legendary eatery, Stefano's. These days there is a crop of gourmet spots running along Langtree Ave, aka 'Feast Street'.

National Parks

The Murray region is also home to national parks with abundant flora and fauna, and plenty of walking trails. Admire the majestic red gums in Barmah National Park, the largest remaining red-gum forest in Australia. Explore the superb Gunbower Island keeping an eye out for kangaroos, turtles and over 200 bird species.

p307

On the Road

Melbourne

POP 4,530,000 / ☎03

Includes ➡

Best Places to Eat

- ➡ Attica (p110)
- ➡ Lee Ho Fook (p95)
- ➡ Supernormal (p92)
- ➡ Hakata Gensuke (p92)
- ➡ Chin Chin (p93)

Best Places to Sleep

- ➡ Treasury on Collins (p85)
- ➡ Ovolo Laneways (p86)
- ➡ QT Melbourne (p86)
- ➡ Tyrian Serviced Apartments (p89)
- ➡ Nunnery (p88)

Why Go?

Stylish, arty Melbourne is both dynamic and cosmopolitan, and it's proud of its place as Australia's sporting and cultural capital. More than 230 laneways penetrate into the heart of the city blocks and it's here that the inner city's true nature resides, crammed into narrow lanes concealing world-beating restaurants, bars and street art.

Melbourne is best experienced as a local would, with its character largely reliant upon its diverse collection of inner-city neighbourhoods. Despite a long-standing north–south divide (flashy South Yarra versus hipster Fitzroy), there's a coolness about its bars, cafes, restaurants, festivals and people that transcends the borders.

Sport is a crucial part of the social fabric here, taking on something of a religious aspect. Melburnians are passionate about AFL football ('footy'), cricket and horse racing, while grand-slam tennis and Formula One car racing draw visitors in droves.

When to Go

Melbourne

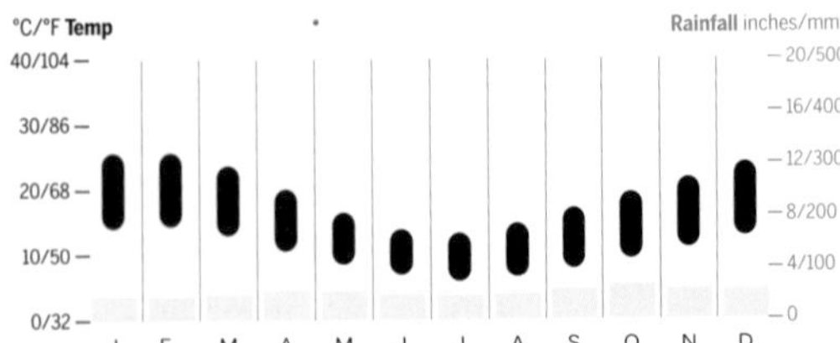

Sept–Nov Footy-finals fever hits before the lead-up to the Melbourne Cup.

Dec– Feb Summer brings balmy nights, grand-slam tennis, Formula One cars and music festivals.

April–Sept April has arguably has the best weather, before cold nights and crisp winter days.

Melbourne Highlights

❶ Royal Botanic Gardens (p74) Victorian-era garden landscaping.

❷ City Laneways & Arcades (p51) Graffiti-as-art in narrow city laneways.

❸ National Gallery of Victoria (p50) National and international art treasures.

❹ Melbourne Cricket Ground (p64) Home to the sacred AFL Grand Final.

❺ Shrine of Remembrance (p74) Prominent secular civic War Memorial shrine.

❻ Melbourne Museum & Royal Exhibition Building (p69) Victoria's cultural, social and natural history.

❼ St Kilda (p75) Roguish seaside surburb with Victorian-era pier

❽ Abbotsford Convent (p66) Converted historic buildings with galleries, cafés and markets.

❾ Cult of Coffee (p117) Get the perfect cup of Melbourne coffee.

Sights

City Centre

The city centre's wide main streets and legion of laneways pop and fizz day and night, seven days a week. Not just a business and shopping district, the city grid houses many of Melbourne's top eateries and bars. Flanking the river, Federation Sq is Melbourne's civic heart and home to several high-profile sights. The political precinct is to the east, on Spring St, while the constant buzz of retail radiates along Swanston and Elizabeth Sts towards the enormous Queen Victoria Market.

★Federation Square SQUARE

(Map p56; www.fedsquare.com; cnr Flinders & Swanston Sts; Flinders St) While it's taken some time, Melburnians have come to embrace Federation Sq, accepting it as the congregation place it was meant to be – somewhere to celebrate, protest, watch major sporting events or hang out on its deckchairs. Occupying a prominent city block, 'Fed Square' is far from square: its undulating and patterned forecourt is paved with 460,000 hand-laid cobblestones from the Kimberley region in Western Australia, with sight lines to important Melbourne landmarks. Its buildings are clad in a fractal-patterned reptilian skin.

Set within the square are cultural heavyweights such as the **Ian Potter Centre**, the **Australian Centre for the Moving Image** and the Koorie Heritage Trust (p62), as well as restaurants and bars. Free public events are staged here most days, particularly at weekends. Highly recommended free tours depart Monday to Saturday at 11am; spaces are limited, so get there 10 to 15 minutes early.

★Ian Potter Centre: NGV Australia GALLERY

(Map p56; 03-8620 2222; www.ngv.vic.gov.au; Federation Sq; 10am-5pm; Flinders St) FREE The National Gallery of Victoria's impressive Fed Sq offshoot was set up to showcase its extraordinary collection of Australian works. Set over three levels, it's a mix of permanent (free) and temporary (ticketed) exhibitions, comprising paintings, decorative arts, photography, prints, sculpture and fashion. Free tours are conducted daily at 11am, noon, 1pm and 2pm.

Indigenous art is prominently featured, and there are permanent displays of colonial paintings and the work of Melbourne's own Heidelberg School, most notably Tom Roberts' famous *Shearing the Rams* (1890) and Frederick McCubbin's monumental triptych *The Pioneer* (1904). The modernist 'Angry Penguins' are also well represented: the gallery houses the work of Sir Sidney Nolan, Arthur Boyd, Joy Hester and Albert Tucker. Other prominent artists whose work is displayed include Grace Cossington Smith, Sir Russell Drysdale, James Gleeson, Jeffrey Smart, Fred Williams and Brett Whiteley.

Australian Centre for the Moving Image MUSEUM

(ACMI; Map p56; 03-8663 2200; www.acmi.net.au; Federation Sq; 10am-5pm; Flinders St) FREE Managing to educate, enthrall and entertain in equal parts, ACMI is a visual feast that pays homage to Australian cinema and TV, offering an insight into the modern-day Australian psyche perhaps as no other museum can. Its screens don't discriminate against age, with TV shows, games and movies on call, making it a great place to spend a day watching TV and not feel guilty about it. Free tours are conducted daily at 11am and 2.30pm.

Screen Worlds is the main focus here, an interactive exhibition that celebrates Australian cinema and TV, along with gaming and small-screen media. The collection includes props, costumes, a trippy zoetrope, interactive editing displays and clips of everyone from Crocodile Dundee to Dame Edna. Upstairs you'll find the **Australian Mediatheque**, a series of free booths set aside for viewing clips from the National Film and Sound Archive – it's the perfect hideaway on a rainy day.

Birrarung Marr PARK

(Map p56; Batman Ave; Flinders St) Multiterraced Birrarung Marr is a welcome addition to Melbourne's patchwork of parks and gardens, featuring grassy knolls, river promenades, thoughtful planting of indigenous flora, and great viewpoints of the city and the river. There's also a scenic route to the MCG (p64) via the 'talking' William Barak Bridge – listen out for songs, words and sounds representing Melbourne's cultural diversity as you walk.

As a sign of respect to the Wurundjeri people, the traditional owners of the area (in their language, 'Birrarung Marr' means 'river of mists'), the park features a snaking eel path with Indigenous Australian art, a shield-and-spear sculpture and an audio installation outside ArtPlay that tells the story of contemporary Wurundjeri people.

Within an old railway building, **ArtPlay** (Map p56; 03-9664 7900; www.artplay.com.au; Birrarung Marr; 10am-4pm Wed-Sun; ; Flinders St) hosts creative workshops for babies, toddlers and preteens, getting them sewing, singing, painting and puppeteering; there's also a very cool playground out the back.

The sculptural **Federation Bells** (Map p56; www.federationbells.com.au; Birrarung Marr; performances 8-9am, 12.30-1.30pm & 5-6pm; Flinders St) perch on the park's upper level and ring out daily like a robotic orchestra, with 39 brass bells of various sizes and shapes, all with impressive acoustics, and specially commissioned contemporary compositions.

Other highlights are the 10m-high, three-legged mosaic **Angel** (1988), a vivid abstract sculpture by Deborah Halpern; **Speakers Corner**, featuring original mounds used as soapboxes in the early 20th century; and a dried riverbed lined with ghost gums and palms, giving it a tranquil billlabong feel.

★Hosier Lane — PUBLIC ART

(Map p56; Flinders St) Melbourne's most celebrated laneway for street art, Hosier Lane's cobbled length draws camera-wielding crowds snapping edgy graffiti, stencils and art installations. Subject matter runs to the mostly political and countercultural, spiced with irreverent humour; pieces change almost daily (not even a Banksy is safe here). Be sure to see Rutledge Lane (which horseshoes around Hosier), too.

Flinders Street Station — HISTORIC BUILDING

(Map p56; cnr Flinders & Swanston Sts; Flinders St) If ever there were a true symbol of the city, Flinders St station would have to be it. Built in 1854, it was Melbourne's first railway station, and you'd be hard-pressed to find a Melburnian who hasn't uttered the phrase 'Meet me under the clocks' at one time or another (the popular rendezvous spot is located at the front entrance of the station). Stretching along the Yarra, it's a beautiful neoclassical building topped with a striking octagonal dome.

St Paul's Cathedral — CHURCH

(Map p56; 03-9653 4333; www.cathedral.org.au; cnr Flinders & Swanston Sts; 7.30am-7.30pm Sun, 8am-6pm Mon-Fri, 9am-4pm Sat; Flinders St) Services were celebrated on this prominent site from the city's first days, but work on Melbourne's Anglican cathedral wasn't commenced until 1880. Consecrated in 1891, the present Gothic Revival church is the work of distinguished ecclesiastical architect William Butterfield (a case of architecture by proxy, as he did not condescend to visit

MELBOURNE IN...

Two Days

Grab a coffee at **Degraves Espresso** (p113) then head over to check out the **Ian Potter Centre: NGV Australia** (p50) art collection and have a look around **Federation Square** (p50) before joining a **walking tour** (p84) to see Melbourne's street art. Enjoy lunch at **MoVida** (p93) then find a **rooftop bar** (p112) to test the city's cocktails and take in the views before an evening **kayak tour** (p80) down the Yarra River. Finish the night off dining at one of Melbourne's best **restaurants** (p93). Start day two with a stroll along **Birrarung Marr** (p50) and into the **Royal Botanic Gardens** (p74), then discover the gastronomic delights of the **Queen Victoria Market** (p60). Catch a tram to St Kilda (p75) to wander along the foreshore and pier before propping up at a bar in lively **Acland Street** for the evening.

One Week

Spend a couple of hours at the **Melbourne Museum** (p69) then head into Fitzroy to boutique shop along **Gertrude Street** and grab lunch and coffee at **Proud Mary** (p115) in Collingwood. Back in the city centre, wander through **Chinatown** (p55) and check out Ned Kelly's armour at the **State Library** (p60) before grabbing some dumplings at **HuTong** (p94) for dinner. Spend the rest of the week exploring the shopping and cafe-hopping in hip Windsor and **Prahran** (p132), hitting the market in **South Melbourne** (p73) and heading out to the **Abbotsford Convent** (p66). Make sure to fit in a meal at **Supernormal** (p92) and a drink at **Bar Americano** (p111).

Melbourne

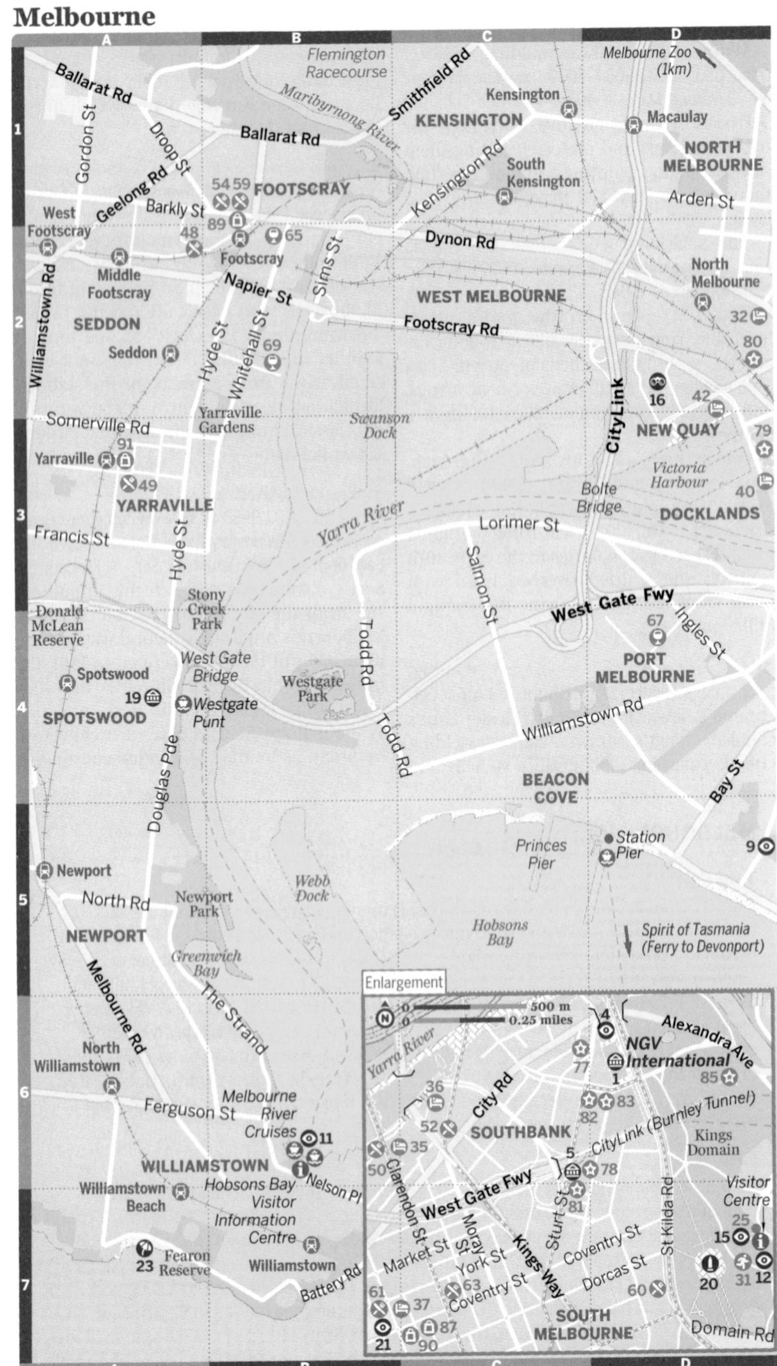
A
B
C
D
1
2
3
4
5
6
7
Flemington Racecourse
Maribyrnong River
Smithfield Rd
Ballarat Rd
Ballarat Rd
Gordon St
Droop St
Geelong Rd
Kensington
KENSINGTON
Macaulay
Melbourne Zoo (1km)
NORTH MELBOURNE
South Kensington
Kensington Rd
FOOTSCRAY
54
59
Barkly St
89
48
65
Footscray
West Footscray
Middle Footscray
Arden St
Dynon Rd
North Melbourne
Williamstown Rd
Napier St
Sims St
WEST MELBOURNE
SEDDON
Footscray Rd
32
80
Seddon
Hyde St
Whitehall St
69
16
42
CityLink
Somerville Rd
Yarraville Gardens
Swanson Dock
NEW QUAY
79
91
Yarraville
49
Victoria Harbour
40
YARRAVILLE
Bolte Bridge
DOCKLANDS
Yarra River
Francis St
Lorimer St
Hyde St
Salmon St
Stony Creek Park
Donald McLean Reserve
West Gate Fwy
Ingles St
67
Todd Rd
West Gate Bridge
PORT MELBOURNE
Spotswood
Westgate Park
19
Westgate Punt
SPOTSWOOD
Todd Rd
Williamstown Rd
Douglas Pde
BEACON COVE
Bay St
Station Pier
9
Princes Pier
Newport
Webb Dock
North Rd
Newport Park
NEWPORT
Hobsons Bay
Spirit of Tasmania (Ferry to Devonport)
Greenwich Bay
Melbourne Rd
The Strand
North Williamstown
Ferguson St
Melbourne River Cruises
11
WILLIAMSTOWN
Nelson Pl
Williamstown Beach
Hobsons Bay Visitor Information Centre
23
Fearon Reserve
Williamstown
Battery Rd
Enlargement
500 m
0.25 miles
Yarra River
4
Alexandra Ave
77
NGV International
1
85
36
City Rd
83
82
CityLink (Burnley Tunnel)
52
SOUTHBANK
Kings Domain
35
5
78
50
Clarendon St
West Gate Fwy
81
St Kilda Rd
Visitor Centre
25
15
Market St
Moray St
York St
Sturt St
Kings Way
Coventry St
Dorcas St
20
31
12
61
63
Coventry St
60
37
87
21
90
SOUTH MELBOURNE
Domain Rd

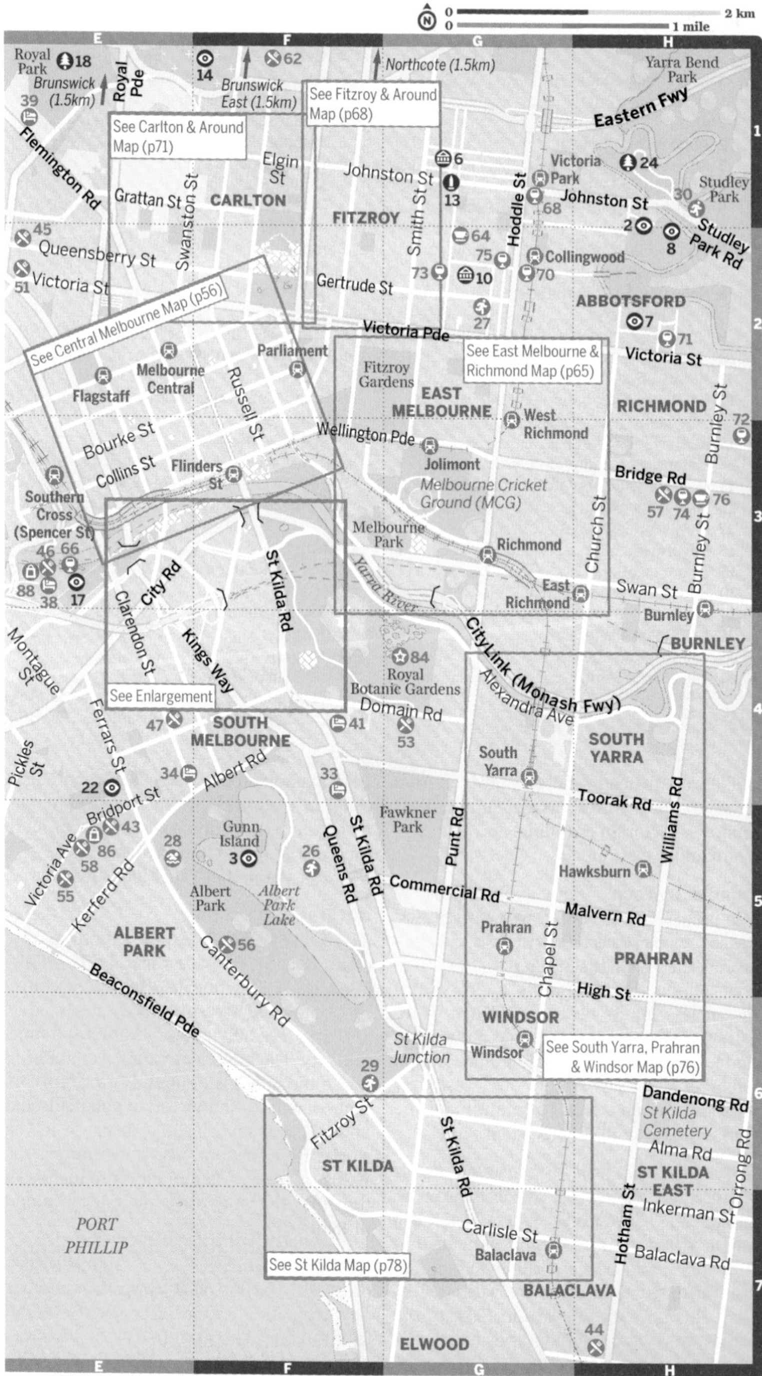

0 2 km
0 1 mile
Royal Park
18
Brunswick (1.5km)
Royal Pde
14
62
Brunswick East (1.5km)
Northcote (1.5km)
Yarra Bend Park
Eastern Fwy
39
See Carlton & Around Map (p71)
See Fitzroy & Around Map (p68)
Flemington Rd
Elgin St
6
Johnston St
13
Victoria Park
24
Studley Park
30
Grattan St
Swanston St
CARLTON
FITZROY
Smith St
Hoddle St
Johnston St
68
2
8
Studley Park Rd
45
Queensberry St
64
75
Collingwood
Victoria St
51
73
10
70
Gertrude St
ABBOTSFORD
27
See Central Melbourne Map (p56)
7
Victoria Pde
71
Parliament
See East Melbourne & Richmond Map (p65)
Victoria St
Melbourne Central
Flagstaff
Russell St
Fitzroy Gardens
EAST MELBOURNE
RICHMOND
Burnley St
72
West Richmond
Bourke St
Wellington Pde
Jolimont
Collins St
Flinders St
Melbourne Cricket Ground (MCG)
Bridge Rd
Southern Cross (Spencer St)
57
74
76
Melbourne Park
Church St
Burnley St
46
66
Richmond
St Kilda Rd
88
38
17
City Rd
Yarra River
East Richmond
Swan St
Clarendon St
Burnley
Montague St
Kings Way
84
BURNLEY
Royal Botanic Gardens
CityLink (Monash Fwy)
Alexandra Ave
See Enlargement
Domain Rd
47
SOUTH MELBOURNE
41
53
SOUTH YARRA
Ferrars St
South Yarra
Pickles St
34
Albert Rd
33
Williams Rd
22
Toorak Rd
Bridport St
43
Fawkner Park
Victoria Ave
86
28
Gunn Island
3
Queens Rd
St Kilda Rd
26
Punt Rd
58
Hawksburn
55
Kerferd Rd
Albert Park
Albert Park Lake
Commercial Rd
Malvern Rd
ALBERT PARK
56
Prahran
Chapel St
PRAHRAN
Canterbury Rd
Beaconsfield Pde
High St
WINDSOR
St Kilda Junction
Windsor
See South Yarra, Prahran & Windsor Map (p76)
29
Dandenong Rd
St Kilda Cemetery
Fitzroy St
Alma Rd
Orrong Rd
ST KILDA
St Kilda Rd
ST KILDA EAST
Hotham St
Inkerman St
PORT PHILLIP
Carlisle St
Balaclava
Balaclava Rd
See St Kilda Map (p78)
BALACLAVA
44
ELWOOD

Melbourne

Top Sights
1 NGV International D6

Sights
2 Abbotsford Convent H1
3 Albert Park Lake F5
4 Arts Centre Melbourne D6
5 Australian Centre for Contemporary Art C6
6 Backwoods Gallery G1
7 Carlton Brewhouse H2
8 Collingwood Children's Farm H2
Farmers Market (see 8)
9 Gasworks Arts Park D5
10 Gertrude Glasshouse G2
11 HMAS Castlemaine B6
12 Ian Potter Foundation Children's Garden D7
13 Keith Haring Mural G1
14 Melbourne General Cemetery F1
15 Melbourne Observatory D7
16 Melbourne Star D2
17 Polly Woodside E3
18 Royal Park E1
19 Scienceworks A4
20 Shrine of Remembrance D7
21 South Melbourne Market B7
22 St Vincent Place E4
23 Williamstown Beach A7
24 Yarra Bend Park H1

Activities, Courses & Tours
25 Aboriginal Heritage Walk D7
26 Albert Park Golf Course F5
27 Japanese Bath House G2
28 Melbourne Sports & Aquatic Centre E5
29 St Kilda Sports Club F6
30 Studley Park Boathouse H1
31 Tan D7

Sleeping
32 Bev & Mick's Backpackers D2
33 Blackman F4
34 Coppersmith E4
35 Crown Metropol B6
36 Crown Promenade C6
37 Drop Bear Inn C7
38 Hilton Melbourne South Wharf E3
39 Larwill Studio E1
40 Quest Docklands D3
41 Royce on St Kilda Road F4
42 Sebel & Grand Mercure Melbourne Docklands D2

Eating
43 Andrew's Burgers E5
44 Attica H7
45 Auction Rooms E2
46 Bangpop E3
47 Bellota Wine Bar E4
48 Cafe Lalibela A2
49 Cobb Lane A3
50 Colonial Tramcar Restaurant B6

Melbourne, instead sending drawings from England). It features ornate stained-glass windows, Victorian-era tiling, and stripes of cream and grey stone.

Young & Jackson HISTORIC BUILDING
(Map p56; ☎03-9650 3884; www.youngandjacksons.com.au; cnr Flinders & Swanston Sts; ⏲Chloe's Bar 2pm-late; 🚉Flinders St) Across the street from Flinders St station is a pub (p114) known less for its beer (served here since 1861) than for its famous nude painting of the teenaged *Chloe*, painted by Jules Joseph Lefebvre. Chloe's yearning gaze, cast over her shoulder and out of the frame, made the work a hit at the 1875 Paris Salon.

Melbourne Town Hall NOTABLE BUILDING
(Map p56; ☎03-9658 9658; www.thatsmelbourne.com.au; 90-130 Swanston St; ⏲tours 11am & 1pm Mon-Fri; 🚉Flinders St) FREE Since it opened in 1870, this grand neoclassical civic building has welcomed everyone from Queen Elizabeth II, who took tea here in 1954, to the Beatles, who waved to thousands of screaming fans from the balcony in 1964. Take the free one-hour tour to see the Grand Organ (built in 1929, and the largest grand romantic organ in the southern hemisphere), sit in the Lord Mayor's chair or tickle the keys of the same piano that Paul McCartney played.

Old Treasury Building MUSEUM
(Map p56; ☎03-9651 2233; www.oldtreasurybuilding.org.au; 20 Spring St; ⏲10am-4pm Sun-Fri; 🚉Parliament) FREE The fine neoclassical architecture of the Old Treasury (1862), designed by JJ Clarke, is a telling mix of hubris and functionality. The basement vaults were built to house the millions of pounds' worth of loot that came from the Victorian goldfields and now feature multimedia displays telling stories from that era. Also downstairs is the 1920s caretaker's flat and a reproduction of the 70kg *Welcome Stranger* nugget, found in 1869.

Parliament House HISTORIC BUILDING
(Map p56; ☎03-9651 8568; www.parliament.vic.gov.au; Spring St; ⏲8.30am-5.30pm Mon-Fri; 🚉Parliament) FREE The grand steps of Victoria's parliament (1856) are often dotted with

Convent Bakery ....(see 2)
Easey's ....(see 6)
51 El Sabor E2
52 Enlightened Cuisine C6
53 Gilson G4
54 Hung Vuong B1
55 Jock's Ice-Cream E5
Lentil as Anything ....(see 2)
56 Mart 130 ....F5
57 Minamishima H3
58 Misuzu's E5
59 Nhu Lan B1
60 Orient East D7
61 Paco y Lola B7
Simply Spanish ....(see 61)
62 Small Victories F1
Son in Law ....(see 13)
63 St Ali C7

Drinking & Nightlife

64 Aunty Peg's G2
65 Back Alley Sally's B2
66 Boatbuilders Yard E3
Clement ....(see 61)
67 Colonial Brewery Co D4
68 Dr Morse Bar & Eatery G1
69 Hop Nation B2
70 Laird G2
71 Moon Dog Bar & Brewery H2
72 Mountain Goat Brewery H3
Padre Coffee ....(see 21)
73 Peel Hotel G2
74 Slowbeer H3
St Kilda Bowling Club ....(see 29)
75 Stomping Ground Brewery & Beer Hall G2
76 Touchwood H3
Town Hall Hotel ....(see 51)

Entertainment

77 Australian Ballet C6
78 Chunky Move D6
Comic's Lounge ....(see 51)
79 Etihad Stadium D3
80 Festival Hall D2
81 Malthouse Theatre C7
82 Melbourne Recital Centre C6
83 Melbourne Theatre Company D6
84 Moonlight Cinema G4
Opera Australia ....(see 4)
85 Sidney Myer Music Bowl D6
The Tote ....(see 13)

Shopping

86 Avenue Books E5
87 Coventry Bookstore C7
88 DFO South Wharf E3
89 Footscray Market B1
90 Nest C7
NGV Design Store ....(see 1)
Shirt & Skirt Market ....(see 2)
91 Sun Bookshop A3
Vincent 2 ....(see 87)

slow-moving, tulle-wearing brides smiling for the camera, or placard-holding protesters doing the same. On sitting days the public is welcome to view proceedings from the galleries. On nonsitting days, there are eight guided tours a day; times are posted online and on a sign by the door. Numbers are limited, so aim to arrive at least 15 minutes before time.

The building's interiors are bursting with gold-rush-era pride and optimism, expressed through exuberant use of ornamental plasterwork, stencilling and gilt. Tours head through the lower house (legislative assembly), the upper house (legislative council) and the library. Fascinating design features and the symbolism underlying much of the ornamentation are illuminated by the knowledgeable guides. Ask about the mystery of the stolen ceremonial mace that disappeared from the lower house in 1891 – it's rumoured to have ended up in a brothel.

Australia's first federal parliament sat here from 1901 until 1927, when it moved to Canberra (the Victorian parliament temporarily relocated to the Royal Exhibition Building). Though they've never been used, gun slits are visible just below the roof, and a dungeon is now the cleaners' tearoom.

★Chinatown AREA

(Map p56; www.chinatownmelbourne.com.au; Little Bourke St, btwn Swanston & Exhibition Sts; Melbourne Central, Parliament) For over 150 years this section of central Melbourne, now flanked by five traditional arches, has been the focal point for the city's Chinese community and it remains a vibrant neighbourhood of historic buildings filled with Chinese (and other Asian) restaurants. Come here for yum cha (dim sum) or to explore the attendant laneways for late-night dumplings or cocktails. Chinatown also hosts the city's **Chinese New Year** (www.chinatownmelbourne.com.au; Little Bourke St; Jan or Feb) celebrations.

Chinese miners arrived in Victoria in search of the 'new gold mountain' in the 1850s and started to settle in this strip of Little Bourke St from the 1860s. To learn more

Central Melbourne

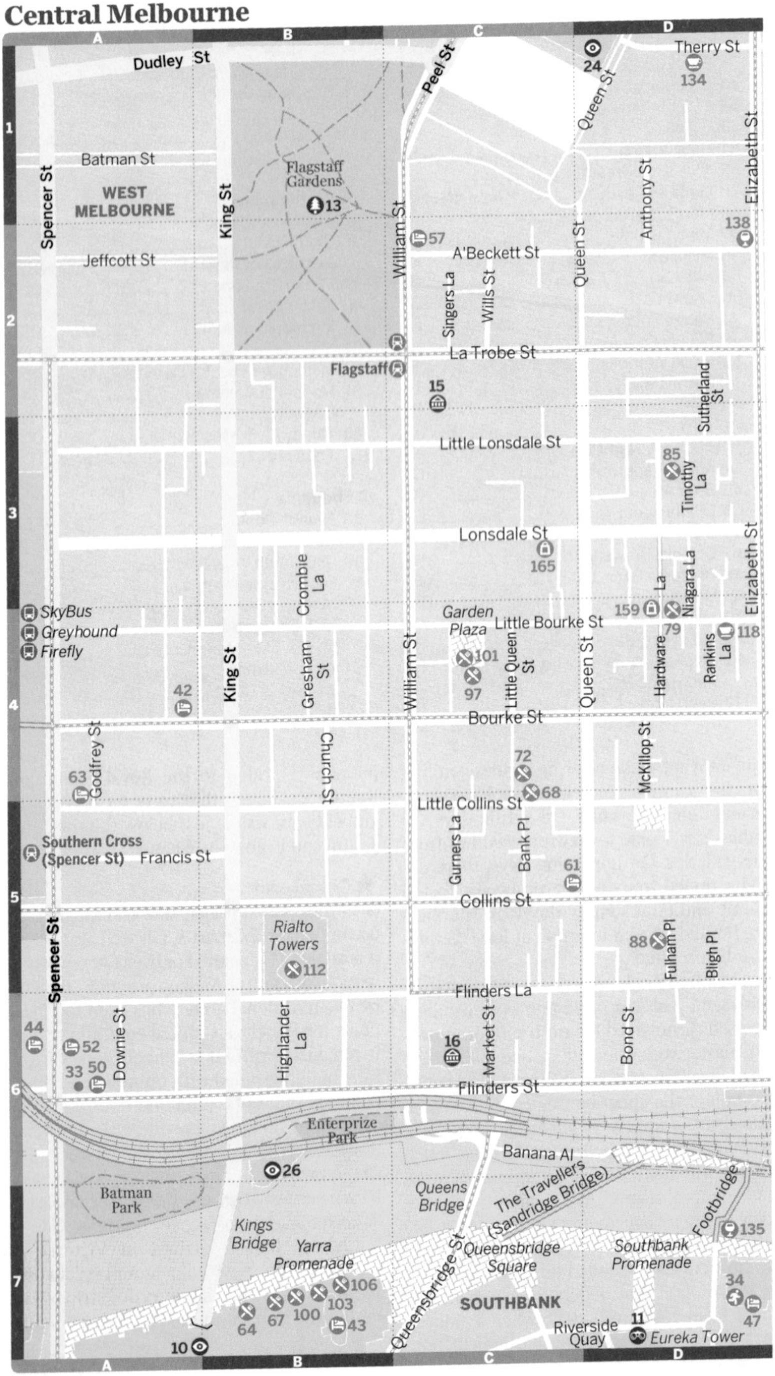

Dudley St
Peel St
Queen St
Therry St
Batman St
WEST MELBOURNE
Spencer St
King St
Flagstaff Gardens
13
Jeffcott St
William St
57
A'Beckett St
Singers La
Wills St
Anthony St
Elizabeth St
138
134
24
La Trobe St
Flagstaff
15
Sutherland St
Little Lonsdale St
85
Timothy La
Lonsdale St
165
Crombie La
Niagara La
159
79
118
SkyBus
Greyhound
Firefly
Garden Plaza
Little Bourke St
101
97
Little Queen St
Hardware La
Rankins La
Gresham St
42
Bourke St
Godfrey St
63
Church St
72
68
McKillop St
Little Collins St
Southern Cross (Spencer St)
Francis St
Gurners La
Bank Pl
61
Collins St
Rialto Towers
112
88
Fulham Pl
Bligh Pl
Flinders La
44
52
33
50
Downie St
Highlander La
16
Market St
Bond St
Flinders St
Enterprize Park
Banana Al
26
Batman Park
Queens Bridge
The Travellers (Sandridge Bridge)
Footbridge
135
Kings Bridge
Yarra Promenade
Queensbridge St
Queensbridge Square
Southbank Promenade
106
103
100
67
64
43
SOUTHBANK
34
47
10
Riverside Quay
11
Eureka Tower

0 200 m
0 0.1 miles
RMIT University
Cardigan St
Earl St
Lygon St
Queensberry St
Royal Exhibition Building
Aldi
Franklin St
Victoria St
CARLTON
Rathdowne St
Mackenzie St
A'Beckett St
Little La Trobe St
Swanston St
Bowen St
Russell St
Carlton Gardens South
Melbourne Central
La Trobe St
Victoria Pde
Davisons Pl
Bennetts La
Exploration La
Hayward La
Little Lonsdale St
Spring St
Red Cape La
Woolworths
QV Square
Artemis La
Jones La
Lonsdale St
Caledonian La
CHINATOWN
Chinatown
Parliament
Crossley St
Parliament Gardens
Little Bourke St
Exhibition St
La Trobe Pl
Coverlid Pl
Melbourne Visitor Booth
Bourke St
Union La
Royal La
Russell Pl
Little Collins St
Baptist Pl
Scots Church
St Michael's Uniting Church
Alfred Pl
Collins St
Centre Pl
Manchester La
Regent Pl
George Pde
City Library
Flinders La
Hosier Lane
Oliver La
ACDC La
Treasury Gardens
Flinders St
Melbourne Visitor Centre
Wellington Pde S
Melbourne Cricket Ground (1km)
Federation Square
Ian Potter Centre: NGV Australia
Yarra River
Princes Bridge
Birrarung Marr
Batman Ave
St Kilda Rd
Alexandra Gardens

Central Melbourne

Top Sights
1 Chinatown F4
2 Federation Square F6
3 Hosier Lane F6
4 Ian Potter Centre: NGV Australia F6

Sights
5 Anna Schwartz Gallery F6
6 Australian Centre for the Moving Image F6
7 Birrarung Marr G7
8 Block Arcade E5
9 Chinese Museum G3
10 Crown A7
11 Eureka Skydeck D7
12 Federation Bells G7
13 Flagstaff Gardens B1
14 Flinders Street Station E6
15 Hellenic Museum C2
16 Immigration Museum C6
17 Koorie Heritage Trust F7
18 Manchester Unity Building E5
19 Melbourne Town Hall F5
20 Nicholas Building E6
21 Old Melbourne Gaol F2
22 Old Treasury Building H5
23 Parliament House H4
24 Queen Victoria Market D1
25 Royal Arcade E4
26 Sea Life B6
27 St Paul's Cathedral F6
28 State Library of Victoria F2
29 Tolarno Galleries G5
30 West Space F4
31 Young & Jackson E6

Activities, Courses & Tours
32 ArtPlay G7
33 Bunyip Tours A6
34 Chuan Spa D7
35 Kayak Melbourne F7
36 Melbourne By Foot F6
37 Melbourne City Baths F1
38 Melbourne Greeter Service F6
39 Rentabike F7

Sleeping
40 Adelphi Hotel F6
41 Adina Apartment Hotel G6
42 Alto Hotel on Bourke A4
43 Crown Towers B7
44 Grand Hotel Melbourne A6
45 Grand Hyatt Melbourne G5
46 Hotel Lindrum H6
47 Langham Hotel D7
48 Majorca Apartment 401 E5
49 Mantra 100 Exhibition G5
50 Melbourne Central YHA A6
51 Ovolo Laneways H4
52 Pensione Hotel A6
53 Punthill Flinders Lane E6
54 Punthill Little Bourke G3
55 Punthill Manhattan H6
56 QT Melbourne F4
57 Radisson on Flagstaff Gardens C2
58 Sofitel H5
59 Space Hotel F2
60 St Jerome's The Hotel E3
61 Treasury on Collins C5
62 United Backpackers E6
63 Vibe Savoy Hotel A4

Eating
64 Atlantic B7
65 Bar Lourinhã H5
66 Belleville F4
67 Bistro Guillaume B7
68 Bistro Vue C5
69 Bluetrain E7
70 Bomba G3
71 Bowery to Williamsburg G6
72 Café Vue C4
73 Chin Chin G6
74 Coda F6
75 Coles E3
76 Cumulus Inc H6
77 Don Don E3
78 Flower Drum G4
79 French Saloon D4
80 Gazi G6
81 Gingerboy G4
82 Gopals Pure Vegetarian E4
83 Grossi Florentino G4
84 Hakata Gensuke F4
85 Hardware Société D3
86 Hopetoun Tea Rooms E5
87 HuTong Dumpling Bar G4
88 Huxtaburger D5
89 IGA X-Press G2
90 Izakaya Chuji F3

about the Chinese Australian story, visit the excellent **Chinese Museum**.

Chinese Museum MUSEUM

(Map p56; 03-9662 2888; www.chinesemuseum.com.au; 22 Cohen Pl; adult/child $10/8.50; 10am-4pm; Parliament) The fascinating and often fraught history of Chinese people in Australia is showcased in this wonderful little museum at the heart of Chinatown. Start on level three, which features displays and artefacts relating to the gold-rush era and the xenophobic White Australia policy. Work your way down to the basement, where there are recreations of the hold of an immigrant boat, a temple and a typical house. Then follow the dragon's tail up to the Dragon Gallery on the ground floor.

The astounding 63m-long Millennium Dragon bends around the building and is the largest processional dragon in the world. In full flight during Chinese New Year, it needs eight people just to hold up its 200kg head.

Royal Arcade HISTORIC BUILDING

(Map p56; www.royalarcade.com.au; 335 Bourke St Mall; 86, 96) Built between 1869 and 1870, this Parisian-style shopping arcade is Melbourne's oldest and it's managed to retain much of its charming 19th-century detail. A black-and-white chequered path leads to the mythological figures of giant brothers Gog and Magog, perched with hammers within the domed exit to Little Collins St. They've been striking the hour here since 1892.

State Library of Victoria LIBRARY

(Map p56; ☎03-8664 7002; www.slv.vic.gov.au; 328 Swanston St; ⊙10am-9pm Mon-Thu, to 6pm Fri-Sun, galleries 10am-5pm; ⓡMelbourne Central) This grand neoclassical building has been at the forefront of Melbourne's literary scene since it opened in 1856. When its epicentre, the gorgeous octagonal **La Trobe Reading Room**, was completed in 1913, its reinforced-concrete dome was the largest of its kind in the world; its natural light illuminates the ornate plasterwork and the studious Melbourne writers who come here to pen their works. For visitors, the highlight is the fascinating collection showcased in the **Dome Galleries**.

Start on the dome viewing balcony on the 6th floor and then work your way down to the Dome Galleres, spread over the next two floors. The 5th floor has the *Changing Face of Victoria* exhibition. Its most notable items are the bullet-dented armour and death mask of Ned Kelly, Australia's most infamous bushranger; the menacing helmet was cobbled together from a plough with a slit cut out for the eyes. There's also numerous original Burke and Wills memorabilia and John Batman's controversial land treaty (read: land grab), in which he's believed to have forged the signatures of the Wurundjeri people.

Bibiliophiles won't want to miss the *Mirror of the World* exhibition on the 4th floor, featuring a weird and wonderful collection of books through the ages, including a 4000-year-old Sumerian cuneiform tax receipt, significant religious tomes and beautifully rendered nature studies. There are also a couple of galleries on the ground floor near the main entrance.

For more information, join a free hour-long themed tour (departing at 11.30am, 1pm and 2pm).

The lawns in front of the library are a popular lunching and blogging spot; protests and free events are often held here.

Old Melbourne Gaol HISTORIC BUILDING

(Map p56; ☎03-8663 7228; www.oldmelbournegaol.com.au; 337 Russell St; adult/child/family $25/14/55; ⊙9.30am-5pm; ⓡMelbourne Central) Built in 1841, this forbidding bluestone prison was in operation until 1929. It's now one of Melbourne's most popular museums, where you can tour the tiny, bleak cells. Around 135 people were hanged here, including Ned Kelly, Australia's most infamous bushranger, in 1880; one of his death masks is on display. Visits include the Police Watch House Experience, where you get 'arrested' and thrown in the slammer (more fun than it sounds).

The dire social conditions that motivated criminals in 19th-century Melbourne are also highlighted, including the era's obsession with phrenology. During school holidays you can visit the Old Magistrates' Court, where notorious gangster Squizzy Taylor stood trial.

You can also join one of three creepy night tours: A Night in the Watch House, the Hangman's Night Tour or Ghosts? What Ghosts! (all $38, check the website for the schedule). The latter two are not recommended for children under 12, while the pitch-black Watch House tour isn't recommended for under 16s.

Queen Victoria Market MARKET

(Map p56; www.qvm.com.au; 513 Elizabeth St; ⊙6am-2pm Tue & Thu, to 5pm Fri, to 3pm Sat, 9am-4pm Sun; ⓡFlagstaff) With over 600 traders, the Vic Market is the largest open-air market in the southern hemisphere and attracts thousands of shoppers. It's where Melburnians sniff out fresh produce among the booming cries of spruiking fishmongers and fruit-and-veg vendors. The wonderful deli hall (with art-deco features) is lined with everything from soft cheeses, wines and Polish sausages to Greek dips, truffle oil and kangaroo biltong.

Saturday morning is particularly buzzing, with marketgoers breakfasting to the sounds and shows of buskers. Clothing and knickknack stalls dominate on Sunday; they're big on variety, but don't come looking for style. (If you're in the market for sheepskin moccasins or cheap T-shirts, you'll be in luck.)

On Wednesday evenings from mid-November to the end of February, the **Summer Night Market** takes over. It's a lively social event featuring hawker-style food stalls, bars, and music and dance performances. There's also a **Winter Night Market** each Wednesday evening from June to August.

The market has been here for more than 130 years; from 1837 to 1854, it was the old Melbourne Cemetery (remarkably, around 9000 bodies remain buried here, from underneath Shed F to the car park leading to Franklin St). There's a small memorial on the corner of Queen and Therry Sts.

Major restoration and redevelopment works are planned for the market, which are

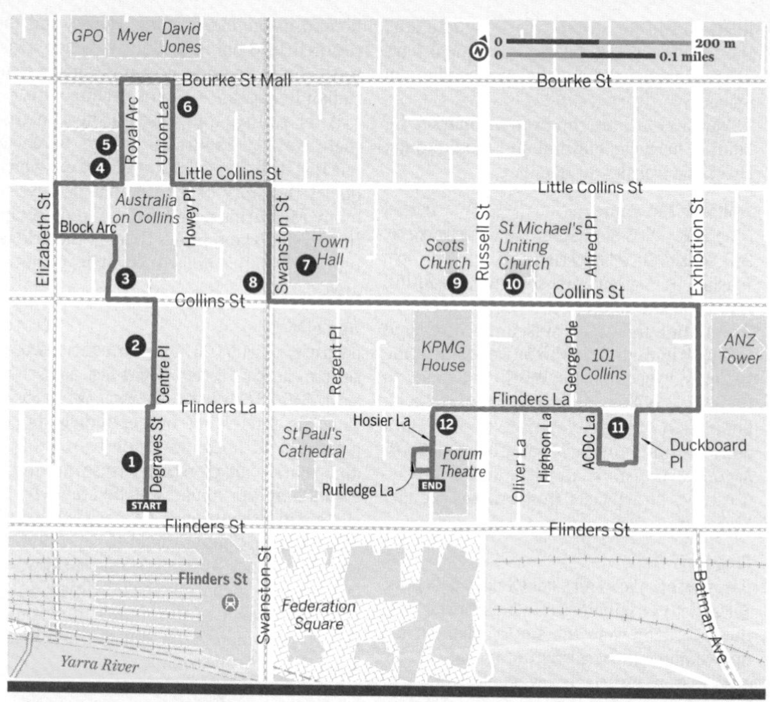

Walking Tour
City Arcades & Laneways

START DEGRAVES ST
END MOVIDA
LENGTH 3KM; 2½ HOURS

Central Melbourne is a warren of 19th-century arcades and cobbled laneways featuring street art, basement restaurants, boutiques and bars.

Start on **1 Degraves St**, an archetypal street lined with interesting shops and cafes. Grab a coffee at Degraves Espresso, then continue north, crossing over Flinders Lane to cafe-and-art-filled **2 Centre Place**.

Cross Collins St, turn left and enter the **3 Block Arcade** (p63); built in 1891 with ornate mosaic floors, it's based on Milan's Galleria Vittorio Emanuele II arcade. Ogle Hopetoun Tea Rooms' windows before continuing through the arcade, turning left and exiting onto Elizabeth St.

At the next corner cross the road and turn right into Little Collins St. Pause for an afternoon tipple at kooky **4 Chuckle Park** (p112), then continue on and turn left into wonderfully ornate **5 Royal Arcade** (p59); look out for Gog and Magog under the dome. Wander through to Bourke St Mall, then turn right and continue until you find **6 Union Lane** on the right.

Follow Union Lane to the end, turn left onto Little Collins St, then take a right on Swanston St. Walk past **7 Melbourne Town Hall** (p54), on the other side of Swanston St, and pop into the 1932 **8 Manchester Unity Building** for its impressive foyer, then cross Swanston St and head uphill to the 'Paris End' of Collins St. You'll pass the 1873 Gothic **9 Scots Church** (the first Presbyterian church in Victoria) and the 1866 **10 St Michael's Uniting Church**, built in Lombardic Romanesque style.

Turn right into Exhibition St, then right into Flinders Lane, and continue until you see **11 Duckboard Place**. Head down the laneway and take your time to soak up the street art before bending around into AC/DC Lane, past rock 'n' roll dive bar Cherry.

Continue on down Flinders Lane to the street-art meccas of **12 Hosier Lane** (p51) and Rutledge Lane before finishing with tapas and a hard-earned drink at MoVida.

likely to run for several years. By late 2017 the fruit and vegetable traders should have moved into a striking new glass pavilion on Queen St.

Various tours are run from the market, including heritage, cultural and foodie tours; check the website for details.

Hellenic Museum MUSEUM

(Map p56; ☎03-8615 9016; www.hellenic.org.au; 280 William St; adult/child $10/5; ⏰10am-4pm Tue-Sun; 🚊Flagstaff) Housed in a beautiful neoclassical building that was formerly the Royal Mint, this small museum is dedicated to Greek immigrants who moved here in the 1950s and the contribution they've made to the city – Melbourne has the largest Greek population of any city outside Greece. Until 2024 the museum is playing host to *Gods, Myths & Monsters*, an extraordinary treasure trove of artefacts from Athens' Benaki Museum.

Flagstaff Gardens PARK

(Map p56; btwn William, La Trobe, Dudley & King Sts; 🚊Flagstaff) Originally known as Burial Hill, these gardens were the site of Melbourne's first cemetery, where eight of the city's early settlers were buried. Today its pleasant open lawns are popular with workers taking a lunchtime break. The gardens contain trees that are well over 100 years old, including Moreton Bay figs and a variety of eucalypts, among them spotted, sugar and river red gums. There are plenty of possums about, but don't feed them.

Koorie Heritage Trust CULTURAL CENTRE

(Map p56; ☎03-8662 6300; www.koorieheritagetrust.com; Yarra Building, Federation Sq; tours adult/child $33/17; ⏰10am-5pm; 🚊Flinders St) FREE Devoted to southeastern Aboriginal culture, this centre houses interesting artefacts and oral history. There's a shop and gallery downstairs while, upstairs, carefully preserved significant objects can be viewed in display cases and drawers. It also runs hour-long tours along the Yarra during summer, evoking the history and memories that lie beneath the modern city (book online).

Immigration Museum MUSEUM

(Map p56; ☎13 11 02; www.museumvictoria.com.au/immigrationmuseum; 400 Flinders St; adult/child $14/free; ⏰10am-5pm; 🚋55) The Immigration Museum uses voices, images and memorabilia to tell the many stories of Australian immigration. It's symbolically housed in the old Customs House, and the restored 1876 building alone is worth a visit: the Long Room is a magnificent piece of Italian Renaissance–revival architecture.

After exiting the museum, head across the river via Sandridge Bridge to check out the steel **Travellers sculptures**, which depict the story of arrival that belongs to many Melburnians; *Gayip*, the only sculpture to sit on land rather than on the bridge, represents Indigenous Australians from the area.

Sea Life AQUARIUM

(Map p56; ☎1800 026 576; www.melbourneaquarium.com.au; cnr Flinders & King Sts; adult/child/family $46/26/99; ⏰9.30am-6pm; 👪; 🚋35, 70, 75) This interesting but extremely pricey aquarium is home to giant rays, gropers and sharks, all of which cruise around a 2.2-million-litre tank, watched closely by visitors in a see-through tunnel. Gentoo and king penguins potter about in icy 'Antarctica', while one of Australia's largest saltwater crocs casts a menacing eye over his lair. Divers are thrown to the sharks three times a day; for a mere $299 you can join them. Tickets are cheaper online.

St Patrick's Cathedral CHURCH

(Map p65; ☎03-9662 2233; www.stpatrickscathedral.org.au; 1 Cathedral Pl, East Melbourne; ⏰9am-5pm Mon-Fri; 🚊Parliament) Designed by William Wardell, Melbourne's Catholic cathedral is among the world's finest examples of Gothic Revival architecture and the largest church building in Australia. Building began in 1858 and continued until the spires were added in 1939. The imposing bluestone exterior and grounds are but a preview of its contents: inside are several tonnes of bells, an organ with 4500 pipes, ornate stained-glass windows, and exquisite mosaics in the Blessed Sacrament chapel.

Nicholas Building NOTABLE BUILDING

(Map p56; www.thenicholasbuilding.blogspot.co.nz; 31-41 Swanston St; 🚊Flinders St) Designed by Harry Norris in 1926, this classical palazzo in terracotta tile was built as a demonstration of the wealth of the Nicholas family. Today the building is full of artists' studios and designers. Having managed to escape being turned into apartments, it's one of the few unrenovated buildings of its type left in the city. Call into the Cathedral Arcade downstairs to admire the arched stained-glass ceiling.

Tolarno Galleries GALLERY

(Map p56; ☎03-9654 6000; www.tolarnogalleries.com; 4th fl, 104 Exhibition St; ⏰10am-5pm Tue-Fri, 1-5pm Sat; 🚉Parliament) FREE Tolarno was an integral player in Melbourne's most famous midcentury artistic marriage: that between Georges and Mirka Mora. The gallery was once raucously bohemian, but now, many years and several sites later, it's a serious, cerebral, contemporary space, with exhibitions changing monthly. It's not well signed; look for it in the art-deco Centenary Hall building.

Block Arcade NOTABLE BUILDING

(Map p56; ☎03-9654 5244; www.theblock.com.au; 282 Collins St; 🚉Flinders St) This beautiful Victorian shopping arcade was built in 1891 and features ornate plasterwork and mosaic floors. Doing 'the Block' (walking around the block) was a popular pastime in 19th-century Melbourne, as it was the place to shop and be seen.

West Space GALLERY

(Map p56; ☎03-9662 3297; www.westspace.org.au; 1st fl, 225 Bourke St; ⏰noon-6pm Tue-Sat; 🚋86, 96) FREE One of Melbourne's oldest nonprofit, artist-run galleries, West Space has a varied exhibition schedule featuring young and emerging artists. Expect a range of mediums, from traditional forms to digital technologies and highly conceptual installations; push the buzzer for admittance.

Anna Schwartz Gallery GALLERY

(Map p56; ☎03-9654 6131; www.annaschwartzgallery.com; 185 Flinders Lane; ⏰noon-6pm Tue-Fri, 1-5pm Sat; 🚉Flinders St) FREE Redoubtable Anna Schwartz keeps some of the city's most respected contemporary artists in her stable, as well as representing midcareer names from around the country. The work is often fiercely conceptual.

Southbank & Docklands

The reinvention of Southbank as a glitzy tourist precinct is so complete that it's hard to imagine that, before the 1980s, it was a gritty industrial zone supporting a major port. Now its pleasant riverside promenade is peppered with famous restaurants and hotels, while the presence of some of the city's top arts institutions makes it an essential part of any Melbourne itinerary. To the city's west, the once working wharves of Docklands have given birth to a mini city of apartments, offices, restaurants, plazas, public art and parks.

★NGV International GALLERY

(☎03-8662 1555; www.ngv.vic.gov.au; 180 St Kilda Rd, Southbank; ⏰10am-5pm; 🚉Flinders St) FREE Housed in a vast, brutally beautiful, bunker-like building, the international branch of the National Gallery of Victoria has an expansive collection that runs the gamut from the ancient to the bleeding edge. Regular blockbuster exhibitions (prices vary) draw the crowds, and there are free 45-minute highlights tours at 11am and 1pm daily, and hour-long tours at midday and 2pm.

Key works include a Rembrandt self-portrait, Tiepolo's *The Banquet of Cleopatra* and Turner's otherworldly *Falls of Schaffhausen*. It's also home to Picasso's *Weeping Woman*, which was the victim of an art heist in 1986. The 1st floor is given over to Asian art, with exquisite pieces from China, Japan, India and Southeast Asia. The gallery also has an excellent decorative arts and furniture collection, which is showcased alongside contemporaneous paintings rather than being quarantined in its own section.

Designed by architect Sir Roy Grounds, the NGV building was controversial when it was completed in 1967 but has come to be respected as a modernist masterpiece. Make sure you wander through the foyer to the Great Hall, with its extraordinary stained-glass ceiling, and continue out onto the sculpture lawn.

The NGV's Australian art collection is on display at the Ian Potter Centre (p50) at nearby Federation Sq.

Eureka Skydeck VIEWPOINT

(Map p56; ☎03-9693 8888; www.eurekaskydeck.com.au; 7 Riverside Quay, Southbank; adult/child $20/12, Edge extra $12/8; ⏰10am-10pm; 🚉Flinders St) Melbourne's tallest building, the 297m-high Eureka Tower was built in 2006, and a wild elevator ride takes you to its 88 floors in less than 40 seconds (check out the photo on the elevator floor if there's time). The Edge – a slightly sadistic glass cube – cantilevers you out of the building; you've got no choice but to look down.

Australian Centre for Contemporary Art GALLERY

(ACCA; ☎03-9697 9999; www.accaonline.org.au; 111 Sturt St, Southbank; ⏰10am-5pm Tue-Sun; 🚋1) FREE ACCA is one of Australia's most exciting and challenging contemporary galleries, showcasing the work of a range of local and international artists. The building is, fittingly, sculptural, with a rusted exterior evoking the factories that once stood on the site, and a soaring interior designed to house often massive installations.

Polly Woodside SHIP

(☎03-9699 9760; www.pollywoodside.com.au; 21 South Wharf Promenade, South Wharf; adult/child/family $16/9.50/43; ⏰10am-4pm Sat & Sun, daily school holidays; 🚊12, 96, 109) The *Polly Woodside* is a restored iron-hulled tall ship, dating from 1885, that now rests in a basin off the Yarra River. A glimpse of the rigging makes for a tiny reminder of what the Yarra would have looked like in the 19th century, dense with ships at anchor.

Arts Centre Melbourne ARTS CENTRE

(☎1300 182 183; www.artscentremelbourne.com.au; 100 St Kilda Rd, Southbank; ⏰box office 9am-8.30pm Mon-Fri, 10am-5pm Sat; 🚆Flinders St) The Arts Centre is made up of two separate buildings, Hamer Hall and the **Theatres Building** (under the spire, including a free gallery space with changing exhibitions), linked by a series of landscaped walkways. Tours of the theatres and exhibitions leave daily at 11am (adult/child $20/15); the Sunday tour includes the backstage areas.

Melbourne Star VIEWPOINT

(☎03-8688 9688; www.melbournestar.com; 101 Waterfront Way, Docklands; adult/child $36/22; ⏰11am-7.30pm Sun-Thu, to 9pm Fri & Sat May–mid-Sep, to 10pm mid-Sep–Apr; 🚊35, 70, 86) Joining the London Eye and Singapore Flyer, this giant observation wheel has glass cabins that take you up 120m for 360-degree views of the city, Port Phillip Bay and even further afield to Geelong and the Dandenongs. Rides last 30 minutes. For an extra $10 you can head back for another ride at night to see the bright lights of the city.

Richmond & East Melbourne

Melbourne is one of the world's great sporting cities, and Richmond and East Melbourne are the absolute nexus for all things sporting. The neighbourhood's southeastern skyline is dominated by the angular shapes of sporting stadia, none more hulking than the mighty Melbourne Cricket Ground. North from here are the genteel streets of East Melbourne, centred on pretty Fitzroy Gardens. Taking up the eastern flank, Richmond is a part-gentrified, part-gritty residential and commercial expanse peppered with interesting eateries, both budget and top end.

★ **Melbourne Cricket Ground** STADIUM

(MCG; Map p65; ☎03-9657 8888; www.mcg.org.au; Brunton Ave, East Melbourne; tour adult/child/family $23/12/55, incl museum $32/16/70; ⏰tours 10am-3pm; 🚆Jolimont) With a capacity of 100,000 people, the 'G' is one of the world's great sporting venues, hosting cricket in summer and AFL (Australian Football League; Aussie rules) footy in winter. For many Australians it's considered hallowed ground. Make it to a game if you can (highly recommended), but otherwise you can still make your pilgrimage on nonmatch-day **tours** that take you through the stands, media and coaches' areas, change rooms and members' lounges. The MCG houses the state-of-the-art **National Sports Museum.**

The stadium is ringed by gigantic sporting sculptures facing the tidy lawns of Yarra Park. Also look out for the **scarred tree**, whose bark was removed in pre-colonial times by the local Wurundjeri people for artisanal purposes.

National Sports Museum MUSEUM

(Map p65; ☎03-9657 8879; www.nsm.org.au; Gate 3, MCG, Brunton Ave, East Melbourne; adult/child/family $23/12/55; ⏰10am-5pm; 🚆Jolimont) Hidden away in the bowels of the Melbourne Cricket Ground, this sports museum features exhibits focusing on Australia's favourite sports and historic sporting moments. Kids will love the interactive section where they can test their footy, cricket or netball skills. There's even a hologram of cricketer Shane Warne.

Objects on display include the handwritten notes used to define the rules of Australian Rules football in 1859; a collection of baggy green caps worn by a who's who of Aussie cricket (including the legendary Don Bradman); olive branches awarded to Edwin Flack, Australia's first Olympic medallist, in 1886; various Olympic medals; and sprinter Cathy Freeman's famous Sydney Olympics swift suit.

Fitzroy Gardens PARK

(Map p65; www.fitzroygardens.com; Wellington Pde, East Melbourne; 🚆Jolimont) The city drops away suddenly just east of Spring St, giving way to Melbourne's beautiful backyard, Fitzroy Gardens. The park's stately avenues are lined with English elms, flowerbeds, expansive lawns, strange fountains and a creek. A highlight is Cooks' Cottage (p66), which belonged to the parents of navigator Captain James Cook. The cottage was shipped brick by brick from Yorkshire and reconstructed here in 1934. Nearby is a **visitor centre** (Map

East Melbourne & Richmond

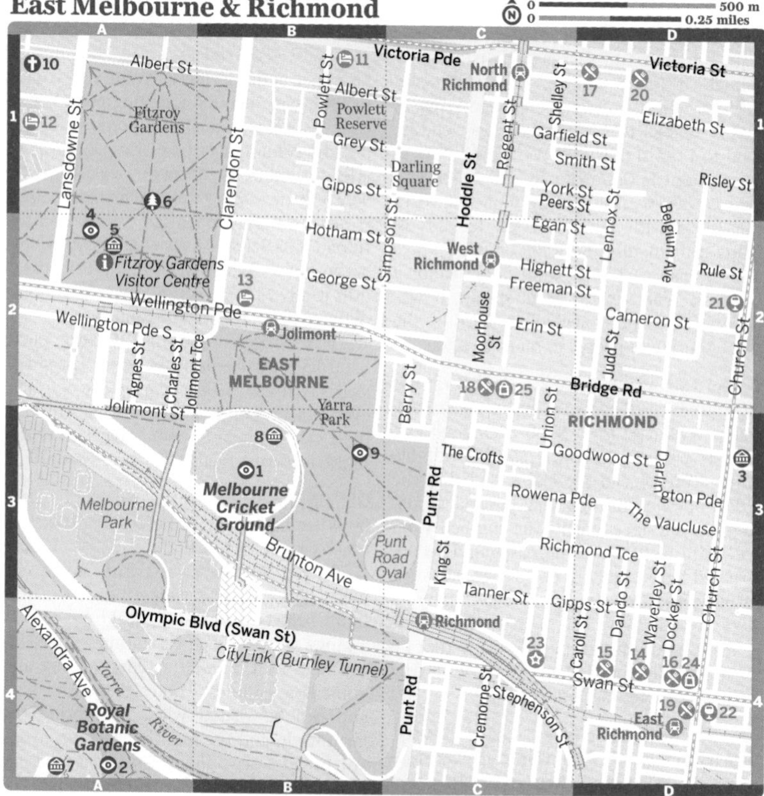

East Melbourne & Richmond

Top Sights

1 Melbourne Cricket Ground B3
2 Royal Botanic Gardens A4

Sights

3 Charles Nodrum Gallery D3
4 Conservatory A2
5 Cooks' Cottage A2
6 Fitzroy Gardens A1
7 Government House A4
8 National Sports Museum B3
9 Scarred Tree B3
10 St Patrick's Cathedral A1

Sleeping

11 Aberlour Court B1
12 Park Hyatt A1
13 Pullman Melbourne on the Park B2

Eating

14 Demitri's Feast D4
15 Meatball & Wine Bar D4
16 Meatmother D4
17 Minh Minh D1
18 Richmond Hill Cafe & Larder C2
19 Sabai D4
20 Thy Thy D1

Drinking & Nightlife

21 DT's Hotel D2
22 Public House D4

Entertainment

23 Corner C4
Melbourne Cricket Ground .... (see 1)

Shopping

24 Lily & the Weasel D4
25 Pookipoiga C2

p65; ☎03-9658 9658; www.thatsmelbourne.com.au; ⏰9am-5pm) with a cafe attached and the delightful 1930s **Conservatory**.

In the centre of the gardens is a cutesy miniature **Tudor village**. This well-meaning gift was a London pensioner's way of saying thanks to Melburnians for sending food to Britain during WWII. Right next to it is writer Ola Cohn's kooky carved **Fairies' Tree**, a 300-year-old stump embellished in the 1930s with fairies, pixies, kangaroos, emus and possums. Between Cooks' Cottage and the Fairies Tree is what is known as a **Scarred Tree**: now a large stump, it was once stripped of a piece of its bark by the local Aboriginal people to make a canoe.

Cooks' Cottage HISTORIC BUILDING
(Map p65; Fitzroy Gardens, Wellington Pde, East Melbourne; adult/child/family $6.50/3.50/18; ⏰9am-5pm; Jolimont) Built in 1755, this humble family cottage can lay claim to being the oldest building in Australia, but that's sidestepping the fact that it was shipped from Yorkshire in 253 packing cases and reconstructed here in 1934. The cottage belonged to navigator Captain James Cook's parents later in their lives. The great explorer never lived here himself, but it's likely that he visited it. Buy your tickets from the nearby visitor centre to take a look inside.

Charles Nodrum Gallery GALLERY
(Map p65; ☎03-9427 0140; www.charlesnodrumgallery.com.au; 267 Church St, Richmond; ⏰11am-6pm Tue-Sat; 48, 75, 78) Situated in a lovely old house, this quality commercial gallery specialises in the Australian abstract and alternative art movements from the 1950s to the 1970s.

Fitzroy, Collingwood & Abbotsford

A short tram ride from the city centre delivers you to the doorstep of some of the hippest enclaves in Melbourne, where up-to-the-minute eateries and midcentury furniture stores sit comfortably next to century-old classic pubs and divey live-music venues. Fitzroy, Melbourne's first suburb, and Collingwood have long had a reputation for vice and squalor and, despite ongoing gentrification, there's still enough grit holding these areas in check. Beyond Collingwood is largely industrial Abbotsford, bordered by a scenic stretch of the Yarra River, where more cafes and restaurants have started sprouting.

Abbotsford Convent HISTORIC SITE
(☎03-9415 3600; www.abbotsfordconvent.com.au; 1 St Heliers St, Abbotsford; tours $15; ⏰7.30am-10pm; 200, 207, Victoria Park) FREE The nuns are long gone at this former convent, which dates to 1861, but today its rambling collection of ecclesiastical architecture is home to a thriving arts community of galleries, studios, eateries (including the **Convent Bakery** (☎03-9419 9426; www.conventbakery.com; mains $10-20; ⏰7am-5pm) and vegetarian **Lentil as Anything** (☎03-9419 6444; www.lentilasanything.com; by donation; ⏰9am-9pm;) and a bar, spread over nearly 7 hectares of riverside land. Tours of the complex run at 2pm Sunday.

There's a Slow Food Market every fourth Saturday, a **clothes market** (www.shirtandskirtmarkets.com.au; ⏰10am-4pm 3rd Sun of month) every third Sunday, and during summer there's the popular Supper Market on Friday night, featuring food stalls and live music.

Collingwood Children's Farm FARM
(www.farm.org.au; 18 St Heliers St, Abbotsford; adult/child/family $10/5/20; ⏰9.15am-4.30pm; 200, 207, Victoria Park) The inner city melts away at this rustic riverside retreat that's beloved not just by children. There's a range of frolicking farm animals that kids can help feed, as well as cow milking and guinea-pig cuddles! The cafe opens at 9am and can be visited without entering the farm itself, and the monthly **farmers market** (www.mfm.com.au/markets/collingwood-childrens-farm; adult/child $2/free; ⏰8am-1pm 2nd Sat of month) is a local highlight.

Yarra Bend Park PARK
(www.parkweb.vic.gov.au; Yarra Blvd, Fairfield; Victoria Park) Escape the city without leaving town in this large area of native bushland flanking the river, about 5km northeast of the city centre. It's an area cherished by runners, rowers, cyclists, picnickers and strollers. You can hire rowing boats, canoes and kayaks from the Studley Park Boathouse (p80), which has a kiosk, cafe and restaurant, and BBQ facilities nearby.

Carlton Brewhouse BREWERY
(☎03-9420 6800; www.carltonbrewhouse.com.au; cnr Nelson & Thompson Sts, Abbotsford; tours adult/concession $29/25; 109, 12) Foster's beer-brewing empire runs 1½-hour tours of its Abbotsford operations, where you'll encounter enormous 30m-wide vats of beer and a superfast bottling operation – and yes: samples are included in the price. Tours run daily; times vary, so check the website.

WORTH A TRIP

HEIDE MUSEUM OF MODERN ART

The former home of John and Sunday Reed, **Heide Museum of Modern Art** (☎03-9850 1500; www.heide.com.au; 7 Templestowe Rd, Bulleen; adult/child $22/18; ⏲10am-5pm Tue-Sun; 🚌903, 🚆Heidelberg) is a prestigious not-for-profit art gallery with a sculpture garden in its wonderful grounds. It holds regularly changing exhibitions, many of which include works by the famous artists that called Heide home, including Sir Sidney Nolan and Albert Tucker. The collection is spread over three buildings: a large purpose-built gallery, the Reeds' original farmhouse and the wonderful modernist house they built in 1963 as 'a gallery to be lived in'.

There's a cafe, or you can pack a picnic to eat by the Yarra. The free tours (Tuesday 2pm) are a great introduction to Melbourne's 20th-century painting scene.

Bulleen is 14km northeast of the city centre.

Visitors need to be aged over 18 and wear closed-toed shoes. Bookings essential.

Centre for Contemporary Photography GALLERY
(CCP; Map p68; ☎03-9417 1549; www.ccp.org.au; 404 George St, Fitzroy; ⏲11am-5pm Wed-Fri, noon-5pm Sat & Sun; 🚋86) FREE This not-for-profit centre exhibits contemporary photography exhibitions across five galleries. Shows traverse traditional techniques and the highly conceptual, and exhibitions change approximately every six weeks. There's a particular fascination with work involving video projection, including a nightly after-hours screening in a window, which can be seen at the corner of George and Kerr Sts.

Gertrude Contemporary Art Space GALLERY
(Map p68; ☎03-9419 3406; www.gertrude.org.au; 200 Gertrude St, Fitzroy; ⏲11am-5.30pm Tue-Fri, to 4.30pm Sat; 🚋86) This nonprofit gallery and studio complex has been going strong for nearly 30 years; many of its alumni are now certified famous artists. The monthly exhibition openings often see crowds spilling out onto the street. The gallery will be relocating in mid-2017, and its new venue is yet to be confirmed. Also check out its new space nearby, **Glasshouse**.

Alcaston Gallery GALLERY
(Map p68; ☎03-9418 6444; www.alcastongallery.com.au; 11 Brunswick St, Fitzroy; ⏲10am-6pm Tue-Fri, 11am-5pm Sat; 🚋11) FREE Set in an imposing boom-style terrace, the Alcaston showcases international and Australian art, with a focus on the work of living Indigenous Australian artists. The gallery works directly with Indigenous communities and is particularly attentive to cultural sensitivities; it shows a wide range of styles from traditional to contemporary. Check the website for exhibitions.

Backwoods Gallery GALLERY
(☎03-9041 3606; www.backwoods.gallery; 25 Easey St, Collingwood; ⏲noon-6pm Tue-Sun; 🚋86) Set up in 2010 by a team of Melbourne street artists, the Backwoods Gallery promotes and exhibits works by Australian and international artists, with a focus on urban contemporary art, stencil, street art and illustration in its warehouse space in a Collingwood backstreet.

Keith Haring Mural PUBLIC ART
(Smith St, Collingwood; 🚋86) Anyone with an interest in street art will want to check out the Keith Haring mural, painted by the late New York artist on his visit in 1984. It adorns the side of the former Collingwood Technical School next door to The Tote (p122) on Johnston St.

Gertrude Glasshouse GALLERY
(www.gertrude.org.au; 44 Glasshouse Rd, Collingwood; ⏲noon-5pm Tue-Sat; 🚋109, 86) Established in 2015, this architecturally designed, versatile project space is the newest venue for the **Gertrude Contemporary gallery**, giving artists undertaking the gallery's Studio Artists program the chance to exhibit new work during their tenure.

James Makin Gallery GALLERY
(Map p68; ☎03-9416 3966; www.jamesmakingallery.com; 67 Cambridge St, Collingwood; ⏲11am-5pm Wed-Sat; 🚋86, 109) Set in an inspiring converted warehouse in the backstreets of Collingwood, the James Makin Gallery showcases innovative contemporary works by a largely Australian roster of artists across a mix of mediums from painting and printmaking to sculpture and photography.

Fitzroy & Around

Fitzroy & Around

Sights

1 Alcaston Gallery B7
2 Australian Galleries D7
3 Centre for Contemporary Photography C3
4 Gertrude Contemporary Art Space C6
5 James Makin Gallery D6

Activities, Courses & Tours

6 Fitzroy Swimming Pool C1

Sleeping

7 Brooklyn Arts Hotel C7
8 Home @ The Mansion A7
9 Melbourne Metropole Central B6
10 Nunnery A5
11 Tyrian Serviced Apartments B3

Eating

12 Añada C6
13 Archie's All Day C6
14 Babka Bakery Cafe B2
15 Belle's Hot Chicken C6
16 Charcoal Lane B6
17 Cutler & Co A6
18 Gelato Messina D4
19 Hinoki Japanese Pantry D4
20 Horn D3
21 Hotel Jesus D5
22 Huxtaburger D6
23 IDES D6
24 Lazerpig D6
25 Lune Croissanterie B2
26 Marios B3
27 Po' Boy Quarter D3
28 Project Forty Nine D5
29 Robert Burns Hotel D3
30 Saint Crispin D4
31 Smith & Daughters B5
32 Smith & Deli B4
33 Smith Street Alimentari D4
34 South of Johnston D6
35 Transformer B2
36 Vegie Bar B2

Drinking & Nightlife

37 Bar Liberty C3
38 Bar Open B3
39 Black Pearl B3
40 Craft & Co D2
41 Everleigh B6
42 Forester's Hall D6
43 Grace Darling D6
44 Industry Beans B2
45 Marion A6
46 Naked for Satan B3
47 Napier Hotel C4
48 Noble Experiment D4
49 Panama Dining Room & Bar D5
50 Proud Mary D5
51 Sircuit D6
52 Standard Hotel A4
53 Union Club Hotel C5

Entertainment

54 Gasometer D1
55 Night Cat B3
56 Old Bar B3
57 Workers Club B6
58 Yah Yah's D6

Shopping

59 Aesop D6
60 Brunswick Street Bookstore B3
61 Crumpler D6
62 Ess B6
63 Gorman B4
64 Happy Valley D4
65 Mud Australia C6
66 Northside C6
67 Obüs C6
68 Poison City Records B2
69 Polyester Records B2
70 Rose Street Artists' Market B2
71 Smith Street Bazaar D4
72 SpaceCraft C6
73 Tanner + Teague B3
74 Third Drawer Down C6

Australian Galleries GALLERY

(Map p68; 03-9417 4303; www.australiangalleries.com.au; 35 Derby St, Collingwood; 10am-6pm; 86) Around since the 1950s, this gallery in the backstreets of Collingwood showcases contemporary Australian art with monthly-changing exhibitions. Across the road is its stock room, with a huge, varied collection (also open 10am to 6pm).

Carlton & Brunswick

Home to Melbourne's Italian community and the University of Melbourne, Carlton dishes up a heady mix of intellectual activity, espresso and excellent food – the same things that lured bohemians to the area in the 1950s. You'll see the *tricolori* unfurled with characteristic passion come soccer finals and the Grand Prix.

Head west to multicultural-meets-hipster Brunswick to feast on Middle Eastern cuisine along Sydney Rd before bar-hopping home.

★**Melbourne Museum** MUSEUM

(Map p71; 13 11 02; www.museumvictoria.com.au; 11 Nicholson St, Carlton; adult $14, child & student free, exhibitions extra; 10am-5pm;

Tourist Shuttle, City Circle, 86, 96, Parliament) This museum provides a grand sweep of Victoria's natural and cultural histories, incorporating dinosaur fossils, giant-squid specimens, a taxidermy hall, a 3D volcano and an open-air forest atrium of Victorian flora. Become immersed in the legend of champion racehorse and national hero Phar Lap. The excellent **Bunjilaka**, on the ground floor, presents Indigenous Australian stories and history told through objects and Aboriginal voices with state-of-the-art technology. There's also an **IMAX cinema**.

★ Royal Exhibition Building HISTORIC BUILDING

(Map p71; 13 11 02; www.museumvictoria.com.au/reb; 9 Nicholson St, Carlton; tours adult/child $10/7; Tourist Shuttle, City Circle, 86, 96, Parliament) Built for the 1880 International Exhibition, and winning Unesco World Heritage status in 2004, this beautiful Victorian edifice symbolises the glory days of the Industrial Revolution, the British Empire and 19th-century Melbourne's economic supremacy. It was the first building to fly the Australian flag, and Australia's first parliament was held here in 1901; it now hosts everything from trade fairs to car shows, as well as the biennial Melbourne Art Fair. Tours of the building leave from Melbourne Museum (opposite) at 2pm.

Ian Potter Museum of Art GALLERY

(Map p71; 03-8344 5148; www.art-museum.unimelb.edu.au; Melbourne University, 800 Swanston St, Parkville; 10am-5pm Tue-Fri, noon-5pm Sat & Sun; 6, 8, 72) FREE The Ian Potter Museum of Art manages Melbourne University's extensive art collection, which ranges from antiquities to contemporary Australian work. It's a thoughtfully designed space and always has an exciting exhibition program. Pick up the *Sculpture on Campus* map here for a walking tour taking in Melbourne Uni's sculptures, set amid heritage-listed buildings.

Grainger Museum MUSEUM

(Map p71; 03-8344 5270; www.grainger.unimelb.edu.au; Gate 13, Melbourne University, Royal Pde, Parkville; noon-4pm Sun-Fri; 19) FREE A tribute to one of Australia's great musical exports, this museum housed in an art deco building lays bare the fascinating life of Percy Grainger. Leaving Australia aged nine, Grainger became an internationally renowned composer and pianist in Europe and the USA, as well as a forerunner in experimental music. Exhibits from all points of his life are on display, from his sound machines to a collection of fetish whips.

Melbourne General Cemetery CEMETERY

(03-9349 3014; www.mgc.smct.org.au; College Cres, Parkville; 8am-6pm Apr-Sep, to 8pm Oct-Mar; 1, 8) Melbourne has been burying its dead in this cemetery since 1852. It's worth a stroll to see the final resting place of three Australian prime ministers, the ill-fated explorers Burke and Wills, Walter Lindrum's billiard-table tombstone and a shrine to Elvis erected by fans. Check the website about guided day and night tours.

University of Melbourne UNIVERSITY

(Map p71; 03-8344 4000; www.unimelb.edu.au; Grattan St, Carlton; 6, 8, 72) The esteemed University of Melbourne was established in 1853 and remains one of Australia's most prestigious universities. Its blend of Victorian Gothic stone buildings, midcentury international-style towers and postmodern showpieces provides a snapshot of changing architectural aspirations. The campus sprawls from Carlton through to the neighbouring suburb of Parkville, and its extensive grounds house the university colleges. Most notable is the Walter Burley Griffin–designed **Newman College**. Pick up a *Sculpture on Campus* map from the **Ian Potter Museum of Art**.

Museo Italiano MUSEUM

(Map p71; 03-9349 9000; www.museoitaliano.com.au; 199 Faraday St, Carlton; 10am-5pm Tue-Fri, noon-5pm Sat; Tourist Shuttle, 1, 8) FREE Telling the story of Melbourne's Italian community, this museum offers a good starting point to put the history of Lygon St into both historical and contemporary context.

Ceres CULTURAL CENTRE

(03-9389 0100; www.ceres.org.au; cnr Roberts & Stewart Sts, East Brunswick; 9am-5pm, cafe 9am-3pm Mon-Fri, to 4pm Sat & Sun; 96) FREE Ceres, the name of the Roman goddess of agriculture and fertility, also stands for Centre for Education & Research in Environmental Strategies, a two-decades-old community environment built on a former rubbish tip. Stroll around the permaculture and bush-food nursery before refuelling with an organic homemade chai and lunch at Merri Table cafe.

There's a grocery store and community market where you can buy organic and backyard-produced goodies, and the info centre

Carlton & Around

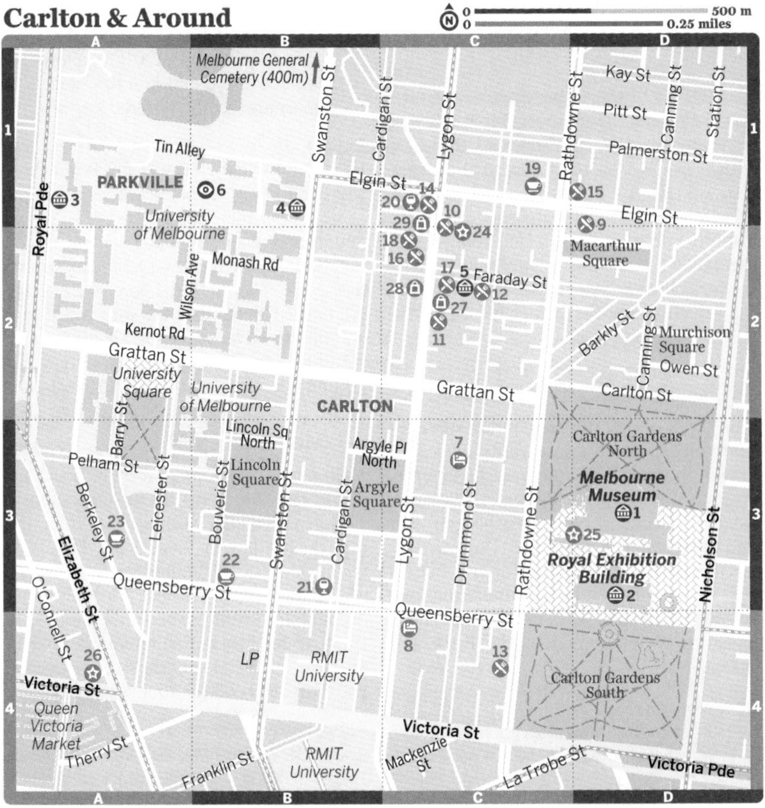

Carlton & Around

Top Sights

1 Melbourne Museum D3
2 Royal Exhibition Building D3

Sights

3 Grainger Museum A1
4 Ian Potter Museum of Art B1
5 Museo Italiano C2
6 University of Melbourne B1

Sleeping

7 169 Drummond C3
8 Downtowner on Lygon C4

Eating

9 Abla's D1
10 Brunetti C2
D.O.C Delicatessen .... (see 11)
11 D.O.C Espresso C2
12 D.O.C Pizza & Mozzarella Bar C2
13 Epocha C4
14 Heartattack and Vine C1
15 Longhorn Saloon D1
Milk the Cow .... (see 14)
16 Pidapipo C2
17 Shakahari C2
18 Tiamo C2

Drinking & Nightlife

19 Campos Coffee C1
20 Jimmy Watson's C1
21 Lincoln B3
22 Queensberry Pourhouse B3
23 Seven Seeds A3

Entertainment

24 Cinema Nova C2
25 Imax D3
La Mama .... (see 17)
26 Last Chance Rock & Roll Bar A4

Shopping

27 Gewürzhaus C2
28 Poppy Shop C2
29 Readings C1

has a great bookstore on sustainability-related matters and organic gardening.

Counihan Gallery GALLERY

(☎03-9389 8622; www.moreland.vic.gov.au/events-recreation/arts-and-gallery/counihan-gallery-in-brunswick; Brunswick Town Hall, 233 Sydney Rd, Brunswick; ⏲11am-5pm Wed-Sat, 1-5pm Sun; 19, Jewell, Brunswick) FREE While strolling down Sydney Rd, drop into this contemporary art gallery inside the Brunswick Town Hall. Named after Australian activist and artist Noel Counihan, the focus here is on political, social and cultural themes, and the gallery presents challenging ideas and works.

North Melbourne & Parkville

This strip of central Melbourne stretches from the shabby railway yards and gridlocked thoroughfares of West Melbourne, through the surprisingly quiet Victorian neighbourhood of North Melbourne and into the ample green spaces of Parkville.

The big attraction here is the zoo, but it's also worth stopping by to sample the low-key neighbourhood pubs, eateries and shops of North Melbourne's Victoria, Errol and Queensberry Sts.

★ **Melbourne Zoo** ZOO

(☎1300 966 784; www.zoo.org.au; Elliott Ave, Parkville; adult/child $33/17, children weekends & holidays free; ⏲8am-5pm; ; Royal Park) Established in 1861, this compact zoo is the oldest in Australia and the third oldest in the world. It remains one of the city's most popular attractions and it continues to innovate, recently becoming the world's first carbon-neutral zoo. Set in prettily landscaped gardens, the zoo's enclosures aim to simulate the animals' natural habitats and give them the option to hide if they want to (the gorillas and the tigers are particularly good at playing hard to get).

There's a large collection of native animals in natural bush settings, a platypus aquarium, fur seals, plenty of reptiles, and an entire faux–South East Asian jungle village built around the elephant enclosures. In some cases walkways pass through the enclosures: you can stroll through some of the aviaries and enter a tropical hothouse full of colourful butterflies. See if you can pass through Lemur Island without an internal soundtrack of 'I like to move it, move it' turning over in your mind. Sadly, the lion enclosure remains out of bounds.

In summer, the zoo hosts twilight concerts, while from September to May **Roar 'n' Snore** (adult/child $190/150) allows you to camp at the zoo and join the keepers on their morning feeding rounds.

Royal Park PARK

(Elliott Ave, Parkville; Royal Park) Royal Park's vast open spaces are perfect for a run or power walk, and there are sports fields, netball and hockey stadiums, a golf course and tennis courts. In the northwestern section of the park, Trin Warren Tam-boore is a recently established wetlands area, with boardwalks and interpretive signs for spotting native plants and animals. There's also a great playground near the Royal Children's Hospital.

Melbourne's West

Melbourne's remaining working docklands divide the city from the western suburbs. This once solidly working-class area has, over the last 15 years or so, started to attract young professional families taking advantage of its cute cottages, cheaper prices and sense of community. Venture here for multicultural feasts, technology-driven museums, bohemian bars, one of Melbourne's better beaches and a distinctly off-the-tourist-path feel.

Williamstown Beach BEACH

(Esplanade, Williamstown; Williamstown Beach) Forget St Kilda – the pleasant lopsided grin of coarse golden sand at Williamstown is a much more appealing place for a dip. It has its own surf-lifesaving club, and a swimming pool down one end and a pavilion at the other.

HMAS Castlemaine SHIP

(☎03-9397 2363; www.hmascastlemaine.org.au; Gem Pier, Williamstown; adult/child $6/3; ⏲noon-4pm Sat & Sun; Williamstown) Take a look around the last of 60 Australian-built Bathurst Class corvettes still afloat. This one did time as an escort ship and minesweeper along the Australian coast, New Guinea, Timor and the Philippines during WWII.

Scienceworks MUSEUM

(☎13 11 02; www.museumvictoria.com.au/scienceworks; 2 Booker St, Spotswood; adult/child $14/free, plus Planetarium & Lightning Room $10/6; ⏲10am-4.30pm; Spotswood) Incorporating an old brick sewage-pumping station that resembles a French chateau, this engrossing museum keeps inquisitive grey matter occupied with interactive displays. Figure out the mysteries of the universe (or your own

WORTH A TRIP

WERRIBEE ZOO & RAAF MUSEUM

A 225-hectare, African-safari-style experience run by Melbourne Zoo, **Werribee Open Range Zoo** (☎1300 966 784; www.zoo.org.au/werribee; K Rd, Werribee South; adult/child $33/17; ⏲9am-5pm, last entry 3.30pm; 🚌439, 🚆Werribee)is located a 30-minute drive down the Princes Hwy en route to the Great Ocean Road. Admission includes a 45-minute safari tour, where you'll see grazing rhinos, giraffes, antelopes and zebras on savannah-like plains. The walking trail has enclosures for lowland gorillas, lions, hippos, cheetahs and meerkats, among others.

Down the road is Point Cook, birthplace of the Royal Australian Air Force. It's now home to the **RAAF Museum** (www.airforce.gov.au/raafmuseum/; RAAF Base Williams, Point Cook Rd, Point Cook; ⏲10am-3pm Tue-Fri, to 5pm Sat & Sun; 🚌497, 🚆Williams Landing) FREE, an essential visit for aviation fans and war buffs. There's plenty of awesome aircraft on display to enthrall kids and adults alike, from flimsy box-kite planes to sleek F-111 fighters. There's also a comprehensive exhibit on Australia at war, featuring memorabilia such as shrapnel from the Red Baron's German plane, shot down by Australians in WWI. The museum is located at the RAAF Williams base, so you'll need to bring ID.

If you don't have a car, **Werribee Park Shuttle** (☎03-9748 5094; www.werribeeparkshuttle.com.au; departs NGV Australia, 180 St Kilda Rd; return adult/child $35/25) departs from NGV International in Melbourne at 9.20am, heading to the above sights and returning to Melbourne around 3pm. Bookings are essential.

anatomy) by poking buttons, pulling levers, lifting flaps and learning all sorts of weird facts. The planetarium splashes the universe onto a 16m-domed ceiling during 40-minute shows.

South Melbourne, Port Melbourne & Albert Park

The well-heeled trio of South Melbourne, Port Melbourne and Albert Park isn't short on lunching ladies, AFL stars and Porsche-steering Lotharios living it up in grandiose Victorian terraces and bayside condos. Leafy and generally sedate, the area boasts some of Melbourne's most beautiful heritage architecture, both civic and domestic. South Melbourne is the busiest neighbourhood, with a bustling market, cult-status cafes and sharply curated design stores. Albert Park offers culture in a former gasworks, while Port Melbourne's home to Station Pier, from where ferries shoot south to Tasmania.

South Melbourne Market MARKET

(☎03-9209 6295; www.southmelbournemarket.com.au; cnr Coventry & Cecil Sts, South Melbourne; ⏲8am-4pm Wed, Sat & Sun, to 5pm Fri; 🚊12, 96) Trading since 1864, this market is a neighbourhood institution, its labyrinthine guts packed with a brilliant collection of stalls selling everything from organic produce and deli treats to hipster specs, art and crafts. The place is famous for its dim sims (sold here since 1949), and there's no shortage of atmospheric eateries. From early January to late February, there's a lively night market on Thursday. The site is also home to a cooking school – see the website for details.

Albert Park Lake LAKE

(btwn Queens Rd, Fitzroy St, Aughtie Dr & Albert Rd, Albert Park; 🚊96) Elegant black swans give their inimitable bottoms-up salute as you jog, cycle or walk the 5km perimeter of this constructed lake. Lakeside Dr was used as an international motor-racing circuit in the 1950s, and since 1996 the revamped track has been the venue for the **Australian Formula One Grand Prix** (☎1800 100 030; www.grandprix.com.au; Albert Park Lake, Albert Park; tickets from $55; ⏲Mar) each March. Also on the periphery is the Melbourne Sports & Aquatic Centre (p81), with an Olympic-size pool and child-delighting wave machine.

St Vincent Place ARCHITECTURE

(St Vincent Pl, Albert Park; 🚊1) For a taste of Victorian-era finery, take a stroll in St Vincent Pl, a heritage precinct in Albert Park. Consisting of a long, arch-shaped street skirting a central landscaped garden, it's considered Australia's finest example of a 19th-century residential square. The street itself is flanked by some of Melbourne's grandest Victorian terraces, many of which date to the 1860s. Such elegance and boldness reflect Melbourne's blooming confidence during the gold rush. The precinct is 700m south of South Melbourne Market.

Gasworks Arts Park ARTS CENTRE
(☎03-8606 4200; www.gasworks.org.au; cnr Graham & Pickles St, Albert Park; tours adult/child $25/15; ⏲tours 10.30am & 2pm Mon-Thu; 🚊1, 109) This former gas plant lay derelict from the 1950s before finding new purpose in life as an arts precinct, with red-brick galleries, a **theatre company** (check website for shows) and ultra-dog-friendly parkland. You can meet the artists on a guided tour or come for the **farmers market** (third Saturday of each month). The venue also hosts an **open-air cinema** season, usually in November.

South Yarra, Prahran & Windsor

South Yarra, Prahran and Windsor are Melbourne's perennial cool kids: fashion obsessed, body conscious and party loving. While the South Yarra end of Chapel St has sold its soul to high-street chains, the Prahran and Windsor end rocks with of-the-moment eateries, bars, boutiques and street art that pull trendy, eye-candy crowds. Kissing South Yarra's northwestern edge are Melbourne's showpiece Botanic Gardens, while Prahran itself is home to an extraordinary private house museum of art.

★ **Royal Botanic Gardens** GARDENS
(Map p65; www.rbg.vic.gov.au; Birdwood Ave, South Yarra; ⏲7.30am-sunset; 🚌Tourist Shuttle, 🚊1, 3, 5, 6, 8, 16, 64, 67, 72) FREE Melbourne's Royal Botanical Gardens are simply glorious, a 94-acre green lung in the middle of the city. Drawing over 1.5 million visitors annually, the gardens are considered one of the finest examples of Victorian-era landscaping in the world. You'll find a global selection of plantings and endemic Australian flora. Mini ecosystems, such as a cacti and succulents area, a herb garden and an indigenous rainforest, are set amid vast lawns.

In summer the gardens play host to Moonlight Cinema (p122) and theatre performances. Other features include the 19th-century **Melbourne Observatory** (☎03-9252 2429; adult/child/family $24/20/70; ⏲tours by appointment 9pm Mon; 🚊3, 5, 6, 8, 16, 64, 67, 72) for tours of the night sky, and the excellent, nature-based **Ian Potter Foundation Children's Garden** (☎03-9252 2300; www.rbg.vic.gov.au/visit-melbourne/attractions/children-garden; ⏲10am-dusk Wed-Sun, daily Victorian school holidays; 🚊8), a whimsical, child-scaled place that invites kids and their parents to explore, discover and imagine.

The **visitor centre** (☎03-9252 2429; Observatory Gate, Birdwood Ave, South Yarra; ⏲9am-5pm Mon-Fri, from 9.30am Sat & Sun; 🚌Tourist Shuttle, 🚊3, 5, 6, 8, 16, 64, 67, 72) is the departure point for tours, some of which are free and all of which should be booked by calling ahead (see the website for details). Close by, the National Herbarium, established in 1853, contains over a million dried botanical specimens used for plant-identification purposes.

For visitors who can't get enough, the Royal Botanical Gardens has recently developed the **Australian Garden** (☎03-5990 2220; www.rbg.vic.gov.au; 1000 Ballarto Rd, Cranbourne; ⏲9am-5pm; 🚌796, 🚆Cranbourne) FREE in the outlying suburb of Cranbourne.

Shrine of Remembrance MONUMENT
(☎03-9661 8100; www.shrine.org.au; Birdwood Ave, South Yarra; ⏲10am-5pm; 🚌Tourist Shuttle, 🚊3, 5, 6, 8, 16, 64, 67, 72) FREE One of Melbourne's icons, the Shrine of Remembrance is a commanding memorial to Victorians killed in WWI. Built between 1928 and 1934, much of it with Depression-relief, or 'susso' (sustenance), labour, its stoic, classical design is partly based on the Mausoleum of Halicarnassus, one of the seven ancient wonders of the world. The shrine's upper balcony affords epic panoramic views of the Melbourne skyline and all the way up tram-studded Swanston St.

The shrine itself draws thousands to its annual Anzac Day (25 April) dawn service, while the Remembrance Day service at 11am on 11 November commemorates the signing of the 1918 Armistice marking the formal end to WWI. At this precise moment a shaft of light shines through an opening in the ceiling, passing over the Stone of Remembrance and illuminating the word 'love'; on all other days this effect is demonstrated using artificial lighting on the hour.

With its cenotaph and eternal flame (lit by Queen Elizabeth II in 1954), the forecourt was built as a memorial to those who died in WWII, and several other specific memorials surround the shrine. Below the shrine, a stunningly conceived architectural space houses the Galleries of Remembrance, a museum dedicated to telling the story of Australians at war via its 800-plus historical artefacts and artworks.

The complex is under 24-hour police guard; during opening hours the police are quaintly required to wear uniforms resembling those worn by WWI light-horsemen. Download the free Shrine of Remembrance app for a self-guided tour, or consider joining the **free guided tours** daily at 11am and 2pm, often conducted by returned soldiers.

Government House HISTORIC BUILDING
(Map p65; ☎03-9656 9889; www.nationaltrust.org.au; Kings Domain, South Yarra; tours $18; ⏱tours 10am Mon & Thu; Tourist Shuttle, 1, 3, 5, 6, 8, 16, 64, 67, 72) On the outer edge of the Botanic Gardens, the Italianate Government House dates to 1872. A replica of Queen Victoria's Osborne House on England's Isle of Wight, it has served as the residence of all Victorian governors, as well as being the royal pied-à-terre. Unfortunately, the two-hour tour of the property is only available to groups of 10 or more. Tours should be booked at least two weeks ahead, by phone or email.

Como House HISTORIC BUILDING
(Map p76; ☎03-9827 2500, tour bookings 03-9656 9889; www.nationaltrust.org.au; cnr Williams Rd & Lechlade Ave, South Yarra; adult/child/family $15/9/35; ⏱gardens 9am-5pm Mon-Sat, from 10am Sun, house tours 11am, 12.30pm & 2pm Sat & Sun; 8) A wedding cake of Australian Regency and Italianate architecture, this elegant colonial residence is among Melbourne's heritage royalty. Dating to 1840, it houses numerous belongings of the high-society Armytage family, the last and longest owners, who lived in the house for 95 years. House tours run every Saturday and Sunday and tickets can be purchased online or by phone.

The **Stables of Como** (p107) cafe, located in the former stables, can pack a picnic hamper for you to enjoy on the stately lawns; it also hosts high tea.

Herring Island PARK
(Map p76; http://parkweb.vic.gov.au/explore/parks/herring-island; Alexandra Ave, South Yarra; 605, 8, 78) This prelapsarian river island is a sanctuary for the Yarra's original trees, grasses and indigenous animals. Within is an impressive collection of environmental sculpture, including work by Brit Andy Goldsworthy and numerous Australian artists, among them Julie Collins, Robert Jacks, Robert Bridgewater, John Davis and Ellen José. There are designated picnic and BBQ areas. On summer weekends, a Parks Victoria punt operates from Como Landing on Alexandra Ave in South Yarra; at other times you'll need a kayak to get here.

Prahran Market MARKET
(Map p76; ☎03-8290 8220; www.prahranmarket.com.au; 163 Commercial Rd, South Yarra; ⏱7am-5pm Tue & Thu-Sat, 10am-3pm Sun; 72, 78, Prahran) Prahran Market is a Melbourne institution, whetting appetites since 1881. While much of the current structure dates to the 1970s and '80s, the Commercial Rd facade – designed by Charles D'Ebro in a Queen Anne–revival style – dates to 1891. Grab a speciality coffee from Market Lane (p120) and trawl stalls heaving with organic produce, seafood, meat, handmade pasta, gourmet deli items and more. The market is also home to culinary store and cooking school **Essential Ingredient** (Map p76; ☎03-9827 9047; www.essentialingredient.com.au; Prahran Market, Elizabeth St, South Yarra; classes $175-275).

★**Justin Art House Museum** GALLERY
(JAHM; Map p76; ☎0411 158 967; www.jahm.com.au; cnr Williams Rd & Lumley Ct, Prahran; adult/child $25/free; ⏱by appointment; 5, 6, 64) The geometric, zinc-clad home of Melbourne art collectors Charles and Leah Justin doubles as the Justin Art House Museum. Book ahead for a private tour of the couple's dynamic collection of contemporary art, consisting of more than 250 pieces amassed over four decades. There's a strong emphasis on video and digital art, with the works rotated regularly. Guided tours take around two hours. The house was designed by the couple's daughter, Elisa.

Artists Lane PUBLIC ART
(Map p76; Artists Lane, Windsor; 5, 6, 64, 78, Windsor) Running parallel to Chapel St is Artists Lane (Aerosol Alley to south-siders), a long bluestone alley soaked in street art. The project was initiated by artist Wayne Tindall, who started by painting himself and his wife outside his studio in the laneway before getting other artists involved, with the blessing of the local council. In the corner of the car park that spills off the laneway, look out for childlike human-animal hybrids by internationally renowned Melbourne artist Kaff-eine.

St Kilda

St Kilda is Melbourne's slightly tattered bohemian heart, a place where a young Nick Cave played gloriously chaotic gigs at the George Hotel (formerly the Crystal Ballroom) and a place featured in countless songs, plays, novels, TV series and films.

South Yarra, Prahran & Windsor

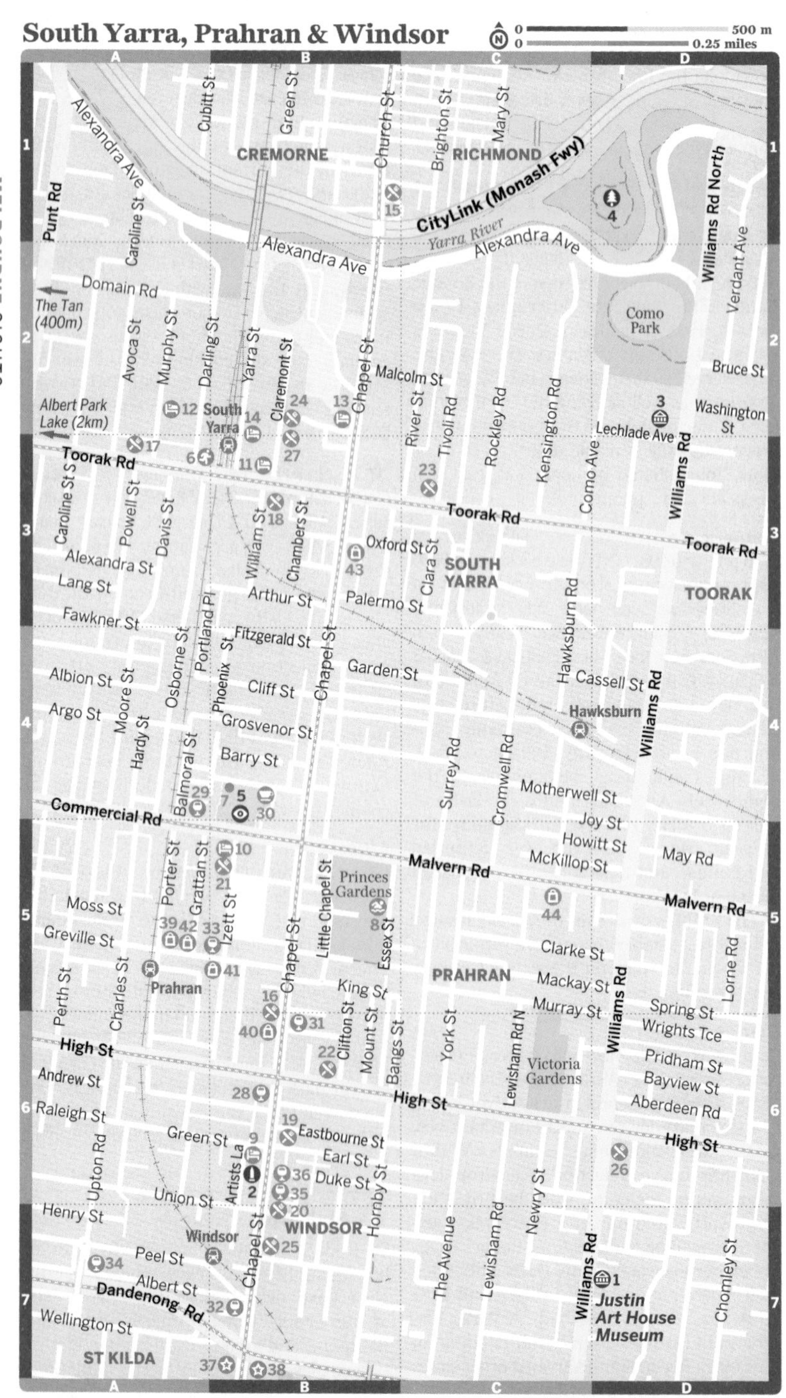

South Yarra, Prahran & Windsor

Top Sights
1 Justin Art House Museum.......D7

Sights
2 Artists Lane.......B6
3 Como House.......D2
4 Herring Island.......D1
5 Prahran Market.......B4

Activities, Courses & Tours
6 Aesop Spa.......A3
7 Essential Ingredient.......B4
8 Prahran Aquatic Centre.......B5

Sleeping
9 Back of Chapel.......B6
10 Cullen.......B5
11 Hotel Claremont.......B3
12 Lyall.......A2
13 Olsen.......B2
14 Punthill South Yarra Grand.......B2

Eating
15 Baby.......B1
16 Colonel Tan's.......B5
17 Da Noi.......A3
18 Drugstore Espresso.......B3
19 Fonda.......B6
20 Hawker Hall.......B7
21 HuTong Dumpling Bar.......B5
22 Huxtaburger.......B6
Stables of Como.......(see 3)
23 Tivoli Road Bakery.......C3
24 Two Birds One Stone.......B3
25 Uncommon.......B7
26 WoodLand House.......D6
27 Zumbo.......B2

Drinking & Nightlife
28 Borsch, Vodka & Tears.......B6
29 Emerson.......A4
30 Market Lane Coffee.......B4
31 Montereys.......B6
32 Railway Hotel.......B7
Revolver Upstairs.......(see 16)
33 Rufus.......B5
34 Windsor Castle Hotel.......A7
35 Woods of Windsor.......B6
36 Yellow Bird.......B6

Entertainment
37 Astor.......B7
38 Red Stitch Actors Theatre.......B7

Shopping
39 ArtBoy Gallery.......A5
40 Chapel Street Bazaar.......B6
41 Greville Records.......B5
42 Lunar Store.......A5
43 Scanlan Theodore.......B3
44 Shelley Panton.......C5
Signed & Numbered.......(see 33)
Third Drawer Down.......(see 33)

Starting life as a 19th-century seaside resort, the neighbourhood has played many roles: post-war Jewish enclave, red-light district, punk-rocker hub and real-estate hot spot. It's a complex, hypnotic jumble of boom-style Victorian mansions, raffish Spanish Moorish apartments, seedy side streets, cosmopolitan wine bars, crusty pubs, rickety roller coasters and nostalgia-inducing theatres.

St Kilda Foreshore BEACH
(Map p78; Jacka Blvd, St Kilda; 3, 12, 16, 96) Despite the palm-fringed promenades and golden stretch of sand, St Kilda's seaside appeal is more Brighton, England, than Venice, LA. The kiosk at the end of St Kilda Pier is as much about the journey as the destination: the pier offers a knockout panorama of the Melbourne skyline.

During summer **Port Phillip EcoCentre** (Map p78; 03-9534 0670; www.ecocentre.com; 55a Blessington St, St Kilda) runs a range of tours, including urban wildlife walks and coastal discovery walks, and offers information on the little-penguin colony that lives in the breakwater behind the pier's kiosk.

On the foreshore south of the pier, the Moorish-style St Kilda Sea Baths (p81) houses a heated indoor saltwater pool, but, at $13 a dip, it's really only attractive on frosty days. Behind it, the Esplanade is home to Sunday art-and-craft staple **St Kilda Esplanade Market** (p133).

St Kilda Pier PIER
(Map p78; Jacka Blvd, St Kilda; 3, 12, 16, 96) Jutting out over the bay, St Kilda Pier offers a smashing view of the Melbourne skyline (best seen at sunset). The Edwardian-style kiosk at the end of the pier is a replica of the original, which burnt down in 2003, a year short of its centenary. Behind it, the breakwater is home to a colony of **little penguins**. Visit them at dusk, but if you're taking photos of them, don't use your flash.

The breakwater was built in the 1950s as a safe harbour for boats competing in the Olympic Games.

St Kilda

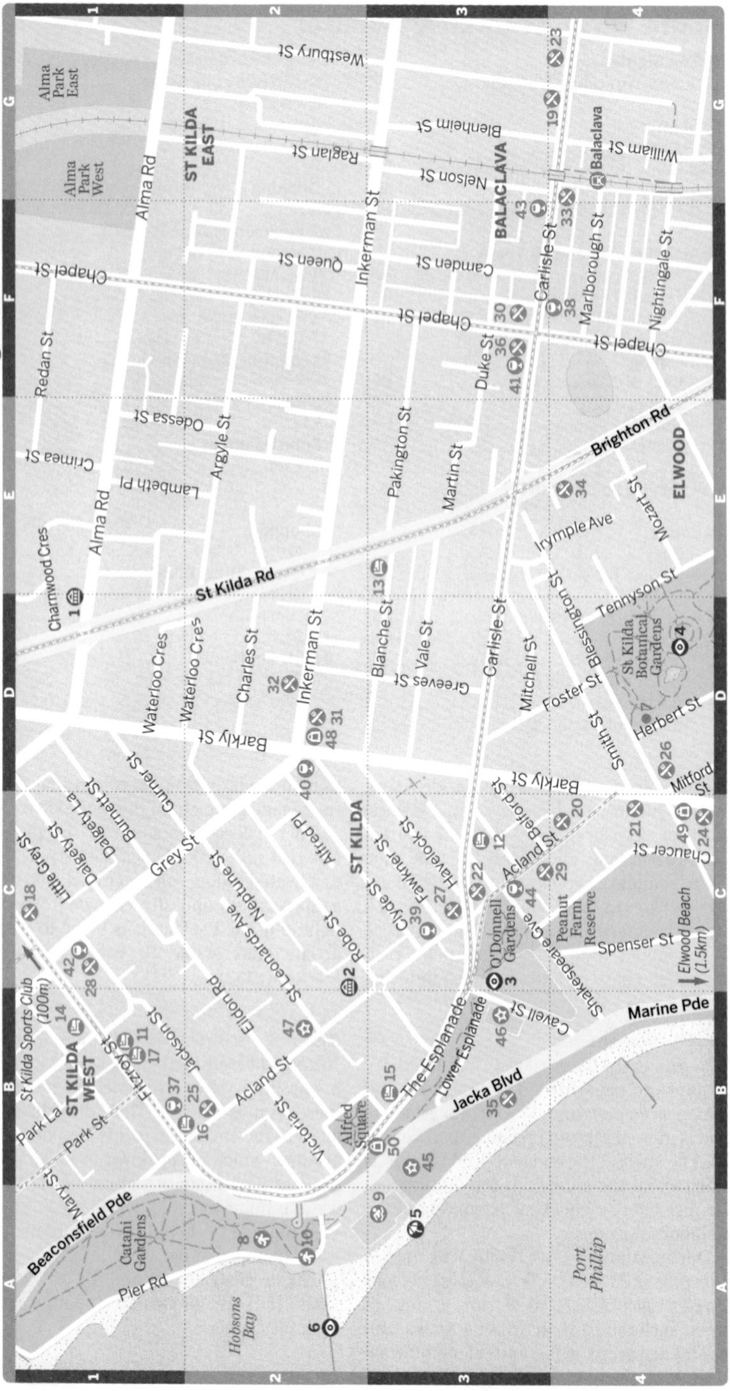

Port Phillip
Hobsons Bay
Catani Gardens
Beaconsfield Pde
Pier Rd
Mary St
Park La
Park St
ST KILDA WEST
St Kilda Sports Club (100m)
Fitzroy St
Jackson St
Little Grey St
Dalgety St
Dalgety La
Burnett St
Gurner St
Grey St
Eildon Rd
St Leonards Ave
Neptune St
Acland St
Victoria St
Alfred Square
The Esplanade
Lower Esplanade
Jacka Blvd
Marine Pde
Cavell St
O'Donnell Gardens
Shakespeare Gve
Peanut Farm Reserve
Spenser St
Elwood Beach (1.5km)
Robe St
Clyde St
Fawkner St
Havelock St
Alfred Pl
ST KILDA
Chaucer St
Acland St
Belford St
Barkly St
Mitford St
Herbert St
Smith St
St Kilda Botanical Gardens
Foster St
Blessington St
Tennyson St
Mitchell St
Carlisle St
Greeves St
Vale St
Blanche St
Inkerman St
Charles St
Waterloo Cres
Barkly St
St Kilda Rd
Charnwood Cres
Alma Rd
Lambeth Pl
Crimea St
Argyle St
Odessa St
Redan St
Chapel St
Pakington St
Martin St
Irymple Ave
Mozart St
ELWOOD
Brighton Rd
Duke St
Chapel St
Nightingale St
Marlborough St
Camden St
Queen St
BALACLAVA
Balaclava
William St
Nelson St
Raglan St
ST KILDA EAST
Blenheim St
Westbury St
Alma Park West
Alma Park East

0 — 500 m
0 — 0.25 miles

1 2 3 4 5 6 7 8 9 10 11 12 13 14 15 16 17 18 19 20 21 22 23 24 25 26 27 28 29 30 31 32 33 34 35 36 37 38 39 40 41 42 43 44 45 46 47 48 49 50

A B C D E F G
1 2 3 4

St Kilda & Around

Sights

1 Jewish Museum of Australia D1
2 Linden New Art C2
3 Luna Park C3
4 St Kilda Botanical Gardens D4
5 St Kilda Foreshore A3
6 St Kilda Pier A2

Activities, Courses & Tours

Aurora Spa Retreat .... (see 16)
Kite Republic .... (see 9)
7 Port Phillip EcoCentre D4
8 Royal Melbourne Yacht Squadron A2
9 St Kilda Sea Baths A3
10 Stand Up Paddle HQ A2

Sleeping

11 Abode St Kilda B1
12 Base C3
13 Habitat HQ E3
14 Hotel Tolarno B1
15 Novotel St Kilda B3
16 Prince B2
17 Rydges St Kilda B1

Eating

18 Banff C1
19 Batch Espresso G4
20 Cicciolina C4
21 Claypots C4
22 Galleon Cafe C3
23 Glick's G4
24 I Carusi II C4
25 Lau's Family Kitchen B2
26 Lentil as Anything D4
27 Matcha Mylkbar C3
28 Miss Jackson C1
29 Monarch Cake Shop C3
30 Monk Bodhi Dharma F3
31 Mr Wolf D2
32 Newmarket Hotel D2
33 Si Señor G4
34 St Kilda Dispensary E4
35 Stokehouse B3
36 Uncle F3

Drinking & Nightlife

37 Bar Di Stasio B1
38 Carlisle Wine Bar F4
39 Dogs Bar C3
40 Hotel Barkly D2
41 Local Taphouse F3
42 Misery Guts C1
43 Pause Bar F3
Pontoon .... (see 35)
Republica .... (see 9)
44 Vineyard C3

Entertainment

45 Ben & Jerry's Openair Cinemas B3
46 Palais Theatre B3
Prince Bandroom .... (see 16)
47 Theatre Works B2

Shopping

48 Bitch Is Back D2
49 Dot Herbey C4
Readings .... (see 20)
50 St Kilda Esplanade Market B3

Linden New Art — GALLERY

(Map p78; ☎03-9534 0099; www.lindenarts.org; 26 Acland St, St Kilda; ⏰11am-4pm Tue & Thu-Sun, to 8pm Wed; 🚊3, 12, 16, 96) Housed in a wrought iron–clad 1870s mansion, Linden mainly champions new contemporary art by midcareer artists. The annual postcard show (generally held from late October to January) is a highlight.

Luna Park — AMUSEMENT PARK

(Map p78; ☎03-9525 5033; www.lunapark.com.au; 18 Lower Esplanade, St Kilda; single ride adult/child $11/10, unlimited rides $50/40; ⏰hrs vary; 🚊3, 16, 96) Luna Park opened in 1912 and still has the feel of an old-style amusement park, with creepy Mr Moon's gaping mouth swallowing you up as you enter. There's a heritage-listed 'scenic railway' (the oldest operating roller coaster in the world), a beautifully baroque carousel with hand-painted horses, swans and chariots, as well as the full complement of gut-churning rides.

St Kilda Botanical Gardens — GARDENS

(Map p78; ☎03-9209 6777; www.portphillip.vic.gov.au; cnr Blessington & Tennyson Sts, St Kilda; ⏰sunrise-sunset, conservatory 10.30am-3.30pm Mon-Fri, sunrise-sunset Sat & Sun; 🚊96,) Taking pride of place on the southern line of the Barkly, Carlisle and Blessington St triangle, the Botanical Gardens are an unexpected haven from the St Kilda hustle. Wide gravel paths invite a leisurely stroll, and there are plenty of shady spots to sprawl on the open lawns. Features include local indigenous plants, a subtropical-rainforest conservatory and a giant chessboard for large-scale plotting.

Jewish Museum of Australia — MUSEUM

(Map p78; ☎03-9834 3600; www.jewishmuseum.com.au; 26 Alma Rd, St Kilda; adult/child/family $10/5/20; ⏰10am-4pm Tue-Thu, to 3pm Fri, to 5pm Sun, closed Jewish holy days; 🚊3, 67) Interactive displays tell the history of Australia's Jewish community from the earliest days of European settlement, while permanent exhibitions celebrate Judaism's rich cycle of festivals and holy days. The museum also has a good curatorial reputation for its contemporary art exhibitions. By car, follow St Kilda Rd from St Kilda Junction, then turn left at Alma Rd.

Jewish Holocaust Centre MUSEUM
(03-9528 1985; www.jhc.org.au; 13-15 Selwyn St, Elsternwick; by donation; 10am-4pm Mon-Thu, to 2pm Fri, noon-4pm Sun; 67, Elsternwick) FREE Dedicated to the memory of the six million Jews who lost their lives during the Holocaust, this well-presented museum was set up by survivors as a sobering reminder of the atrocities they endured. Guided tours are available, often led by Holocaust survivors themselves.

Activities

Boating, Canoeing & Kayaking

★ **Kayak Melbourne** KAYAKING
(Map p56; 0418 106 427; www.kayakmelbourne.com.au; Alexandra Gardens, Boathouse Dr, Southbank; tours $82-110; 11, 48) Ninety-minute City Sights tours paddle past Southbank to Docklands, while two-hour River to Sky tours include entry to the Eureka Skydeck (p63). You can also start your day saluting the sun on a two-hour Yoga Sunrise tour, or end it with a 2½-hour Moonlight tour starting from Docklands.

Studley Park Boathouse BOATING, CANOEING
(03-9853 1828; www.studleyparkboathouse.com.au; 1 Boathouse Rd, Kew; 2-person vessel per hr $36; 9am-5pm) Melbourne's oldest operating boathouse dates back to the 1860s, and has a restaurant, a kiosk and a cafe. There are rowing boats, canoes and kayaks available for hire.

Royal Melbourne Yacht Squadron BOATING
(RMYC; Map p78; 03-9534 0227; www.rmys.com.au; Pier Rd, St Kilda; 3, 16, 96) Here anyone can have a go on a yacht ($20) on Wednesday night during daylight-saving time (October to April); arrive by 4.30pm. Wear nonmarking shoes (with white soles) and bring sunscreen and waterproof gear. In winter, races take place on Wednesday afternoon, so you'll need to arrive by noon. Races also take place most Saturdays, though times vary; call ahead.

Running

Princes Park RUNNING
(Princes Park Dr, North Carlton; 19) Joggers and walkers pound the 3.2km gravel path around the perimeter of the park, while cricket, soccer and dog walking fill up the centre. It's the former home of the Carlton Football Club (and its current training ground).

Tan RUNNING
(Royal Botanic Gardens, Birdwood Ave, South Yarra; Tourist Shuttle, 8) What was once a horse-exercising track is now the city's most famous running spot, stretching 3.8km around the Royal Botanic Gardens and King's Domain. Join the daily stream of fitness freaks and eye-candy fans for a pulse-raising serve of daily Melbourne life.

Wellness & Relaxation

Japanese Bath House BATHHOUSE
(03-9419 0268; www.japanesebathhouse.com; 59 Cromwell St, Collingwood; bath $32, shiatsu 30/60min $48/82; 11am-last entry 8pm Tue-Fri, last entry 6pm Sat & Sun; 109) Urban as the setting is, it's as serene as can be inside this authentic *sentō* (bathhouse). Partake in some communal skinship (it's nude, segregated bathing), a shiatsu and a postsoak sake or tea in the tatami lounge. Bookings are recommended and there's a useful how-to guide on the website for the uninitiated.

Aurora Spa Retreat SPA
(Map p78; 03-9536 1130; www.aurorasparetreat.com; 2 Acland St, St Kilda; 1hr massage $175; 10am-6pm Mon, Tue, Thu & Fri, 11.30am-7.30pm Wed, 9am-5.30pm Sat, 10am-3pm Sun; 3, 12, 16, 96) Treatments at this chichi oasis inside the Prince hotel (p91) range from body massages and exfoliations to facials, manicures and pedicures. The award-winning Kitya Karnu signature treatment ($225) is especially popular, consisting of an hour of scrubbing, rubbing and smoothing in a private steam room. Treatments lasting two or more hours attract a 30% discount Monday to Thursday.

Aesop Spa SPA
(Map p76; 03-9866 5250; www.aesop.com/au/facialappointments; 153 Toorak Rd, South Yarra; 60/75min treatment $175/220; by appointment 10am-4pm Wed-Sun; 8, South Yarra) Melbourne's most famous skincare brand takes it up a notch at its South Yarra store, with a dedicated space for sophisticated

pampering. Each of the six basic treatments – from the Lactate Surge to the Detox Anew – is tailored to your skin using specially developed active ingredients from concentrated formulations. A perfect pick-me-up before hitting the South Yarra scene.

Chuan Spa SPA

(Map p56; ☎03-8696 8111; www.chuanspa.com.au; Langham Hotel, 1 Southgate Ave, Southbank; 75min $199; ⏰6am-9pm Mon-Fri, 8am-9pm Sat & Sun; 🚂Flinders St) A spin-off from the Hong Kong spa of the same name, Chuan has a Chinese-garden ambience and focuses on the principles of traditional Chinese medicine. It offers a full range of beauty and relaxation treatments.

Swimming

Fitzroy Swimming Pool SWIMMING

(Map p68; ☎03-9205 5180; 160 Alexandra Pde, Fitzroy; adult/child/under 5yr $6.50/3.30/free; ⏰6am-9pm Mon-Thu, to 8pm Fri, 8am-6pm Sat & Sun; 🚋11) Between laps, locals love catching a few rays up in the bleachers or on the lawn; there's also a toddler pool.

Melbourne Sports & Aquatic Centre SWIMMING

(MSAC; ☎03-9926 1555; www.msac.com.au; Albert Rd, Albert Park; adult/child from $8.20/5.60; ⏰5.30am-10pm Mon-Fri, 7am-8pm Sat & Sun; 🚋96, 112) Flanking Albert Park Lake (p73), Melbourne's premier aquatic centre was a venue for the 2006 Commonwealth Games. Facilities include indoor and outdoor 50m pools, an indoor 25m pool, a wave pool, water slides, a spa, sauna and steam room, and spacious common areas. Childcare is available.

Prahran Aquatic Centre SWIMMING

(Map p76; ☎03-8290 7140; www.facebook.com/prahranaquaticcentre; 41 Essex St, Prahran; adult/child $6.20/3.50; ⏰5.45am-7.45pm Mon-Fri, 6am-6.15pm Sat, 7am-6.15pm Sun; 🚋72, 78, 🚂Prahran) More than just a 50m heated outdoor pool, this place is a total scene in summer, with no shortage of buffed south-side bods soaking up some rays on the poolside lawn. Centre facilities include a spa, a sauna, a steam room and (in summer) a toddler pool.

St Kilda Sea Baths SWIMMING

(Map p78; ☎03-9525 4888; www.stkildaseabaths.com.au; 10-18 Jacka Blvd, St Kilda; pool adult/child $13/6; ⏰5am-10.45pm Mon-Thu, to 9.45pm Fri, 7am-7.45pm Sat & Sun; 🚋3, 16, 96) South of St Kilda Pier, the Moorish-style sea baths contains cafes and restaurants, a gym and a pricey 25m saltwater pool best enjoyed on chilly days.

Melbourne City Baths SWIMMING

(Map p56; ☎03-9658 9011; www.melbourne.vic.gov.au/mcb; 420 Swanston St; adult/child $6.40/3.80; ⏰6am-10pm Mon-Thu, to 8pm Fri, 8am-6pm Sat & Sun; 🚂Melbourne Central) When they first opened in 1860, these public baths were intended to stop people bathing in and drinking from the seriously polluted Yarra River. The current baroque-style building dates from 1903 and boasts the city centre's largest pool (30m).

Water Sports

Kite Republic KITESURFING

(Map p78; ☎03-9537 0644; www.kiterepublic.com.au; St Kilda Sea Baths, 4/10-18 Jacka Blvd, St Kilda; 1hr lesson $90; ⏰10am-6pm Mon-Fri, to 5pm Sat & Sun; 🚋96) Offers kiteboarding lessons, tours and

MELBOURNE FOR FREE

City Circle Trams (p85) Heritage trams that loop around the free tram zone, which covers the entire central city.

Koorie Heritage Trust (p62) Cultural centre devoted to southeastern Aboriginal culture.

Federation Square (p50) 'Fed Square' is a popular gathering spot and home to two significant free museums.

Australian Centre for the Moving Image (p50) A visual feast that pays homage to Australian cinema and TV.

State Library of Victoria (p60) A great place to browse or check out an exhibition.

Wheeler Centre (p125) A unique literary centre with free lunchtime talks.

Greeter Service (Map p56; ☎03-9658 9658; www.thatsmelbourne.com.au; ⏰9.30am; 🚂Flinders St) FREE Offers a free volunteer-run two-hour orientation tour; bookings required.

1

WAYNE FOGDEN / GETTY IMAGES ©

4

MAYDAYS / GETTY IMAGES ©

1. Southbank pedestrian bridge over the Yarra River
Stroll along and through Melbourne CBD, to experience the city's culture and architecture.

2. Beach huts at Brighton Beach
Melbourne's beach suburbs offer the perfect getaway, just a tram ride away from the city.

3. Graffiti art in Hosier Lane (p51)
Melbourne's network of laneways and alleys are bedecked in colourful street art.

4. Aerial view of Melbourne's CBD (p51)
Melbourne lights up at night and keeps bustling until the early hours; plunge into its wealth of dining and nightlife options.

PATJO / SHUTTERSTOCK ©

equipment; also a good source of info. In winter it can arrange snow-kiting at Mt Hotham. Also rents stand-up paddleboards (SUPs).

Stand Up Paddle HQ WATER SPORTS
(Map p78; ☎0416 184 994; www.supb.com.au; St Kilda Pier, St Kilda; hire per hr $30, 1½hr tour $99; 96) Arrange a lesson or hire SUP equipment from St Kilda Pier, or join its Yarra River tour.

Golf

Albert Park Golf Course GOLF
(☎03-9510 5588; www.albertparkgolf.com.au; Queens Rd, Albert Park; 18 holes weekdays/weekend $34/39, driving range 50/100 balls $9.90/17.90; golf course dawn-dusk, driving range 10am-10pm Mon, 7am-10pm Tue-Fri, 7am-9pm Sat & Sun; 3, 5, 6, 16, 64, 67) This 18-hole championship golf course is set on the fringes of Albert Park Lake, just 2km from the city. Located alongside the Australian Formula One Grand Prix racing circuit, a separate driving range (www.albertparkdrivingrange.com.au) allows golfers to hit off from 65 two-tier all-weather bays.

Royal Melbourne Golf Club GOLF
(☎03-9599 0500; www.royalmelbournegc.com; Cheltenham Rd, Black Rock; 922, Sandringham) This 36-hole course has been rated as one of the best in the world; it's played host to the Australian Open over a dozen times.

Lawn Bowls

North Fitzroy Bowls LAWN BOWLS
(☎03-9481 3137; www.barefootbowling.com.au; 578 Brunswick St, North Fitzroy; barefoot bowls lane hire $150; 9.30am-10pm; 11) Head north on Brunswick St over Alexandra Pde and you'll find this bowls club, a good spot for a beer and a game of barefoot bowls (groups of 10 maximum). BBQs are available for hire ($60) and night bowling is open till 10pm. Phone to make a booking; walk-ins are accepted if it's quiet.

St Kilda Sports Club LAWN BOWLS
(☎03-9534 5229; www.stkildasportsclub.com.au; 66 Fitzroy St, St Kilda; 2hr lawn bowls $20; lawn bowls noon-4pm Tue & Thu, to 8pm Wed, Fri & Sun; 16, 96) The only dress code at this popular bowling club is 'shoes off'. First-timers can get some friendly instruction. Great place for a beer (p121).

Other Activities

Global Ballooning BALLOONING
(☎03-9428 5703; www.globalballooning.com.au; adult/child from $440/340) Wake up at the crack of dawn to view the city from another angle on this one-hour ride.

Tours

Melbourne Street Tours WALKING
(☎03-9328 5556; www.melbournestreettours.com; tours $69; city centre 1.30pm Tue, Thu & Sat, Fitzroy 11am Sat) Three-hour tours exploring the street art of the city centre or Fitzroy. The tour guides are street artists themselves, so you'll get a good insight into this art form.

★ **Rentabike** CYCLING
(Map p56; ☎0417 339 203; www.rentabike.net.au; Federation Wharf; rental per hr/day $15/40, 4hr tour incl lunch adult/child $110/79; 10am-5pm; Flinders St) Rents bikes and runs **Real Melbourne Bike Tours**, offering a local's insight into the city, with a foodie focus.

Chocoholic Tours FOOD & DRINK
(☎1300 915 566; www.chocoholictours.com.au; tours from $99) Sure, you can check out Melbourne's chocolate shops yourself, but why not join a large bunch of fellow addicts and make a meal of it?

Melbourne By Foot WALKING
(Map p56; ☎1300 311 081; www.melbournebyfoot.com; departs Federation Sq; tours $40; 1pm; Flinders St) Take a few hours out and experience a mellow, informative three-hour walking tour that covers laneway art, politics, Melbourne's history and diversity. Highly recommended; book online. There's also a Beer Lovers tour ($85).

Hidden Secrets Tours WALKING
(☎03-9663 3358; www.hiddensecretstours.com; tours from $29) Offers a variety of walking tours covering subjects such as lanes and arcades, history, architecture and cafe culture.

Melbourne Visitor Shuttle BUS
(www.thatsmelbourne.com.au; 2 days $10; 9.30am-3.45pm) Hop-on, hop-off bus tour with an audio commentary, stopping at 13 of Melbourne's main sights on a 90-minute loop.

Aboriginal Heritage Walk CULTURAL
(☎03-9252 2429; www.rbg.vic.gov.au; Royal Botanic Gardens, Birdwood Ave, South Yarra; adult/child $31/12; 11am Sun-Fri; 3, 5, 6, 8, 16, 64, 67, 72) The Royal Botanic Gardens is on a traditional camping and meeting place of the Kulin people, and this tour takes you through their story – from songlines to plant lore, all in 90 fascinating minutes. The tour departs from the gardens' visitor centre (p74).

City Circle Trams TOURS
(☎13 16 38; www.ptv.vic.gov.au; ⊙10am-6pm Sun-Wed, to 9pm Thu-Sat; 🚊35) FREE Designed primarily for tourists, this free tram service travels around the city centre, passing many city sights along the way. It runs every 12 minutes or so and there's a recorded commentary.

Eight refurbished W-class trams operate on this route. Built in Melbourne between 1936 and 1956, they have all been painted a distinctive deep burgundy or green and gold. You can also dine on board the **Colonial Tramcar Restaurant** (☎03-9695 4000; www.tramrestaurant.com.au; tram stop 125, Normanby Rd, Southbank; meals $82-140; ⊙departs 1pm, 5.45pm & 8.35pm; ✍; 🚊12, 96, 109) while scuttling around Melbourne's streets.

Sleeping

As in any big city, accommodation in Melbourne is relatively expensive and you'll need to book well ahead if you're coinciding your trip with a major event such as the Australian Open or the Melbourne Cup. Prices tend to shoot up on Friday and Saturday nights, and are often at their lowest on Sunday night.

Airport & Around

If you've got an early flight to catch – or you're arriving late and jet-lagged and just need a place to crash – there are some decent options near Melbourne Airport. The **Parkroyal** (☎03-8347 2000; www.parkroyalhotels.com; Arrival Dr, Melbourne Airport; r from $323; ❄@🛜🏊) has all the bells and whistles, and direct 'air-bridge' access to the terminal. The smart but slightly further away **Holiday Inn Melbourne Airport** (☎03-9933 5111; www.ihg.com; 10-14 Centre Rd, Melbourne Airport; r from $206; P❄🛜🏊) is a cheaper option, with a free shuttle service.

City Centre

Space Hotel HOSTEL $
(Map p56; ☎03-9662 3888; www.spacehotel.com.au; 380 Russell St; dm from $37, r with/without bathroom from $100/89; ❄🛜; 🚉Melbourne Central) One of Melbourne's few genuine flashpackers, this sleek place walks the line between hostel and budget hotel. The better private rooms have iPod docks and flat-screen TVs, while dorms have thoughtful touches like large lockers equipped with sensor lights and lockable adapters. Some of the doubles have en suites and balconies. The rooftop hot tub is another big tick.

Home @ The Mansion HOSTEL $
(Map p68; ☎03-9663 4212; www.homeatthemansion.com; 80 Victoria Pde, East Melbourne; dm/r from $33/80; @🛜; 🚉Parliament) Located within a castlelike former Salvation Army building with grand double staircases, this is one of Melbourne's few hostels with genuine character. It has 92 dorm beds and a couple of double rooms; all rooms are light and bright and have lovely high ceilings. There are two small TV areas, a courtyard out the front and a sunny kitchen.

Melbourne Central YHA HOSTEL $
(Map p56; ☎03-9621 2523; www.yha.com.au; 562 Flinders St; dm from $36, d with/without bathroom $130/107; @🛜; 🚉Southern Cross) The former Markillie's Hotel has been transformed by the YHA gang: expect a lively reception, handsome rooms, and kitchens and common areas on each of the four levels. Entertainment's high on the agenda, and there's a cafe on the ground floor and a grand rooftop area. Best of all are the two private en-suite rooms on the roof.

Pensione Hotel HOTEL $
(Map p56; ☎03-9621 3333; www.pensione.com.au; 16 Spencer St; s/d from $115/125; P❄@🛜🐾; 🚉Southern Cross) With refreshing honesty, the lovely, boutique Pensione Hotel names some room categories 'matchbox' and 'shoebox' – but what you don't get in size is more than made up for in style and reasonable rates.

★ **Treasury on Collins** APARTMENT $$
(Map p56; ☎03-8535 8535; www.treasuryoncollins.com.au; 394 Collins St; apt from $198; ❄🛜; 🚊11, 12, 48, 109) This imposing stone neoclassical building (1876) once housed a branch of the Bank of Australia. An impressive bar now fills the downstairs space, its impossibly high ceiling supported by gilt-edged columns. The apartments, on the other hand, are modern and restrained, not to mention chic and spacious. Winning extras include coffee machines, laundries and free Netflix.

Alto Hotel on Bourke HOTEL $$
(Map p56; ☎03-8608 5500; www.altohotel.com.au; 636 Bourke St; r/apt from $176/220; P❄🛜; 🚉Southern Cross) 🍃 Environmentally minded Alto has water-saving showers, energy-efficient lights and double-glazed windows, and in-room recycling is encouraged. Rooms are well equipped, with good light and neutral decoration, and even the 'petite' rooms are a reasonable size. Studios have kitchenettes, while larger apartments

have full kitchens. Guests also have access to a full-service gym nearby.

United Backpackers HOSTEL $$
(Map p56; ☎03-9654 2616; www.unitedbackpackers.com.au; 250 Flinders St; dm from $40, r with/without bathroom $170/125; ❄@📶; 🚆Flinders St) Occupying an Edwardian building right in the heart of the action, and opposite Flinders St station, this perpetually buzzing backpackers has been thoughtfully renovated throughout. The prices are steep for a hostel, but it's arguably the best one in the city.

Punthill Flinders Lane APARTMENT $$
(Map p56; ☎03-9631 1199; www.punthill.com.au; 267 Flinders Lane; apt from $158; ❄📶; 🚆Flinders St) The black-walled lobby sets a schmick tone for this well-positioned apartment hotel. The spacious one-bedroom apartments have full kitchens, while the studios are more like hotel rooms with kitchenettes. Plus there's a communal laundry hidden in a cupboard in the corridor.

Radisson on Flagstaff Gardens HOTEL $$
(Map p56; ☎03-9322 8000; www.radisson.com/melbourneau; 380 William St; r from $222; ❄@📶; 🚆Flagstaff) Directly opposite Flagstaff Gardens, this is a great option for those who enjoy a bit of greenery outside their window while being in striking distance of city sightseeing. The rooftop spa is a huge perk.

Punthill Little Bourke APARTMENT $$
(Map p56; ☎03-8680 5900; www.punthill.com.au; 11-17 Cohen Pl; apt from $160; ❄@📶🏊; 🚆Parliament) Neat and modern open-plan apartments have bright colours, balconies, laundries and stainless-steel kitchens. Lots of light, an indoor lap pool and a heart-of-Chinatown laneway location lift this little place above the ordinary.

Punthill Manhattan APARTMENT $$
(Map p56; ☎03-9659 3788; www.punthill.com.au; 57 Flinders Lane; apt from $175; ❄@📶; 🚆Flinders St) While not quite avoiding the serviced-apartment furnishing clichés, these loft spaces are set in a former warehouse and have original industrial-age details. Large marble bathrooms, full kitchens with granite benchtops, a muted palette and a prime laneway location make this a good option; ask for a room at the back for an outlook. There's also a gym and spa.

Vibe Savoy Hotel HOTEL $$
(Map p56; ☎03-9622 8888; www.tfehotels.com; 630 Little Collins St; r from $200; ❄📶; 🚆Southern Cross) With 11 floors, the Savoy was the tallest building in Melbourne when it first opened its doors in the 1920s. Although it's been thoroughly made over, period features still show through. It's a concoction of traditional hotel comforts, bright colours and contemporary furnishings.

Mantra 100 Exhibition APARTMENT $$
(Map p56; ☎03-9631 4444; www.mantra.com.au; 100 Exhibition St; apt from $189; ❄@📶; 🚆Parliament) In a great midcity location, between the bustle of Bourke St and the calm of Little Collins St, Mantra offers streamlined facilities and professional, friendly service. Apartments are quietly stylish and guests have access to a swimming pool at the sister property on Russell St.

Adina Apartment Hotel APARTMENT $$
(Map p56; ☎03-8663 0000; www.adinahotels.com.au; 88 Flinders St; apt from $205; P❄📶; 🚆Flinders St) Quintessentially Melbourne views are on offer at this apartment-style hotel, gazing over the railway tracks to the riverside park at the front and into lanes at the rear. The entry-level apartments are loft style, with high ceilings and full kitchens.

★**QT Melbourne** HOTEL $$$
(Map p56; ☎03-8636 8800; www.qtmelbourne.com.au; 133 Russell St; r from $350; @📶; 🚋86, 96) Rough concrete surfaces, brass trim, lifts with tapestry light boxes that play house music and say random stuff in a Russian accent: this is one of Melbourne's newest, quirkiest and best boutique hotels. The rooms are beautifully kitted out and there's a great plant-draped rooftop bar too.

★**Ovolo Laneways** BOUTIQUE HOTEL $$$
(Map p56; ☎03-8692 0777; www.ovolohotels.com.au; 19 Little Bourke St; r from $219; ❄@📶; 🚆Parliament) This boutique hotel mixes hipster chic with a funky executive vibe. It's friendly, fun and loaded with goodies – there's a free self-service laundry, a free minibar in each room, free booze downstairs at the daily happy hour and a Nespresso machine in the lobby. It's just a shame about the silly little sinks.

Hotel Lindrum BOUTIQUE HOTEL $$$
(Map p56; ☎03-9668 1111; www.hotellindrum.com.au; 26 Flinders St; r from $330; ❄📶; 🚆Parliament) One of the city's most attractive hotels, this was once the snooker hall of the legendary and literally unbeatable Walter Lindrum. Expect minimalist tones, subtle

lighting and tactile fabrics. Spring for a deluxe room and you'll snare either arch or bay windows and marvellous Melbourne views. And yes, there's a billiard table – one of Lindrum's originals, no less.

Adelphi Hotel HOTEL **$$$**
(Map p56; ☎03-8080 8888; www.adelphi.com.au; 187 Flinders Lane; r from $335; ❄📶🏊; 🚊Flinders St) One of Australia's first boutique hotels, this discreet Flinders Lane property has a distinctly glam European feel, with design touches throughout. The lobby looks good enough to eat, although it could just be the dessert-themed Om Nom restaurant and cocktail bar that's making us salivate. You'll also find free lollies and nonalcoholic beverages in the well-stocked minibars.

St Jerome's The Hotel TENTED CAMP **$$$**
(Map p56; ☎0406 118 561; www.stjeromesthehotel.com.au; Melbourne Central rooftop, 3/300 Lonsdale St; tents $420-480; 🚊Melbourne Central) Each of the canvas glamping tents here has a double or a queen bed with funky bedspreads, reverse-cycle air-conditioners, a complimentary cooler of craft beer and cider, and free 10-pin bowling at Strike next door. Come morning, there's an on-site barista and brekky box. It's a great experience, but then it would need to be for these prices.

Park Hyatt HOTEL **$$$**
(Map p65; ☎03-9224 1234; www.melbourne.park.hyatt.com; 1 Parliament Sq, East Melbourne; r from $375; ❄@📶🏊; 🚊Parliament) Resembling a Californian shopping mall from the outside, the Park Hyatt has a luxurious interior with wood panelling, shiny surfaces and miles of marble. Rooms are elegantly subdued, and most have supersized baths, clever layouts that maximise your chance of seeing natural light and lovely treetop-level views. There's a lavish indoor pool, plus a great tennis court.

Sofitel HOTEL **$$$**
(Map p56; ☎03-9653 0000; www.sofitel-melbourne.com; 25 Collins St; r from $352; P❄@📶🏊; 🚊Parliament) Guest rooms at the Sofitel start on the 36th floor, so you're guaranteed views that will make you giddy. The rooms are of a high international style and, though the hotel entrance is relentlessly workaday, you'll soon be a world (or at least 36 floors) away.

Grand Hyatt Melbourne HOTEL **$$$**
(Map p56; ☎03-9657 1234; www.melbourne.grand.hyatt.com; 123 Collins St; r from $445; ❄@📶🏊; 🚊Flinders St) Plenty grand enough to warrant the name, this famous Collins St five-star has over 500 rooms, with marble bathrooms, designated workspaces and floor-to-ceiling windows looking out to the city centre, Yarra River or MCG.

Majorca Apartment 401 APARTMENT **$$$**
(Map p56; ☎0412 068 855; www.apartment401.com.au; 258 Flinders Lane; apt from $275; ❄📶; 🚊Flinders St) This is the ultimate in like-a-local living. The Majorca, a single apartment in one of the city's loveliest art-deco buildings, watches over a bustling vortex of laneways. Stylishly furnished, it has timber floorboards and huge windows. Who needs a concierge when you're right in the centre of things already? There's a two-night minimum.

Southbank & Docklands

Hilton Melbourne South Wharf HOTEL **$$**
(☎03-9027 2000; www.hiltonmelbourne.com.au; 2 Convention Centre Pl, South Wharf; r from $200; P❄📶; 🚋35, 70, 75) Polished wood and natural fibres provide an earthy feel in this luxurious hotel. Suites are huge and some offer dazzling views along the river. There's an in-house Aboriginal art gallery and all of the art in reception is for sale – except for the giant piece above the desk that appears to have been crafted from pot scourers.

Quest Docklands APARTMENT **$$**
(☎03-9630 1000; www.questdocklands.com.au; 750 Bourke St, Docklands; apt from $220; P❄@📶; 🚋35, 70, 75, 🚊Southern Cross) Join the new breed of Melburnians on the Docklands frontier. These apartments are well kept and smartly furnished, and, while the studios are small, they have kitchens and laundry facilities; one-bedroom apartments have balconies. It's on the doorstep of Etihad Stadium, so it's perfect for big-game visits.

Grand Hotel Melbourne HOTEL **$$**
(Map p56; ☎03-9611 4567; www.grandhotelmelbourne.com.au; 33 Spencer St, Docklands; apt from $170; P❄📶🏊; 🚊Southern Cross) This grand Italianate building housed the Victorian Railways administration back in the days when rail ruled the world. The apartments here were originally offices and, although they vary in size and layout (from studios to two-bedroom apartments), they all have high ceilings and some have balconies. Don't expect anything flash, just comfortable and spacious rooms with plenty of character.

Crown Towers HOTEL $$$
(Map p56; ☎03-9292 6868; www.crownhotels.com.au/crown-towers-melbourne; 8 Whiteman St, Southbank; r from $338; P❄📶🏊; 🚋55) Crown's flashest digs, this oversized hotel shrugs off the gaudy glitziness of its reception by the time you reach the quietly elegant rooms, many of which have extraordinary views. The large bathrooms have separate tubs and shower stalls, and the walk-in wardrobe is something you could easily get used to.

Crown Metropol HOTEL $$$
(☎03-9292 8319; www.crownmetropolmelbourne.com.au; 8 Whiteman St, Southbank; r from $258; P❄@📶🏊; 🚋12, 96, 109) Welcome to the biggest hotel in the southern hemisphere, with a staggering 658 rooms spread over 28 floors. Guests have access to Skybar on the top floor and the most extraordinary indoor infinity pool one floor down, offering views over the city to the Dandenongs in the distance. Rooms are suitably luxurious.

Crown Promenade HOTEL $$$
(☎03-9292 6688; www.crownpromenademelbourne.com.au; 8 Whiteman St, Southbank; r from $248; ❄📶🏊; 🚋55) Crown's four-star option is linked to the mother ship (read: casino) by an air bridge. It offers large, modern and gently masculine rooms with luxurious bathrooms, big windows and flat-screen TVs.

Langham Hotel HOTEL $$$
(Map p56; ☎03-8696 8888; www.langhamhotels.com; 1 Southgate Ave, Southbank; r from $250; ❄@📶🏊; 🚆Flinders St) The Langham lobby is as over the top as they come, with water cascading down a marble waterfall under the blaze of crystal chandeliers. The rooms, while comfortable and perfectly equipped, are a little past their prime in the style stakes.

Sebel & Grand Mercure Melbourne Docklands HOTEL $$$
(☎03-9641 7500; www.sebeldocklands.com.au; 18 Aquitania Way, Docklands; apt from $259; P❄@📶; 🚋35, 70, 86) These two Accor offshoots share reception but offer slightly different propositions. The Sebel operates as a hotel, although all the suites are apartment style, with kitchenettes and balconies. The Grand Mercure 'residences' are straight-out apartments and better for longer stays. Floor-to-ceiling windows make the most of the water and city views.

Richmond & East Melbourne

East Melbourne takes you out of the action yet is still walking distance from the city and offers ready access to the MCG. Good places to stay are limited, though, particularly in Richmond.

Aberlour Court APARTMENT $$
(Map p65; ☎03-9039 5310; www.aberlourcourt.com.au; 462 Victoria Pde, East Melbourne; apt from $155; P❄📶🐾; 🚆North Richmond) Built sometime in the latter half of last century, this brick residential block has been thoroughly smartened up and converted into an appealing apartment hotel. The brand-new bathrooms and kitchens are decked out in Italian tiles, and every unit has laundry facilities and separate bedrooms; the better ones have balconies or private terraces too.

Pullman Melbourne on the Park HOTEL $$
(Map p65; ☎03-9419 2000; www.pullmanhotels.com; 192 Wellington Pde, East Melbourne; r from $219; ❄@📶🏊; 🚆Jolimont) 🍃 This brown-brick building on the edge of both Fitzroy Gardens and Yarra Park is a monument to 1970s functionalism. Complete renovations of the rooms have brought in crimson carpets, oversized TVs and simple, stylish artwork. The location is superb for those looking at an MCG-filled weekend.

Fitzroy, Collingwood & Abbotsford

There are a few unique accommodation options in Fitzroy, from a hostel in a former nunnery to an arty boutique hotel in a historic terrace house. If you can't find something to suit in this area, staying at the northern end of Melbourne's CBD is an option, as it's a short walk or tram ride away.

★Nunnery HOSTEL $
(Map p68; ☎1800 032 635; www.nunnery.com.au; 116 Nicholson St, Fitzroy; dm/s/d from $34/95/120; @📶; 🚋96) Built in 1888, the Nunnery oozes atmosphere, with sweeping staircases and many original features; the walls are dripping with religious works of art and ornate stained-glass windows. You'll be giving thanks for the big, comfortable lounges and communal areas. The next-door Nunnery Guesthouse has larger rooms in a private setting (from $130). It's popular, so book ahead. All rates include breakfast.

★ **Tyrian Serviced Apartments** APARTMENT $$
(Map p68; 03-9415 1900; www.tyrian.com.au; 91 Johnston St, Fitzroy; apt from $188; P ❄ ; 11) These spacious modern apartments have a certain Fitzroy-celeb vibe. Big couches, flat-screen TVs, European laundries and balconies add to the appeal, and plenty of restaurants and bars are right at your door. It's rounded off with free wi-fi and parking. Rooms facing Johnston St can get noisy.

Brooklyn Arts Hotel B&B $$
(Map p68; 03-9419 9328; www.brooklynartshotel.com.au; 48-50 George St, Fitzroy; s/d from $115/155; ; 86) There are seven rooms in this character-filled hotel owned by filmmaker and artist Maggie Fooke. Set in a lovely terrace house, rooms vary in size but are all clean, quirky, colourful and beautifully decorated. Spacious upstairs rooms with high ceilings and balconies are the pick (from $220). Expect lively conversation at the included continental breakfast of local sourdough bread and homemade jams.

Melbourne Metropole Central APARTMENT $$
(Map p68; 03-9411 8100; www.metropolecentral.com.au; 44 Brunswick St, Fitzroy; apt $175-265; P ❄ ; 86, 11) If you can forgive the mid-'90s façade blighting this heritage strip at the top of Brunswick St, the Metropole is worth considering for its cracking location: a skip and a jump to the city and right on the doorstep of the best streets in hip Fitzroy and Collingwood. The rooms are large and well equipped, though with some beyond-bland interiors.

Carlton & Brunswick

Both Carlton and Brunswick are short on accommodation options aside from a few generic hotel chains, but they're easily accessed from the city centre so it's not essential to bed down in these neighbourhoods.

169 Drummond B&B $$
(Map p71; 03-9663 3081; www.169drummond.com.au; 169 Drummond St, Carlton; d incl breakfast $135; ❄ ; 1, 8) This privately owned guesthouse in a renovated 19th-century terrace is well located just a block from vibrant Lygon St. Rooms feature fireplaces and Persian rugs, and there's a homey dining area and kitchenette for guests' use. It's gay friendly and welcoming to all.

Downtowner on Lygon HOTEL $$
(Map p71; 03-9663 5555; www.downtowner.com.au; 66 Lygon St, Carlton; r from $149; P ❄ @ ; 1, 8) Well located between the city centre and Lygon St, the Downtowner has a range of rooms, including connecting suites perfect for families. While the rooms are a bit dated and can be on the dark side, they're clean and comfy, and the staff are very helpful.

North Melbourne & Parkville

There aren't many good sleeping options in this area, although there's an excellent, reasonably priced hotel at the Royal Children's Hospital. Otherwise, you're better off staying elsewhere.

Bev & Mick's Backpackers HOSTEL $
(McMahon's Hotel; 03-9328 2423; www.facebook.com/BevAndMicksBackpackers; 575 Spencer St, West Melbourne; dm $28-30; @ ; North Melbourne) On the city's fringe, this rough-around-the-edges backpackers is convenient for balancing sightseeing with local life. Being above an appealing pub means it's always social, with the usual theme nights and a fantastic little beer garden.

Larwill Studio HOTEL $$
(03-9032 9111; www.thelarwillstudio.com.au; 48 Flemington Rd, Parkville; r from $189; P ; 55, 57, 59) Named after artist David Larwill (1956–2011), whose colourful paintings brighten the walls, this highly unusual hotel is within the confines of the Royal Children's Hospital. Don't let that put you off: the rooms are fresh, breezy and, despite being relatively simple, not remotely hospital-like. It's worth paying $30 more for a park view.

Vibe Hotel Carlton HOTEL $$
(03-9380 9222; www.vibehotels.com.au; 441 Royal Pde, Parkville; r from $129; P ; 19) This early-1960s motel was once noted for its glamorous, high-Californian style. Now it's more of a generic business hotel with factory-made 'art' and poky bathrooms, but it's very convenient for parks and the zoo, and the city is a short tram ride away.

South Melbourne, Port Melbourne & Albert Park

This corner of Melbourne is scarce on slumber options. That said, South Melbourne has a decent hostel and one of the city's hottest boutique digs. Both are within walking distance of trams to the city and St Kilda.

Drop Bear Inn HOSTEL $
(☎03-9690 2220; www.dropbearinn.com.au; 115 Cecil St, South Melbourne; dm/d from $24/50; @🛜; 🚊96, 12) Named after Australia's legendary fearsome creature, this hostel is right opposite South Melbourne Market, so it's great for fresh produce – particularly the bargains available at closing time. It's above a pub, so it'll suit those looking to party. Most rooms have good natural light and more charm than is generally found at hostels. Free wi-fi.

★ **Coppersmith** BOUTIQUE HOTEL $$
(☎03-8696 7777; http://coppersmithhotel.com.au; 435 Clarendon St, South Melbourne; r from $230; ❄🛜; 🚊12) Low key, contemporary and elegantly restrained, the 15-room Coppersmith has every right to call itself a boutique property. Designer furniture, heavenly beds and fine woollen rugs set a seductive tone in the muted rooms, each with Nespresso machine, work desk, free wi-fi and recordable cable TV. On-site assets include a smart, locavore bistro-bar and a rooftop deck with skyline views.

Blackman BOUTIQUE HOTEL $$
(☎03-9039 1444, 1800 278 468; www.artserieshotels.com.au/blackman; 452 St Kilda Rd, Melbourne; r from $200; ❄🛜; 🚊3, 5, 6, 16, 64, 67, 72) While it may not have any original Charles Blackman paintings (though there are loads of prints and Blackman room decals), it does have a superb outlook – aim for a corner suite for views of Albert Park Lake and the city skyline. Beds are luxurious, though wear-and-tear is a problem in some rooms.

South Yarra, Prahran & Windsor

This corner of the city makes a good base if you want to be within stumbling distance of kicking bars and clubs. South Yarra offers numerous boutique digs, including two art-themed hotels. The area's also home to a bounty of serviced apartments. Further south, Windsor claims a reputable hostel that's located steps from the cooler, edgier end of Chapel St.

Back of Chapel HOSTEL $
(Map p76; ☎03-9521 5338; www.backofchapel.com; 50 Green St, Windsor; dm $32-36, d $80; ⏲reception 8.30am-5pm; @🛜; 🚊6, 78, 🚆Windsor) Literally 20 steps from the cooler end of Chapel St, Back of Chapel offers budget-conscious slumber in an old Victorian terrace. A clean, laid-back spot with four- and six-bed dorms, it also offers private twins, doubles and triples. Facilities include communal kitchen, BBQ and coin-operated laundry. It's especially popular with those on a working holiday. All rates include breakfast.

Hotel Claremont GUESTHOUSE $
(Map p76; ☎03-9826 8000; www.hotelclaremont.com; 189 Toorak Rd, South Yarra; dm/d from $48/88; 🛜; 🚊8, 78, 79, 🚆South Yarra) In a heritage building dating to 1868, the Claremont offers good value on an exclusive strip. Rooms are simple, clean and comfortable, with high ceilings, wooden floorboards and shared bathrooms. There's a guest laundry and 24-hour reception. Best of all, it's steps from Chapel St and South Yarra station (a mere two stations from the city centre). Rates include breakfast.

Cullen BOUTIQUE HOTEL $$
(Map p76; ☎03-9098 1555; www.artserieshotels.com.au/cullen; 164 Commercial Rd, Prahran; r from $209; ❄@🛜; 🚊72, 78, 79, 🚆Prahran) The work of late grunge painter Adam Cullen drives the decor here: his vibrant and often graphic art provides such visions as Ned Kelly shooting you from the opaque bedroom-bathroom dividers. Rooms are stylish and comfy, with handy kitchenettes, though the standard studios are small. Rooms facing north and west from level four and up offer the best views.

You can borrow the keys for the hotel's smart car ($50 per day) or pedal a Lekker bike (per hour/day $5/35). On the art theme, French street artist Blek Le Rat contributed 17 of his signature rat stencils here, too.

Olsen BOUTIQUE HOTEL $$
(Map p76; ☎03-9040 1222; www.artserieshotels.com.au/olsen; 637 Chapel St, South Yarra; r from $199; P❄🛜≋; 🚊8, 78, 🚆South Yarra) At the top end of Chapel St, steps from svelte South Yarra boutiques and cafes, this 224-suite property honours artist John Olsen. The painter's bold, raw artworks add verve to the open-plan, grey-and-silver rooms, each of which comes with handy kitchenette and sublimely comfortable AH Beard bed. Staff are attentive and the hotel's glass-bottomed pool juts out over Chapel St.

Punthill South Yarra Grand APARTMENT $$
(Map p76; ☎1300 731 299; www.punthill.com.au; 7 Yarra St, South Yarra; studios from $159, 1-/2-bedroom apt from $179/249; P❄🛜; 🚊8, 78, 79, 🚆South Yarra) It's the little things, like a blackboard and chalk in the kitchen for messages,

that make this modern, charcoal-accented place a great choice. The smart, contemporary studios and apartments are equipped with kitchens; the apartments – in one-, two- and three-bedroom configurations – also have laundry facilities. The property has a small number of bikes for hire (per hour/day $4/15).

Royce on St Kilda Road BOUTIQUE HOTEL $$
(03-9677 9900; www.roycehotels.com.au; 379 St Kilda Rd, Melbourne; r from $189; ; 3, 5, 6, 16, 64, 67, 72) Close to the Botanic Gardens, the Royce occupies a Moorish-inspired building from the late 1920s. Originally a Rolls-Royce showroom, it's now a boutique slumber spot, with a mix of period and modern features and a range of room types. Rooms are comfortable – with good bedding, marble bathrooms and large plasma TVs – if somewhat lacklustre. Facilities include a gym.

Lyall BOUTIQUE HOTEL $$$
(Map p76; 03-9868 8222, 1800 338 234; www.thelyall.com; 16 Murphy St, South Yarra; r from $255; ; 8, South Yarra) Just off Toorak Rd, the 40-suite Lyall, with one- and two-bedroom apartments, is all about the good life: on-site spa and champagne bar, original artwork by French-born Thierry B, even a pillow menu. Suites are plush, if a little worn, with a seductive, textural palette of shantung, taffeta, suede, velvet and brocade. Regular guests include Melbourne-raised singer Olivia Newton-John.

St Kilda

St Kilda is a budget-traveller enclave, but you'll find a small selection of nondescript midrange chains as well as more individual options a short walk from the beach.

★ **Base** HOSTEL $
(Map p78; 03-8598 6200; www.stayatbase.com; 17 Carlisle St, St Kilda; dm/d from $34/145; ; 3, 16, 96) Well-run Base has streamlined dorms (each with en suite) and slick doubles. There's a floor – complete with hair straighteners and champagne deals – set aside for female travellers, and a bar and live-music nights keep the good times rolling.

Habitat HQ HOSTEL $
(Map p78; 03-9537 3777; www.habitathq.com.au; 333 St Kilda Rd, St Kilda; dm/d from $34/119; ; 3, 67) There's not much this clean, newish hostel doesn't have. Check off open-plan communal spaces, fully equipped kitchen, bar, beer garden, free breakfast, a travel agent and a pool table, for starters. Follow Carlisle St from St Kilda to St Kilda Rd – it's on your left.

Abode St Kilda MOTEL $$
(Map p78; 03-9536 9700; www.easystay.com.au; 63 Fitzroy St, St Kilda; d from $122; ; 3, 12, 16, 96) A great choice for those who've outgrown hostels but want an affordable private room in the heart of the action. Although the exterior suggests dodgy motel, the rooms are upbeat, contemporary and comfortable, with free wi-fi and in-house movies, handy kitchenettes, and bathrooms with underfloor heating and rain shower heads.

Prince HOTEL $$
(Map p78; 03-9536 1111; www.theprince.com.au; 2 Acland St, St Kilda; r from $175; ; 3, 12, 16, 96) The brooding, David Lynch–esque lobby sets a sexy, stylish tone at this fashionable favourite. Rooms are pared back and chic, if a little tired. Also on-site are the celebrated Prince Bandroom (p123) (be prepared for weekend noise) and the Aurora Spa Retreat (p80). Note that the hotel's (unheated) pool is in a private-function space and so isn't always accessible.

Rydges St Kilda HOTEL $$
(Map p78; 1300 884 373; www.rydges.com; 35-37 Fitzroy St, St Kilda; d from $169; ; 3, 12, 16, 96) Despite their somewhat generic look (and the odd sign of wear and tear), rooms here are comfortable, modern and graced with decent beds. The location is handy for the beach and an easy walk from Acland St's bars and eateries. There's a small gym and complimentary access to the nearby St Kilda Sea Baths (p81).

Hotel Tolarno HOTEL $$
(Map p78; 03-9537 0200; www.tolarnohotel.com.au; 42 Fitzroy St, St Kilda; s/d/ste from $109/119/169; ; 3, 12, 16, 96) Tolarno was once the site of art dealer Georges Mora's seminal gallery, Tolarno. A range of rooms are on offer and all come eclectically furnished, with good beds, bright and bold original artworks, Nespresso machine and free wi-fi. Those at the front of the building might get a bit noisy, but they compensate with balconies and enormous windows overlooking Fitzroy St.

Novotel St Kilda HOTEL $$
(Map p78; 03-9525 5522; www.novotelstkilda.com.au; 14-16 The Esplanade, St Kilda; r from $200;

; 3, 16, 96) Generic and dependable chain hotel in a superb location. Free wi-fi in public areas.

Eating

City Centre

Restaurants are spread throughout the city, with many hidden down alleys, arcades or off the 'Little' streets. There's are particularly notable places in and around Flinders Lane.

★ Hakata Gensuke RAMEN $

(Map p56; 03-9663 6342; www.gensuke.com.au; 168 Russell St; mains $13-14; 11.30am-2.45pm & 5-9.30pm Mon-Fri, noon-9.30pm Sat & Sun; Parliament) Gensuke is one of those places that only does one thing and does it extraordinarily well. In this case it's *tonkotsu* (pork broth) ramen. Choose from three types (signature, sesame-infused 'black' or spicy 'god fire') and then order extra toppings (marinated *cha-shu* pork, egg, seaweed, black fungus). Inevitably there will be a queue, but it's well worth the wait.

Traveller CAFE $

(Map p56; www.sevenseeds.com.au; 2/14 Crossley St; bagels $7-10; 7am-5pm Mon-Fri; 86, 96) This pocket-sized place is a proper stand-and-lean espresso bar, serving top-notch coffee courtesy of local roastery Seven Seeds. However, there are a couple of stools around the edge if you want to settle in with a newspaper and filled bagel (cream cheese; avocado and lemon; pastrami and Dijon etc). The sweet things at the counter are enticing too.

Gopals Pure Vegetarian VEGETARIAN $

(Map p56; 03-9650 1578; www.gopalspure vegetarian.com.au; 1st fl, 139 Swanston St; mains $4.50-7; 11.30am-9pm; ; Flinders St) For the best-value veg meal in town, you can't go past this humble Hare Krishna–run institution. The food is both tasty and cheap: the 'feast plate' gives you soup, main, salad, dessert and drink for $13. Everything is vegetarian and there are many vegan options, which are clearly marked.

Wonderbao CHINESE $

(Map p56; 03-9654 7887; www.wonderbaokitchen.com.au; Literature Lane; bao $2.70-5.20; 8am-6pm Mon-Fri, 11am-4pm Sat; Melbourne Central) Wonderbao does only one thing – no prizes for guessing what. Its *bao* (steamed buns) range from the traditional sticky-barbecue-pork variety to oddities like the breakfast *bao*. There are a few stools by the window but no tables.

Spring Street Grocer DELI $

(Map p56; 03-9639 0335; www.springstreetgrocer.com.au; 157 Spring St; rolls $12-13, ice cream $5; 9am-9pm; Parliament) Join the queue at **Gelateria Primavera** for fresh gelati, with a daily-changing selection scooped from traditional *pozzetti* (metal tubs fitted into the benchtops). Next door, the **sandwich bar** serves coffee and made-to-order rolls. Head down the winding staircase to reach the pungent **cheese cave**, an atmospheric maturation cellar with an impressive selection of international cheeses.

Stalactites GREEK $

(Map p56; 03-9663 3316; www.stalactites.com.au; 177-183 Lonsdale St; mains $11-18; 24hr; Melbourne Central) What's not to love about a 24-hour 'souva' joint? Especially when it's been doling out late-night lamb souvlakis in Melbourne for nearly 40 years. Located in the heart of what remains of the central city's little Greek precinct, it's an institution for an early-hours feed. The cavelike interior is hilarious too.

Huxtaburger BURGERS $

(Map p56; www.huxtaburger.com.au; Fulham Pl; burgers $7-14; 11.30am-10pm; Flinders St) Burgers, chips and shakes are the mainstays here, devoured on the bench seating or at a handful of little tables on the lane.

Don Don JAPANESE $

(Map p56; 03-9662 3377; 198 Little Lonsdale St; mains $6.50-9.80; 11am-9pm; Melbourne Central) This humble Japanese eatery fills up fast. Grab a big bowl of udon noodles or a bento box full of assorted goodies and either wolf it down indoors or join the masses eating on the State Library's lawns.

★ Supernormal ASIAN $$

(Map p56; 03-9650 8688; www.supernormal.net.au; 180 Flinders Lane; dishes $16-39; 11am-11pm; Flinders St) Drawing on his years spent in Shanghai and Hong Kong, chef Andrew McConnell presents a creative selection of pan-Asian sharing dishes, from dumplings to raw seafood to slow-cooked Sichuan lamb. Even if you don't dine in, stop by for his now-famous takeaway New England lobster roll. No dinner bookings, so get here early to put your name on the list.

★Chin Chin SOUTHEAST ASIAN $$
(Map p56; ☎03-8663 2000; www.chinchinrestaurant.com.au; 125 Flinders Lane; mains $20-39; ⏰11am-late; 🚉Flinders St) Insanely popular, and for good reason, chic Chin Chin serves delicious Southeast Asian hawker-style food designed as shared plates. It's housed in a glammed-up old warehouse with a real New York feel, and while there are no bookings, you can fill in time at the **Go Go Bar** downstairs until there's space.

Hardware Société CAFE $$
(Map p56; ☎03-9078 5992; 120 Hardware St; mains $14-26; ⏰7.30am-2.30pm; 🚉Melbourne Central) If you're not prepared for a lengthy queue, go elsewhere, as this wonderful little cafe is always heaving. Once you're finally seated – either outdoors under the awnings or beneath the butterfly wallpaper in the cute interior – an inventive menu of mouth-watering French-influenced cafe fare awaits.

Gazi GREEK $$
(Map p56; ☎03-9207 7444; www.gazirestaurant.com.au; 2 Exhibition St; mains $12-28; ⏰11.30am-late; 🚉Parliament) The latest offering from George Calombaris of *MasterChef* fame, this side project to the fancier Press Club (next door) is set in a designer-industrial space and delivers a menu inspired by Greek street food. Select from authentic shared starters, gourmet mini souvlakis filled with soft-shell crab or duck, chargrilled octopus and spit-roasted meats.

Mamasita MEXICAN $$
(Map p56; ☎03-9650 3821; www.mamasita.com.au; 1st fl, 11 Collins St; tacos $7, quesadillas $15, shared plates $24-27; ⏰5-11pm Sun-Wed, noon-midnight Thu-Sat; 🚉Parliament) The restaurant responsible for kicking off Melbourne's obsession with authentic Mexican street food, Mamasita is still one of the very best. The chargrilled corn sprinkled with cheese and chipotle mayo is a legendary starter, and there's a fantastic range of corn-tortilla tacos and a mammoth selection of tequila. It doesn't take reservations for dinner, so prepare to wait.

Café Vue CAFE $$
(Map p56; ☎03-9691 3843; www.vuedemonde.com.au; 430 Little Collins St; mains $12-18; ⏰7am-4pm Mon-Thu, to late Fri; 🚋55, 86, 96) The most affordable outpost of Shannon Bennett's Vue de Monde empire serves excellent coffee and a wondrous range of cakes, pastries, sandwiches and fancy burgers. Join the cult that's sprung up around the pistachio cupcakes.

MoVida TAPAS $$
(Map p56; ☎03-9663 3038; www.movida.com.au; 1 Hosier Lane; tapas $4-8, raciones $16-34; ⏰noon-late; 🚉Flinders St) MoVida's location in much-graffitied Hosier Lane is about as Melbourne as it gets. Line up by the bar, cluster around little window tables or, if you've booked, take a seat in the dining area for fantastic Spanish tapas and *raciones*. MoVida Next Door – yes, right next door – is the perfect place for preshow beers and tapas.

Pellegrini's Espresso Bar ITALIAN $$
(Map p56; ☎03-9662 1885; 66 Bourke St; mains $18; ⏰8am-11pm Mon-Sat, noon-8pm Sun; 🚉Parliament) The Italian equivalent of a classic 1950s diner, locally famous Pellegrini's has remained genuinely unchanged for decades. There's no menu with prices; the staff will tell you what's available. Expect classic Italian comfort food: lasagne, spaghetti bolognese and big slabs of cake. Service can be brusque, but that's all part of the experience.

Flower Drum CHINESE $$
(Map p56; ☎03-9662 3655; www.flowerdrum.melbourne; 1st fl, 17 Market Lane; mains $18-40; ⏰noon-3pm & 6-11pm Mon-Sat, 6-10.30pm Sun; 📶; 🚉Parliament) Established in 1975, Flower Drum continues to be Melbourne's most celebrated Chinese restaurant, imparting a charmingly old-fashioned ambience through its dark wood, lacquerwork and crisp white linen. The sumptuous but ostensibly simple Cantonese food (from a menu that changes daily) is delivered with the top-notch service you'd expect in such elegant surroundings.

NO RESERVATIONS

A widespread trend in Melbourne's fine-dining scene has many of the city's hottest restaurants (MoVida, Mamasita, Longrain, Supernormal and Chin Chin, to name a few) adopting a 'no bookings' policy. The move has received its share of love and criticism but is mostly aimed at delivering more flexibility and spontaneity. Most places will take your number and call once a spot has opened so you're not awkwardly hanging around waiting – or else people make a drink at the bar or a predinner stroll part of their night out.

Bar Lourinhã TAPAS $$

(Map p56; ☎03-9663 7890; www.barlourinha.com.au; 37 Little Collins St; tapas $4-8, raciones $16-30; ⏰noon-11pm Mon-Thu, to 1am Fri & Sat; 🚉Parliament) Grab a seat at the bar and let the charming waitstaff lead you through a menu of modern Portuguese and Spanish dishes and a corresponding list of Iberian wine. The zingy kingfish pancetta is a very good place to start.

New Shanghai CHINESE $$

(Map p56; ☎03-9994 9386; www.newshanghai.com.au; 3rd fl, Emporium, 287 Lonsdale St; mains $12-39; ⏰11am-7pm Sat-Wed, to 9pm Thu & Fri; 🚉Melbourne Central) According to local dumpling experts, New Shanghai, in a flash corner of the Emporium shopping complex's food hall, serves up Melbourne's best *xiao long bao* (soup-filled dumplings). We're not quite ready to shift the crown from **HuTong Dumpling Bar**, but if you like the genre (and have a decent chopstick technique), why not try both?

ShanDong MaMa CHINESE $$

(Map p56; ☎03-9650 3818; www.facebook.com/shandongmama; Mid City Arcade, 200 Bourke St; mains $8-24; ⏰11am-9pm; 🚋86, 96) Melbourne's passion for dumplings finds its truest expression in this simple little place, where the dumplings are boiled rather than steamed. If there are two of you, order a plate of Little Rachaels and another of King Prawn dumplings – bliss! Arrive any later than noon for lunch and you may have to wait.

Mrs Parma's AUSTRALIAN $$

(Map p56; ☎03-9639 2269; www.mrsparmas.com.au; 25 Little Bourke St; mains $24-29; ⏰11.30am-10pm; 🚉Parliament) Melburnians have long adopted the humble chicken parmigiana as their own, but Mrs Parma's takes things to a whole new level with 14 types of parma, of the chicken, veal or eggplant variety – and some downright weird ones (Karma Parma, Parma'geddon). The huge selection of Victorian craft beers is another reason to visit.

Bowery to Williamsburg CAFE $$

(Map p56; ☎03-9077 0162; www.facebook.com/bowerytowilliamsburg; 16 Oliver Lane; mains $13-18; ⏰7.30am-3pm; 🚉Flinders St) This basement deli is true to its NYC name, with central Melbourne's best bagels, served with schmear from traditional (caviar) to local (Vegemite). It also serves pastrami sandwiches with pretzel and pickle sides, and waffles for something sweet. The single-origin coffees come with a Hershey kiss.

Mesa Verde MEXICAN $$

(Map p56; ☎03-9654 4417; www.mesaverde.net.au; 6th fl, Curtin House, 252 Swanston St; mains $12-20; ⏰4pm-late Tue-Sun; 🚉Melbourne Central) Part of the wonderful Curtin House complex, Mesa Verde does great Mexican food to a backdrop of Sergio Leone screenings. As well as street-food dishes, there's a vast selection of tequilas and mezcals, and an exotic choice of salts for margaritas, including black truffle.

Izakaya Chuji JAPANESE $$

(Map p56; ☎03-9663 8118; www.izakayachuji.com; 165 Lonsdale St; mains $12-19; ⏰5-10.30pm; 🚉Melbourne Central) One of Melbourne's most authentic izakayas, no-frills Chuji is popular for its well-priced and delicious traditional Japanese pub-style dishes, from grilled skewers to deep-fried chicken, squid and pork.

HuTong Dumpling Bar CHINESE $$

(Map p56; ☎03-9650 8128; www.hutong.com.au; 14-16 Market Lane; mains $14-31; ⏰11.30am-3pm & 5.30-10.30pm; 🚉Parliament) HuTong's reputation for divine *xiao long bao* means getting a lunchtime seat anywhere in this three-level building isn't easy. Downstairs, watch chefs make the delicate dumplings, then hope they don't watch you making a mess eating them.

Belleville INTERNATIONAL $$

(Map p56; ☎03-9663 4041; www.belleville-melbourne.com; Globe Alley; mains $17-25; ⏰11am-1am; 🚉Melbourne Central) Billing itself as 'the home of worldly eats, drinks and beats', Belleville has an enormous Brazilian rotisserie that barbecues 90 chickens at once. The rest of the sharing-style menu bounces around the globe but centres on Asia, with a few North American dishes (poutine, s'mores) thrown in for good measure.

Seamstress CHINESE $$

(Map p56; ☎03-9663 6363; www.seamstress.com.au; 113 Lonsdale St; mains $18-35; ⏰noon-2.30pm & 5.30-10pm Mon-Fri, 5.30-10pm Sat; 🚉Parliament) Start off with a cocktail under a canopy of tiny *qipao* dresses on the top floor, then make your way downstairs to the dining room for some contemporary Chinese cooking. The 19th-century warehouse, complete with rickety wooden stairs, is fabulously atmospheric.

Paco's Tacos MEXICAN $

(Map p56; ☎03-9663 3038; http://pacostacos.com.au; 1st fl, Garden Plaza, rear 500 Bourke St; tacos $6.50; ⏱noon-9pm; 🚆Flagstaff) Paco's Tacos serves up fine soft tacos in a garden setting, as well as barbecued corn and other Mexican favourites.

MoVida Aqui TAPAS $$

(Map p56; ☎03-9663 3038; www.movida.com.au; 1st fl, Garden Plaza, rear 500 Bourke St; tapas $4.50-8.50, raciones $14-29; ⏱noon-late Mon-Fri, 6pm-late Sat; 🚆Flagstaff) The vibe couldn't be more different than that of the much-loved original MoVida (p93) at this financial-district outpost. Darkened, bohemian and intimate have been traded for sunny, besuited and vast, and the service can be woeful. However, the food's of the same high quality, the garden is lovely and you're much more likely to get a table here.

Waiters Restaurant ITALIAN $$

(Map p56; ☎03-9650 1508; 1st fl, 20 Meyers Pl; mains $17-27; ⏱noon-2.30pm & 6pm-late Mon-Fri, 6pm-late Sat; 🚆Parliament) Head down a laneway and up some stairs to step into this restaurant – and into another era. Opened in 1947, it still has 1950s drapes, wood panelling and Laminex tables. Once only for Italian and Spanish waiters to unwind after work over a game of *scopa* (a card game), now everyone is welcome to enjoy its hearty plates of pasta.

Bistro Vue FRENCH $$$

(Map p56; ☎03-9691 3838; www.bistrovue.com.au; 430 Little Collins St; mains $31-50; ⏱noon-late Mon-Sat; 🚋55, 86, 96) While big sister Vue de Monde sits on top of the world in the Rialto Tower, Melbourne legend Shannon Bennett's bistro is rather more down-to-earth (even if the prices still verge on the astronomical). Expect classic French cooking with flair and finesse.

Hopetoun Tea Rooms CAFE $$

(Map p56; ☎03-9650 2777; www.hopetountearooms.com.au; Block Arcade, 282 Collins St; mains $18-26; ⏱8am-5pm; 🚆Flinders St) Since 1892 patrons have been nibbling pinwheel sandwiches here, taking tea (with pinkies raised) and delicately polishing off a lamington. Hopetoun's venerable status results in almost perpetual queues. Salivate over the window display while you wait.

★ **Lee Ho Fook** CHINESE $$$

(Map p56; ☎03-9077 6261; www.leehofook.com.au; 11-15 Duckboard Pl; mains $32-42; ⏱noon-2.30pm & 6-11pm Mon-Fri, 6-11pm Sat & Sun; 🚆Parliament) Occupying an old brick warehouse down a fabulously skungy laneway, Lee Ho Fook is the epitome of modern Chinese culinary wizardry. The kitchen packs an extraordinary amount of flavour into signature dishes such as crispy eggplant with red vinegar, chicken crackling, liquorice wagyu beef, and crab and scallop rice with homemade XO sauce. The service is terrific too.

Tonka INDIAN $$$

(Map p56; ☎03-9650 3155; www.tonkarestaurant.com.au; 20 Duckboard Pl; mains $26-40; ⏱noon-3pm & 6pm-late Mon-Sat; 🚆Parliament) Tonka's dining room is long, elegant and very white, with billowy white mesh forming clouds overhead. The food, however, is gloriously technicolour. The punchy flavours of Indian cuisine are combined with unexpected elements – burrata, for instance, served with coriander relish and charred roti. Get the clued-up sommelier to recommend appropriate matches from the extraordinary wine list.

Coda SOUTHEAST ASIAN $$$

(Map p56; ☎03-9650 3155; www.codarestaurant.com.au; basement, 141 Flinders Lane; larger plates $39-46; ⏱noon-3pm & 6pm-late; 🚆Flinders St) Coda has a wonderful basement ambience, with exposed light bulbs and roughly stripped walls. Its innovative menu leans heavily towards Southeast Asian flavours, but Japanese, Korean, French and Italian influences are all apparent. While there are larger dishes made for sharing, the single-serve bites – such as the crispy prawn and tapioca betel leaf – are particularly good.

Cumulus Inc MODERN AUSTRALIAN $$$

(Map p56; ☎03-9650 1445; www.cumulusinc.com.au; 45 Flinders Lane; breakfast $14-18, mains $36-44; ⏱7am-11pm; 🚆Parliament) This bustling informal eatery focuses on beautiful produce and simple but artful cooking, served at the long marble bar and at little round tables dotted about. Dinner reservations are only taken for groups, so expect to queue. Upstairs is the Cumulus Up wine bar.

Longrain THAI $$$

(Map p56; ☎03-9671 3151; www.longrain.com; 44 Little Bourke St; mains $30-40; ⏱6-10pm Mon-Thu, noon-3pm & 5.30pm-late Fri, 5.30pm-late Sat & Sun; 🚆Parliament) Get in early or expect a long wait (sip a drink and relax, they suggest) before sampling Longrain's innovative Thai cuisine. The communal tables don't exactly work for a romantic date, but they're great for checking out everyone else's meals. Dishes are designed to be shared; try the pork-and-prawn eggnet, the amazing seafood dishes and the coconut sorbet.

Vue de Monde MODERN AUSTRALIAN $$$

(Map p56; ☎03-9691 3888; www.vuedemonde.com.au; 55th fl, Rialto, 525 Collins St; set menu $230-275; ⏰6-11pm Mon-Wed, noon-2pm & 6-11pm Thu-Sun; 🚉Southern Cross) Surveying the world from the old observation deck of the Rialto tower, Melbourne's favoured spot for occasion dining has views to match its storied reputation. Visionary chef Shannon Bennett, when he's not mentoring on *MasterChef*, produces sophisticated set menus showcasing the very best Australian ingredients. Book well – months – ahead.

Grossi Florentino ITALIAN $$$

(Map p56; ☎03-9662 1811; www.grossiflorentino.com; 1st fl, 80 Bourke St; 2-course lunch $65, 3-course dinner $140; ⏰noon-2.30pm & 6pm-late Mon-Fri, 6pm-late Sat; 🚉Parliament) Over-the-top gilded plasterwork, chandeliers and 1930s Florentine Renaissance murals engender a real sense of occasion at this top-notch Italian restaurant. Decadent set menus are accompanied by exquisite canapés and delicious bread, and the service is extremely slick. The Grill and Cellar Bar below offer more affordable options.

French Saloon EUROPEAN $$$

(Map p56; ☎03-9600 2142; www.frenchsaloon.com; 1st fl, 380-384 Little Bourke St; mains $36-39; ⏰noon-late Mon-Fri; 🚉Melbourne Central) Accessed via the unmarked door on Hardware Lane beside Kirk's Wine Bar, this *très chic* space features a zinc-topped bar all the way from France, distressed white floorboards and warehouse windows flooded with light from Little Bourke St. Beneath the red ceilings some customers pair snacks, oysters and caviar with aperitifs, while others dive straight into the dry-aged steak.

Bomba TAPAS $$$

(Map p56; ☎03-9077 0451; www.bombabar.com.au; 103 Lonsdale St; tapas $3.50-8, mains $26-36; ⏰noon-3pm & 5pm-late Mon-Fri, 5pm-late Sat & Sun; 🚉Parliament) Reminiscent of a buzzing Spanish *bodega*, Bomba offers up tasty authentic tapas, *raciones* for those who are hungrier, and Catalan stews and paellas. The wine list is predominantly Spanish and the vermouth flows freely, as does the cold Estrella. Afterwards, head up to the rooftop bar for a nightcap.

Kenzan JAPANESE $$$

(Map p56; ☎03-9654 8933; www.kenzan.com.au; 56 Flinders Lane; mains lunch $33, dinner $38-48; ⏰noon-2.15pm & 6-10pm Mon-Sat; 📶; 🚉Parliament) Kenzan has an unpromising setting on the edge of a shopping mall but serves up sublime sashimi and sushi, with the *nabe ryori* (which you cook at your table) another fine option. Can't choose? Lunch or dinner set menus are outstanding.

Gingerboy ASIAN $$$

(Map p56; ☎03-9662 4200; www.gingerboy.com.au; 27-29 Crossley St; dishes $33-44; ⏰noon-2.30pm & 5.30pm-late Mon-Fri, 5.30pm-late Sat, noon-2.30pm Sun; 🚉Parliament) Brave the trendy surrounds and weekend bustle to feast on delicious dumplings and next-level Southeast Asian hawker food and shared plates. Upstairs there's a long, cool cocktail bar.

Southbank & Docklands

Crown (Map p56; ☎03-9292 8888; www.crownmelbourne.com.au; 8 Whiteman St, Southbank; 🚋12, 55, 96, 109) has done a good job of luring people into its casino complex by installing some of Australia's most famous restaurateurs in glamorous riverside venues. While prices are steep, quality is high – unlike at some other eateries in this touristy stretch. South Wharf also has some interesting dining options right at the river's edge.

Bangpop THAI $$

(☎03-9245 9800; www.bangpop.com.au; 35 South Wharf Promenade, South Wharf; mains $21-29; ⏰noon-late; 🖉; 🚋35, 70, 75) Bangpop breathes a bit of colour and vibrancy into the area with its bar made from Lego and dangling filament bulbs. Flavour-packed hawker-style dishes and curries are served at communal cafe tables and accompanied by Thai-inflected cocktails.

Enlightened Cuisine VEGETARIAN, CHINESE $$

(☎03-9686 9188; 113 Queensbridge St, Southbank; mains $12-23; ⏰11.30am-2.30pm Mon, 11.30am-2.30pm & 5.30-10pm Tue-Sat, 5-10pm Sun; 🖉; 🚋55) Every imaginable variety of mock meat (generally made from wheat gluten or soy) is on offer here, served up in traditional Chinese style, from *kung pao* 'chicken' to king 'pork ribs' to buttered 'prawns'. All dishes are vegetarian and most can be made vegan on request.

Bluetrain INTERNATIONAL **$$**
(Map p56; ☎03-9696 0111; www.bluetrain.com.au; 1st fl, South Gate, Southbank; mains $18-34; ; Flinders St) Semi-al fresco with great river and city views, this family-friendly place serves salads, pasta and wood-fired pizza at reasonable prices.

★ **Spice Temple** CHINESE **$$$**
(Map p56; ☎03-8679 1888; www.rockpool.com; Crown, Yarra Promenade, Southbank; mains $15-52; 6-11pm Mon-Wed, noon-3pm & 6-11pm Thu-Sun; ; 55) When he's not at **Rockpool** next door or in one of his Sydney restaurants, well-known chef Neil Perry pays homage to the spicy cuisines of China's central provinces at this excellent waterfront eatery. By day you can gaze at the river while you tuck into the $49 yum cha banquet. By night, descend to the atmospheric darkened tabernacle beneath.

Rockpool Bar & Grill STEAK **$$$**
(Map p56; ☎03-8648 1900; www.rockpool.com; Crown, Yarra Promenade, Southbank; mains $35-70; noon-2.30pm & 6-11pm Sun-Fri, 6-11pm Sat; 55) The Melbourne outpost of Neil Perry's empire offers his signature seafood raw bar, but the star is the dry-aged beef. The masculine space is simple and stylish, as is the menu. The bar offers the same menu and service with the bonus of an additional, cheaper menu ($24 to $29).

Nobu JAPANESE **$$$**
(Map p56; ☎03-9292 7879; www.noburestaurants.com; Crown, Yarra Promenade, Southbank; dishes $29-64; noon-11pm; 55) The jury's out on whether Melbourne really needed a Nobu in the first place, but it's a seductive space for those out to impress.

Bistro Guillaume FRENCH **$$$**
(Map p56; ☎03-9292 4751; www.bistroguillaume-melbourne.com.au; Crown, Yarra Promenade, Southbank; mains $38-42; noon-late; 55) Sydney's famed Frenchman does bistro food with fine-dining flair.

Atlantic SEAFOOD **$$$**
(Map p56; ☎03-9698 8888; www.theatlantic.com.au; Crown, Yarra Promenade, Southbank; mains $38-51; noon-3pm & 6-11pm; 12, 96, 109) 'Simple sustainable seafood' is the mantra at this upmarket eatery in the casino complex.

Richmond & East Melbourne

Richmond's main draw has traditionally been restaurant-packed Victoria St, with its long strip of cheap Vietnamese and other Asian eateries. However, standards are arguably higher on Swan St, Church St and Bridge Rd.

Thy Thy VIETNAMESE **$**
(Map p65; ☎03-9429 1104; 1st fl, 142 Victoria St, Richmond; mains $9-16; 9am-10pm; North Richmond) Head upstairs to this Victoria St original (unchanged since 1987) for cheap and delicious Vietnamese food. No corkage for BYO booze.

Minh Minh SOUTHEAST ASIAN **$**
(Map p65; ☎03-9427 7891; 94 Victoria St, Richmond; mains $7-19; 4-10pm Tue, 11.30am-10.30pm Wed-Sun; North Richmond) Minh Minh specialises in fiery Laotian dishes – the herby green-and-red-chilli beef salad is a favourite – but it serves plenty of Vietnamese and Thai staples, too.

Sabai THAI **$$**
(Map p65; ☎03-8528 6884; www.sabairichmond.com.au; 460 Church St, Richmond; mains $17-24; 11.30am-9.30pm Mon-Fri, 4-9.30pm Sat & Sun; East Richmond) The traditional wisdom is that Sydney does Thai and Melbourne does Vietnamese, but this little neighbourhood restaurant bucks the trend, serving a delicious mix of classic and modern Thai dishes in smart surrounds. The service is excellent too.

Meatmother AMERICAN **$$**
(Map p65; ☎03-9041 5393; www.meatmother.com.au; 167 Swan St, Richmond; mains $20-28; 5pm-late Wed & Thu, noon-3pm & 5pm-late Fri-Sun; 70) Vegetarians, beware; this eatery is a shrine to the slaughterhouse, as is evident in the meat cleavers hanging on the walls. All meat is smoked over oak, from the 12-hour pulled-pork sandwich to the 20-hour beef brisket. At lunchtime it offers a range of $15 burgers and sandwiches, including a delicious burnt-end bun. Wash it down with some American whiskey.

Demitri's Feast GREEK **$$**
(Map p65; ☎03-9428 8659; www.demitrisfeast.com.au; 141 Swan St, Richmond; mains $10-24; 8am-4pm Tue-Sun; East Richmond) This down-to-earth cafe may be tiny, but it's full of huge Greek flavours in dishes such as spanakopita, souvlaki and meze platters. There's an interesting breakfast menu (the zucchini and feta fritters are a standout),

and the coffee's excellent too, especially when paired with a traditional Greek sweet.

Richmond Hill Cafe & Larder CAFE **$$**
(Map p65; ☎03-9421 2808; www.rhcl.com.au; 48-50 Bridge Rd, Richmond; lunch $12-27; ⏰7am-5pm; 🚋48, 75) Once the domain of well-known cook Stephanie Alexander, this deli-cafe may be looking a little dated, but it's still excellent. It boasts a top-notch cheese room and a menu ranging from the simple (cheesy toast) to little works of art (bircher muesli with chia-seed cubes and raspberry dust). There are breakfast cocktails for the adventurous.

Baby ITALIAN **$$**
(Map p76; ☎03-9421 4599; www.babypizza.com.au; 631-633 Church St, Richmond; mains $22-35; ⏰7am-11pm; 🚋78) Arguably the most painfully fashionable spot in Richmond, this bold and buzzy pizzeria has a good vibe and cheery service – and you might spot the odd Aussie TV star.

Meatball & Wine Bar AMERICAN **$$**
(Map p65; ☎03-9428 3339; www.meatballandwinebar.com.au; 105 Swan St, Richmond; mains $20-22; ⏰5pm-late Mon & Tue, noon-late Wed-Sun; 🚋70) A branch of a Melbourne chain serving an American take on Italian meatballs.

Minamishima JAPANESE **$$$**
(☎03-9429 5180; www.minamishima.com.au; 4 Lord St, Richmond; per person $150; ⏰6-10pm Tue-Sat; 🚋48, 75) Hidden down a side street, Minamishima offers possibly the most unique Japanese dining experience this side of the equator. Sit at the bar seats and watch sushi master Koichi Minamishima prepare seafood with surgical precision and serve it one piece at a time. There's only a handful of seats, so book well in advance.

Fitzroy, Collingwood & Abbotsford

Smith St's astounding food scene just keeps evolving and has now extended into the surrounding backstreets, with cafes and restaurants setting up shop in converted warehouses. Gertrude St is packed side-by-side with cafes and some excellent fine-dining options, while Brunswick St has a few well-established favourites (the rest is a little hit-and-miss). A good scene is starting to develop on the Abbotsford side of Johnston St, too.

★ **Lune Croissanterie** BAKERY **$**
(Map p68; www.lunecroissanterie.com; 119 Rose St, Fitzroy; pastries $5.50-12.50; ⏰7.30am-3pm Mon, Thu & Fri, from 8am Sat & Sun; 🚋11) The queues may have you turning on your heel, but good things come to those who wait, and here they come in the form of some of the best pastries you'll ever taste – from the lemon-curd cruffin to a classic almond croissant. In the centre of this warehouse space sits a climate-controlled glass cube, the Lune Lab, where the magic happens.

You can buy tickets online for the Lune Lab experience, where you sit at the bar looking into 'the lab' while sampling three courses of Lune's experimental pastries and getting an overview of the processes involved.

★ **Smith & Deli** DELI, VEGAN **$**
(Map p68; ☎03-9042 4117; www.smithanddaughters.com; 111 Moor St, Fitzroy; sandwiches $10-15; ⏰8am-6pm Tue-Sat; 🌿; 🚋11) Full of '50s-NYC-deli charm with a vegan twist, this little takeaway creates what might be the closest vegetarians will get to eating meat – it's even been known to fool a few carnivores. Sandwiches are made to order and filled with all the favourites; try the Rubenstein, loaded with 'pastrami', sauerkraut and pickles, or opt for the Club Sandwiches Not Seals.

★ **Gelato Messina** GELATO **$**
(Map p68; www.gelatomessina.com; 237 Smith St, Fitzroy; 1 scoop $4.80; ⏰noon-11pm Sun-Thu, to 11.30pm Fri & Sat; 🚋86) Messina is hyped as Melbourne's best ice-creamery and its popularity is evident in the queues of people in summer waiting to wrap their smackers around such smooth flavours as salted coconut and mango, poached figs in marsala, or blood-orange sorbet. You can watch the ice-cream makers at work through glass windows inside.

Huxtaburger BURGERS **$**
(Map p68; ☎03-9417 6328; www.huxtaburger.com.au; 106 Smith St, Collingwood; burgers $10-14.50; ⏰11.30am-10pm Sun-Thu, to 11pm Fri & Sat; 🚋86) This American-style burger joint is a hit for its crinkle-cut chips in old-school containers (go the spicy chipotle salt), tasty burgers (veg options available) on glazed brioche buns, and bottled craft beers. Other branches are in the city (p92) and Prahran (p106).

Babka Bakery Cafe BAKERY, CAFE **$**
(Map p68; ☎03-9416 0091; 358 Brunswick St, Fitzroy; mains $11-19; ⏰7am-7pm Tue-Sun; 🚋11) From borscht to dumplings, Russian

flavours infuse the lovingly prepared breakfast and lunch dishes at little local institution Babka. It also has its own bakery, and the heady aroma of cinnamon and freshly baked sourdough bread, pies and cakes makes even just a coffee worth queuing for.

Hinoki Japanese Pantry SUSHI **$**
(Map p68; http://hinoki.com.au; 279 Smith St, Fitzroy; sushi sets from $10; ⌚10am-6pm Tue-Thu, to 7pm Fri & Sat, to 4pm Sun; 🚋86) For all your favourite Japanese snacks and groceries head straight to Hinoki, where the shelves are stocked with everything from black-sesame ice cream and Pocky sticks to mini kegs of Asahi, sake bottles and Kewpie mayonnaise. The sushi bar is a great lunch pit stop for its made-to-order sushi and sashimi, including a speciality *nosé-maki* of salmon with aioli topping.

Po' Boy Quarter AMERICAN **$**
(Map p68; ☎03-9419 2130; www.poboyquarter.com.au; 295 Smith St, Fitzroy; rolls $12-15; ⌚11.30am-11pm Sun-Wed, to 1am Thu-Sat; 🚋86) The boys behind the Gumbo Kitchen truck have parked permanently on Smith St with this smart canteen-style eatery. Wolf down one of their rolls of pulled pork, shrimp with Louisiana hot sauce or fried green tomatoes with Cajun slaw while people-watching out the front. Finish it off with a gin fizz in Huey Long's bar out the back.

Lazerpig PIZZA **$$**
(Map p68; ☎03-9417 1177; www.lazerpig.com.au; 9-11 Peel St, Collingwood; pizza $16-24; ⌚4pm-late Mon-Wed, noon-late Thu-Sun; 🚋86) From the neon-pink pig sign out the front to the pub-style interior, disco ball and red-gingham tablecloths, hip Lazerpig is a hard one to get your head around. It's a bit rock 'n' roll and disco meets trattoria, where people pile in to scoff the excellent wood-fired pizzas and booze on craft beer or cocktails to DJs doin' their thing.

Easey's BURGERS **$$**
(http://easeys.com.au; 48 Easey St, Collingwood; burgers $10-23; ⌚11am-10pm Sun-Thu, to 11pm Fri & Sat; 🚋86) Biting into burgers and gulping back beers in a graffiti-covered old train carriage perched on top of a backstreet rooftop – it doesn't get much more Collingwood than this. Easey's does a handful of no-holds-barred burgers that will have your cholesterol rising faster than you can say 'gimme the side of triple-fried dim sims'.

It also does one of the best veggie burgers around: a potato-and-zucchini rösti with all the usual burger trimmings and not a dollop of hummus or slice of avocado in sight.

Horn AFRICAN **$$**
(Map p68; ☎03-9417 4670; www.thehorncafe.com.au; 20 Johnston St, Collingwood; mains $16-21; ⌚6pm-late Wed-Sat, 3-10pm Sun; 🚋86) Straight outta Addis Ababa, the flavours and feel of this Ethiopian restaurant are as authentic as its homemade *injera* (soft bread; prepared fresh daily). Tear it into your meal using your fingers and wash it down with Ethiopian beer. There's jazz on Thursday evening, and on Sunday the eight-piece Black Jesus Experiment plays traditional Ethiopian music with a modern take.

Charcoal Lane MODERN AUSTRALIAN **$$**
(Map p68; ☎03-9418 3400; www.charcoallane.com.au; 136 Gertrude St, Fitzroy; mains $19-31; ⌚noon-3pm & 6-9pm Tue-Sat; 🚋86) 🍃 Housed in an old bluestone former bank, this training restaurant for Indigenous and disadvantaged young people is one of the best places to try native flora and fauna; menu items may include pan-seared emu fillet with lemon-myrtle risotto and wattleseed crème brûlée. The chef's native tasting plate for two ($30) is a great place to start. Weekend bookings advised.

Moroccan Soup Bar MOROCCAN **$$**
(☎03-9482 4240; www.moroccansoupbar.com.au; 183 St Georges Rd, North Fitzroy; banquet per person $23; ⌚6-10pm Tue-Sun; 🌱; 🚋11) Prepare to queue before being seated by stalwart Hana, who will then go through the vegetarian menu verbally while you sip a mint tea (it's an alcohol-free zone). The banquet is great value and the sublime chickpea bake is a favourite, driving locals to queue with their own pots and containers for takeaway.

Horn Please INDIAN **$$**
(http://hornplease.com.au; 167 St Georges Rd, North Fitzroy; dishes $12-23; ⌚6-9pm Sun-Wed, to late Thu-Sat; 🚋11) The regularly changing menu at this stylish spot spans street food, curries, dal and tandoor dishes. You might find charred trout cooked on the tandoor, creamy black-lentil dal or smoked-lamb curry, and don't miss the homemade *kulfi* (Indian ice cream). The beer fridge is stocked with a great selection of craft brews.

Project Forty Nine CAFE, DELI $$

(Map p68; ☎03-9419 4449; www.projectfortynine.com.au; 107 Cambridge St, Collingwood; cafe mains $13-16, restaurant mains $26-31; ⏰cafe 7am-4pm, deli 9am-6pm Wed-Mon; 🚋86) Project Forty Nine brings a slice of the country to Collingwood's industrial backstreets with this outpost of its original cafe in Beechworth, regional Victoria. The huge, airy warehouse incorporates deli, cafe, restaurant and wine bar, focusing on a fusion of country Victorian produce and Italian flavours in the cafe and restaurant, while the wine bar showcases northeastern Victorian wines.

The deli shelves are stocked with olive oils, pastas and sauces, and the fridges are piled high with meats and cheeses to take home.

South of Johnston CAFE $$

(Map p68; ☎03-9417 2741; http://southofjohnston.com.au; 46 Oxford St, Collingwood; mains $12-22; ⏰7.30am-5pm; 📶; 🚋86) In a neighbourhood crammed with cafes, South of Johnston may not be trailblazing, but it does stand out from the pack for its charming rustic space in a warehouse conversion with plenty of room to move. The menu covers all-day breakfasts, brunch and lunch, with chilli scrambled eggs, steak sandwiches and semolina gnocchi.

Transformer VEGETARIAN $$

(Map p68; ☎03-9419 2022; www.transformerfitzroy.com; 99 Rose St, Fitzroy; mains $16-24; ⏰5.30-10pm Mon-Thu, 11.30am-11pm Fri, 9am-11pm Sat, 9am-10.30pm Sun; 📶🌶; 🚋11) This is haute vegetarian cuisine (think ricotta and rye gnocchi rather than tofu stir-fry) in a sophisticated, plant-filled warehouse space that's perfect for breakfast, dinner dates or cocktails.

Smith & Daughters LATIN AMERICAN, VEGAN $$

(Map p68; ☎03-9939 3293; www.smithanddaughterscom; 175 Brunswick St, Fitzroy; dishes $10-18; ⏰6pm-1am Tue-Fri, 10am-1am Sat, 10am-11pm Sun; 🌶; 🚋11) This cosy corner restaurant has an all-vegan menu and a subtle punk sensibility. Latin flavours are present in dishes such as paella fritters and 'chorizo' tacos, and extend to the cocktail menu, with jalapeño, cucumber and coriander margaritas and sangria by the jug.

Hotel Jesus MEXICAN $$

(Map p68; www.hoteljesus.com.au; 174 Smith St, Collingwood; dishes $6-16; ⏰noon-late Wed-Sun, Taco Wey shop noon-5pm Tue, to 6pm Wed-Sat; 🚋86) Set in an old post-office building, this brash retro cantina is going for fun, with gleaming tiles, red folding chairs and a daggy picture menu. Street food is the focus, particularly tostadas, topped with flavours that are a bit hit-and-miss, sadly. The tick-the-box paper ordering system and the service need a little finessing, and the menu could be clearer.

Son in Law THAI $$

(☎03-9410 0399; www.soninlaw.com.au; 56 Johnston St, Collingwood; dishes $7-18; ⏰5.30-11.30pm Mon-Thu, noon-4.30pm & 5.30-11.30pm Fri-Sun; 🚋86) Brightening up Johnston St is this Thai-owned eatery where the fun, fresh vibe permeates throughout, from the brightly coloured decor to the creatively presented dishes. The menu is split between classic, fusion, small plates and bigger dishes; go the crispy barramundi fillets, the namesake son-in-law chilli eggs or a classic pad thai paired with a cocktail, craft beer or chilled Singha.

Smith Street Alimentari CAFE, DELI $$

(Map p68; ☎03-9416 1666; www.alimentari.com.au/smith-street; 302 Smith St, Collingwood; panini $9.50-11.50, mains $10-24; ⏰8am-6pm Mon-Wed & Sat, to 7pm Thu & Fri; 📶; 🚋86) A winning Italian deli-cafe combo offering take-home meals, panini, salads, fresh pasta and rotisserie meats. The expansive space extends to a dining area with a Mediterranean-inspired menu and lovely rear courtyard.

Belle's Hot Chicken AMERICAN $$

(Map p68; ☎03-9077 0788; http://belleshotchicken.com; 150 Gertrude St, Fitzroy; chicken & a side from $17; ⏰noon-10pm Sun-Thu, to 11pm Fri & Sat; 🚋86) Chef Morgan McGlone knew he was onto a good thing while honing his kitchen skills in the States. But ever since he brought Nashville fried chicken back to Australia and paired it with natural wine, it's been a finger-lickin' revolution. Launch into tenders, drumsticks or wings with your preference of heat (note: 'Really F**kin Hot' is so named for good reason).

Robert Burns Hotel SPANISH $$

(Map p68; ☎03-9417 2233; www.robertburnshotel.com.au; 376 Smith St, Collingwood; paella per person from $20, mains from $27; ⏰5-11pm Mon & Tue, noon-midnight Wed-Sat, noon-11pm Sun; 🚋86) A slick makeover several years back meant the loss of its appealing dingy charm, but thankfully the authenticity of its Spanish flavours remain: the Burns' seafood paella is still one of Melbourne's best. The $17 lunch menu with a drink Wednesday to Saturday is great value.

Archie's All Day CAFE $$
(Map p68; ☎03-9417 0066; www.archiesallday.com; 189 Gertrude St, Fitzroy; mains $12-26; ⏰7.30am-4pm Mon & Tue, 7.30am-4pm & 5-10pm Wed-Sun; 📶; 🚋86) A light, airy, welcoming space in the heart of hip Gertrude St, Archie's is the place to head for brekky, a midmorning burger, Korean BBQ pork belly for dinner or an in-between-meals snack. Or you could forgo food altogether and sip a craft beer or cocktail (negronis on tap for $10!) in the sunny courtyard.

Vegie Bar VEGETARIAN $$
(Map p68; ☎03-9417 6935; www.vegiebar.com.au; 380 Brunswick St, Fitzroy; mains $13-18; ⏰11am-10pm Sun-Thu, to 10.30pm Fri & Sat; 📶🌱; 🚋11) An oldie but a goodie, this cavernous warehouse eatery has been feeding droves of Melbourne's veggie-loving residents for over 20 years. Expect inventive fare and big servings from its menu of delicious thin-crust pizzas, tasty salads, burgers and curries, as well as great smoothies and fresh juices. Also has a fascinating selection of raw food dishes, and plenty of vegan choices.

Añada TAPAS $$
(Map p68; ☎03-9415 6101; www.anada.com.au; 197 Gertrude St, Fitzroy; tapas from $4, raciones $10-28; ⏰6pm-late Mon-Sat, noon-late Sun; 🚋86) Dishes in this lovely little restaurant are alive with hearty Spanish and Muslim-Mediterranean flavours and feature a lot of seafood. It has a great tapas selection and a larger *raciones* menu, or go the nine-course tasting menu (chef's choice, for groups of seven or more) for $58.

Marios CAFE $$
(Map p68; ☎03-9417 3343; www.marioscafe.com.au; 303 Brunswick St, Fitzroy; mains $15-30; ⏰7am-10.30pm Mon-Sat, 8am-10.30pm Sun; 🚋11) Mooching at Marios is part of the Melbourne 101 curriculum. Breakfasts are big and served all day, the service is swift, the dishes are simple, classic Italian and the coffee is old-school strong.

★ **Cutler & Co** MODERN AUSTRALIAN $$$
(Map p68; ☎03-9419 4888; www.cutlerandco.com.au; 55 Gertrude St, Fitzroy; mains $36-48; ⏰6pm-late Tue-Sun, lunch from noon Sun; 🚋86) Hyped for all the right reasons, this is Andrew McConnell's flagship Melbourne restaurant and its atten tive, informed staff and joy-inducing dishes have quickly made it one of Melbourne's top places for fine dining. The menu strives to incorporate the best seasonal produce across the à la carte offering, the degustation menu (from $150), and the casual Sunday lunch designed for sharing.

Saint Crispin MODERN AUSTRALIAN $$$
(Map p68; ☎03-9419 2202; www.saintcrispin.com.au; 300 Smith St, Collingwood; 2/3 courses $50/65; ⏰6pm-late Tue-Thu, noon-late Fri-Sun; 🚋86) The stylish interiors, light-filled space, prompt service and excellent food make this one of the best places for fine dining in the inner city. You can choose from two or three courses, or opt for the chef's tasting menu (from $100). The duo behind the restaurant spent time working together at Michelin-starred The Square in London.

IDES MODERN AUSTRALIAN $$$
(Map p68; ☎03-9939 9542; www.idesmelbourne.com.au; 92 Smith St, Collingwood; 6-course degustation $110; ⏰from 6pm Wed-Sun; 🚋86) What started as a pop-up is now a permanent restaurant in Smith St. Word spread quickly that Attica (p110) sous chef Peter Gunn had started his own establishment, where he does the term 'creative' justice with a contemporary take on fine dining. It's a six-course, seasonal affair preceded by hot bread with dangerously good house peanut butter.

Inside it's dark but comfortable, with tactile leather-covered tables, felt-adorned walls that muffle ambient noise, and privacy offered by the lattice covering the front window. IDES serves the kind of food that you'll still be discussing the next day. The drinks match, which ventures well beyond wine, takes dinner from excellent to extraordinary.

Carlton & Brunswick

Sydney Rd in Brunswick is Melbourne's Middle Eastern hub, with plenty of bakeries and long-time favourite restaurants spread out along the thoroughfare. Since the arrival of Mediterranean immigrants in the 1950s, Lygon St in Carlton has been synonymous with Italian cuisine. For a mix of both cuisines, head to the East Brunswick end of Lygon St, where a couple of excellent Italian and Middle Eastern restaurants can be found, along with some well-loved cafes.

Heartattack and Vine ITALIAN $
(Map p71; ☎03-9005 8674; www.heartattackandvine.com.au; 329 Lygon St, Carlton; ⏰7am-11pm Mon-Fri, from 8am Sat & Sun; 📶; 🚌Tourist Shuttle, 🚋1,8) Heartattack and Vine is a relaxed space with a neighbourhood feel all centred

on a long wooden bar. Drop in for a coffee morning or night, prop up at the bar for an Aperol spritz or glass of wine, grab a brekky pastry or prawn brioche roll for lunch, or spend the evening sampling the *cicchetti,* a Venetian take on tapas.

Los Hermanos MEXICAN **$**
(www.los-hermanos.com.au; 339 Victoria St, Brunswick; tacos from $5; 6-11pm Mon-Thu, to 1am Fri & Sat; 19, Brunswick) Mexican-born owner Carreto brings Mexican street food to Brunswick with this casual neighbourhood taqueria. Tacos come cheap and tasty, but you'll need a few to fill up. Try the slow-cooked lamb, beer-battered fish or smoky mushrooms with grilled Manchego cheese. There's plenty of tequila to round the night off, too.

Very Good Falafel FELAFEL **$**
(03-9383 6479; www.shukiandlouisa.com; 626 Sydney Rd, Brunswick; felafel from $8.50; 11am-10pm Mon-Sat; ; 19, Anstey) They started off selling dips at markets and now Louisa and Shuki have set up permanent shop here. Their backgrounds combine perfectly: Shuki grew up on Middle Eastern home cooking in Israel, while Louisa's family has a farm in the Mallee growing chickpeas! On offer are Israeli-style pita with fresh (and indeed very good!) felafel, tasty salads and filter coffee.

Pidapipo GELATO **$**
(Map p71; 03-9347 4596; http://pidapipo.com.au; 299 Lygon St, Carlton; 1 scoop $4.50; noon-11pm; Tourist Shuttle, 1, 8) Pidapipo is the perfect precinema, pretheatre, postpizza – whenever! – treat when you're hanging out on Lygon St. Owner Lisa Valmorbida learned from the best in the world at the Carpigiani Gelato University and now whips up her own handmade creations on-site from local and imported Italian ingredients.

Sugardough Panificio & Patisserie BAKERY **$**
(03-9380 4060; www.sugardough.com.au; 163 Lygon St, East Brunswick; meals from $8.80; 7.30am-5pm Tue-Fri, to 4pm Sat, 8am-4pm Sun; ; 1, 8) Sugardough does a roaring trade in homemade pies (including vegetarian ones), panini, homebaked bread and pastries. Mismatched cutlery and cups and saucers make it rather like being at Grandma's on family-reunion day.

Small Victories CAFE **$$**
(03-9347 4064; www.smallvictoriescafe.com.au; 617 Rathdowne St, North Carlton; from $13; 8am-5pm Mon-Sat, 9am-5pm Sun; 1, 8) Not your ordinary posh North Carlton cafe, Small Victories is big on DIY: preparing and smoking its own smallgoods, churning its own butter and making pastas from scratch. It rounds it all off with single-origin coffee and craft beers.

A1 Lebanese Bakehouse MIDDLE EASTERN **$**
(http://a1bakery.com.au; 643-5 Sydney Rd, Brunswick; pastries from $1.40, plates from $7; 7am-7pm Sun-Wed, to 9pm Thu-Sat; 19, Anstey) This huge, classic Sydney Rd eatery and bakery is perfect for dining in on hearty Lebanese food including falafel and chicken tawouk plates, or takeaway piping-hot pastries and pizzas: spinach-and-cheese triangles, labne pizza and *kaak* (sesame buns filled with halloumi cheese).

Brunetti ITALIAN **$**
(Map p71; 03-9347 2801; www.brunetti.com.au; 380 Lygon St, Carlton; panini around $10, mains from $17; cafe 6am-11pm Sun-Thu, to midnight Fri & Sat; ; Tourist Shuttle, 1, 8, 96) Bustling from dawn to midnight, Brunetti is a mini-Roman empire with a drool-inducing display of cakes and sweets. It's famous for its coffee, granitas and authentic *pasticceria* (pastries), and also does a menu of pizzas, pastas and panini.

★**D.O.C. Espresso** ITALIAN **$$**
(Map p71; 03-9347 8482; www.docgroup.net; 326 Lygon St, Carlton; mains $12-20; 7.30am-late Mon-Sat, 8am-late Sun; Tourist Shuttle, 1, 8) Run by third-generation Italian Australians, authentic D.O.C. has breathed new life into Lygon St. The espresso bar features homemade pasta specials, Italian microbrewery beers and *aperitivo* time (4pm to 7pm), when you can enjoy a negroni with complimentary nibble board.

The affiliated **deli** (Map p71; panini from $7; 9am-7pm Mon-Sat, from 10am Sun) next door does great cheese boards and panini, while around the corner is the original pizzeria (p103).

★**Rumi** MIDDLE EASTERN **$$**
(03-9388 8255; www.rumirestaurant.com.au; 116 Lygon St, East Brunswick; dishes $13-28; 6-10pm; 1, 8) A fabulously well-considered place that serves up a mix of traditional Lebanese cooking and contemporary

interpretations of old Persian dishes. The *sigara boregi* (cheese and pine-nut pastries) are a local institution, and tasty mains from the charcoal BBQ are balanced with a large and interesting selection of vegetable dishes.

★D.O.C. Pizza & Mozzarella Bar PIZZA **$$**

(Map p71; ☎03-9347 2998; www.docgroup.net; 295 Drummond St, Carlton; pizzas $17-25; ⏲5pm-late Mon-Wed, noon-late Fri-Sun; Tourist Shuttle, 1, 8) D.O.C. has jumped on the Milanese-led mozzarella-bar trend and serves up the milky-white balls – your choice of local cow or imported *buffala* – as entrees, in salads or atop fabulous pizzas. Pizza toppings include bitter-sweet *cicoria* (chicory) and lemon, and wild mushrooms and truffle oil; the litmus-test margherita gets rave reviews.

400 Gradi PIZZA **$$**

(☎03-9380 2320; www.400gradi.com.au; 99 Lygon St, East Brunswick; pizza $14-29, mains $27-45; ⏲noon-11pm; 1, 8) Named after the temperature the wood-fired oven gets cranked up to, 400 Gradi rolls out some of the best pizzas in the city. It's headed by *pizzaiolo* Johnny Di Francesco, whose family hails from Naples. Johnny trained at Naples' Associazione Verace Pizza Napoletana – the first Australian to do so. Don't miss the signature margherita with generous dollops of buffalo mozzarella.

Babajan TURKISH **$$**

(☎03-9388 9814; www.babajan.com.au; 713 Nicholson St, North Carlton; mains $12-26; ⏲Tues-Fri 7am-7pm, Sat & Sun to 5pm; 96) For a small corner cafe, Babajan whips up some big Turkish flavours. Kirsty Chiaplias, who runs the show, has culinary cred going back years from working with noteworthy chefs such as Gordon Ramsay. Drop in for a deliciously flaky *borek* or a grain- and pulse-filled salad, or feast on cumin-and-mint-rubbed lamb shanks or a crab and halloumi omelette.

Longhorn Saloon AMERICAN **$$**

(Map p71; ☎03-9348 4794; www.longhornsaloon.com.au; 118 Elgin St, Carlton; mains $16-44; ⏲from 5pm Tue-Thu, noon-late Fri-Sun; 1, 8) Longhorn Saloon is an upmarket Wild West saloon-style restaurant-bar with lots of pressed copper, exposed brick, dark wood and low lighting. The menu features Southern-style flavours, from steaks cooked on the wood-fire grill to a brisket Reuben sandwich and a side of jalapeño-spiced mac 'n cheese. Pair it with a hoppy US IPA or a classic Dark 'n' Stormy cocktail.

Milk the Cow EUROPEAN **$$**

(Map p71; ☎03-9348 4771; www.milkthecow.com.au; 323 Lygon St, Carlton; cheeseboards from $27, flights & fondue from $17; ⏲noon-late; 1, 8) When a cheese craving strikes, head to licensed fromagerie Milk the Cow for baked camembert with a crusty baguette or a farmer's board of country-style bites. The electric milking chandeliers are a talking point, as is the giant glass cabinet filled with more than 150 unique, hard-to-find cheeses from all over the world.

Epocha EUROPEAN **$$**

(Map p71; ☎03-9036 4949; www.epocha.com.au; 49 Rathdowne St, Carlton; small/large sharing plates from $16/27; ⏲noon-3pm & 5.30-10pm Tue-Sat, noon-3pm Sun; City Circle, 30) Set within a grand Victorian double-storey terrace dating from 1884, elegant Epocha creates an interesting mix of Greek- and English-inspired dishes that's reflective of each of the co-owners' successes in previous restaurants. It all comes together beautifully on the $68 sharing menu. Head upstairs for fantastic cocktails at **Hannah's Bar**.

Pope Joan CAFE **$$**

(☎03-9388 8858; www.popejoan.com.au; 75-79 Nicholson St, East Brunswick; mains $15; ⏲7.30am-3pm; ; 96) This East Brunswick favourite is the perfect place to drop in, offering a comfort-food menu featuring all-day breakfasts, sensational sandwiches, St Ali coffee and 'liquid breakfasts' of Bloody Marys, as well as craft beer. A few doors up you'll find its bright produce store, Hams & Bacon, where you can grab a takeaway sandwich.

Hellenic Republic GREEK **$$**

(☎03-9381 1222; www.hellenicrepublic.com.au; 434 Lygon St, East Brunswick; mains $12-32; ⏲5.30-10pm Mon-Thu, noon-10pm Fri-Sun; ; 1, 8) The ironbark grill at George Calombaris' northern outpost works overtime grilling up pita, king prawns, calamari and whole fish, and luscious lamb. The *taramasalata* (white-cod-roe dip) is unbelievably good. Choose from à la carte or sharing menus and wash it all down with a warming ouzo from the long list.

Bar Idda ITALIAN **$$**

(☎03-9380 5339; www.baridda.com.au; 132 Lygon St, East Brunswick; mains $18-30; ⏲6-10pm Mon-Sat, 5.30-10pm Sun; 1, 8) This cosy Sicilian restaurant is intimate and relaxed, with a share-plates menu ranging from barbecued swordfish to vegetarian layered eggplant, and classic Italian desserts of tiramisu, affogato and cannoli.

Ray CAFE $$
(332 Victoria St, Brunswick; meals $13-21; 7.30am-4pm Mon-Fri, 8.30am-4pm Sat & Sun; ; 19, Brunswick) Its graffitied facade makes it look like an abandoned house… before opening up to reveal the cafe as an inviting space with exposed brick and friendly service. The inspired menu reflects Brunswick by mixing Middle Eastern flavours with classic cafe fare named after bands: Rage Against the Tagine, God Speed You Black Lentil. There's also a vegan menu.

Shakahari VEGETARIAN $$
(Map p71; 03-9347 3848; www.shakahari.com.au; 201 Faraday St, Carlton; mains $19-22; noon-3pm & 6-9.30pm Mon-Fri, 6-10.30pm Sat & Sun; ; Tourist Shuttle, 1, 8, 96) Shakahari's limited, seasonal menu reflects both Asian and European influences, and dishes are made using great produce. Established over 40 years ago, and bedecked with a wonderful collection of Asian antiques, Shakahari takes its mission seriously. If the weather is in your favour, ask to be seated in the palm-fringed courtyard.

Tiamo ITALIAN $$
(Map p71; 03-9347 5759; www.tiamo.com.au; 303 Lygon St, Carlton; mains $15-26; 6am-10.30pm; Tourist Shuttle, 1, 8) When you've had enough of pressed, siphoned, Slayer-machined, poured-over, filtered and plunged coffee, head here to one of Lygon St's original Italian cafe-restaurants. There's the laughter and relaxed joie de vivre that only a well-established restaurant can offer. Great pastas and pizza, too. Also has the upmarket Tiamo 2 next door.

Abla's LEBANESE $$
(Map p71; 03-9347 0006; www.ablas.com.au; 109 Elgin St, Carlton; mains $28-30; 6-10pm Mon-Sat, noon-3pm Thu & Fri; 1, 8, 96) The kitchen here is steered by Abla Amad, whose authentic, flavour-packed food has inspired a whole generation of local Lebanese chefs. The banquet menu (from $60) is compulsory on Friday and Saturday nights. BYO wine Monday to Thursday.

North Melbourne & Parkville

Not one of Melbourne's famous dining neighbourhoods, but there are a few places that are worth travelling to North Melbourne for.

El Sabor MEXICAN $$
(03-9329 9477; www.elsabor.com.au; 500 Victoria St, North Melbourne; dishes $15-27; 6-11pm Mon-Sat; 57) This excellent little eatery serves authentic Mexican street food and home cooking, all designed to be shared. Wash it down with a cocktail, a shot of tequila, a jug of sangria or a glass of Spanish or South American wine.

Auction Rooms CAFE $$
(03-9326 7749; www.auctionroomscafe.com.au; 103-107 Errol St, North Melbourne; mains $11-21; 7am-5pm; ; 57) This industrial-chic former auction house turned North Melbourne success story serves up some of Melbourne's best coffee, both espresso and filter, using ever-changing, house-roasted, single-origin beans. Then there's the food, with a highly seasonal menu of creative breakfasts and lunches.

Melbourne's West

From authentic ethnic cuisine to cafes with more than just the usual staples, the west offers plenty to lure itinerant foodies. Footscray is the best for Vietnamese, African, Indian and Italian eats; Williamstown has an upmarket Croatian restaurant, while Yarraville has an excellent bakery-cafe and a Mediterranean deliwine bar.

Nhu Lan VIETNAMESE, BAKERY $
(03-9689 7296; 116 Hopkins St, Footscray; rolls $5; 5am-6pm; Footscray) That classic marriage of French and Vietnamese cuisine, the *bánh mì* (filled baguette), finds its Melbourne apotheosis at this humble neighbourhood bakery. Choose between barbecue pork, barbecue chicken, meatballs and salad, and make sure you grab a cassava cake or profiterole for afterwards.

Hung Vuong VIETNAMESE $
(03-9689 6002; 128 Hopkins St, Footscray; mains $10-13; 9am-8.30pm; 82, Footscray) If you try just one of Footscray's authentic Vietnamese restaurants, this is the pick. The menu is limited to rice-paper rolls, various types of noodle soup and a handful of rice dishes, and green tea is provided for the ta-

ble. It's bustling and brightly lit, and you'll be hurried out as soon you've finished – it's just like being in Saigon.

Cafe Lalibela ETHIOPIAN $

(☎03-9687 0300; 91 Irving St, Footscray; mains $14-15; ⏰11am-10pm; ✍; 🚆Footscray) Spongy *injera* bread serves as both platter and cutlery at this traditional Ethiopian restaurant. Choose from a range of beef, lamb, chicken and vegetarian stews, and they'll be served on a large expanse of bread; break off chunks to scoop up the stew.

★Cobb Lane CAFE, BAKERY $$

(☎03-9687 1538; www.cobblane.com.au; 13 Anderson St, Yarraville; mains $12-20; ⏰7am-4.30pm Tue-Fri, 8.30am-4.30pm Sat & Sun; 🚆Yarraville) There's a tempting array of sourdough sandwiches and sweet stuff in the cabinet here, but an even better idea is to settle yourself at one of the half-dozen wooden tables and peruse the menu, stacked with such interesting dishes as the salmon-and-egg choux pastry. Save room for the superlatively light and delicious doughnuts.

South Melbourne, Port Melbourne & Albert Park

All three neighbourhoods are perfect for casual footpath dining on sunny weekends, with a good number of casual cafes and restaurants. There's a slew of places to eat at on and off Clarendon St in South Melbourne, though not all are especially noteworthy. You'll find fabulous fresh produce, decent coffee and quality sit-down eateries at South Melbourne Market. Restaurants and cafes dot Bridport St and Victoria Ave in Albert Park, as well as Bay St in Port Melbourne. There's a small handful of restaurants overlooking the bay, though many serve nondescript food.

St Ali CAFE $

(☎03-9686 2990; www.stali.com.au; 12-18 Yarra Pl, South Melbourne; dishes $8-25; ⏰7am-6pm; 🚋12) A hideaway warehouse conversion where the coffee's carefully sourced and guaranteed to be good. If you can't decide between house blend, speciality, black or white, there's a six-coffee tasting 'adventure' ($20). The food menu covers all bases with competence and creativity, from virtuous vanilla-and-maple quinoa pudding with baby Thai basil to cult-status corn fritters with poached eggs and grilled halloumi.

Andrew's Burgers BURGERS $

(☎03-9690 2126; www.andrewshamburgers.com.au; 144 Bridport St, Albert Park; burgers from $8.50; ⏰11am-9pm Mon-Sat; 🚋1) Andrew's is a family-run, wildly popular institution that's been around since the '50s. It's walls are still wood-panelled, and now they're covered with photos of local celebs who, like many, drop in for a classic burger with the lot and a big bag of chips to take away. Veg option available.

Jock's Ice-Cream ICE CREAM $

(☎03-9686 3838; 83 Victoria Ave, Albert Park; single cone $4; ⏰noon-8pm Mon-Thu, to 10pm Fri & Sat, to 9pm Sun; 🚋1) For almost two decades Jock has been scooping up his made-on-site sorbets and ice creams for baysiders (and the odd Canadian teen-pop icon). Cult-status flavours include hokey-pokey and a star-spangled jam-and-peanut-butter combo. Take-home tubs also available.

Simply Spanish SPANISH $$

(☎03-9682 6100; www.simplyspanish.com.au; South Melbourne Market, cnr Coventry & Cecil Sts, South Melbourne; gourmet paellas from $20.50, tapas $8-16; ⏰8am-9pm Wed-Sat, to 4pm Sun; 🚋12, 96) When a Melbourne restaurant wins the title of 'Best Paella Outside of Spain' in Valencia, you know you're on to a good thing. This casual market eatery is *the* place to go for paella, which is available here in numerous combos. While you wait, nibble on a tapas dish or two; the chilli-spiked garlic prawns are a top pick.

Paco y Lola MEXICAN $$

(☎03-9696 5659; http://pacoylola.com.au; shop 99, South Melbourne Market, cnr Coventry & Cecil Sts, South Melbourne; burritos $13-14, mains $15-30; ⏰8.30am-10.30pm Wed & Fri, 9am-11pm Thu, 7.30am-11pm Sat, 7.30am-5pm Sun; 🚋12, 96) Upbeat and casual, Paco y Lola cooks up a storm of zingy, fresh, generous Mexican flavours, from juicy burritos, quesadillas and tacos to more substantial options like Mexican pork ribs and refreshing soft-shell-crab salad. If there are two of you, don't miss the *caldo de pescado*, a fragrant Mexican fish soup made with super-fresh seafood from the adjoining market.

Misuzu's JAPANESE $$

(☎03-9699 9022; www.misuzus.com.au; 3-7 Victoria Ave, Albert Park; mains $17-32; ⏰noon-10pm; 🚋1) Misuzu's menu includes whopping noodle, rice and curry dishes, tempuras and takeaway options from the neatly displayed sushi bar. Sit outside under a lantern-hung tree, or inside surrounded by murals and dark wood.

Orient East MALAYSIAN **$$**

(☎03-9685 2900; www.orienteast.com.au; 348 St Kilda Rd, Melbourne; mains $17-27; ⊙6.30am-10pm Mon-Fri, 7-11am & 5-9pm Sat & Sun; 🚊3, 5, 6, 8, 16, 64, 67, 72) A convenient lunch spot if you're visiting the Shrine of Remembrance and Botanic Gardens across the road, Orient East whips up British-colonial Straits cuisine in a setting reminiscent of a 1960s foreign-correspondent cafe. Enjoy hawker-style grub such as black-pepper soft-shell-crab buns, prawn *char kuey teow* (fried flat noodles) and fragrant laksas, best washed down with some cold craft suds.

Mart 130 CAFE **$$**

(☎03-9690 8831; 107 Canterbury Rd, Middle Park; mains $13-20; ⊙7.30am-3pm; 📶; 🚊96) A quirky location within the Federation-style Middle Park tram station, Mart 130 is a cute, sun-filled cafe that serves up corn fritters, toasted pide and big salads. Its deck overlooks the park with city views in the background. Weekend waits can be long.

Bellota Wine Bar ITALIAN **$$$**

(☎03-9078 8381; http://bellota.com.au; 181 Bank St, South Melbourne; mains $28-34; ⊙11am-11pm Tue-Sat; 🚊1, 12) This handsome wine bar and bistro is an extension of the adjoining Prince Wine Store, with an ever-changing wine list and beautiful dishes to match. Whether you're dining at the bar or at one of the intimate back tables (the latter require a reservation), expect to swoon over perfect grilled octopus, *vitello tonnato* (thinly sliced veal) and elegant, nuanced pastas. Lunch is served until 3pm and dinner service usually wraps up between 9pm and 9.30pm.

South Yarra, Prahran & Windsor

The three neighbourhoods are packed with great eateries, spanning all price ranges and countless cuisines. Toorak Rd in South Yarra has a number of fine-dining options, along with trendier cafes and bistros. Chapel St heaves with cafes and hotspot eateries, the best of which lie south of Commercial Rd. Commercial Rd itself is home to Prahran Market, a must for fresh produce, pasta and deli treats. Both Greville and High Sts also host a number of decent nosh spots.

★ **Zumbo** DESSERTS **$**

(Map p76; ☎1800 858 611; http://zumbo.com.au; 14 Claremont St, South Yarra; macarons $2.80, cakes from $6; ⊙7am-7pm; 🚊8, 78, 🚆South Yarra) Aussie pâtissier Adriano Zumbo is hot property, famed for his outrageously creative, technically ambitious concoctions. Here, cheesecake might be made with yuzu-cream-cheese mousse and shaped like a Swiss cheese, and a tart might get spicy with churros-custard crème and Mexican-hot-chocolate crème. And then there's the '70s disco-chamber-like fit-out. Fine print: the coffee's better next door.

Two Birds One Stone CAFE **$**

(Map p76; ☎03-9827 1228; www.twobirdsonestonecafe.com.au; 12 Claremont St, South Yarra; dishes $14-22.50; ⊙7am-3.30pm Mon-Fri, from 8am Sat & Sun; 🚊8, 78, 🚆South Yarra) Sandblasted oak stools, whitewashed timber and a wintry forest mural evoke Scandinavia at Two Birds One Stone, a crisp, contemporary cafe with smooth third-wave coffee and a smart, produce-driven menu. Find your happy place tucking into soul-nourishing dishes like ricotta pancakes with figs, marmalade syrup and pistachio cream, or pan-seared salmon with potato rösti, truffled cauliflower puree and poached eggs.

Uncommon CAFE **$**

(Map p76; ☎03-9510 6655; www.uncommonfood.com; 60 Chapel St, Windsor; dishes $11-23; ⊙7am-3.30pm Mon-Fri, from 8am Sat & Sun; 🚊5, 64, 78, 🚆Windsor) White-on-white interiors and cascading plants await at Uncommon, a cool, light-filled cafe singing the praises of local, seasonal produce and out-of-the-box dishes. Highlights include the sublime sliced salmon with mild green chilli, soft-herb scramble and whipped honey, and the coffee-rubbed short rib with potato croquette, pickled green tomato and egg. Serves are on the smaller size but feel just right.

Tivoli Road Bakery CAFE **$**

(Map p76; ☎03-9041 4345; http://tivoliroad.com.au; 3 Tivoli Rd, South Yarra; dishes $7-12; ⊙7.30am-4pm; 🚊8, 78, 🚆South Yarra) Join fashionistas, realtors and upmarket hipsters at this contemporary, side-street bakery-cafe, serving everything from impossibly light custard doughnuts to generously stuffed sandwiches, made-from-scratch pies and sausage rolls, and fashionable salads. Its cult-status artisanal loaves are also on offer, as well as a small selection of other local treats, from jam to nougat.

Huxtaburger BURGERS $

(Map p76; www.huxtaburger.com.au; 203 High St, Prahran; burgers from $10; ⏲11.30am-10pm Sun-Thu, to 11pm Fri & Sat; 🚊6, 78, 🚆Prahran) The south-side branch of Fitzroy burger royalty (p106), Huxtaburger is famed for its sweet brioche buns, grass-fed wagyu patties and crinkle-cut chips (best sprinkled with spicy chipotle salt). There are a couple of veggie burgers, too, as well as an ice-cream burger for those who don't know when to stop – no judgement.

Drugstore Espresso CAFE $

(Map p76; ☎03-9827 5058; www.drugstoreespresso.com.au; 194 Toorak Rd, South Yarra; dishes $15-22; ⏲7am-4pm Mon-Fri, 8am-4pm Sat & Sun; 📶; 🚊8, 🚆South Yarra) A split-level, graffiti-pimped hipster haven, Drugstore trades in serious coffee and smashing brekky and lunchtime grub. Lick your whiskers over buttermilk hotcakes with maple bacon, stone fruit and whipped espresso ricotta, or lunch on canned sardines with sourdough, local stracciatella cheese, heirloom tomatoes, basil, chilli oil, fried capers and poached egg. It's Toorak Rd, Jim, but not as we know it.

Gilson MODERN AUSTRALIAN $$

(☎03-9866 3120; http://gilsonrestaurant.com.au; 171 Domain Rd, South Yarra; pizzas $18-25 , mains $24-34; ⏲6am-11pm Mon-Fri, from 7am Sat & Sun; 🚊8) Sassy new kid Gilson straddles the line between cafe and restaurant. Directly opposite the Botanic Gardens, it has a concrete and Italian-marble fit-out inspired by midcentury French modernism and contemporary, Italian-influenced food. Forgo the famous (and underwhelming) grilled cucumber for the outstanding pasta dishes and interesting wood-fired pizzas. Rounding things off are intriguing wines and cocktails, and attentive, knowledgeable staff.

Colonel Tan's THAI $$

(Map p76; ☎03-9521 5985; http://revolverupstairs.com.au/colonel-tans; 229 Chapel St, Prahran; mains $15-29; ⏲5-11pm Tue-Thu & Sat, from noon Fri; 🚊6, 78, 🚆Prahran) In the back corner of pumping Revolver Upstairs (p120), retro-licious Colonel Tan's dishes out top-notch Thai-American fusion. Expect such things as corn, coriander and pickled-chilli doughnuts, soft-shell-crab burgers with curried egg, and a Bangkok bolognese that tastes a hell of a lot better than it sounds.

Fonda MEXICAN $$

(Map p76; ☎03-9521 2660; http://fondamexican.com.au; 144 Chapel St, Windsor; tacos from $6.50, burritos from $14; ⏲11.30am-10.30pm Sun-Thu, to 11pm Fri & Sat, rooftop from 5.30pm Mon-Wed, from noon Thu-Sun; 🚊6, 78, 🚆Windsor) Fun, thumping Fonda serves Mexican-with-a-twist street food. The emphasis is on fresh, local ingredients, from Queen Vic Market produce to authentic, made-from-scratch tacos from La Tortilleria. Order the prawn taco with kimchi and caramelised pineapple and wash it down with a burnt-orange margarita. Dine downstairs or try your luck on the see-and-be-seen rooftop (ridiculously busy at weekends).

Hawker Hall SOUTHEAST ASIAN $$

(Map p76; ☎03-8560 0090; http://hawkerhall.com.au; 98 Chapel St, Windsor; dishes $8-34; ⏲11am-late; 🚊5, 6, 64, 78, 🚆Windsor) Did you hear the one about the turn-of-the-century stable turned hipster take on a Southeast Asian food hall? Decked with playful Chinatown-style signage, ever-popular Hawker Hall serves up spicy, punchy share-style dishes like barbecue pork and lychee salad and fiery Portuguese devil chicken curry. No reservations, so head in before 6pm or after 9.30pm to minimise the wait.

Stables of Como CAFE $$

(Map p76; ☎03-9827 6886; www.thestablesofcomo.com.au; Como House & Garden, cnr Williams Rd & Lechlade Ave, South Yarra; sandwiches $13-20, mains $23-29; ⏲9am-5pm Mon-Sat, from 10am Sun; 🚊8) This studiously rustic cafe occupies the former stables at heritage-listed Como House (p75). Nibble gourmet sandwiches, salads or more substantial creations like corn and zucchini fritters with roasted tomatoes, bacon and herb-spiked ricotta. Afternoon high tea includes a free-flow mimosas option ($65), and the cafe also offers gourmet picnic hampers (per person $60; book at least 48 hours ahead).

WoodLand House MODERN AUSTRALIAN $$$

(Map p76; ☎03-9525 2178; www.woodlandhouse.com.au; 78 Williams Rd, Prahran; tasting menus from $125; ⏲6.30-9pm Tue, Wed & Sat, noon-3pm & 6.30-9pm Thu & Fri, noon-3pm Sun; 🚊6) In a glorious Victorian villa, WoodLand House is home turf for young-gun chefs Thomas Woods and Hayden McFarland, former sous chefs for lauded Melbourne restaurateur Jacques

Reymond. The menu spotlights quality local produce, cooked confidently and creatively in dishes like wood-roasted mussels with asparagus and salted yolk. Thursday and Friday offer a good-value three-course lunch with a glass of wine for $55.

Sunday lunch also offers a good deal: a chef's set menu of four/six courses for $80/110.

Da Noi ITALIAN **$$$**

(Map p76; ☎03-9866 5975; http://danoi.com.au; 95 Toorak Rd, South Yarra; mains $30-40, 4-course tasting menu $75-95; ⏰noon-10.30pm; 🚋8, 🚆South Yarra) Elegant Da Noi serves up beautiful dishes from Sardinia, the island home of owner-chef Pietro Porcu. Offerings change daily, with the chef's special reinterpreted several times a night on some occasions. Just go with it. For the full effect, opt for the four-course set menu, which sees the chef decide your dishes based on whatever's best that day. Bookings advised.

St Kilda

Despite having seen better days, Fitzroy St remains a popular eating strip, and you'll find the good, the very good and the downright ugly along its length. Acland and Barkly Sts also hum with dining options, the former also famed for its historic cake shops. Over the Nepean Hwy, Carlisle St in Balaclava has its fair share of hipster cafes and trendy eateries, catering to a mostly local crowd.

St Kilda Dispensary CAFE **$**

(Map p78; ☎03-9077 4989; www.facebook.com/TheStKildaDispensary; 13 Brighton Rd, St Kilda; dishes $6.50-18; ⏰7am-3.30pm Mon-Fri, from 8am Sat & Sun; 🚋16, 67, 79) In what was the first dispensary in the southern hemisphere during the 1940s, this cafe keeps with the medical theme with tiled counters, test tubes and beakers, and a menu that prescribes the good stuff: house-made cold drip, corn fritters and comforting bubble and squeak.

Monk Bodhi Dharma CAFE **$**

(Map p78; ☎03-9534 7250; rear 202 Carlisle St, Balaclava; dishes $9-19; ⏰7am-5pm Mon-Fri, from 8am Sat & Sun; 🌿; 🚋3, 16, 78) Monk Bodhi Dharma's location, down an alley off Carlisle St (next to Woolworths), means it doesn't get much foot traffic, which is lucky given that this cosy brick cafe has enough devotees as it is. A former 1920s bakehouse, it's now all about transcendental vegetarian food, from house-made bircher muesli to zucchini and mint hotcakes. House-roasted single-estate coffee tops things off.

Si Señor MEXICAN **$**

(Map p78; ☎03-9995 1083; www.sisenor.com.au; 193 Carlisle St, Balaclava; tacos $6-6.50, burritos $13-14.50; ⏰noon-3pm & 5-10pm Mon-Thu, noon-10pm Fri-Sun; 📶; 🚋3, 16, 78, 🚆Balaclava) Si Señor is one of the most authentic Mexican joints in the city. Tasty spit-and-grilled meats are heaped onto soft corn tortillas under the direction of the place's Mexican owner. If you've overdone the hot sauce, cool it down with an authentic *horchata* (a delicious rice-milk and cinnamon drink).

Glick's BAGELS **$**

(Map p78; www.glicks.com.au; 330a Carlisle St, Balaclava; bagels from $4; ⏰6am-8pm Sun-Thu, 6am-30min before sunset Fri, 30min after sunset-midnight Sat; 🚋3, 16, 78, 🚆Balaclava) A staple for the local Jewish community, kosher bakery Glick's sells bagels baked and boiled in-house. Stick with the classics and try the 'New Yorker' with cream cheese and egg salad.

Monarch Cake Shop DESSERTS **$**

(Map p78; ☎03-9534 2972; www.monarchcakes.com.au; 103 Acland St, St Kilda; slice of cake from $5; ⏰8am-9.30pm Sun-Thu, to 10pm Fri & Sat; 🚋96) Monarch is a favourite among St Kilda's Eastern European cake shops, and its *kugelhopf* (marble cake), plum cake and Polish baked cheesecake can't be beaten. In business since 1934, the shop doesn't seem to have changed much, with a soft, old-time atmosphere and wonderful buttery aromas. It also does good coffee.

Banff PIZZA **$**

(Map p78; ☎03-9525 3899; www.banffstkilda.com; 145 Fitzroy St, St Kilda; mains $9; ⏰8am-10pm; 🚋3, 16) It's not just the daily happy hour (drinks $3 to $6) that keeps Banff's Fitzroy St–fronting chairs occupied, it's also the $9 pizzas. And if you thought that was a bargain, the house pizzas are slashed to $6 all day Monday and Tuesday and till 5.30pm Wednesday to Friday. The pizzas won't win any prizes, but at this price who cares?

Galleon Cafe CAFE **$**

(Map p78; ☎03-9534 8934; 9 Carlisle St, St Kilda; mains from $10; ⏰7am-5pm; 🚋3, 16, 96) Affable and reassuringly worn, this '80s veteran is a true St Kilda institution, having pumped caffeine, grub and Bloody Marys into generations of local writers, musos and eccentrics. Especially hectic at weekends, the cafe serves a decent choice of tasty, straightforward dishes, from French toast, porridge and pancakes to scrambled tofu and house-baked muffins and cakes.

Lentil as Anything VEGETARIAN $
(Map p78; ☎0424 345 368; www.lentilasanything.com; 41 Blessington St, St Kilda; by donation; ⊙noon-9pm; ☑; 🚊3,16,96) Choosing from the vegetarian menu is easy. Deciding what to pay can be hard. This unique not-for-profit operation provides training and educational opportunities for marginalised people, as well as tasty flesh-free grub. Whatever you pay for your meal goes towards helping new migrants, refugees, people with disabilities and the long-term unemployed. There are several branches, including one at Abbotsford Convent (p66).

Claypots SEAFOOD $$
(Map p78; ☎03-9534 1282; www.facebook.com/claypotsstkilda; 213 Barkly St, St Kilda; claypots $20, mains $24-45; ⊙noon-1am; 🚊96) A local favourite, Claypots serves up fresh, share-style plates of seafood. Its namesake dish is available in a number of options, including a beautifully spiced Moroccan (mussels and fish fillet cooked with couscous, tomato, eggplant, harissa, zaatar and chickpeas). Get in early to both nab a seat and ensure the good stuff is still available, as hot items go fast.

Matcha Mylkbar CAFE, VEGETARIAN $$
(Map p78; ☎03-9534 1111; www.matchamylkbar.com; 72a Acland St, St Kilda; dishes $15-22; ⊙8am-3pm; ☑; 🚊3, 16, 96) If you've spied anything from Matcha Mylkbar in your Instagram feed, it's likely you've been left green with envy. This small, contemporary St Kilda cafe is known for its matcha-heavy menu, which is also 100% plant based and vegan friendly.

Favourite dishes include vibrant green pancakes and burger buns, as well as social-media-inclined smoothies served in skull-shaped glasses, healthy breakfast bowls scattered with edible flowers, and trademarked vegan eggs made from agar, sweet potato, coconut milk and linseed protein.

Miss Jackson CAFE $$
(Map p78; ☎03-9534 8415; www.facebook.com/missjacksoncafe; 2/19 Grey St, St Kilda; mains from $15; ⊙7am-4pm Tue-Sun; 🚊3, 16, 96) The casual set-up and atmosphere here makes it feel a bit like you've been invited around to a friend's house for brunch – a friend with good enough taste to cook things like crab scrambled eggs, panko-crumbed chicken-schnitzel burgers or house-smoked Portarlington sardines with romesco sauce, avocado, cos and fennel on rye toast.

Uncle VIETNAMESE $$
(Map p78; ☎03-9041 2668; www.unclestkilda.com.au; 188 Carlisle St, St Kilda; mains $30-34; ⊙5pm-late Mon & Tue, noon-late Wed-Sun; 🚊3, 16, 78, 🚆Balaclava) Uncle delivers stellar Vietnamese cooking in a quintessentially St Kilda space, complete with popular rooftop dining area. The *pho* (noodle soup) is fragrant and herbaceous, and best ordered as a small portion so you have room to try the golden, crunchy deliciousness of the DIY chicken-tenderloin steamed *bao*. Wash it all down with Viet sangria or a can of Vietnamese beer.

Newmarket Hotel AMERICAN $$
(Map p78; ☎03-9537 1777; www.newmarketstkilda.com.au; 34 Inkerman St, St Kilda; sharing plates from $13; ⊙noon-3pm & 6-10.30pm; 🚊3, 16, 67) Sporting interiors by renowned architects Six Degrees, this historic pub channels the California–Mexico border with tasty dishes like tacos, smoked-chicken quesadillas and scallop ceviche with salt-water cream and chilli. There's no shortage of quality wood-fired meats, and the weekday lunch specials are excellent value. There's a top-shelf bar to boot.

I Carusi II PIZZA $$
(Map p78; ☎03-9593 6033; 231 Barkly St, St Kilda; pizza $19-26; ⊙6-10pm Mon-Fri, from 5pm Sat & Sun; 🚊3, 16, 96) Located around the corner from the Acland St chaos, this casually elegant Italian is well loved for its thin-based pizzas. While quality isn't always consistent, when they're done well the pizzas are smashing. Check the board for creative pasta specials, and flaunt your sophistication by ordering a Cynar *spritz* – Venice's less-sweet take on the ubiquitous Aperol *spritz*. Bookings advised.

HuTong Dumpling Bar CHINESE $$
(Map p76; ☎03-9098 1188; www.hutong.com.au; 162 Commercial Rd, Prahran; dumplings $9-14, mains $19-50; ⊙11.30am-3pm & 5.30-10.30pm Sun-Thu, to 11pm Fri & Sat; 🚊72, 78, 🚆Prahran) This Prahran outpost of the city restaurant (p94) of the same name is best known for its flawless, made-from-scratch *xiao long bao*. Other bite-size favourites include wontons with vinegary chilli sauce and prawn dumplings. The steamed-spinach dumplings are less impressive.

Mr Wolf PIZZA $$
(Map p78; ☎03-9534 0255; www.mrwolf.com.au; 9-15 Inkerman St, St Kilda; pizza $20-25; ⊙5pm-late Tue-Sun, from noon Fri-Sun; 🚊3, 16, 67) Local celeb chef Karen Martini's casual but stylish space is renowned for its crisp Roman-style pizzas. There's also a great menu of antipasti and pastas that display her flair for matching ingredients.

Batch Espresso CAFE $$
(Map p78; ☎03-9530 3550; 320 Carlisle St, Balaclava; mains $16; ⊙7am-4.30pm, kitchen to 3pm Mon-Fri, to 3.30pm Sat & Sun; 🚊3, 3a, 16, 🚆Balaclava) Like a pair of well-worn slippers, Batch feels snug and familiar. Upcycled artworks by Melbourne-based artists Joost Bakker and Peter James Smith share the limelight with trinkets from loyal regulars, many of whom keep coming back for the cafe's dark-roasted coffee, kedgeree (an Indian dish with house-smoked fish, coriander and egg) and potato-and-spinach hash. Good luck getting a seat at weekends!

★ **Attica** MODERN AUSTRALIAN $$$
(☎03-9530 0111; www.attica.com.au; 74 Glen Eira Rd, Ripponlea; tasting menu $250; ⊙6pm-late Tue-Sat; 🚊67, 🚆Ripponlea) The only Australian restaurant on the San Pellegrino World's Top 50 Restaurants list, Attica is home to prodigious Kiwi import Ben Shewry and his extraordinary culinary creations. Native ingredients shine in dishes like bunya bunya with salted red kangaroo, or bush-currant granité with lemon aspen and rosella flower. Reservations accepted three months ahead, on the first Wednesday of each month at 9am. Note that tables of two can go within a couple of hours, especially for Friday and Saturday nights. You'll have a better chance with a table for four or more, or trying for dinner midweek. It's also worth emailing or calling to check if availability isn't showing online. If driving, follow Brighton Rd south and turn left onto Glen Eira Rd.

Lau's Family Kitchen CHINESE $$$
(Map p78; ☎03-8598 9880; www.lauskitchen.com.au; 4 Acland St, St Kilda; mains $26-45; ⊙noon-3pm Mon-Fri, 12.30-3.30pm Sun, dinner sittings 6pm & 8pm daily; 🚊16, 96) This polished nosh spot serves beautiful, home-style Cantonese with a few Sichuan surprises, including a seductive braised eggplant with spiced minced pork. Reserve for one of the two dinner sittings, and check out the elegant wall panels, made from 1930s kimonos.

Stokehouse SEAFOOD $$$
(Map p78; ☎03-9525 5555; www.stokehouse.com.au; 30 Jacka Blvd, St Kilda; mains $36-42; ⊙noon-3pm & 6pm-late; 🚊3a, 16, 96) After a devastating fire, the lauded Stokehouse is back, brighter and better than ever. Striking contemporary architecture and floor-to-ceiling bay views set the right tone for fresh, modern, seafood-centric dishes, not to mention a stuff-of-legend bombe Alaska. This is one of Melbourne's hottest restaurants, so always book ahead.

Downstairs at beach level is the Stokehouse's casual, walk-in bar-bistro Pontoon (p121), as well as a fish-and-chip kiosk.

Cicciolina ITALIAN $$$
(Map p78; ☎03-9525 3333; www.cicciolinastkilda.com.au; 130 Acland St, St Kilda; mains lunch $18-30, dinner $27-45; ⊙noon-10pm; 🚊3, 16, 96) This hideaway of dark wood, subdued lighting and pencil sketches is a St Kilda institution. The menu is modern Italian, with dishes that might see tortellini paired beautifully with Persian feta, ricotta, pine nuts, lime zest, asparagus and burnt sage butter. Bookings only for lunch; for dinner, eat very early or while away your wait in the moody back bar.

Drinking & Nightlife

Melbourne's drinking scene is easily the best in Australia and as good as any in the world. There's a huge diversity of venues, ranging from hip basement dives hidden down laneways to sophisticated cocktail bars perched on rooftops. Many pubs have pulled up the beer-stained carpet and polished the concrete, but don't dismiss the character-filled oldies that still exist.

City Centre

The city's best bars are an eclectic bunch, with many lurking down laneways or brazenly basking in the open air at the top of city buildings. There's a particularly good batch around Spring St and Chinatown. Curtin House on Swanston St offers more cool per square metre than anywhere else in Australia.

★ **Heartbreaker** BAR
(Map p56; ☎03-9041 0856; www.heartbreakerbar.com.au; 234a Russell St; ⊙5pm-3am Mon-Sat, to 11pm Sun; 🚆Melbourne Central) Black walls, red lights, skeleton handles on the beer taps, random taxidermy, craft beer, a big selection of bourbon, rock and punk on the sound sys-

MEALS ON WHEELS: MELBOURNE'S FOOD TRUCKS

Melbourne's long had an association with food vans; a game of suburban footy isn't complete without someone dishing out hot jam doughnuts, meat pies and chips to freezing fans over a truck counter – and what would a trip to the beach be without an ice-cream van playing its tune? But getting quality food from a van is a different matter. Taking a cue from LA's food-truck revolution, fabulous options have begun plying the streets of Melbourne. Each day the trucks post to let their Twitter and Facebook followers know where they'll be, and hungry folk dutifully respond by turning up street-side for a meal. Favourite Melbourne food trucks (and their Twitter handles and websites) to chase down:

Cornutopia (@cornutopia; www.cornutopia.com.au) Mexican street food

Gumbo Kitchen (@GumboKitchen; www.gumbokitchen.com.au) New Orleans–style po' boys

Beatbox Kitchen (@beatboxkitchen; www.beatboxkitchen.com) Gourmet burgers and fries

Mr Burger (@MrBurgerTruck; www.mrburger.com.au) As the name suggests

Smokin' Barry's (@Smokinbarrys; www.smokinbarrys.com.au) Smoky BBQ meats

GrumbleTumms (@GrumbleTumms; www.grumbletumms.com) Aussie bush tucker: croc or emu pies and roo burgers

Also check out www.wherethetruck.at for more food trucks around town.

tem, and tough-looking sweethearts behind the bar – all the prerequisites, in fact, for a hard-rocking good time.

★Madame Brussels ROOFTOP BAR

(Map p56; ☎03-9662 2775; www.madamebrussels.com; 3rd fl, 57-59 Bourke St; ⏰noon-11pm Sun-Wed, to 1am Thu-Sat; 🚉Parliament) Head up to this wonderful rooftop terrace if you've had it with Melbourne-moody and all that dark wood. Although it's named for a famous 19th-century brothel owner, it feels like a camp 1960s country club, with much Astro-turfery and wisteria, and staff dressed for a spot of tennis.

★Croft Institute BAR

(Map p56; www.thecroftinstitute.com.au; 21 Croft Alley; ⏰5pm-midnight Mon-Thu, 5pm-3am Fri, 8pm-3am Sat; 🚋86, 96) Hidden in a graffitied laneway off a laneway, the slightly creepy Croft is a laboratory-themed bar downstairs, while upstairs at weekends the 1950s-themed gymnasium opens as a club. There's a $5 cover charge for DJs Friday and Saturday nights.

★Bar Americano COCKTAIL BAR

(Map p56; www.baramericano.com.au; 20 Presgrave Pl; ⏰5pm-1am Mon-Sat; 🚉Flinders St) A hideaway bar in a lane off Howey Pl, Bar Americano is a teensy standing-room-only affair with black-and-white chequered floors complemented by classic 'do not spit' subway-tiled walls and a subtle air of speakeasy. Once it hits its 14-person max, the grille gets pulled shut. The cocktails here don't come cheap, but they do come superb.

★Siglo ROOFTOP BAR

(Map p56; ☎03-9654 6631; www.siglobar.com.au; 2nd fl, 161 Spring St; ⏰5pm-3am; 🚉Parliament) Siglo's sought-after terrace comes with Parisian flair, wafting cigar smoke and serious drinks. It fills with suits on Friday night, which may lure or horrify you. Regardless, pick a time to mull over a classic cocktail, snack on upper-crust morsels and admire the 19th-century vista over Parliament and St Patrick's Cathedral. Entry is via the similarly unsigned Supper Club (p112).

Boilermaker House BAR

(Map p56; www.boilermakerhouse.com.au; 209-211 Lonsdale St; ⏰4pm-3am; 🚉Melbourne Central) A real surprise on busy, workaday Lonsdale St, this dimly lit haven of urbanity has a phenomenal 850 whiskies on its list, along with 12 craft beers on tap and a further 40 by the bottle. Snack on cheese, charcuterie and jalapeño poppers as you make your way through them.

Cookie BAR

(Map p56; ☎03-9663 7660; www.cookie.net.au; 1st fl, Curtin House, 252 Swanston St; ⏰noon-3am; 🚉Melbourne Central) Part bar, part Thai restaurant, this kooky-cool venue with grand bones is one of the more enduring rites of passage of the Melbourne night. The bar is unbelievably well stocked with fine whiskies, wines, and plenty of craft beers among the more than 200 brews on offer. The staff also knows how to make a serious cocktail.

Melbourne Supper Club BAR

(Map p56; ☎03-9654 6300; www.melbournesupperclub.com.au; 1st fl, 161 Spring St; ⏰5pm-4am Sun-Thu, to 6am Fri & Sat; 🚊Parliament) Let's face it, late-night bars can be shady places, but that's not the case at this sophisticated hideaway by the Princess Theatre, entered via an unsigned wooden door. It's a favoured after-work destination for performers and hospitality types. Cosy into a chesterfield, browse the encyclopaedic wine menu and relax; the sommeliers will cater to any liquid desire.

Rooftop Bar ROOFTOP BAR

(Map p56; ☎03-9654 5394; www.rooftopcinema.com.au; 6th fl, Curtin House, 252 Swanston St; ⏰noon-1am; 🚊Melbourne Central) This bar sits at dizzying heights atop happening Curtin House. In summer it transforms into an outdoor cinema with striped deckchairs and a calendar of new and classic favourite flicks.

Garden State Hotel BAR

(Map p56; ☎03-8396 5777; www.gardenstatehotel.com.au; 101 Flinders Lane; ⏰11am-late; 📶; 🚊Flinders St) Just as in a grand English garden, there are orderly bits, wild bits and little dark nooks in this so-hot-right-now multipurpose venue. Shuffle past the suits into the main bar area, which is backed by shiny copper vats and a three-storey void filled with mature trees. The best part is the chandelier-festooned Rose Garden cocktail bar in the basement.

Arbory BAR

(Map p56; ☎03-8648 7644; www.arbory.com.au; 1 Flinders Walk; ⏰7.30am-late; 🚊Flinders St) Situated as close as a venue can get to the Yarra without toppling in, Arbory occupies the decommissioned platform for the Sandridge train line at the edge of Flinders St station. At over 100m long, it's Melbourne's broadest bar. Come for the view of the Arts Centre across the water, stay for the espresso martinis. The food's not bad either.

Magic Mountain Saloon BAR

(Map p56; ☎03-9078 0078; www.magicmountainsaloon.com.au; 62 Little Collins St; ⏰7am-3am; 📶; 🚊Parliament) Too hip to have a sign (look for the stylised mountain/M-shaped neon), this slick venue spills over two levels where visitors can order cocktails from burnt-orange booths, socialise at the marble bars and dance to DJs from Wednesday to Sunday. It's also open for Asian-inflected meals throughout the day, starting with Chinese doughnuts and black sticky rice for breakfast.

Market Lane Coffee CAFE

(Map p56; www.marketlane.com.au; 109-111 Therry St; ⏰7am-4pm; 🚊Melbourne Central) It's all about the super-strong coffee at this branch of Market Lane. It serves a few pastries, too, but as it's right opposite Queen Victoria Market there's no shortage of snacks at hand to enjoy with your takeaway cup. There's another branch in the market's deli hall.

Lui Bar COCKTAIL BAR

(Map p56; ☎03-9691 3888; www.vuedemonde.com.au; 55th fl, Rialto, 525 Collins St; ⏰5.30pm-midnight Mon-Wed, 11.30am-1am Thu, 11.30am-3am Fri & Sat, 11.30am-midnight Sun; 🚊Southern Cross) Some people are happy to shell out $36 for the view from the 120m-high Melbourne Star, but we'd much rather spend $25 on a cocktail at this sophisticated bar perched 236m up the Rialto tower. Suits and jet-setters cram in most nights, so get there early (and nicely dressed) to claim your table.

Chuckle Park BAR

(Map p56; ☎03-9650 4494; www.chucklepark.com.au; 322 Little Collins St; ⏰11am-1am; 🚋86, 96) Creating a park out of a narrow laneway and an expanse of astroturf, this kooky crew serves huge jars of cocktails and pulled-pork rolls from a little 1970s caravan parked down one end. Hanging plant jars double as swaying lights, and indie and rock music entertain the in-the-know crowd.

Hells Kitchen BAR

(Map p56; ☎03-9654 5755; www.hellskitchenmelbourne.com; 1st fl, 20 Centre Pl; ⏰noon-11pm Sun-Tue, to 1am Wed-Sat; 🚊Flinders St) Head up to Hells via the narrow stairway from beautiful Centre Pl. It attracts a hip, young crowd who sip classic cocktails, wine, beer or cider and people-watch from the large windows. Also serves food.

Lounge BAR

(Map p56; ☎03-9663 2916; www.lounge.com.au; 1st fl, 243 Swanston St; ⏰noon-midnight Sun & Mon, to 2am Tue-Thu, to 4am Fri, to 6am Sat; 📶; 🚊Melbourne Central) The Lounge has seen a lot of years and still feels like a share house from the early 1990s – in a good way, of course. Evenings are filled with the sound of DJs and live music. Escape to the big balcony with some American diner–style grub.

Ferdydurke BAR

(Map p56; ☎03-9639 3750; www.ferdydurke.com.au; 1st fl, 31 Tattersalls Lane; ⏰4pm-1am Sun-Thu, noon-1am Fri & Sat; 📶; 🚉Melbourne Central) This dive bar and art space is set over two levels, and within its gritty confines they play everything from electronic to live Polish jazz. Also sells hot dogs.

Riverland BAR

(Map p56; ☎03-9662 1771; www.riverlandbar.com; vaults 1-9, Federation Wharf; ⏰8am-late; 🚉Flinders St) Perched below Princes Bridge alongside the Yarra River, this bluestone beauty keeps things simple with good wine, beer on tap and bar meals that hit the mark: burgers, ribs, fish and chips. The outside tables are a treat when the weather is kind. Be prepared for rowdiness before and after footy matches at the nearby MCG.

Brother Baba Budan CAFE

(Map p56; www.sevenseeds.com.au; 359 Little Bourke St; ⏰7am-5pm Mon-Sat, 9am-5pm Sun; 📶; 🚉Melbourne Central) This small cafe has just a few seats (most are hangin' from the ceiling), but it does a roaring takeaway-coffee trade for inner-city workers and is a great spot to acquire a midshopping caffeine buzz. Don't be put off by queues; service is fast and friendly. Food is limited to croissants, muffins, scones and cookies.

Carlton Hotel BAR

(Map p56; ☎03-9663 3246; www.thecarlton.com.au; 193 Bourke St; ⏰3pm-late Sun-Wed, noon-late Thu-Sat; 🚋86, 96) Over-the-top Melbourne rococo gets another workout here and never fails to raise a smile. The tropical deck on the 1st floor is shrouded in jasmine and bougainvillea. Check out the rooftop **Palmz** if you're looking for some Miami-flavoured vice, or just a great view.

Loop BAR, CLUB

(Map p56; ☎03-9654 0500; www.looponline.com.au; 23 Meyers Pl; ⏰4pm-late; 🚉Parliament) At weekends, DJs perform here in a project space with a large double screen and scattered projectors; find yourself a dark seat or a spot at the bar. There's something on most nights, from beats to heartfelt docos. Best of all is the plant-filled rooftop bar, offering great urban views.

Gin Palace COCKTAIL BAR

(Map p56; ☎03-9654 0533; www.ginpalace.com.au; 10 Russell Pl; ⏰4pm-3am; 🚋86, 96, 🚉Flinders St) With a drinks list to make your liver quiver, Gin Palace is the perfect place to grab a soft couch, secluded alcove or bathtub filled with cushions, sip, and take it slow. The martinis here are legendary and it's open super late most nights.

Double Happiness COCKTAIL BAR

(Map p56; ☎03-9650 4488; www.double-happiness.com.au; 21 Liverpool St; ⏰4pm-1am Mon-Wed, 4pm-3am Thu & Fri, 6pm-3am Sat, 6pm-1am Sun; 🚋86, 96, 🚉Parliament) This stylish hole-in-the-wall is decked out in Chinese propaganda posters and Mao statues, and serves an excellent range of Asian-influenced chilli- and coriander-flavoured cocktails, along with a legendary espresso martini.

Section 8 BAR

(Map p56; www.section8.com.au; 27-29 Tattersalls Lane; ⏰noon-11pm Sun, 10am-11pm Mon-Wed, 10am-1am Thu & Fri, noon-1am Sat; 🚉Melbourne Central) Enclosed within a cage full of shipping containers, graffiti and wooden-pallet seating, Section 8 remains one of the city's hippest bars. It's quite a scene, with DJs playing regularly.

Degraves Espresso CAFE

(Map p56; ☎03-9654 1245; 23-25 Degraves St; ⏰7am-10pm Mon-Sat, 8am-5pm Sun; 🚉Flinders St) In atmospheric Degraves St, this institution is a good spot to grab a quick takeaway coffee and wander the laneways.

Crafty Squire BREWERY

(Map p56; ☎03-9810 0064; www.thecraftysquire.com.au; 127 Russell St; ⏰11am-3am Sun-Thu, noon-5am Fri & Sat; 🚋86, 96) This vast booze barn houses a James Squire microbrewery, although it's debatable whether a brand owned by a giant multinational brewery can really be called 'craft'. Free brewery tours can be arranged.

New Gold Mountain COCKTAIL BAR

(Map p56; ☎03-9650 8859; www.newgoldmountain.com.au; 1st fl, 21 Liverpool St; ⏰5pm-1am Mon-Wed, to 3am Thu, to 5am Fri & Sat; 🚉Parliament) Unsignposted above Double Happiness (p113), New Gold Mountain's intense chinoiserie interior overloads the senses, with decoration so relentless you may feel as if you're trapped in an art-house dream sequence. Service can be variable, but it's a pleasant bolthole regardless. At weekends Red Devil on the upper floor provides further nooks to hide in.

Workshop BAR
(Map p56; ☎03-9326 4365; www.workshopbar.com.au; 1st fl, 413 Elizabeth St; ⏰11am-2am Mon-Fri, 2pm-3am Sat, 3pm-1am Sun; 📶; 🚉Melbourne Central) Popular with students and young, arty types, this grungy bar has a lively party atmosphere, with DJs playing mainly hip-hop, bass, electro and grime. It's a good cheap lunch spot, too, with sandwiches, $9 pizzas and $2 student coffees consumed on its flora-filled balcony.

Young & Jackson PUB
(Map p56; ☎03-9650 3884; www.youngandjacksons.com.au; cnr Flinders & Swanston Sts; ⏰10am-late; 📶; 🚉Flinders St) Opposite Flinders St station, this heritage pub has been pouring beer since 1861 and makes for a popular meeting spot. Head to the 1st-floor Chloe's Bar (home to a famous nude painting) or continue to the rooftop cider bar, where there's a good selection of Australian craft ciders on tap.

Southbank & Docklands

Boatbuilders Yard BAR
(☎03-9686 5088; www.theboatbuildersyard.com.au; 23 South Wharf Promenade, South Wharf; ⏰7am-late; 🚋12, 96, 109) Occupying a slice of South Wharf next to the historic *Polly Woodside* ship, Boatbuilders attracts a mixed crowd of office workers, travellers and Melburnians keen to discover this developing area. It's made up of 'zones' running seamlessly from the indoor cafe-bar to the outdoor BBQ and bocce pit. There are usually live bands or DJs at weekends.

Ponyfish Island BAR
(Map p56; www.ponyfish.com.au; Southbank Pedestrian Bridge, Southbank; ⏰11am-late; 🚉Flinders St) Not content with hiding bars down laneways or on rooftops, Melburnians are finding ever more creative spots to do their drinking. Where better than a little open-air nook on the pylon of a bridge arcing over the Yarra? It's a surprisingly good spot to knock back beers while snacking on toasted sandwiches or cheese plates.

Richmond & East Melbourne

Richmond's coolest drinking venues are grouped around Swan St and Church St.

Mountain Goat Brewery MICROBREWERY
(☎03-9428 1180; www.goatbeer.com.au; 80 North St, Richmond; ⏰5-10pm Wed & Fri; 🚋48, 75) This local microbrewery occupies a large warehouse in Richmond's backstreets. Sample its range of beers with an $11 tasting paddle while nibbling pizza. There are free brewery tours at 6.30pm on Wednesday. It's tricky to reach: head east on Bridge Rd, then turn left at Burnley St and right at North St.

Slowbeer CRAFT BEER
(☎03-9421 3838; www.slowbeer.com.au; 468 Bridge Rd, Richmond; ⏰2-8pm Mon-Wed, noon-9pm Thu-Sat, noon-8pm Sun; 🚋48, 75) The walls of this little shop are lined with craft beer for sale, but you can pull up a seat at the central wooden table and settle in for a drink and a snack.

DT's Hotel GAY
(Map p65; ☎03-9428 5724; www.facebook.com/dtspub/; 164 Church St, Richmond; ⏰6pm-midnight Tue, 4pm-1am Wed-Sat, 2-11pm Sun; 🚋78) This long-standing gay pub hosts drag shows, karaoke, pool competitions and happy hours.

Public House BAR
(Map p65; ☎03-9421 0187; www.publichouse.com.au; 433-435 Church St, Richmond; ⏰noon-late Tue-Sun; 🚉East Richmond) Not in any way resembling a public house from any discernible period in history, this swanky bar has been given a striking fit-out using raw and recycled materials. The food's excellent and DJs set up at weekends, attracting a young, good-looking crowd ready to, uh, mingle.

Touchwood CAFE
(☎03-9429 9347; www.touchwoodcafe.com; 480 Bridge Rd, Richmond; ⏰7am-4pm; 🚋48, 75) There's plenty of space both indoors and in the courtyard of this light, airy cafe housed in a former recycled-furniture store (hence the name). The coffee's single origin and the doughnuts at the counter are difficult to resist.

Fitzroy, Collingwood & Abbotsford

You won't go thirsty for long in these hip neighbourhoods, as they're home to some of the city's best bars, pubs and coffee roasters. Smith and Gertrude Sts are loaded with intimate wine bars, cool cocktail spots and cafes, while the best local pubs can be found in the backstreets of Fitzroy. Brunswick St can be patchy but has some real gems hidden among it all.

★ **Black Pearl** COCKTAIL BAR
(Map p68; ☎03-9417 0455; www.blackpearlbar.com.au; 304 Brunswick St, Fitzroy; ⏲5pm-3am, Attic Bar 7pm-2am Thu-Sat; 🚋11) After 15 years in the game, Black Pearl goes from strength to strength, winning awards and receiving global accolades along the way. Low lighting, leather banquettes and candles set the mood downstairs. Prop at the bar to study the extensive cocktail list or let the expert bartenders concoct something to your taste. Upstairs is the table-service Attic Bar; book ahead.

★ **Marion** WINE BAR
(Map p68; ☎03-9419 6262; www.marionwine.com.au; 53 Gertrude St, Fitzroy; ⏲5-11pm Mon-Thu, noon-11pm Fri, 8am-11pm Sat & Sun; 🚋86) Melbourne's poster-boy chef, Andrew McConnell, knew what he was doing when he opened Marion. The wine list is one of the area's most impressive and the space – catering to both stop-ins and long, romantic chats – is a pleasure to be in. Food changes regularly, but expect charcuterie from McConnell's butcher Meatsmith and specials with a European bent (dishes $10 to $34).

★ **Everleigh** COCKTAIL BAR
(Map p68; www.theeverleigh.com; 150-156 Gertrude St, Fitzroy; ⏲5.30pm-1am; 🚋86) Sophistication and bartending standards are off the charts at this upstairs hidden nook. Settle into a leather booth in the intimate setting with a few friends for conversation, and exclaiming over classic 'golden era' cocktails like you've never tasted before.

★ **Naked for Satan** BAR
(Map p68; ☎03-9416 2238; www.nakedforsatan.com.au; 285 Brunswick St, Fitzroy; ⏲noon-midnight Sun-Thu, to 1am Fri & Sat; 🚋11) Vibrant, loud and reviving an apparent Brunswick St legend (a man nicknamed Satan who would get down and dirty, naked because of the heat, in an illegal vodka distillery under the shop), this place packs a punch with its popular *pintxos* (Basque tapas; $1 to $2), huge range of beverages, and unbeatable roof terrace (Naked in the Sky) with wraparound balcony.

★ **Proud Mary** CAFE
(Map p68; ☎03-9417 5930; 172 Oxford St, Collingwood; ⏲7.30am-4pm Mon-Fri, 8.30am-4pm Sat & Sun; 📶; 🚋86) A champion for direct-trade, single-origin coffee, this quintessential industrial Collingwood red-brick space takes its caffeine seriously. It's consistently packed, not only for the excellent brew but also for the equally top-notch food, such as ricotta hotcakes or free-range pork with fennel crackling.

For a further coffee education, check out **Aunty Peg's** (p116), its roastery nearby.

Stomping Ground Brewery & Beer Hall BREWERY
(☎03-9415 1944; www.stompingground.beer; 100 Gipps St, Collingwood; ⏲11.30am-11pm Mon-Thu, to 1am Fri & Sat; 📶👪; 🚋109, 🚆Collingwood) This inviting brewery set in a former textile factory is a relaxed, leafy retreat with exposed-brick walls, hanging plants, a kids' play area and a large central bar. There are 15 to 25 Stomping Ground beers on tap, as well as rotating guest beers, and a menu of wood-fired pizzas, burgers and salads.

The beer menu is split into helpful categories: easy drinking, intermediate or challenging. If beer's not your thing, never fear, as it also offers wine on tap, cocktails, and whisky boilermakers. Brewery tours run on weekends from midday; check the website for updates.

Bar Liberty BAR
(Map p68; http://barliberty.com; 234 Johnston St, Fitzroy; ⏲5pm-late Mon-Sat & from noon Sun; 🚋86) From a team of hospitality heavyweights, Bar Liberty is bringing carefully selected wines (over 300 on the list) and expertly crafted cocktails to Fitzroy minus any pretentiousness. The approach is laid-back, the atmosphere is relaxed and the dining focus is on bold, refined food. There are monthly wine dinners upstairs and a rear courtyard beer garden, Drinkwell.

Industry Beans CAFE
(Map p68; ☎03-9417 1034; www.industrybeans.com; 3/62 Rose St, Fitzroy; ⏲7am-4pm Mon-Fri, 8am-4pm Sat & Sun; 📶; 🚋96, 11) It's all about coffee chemistry at this warehouse cafe tucked in a Fitzroy side street. The coffee guide takes you through the speciality styles on offer (roasted on -ite), from AeroPress and pourover to cold drip and espresso, and helpful staff take the pressure off deciding. The food menu (brunch $12 to $35) is ambitious but doesn't always hit the mark.

Sircuit GAY
(Map p68; www.sircuit.com.au; 103 Smith St, Fitzroy; ⏲7.30pm-late Wed-Sun; 🚋86) Hugely popular with a big cross section of gay men, Sircuit is an old-school gay bar with pool tables, drag

shows, a back room and, as the night progresses, a heaving dance floor.

Dr Morse Bar & Eatery BAR

(☎03-9416 1005; www.drmorse.com.au; 274 Johnston St, Abbotsford; ⏰7am-11pm Mon-Thu, to 1am Fri, 8am-1am Sat, 8am-11pm Sun; 📶; 🚆Victoria Park) Dr Morse is a classic all-rounder, keeping everyone happy at any time of day. The Asian-influenced cuisine is a winner from morning to night, you can wet your whistle on craft beer and cocktails, the beer garden is the perfect Sunday lingering spot, or you can simply grab a coffee from the takeaway window on your way to/from Victoria Park station.

Moon Dog Bar & Brewery BREWERY

(☎03-9428 2307; www.moondogbrewing.com.au; 1 Duke St, Abbotsford; ⏰4-11pm Wed-Fri, noon-11pm Sat, noon-8pm Sun; 🚋12, 109) It's a bit of a hike to get here, but you'll be rewarded with excellent and experimental craft beer at this functioning microbrewery. Don't be put off by the nondescript industrial backstreet: inside it's an inviting, eclectic atmosphere with projector screens, secondhand couches and wooden barrels. Snack on free popcorn or grab a pizza from the van out the front.

Noble Experiment BAR

(Map p68; ☎03-9416 0058; www.thenobleexperiment.com.au; 284 Smith St, Collingwood; ⏰5pm-late Wed & Thu, noon-late Fri-Sun; 🚋86) If 1920s Prohibition-era cocktails are your tipple then swing by the Noble Experiment for a bottle-aged negroni, a bootleggers iced tea or a Kentucky cobbler. Spread over three levels, the decor hints at New York old-world charm and there's a seriously good food offering, from a chef's menu to slow-cooked meats designed for sharing.

Aunty Peg's COFFEE

(☎03-9417 1333; www.auntypegsbypmc.com.au; 200 Wellington St, Collingwood; ⏰8am-5pm; 🚋86) For a peek behind the scenes of Proud Mary (p115) – producer of some of the city's best coffee – swing by Aunty Peg's roasting house. The warehouse shows off the production side and hosts workshops and barista boot camps; it also has a tasting bar (black coffee only) with a one-on-one barista experience. Coffee merchandise and Proud Mary beans are for sale, too.

Free cuppings are held Tuesday from 6.30pm.

Craft & Co MICROBREWERY

(Map p68; ☎03-9417 4755; www.thecraftandco.com.au; 390 Smith St, Collingwood; ⏰7am-4pm Mon-Wed, 7am-late Thu & Fri, 8am-late Sat, 8am-6pm Sun; 🚋86) Take time to explore this two-storey warehouse – there's lots going on, from cafe, coffee roaster, bakery and deli to brewery and distillery. Most of the cafe menu's ingredients are produced in-house and are also for sale, among them bread, cheese, charcuterie, coffee, beer, gin and vodka. Come evening it's a bar with an almost exclusively Australian booze list.

Growers Espresso & Eureka Coffee CAFE

(☎03-9486 1886; www.eurekacoffee.com.au; 332 St Georges Rd, North Fitzroy; ⏰7.30am-3pm Mon-Fri, from 8am Sat; 🚋11) Specialising in Australian-grown coffee, Eureka roasts its own beans and has a great selection of single-origins, too. Ask about free cupping sessions and tastings on Thursday.

Forester's Hall BAR

(Map p68; www.forestershall.com.au; 64 Smith St, Collingwood, cnr Smith & Gertrude Sts; ⏰4pm-2am Tue-Thu, 4pm-4am Fri, 2pm-4am Sat, 2pm-2am Sun; 🚋86) The former nightclub here has been transformed into a haven for beer lovers, with 32 well-curated taps on offer from Australia and around the world. Pair this with pizzas served 'til 2am, ping-pong tables, street-side seating, a mezzanine space and an upstairs dive bar, and you've got a winning combo for a night out.

Grace Darling PUB

(Map p68; ☎03-9416 0055; www.thegracedarlinghotel.com.au; 114 Smith St, Collingwood; mains $18-30; ⏰noon-1am Mon-Sat, to 11pm Sun; 🚋86) Adored by Collingwood football fans as the birthplace of the club, these days the Grace has been given a spit-and-polish and attracts a clientele of pretty young things. The bluestone beauty has a cosy restaurant, street-side tables, and live music, mainly aimed at the young indie crowd.

Laird GAY, PUB

(☎03-9417 2832; www.lairdhotel.com; 149 Gipps St, Abbotsford; ⏰5pm-late Mon-Sat, from 4pm Sun; 🚆Collingwood) This long-running men-only pub comes with lots of leather, beer and brawn. Who's yer daddy? And you don't have to worry about getting home: there's accommodation on-site (from $120). There's a calendar of events; check the website for details.

Peel Hotel GAY, CLUB

(03-9419 4762; www.thepeel.com.au; 113 Wellington St, Collingwood; 11pm-5am Thu, to 7am Fri & Sat; 86) The Peel is one of the best-known and most popular gay venues in Melbourne. It's the last stop of a big night.

Panama Dining Room & Bar BAR

(Map p68; 03-9417 7663; www.thepanama.com.au; 3rd fl, 231 Smith St, Fitzroy; bar 5pm-late, restaurant from 6pm; 86) Disappear up the stairs to where Smith St's traded in for a Manhattan feel at this warehouse space with huge arched windows. Sip serious cocktails, such as a barrel-aged negroni or a pineapple-and-chipotle daiquiri, while snacking on BBQ king prawns or grilled saganaki. For a more serious feed, park yourself in the dining area for the Euro-inspired menu with an Australian twist.

Napier Hotel PUB

(Map p68; 03-9419 4240; www.thenapierhotel.com; 210 Napier St, Fitzroy; 3-11pm Mon-Thu, noon-1am Fri, noon-11pm Sat, 1-11pm Sun; 86, 11) The Napier has stood on this corner for over a century; many pots have been pulled as the face of the neighbourhood has changed, as demonstrated by the memorabilia of the sadly departed Fitzroy footy team. Worm your way around the central bar to the boisterous dining room for an iconic Bogan burger. Head upstairs to check out the gallery, too.

Union Club Hotel PUB

(Map p68; 03-9417 2926; www.unionclubhotel.com.au; 164 Gore St, Fitzroy; 3pm-late Mon-Wed, noon-late Thu-Sat, noon-11pm Sun; 86) A die-hard local with a retro feel and happy chatter from a relaxed indie crowd. The large curved bar is one of Melbourne's best spots to park yourself; the food is good, honest pub nosh; and the beer garden and roof deck beg you to make a lazy afternoon of it on a hot day.

Standard Hotel PUB

(Map p68; 03-9419 4793; 293 Fitzroy St, Fitzroy; 3-10pm Mon, to 11pm Tue, noon-11pm Wed-Sat, noon-10pm Sun; 96, 11) Flaunting a great beer garden, the Standard is anything but its moniker. The Fitzroy backstreet local has down-to-earth bar staff and a truly eclectic crowd enhancing an atmosphere defined by live music on Sunday, footy on the small screen, and loud and enthusiastic chatter.

Bar Open BAR

(Map p68; 03-9415 9601; www.baropen.com.au; 317 Brunswick St, Fitzroy; 3pm-3am; 11) This long-established bar is often open when everything else is closed, as the name suggests. The bar attracts a relaxed, young local crowd and bands play in the upstairs loft most nights and are almost always free.

Carlton & Brunswick

Carlton has plenty of bars and pubs catering to a university crowd, as well as a good bunch of intimate wine bars perfect for a pre- or postcinema or theatre tipple. East Brunswick is the spot to mingle with locals in cosy bars, while around Sydney Rd in Brunswick you'll find plenty of late-night choices and classic pubs.

Wide Open Road CAFE

(03-9010 9298; http://wideopenroad.com.au; 274 Barkly St, Brunswick; 7am-4pm Mon-Fri, to 5pm Sat, 8am-5pm Sun; ; 19, Jewell) Wide Open in name translates to wide open in space at this inviting converted-warehouse cafe-roastery just off hectic Sydney Rd. There's plenty of elbow room at the communal tables, where you can tuck into dishes from a refreshingly inventive menu. Try the fish-finger sandwich with pickled cucumbers while sipping a Bathysphere house-blend espresso or weekly-changing filter coffee.

Seven Seeds CAFE

(Map p71; 03-9347 8664; www.sevenseeds.com.au; 114 Berkeley St, Carlton; 7am-5pm Mon-Sat, 8am-5pm Sun; 19, 59) The most spacious location in the Seven Seeds coffee empire, this rather out-of-the-way warehouse cafe has plenty of room to store your bike and sip a splendid coffee. Public cuppings are held 9am Friday. It also owns Traveller (p92) and Brother Baba Budan (p113) cafes in the CBD.

Queensberry Pourhouse CAFE

(Map p71; 03-9347 1277; www.queensberryph.com.au; 210 Queensberry St, Carlton; 7am-4.30pm; 1, 8) A relaxed corner coffeehouse inspired by American diners where the filter coffee is bottomless and lingering is welcomed – it's perfect for students at nearby Melbourne Uni. The beans are roasted onsite and there's a short menu of tasty food; try the mushroom toasties or the house-made granola.

Lincoln PUB

(Map p71; ☎03-9347 4666; http://hotellincoln.com.au/; 91 Cardigan St, Carlton; ⏰noon-11pm Sun-Thu, to midnight Fri & Sat; 🚋1, 8) A bit posher than your average old Carlton boozer, the Lincoln hints at historical charm with art-deco features and a dark-wood curved bar. It offers an impressive wine list and a rotating selection of craft beer on tap, alongside the classic Carlton Draught, of course. The kitchen does gastropub meals (coffee-cured salmon, whole baby snapper) and does them well.

Alehouse Project BAR

(☎03-9387 1218; www.thealehouseproject.com.au; 98-100 Lygon St, East Brunswick; ⏰3pm-late Mon-Fri, noon-late Sat & Sun; 📶; 🚋1, 8) Brunswick venue for beer snobs to convene and compare notes, or just rock up to taste test from a great selection of 12 rotating craft beers on tap.

Padre Coffee CAFE

(☎03-9381 1881; www.padrecoffee.com.au; 438 Lygon St, East Brunswick; ⏰7am-2pm Mon, to 4pm Tue-Sat, 8am-4pm Sun; 📶; 🚋1, 8) A big player in Melbourne's coffee movement, this East Brunswick warehouse-style cafe is the original roaster for Padre Coffee and brews its premium single-origins and blends.

Campos Coffee CAFE

(Map p71; ☎03-9347 7445; www.camposcoffee.com; 144 Elgin St, Carlton; ⏰7am-4pm Mon-Fri, from 8am Sat; 📶; 🚋1, 8) Pourovers, AeroPress, siphon, cold drips and daily-changing single-origin African, Asian and Latin American coffees – Campos has it all covered for the modern-day caffeine addict, along with baguettes and pastries for a light lunch.

Jimmy Watson's WINE BAR

(Map p71; ☎03-9347 3985; www.jimmywatsons.com.au; 333 Lygon St, Carlton; ⏰wine bar 11am-11pm, Wolf's Lair rooftop 4-11pm; 🚌Tourist Shuttle, 🚋1, 8) If this Robin Boyd–designed midcentury building had ears, there'd be a few generations of writers and academics in trouble. Keep it tidy at Watson's wine bar with something nice by the glass, go a bottle of dry and dry (vermouth and ginger ale) and settle in the leafy courtyard, or head up to the Wolf's Lair rooftop for cocktails with a view.

Mr Wilkinson BAR

(295 Lygon St, East Brunswick; ⏰4pm-late Mon, Wed & Thu, 4pm-1am Fri, 2pm-1am Sat, 2pm-late Sun; 🚋1, 8) The owners decked this place out in recycled timber themselves and now concentrate on keeping things mellow and their customers well watered. It's a great place for a natter to the bar staff, and a menu of pizzas, cheese plates and charcuterie boards is on offer.

Alderman WINE BAR

(☎03-9380 9003; 134 Lygon St, East Brunswick; ⏰5-11pm Tue-Thu, to 1am Fri, 3pm-1am Sat, 3-11pm Sun; 📶; 🚋1, 8) A classic East Brunswick local, the Alderman has an inviting traditional heavy wooden bar, an open fireplace, a good beer and cocktail selection, and welcoming staff. There's a small courtyard and you can order from restaurant Bar Idda (p103) next door.

Gerald's Bar WINE BAR

(☎03-9349 4748; http://geraldsbar.com.au; 386 Rathdowne St, North Carlton; ⏰5-11pm Mon-Sat; 🚋1, 8) Wine by the glass is democratically selected at this neighbourhood favourite, and they spin some fine vintage vinyl from behind the curved wooden bar. Gerald himself is out the back preparing to feed you whatever he feels like on the day with produce sourced mainly from local producers.

Retreat PUB

(☎03-9380 4090; www.retreathotelbrunswick.com.au; 280 Sydney Rd, Brunswick; ⏰noon-1am Mon-Thu & Sun, to 3am Fri & Sat; 🚋19, 🚆Brunswick) This pub is so big that it's a tad overwhelming. Find your habitat – garden backyard, grungy band room or intimate front bar – and settle in for the long haul. A long-time champion of live music, it hosts nightly free gigs, which might include acoustic sets in the front bar earlier in the week or bands in the band room Thursday to Sunday.

North Melbourne & Parkville

Town Hall Hotel PUB

(☎03-9328 1983; www.townhallhotelnorthmelbourne.com.au; 33 Errol St, North Melbourne; ⏰4pm-1am Mon-Thu, noon-1am Fri & Sat, noon-11pm Sun; 🚋57) Sure, it's more than a bit grungy, but that's part of the charm of this endearingly unfussy local that's festooned with rock iconography (Bowie and Iggy feature prominently). Other more traditionally religious figures adorn the rear dining room, and there's a beer garden, too. There's often live music from Thursday to Sunday; otherwise they'll be spinning some classic vinyl.

Melbourne's West

★Back Alley Sally's BAR

(☎03-9689 6260; www.backalleysallys.com.au; 1st fl, 4 Yewers St, Footscray; ⏰5-10pm Mon-Thu, noon-10pm Fri-Sun; Ⓡ Footscray) Here's how you do a dodgy-back-alley warehouse conversion: plonk a stonking great bar in the middle, expose the brick walls, fill it with steam-punky wrought iron and light bulbs in lab jars, and offer a terrific selection of beer, gin and rum. Finishing touch: Slice Girls West downstairs to fill your patrons' bellies with pizza. Hipster heaven.

Hop Nation MICROBREWERY

(www.hopnation.com.au; 6/107-109 Whitehall St, Footscray; ⏰3-10pm Fri, noon-10pm Sat, noon-6pm Sun; 🐾; Ⓡ Seddon) Follow the smell of fish down an unlikely industrial lane to this veritable cathedral of beer, located in a cavernous brick warehouse. There's usually six of its own and two guest brews on tap, and a food truck parked out the front.

South Melbourne, Port Melbourne & Albert Park

Although this corner of Melbourne isn't especially known for its nightlife, all three neighbourhoods harbour a number of polished pubs and wine bars. Port Melbourne is home to a microbrewery, while South Melbourne claims some of Melbourne's most respected coffee purveyors. South Melbourne also has the area's widest range of drinking options.

Clement CAFE

(www.clementcoffee.com; shop 89, South Melbourne Market, cnr Coventry & Cecil Sts, South Melbourne; ⏰7am-5pm; 🚋12, 96) There's a buzz about this tiny cafe at the perimeter of South Melbourne Market, not only for its expertly crafted brew but also for its homemade salted-caramel or jam-and-custard doughnuts. Grab a streetside stool or get a takeaway and wander the market stalls.

Padre Coffee CAFE

(☎03-9699 8348; www.padrecoffee.com.au; shop 33, South Melbourne Market, cnr Coventry & Cecil Sts, South Melbourne; ⏰8am-4pm Wed, Fri, Sat & Sun; 🚋12, 96) Offers a perfect (and popular) caffeine-enhanced respite from mad market shopping.

Colonial Brewery Co BREWERY

(☎03-8644 4044; www.colonialbrewingco.com.au/port-melbourne; 89 Bertie St, Port Melbourne; ⏰noon-11pm Thu & Fri; 🚋109) This east coast outpost of Western Australian craft brewery Colonial pours smooth, thirst-crushing suds in a huge warehouse decked out with steel tanks, ping-pong table and food trucks. Staff are passionate and knowledgeable about the beers (which include seasonal drops), and the Kolsch goes down especially well.

South Yarra, Prahran & Windsor

Bars, pubs and clubs line Chapel St, with a handful of options on Commercial Rd and Greville St too. Venues range from posh pubs and upstairs cocktail bars to hipster rooftop hangouts and dark, grungy hideaways.

★Rufus COCKTAIL BAR

(Map p76; ☎03-9525 2197; www.rufusbar.com.au; 1st fl, 143 Greville St, Prahran; ⏰4pm-late; 🚋6, 72, 78, Ⓡ Prahran) Hidden above Greville St, Rufus is deliciously posh and proper, dripping with chandeliers, tinted mirrors and swagged drapes. That the place is named after Sir Winston Churchill's beloved poodle is no coincidence: the late British prime minister is Rufus' muse, hence the emphasis on quality champagnes, martinis and whiskies, the standout Yorkshire-pudding

CRAFT BEER & MICROBREWERIES

Until recently, thirsty Melburnians were given the choice of only two or three mainstream beers on tap (and perhaps an interstate lager if they were feeling adventurous). But the last decade has seen the emergence of microbreweries and craft-beer bars, primed to meet the demands of beer geeks who treat their drinking more seriously.

The big event on the Melbourne beer calendar is **Good Beer Week** (www.goodbeerweek.com.au; ⏰May), held in May, showcasing local, national and foreign craft beers. **Aussie Brewery Tours** (☎1300 787 039; www.aussiebrewerytours.com.au; tour incl transport, lunch & tastings $160; ⏰Thu-Mon) will help you get around, offering a tour of several inner-city breweries and prestigious pubs.

roll, and your butlerlike waiter. Enter from the laneway.

Woods of Windsor BAR

(Map p76; ☎03-9521 1900; www.woodsofwindsor.com.au; 108 Chapel St, Windsor; ⏰5.30pm-1am Tue-Sat; 🚋78, 5, 6, 64, 🚉Windsor) Dark timber, kooky taxidermy and a speakeasy vibe make the Woods a suitable place to hide on those brooding, rainy Melbourne nights. Bunker down for a standout selection of whiskies (including rarer drops), or ditch them altogether for a little Italian subversion: the drinks list includes a string of variations on the classic negroni apéritif. *Cin cin!*

Market Lane Coffee CAFE

(Map p76; ☎03-9804 7434; www.marketlane.com.au; Prahran Market, 163 Commercial Rd, South Yarra; ⏰7am-5pm Tue & Thu-Sat, to 4pm Wed, 8am-5pm Sun; 🚋72, 78, 79, 🚉Prahran) This is one of Melbourne's top speciality coffee roasters, hiding away at the back of Prahran Market. The beans here are strictly seasonal, producing cups of joe that are beautifully nuanced...and best paired with one of the scrumptious pastries. Free one-hour cuppings run at 10am on Saturday (get in by 9.30am to secure your place).

Emerson BAR, CLUB

(Map p76; ☎03-9825 0900; www.theemerson.com.au; 143-145 Commercial Rd, South Yarra; ⏰5pm-midnight Thu, noon-5am Fri & Sat, noon-3.30am Sun; 🚋72, 78, 🚉Prahran) A swanky three-level venue with cocktail bar, club and rooftop bar. On Sunday afternoon the rooftop's a huge hit with gay revellers, who head up to sip skinny bitches (vodka and soda), catch up on the goss and show off all that gym work.

Railway Hotel BAR

(Map p76; ☎03-9510 4050; www.therailway.com.au; 29 Chapel St, Windsor; ⏰noon-late; 🚋5, 64, 78, 🚉Windsor) This smart, casual gastropub is divided into numerous design-savvy spaces. The upstairs bar and deck runs one of the area's two gay-oriented Sunday sessions, this one attracting a slightly older, more down-to-earth crowd. Check out the talent (or at least the great skyline view).

Montereys BAR

(Map p76; ☎03-9525 0980; 218 Chapel St, Prahran; ⏰noon-1am Tue-Sat, 11am-11pm Sun; 📶; 🚋6, 78, 🚉Prahran) This corner bar was inspired by a US road trip, a fact reflected in such cocktails as the Palm Beach Paloma (cucumber, jalapeños, smoky Mezcal, grapefruit, lime) and nosh like lobster rolls (which could use a little more lobster). The real draw, however, is the daily happy hour (5pm to 7pm), with $2 freshly shucked oysters and $6 glasses of bubbles.

Windsor Castle Hotel PUB

(Map p76; ☎03-9525 0239; www.windsorcastle.com.au; 89 Albert St, Windsor; ⏰3pm-late Mon-Thu, from noon Fri-Sun; 🚋5, 64, 🚉Windsor) What's not to love about a lime-hued pub with a herd of pink elephants on the roof? The Windsor Castle is a backstreet veteran, full of cosy nooks, sunken pits, fireplaces and flocked wallpaper. Top billing goes to the tiki-themed beer garden, especially fun on hot summer weekend nights.

Yellow Bird BAR

(Map p76; ☎03-9533 8983; www.yellowbird.com.au; 122 Chapel St, Windsor; ⏰7.30am-late Mon-Fri, from 8am Sat & Sun; 🚋6, 78, 🚉Windsor) This little bird keeps Windsor's cool kids happy with all-day drinks and diner-style food. It's owned by the drummer from Something for Kate, so the loud, dark rock 'n' roll ambience is genuine, with a passing cast of musos, a fantastic playlist of underground bands and one of the most outrageously kitsch bars in town.

Borsch, Vodka & Tears BAR

(Map p76; ☎03-9530 2694; www.borschvodkaandtears.com; 173 Chapel St, Windsor; ⏰8am-late Mon-Fri, from 9am Sat & Sun; 🚋6, 78, 🚉Prahran) A Chapel St classic, Borsch, Vodka & Tears is a nod to the area's Eastern European influences. The more than 100 vodkas include clear, oak-matured, fruit-infused and traditional *nalewka kresowa* (made according to old Russian and Polish recipes). Staff are clued-up, and the menu includes borscht and blintzes good enough to make your Polish grandpa weep. *Na zdrowie!* (Cheers!)

Revolver Upstairs CLUB

(Map p76; ☎03-9521 5985; www.revolverupstairs.com.au; 229 Chapel St, Prahran; ⏰5pm-4am Tue & Wed, 5pm-6am Thu, 5pm Fri to noon Sat, 24hr 5pm Sat-9am Mon; 🚋6, 78, 🚉Prahran) Rowdy Revolver can feel like an enormous version of your lounge room, but with 54 hours of nonstop music come the weekend, you're probably glad it's not. Live music, art exhibitions, not to mention interesting local, national and international DJs keep the mixed crowd wide awake.

St Kilda

Both St Kilda and Balaclava have thriving cafe scenes. After dark, Fitzroy and Acland Sts in St Kilda are the main activity hubs, with no shortage of buzzing bars and pubs, from boozy, free-and-easy backpacker joints to more discerning wine and cocktail bars. St Kilda is home to some of Melbourne's most notable live-music venues, including the Prince Bandroom and the Palais Theatre.

★Bar Di Stasio WINE BAR
(Map p78; ☎03-9525 3999; http://distasio.com.au/about/bar-di-stasio; 31 Fitzroy St, St Kilda; ⊙11.30am-midnight; 🚋3, 12, 16, 96) Within Pompidou-style scaffolding – the work of artist Callum Morton – lies this buzzing, grown-up bar, dominated by a floor-to-ceiling mural of Caravaggio's *Flagellation of Christ*. Behind the deep marble bar, waiters seemingly plucked from Venice's Caffè Florian mix perfect Campari *spritzes* while dishing out gorgeous bites, from lightly fried local seafood to elegant pastas (available until 11pm). Book: the place is extremely popular.

★Pontoon BAR
(Map p78; ☎03-9525 5445; http://pontoonstkildabeach.com.au; 30 Jacka Blvd, St Kilda; ⊙noon-midnight; 🚋3, 16, 96) Beneath the fine-dining Stokehouse (p110) is its casual, buzzing bar-bistro, a light-soaked space with floor-to-ceiling windows and a deck looking right out at the beach and sunset. Slip on the shades and sip craft suds or a local prosecco while eyeing the crowd for the odd local celeb. A shared-plates menu delivers some decent bites, overpriced and undersized pizzas aside.

Misery Guts BAR
(Map p78; ☎03-8590 6431; http://miserygutsbar.com; 19 Grey St, St Kilda; ⊙4-11pm Wed, to midnight Thu, 2pm-1am Fri & Sat, 2pm-midnight Sun; 🚋3, 16, 96) There's nothing cantankerous about this unruffled local, a few steps (and a million miles) away from Fitzroy St's backpacker bars. Punctuated with various oddities – including a menacing vintage police sign – it's where the locals actually lounge, gossiping over decent beers, interesting wines by the glass and tweaked cocktails like a limoncello *spritz*. There's live blues or jazz from 6pm Sunday.

Dogs Bar BAR
(Map p78; ☎03-9593 9535; http://dogsbar.com.au; 54 Acland St, St Kilda; ⊙11.30am-1am; 📶; 🚋3, 16, 96) You're guaranteed a good time at this St Kilda veteran, a joint that's rarely short of berets, boozy debates and raucous banter from local old-timers. Soaked in afternoon sunshine, the outdoor tables are a prime people-watching spot (especially at weekends), while the golden-hued interior is the setting for nightly live blues, rock or funk, usually from 9pm.

Republica BAR
(Map p78; ☎03-8598 9055; www.republica.net.au; St Kilda Sea Baths, 10-18 Jacka Blvd, St Kilda; ⊙11.30am-late Mon-Fri, from 9am Sat & Sun; 📶; 🚋3, 16, 96) Opening right up to St Kilda Beach, Republica is about as close as you'll get to a beach bar in Melbourne. Ditch the daytime food and head in later in the afternoon or in the evening for sunset beers, cocktail lounging and the odd flirtatious glance.

St Kilda Bowling Club PUB
(☎03-9534 5229; www.stkildasportsclub.com.au; 66 Fitzroy St, St Kilda; ⊙noon-late; 🚋12, 16, 96) This fabulously intact old clubhouse is tucked behind a trimmed hedge and a splendid bowling green. The long bar serves drinks at 'club prices' (ie cheap) and you'll be joined by St Kilda's hippest on Sunday afternoons. Kick off your shoes, roll a few bowls, knock back beers and watch the sun go down along with your bowling accuracy.

Carlisle Wine Bar WINE BAR
(Map p78; ☎03-9531 3222; www.carlislewinebar.com.au; 137 Carlisle St, Balaclava; ⊙4pm-late Tue-Fri, from 2pm Sat & Sun; 🚋3, 16, 78, 🚆Balaclava) Locals love this often rowdy, wine-worshipping former butcher's shop. The staff will treat you like a regular and find you a glass of something special, or effortlessly throw together a cocktail amid the weekend rush. A sharp, seasonal menu includes creative snacks (such as chicken skins with kale and smoked eel) and larger, mainly meaty dishes like pork cutlet with provolone.

Local Taphouse BAR
(Map p78; ☎03-9537 2633; www.thelocal.com.au; 184 Carlisle St, St Kilda; ⊙noon-late; 🚋3, 16, 78, 🚆Balaclava) Reminiscent of an old-school Brooklyn bar, the warm, wooden Local has a rotating cast of craft beers and an impressive bottle list. There's a beer garden upstairs, and a snug drawing-room mix of leather couches and open fires inside. Weekly events include live comedy (including well-established acts) on Monday, and live soul, funk, blues or reggae on Friday and Saturday.

Hotel Barkly PUB
(Map p78; ☎03-9525 3371; www.hotelbarkly.com; 109 Barkly St, St Kilda; ⏰4pm-late Tue, from 11.30am Wed-Sun; 🚊3, 16, 67) The street-level public bar is the place to go if you're up for sinking a few pints, wiggling to whatever comes on the jukebox and snogging a stranger before last drinks. The rooftop bar (open Friday only) feigns a bit of class, but things get messy up there, too. It's worth it for the spectacular sunset views across St Kilda, though.

Pause Bar BAR
(Map p78; ☎03-9537 0511; www.pausebar.com.au; 268 Carlisle St, Balaclava; ⏰4pm-late Mon-Fri, from 2pm Sat & Sun; 📶; 🚊3, 16, 78, 🚆Balaclava) Pause has been around since 2001 and draws a loyal local crowd, who settle into the dim North African–inspired bar for cocktails (two for $22!), pints of beer and meze. The bar also serves up live tunes every Friday and Saturday night, as well as on Sunday afternoon once a month (see the website for dates).

After the Tears Elsternwick BAR
(☎03-9523 0969; www.afterthetears.net; 9b Gordon St, Elsternwick; ⏰3.30pm-late; 🚊67, 🚆Elsternwick) Next to the Classic Cinema, After the Tears serves an astonishing range of vodkas (at last count at least 100) and radiates an authentic Polish feel. Follow Brighton Rd to Glen Huntly Rd.

Vineyard BAR
(Map p78; www.thevineyard.com.au; 71a Acland St, St Kilda; ⏰10.30am-3am Mon-Fri, from 10am Sat & Sun; 🚊3, 16, 96) An old favourite, the Vineyard has the perfect corner position and picket-fenced outdoor seating to attract crowds of backpackers and scantily clad young locals, who enjoy themselves so much they drown out the neighbouring roller coaster. Sunday-afternoon sessions are big here.

☆ Entertainment

Cinemas

Moonlight Cinema CINEMA
(www.moonlight.com.au; Gate D, Royal Botanic Gardens, Birdwood Ave, South Yarra; 🚊1, 3, 5, 6, 8, 16, 64, 67, 72) Melbourne's original outdoor cinema hits the Royal Botanic Gardens from early December to early April, screening a mix of current mainstream releases and retro classics. Bring your own picnic hamper or buy light eats and booze at the venue; 'Gold Grass' tickets include waitstaff service and a reserved beanbag bed in the premium viewing area.

Astor CINEMA
(Map p76; ☎03-9510 1414; www.astortheatre.net.au; cnr Chapel St & Dandenong Rd, Windsor; tickets $17; 🚊5, 64, 78, 🚆Windsor) This 1936 art-deco darling has had more ups and downs than a Hollywood diva. Recently saved from permanent closure, it's one of Melbourne's best-loved landmarks, with double features most nights and a mixed bag of recent releases, art-house films and cult classics. Discount tickets ($12 to $13) are available Monday, Wednesday and Thursday.

Cinema Nova CINEMA
(Map p71; ☎03-9347 5331; www.cinemanova.com.au; 380 Lygon St, Carlton; 🚌Tourist Shuttle, 🚊1, 8) See the latest in art-house, docos and foreign films at this locals' favourite. Cheap Monday screenings ($7 before 4pm, $9 after 4pm).

Ben & Jerry's Openair Cinemas CINEMA
(Map p78; http://openaircinemas.com.au/melbourne/home; South Beach Reserve, Jacka Blvd, St Kilda; tickets from $16; ⏰late Nov–mid-Dec; 🚊3, 16, 96) Recent releases and cult classics by the sea, with bar service and the option of renting blankets ($4) and bean-bag lounges ($9). Sunday screenings include live music and free ice cream.

Kino Cinemas CINEMA
(Map p56; ☎03-9650 2100; www.palacecinemas.com.au; Collins Pl, 45 Collins St; 🚊11, 31, 48, 109, 112) The Kino screens art-house films in its comfy licensed cinemas.

IMAX CINEMA
(Map p71; ☎03-9663 5454; www.imaxmelbourne.com.au; Melbourne Museum, Rathdowne St, Carlton; adult/child $20/14; 🚌Tourist Shuttle, 🚊86, 96) Animal and adventure films in 3D screen on a grand scale here, with movies specially made for these giant screens.

Live Music

There's a constant procession of big international acts hitting local stadiums, arenas and theatres, and many of Melbourne's smaller character-filled drinking dens and pubs double as live-music venues.

Check daily papers and street magazines **Beat** (www.beat.com.au) and **The Music** (www.themusic.com.au) for gig info. Radio station **3RRR** (102.7FM; www.rrr.org.au) broadcasts a gig guide at 7pm from Wednesday to Friday, and at 6pm on weekends. Mess+Noise (www.messandnoise.com) is an Australian-focused music website, with an informed, irreverent chat forum. Faster-

Louder (www.fasterlouder.com.au) also has a gig guide and music news.

The Tote LIVE MUSIC

(03-9419 5320; www.thetotehotel.com; cnr Johnston & Wellington Sts, Collingwood; 4pm-late Wed-Sun; 86) One of Melbourne's most iconic live-music venues, this divey Collingwood pub has a great roster of local and international punk and hardcore bands, and one of the best jukeboxes in the universe. Its temporary closure in 2010 brought Melbourne to a stop, literally: people protested on city-centre streets against the liquor-licensing laws that were blamed for the closure.

Cherry LIVE MUSIC

(Map p56; www.cherrybar.com.au; AC/DC Lane; 6pm-late Mon-Sat, 2pm-late Sun; Flinders St) Of course Melbourne's most legendary live-rock bar is located in a black-walled, neon-lit basement on AC/DC Lane. There's often a queue, but once you're inside a welcoming, slightly anarchic spirit prevails. Live music and DJs play seven nights a week, and there's a long-standing soul night on Thursday.

Forum CONCERT VENUE

(Map p56; 1300 111 011; www.forummelbourne.com.au; 150-152 Flinders St; Flinders St) One of the city's most atmospheric live-music venues, the Forum does double duty as a cinema during the Melbourne Film Festival. The striking Moorish exterior (an over-the-top fantasia with minarets, domes and dragons) houses an equally interesting interior, with the southern night sky rendered on the domed ceiling.

Prince Bandroom LIVE MUSIC

(Map p78; 03-9536 1168; www.princebandroom.com.au; 29 Fitzroy St, St Kilda; 12, 16, 96) The Prince is a legendary St Kilda venue, with a solid line-up of local and international acts spanning hip-hop, dance, rock and indie. It's an eclectic mix, with recent guests including UK rapper Tinie Tempah, American roots-rock trio Moreland & Arbuckle and Nordic hardcore-punk outfit Refused.

Toff in Town LIVE MUSIC

(Map p56; 03-9639 8770; www.thetoffintown.com; 2nd fl, Curtin House, 252 Swanston St; 5pm-3am Sun-Thu, to 5am Fri & Sat; Melbourne Central) An atmospheric venue well suited to cabaret, the Toff also works for intimate gigs by rock gods, avant-folksters or dance-hall queens. The moody bar next door serves post-set drinks of the French wine and cocktail variety.

Palais Theatre CONCERT VENUE

(Map p78; 03-9525 3240, tickets 136 100; Lower Esplanade, St Kilda; 3, 16, 96) Standing gracefully next to Luna Park, the heritage-listed Palais (c 1927) is a St Kilda icon. Scheduled to reopen in May 2017 after a nip and tuck (which includes repainting the building in its original colours), the deco giant hosts some of the biggest names in local and international music and comedy.

Corner LIVE MUSIC

(Map p65; 03-9427 7300; www.cornerhotel.com; 57 Swan St, Richmond; 4pm-late Mon-Fri, noon-3am Sat, noon-1am Sun; Richmond) The band room here is one of Melbourne's most popular midsize venues, and it's seen plenty of loud and live action over the years, from Dinosaur Jr to the Buzzcocks. If your ears need a break, there's a friendly front bar. The rooftop has city views but gets packed, and often with a different crowd from the music fans below.

Ding Dong Lounge LIVE MUSIC

(Map p56; 03-9514 4599; www.dingdonglounge.com.au; 1st fl, 18 Market Lane; 9pm-late Wed-Sat; Parliament) Long-standing Ding Dong is one of the city centre's premier venues for smaller touring acts and local bands.

Yah Yah's LIVE MUSIC

(Map p68; http://yahyahs.com.au; 99 Smith St, Fitzroy; 5pm-5am Thu-Sat; 86) Yah Yah's has always had a reputation for general late-night messiness – good or bad depending on your goals. Bands play upstairs every Friday and Saturday. Thursgay is the weekly gay-friendly night.

Night Cat LIVE MUSIC

(Map p68; 03-9417 0090; www.thenightcat.com.au; 141 Johnston St, Fitzroy; 9pm-3am Fri & Sat, 7pm-3am Sun; 11) The Night Cat is a barn-sized space with a dance floor that sees lots of action. Music is generally in the Latin, jazz or funk vein. Offers salsa dance classes ($20) on Sunday night.

Workers Club LIVE MUSIC

(Map p68; 03-9415 6558; www.theworkersclub.com.au; cnr Brunswick & Gertrude Sts, Fitzroy; 4pm-1am Mon-Wed, noon-1am Thu-Sun; 86, 11) The Workers Club pulls in some decent live gigs in the band room most nights, while the front bar and beer garden pack out with punters knocking back beer and cocktail jugs and fuelling up on comfort pub grub.

Festival Hall CONCERT VENUE
(☎03-9329 9699; www.festivalhall.com.au; 300 Dudley St, West Melbourne; 220, North Melbourne) This former boxing stadium – aka 'Festering Hall' (especially on hot summer nights) – is a fave for live international acts. The Beatles played here in 1964.

Last Chance Rock & Roll Bar LIVE MUSIC
(Map p71; ☎03-9329 9888; www.thelastchance.com.au; 238 Victoria St, North Melbourne; 4pm-late Mon-Thu, noon-7am Fri & Sat, noon-11pm Sun; 19, 57, 55) The Public Bar, a much-loved local institution, closed recently and Last Chance took over in the same spirit – it's clear there's been no spit-and-polish here and it's just as perfectly divey as ever. Live bands play most nights and lean towards the punk genre.

Gasometer LIVE MUSIC
(Map p68; ☎03-9416 3335; www.thegasometerhotel.com.au; 484 Smith St, Collingwood; 4pm-midnight Tue & Wed, 4pm-2am Thu, noon-3am Fri & Sat, noon-midnight Sun; 86) This corner bluestone pub features a cosy front bar, an excellent line-up of bands most nights – from up-and-coming local acts to punk and indie big names – and one of the best band rooms in the city, with a mezzanine level and a retractable roof for open-air gigs.

Howler LIVE MUSIC
(☎03-9077 5572; https://h-w-l-r.com; 7 Dawson St, Brunswick; noon-1am; 19, Jewell, Brunswick) At the back of a car park near the train tracks is not usually a recommendable spot to hang out, but behind a street-art-covered warehouse facade is this leafy oasis of a bar and arts hub. The purpose-built theatre hosts everything from international DJs and stand-up comedy to a great line-up of noise, indie and electronica bands. Opposite the Brunswick Baths.

Old Bar LIVE MUSIC
(Map p68; ☎03-9417 4155; www.theoldbar.com.au; 74-76 Johnston St, Fitzroy; 4pm-3am Mon-Fri, 2pm-3am Sat & Sun; ; 96, 11) With live bands seven days a week and a licence till 3am, the Old Bar's another reason that Melbourne is the rock 'n' roll capital of Australia. It gets great local bands and a few internationals in its grungy band room with a house-party vibe.

Bennetts Lane JAZZ
(Map p56; ☎03-9663 2856; www.bennettslane.com; 25 Bennetts Lane; Melbourne Central) Bennetts Lane has long been the boiler room of Melbourne jazz. It attracts the cream of local and international talent and an audience that knows when it's time to applaud a solo. Beyond the cosy front bar is another space reserved for big gigs.

GAY & LESBIAN MELBOURNE

While there's still a handful of specifically gay venues scattered around the city, some of the best hangouts are weekly takeovers of mainstream bars (especially Sunday afternoon at the **Railway Hotel** (p120) in Windsor, Sunday evening at the **Emerson** (p120) in South Yarra and Thursday night at **Yah Yah's** (p123) in Fitzroy). Semiregular themed gay party nights are also popular, such as **Woof** (www.woofclub.com), **DILF** (www.iwantadilf.com), **Closet** (www.facebook.com/closetpartyoz), **Fabuland** (www.fabuland.com.au) and **Swagger** (www.facebook.com/swaggerparty). For lesbians, there's **Fannys at Franny's** (www.francescasbar.com.au/fannys-frannys) and **Mother Party** (www.facebook.com/sojuicysaturdays).

The big event on the queer calendar is the annual **Midsumma Festival** (www.midsumma.org.au; Jan-Feb). It has a diverse program of cultural, community and sporting events, including the popular Midsumma Carnival at Alexandra Gardens, St Kilda's Pride March and much more. Australia's largest GLBT film festival, the **Melbourne Queer Film Festival** (www.melbournequeerfilm.com.au; Mar), screens more than 100 films from around the world.

For more local info, pick up a copy of the free magazines **Star Observer** (www.starobserver.com.au), **MCV** (www.gaynewsnetwork.com.au) and **LOTL** (Lesbians on the Loose; www.lotl.com). Gay and lesbian radio station **JOY 94.9FM** (www.joy.org.au) is another important resource for visitors and locals.

Opera

Chamber Made Opera OPERA
(☎03-9090 7095; www.chambermadeopera.com) Founded in 1988, Chamber Made Opera showcases contemporary music and music-based performance art at various venues around the city and state.

Melbourne Opera OPERA
(Map p56; ☎03-9614 4188; www.melbourneopera.com) A not-for-profit company that performs classic and light opera in various venues, including the Regent Theatre.

Opera Australia OPERA
(☎03-9685 3777; www.opera.org.au; Arts Centre, 100 St Kilda Rd, Southbank; Flinders St) The national opera company performs with some regularity at the Arts Centre (p64).

Victorian Opera OPERA
(☎03-9001 6400; www.victorianopera.com.au) Dedicated to innovation and accessibility, this opera company's program, pleasingly, doesn't always play it safe. It performs mainly at the Arts Centre (p64) and the Recital Centre (p126).

Theatre & Arts

Red Stitch Actors Theatre THEATRE
(Map p76; ☎03-9533 8082; www.redstitch.net; rear 2 Chapel St, Windsor; 5, 64, 78, Windsor) Featuring prolific national talent, Red Stitch is one of Australia's most respected actors' ensembles, staging new international works that are often premieres in Australia. The company's intimate black-box theatre is located opposite the historic Astor cinema, down the end of a driveway.

Her Majesty's Theatre THEATRE
(Map p56; ☎03-8643 3300; www.hmt.com.au; 219 Exhibition St; Parliament) On the outside Her Maj is painted-brick Second Empire; on the inside it's 1930s Moderne. It's been the home of musical comedy since 1880 and it's still going strong.

Princess Theatre THEATRE
(Map p56; ☎Ticketmaster 1300 111 011; www.marrinertheatres.com.au; 163 Spring St; Parliament) This beautifully renovated 1854 theatre is the venue for super-slick musicals. It even has a resident ghost, that of opera singer Federici.

Regent Theatre THEATRE
(Map p56; ☎1300 111 011; www.marrinertheatres.com.au; 191 Collins St; Flinders St) The opulent Regent, built as a picture palace in 1929, hosts musicals, opera, comedy and concerts.

Theatre Works THEATRE
(Map p78; ☎03-9534 3388; www.theatreworks.org.au; 14 Acland St, St Kilda; 3, 16, 96) Theatre Works is one of Melbourne's veteran independent theatre companies. With award-winning creative director John Sheedy at the helm, the company's focus is firmly on new Australian works.

Butterfly Club CABARET
(Map p56; ☎03-9663 8107; www.thebutterflyclub.com; Carson Pl; 5pm-late Tue-Sun; Flinders St) Down a quintessential Melbourne laneway, this eccentric little cabaret club stages acts that aren't really theatre, aren't quite straight comedy either and might just throw in a song. The rooms display an extraordinary collection of kitsch, which adds to the feeling that you're never quite sure what you're in for.

Melbourne Theatre Company THEATRE
(MTC; ☎03-8688 0800; www.mtc.com.au; 140 Southbank Blvd, Southbank; 1) Melbourne's major theatrical company stages around a dozen productions each year, ranging from contemporary (including many new Australian works) to Shakespeare and other classics. Performances take place in its award-winning Southbank Theatre, a striking black building enclosed within angular white tubing.

La Mama THEATRE
(Map p71; ☎03-9347 6948; www.lamama.com.au; 205 Faraday St, Carlton; tickets $10-25; box office 10.30am-5pm Mon-Fri, 2-3pm Sat & Sun; Tourist Shuttle, 1, 8) La Mama is historically significant in Melbourne's theatre scene. This tiny, intimate forum produces new Australian works and experimental theatre, and has a reputation for developing emerging playwrights. It's a ramshackle building with an open-air bar. Shows also run at its larger **Courthouse theatre** at 349 Drummond St, so check tickets carefully for the correct location.

Wheeler Centre ARTS CENTRE
(☎03-9094 7800; www.wheelercentre.com; 176 Little Lonsdale St; Melbourne Central) Set up by Lonely Planet founders Maureen and Tony Wheeler to showcase 'books, writing and ideas', this centre has become an important part of the city's intellectual life, hosting regular talks by distinguished speakers on

TICKETS

Tickets for concerts, theatre, comedy, sports and other events are usually available from one of the following agencies:

Halftix (Map p56; www.halftixmelbourne.com; Melbourne Town Hall, 90-120 Swanston St; ⏲10am-2pm Mon, 11am-6pm Tue-Fri, 10am-4pm Sat; 🚉Flinders St) Discounted theatre tickets are sold on the day of performance.

Moshtix (www.moshtix.com.au)

Ticketek (Map p56; www.ticketek.com.au; 252 Exhibition St; ⏲9am-5pm Mon-Fri, 10am-3pm Sat)

Ticketmaster (Map p56; ☎1300 111 011; www.ticketmaster.com.au; Forum, 150-152 Flinders St; ⏲9am-6pm Mon-Fri)

a vast range of subjects. Its free Lunchbox/Soapbox sessions on Thursday make for a great lunchtime diversion; $10 lunchboxes can be purchased from 12.20pm.

Malthouse Theatre THEATRE
(☎03-9685 5111; www.malthousetheatre.com.au; 113 Sturt St, Southbank; 🚋1) Dedicated to promoting Australian works, this exciting company stages interesting productions in its own theatre, converted from an atmospheric old brick malthouse.

Comedy

Comic's Lounge COMEDY
(☎03-9348 9488; www.thecomicslounge.com.au; 26 Errol St, North Melbourne; ⏲dinner/show from 6.30/8pm Mon-Sat; 🚋57) There's stand-up featuring Melbourne's best-known funny people most nights of the week here. If you like to live dangerously, Tuesday's when professional comedians try out new material. Admission prices vary.

Comedy Theatre THEATRE
(Map p56; ☎1300 111 011; www.marrinertheatres.com.au; 240 Exhibition St; 🚉Parliament) This midsize 1920s Spanish-style venue is dedicated to comic theatre, stand-up and musicals.

Classical Music

Melbourne Recital Centre CLASSICAL MUSIC
(☎03-9699 3333; www.melbournerecital.com.au; 31 Sturt St, Southbank; ⏲box office 9am-5pm Mon-Fri; 📶; 🚋1) This building may look like a framed piece of giant honeycomb, but it's actually the home (or hive?) of the **Melbourne Chamber Orchestra** (www.mco.org.au) and lots of small ensembles. Its two halls are said to have some of the best acoustics in the southern hemisphere. Performances range from chamber music to contemporary classical, jazz, world music and dance.

Melbourne Symphony Orchestra LIVE PERFORMANCE
(MSO; Map p56; ☎03-9929 9600; www.mso.com.au; Hamer Hall, 100 St Kilda Rd, Southbank; 🚉Flinders St) The MSO has a broad reach: while not afraid to be populist (it's done sell-out performances with Burt Bacharach and Kiss), it usually performs classical symphonic masterworks. It plays regularly at its **Hamer Hall** (Map p56; ☎1300 182 183; www.artscentremelbourne.com.au; 100 St Kilda Rd, Southbank; 🚋1, 3, 6, 8, 16, 64, 67, 72, 🚉Flinders St) home, but it also runs a summer series of free concerts at the **Sidney Myer Music Bowl** (☎1300 182 183; www.artscentremelbourne.com.au; Kings Domain, 21 Linlithgow Ave, Southbank; 🚋3, 5, 6, 8, 16, 64, 67, 72).

Dance

Australian Ballet BALLET
(☎1300 369 741; www.australianballet.com.au; 2 Kavanagh St, Southbank; 🚋1) More than 50 years old, the Melbourne-based Australian Ballet performs traditional and new works in the Arts Centre and all around the country. You can take an hour-long tour of the Primrose Potter Australian Ballet Centre ($39, bookings essential) that includes a visit to the production and wardrobe departments as well as watching the dancers practise in the studios.

Chunky Move DANCE
(☎03-9645 5188; www.chunkymove.com.au; 111 Sturt St, Southbank; 🚋1) This acclaimed contemporary-dance company performs mainly at the Malthouse Theatre (p126). It also runs a variety of public dance classes; check the website.

Spectator Sports

★**Melbourne Cricket Ground** SPECTATOR SPORT
(MCG; Map p65; ☎03-9657 8888; www.mcg.org.au; Brunton Ave, East Melbourne; 🚉Jolimont) Melbourne's sporting mecca, the 'G' (p64) hosts cricket in summer and AFL footy in winter.

Etihad Stadium STADIUM
(☎tours 03-8625 7277; www.etihadstadium.com.au; 740 Bourke St, Docklands; tours adult/child $15/8; 🚆Southern Cross) This easy-to-access Docklands stadium seats around 50,000 people for regular AFL games and the odd one-day cricket match, Rugby Union test and Justin Bieber concert – with the advantage of a retractable roof to keep spectators dry. Also runs tours for sporting tragics.

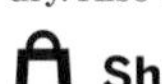

Shopping

City Centre

Swanston St, Elizabeth St and the blocks in between them (particularly those bordered by Bourke St Mall and Collins St) form the heart of Melbourne's retail precinct. Here you'll find all the ritziest department stores, arcades and shopping centres.

★**Craft Victoria** ARTS & CRAFTS
(Map p56; ☎03-9650 7775; www.craft.org.au; 31 Flinders Lane; ⊙11am-6pm Mon-Sat; 🚆Parliament) This retail arm of Craft Victoria showcases handmade goods, mainly by Victorian artists and artisans. Its range of jewellery, textiles, accessories, glass and ceramics bridges the art–craft divide and makes for some wonderful mementos of Melbourne. There are also a few galleries with changing exhibitions; admission is free.

Alpha60 FASHION & ACCESSORIES
(Map p56; ☎03-9663 3002; www.alpha60.com.au; 2nd fl, 209 Flinders Lane; ⊙10am-6pm; 🚆Flinders St) Melbourne has a reputation for top-notch retail spaces, but this place is just showing off. Alpha60's signature store is hidden within the Hogwartsian chapter house of St Paul's Cathedral, where fresh, casual women's clothing is displayed on a phalanx of mannequins while giant projections of roosters keep watch. There's another store below at ground level.

Oscar Hunt Tailors CLOTHING
(Map p56; ☎03-9670 6303; www.oscarhunt.com.au; 3rd fl, 43 Hardware Lane; ⊙8.30am-6.30pm Mon-Fri, 9am-5pm Sat; 🚆Melbourne Central) Make like a gentleman in this tailoring showroom and workshop, where you can have a suit designed, pick up ties, pocket squares and alpaca scarves, and enjoy a spot of whisky at the lounge bar while you wait. The tailors use traditional methods, working closely with each client for an approach as tailored as the end result.

Melbournalia GIFTS & SOUVENIRS
(Map p56; ☎03-9663 3751; www.melbournalia.com.au; 50 Bourke St; ⊙10am-7pm; 🚆Parliament) This is the place to stock up on interesting souvenirs by more than 100 local designers – prints featuring city icons, crazy socks and great books on Melbourne.

Original & Authentic Aboriginal Art ART
(Map p56; ☎03-9663 5133; www.originalandauthenticaboriginalart.com; 90 Bourke St; ⊙10am-6pm; 🚆Parliament) For over 20 years this centrally located gallery has sourced Indigenous art from the Central and Western Deserts, the Kimberleys and Arnhem Land. It subscribes to the City of Melbourne's code of practice for Indigenous art, ensuring authenticity and ethical dealings with artists.

Somewhere FASHION & ACCESSORIES
(Map p56; ☎03-9663 3003; www.someplace.com.au; 2nd fl, Royal Arcade, 314 Little Collins St; ⊙10am-6pm Mon-Thu & Sat, 10am-8pm Fri, noon-5pm Sun; 🚋86, 96) Somewhere is an apt name for this hard-to-find treasure located at the Little Collins St end of the glorious Royal Arcade (look for the Marais sign and take the stairs). The whitewashed warehouse space stocks predominantly Scandinavian labels, as well as local designers for men and women, along with leather tote bags, jewellery, sunglasses and a good range of denim.

NGV Shop DESIGN
(Map p56; ☎03-8662 1543; www.ngv.vic.gov.au; Ian Potter Centre, Federation Sq; ⊙10am-5pm; 🚆Flinders St) This gallery shop has a wide range of international design magazines, a kids' section and a good selection of artsy objects.

Hill of Content BOOKS
(Map p56; ☎03-9662 9472; www.hillofcontentbookshop.com; 86 Bourke St; ⊙10am-6pm Sat-Thu, to 8pm Fri; 🚆Parliament) Melbourne's oldest bookshop (established 1922) has a range of general titles and an extensive stock of books on art, classics and poetry.

Metropolis BOOKS
(Map p56; ☎03-9663 2015; www.metropolisbookshop.com.au; 3rd fl, Curtin House, 252 Swanston St; 🚆Melbourne Central) Lovely bookish eyrie with a focus on art, architecture, fashion and film.

Basement Discs MUSIC
(Map p56; ☎03-9654 1110; www.basementdiscs.com.au; 24 Block Pl; ⊙10am-6pm; 🚆Flinders St) Apart from a range of CD titles across all

genres, Basement Discs has regular in-store performances by big-name touring and local acts. Descend to the basement for a browse; you never know who you might find playing.

Wunderkammer ANTIQUES
(Map p56; ☎03-9642 4694; www.wunderkammer.com.au; 439 Lonsdale St; ⏰10am-6pm Mon-Fri, to 4pm Sat; 🚉Flagstaff) Surprises abound in this 'Wonder Chamber'. The strangest of shops, it stocks taxidermy, insects in jars, antique scientific tools and surgical equipment.

RM Williams CLOTHING
(Map p56; ☎03-9663 7126; www.rmwilliams.com; Melbourne Central, cnr La Trobe & Swanston Sts; ⏰10am-7pm Sat-Wed, to 9pm Thu & Fri; 🚉Melbourne Central) An Aussie icon, even for city slickers, this brand will kit you out in stylish essentials for working the land, including a pair of its famous boots. The Melbourne Central branch occupies the historic brick shot tower at the centre of the complex and has a mini museum inside.

Sticky Institute BOOKS
(Map p56; ☎03-9654 8559; www.stickyinstitute.com; shop 10, Campbell Arcade, Flinders St station; ⏰noon-6pm Mon-Sat; 🚉Flinders St) They take the whole underground-press ethos literally here, stocking a range of hand-photocopied zines in the dingy subway that connects Degraves St to the middle of the Flinders St station platforms.

Paperback Books BOOKS
(Map p56; ☎03-9662 1396; www.paperbackbooks.com.au; 60 Bourke St; ⏰9.30am-10pm Mon-Thu, to 11.30pm Fri, 11am-11.30pm Sat, noon-7pm Sun; 🚉Parliament) A small space jam-packed with carefully selected titles, including a good selection of Australian literature – great when you need a novel late at night.

City Hatters HATS
(Map p56; ☎03-9614 3294; www.cityhatters.com.au; 211 Flinders St; ⏰9am-5pm; 🚉Flinders St) Located beside the main entrance to Flinders St station, this evocatively old-fashioned store is the most convenient place to purchase an iconic Akubra hat, a kangaroo-leather sun hat or something a little more unique.

Southbank & Docklands

'Tourist precinct' and 'bargains' aren't terms you usually expect to see together, but South Wharf's outlet mall is great for discounted clothes and shoes. There's also a good shopping centre near the Metropol hotel in the vast casino complex.

DFO South Wharf MALL
(www.dfo.com.au; 20 Convention Centre Pl, South Wharf; ⏰10am-6pm Sat-Thu, to 9pm Fri; 🚋12, 96, 109) Set over two floors, this large centre offers factory-outlet shopping at its most tempting. Big brands represented include Ben Sherman, Tumi, Lacoste, Victoria's Secret, Vans and Converse.

NGV Design Store DESIGN
(☎03-8620 2243; www.ngv.vic.gov.au; NGV International, 180 St Kilda Rd, Southbank; ⏰10am-5pm; 🚉Flinders St) This large store sells well-designed and thoughtful show-based merchandise, arty T-shirts, a beautifully produced range of posters, and a hefty collection of art and design books.

Richmond & East Melbourne

Bridal shops alternate with midrange fashion outlet stores on Bridge Rd. The bottom end of Church St is lined with upmarket homewares stores selling kooky lighting fixtures, furniture and decorative objects.

Pookipoiga GIFTS & SOUVENIRS
(Map p65; ☎03-8589 4317; www.pookipoiga.com; 64 Bridge Rd, Richmond; ⏰9.30am-5pm; 🚋48, 75) 🍃 Everything is ethically produced, sustainable and animal friendly at this cute little gift store, packed with interesting things. There's a great selection of quirky greeting cards, loud socks, toiletries and scarves.

Lily & the Weasel GIFTS & SOUVENIRS
(Map p65; ☎03-9421 1008; www.lilyandtheweasel.com.au; 173 Swan St, Richmond; ⏰11am-5pm Tue-Sun; 🚋70) A mix of beautiful things from around the globe is stocked at this interesting store, alongside the work of local designers such as children's toys, scarves, toiletries and Robert Gordon ceramics.

Fitzroy, Collingwood & Abbotsford

Cutting-edge fashion boutiques, homewares stores and vintage-clothing shops line Gertrude St, including a good array of local designers. For midcentury furniture and homewares, look no further than Smith St, while for a fine selection of books, music and clothing, Brunswick St delivers.

★Third Drawer Down HOMEWARES

(Map p68; www.thirddrawerdown.com; 93 George St, Fitzroy; ⊙10am-6pm; 🚋86) It all started with its signature tea-towel designs (now found in MoMA in New York) at this 'museum of art souvenirs'. It makes life beautifully unusual by stocking absurdist pieces with a sense of humour as well as high-end art by well-known designers. Giant watermelon stools sit next to Yayoi Kusama's ceramic plates and scarves by Ai Weiwei.

Mud Australia CERAMICS

(Map p68; ☎03-9419 5161; www.mudaustralia.com; 181 Gertrude St, Fitzroy; ⊙10am-6pm Mon-Fri, to 5pm Sat, noon-5pm Sun; 🚋86) You'll find some of the most aesthetically beautiful – as well as functional – porcelainware at Australian-designed Mud. Coffee mugs, milk pourers, salad bowls and serving plates come in muted pastel colours with a raw matte finish.

Polyester Records MUSIC

(Map p68; ☎03-9419 5137; www.polyesterrecords.com; 387 Brunswick St, Fitzroy; ⊙10am-8pm Mon-Thu & Sat, to 9pm Fri, 11am-6pm Sun; 🚋11) This popular record store has been selling Melburnians independent music from around the world for decades, and it also has a great range of local stuff. The knowledgeable staff will help you find what you're looking for and can offer great suggestions.

Tanner + Teague FASHION & ACCESSORIES

(Map p68; ☎03-9417 5659; www.tannerandteague.com.au; 266 Brunswick St, Fitzroy; ⊙10am-6pm Mon-Fri, to 5pm Sat, 11am-5pm Sun; 🚋11) Spread over three floors, this lifestyle concept store stocks a carefully curated selection of homewares, accessories and fragrances, along with clothing for adults and children designed by husband-and-wife team Kyleigh and Sam Fisher. Sam did a stint as a pattern-maker at Vivienne Westwood in London, so you can expect interesting cuts in European tones well suited to a Melbourne crowd.

Happy Valley GIFTS & SOUVENIRS

(Map p68; ☎03-9077 8509; www.happyvalleyshop.com; 294 Smith St, Collingwood; ⊙10.30am-6pm Mon-Fri, 10am-6pm Sat, 11am-5pm Sun; 🚋86) It's difficult to pigeonhole Happy Valley: it's an art store, bookshop and gallery of wonderful things you didn't realise you needed, from laugh-out-loud cards to beautiful jewellery and locally designed homewares. The well-curated range of books includes hardback art titles and a great selection of cookbooks from some of the city's top restaurants and chefs.

Poison City Records MUSIC

(Map p68; www.poisoncityrecords.com; 400 Brunswick St, Fitzroy; ⊙noon-5pm Mon, 11am-5.30pm Wed-Fri, to 5pm Sat & Sun; 🚋11) Independent record/skate shop with its own Poison City label releasing excellent indie, punk and fuzz-rock Melbourne bands such as the Nation Blue, the Meanies, White Walls and Smith Street Band.

Obüs FASHION & ACCESSORIES

(Map p68; ☎03-9416 0012; www.obus.com.au; 226 Gertrude St, Fitzroy; ⊙10am-6pm Mon-Sat, 11am-5pm Sun; 🚋86) Melbourne-based designer Kylie Zerbst set up Obüs over 15 years ago with this, her first store. Known for bright geometric patterns and soft bamboo-cotton travel essentials, the clothing is sophisticated yet fun and offers pieces that get you from work to going out without a change.

Ess CLOTHING

(Map p68; ☎03-9495 6112; www.ess-laboratory.com; 114 Gertrude St, Fitzroy; ⊙11am-5.30pm Mon-Fri, to 5pm Sat, 12.30-4.30pm Sun; 🚋86) Japanese design duo Hoshika Oshimie and her sound-artist collaborative partner, Tatsuyoshi Kawabata, have created waves in Melbourne since Hoshinka established Ess Laboratory in 2001. The National Gallery of Victoria has Ess designs in its collection, but don't let that stop you claiming one for yourself.

Smith Street Bazaar VINTAGE, HOMEWARES

(Map p68; ☎03-9419 4889; 305 Smith St, Fitzroy; ⊙11am-6pm Mon-Fri, noon-6pm Sat, 12.30-5pm Sun; 🚋86) A great place to find midcentury furniture (the occasional Grant Featherston chair), Danish pottery, lamps of all shades and sizes, as well as vintage clothing and shoes. Best of all, it's well organised.

Aesop COSMETICS

(Map p68; ☎03-9419 8356; www.aesop.com; 242 Gertrude St, Fitzroy; ⊙11am-5pm Sun & Mon, 10am-6pm Tue-Fri, 10am-5pm Sat; 🚋86) This homegrown empire specialises in citrus- and botanical-based aromatic balms, hair masques, scents, cleansers and oils in beautifully simple packaging for both men and women. There are plenty of branches around town (and plenty of opportunities to sample the products in most of Melbourne's cafe bathrooms).

Rose Street Artists' Market MARKET

(Map p68; www.rosestmarket.com.au; 60 Rose St, Fitzroy; ⏲11am-5pm Sat & Sun; 🚋11) One of Melbourne's most popular art-and-craft markets showcases the best of local designers. Here you'll find up to 70 stalls selling matte silver jewellery, clothing, ceramics and iconic Melbourne screen prints. After shopping, head to the attached Young Blood's Diner (7am to 5pm Wednesday to Sunday) for rooftop cocktails or brunch, or both.

SpaceCraft HOMEWARES

(Map p68; ☎03-9486 0010; www.spacecraftaustralia.com; 255 Gertrude St, Fitzroy; ⏲10am-5.30pm Mon-Sat, 11am-5pm Sun; 🚋86) An excellent place to find a made-in-Melbourne souvenir that won't end up at the back of the cupboard. Textile artist Stewart Russell's botanical and architectural designs adorn everything from stools to socks to bed linen.

Gorman FASHION & ACCESSORIES

(Map p68; www.gormanshop.com.au; 235 Brunswick St, Fitzroy; ⏲10am-6pm Mon-Sat, 11am-5pm Sun; 🚋11) Lisa Gorman makes everyday clothes that are far from ordinary and that are cut from bright, vibrant fabrics. Plenty of other branches around town.

Crumpler FASHION & ACCESSORIES

(Map p68; ☎03-9417 5338; www.crumpler.com; 87 Smith St, Fitzroy; ⏲10am-6pm Mon-Sat, to 5pm Sun; 🚋86) Crumpler's bike-courier bags – designed by two former couriers looking for a bag they could hold their beer in while cycling home – are what started it all. The brand's durable, practical designs now extend to bags for cameras, laptops and iPads, and can be found around the world. The original messenger bags start at around $150.

Northside MUSIC

(Map p68; ☎03-9417 7557; www.northsiderecords.com.au; 236 Gertrude St, Fitzroy; ⏲11am-6pm Mon-Wed & Sat, to 7pm Thu & Fri, 1-5pm Sun; 🚋86) Northside's stock is DJ-mash-up eclectic, from NY hard salsa to hip-hop, from straight-up funk to Bollywood soundtrack, much of it on vinyl. Despite appearances to the contrary, staff are never too cool for school, and are happy to track down rare albums on request.

Brunswick Street Bookstore BOOKS

(Map p68; ☎03-9416 1030; www.brunswickstreetbookstore.com; 305 Brunswick St, Fitzroy; ⏲10am-9pm; 🚋11) Lovely store with knowledgeable staff and a good selection of children's books.

WORTH A TRIP

CAMBERWELL MARKET

Filled with secondhand and handcrafted goods, **Camberwell Sunday Market** (www.camberwellsundaymarket.org; Market Pl, Camberwell; ⏲6.30am-12.30pm Sun; 🚆Camberwell) is where Melburnians come to offload their unwanted items and where antique hunters come to find them. It's great for discovering preloved (often rarely worn) items of clothing, restocking a bookcase and finding unusual curios.

Carlton & Brunswick

Lygon St isn't just full of Italian restaurants and coffee spots: you'll find a good number of stores where you can offload your hard-earned cash, from boutiques and gourmet food shops to one of the city's best-loved bookstores. The long stretch of Sydney Rd in Brunswick offers continental grocers, secondhand clothes and vintage threads.

Mr Kitly HOMEWARES

(☎03-9078 7357; http://mrkitly.com.au; 381 Sydney Rd, Brunswick; ⏲11am-6pm Mon & Wed-Fri, to 4pm Sat & Sun; 🚋19, 🚆Brunswick) Head up the narrow stairs to a treasure trove of carefully curated homewares, indoor plants and accessories with a heavy Japanese influence. Get lost in time in this beautiful store as you covet everything from Hasami porcelain and copper gardening tools to Lithuanian bed linen and self-watering pot plants by Decor in pretty pastel colours.

Readings BOOKS

(Map p71; www.readings.com.au; 309 Lygon St, Carlton; ⏲9am-11pm Mon-Sat, 10am-9pm Sun; 🚌Tourist Shuttle, 🚋1, 8) A potter around this defiantly prosperous indie bookshop can occupy an entire afternoon if you're so inclined. There's a dangerously loaded (and good-value) specials table and switched-on, helpful staff. Just next door is its speciality children's store.

Also in the **city centre** (Map p56; ☎03-8664 7540; www.readings.com.au; State Library, 328 Swanston St; ⏲10am-6pm; 🚆Melbourne Central) and St Kilda (p133).

Gewürzhaus FOOD

(Map p71; ☎03-9348 4815; www.gewurzhaus.com.au; 342 Lygon St, Carlton; ⏲10am-6pm Mon-Sat, 11am-5pm Sun; 🚌Tourist Shuttle, 🚋1, 8) Set up by two enterprising young German girls, this store is a chef's dream with its displays of spices from around the world, including Indigenous Australian blends, flavoured salts and sugars. It has high-quality cooking accessories and gifts, and cooking classes, too. There's a city store inside the **Block Arcade** (Map p56; 03-9639 6933; Block Arcade, 282 Collins St; 9.30am-6pm; Flinders St).

Poppy Shop TOYS
(Map p71; 03-9347 6302; http://poppyshop.com.au; 283 Lygon St, Carlton; 9.30am-5.30pm Mon-Thu, to 6pm Fri, to 5pm Sat, 11am-4pm Sun; Tourist Shuttle, 1, 8, 16) A Carlton stalwart, tiny Poppy is a riot of intriguing toys, decorative objects and other happy-making paraphernalia. From beautiful handcrafted wooden toys to mechanical wind-up robots and tiny kewpie dolls for a few dollars, there's plenty to keep whole families entertained (if you can all fit at the same time).

Melbourne's West

Yarraville's Anderson and Ballarat Sts offer the west's best shopping, with lots of quirky independent stores. Footscray's main drag is more about the Little Saigon experience; it's great fun, but you're unlikely to want to buy anything other than food. The shop at Scienceworks is good for interesting, mind-expanding gifts.

★ **Footscray Market** MARKET
(03-9687 1205; www.footscraymarketvictoria.com.au; cnr Hopkins & Leeds Sts, Footscray; 7am-4pm Tue, Wed & Sat, to 6pm Thu & Fri; Footscray) Across from the station, this place is loud, pungent, and chock-a-block with food: meat, fish, fruit, vegetables, deli goods and a whole lot of stuff that may be new to you. Various international cuisines are available from the outlets that circle the main market space.

Sun Bookshop BOOKS
(03-9689 0661; www.sunbookshop.com; 10 Ballarat St, Yarraville; 9am-9.30pm Mon-Sat, to 7.30pm Sun; Yarraville) Perfectly located off the foyer of the Sun Theatre, this wonderful little bookshop has the kind of passionate staff that can recommend a tome to suit any taste, particularly if that taste tends towards the interesting, intellectual and literary. It also has a children's branch, Younger Sun, within throwing distance.

South Melbourne, Port Melbourne & Albert Park

In South Melbourne, Coventry St is notable for well-curated homewares, design objects and books. Close by, South Melbourne Market stocks a bounty of specialist foods, deli goods and fresh produce, as well as textiles and locally made gifts. In Albert Park, Bridport St harbours a handful of stylish boutiques and a wonderful bookshop.

Coventry Bookstore BOOKS
(03-9686 8200; www.coventrybookstore.com.au; 265 Coventry St, South Melbourne; 9.30am-5.30pm Mon-Fri, 9am-5pm Sat, 9.30am-4.30pm Sun; 1, 12) Despite its modest size, this independent trader packs a punch with a clued-up selection of books. Lose track of time while leafing through local and international fiction and biographies, not to mention beautiful tomes on travel, design, fashion, architecture and more. Little bookworms will appreciate the dedicated children's book room out the back.

Vincent 2 HOMEWARES
(03-9686 7702; www.vincentdesign.com.au; 269 Coventry St, South Melbourne; 10am-5pm Mon-Sat, 11am-4pm Sun; 1, 12) Nordic-inspired Vincent 2 ensures that every aspect of your day is aesthetically pleasing. Shop for local and international design objects, from striking takes on placemats, rugs, umbrellas and cognac glasses to stylish leather goods, iPhone docking stations and playfully themed bed linen.

Nest HOMEWARES
(03-9699 8277; www.nesthomewares.com.au; 289 Coventry St, South Melbourne; 9.30am-5.30pm Mon-Sat, to 5pm Sun; 12, 96) In a soothing, light-filled space, Nest stocks a gorgeous range of homewares and gifts, from 100%-linen bedding to soy candles, Aesop skincare and a range of cotton-knit 'comfort wear' that's way too nice to hide at home in. Staff are delightful. From South Melbourne Market head along Coventry St.

Avenue Books BOOKS
(03-9690 2227; www.avenuebookstore.com.au; 127 Dundas Pl, Albert Park; 9am-7pm; 1) Everyone needs a neighbourhood bookshop like this one, full of nooks and crannies to perch with literary fiction, cooking, gardening, art and children's books. Cluey staff make spot-on recommendations too.

South Yarra, Prahran & Windsor

Chapel St is the area's main retail spine. The stretch between Toorak and Commercial Rds offers mainly mainstream, midrange local and international chains. South of Commercial Rd, Chapel St becomes more interesting, with an eclectic mix of independent local designers, vintage shops and design stores. Smaller Greville St is even cooler, packed with an especially intriguing mix of retailers selling everything from kooky designer accessories to niche streetwear, limited-edition prints and collectable records.

ArtBoy Gallery ART

(Map p76; ☎03-9939 8993; http://artboygallery.com; 99 Greville St, Prahran; ⏰10am-6pm Mon-Thu, to 5pm Sat, 11am-4pm Sun; 🚋6, 72, 78, 🚆Prahran) ArtBoy displays the talent of up-and-coming and established Melbourne artists. Artworks are affordable, unique and edgy, ranging from stencil to abstract, pop and photography. Even the gallery's rear roller door is a showcase for local creativity, with a feline-themed aerosol portrait by street artist Silly Sully. To see it, head around the corner onto Porter St and then into Brenchley Pl.

Lunar Store DESIGN

(Map p76; ☎03-9533 7668; www.lunarstore.com.au; 2/127 Greville St, Prahran; ⏰11am-5pm Mon-Wed, 10am-6pm Thu & Fri, 10am-5pm Sat, 11am-4pm Sun; 🚋6, 72, 78, 🚆Prahran) This adorable space belongs to Jules Unwin, who fills it up with her favourite things. It's a great place to score quirky, offbeat design objects by both local and foreign artisans. Snoop around and you might find anything from Danish earthenware pencil holders to Melbourne-made ceramic necklaces and pooch-themed pouches from LA. Fun, contemporary, yet strangely nostalgic.

Signed & Numbered ART

(Map p76; ☎03-9077 6468; http://signedandnumbered.com.au; 153 Greville St, Prahran; ⏰11am-5pm Wed-Fri & Sun, from 10am Sat; 🚋6, 72, 78, 🚆Prahran) Art at its democratic best: Signed & Numbered deals in affordable limited-edition prints from more than 60 local and international artists, both emerging and established. Displayed pretty much like vinyl in a record store, the works span numerous print mediums, from etchings, letterpress and lino to screen and digital woodblock.

Chapel Street Bazaar VINTAGE

(Map p76; ☎03-9529 1727; www.facebook.com/ChapelStreetBazaar; 217-223 Chapel St, Prahran; ⏰10am-6pm; 🚋6, 78, 79, 🚆Prahran) Calling this a 'permanent undercover collection of market stalls' won't give you any clue to what's tucked away here. Bluntly, this old arcade is a sprawling, retro-obsessive riot. Whether it's Italian art glass, modernist furniture, classic Hollywood posters or Noddy eggcups that float your boat, you'll find it here. Warning: prepare to lose all track of time.

Third Drawer Down DESIGN

(Map p76; ☎03-9988 2390; www.thirddrawerdown.com; 155 Greville St, Prahran; ⏰11am-5pm Mon-Sat; 🚋6, 72, 78, 🚆Prahran) Dressed in a head-turning Camille Walala mural, Third Drawer Down is perfect for those who thought they had it all. Expect to step out with the likes of giant pineapple-shaped pool floats, altered ceramic plates featuring bearded ladies, statement-making socks, or a convertible backpack enlivened by an Echo Peaks Pendleton wool-panel print. Shopping was never quite this much fun.

Scanlan Theodore FASHION & ACCESSORIES

(Map p76; ☎03-9824 1800; www.scanlantheodore.com; 566 Chapel St, South Yarra; ⏰10am-6pm Mon-Thu, to 7pm Fri, to 5.30pm Sat, 11am-5pm Sun; 🚋78, 79, 🚆South Yarra) Scanlan Theodore helped define the Melbourne look in the 1980s and, despite the cut-throat nature of local retail, the label is still going strong with its super-feminine, beautifully tailored everyday and special-occasion wear. Although it's now considered a mature, mainstream label, its creations continue to make a statement, with clean lines and elegant, understated style.

Shelley Panton HOMEWARES

(Map p76; ☎03-9533 9003; http://shop.shelleypanton.com; 440 Malvern Rd, Prahran; ⏰9am-5.30pm Mon-Sat, from 10am Sun; 🚋72, 🚆Hawksburn) Potter Shelley Panton set up this gorgeous concept store, which stocks her own minimalist tableware alongside other local designers' work and imported goods from around the globe. Give your living space a lift with the likes of bone-china table lamps, mohair throws, graphic-print cotton cushions and whimsical bookends.

Greville Records MUSIC
(Map p76; ☎03-9510 3012; www.grevillerecords.com.au; 152 Greville St, Prahran; ⏰10am-6pm Mon-Thu & Sat, to 7pm Fri, 11am-5pm Sun; 🚋78, 79, 🚆Prahran) One of the last bastions of the 'old' Greville St, this banging music shop has such a loyal following that the great Neil Young invited the owners on stage during a Melbourne concert. The forte here is vinyl, with no shortage of eclectic and limited-edition discs (a super-limited Bob Dylan *Live in Sydney 1966* double vinyl has been discovered here…).

St Kilda

St Kilda isn't one of Melbourne's shopping meccas, though you'll find a handful of interesting retailers dotting Acland and Barkly Sts. On Sunday, St Kilda Esplanade plays host to a major art-and-craft market.

Readings BOOKS
(Map p78; ☎03-9525 3852; www.readings.com.au/st-kilda; 112 Acland St, St Kilda; ⏰10am-9pm; 🚋3, 16, 96) Defiantly prospering indie bookshop. There's a dangerously loaded (and good-value) specials table, switched-on staff and everyone from Lacan to Charlie & Lola on the shelves. Best of all, the store supports a string of independent publishers, as well as locally produced journals.

St Kilda Esplanade Market MARKET
(Map p78; www.stkildaesplanademarket.com.au; Esplanade, St Kilda; ⏰10am-4pm Sun May-Sep, to 5pm Oct-Apr; 🚋3, 12, 16, 96) Fancy a Sunday stroll shopping by the seaside? Well, here's the place, with a kilometre of trestle tables joined end to end. Pick up anything from local ceramics, sculpture, glassware and woodwork to photographic prints, organic soaps and tongue-in-cheek, retro tea towels.

Bitch is Back DESIGN
(Map p78; ☎03-9534 8025; www.thebitchisback.com.au; 100a Barkly St, St Kilda; ⏰closed Mon; 🚋3, 16, 67) This bitch offers a fabulous treasure trove of high-end vintage and mid-20th-century furniture and other design objects. There's an emphasis on Danish and Italian pieces from the 1920s to the 1980s, from armchairs and table lamps to glassware and ceramics. You might also stumble across highly sought-after furniture by European-trained, Australian-based designers like the Rosando Brothers, Dario Zoureff and Jakob Rudowski.

Dot Herbey FASHION & ACCESSORIES
(Map p78; ☎03-9593 6309; www.dotandherbey.com; 229 Barkly St, St Kilda; ⏰10.30am-6.30pm Mon-Wed, to 7pm Thu & Fri, 10am-6pm Sat & Sun; 🚋96) Grandma Dot and Grandpa Herb smile down upon this tiny corner boutique from a mural-sized photo, right at home among the vintage floral fabrics, Japanese linen and understated bohemian cool. Scan the racks for grandpa tops, cotton overalls, beautiful knits and other pieces in gorgeous, ethical fabrics.

Information

DANGERS & ANNOYANCES

There are occasional reports of alcohol-fuelled violence in some parts of Melbourne's city centre late on weekend nights – particularly in King St.

EMERGENCY & IMPORTANT NUMBERS

Australia's country code	☎61
International access code	☎0011
Ambulance, fire, police	☎000
Centres Against Sexual Assault	☎1800 806 292
Translating & Interpreting Service	☎131 450

GAY & LESBIAN TRAVELLERS

Melbourne has a large gay and lesbian population, second in Australia only to Sydney, and it's generally a very accepting city. Although same-sex marriage isn't legal, there's equality in most other aspects of the law.

Useful associations and publications include Gay & Lesbian Tourism Australia (www.galta.com.au), Star Observer (www.starobserver.com.au), Gay News Network (www.gaynewsnetwork.com.au), Lesbians on the Loose (www.lotl.com), DNA magazine (www.dnamagazine.com.au) and the Victorian AIDS Council (www.vac.org.au).

INTERNET ACCESS

Free wi-fi is available at central city spots such as Federation Sq, Flinders St station, Crown Casino and the State Library. Free wi-fi is now the norm in most midrange accommodation, although you sometimes have to pay in both budget and top-end places. Many cafes also offer free wi-fi.

If you're not travelling with your own device, there are plenty of libraries around Melbourne with terminals, though you'll need to bring ID to sign up and prebooking is recommended. The **City** (Map p56; ☎03-9658 9500; 253 Flinders Lane; ⊙8am-8pm Mon-Thu, 8am-6pm Fri, 10am-5pm Sat, noon-5pm Sun; Flinders St), **St Kilda** (☎03-9209 6655; http://library.portphillip.vic.gov.au; 150 Carlisle St, St Kilda; ⊙10am-8pm Mon-Thu, to 6pm Fri, to 5pm Sat & Sun; 3, 16, 78, Balaclava) and **Prahran** (☎03-8290 3344; www.stonnington.vic.gov.au/library/Visit-us/Prahran-Library; 180 Greville St, Prahran; ⊙10am-6pm Mon-Fri, to 1pm Sat; 78, 79, Prahran) libraries all offer access.

MEDIA

Newspapers Key publications are the *Age* (www.theage.com.au) and the tabloid *Herald Sun* (www.heraldsun.com.au).

MEDICAL SERVICES

Visitors from Belgium, Finland, Ireland, Italy, Malta, the Netherlands, New Zealand, Norway, Slovenia, Sweden and the UK have reciprocal health-care agreements with Australia and can access some free or subsidised health services through Medicare; see www.humanservices.gov.au for more details.

If you've been bitten by a snake or spider or have consumed something you think might be poisonous, contact the **Victorian Poisons Information Centre** (☎13 11 26; www.austin.org.au/poisons) for advice.

Hospitals

Royal Children's Hospital (☎03-9345 5522; www.rch.org.au; 50 Flemington Rd, Parkville; 57)

Royal Melbourne Hospital (☎03-9342 7000; www.thermh.org.au; 300 Grattan St, Parkville; 19, 55, 59)

Medical Clinics

La Trobe St Medical (☎03-9650 0023; Melbourne Central, 211 La Trobe St; ⊙8.30am-5pm Mon-Fri; Melbourne Central)

QV Medical Centre (☎03-9662 2256; www.qvmedical.com.au; L1 QV, 292 Swanston St; ⊙9am-5pm Mon-Sat, 10.30am-5.30pm Sun)

Travel Doctor (TVMC; ☎03-9935 8100; www.traveldoctor.com.au; L2, 393 Little Bourke St; ⊙9am-5pm Mon-Wed & Fri, to 8pm Thu, to 1pm Sat)

Travel Doctor (☎03-9690 1433; www.traveldoctor.com.au; 3 Southgate Ave, Southbank; ⊙8.30am-5.30pm Mon-Fri)

Wellnation Clinic (☎03-9662 4856; www.wellnationclinics.com.au; 368 Elizabeth St)

Pharmacies

Mulqueeny Midnight Pharmacy (☎03-9510 3977; www.mulqueenypharmacy.com.au/prahran; 416 High St, Prahran; ⊙9am-midnight; 6)

Priceline (☎03-9663 4747; www.priceline.com.au; Melbourne Central, 300 Lonsdale St; ⊙8am-7pm Mon-Wed, 8am-9pm Thu & Fri, 10am-7pm Sat & Sun)

Priceline (☎03-9663 6411; www.priceline.com.au; 58 Franklin St; ⊙9am-5pm Sat-Wed, to 5.30pm Thu & Fri)

Tambassis Pharmacy (☎03-9387 8830; cnr Brunswick & Sydney Rds, Brunswick; ⊙8am-midnight; 19)

Victoria Market Pharmacy (☎03-9329 7703; www.victoriamarketpharmacy.com; 523 Elizabeth St; ⊙8am-5.30pm Mon-Fri, 8am-4pm Sat, 9.30am-3.30pm Sun)

POST

Australia Post offers a very reliable service; visit www.auspost.com.au for up-to-date postage rates and the location of post offices.

Melbourne GPO Post Shop (Map p56; ☎13 13 18; www.auspost.com.au; 250 Elizabeth St; ⊙8.30am-5.30pm Mon-Sat; 19, 57, 59)

Franklin Street Post Shop (Map p56; ☎13 13 18; www.auspost.com.au; 58 Franklin St; ⊙9am-5pm Mon-Fri)

TOURIST INFORMATION

Fitzroy Gardens Visitor Centre (p66)

Hobsons Bay Visitor Information Centre (☎03-9932 4310; www.visithobsonsbay.com.au; cnr Syme St & Nelson Pl, Williamstown; ⊙9am-5pm, tours 11.45am Tue & Fri Mar-May & Sep-Nov; Williamstown) At this centre in Williamstown, friendly staff dispense info, and free tours depart in autumn and spring.

Melbourne Visitor Booth (Map p56; www.thatsmelbourne.com.au; Bourke St Mall; ⊙9am-5pm) Official city booth dispensing free tourist information.

Melbourne Visitor Centre (Map p56; ☎03-9658 9658; www.thatsmelbourne.com.au; Federation Sq; ⊙9am-6pm; ; Flinders St) Comprehensive information on Melbourne and regional Victoria, resources for mobility-impaired travellers, and a travel desk for accommodation and tour bookings. There are power sockets for recharging phones, too. There's a chance the centre might need to move sometime in 2017 due to construction work nearby.

Royal Botanic Gardens Visitor Centre (p74) Located beside the Melbourne Observatory, this information centre stocks maps and information about the adjoining Royal Botanic Gardens, books tours and rents out wheelchairs and umbrellas. It also contains the gardens' shop, which sells quality gifts with botanical and local themes.

Getting There & Away

Most travellers to Melbourne arrive via Melbourne Airport, which is well connected to the city by shuttle bus and taxi. There are also interstate trains and buses, a direct boat from Tasmania, and two minor domestic airports nearby.

Flights, cars and tours can be booked online at lonelyplanet.com/bookings.

AIR

Melbourne Airport

Melbourne Airport (p371) is the city's only international and main domestic airport, located 22km northwest of the city centre in Tullamarine. It has all of the facilities you'd expect from a major airport, including **Baggage Storage** (03-9338 3119; www.baggagestorage.com.au; Terminal 2, International Arrivals, Melbourne Airport; per 24hr $16; 5am-12.30am).

Dozens of airlines fly here from destinations in the South Pacific, Asia, the Middle East and the Americas. The main domestic airlines are **Qantas** (13 11 31; www.qantas.com), **Jetstar** (13 15 38; www.jetstar.com), **Virgin Australia** (13 67 89; www.virginaustralia.com), **Tigerair** (1300 174 266; www.tigerair.com) and **Regional Express** (Rex; 131 713; www.rex.com.au).

Avalon Airport

Some **Jetstar** flights to and from Sydney and Brisbane use **Avalon Airport** (p371), around 55km southwest of Melbourne's city centre.

Essendon Airport

Once Melbourne's main international airport, **Essendon Airport** (p371) is only 11km north of the city centre. Now only small operators fly from here to domestic destinations.

Free Spirit Airlines (03-9379 6122; www.freespiritairlines.com.au) flies to/from Merimbula and Burnie.

Jetgo (1300 328 000; www.jetgo.com) flies to/from to Port Macquarie, Dubbo and Brisbane.

Sharp Airlines (p371) flies to/from Flinders Island, King Island, Portland and Warrnambool.

BOAT

The **Spirit of Tasmania** (p372) ferry crosses Bass Strait from Melbourne to Devonport, Tasmania, at least nightly; there are also day sailings during peak season. The crossing takes 10 hours.

BUS

The main terminus for long-distance buses is within the northern half of Southern Cross station. Here you'll find counters for all the main bus companies, along with **luggage lockers** (03-9619 2588; www.southerncrossstation.net.au; Southern Cross station, 99 Spencer St; per 24hr $10-16; during train-service hours).

Firefly (Map p56; 1300 730 740; www.fireflyexpress.com.au; Southern Cross station, 99 Spencer St) Overnight coaches to/from Sydney ($65, 12 hours), Wagga Wagga ($65, 5¾ hours), Albury ($65, 3½ hours), Ballarat ($50, 1¾ hours) and Adelaide ($60, 9¾ hours).

Greyhound (Map p56; 1300 473 946; www.greyhound.com.au) Coaches to Albury ($55, 3½ hours), Wagga Wagga ($69, 6¼ hours), Gundagai ($75, 7¼ hours), Yass ($85, 8¼ hours) and Canberra ($88, eight hours).

V/Line (p373) Services destinations within Victoria, including Korumburra ($15, two hours), Mansfield ($29, three hours) and Echuca ($29, three hours).

CAR & MOTORCYCLE

The most direct (and boring) route between Melbourne and Sydney is the Hume Hwy (870km). The Princes Hwy hugs the coast and is much more scenic but much longer (1040km). Likewise, the main route to/from Adelaide is the Western/Dukes Hwy (730km), but this misses out on the Great Ocean Road.

TRAIN

Southern Cross station is the terminus for intercity and interstate trains.

Great Southern Rail (1800 703 357; www.greatsouthernrail.com.au) Runs the *Overland* between Melbourne and Adelaide ($149, 10½ hours, twice weekly).

NSW TrainLink (13 22 32; www.nswtrainlink.info) Twice-daily services to/from Sydney ($92, 11½ hours) via Benalla ($24, 2¼ hours), Wangaratta ($34, 2½ hours), Albury ($47, 3¼ hours) and Wagga Wagga ($63, 4½ hours).

V/Line (p373) Operates the Victorian train network; direct services include Geelong ($9, one hour), Warrnambool ($36, 3¾ hours), Ballarat ($15, 1½ hours), Bendigo ($22, two hours) and Albury ($38, four hours).

Getting Around

TO/FROM THE AIRPORT

Melbourne Airport The **SkyBus** (1300 759 287; www.skybus.com.au) departs regularly and connects the airport to Southern Cross station 24 hours a day. There's also a service to St Kilda.

Southern Cross station Long-distance trains and buses arrive at this large station on the Docklands side of the city centre. From here it's easy to connect to metropolitan trains, buses and trams.

Avalon Airport Near the neighbouring city of Geelong, but connected to Melbourne's Southern Cross station by **Sita Coaches** (☎03-9689 7999; www.skybus.com.au; adult/child $22/10).

BICYCLE

- Cycling maps and information are available from the **Melbourne Visitor Centre** (p134) and **Bicycle Network** (☎03-8376 8888; www.bv.com.au).
- Helmets are compulsory.
- Conventional bikes can be taken on trains (but not the first carriage), but only folding bikes are allowed on trams or buses. Front bike racks are being trialled on some bus routes.

Melbourne Bike Share (☎1300 711 590; www.melbournebikeshare.com.au; subscription day/week $3/8) is an automated, self-service bike-share system; look out for the 52 bright-blue stations scattered around the city, central suburbs and St Kilda. They're ideal for short trips as the first half-hour of use is free once you pay for your subscription (which requires a credit card and $50 security deposit). Some but not all bikes have safety helmets left with them; otherwise helmets are available with a $5 subsidy from 7-Eleven, IGA and bike stores around the city.

- For bike hire, try **Humble Vintage** (☎0424 619 262; www.thehumblevintage.com; 2hr/day/week $25/35/90) or **Rentabike** (p84).

BOAT

Melbourne Water Taxis (☎0416 068 655; www.melbournewatertaxis.com.au) travel between landings and jetties on the Yarra River between Abbotsford and Williamstown, and on the Maribyrnong River as far as Essendon.

Westgate Punt (☎0419 999 458; www.westgatepunt.com; weekday/weekend $2.70/5; ⊙6.30-9.10am & 3.40-7pm Mon-Fri, 9am-5pm Sat & Sun) crosses the Yarra between Port Melbourne and Spotswood.

Both **Williamstown Ferries** (☎03-9682 9555; www.williamstownferries.com.au; adult/child 1 way $18/9, return $28/14) and **Melbourne River Cruises** (☎03-8610 2600; www.melbcruises.com.au; adult/child return $29/16) head between the Southbank promenade and Williamstown's Gem Pier several times a day.

BUS

Melbourne has an extensive bus network, with over 300 routes covering all the places that the trains and trams don't go. Most routes operate from about 5.30am until about 11.30pm, but 10 central-city routes run every half hour throughout the night, while a further 11 depart from suburban train stations hourly.

You'll need a myki card (p136) to use the buses; **PTV** (Public Transport Victoria; ☎1800 800 007; www.ptv.vic.gov.au) has timetables, maps and a journey planner on its website.

CAR & MOTORCYCLE

Driving in Melbourne presents its own set of challenges, due to the need to share the road with trams.

TICKETS & PASSES

Melbourne's buses, trams and trains use **myki**, a 'touch on, touch off' travel-pass system. It's not particularly convenient for short-term visitors as it requires you to purchase a $6 plastic myki card and then put credit on it before you travel.

Travellers should consider buying a **myki Explorer** ($15), which includes the card, one day's travel and discounts on various sights; it's available from SkyBus terminals, PTV hubs, the **Melbourne Visitor Centre** (p134) and some hotels. Otherwise, standard myki cards can be purchased at 7-Elevens or newsagents.

The myki can be topped up at 7-Eleven stores, machines at most train stations and at some tram stops in the city centre; frustratingly, online top-ups take at least 24 hours to process. You can either top up with pay-as-you-go **myki Money** or purchase a seven-day unlimited **myki Pass** ($41); if you're staying more than 28 days, longer passes are available.

For zone 1, which is all that most travellers will need, the pay-as-you-go fare is $4.10 for two hours, or $8.20 for the day ($6 on weekends). The fine for travelling without tapping on with a valid myki card is $212, or $75 if you pay on the spot – ticket inspectors are vigilant and unforgiving.

➡ Where the trams run along the centre of the road, drivers cannot pass them once they indicate that they're stopping, as passengers board and alight from the street.

➡ In the city centre many intersections are marked 'right turn from left only'. This is the counter-intuitive 'hook turn', devised so as not to block trams or other cars. Right-turning drivers are required to move into the far left of the intersection and then turn right once the lights on that side of the intersection turn green. See www.vicroads.vic.gov.au for further details.

Car Hire

Most car and campervan hire places have offices at Melbourne Airport and in the city or central suburbs.

Aussie Campervans (p374)

Avis (p374)

Britz Australia (p374)

Budget (☎1300 362 848; www.budget.com.au)

Europcar (☎1300 131 390; www.europcar.com.au)

Hertz (☎03-9663 6244; www.hertz.com.au)

Rent a Bomb (☎03-9428 0088; www.rent-abomb.com.au; 452 Bridge Rd, Richmond; 🚋48, 75)

Thrifty (☎1300 367 227; www.thrifty.com.au)

Travellers Autobarn (p374) Hires and sells vehicles.

Car Sharing

Car-sharing companies that operate in Melbourne include **Flexi Car** (☎1300 363 780; www.flexicar.com.au), **Go Get** (☎1300 769 389; www.goget.com.au) and **Green Share Car** (☎1300 575 878; www.greensharecar.com.au). You rent the cars by the hour (from $9) or the day (from $55) and prices include petrol. Companies vary in terms of joining fees ($12 to $70) and how they charge (insurance fees, per hour and per kilometre). The cars are parked in and around the city centre and inner suburbs in designated 'car share' spots.

Parking

Parking inspectors are particularly vigilant in the city centre. Most of the street parking is metered and it's more likely than not that you'll be fined if you overstay your metered time. Also keep an eye out for 'clearway' zones (prohibited kerbside parking indicated by signs), which can result in sizeable fines. There are plenty of parking garages in the city; rates vary. Motorcyclists are allowed to park on the footpath except in some parts of the city centre where there are signs.

Toll Roads

Both drivers and motorcyclists will need to purchase a Melbourne Pass ($5.50 start-up fee, plus tolls and a 75c vehicle-matching fee per trip) if they're planning on using one of the two toll roads: **CityLink** (p373), from Tullamarine Airport to the city and eastern suburbs, or **EastLink** (☎03-9955 1400; www.eastlink.com.au), which runs from Ringwood to Frankston. Pay online or via phone – but pay within three days of using the toll road to avoid a fine.

Rental cars are sometimes set up for automatic toll payments; check when you hire.

TAXI

Melbourne's taxis are metered and require an estimated prepaid fare when hailed between 10pm and 5am (you may need to pay more or get a refund depending on the final fare). Toll charges are added to fares. Two of the largest taxi companies are **Silver Top** (☎131 008; www.silvertop.com.au) and **13 Cabs** (☎13 22 27; www.13cabs.com.au). **Uber** (www.uber.com) also operates in Melbourne.

TRAIN

Flinders St station is the main city hub for Melbourne's 17 train lines, which run from around 5am to around 11.30pm daily. Many lines spin around the City Loop, which connects the five stations in the inner city (Flinders St, Southern Cross, Flagstaff, Melbourne Central and Parliament), before heading out again.

Payment is via myki card (p136); **PTV** has timetables, maps and a journey planner on its website.

TRAM

Trams are intertwined with the Melbourne identity and an extensive network covers the city. They run roughly every 10 minutes Monday to Friday, every 15 minutes on Saturday and every 20 minutes on Sunday.

The entire city centre is a free tram zone. The zone is signposted on tram stops, with messages broadcast on board when you're nearing its edge to warn you that you should either hop off or pay with a myki card (p136). Note that there's no need to 'touch off' your myki on the trams, as all zone 1 journeys are charged at the same rate – although it won't matter if you do.

PTV has timetables, maps and a journey planner on their website.

Around Melbourne

Includes ➡

Best Places to Eat

- Lake House (p154)
- Sault (p154)
- Du Fermier (p157)
- Giant Steps (p143)
- ezard's @ Levantine Hill (p144)
- Kazuki's (p154)

Best Places to Sleep

- Clifftop at Hepburn (p152)
- 2 Dukes (p152)
- Hepburn Springs Chalet (p152)
- Healesville Hotel (p143)
- Tuck Inn (p143)

Why Go?

Getting out of the city for a day, a weekend or longer is easy – the question is not why, but where to first? Should you spend a day tripping from one winery to the next in the Yarra Valley? Disappear into the tall forest with a pair of walking boots and a keen eye for native wildlife? Indulge in some of Victoria's finest regional produce? Or pamper yourself with a massage and mineral spa?

Just a short drive from Melbourne you can experience historic towns, mountains, rivers, waterfalls, bush, vine-covered hills, cycle paths and wildlife. And don't think you have to rough it – around Daylesford and the Yarra Valley you'll find some of the finest boutique accommodation, cafes and restaurants in regional Victoria, with fresh country air to match.

When to Go

Dandenong

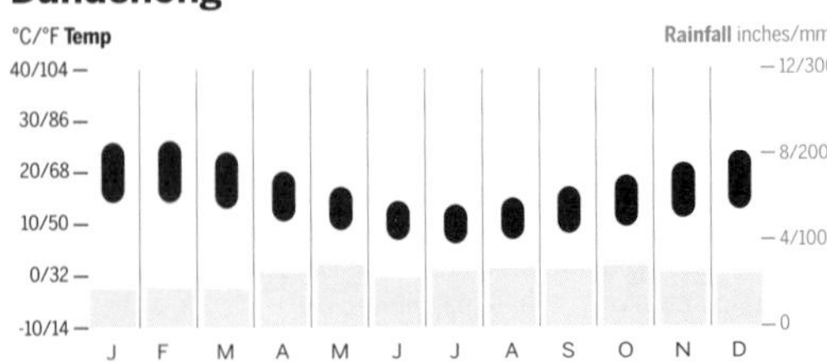

Feb–May The Yarra Valley is at its most colourful; grape harvest starts in February.

Jun–Sep Cross-country skiing at Lake Mountain or a hot winter soak in Spa Country.

Oct–Nov Festivals and spring weather make this a good time to hit the Dandenongs.

Around Melbourne Highlights

1 **Yarra Valley** (p141) Sampling Australia's finest cool-climate pinots in this historic wine-growing region.

2 **Hepburn Springs** (p150) Soaking in the soothing mineral waters at this charming resort town.

3 **Hanging Rock** (p156) Taking in the stunning vistas at this captivating, sacred site.

4 **Healesville Sanctuary** (p141) Meeting native fauna at this famous wildlife park.

5 **Lake House** (p154) Dining in style at this Daylesford institution.

6 **Lake Mountain** (p150) Relaxing in pretty Marysville, then cross-country skiing at this family-friendly resort.

7 **Lilydale to Warburton Rail Trail** (p146) Cycling along this scenic Yarra Valley trail.

8 **Puffing Billy** (p140) Steaming along on this historic train through beautiful eucalyptus and fern forests in the Dandenongs.

THE DANDENONGS

The low ranges of the verdant Dandenongs, just 35km from Melbourne, feel a world away from the city and make a fantastic day trip. Mt Dandenong (633m) is the tallest peak and the landscape is a patchwork of exotic and native flora with a lush understorey of tree ferns. Take care driving on the winding roads – apart from other traffic, you might see a lyrebird wandering across.

The consumption of tea and scones is de rigueur in the many cafes in the hills, or you can stop for lunch at some quality restaurants in towns such as Olinda, Sassafras and Emerald.

On summer weekends, the hills are alive with day trippers – visit for midweek for the best experience.

Sights

Dandenong Ranges National Park NATIONAL PARK
(Map p142; www.parkweb.vic.gov.au; Upper Ferntree Gully, Belgrave) This national park contains the four largest areas of remaining forest in the Dandenongs. The Ferntree Gully Area has several short walks, including the popular **1000 Steps** (Map p142; Mt Dandenong Tourist Rd, Dandenong Ranges National Park, Ferny Creek) up to **One Tree Hill Picnic Ground** (Map p142; www.parkweb.vic.gov.au; Lord Somers Rd, Tremont), two hours return, part of the **Kokoda Memorial Track**, which commemorates Australian WWII servicemen who served in New Guinea. Bring sturdy shoes as its steps get slippery.

SkyHigh Mt Dandenong VIEWPOINT
(Map p142; 03-9751 0443; www.skyhighmtdandenong.com.au; 26 Observatory Rd, Mt Dandenong; per vehicle $6; 9am-10pm Mon-Thu, to 10.30pm Fri, 8am-11pm Sat & Sun; 688) Drive up to SkyHigh for amazing views over Melbourne and Port Phillip Bay from the highest point in the Dandenongs. The view of the city lights at dusk is spectacular. There's a cafe-restaurant, a garden, picnic areas and a maze (adult/child/family $6/4/16).

William Ricketts Sanctuary GARDENS
(Map p142; 13 19 63; www.parkweb.vic.gov.au; 1402 Mt Dandenong Tourist Rd, Mt Dandenong; 10am-4.30pm) FREE This ferny garden features William Ricketts' sculptures of Aboriginal people, inspired by years spent living among them. You can also see his log cottage and gallery. There's an audio guide ($5) from the info office.

Activities

Puffing Billy RAIL
(Map p142; 03-9757 0700; www.puffingbilly.com.au; Old Monbulk Rd, Belgrave; return adult/child/family to Gembrooke $71.50/36/143; Belgrave) Holding fond childhood memories for many a Melburnian, popular *Puffing Billy* is an iconic restored steam train that toots its way through the ferny hills from Belgrave to Emerald Lake Park and Gembrook. Kids love to dangle their legs out the sides of the open-air compartments, and you can hopon and hopoff en route to enjoy a picnic or walk. Check its website for various dining packages and themed trips.

Trees Adventure ADVENTURE SPORTS
(Map p142; 03-9752 5354; www.treesadventure.com.au; Old Monbulk Rd, Belgrave; 2hr session adult/child $40/35; 11am-5pm Mon-Fri, 9am-5pm Sat & Sun; Belgrave) Reminiscent of the Ewok village in *Return of the Jedi*, Trees Adventure is a blast of tree climbs, flying foxes and obstacle courses in a stunning patch of old-growth forest made up of sequoia, mountain ash and Japanese oak trees. The safety system ensures you're always attached to a secure line; beginner sections are suitable for kids as young as five (per two hours $25).

Sleeping

Loft in the Mill GUESTHOUSE $$
(Map p142; 03-9751 1700; www.loftinthemill.com.au; 1602 Mt Dandenong Tourist Rd, Olinda; d $130-375;) In the centre of Olinda, Loft in the Mill is a welcoming place with nine cosy suites in two bluestone buildings modelled on an old flour mill and a 19th-century carriage house.

Monreale Cottages COTTAGE $$$
(Map p142; 03-9755 1773; www.monreale-estate.com.au; 81 the Crescent, Sassafras; cottages $225-380;) This beautifully restored 1920s country house has four luxurious cottages on its grounds and two retreats within the house itself. The fireside spas are a romantic innovation. Rates include welcome hampers which include provisions for breakfast.

Eating & Drinking

Cafe de Beaumarchais CAFE $
(Map p142; 03-9755 1100; 372 Mt Dandenong Tourist Rd, Sassafras; baguettes from $11; 8am-4pm Mon-Fri, to 5pm Sat & Sun;) This dimly lit Parisian style cafe is a great spot for a breakfast pie, freshly baked croissant, baguette or homemade sweet treat.

★Piggery Cafe CAFE $$
(Map p142; ☎03-9691 3858; www.piggerycafe.com.au; 1 Sherbrooke Rd, Sherbrooke; mains $12-25; ⊙10am-5pm Mon-Fri, 9am-5pm Sat & Sun) Set over 23 acres on the 1920s Burnham Beeches estate is this venture by celebrity chef Shannon Bennett. What was a former piggery is now a trendy open-plan cafe-restaurant with chargrilled barbecue dishes, kitchen garden produce and homebaked goods. Expect a menu of wagyu beef burgers, charcoal trout, prawn rolls and pork belly.

Miss Marple's Tearoom TEAHOUSE
(Map p142; ☎03-9755 1610; www.missmarplestearoom.com; 382 Mt Dandenong Tourist Rd, Sassafras; ⊙11am-4pm Mon-Fri, to 4.30pm Sat & Sun) This quaint English tearoom, inspired by the Agatha Christie character, comes with floral tablecloths, Devonshire scones ($9.50 for two) and sticky toffee pudding, as well as lunch mains. It's wildly popular on weekends; two-hour waits are not unusual.

Information

Dandenong Ranges & Knox Visitor Information Centre (Map p142; ☎03-9758 7522; www.visitdandenongranges.com.au; 1211 Burwood Hwy, Upper Ferntree Gully; ⊙11am-3pm Mon, 9.30am-4.30pm Tue-Sat, 10am-2pm Sun; Upper Ferntree Gully) Outside the Upper Ferntree Gully train station; good for walking maps.

Getting There & Away

It's just under an hour's drive from Melbourne's city centre to Olinda, Sassafras or Belgrave. The quickest route is via the Eastern Fwy, exiting on Burwood Hwy or Boronia Rd. Suburban trains from Melbourne (Belgrave Line) head to Belgrave station.

YARRA VALLEY

The lush Yarra Valley is Victoria's premier wine region and weekend getaway – partly for its close proximity to Melbourne, but mainly for the 80-plus wineries, superb restaurants, national parks and wildlife. This is the place to rise at dawn in a hot-air balloon over patchwork fields and vineyards, and to kick back with a pinot noir at world-class wineries.

The Yarra River starts its journey in the upper reaches of the Yarra Ranges National Park, passing through Warburton and close to Healesville before winding into Greater Melbourne and emptying into Port Phillip Bay near Williamstown.

Coldstream is considered the gateway to the Yarra Valley winery region, and most of the wineries are found within the triangle bound by Coldstream, Healesville and Yarra Glen. Further southeast, Warburton is the gateway to the Upper Yarra Valley region. There's another knot of wineries around Wandin and Seville along the Warburton Hwy (B380).

Healesville & the Lower Yarra Valley

Pretty little Healesville is the main town and base for exploring the triangular area of the Lower Yarra Valley. It's famous for its wildlife sanctuary, and perfectly located for easy access to some of the region's finest wineries.

Sights

Healesville & Around

★Healesville Sanctuary ZOO
(Map p144; ☎03-5957 2800, 1300 966 784; www.zoo.org.au/healesville; Badger Creek Rd; adult/child/family $32.50/16.30/82.10; ⊙9am-5pm; 685, 686) One of the best places in southern Australia to see native fauna, this wildlife park is full of kangaroos, dingoes, lyrebirds, Tasmanian devils, bats, koalas, eagles, snakes and lizards. The Platypus House displays the shy underwater creatures, and there's a daily interactive show and wildlife encounters. The exciting Birds of Prey presentation features huge wedge-tailed eagles and owls soaring through the air. Check the website for timings. Admission for kids is free on weekends and holidays.

★TarraWarra Museum of Art GALLERY
(Map p144; ☎03-5957 3100; www.twma.com.au; 311 Healesville-Yarra Glen Rd; adult/child $7.50/free; ⊙11am-5pm Tue-Sun) In a striking contemporary building at TarraWarra Estate, this excellent gallery showcases Australian art from the 1950s onwards and also features regularly changing Australian and international contemporary art exhibitions. The rotating permanent collection includes work from heavyweights Arthur Boyd, Fred Williams, Sidney Nolan and Brett Whiteley.

Yarra Glen

Yarra Valley Chocolaterie & Ice Creamery FACTORY
(Map p144; ☎03-9730 2777; www.yvci.com.au; 35 Old Healesville Rd, Yarra Glen; ⊙9am-5pm) A bit of Willy Wonka has arrived in the Yarra Valley – this is the perfect winery break for

The Dandenongs

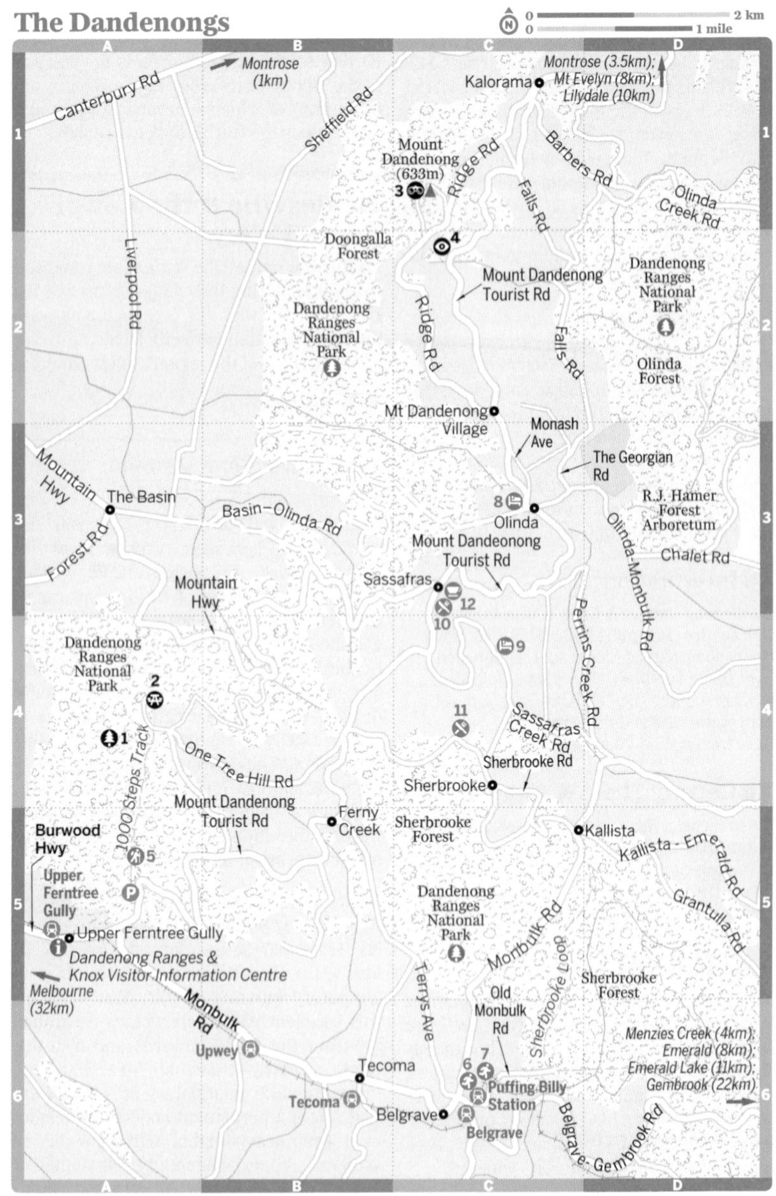

the kids. Brightly uniformed staff carry trays piled high with free samples made with imported Belgian chocolate and you can watch the European chocolatiers at work through floor-to-ceiling glass windows. The Bushtucker range makes for great souvenirs.

Tours

Ballooning over the Yarra Valley is a peaceful way to view the hills and vineyards. One-hour dawn flights with operators **Global Ballooning** (1800 627 661; www.globalballooning.com.au; 1hr flights adult/child from

The Dandenongs

Sights
1 Dandenong Ranges National Park A4
2 One Tree Hill Picnic Ground A4
3 SkyHigh Mt Dandenong C1
4 William Ricketts Sanctuary C2

Activities, Courses & Tours
5 1000 Steps A5
6 Puffing Billy.. C6
7 Trees Adventure C6

Sleeping
8 Loft in the Mill C3
9 Monreale Cottages................................ C4

Eating
10 Cafe de Beaumarchais C3
11 Piggery Cafe... C4

Drinking & Nightlife
12 Miss Marple's Tearoom C3

$285/365) and **Go Wild Ballooning** (☎03-9739 0772; www.gowildballooning.com.au; 621 Maroondah Hwy, Coldstream; 1hr flight adult/child $330/285) include a champagne breakfast and cost about $275 midweek and around $300 on weekends.

Eco Adventure Tours CULTURAL
(☎0418 999 936, 03-5962 5115; www.ecoadventuretours.com.au; walks adult/child from $50/30) A great way to see native animals in the wild is to join one of these nocturnal wildlife-spotting and daytime cultural walks in the Healesville, Toolangi and Dandenongs areas.

Yarra Valley Winery Tours TOURS
(☎1300 496 766; www.yarravalleywinerytours.com.au; tours from Yarra Valley/Melbourne $110/140) Daily tours taking in four or five wineries, plus lunch.

Sleeping

Healesville Hotel HOTEL $$
(☎03-5962 4002; www.yarravalleyharvest.com.au; 256 Maroondah Hwy; d week/weekend without bathroom from $115/135, incl dinner $310;) An iconic Healesville landmark, this restored 1910 hotel offers boutique rooms upstairs with crisp white linen, pressed-metal ceilings and spotless shared bathrooms. Also has chic apartments behind the hotel in Furmston House (studio from $180). Its renowned restaurant and bar is downstairs.

Tuck Inn B&B $$
(☎03-5962 3600; www.tuckinn.com.au; 2 Church St; d week/weekend incl breakfast from $160/180;) This former Masonic lodge has been refitted as a contemporary and stylish five-room guesthouse. Full breakfast included.

BIG4 Yarra Valley Park Lane Holiday Park CAMPGROUND $
(Map p144; ☎03-5962 4328; www.parklaneholidayparks.com.au/yarravalley; 419 Don Rd; unpowered & powered sites from $42, d cabins & tents $122-207;) Among trees and birdlife, this riverside park is well kitted out with comfortable cabins, luxury belle tents and campsites. It's a great spot for kids with an adventure playground and jumping cushion, as well as bike rental, swimming pool, tennis courts and a gym.

Eating

Healesville

Healesville Harvest Cafe CAFE $
(☎03-5962 4002; www.yarravalleyharvest.com.au; 256 Maroondah Hwy; snacks $7-20; 8am-4pm;) Sidling up next to the Healesville Hotel, the Harvest is perfect for fresh coffee and light meals made with local produce – salads, sandwiches, cakes, breakfast rolls, sausage rolls and soups. Head next door to its **Kitchen & Butcher** (☎03-5962 2866; www.yarravalleyharvest.com.au; 258 Maroondah Hwy; 10am-6pm Mon-Fri, 9am-6pm Sat, 10am-4pm Sun) to pick up gourmet picnic goodies and hampers.

★**Giant Steps** MODERN AUSTRALIAN, WINE $$
(☎03-5962 6111; www.giantstepswine.com.au; 336 Maroondah Hwy; small/large plates from $16/26; 11am-late Mon-Fri, 9am-late Sat & Sun;) The massive, refurbed Giant Steps is known for both its cellar door and buzzing restaurant. The delicious wood-fired dishes – featuring anything from a grilled snapper to chicken and tofu – steal the show, followed by slow-cooked lamb shoulder, duck fat chips and a charcuterie selection.

Healesville Hotel MODERN AUSTRALIAN $$
(☎03-5962 4002; www.yarravalleyharvest.com.au; 256 Maroondah Hwy; mains $16-41; noon-3pm & 6-10pm) One of the area's culinary showstoppers, historic Healesville Hotel is split into a formal dining room and the inviting front bar for more casual gastropub fare; the latter is a perfect spot for a pint or a glass of red by the fire. It's known for

Yarra Valley

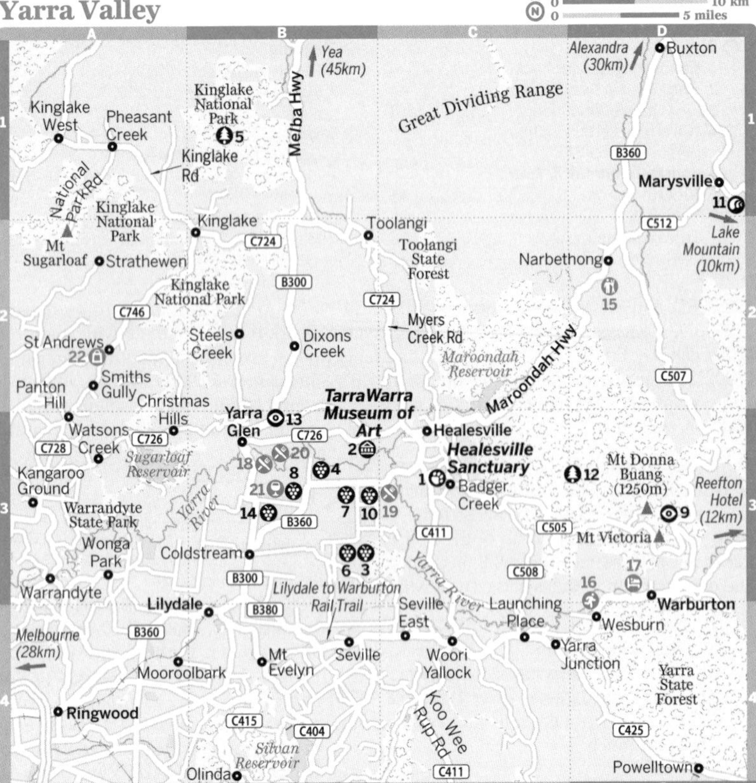

its wood-grilled meats over red-gum coals, slow-cooked lamb and steaks served with buttermilk-fried onion rings.

Yarra Glen

Zonzo ITALIAN **$$**

(Map p144; ☎03-9730 2500; www.zonzo.com.au; 957 Healesville-Yarra Glen Rd; pizza $24, share menu per person $50; ⊙noon-3pm Wed-Sun & 6pm-late Fri-Sun) At the Zonzo Estate Winery is this stylish Italian and traditional pizza restaurant with superb views out over the valley. The thin-crust pizzas just fly off the plate. They also offer tastings of their wines in their cellar door converted from old horse stables. Bookings recommended.

Lower Yarra Valley

Yarra Valley Dairy CHEESE, WINE

(Map p144; ☎03-9739 1222; www.yvd.com.au; 70-80 McMeikans Rd, Yering; cheese platters for 2 $32; ⊙10.30am-5pm) This renowned cheesemaker sells creamy French-style cheeses, produce and wine from its picturesque farm gate. Take part in the free cheese tasting, pick your favourites and order a platter to eat in the dairy's refurbished milking shed.

ezard @ Levantine Hill MODERN AUSTRALIAN **$$$**

(Map p144; ☎03-5962 1333; www.levantinehill.com.au; 882 Maroondah Hwy, Coldstream; 5-/8-course degustation menu $135/195; ⊙11am-5pm Mon & Wed-Fri, 10am-10pm Sat, 10am-5pm Sun) The latest restaurant by acclaimed chef Teage Ezard has him collaborating with the Levantine Hill winery. Within its striking contemporary cellar door overlooking the vineyards, it has wine barrel–inspired booth seating to take a long lunch of creative cuisine from a degustation menu designed specifically to match the wines.

Yarra Valley

Top Sights
1 Healesville Sanctuary C3
2 TarraWarra Museum of Art B3

Sights
3 Coldstream Hills B3
4 Domain Chandon B3
5 Kinglake National Park B1
6 Medhurst Wines B3
7 Oakridge B3
8 Punt Road Wines B3
9 Rainforest Gallery D3
10 Rochford Wines B3
11 Steavenson Falls D1
TarraWarra Estate .... (see 2)
12 Yarra Ranges National Park D3
13 Yarra Valley Chocolaterie & Ice Creamery B3
14 Yering Farm B3

Activities, Courses & Tours
15 Lake Mountain Ski Hire D2
16 Lilydale to Warburton Rail Trail D3

Sleeping
17 Alpine Retreat Hotel D3
BIG4 Yarra Valley Park Lane Holiday Park .... (see 1)

Eating
18 Elenore's Restaurant B3
19 Ezard's @ Levantine Hill C3
Yarra Valley Dairy .... (see 14)
20 Zonzo B3

Drinking & Nightlife
21 Napoleone Brewery & Ciderhouse B3
Yering Station .... (see 18)

Shopping
22 St Andrews Community Market A2

Elenore's Restaurant MODERN AUSTRALIAN $$$
(Map p144; 03-9237 3333; www.chateauyering.com.au; 42 Melba Hwy, Chateau Yering; 2-/3-course menu $85/98; 6-9pm) Within the historic 1850s Yering chateau and winery is this contemporary fine dining restaurant with a reputation as one of the region's best. Featuring a chef who's worked at Michelin-star restaurants, here you can select multiple courses from its à la carte menu with items such as twice-cooked brisket with betel-leaf farci or smoked duck pie with crispy-skin salad.

Bookings are essential. Its high tea ($60) from 1.30pm on Sunday is also very popular.

Drinking & Nightlife

Healesville

★ **Four Pillars** DISTILLERY
(03-5962 2791; www.fourpillarsgin.com.au; 2a Lilydale Rd; tastings & tour $10; 10.30am-5.30pm Sun-Thu, to 9.30pm Fri & Sat) One of Victoria's best-run microdistillers is this class operator that specialises in a range of inventive gins that you can watch being made while sampling the goods. Grab a paddle to taste their range, including an Australian gin, Spiced Negroni, Rare Dry and Navy Strength (58.8%). Staff are enthusiastic, friendly and knowledgeable.

Watts River Brewing MICROBREWERY
(03-5962 1409; www.wattsriverbrewing.com.au; 7 Hunter Rd; 11am-5pm Thu, Sun & Mon, to 9pm Fri & Sat) Run by a couple of brewers from the old White Rabbit (since relocated to Geelong), this small-scale brewery has a distinct man's cave feel to it with a couple of couches strewn about the beer vats. Its core range comprises a blonde, IPA and stout, with more varieties on their way.

Coldstream

★ **Napoleone Brewery & Ciderhouse** BREWERY
(Map p144; 03-9738 9100; www.napoleone-cider.com.au; 12 St Huberts Rd; 10am-5pm) A welcome variation among the ubiquitous wineries is this stop to sample Napoleone's selection of beers and ciders. Set in a contemporary glass atrium looking on to the brewing equipment, here you can sample the range of ales and ciders available by the tasting paddle ($12). Brewery tours are held at 11am each Saturday ($20 including tasting), or by appointment.

Punt Road Wines WINERY
(Map p144; 03-9739 0666; www.puntroadwines.com.au; 10 St Huberts Rd, Coldstream; 10am-5pm) This well-established Yarra Valley winery grows all its grapes on its estate, and features a slick cellar door staffed by a knowledgeable team offering free tastings.

It's a good spot to hang out with giant Jenga and a pétanque (boules) pit.

Yarra Glen

Hargreaves Hill Brewing Co BREWERY
(☎03-9730 1905; www.hargreaveshill.com.au; 25 Bell St; ⊙11.30am-8pm Mon-Sat, to 4pm Sun) Within a historic former bank (c1890), Hargreaves Hill has eight of its beers on tap to be enjoyed by the fire or in the rear courtyard. It doubles as a restaurant too, doing fantastic burgers, southern fried chicken and handmade pastas (mains $12 to $25).

Information

Yarra Valley Visitor Centre (☎03-5962 2600; www.visityarravalley.com.au; Harker St, Healesville; ⊙9am-5pm) Main info centre for the Lower Yarra Valley with loads of brochures as well as maps for sale.

Getting There & Away

Healesville is 65km north of Melbourne, an easy one-hour drive via the Eastern Fwy and Maroondah Hwy/B360.

McKenzie's Bus Line (☎03-5962 5088; www.mckenzies.com.au) runs daily from Melbourne's Southern Cross station to Healesville ($4.10, 1½ hours) en route to Marysville and Eildon; check website for schedule.

From Melbourne, suburban trains run to Lilydale, where there are regular buses to Healesville.

Warburton & the Upper Yarra Valley

The riverside town of Warburton has a very different feel from its Lower Valley neighbours – most visitors here are more interested in communing with nature than sipping chardonnay. The youthful Yarra River flows right through town, and a lovely 6km walking and cycling trail follows both sides of the river.

Sights & Activities

Cyclists can pedal the Rail Trail and other mountain-bike trails; there are additionally plenty of good walks in the area. You can tackle the 30km forested **O'Shannassy Aqueduct Trail**, head up to the **Rainforest Gallery** observation deck among 65m tall mountain ash, or try **La La Falls** or the **Redwood Forest** featuring 1500 Californian redwoods.

Yarra Ranges National Park NATIONAL PARK
(Map p144; ☎13 19 63; www.parkweb.vic.gov.au) Towering above Warburton is the ruggedly beautiful Yarra Ranges National Park. **Mt Donna Buang** (1250m) is the highlight of the park, snow-topped in winter. Toboggans can be rented at the toboggan run. A few kilometres before the summit, the **Rainforest Gallery** (Map p144; ☎03-5966 5996; Acheron Way) FREE, also known as the Mt Donna Buang Skywalk, is a fantastic treetop walk along a 40m observation platform into the rainforest canopy, and a 350m boardwalk through the forest floor.

Lilydale to Warburton Rail Trail CYCLING
(Warby Trail; Map p144; www.railtrails.org.au) Following a disused 1901 railway line, the 40km Lilydale to Warburton Rail Trail is a popular cycling route passing through farmland, the Yarra and wine country. The whole route takes about three to four hours one way, but it's relatively flat. Bike hire is available at **Yarra Valley Cycles** (☎03-9735 1483; www.yarravalleycycles.com; 108 Main St, Lilydale; per day from $50; ⊙Mon-Thu 9am-5.30pm, 9am-7pm Fri, 9am-5pm Sat, 10am-4pm Sun) in Lilydale and Cog (p147) in Warburton.

Warburton Habitat Tree WILDLIFE WATCHING
(☎0409 493 721; www.habitattree.com.au; private tours per hr/half-/full day $80/280/460) A great opportunity to get out into the bush, these private ecotours explore all aspects of the local habitat. Tours are tailor-made to your interests and can range from birdwatching (including lyrebirds) to nocturnal spotlight walks to see wildlife. They also have a wildlife display at the visitor info centre.

Sleeping & Eating

Alpine Retreat Hotel HOTEL $
(Map p144; ☎03-5966 2411; www.alpineretreat.com.au; 3340 Warburton Hwy, Warburton; d without bathroom $50, with bathroom $80-110; 📶) Once catering to Melbourne honeymooners, the sprawling 1920s faux-Tudor Alpine Retreat has cheap and cheerful rooms. It's right on the Warby Trail so it's popular with bike riders. Its pub is also a great place for a beer and a meal with a selection of 15 types of parmas (from $18), including a seafood, pulled beef and veggie variety.

Riverview Cafe CAFE $
(☎03-5966 5888; www.theriverview.com.au; 3373 Warburton Hwy, Warburton; mains $8-23;

YARRA VALLEY WINERIES

The **Yarra Valley** (http://wineyarravalley.com.au) has more than 80 wineries and 50 cellar doors scattered around its rolling, vine-cloaked hills, and is recognised as Victoria's oldest wine region – the first vines were planted at Yering Station in 1838. The region produces cool-climate, food-friendly drops such as chardonnay, pinot noir and pinot gris, as well as not-half-bad, full-bodied reds.

The smaller family-run wineries are equal to the large-scale producers, offering a less pretentious experience; visit www.yarravalleysmallerwineries.com.au for a list.

Some cellars charge a small fee for tasting, which is redeemable on purchase. Top Yarra Valley wineries with cellar door sales and tastings:

Coldstream Hills (Map p144; 03-5960 7000; www.coldstreamhills.com.au; 31 Maddens Lane, Coldstream; 10am-5pm) Chardonnay, pinot noir and velvety merlot are the prime picks.

Domain Chandon (Map p144; 03-9738 9200; www.chandon.com; 727 Maroondah Hwy, Coldstream; 10.30am-4.30pm) Established by the makers of Moët & Chandon, this slick operation with stunning views is worth a visit for the free guided tours at 11am, 1pm and 3pm, which include a peek at its atmospheric riddling hall.

Medhurst Wines (Map p144; 03-5964 9022; www.medhurstwines.com.au; 24-26 Medhurst Rd, Gruyere; cellar door 11am-5pm Thu-Mon, restaurant 11.30am-5pm Fri-Sun) Polished concrete and glass work well together at this modern winery.

Oakridge (Map p144; 03-9738 9900; www.oakridgewines.com.au; 864 Maroondah Hwy, Coldstream; 10am-5pm) The cellar door affords stunning views at this award-winning winery. Contemporary fare is dished up in its chic restaurant.

Rochford (Map p144; 03-5957 3333; www.rochfordwines.com.au; 878-880 Maroondah Hwy, cnr Hill Rd, Coldstream; 9am-5pm) A huge complex with a restaurant, cafe and regular concerts.

TarraWarra Estate (Map p144; 03-5957 3510; www.tarrawarra.com.au; 311 Healesville–Yarra Glen Rd, Healesville; tastings $5; 11am-5pm Tue-Sun) A convivial bistro and winery in a striking building. Sip away while lazing on the grassy knolls and visit the superb adjoining art gallery (p141).

Yering Farm Wines (Map p144; 03-9739 0461; www.yeringfarmwines.com; 19-21 St Huberts Rd, Yering; 10am-5pm) A rustic, family-owned little cellar door in an old hay shed with lovely views.

Yering Station (Map p144; 03-9730 0100; www.yering.com; 38 Melba Hwy, Yering; 10am-5pm) Victoria's first vineyard, and home to the heady shiraz-viognier blend.

8am-5pm Wed-Mon, to 11pm Fri & Sat;) Featuring beautiful forest views from its rear deck is this lovely cafe on the river, with a menu of homemade pies and sandwiches. There are hearty mains too, such as veggie lasagne or seafood chowder. It's a wonderful spot for a drink, with hand-pressed juices, Yarra Valley wines and a great selection of craft beers – including the local Seville Ridge Pale Ale.

Cog Bike Cafe CAFE $

(0418 134 347, 03-5966 2213; www.cogbikecafe.com.au; 42 Station Rd, Warburton; mains $12-18; 9am-4pm Thu-Sun Jun-Sep, 9am-4pm Thu-Mon Oct-May;) Part of the Warby bike trail, Cog is the perfect pit stop for good coffee and lunch snacks. They offer all your bike hire and service needs, and rent electric bikes too (1hr/half-/full-day $15/25/40, e-bike $30/60/80). With a day's notice you can arrange bike hire even if the cafe is closed. It's just up from the visitor info centre, near the old train station.

Information

Warburton Visitor Centre (03-5966 9600; www.warburtoninfo.com; 3400 Warburton Hwy, Warburton; 10am-4pm) Plenty of brochures and info here, including walks and waterfalls to visit. Check out a replica of the old water wheel, home to an eco centre for kids and local handicrafts and arts.

WORTH A TRIP

ST ANDREWS COMMUNITY MARKET

Sleepily ensconced in the hills 35km north of Melbourne is the township of St Andrews, which is synonymous with the weekly hippy **St Andrews Community Market** (Map p144; www.standrewsmarket.com.au; 8am-2pm Sat). Every Saturday morning the scent of eucalypt competes with incense as an alternative crowd comes to mingle and buy handmade crafts, enjoy a shiatsu massage, sip chai, have their chakra aligned or just listen to the street musos To get here, a shuttle bus departs from Hurstbridge train station.

Getting There & Away

Warburton is 80km east of Melbourne, around a 1½-hour drive. Take the Maroondah Hwy or Eastlink to join up to the Warburton Hwy (B380). If you're continuing east through the Yarra Ranges National Park, take Woods Point Rd (C511).

By public transport you catch the train to Lilydale station, from where bus 683 departs throughout the day to Warburton ($4.10, 40 minutes) via Healesville; you'll need a myki card.

Marysville

Spread across a valley between Narbethong and Lake Mountain, Marysville was a private mountain retreat as far back as 1863, and by the 1920s was known as Melbourne's honeymoon capital. Today it's still the main base for the cross-country ski fields at Lake Mountain and is reached via a beautiful drive over the Black Spur from Healesville; look out for lyrebirds on the way.

Marysville was at the epicentre of the tragic 2009 bushfires, during which most of the town's buildings were destroyed and 34 people tragically lost their lives. The town's tight-knit community continues to steadily and courageously rebuild.

Sights

Phoenix Museum MUSEUM
(Black Saturday Museum; 0418 175 090; www.blacksaturdaymuseum.com; 11 Murchison St; $5; 9am-5pm) A must-see sight for any visitor to Marysville is this sobering exhibition that shows the devastating impact the 2009 bushfires had on the town. It includes photos, video and salvaged items. It shares space with the visitor information centre.

Steavenson Falls WATERFALL
(Map p144; Falls Rd) Spectacular Steavenson Falls, about 2km from town, is Victoria's highest waterfall (84m). The infrastructure has been rebuilt since the fires, with a viewing platform spanning the river and floodlights illuminating the falls to 11pm.

Activities

Beeches Rainforest Walk WALKING
The Beeches Rainforest Walk is 4km (return) from the Beeches car park, which takes you through mountain ash and myrtle beech rainforest. It's a relatively easy walk with a few steep hills; look out for platypuses in the river, as well as lyrebirds, wallabies and echidnas.

Keppel Lookout Trail WALKING
The Keppel Lookout Trail is a challenging walk with spectacular views from the lookout point and at the top of the Steavenson Falls.

Sleeping

Marysville Caravan Park CAMPGROUND $
(03-5963 3247; www.marysvillecaravanpark.com.au; 1130 Buxton Rd; powered site from $38, cabins from $99;) Located at the edge of town, Marysville caravan park has excellent self-contained riverside cabins, camping and a play area for kids. Other than the pricier cabins, it's a BYO linen and towels.

The Tower MOTEL $$
(03-5963 3225; www.towermotel.com.au; 33 Murchison St; s/d/f $125/145/165;) One of the few buildings on the main road to survive Black Saturday, the Tower features a 1970s motel facade, which has been stylised with contemporary flair. The owners are friendly, there's a roof deck and a chintzy bar at reception (not always open), while rooms come with minibars and free wi-fi. Rates increase slightly in ski season.

Vibe Hotel HOTEL $$
(03-5957 7700; www.tfehotels.com; 32-42 Murchison St; r $160-250, ste $260-350;) While it has the best rooms in town by far, a slick business-style hotel along Maryville's sleepy main road still seems a bit out of place. Regardless, it makes for a very comfortable stay with modern rooms and large suites with balconies and kitchenettes. Facilities include a heated pool, gym, tennis court and swish restaurant-cafe next door.

Eating & Drinking

Fraga's Café CAFE $$
(☎03-5963 3216; www.facebook.com/fragascafe; 19 Murchison St; meals $9.50-26.50; ⏰9am-4pm Mon-Fri, to 4.30 Sat & Sun) A vibrant, arty cafe serving the town's best coffee, creative mains, pies and cakes, as well as local ciders.

The Duck Inn PUB
(☎03-5963 3437; www.facebook.com/theduckinnmarysvillepub; 6 Murchison St; ⏰Mon & Wed 4-11pm, Thu-Sun 11am-11pm) It's been a long wait in between drinks, but *finally* Marysville has got its pub back. The Duck Inn opened its doors in late 2016 (eight years since the fires) and features local breweries on tap, regional wines and a menu of pub classics ($15 to $34).

Shopping

Marysville Lolly Shop FOOD
(☎03-5963 3644; www.facebook.com/marysvillelollyshop; 8 Murchison St; ⏰10am-4pm Sun-Fri, to 5pm Sat) Symbolic of Marysville's rise from the ashes, this old favourite was one of the first rebuilt after the fires, and is a must-visit for sweet tooths. Also stocks local organic produce.

Information

Marysville Lake Mountain Visitor Information Centre (☎03-5963 4567; www.marysvilletourism.com; 11 Murchison St; ⏰9am-5pm; 📶) The modern tourist office provides helpful service, wi-fi and bike hire (per two hours/day $15/30). There's also a free app to download.

Getting There & Away

Marysville is 100km from Melbourne, a 1½-hour drive via the Maroondah Hwy. It's 40 minutes from Healesville.

McKenzie's Bus Line (p146) has a daily service to/from Melbourne ($11.62, two hours) via Healesville.

Lake Mountain

Part of the Yarra Ranges National Park, Lake Mountain (1433m) is the premier cross-country skiing resort in Australia,

BLACK SATURDAY

Victoria is no stranger to bushfires. In 1939, 71 people died in the Black Friday fires; in 1983 Ash Wednesday claimed 75 lives in Victoria and South Australia. But no one was prepared for the utter devastation of the 2009 bushfires that became known as Black Saturday.

On 7 February, Victoria recorded its hottest temperature on record with Melbourne exceeding 46°C and some parts of the state topping 48°C. Strong winds and tinder-dry undergrowth from years of drought, combined with the record-high temperatures, created conditions in which the risk of bushfires was extreme. The first recorded fires began near Kilmore and strong winds from a southerly change fanned the flames towards the Yarra Ranges. Within a few devastating hours a ferocious firestorm engulfed the tiny bush towns of Marysville, Kinglake, Strathewen, Flowerdale and Narbethong, while separate fires started at Horsham, Bendigo and an area southeast of Beechworth. The fires virtually razed the towns of Marysville and Kinglake, and moved so quickly that many residents had no chance to escape. Many victims of the fires died in their homes or trapped in their cars, some blocked by trees that had fallen across the road.

Fires raged across the state for more than a month, with high temperatures, winds and practically no rainfall making it impossible for fire crews to contain the worst blazes. New fires began at Wilsons Promontory National Park (burning more than 50% of the park area), Dandenong Ranges and in the Daylesford area.

The statistics tell a tragic tale: 173 people died; more than 2000 homes were destroyed; an estimated 7500 people were left homeless; and more than 4500 sq km were burned. What followed from the shell-shocked state and nation was a huge outpouring of grief, humanitarian aid and charity. Strangers donated tonnes of clothing, toys, food, caravans and even houses to bushfire survivors, while an appeal set up by the Australian Red Cross raised more than $300 million.

Today the blackened forests around Kinglake and Marysville are regenerating, and the communities are rebuilding. Tourism remains a big part of the economy, and visiting the shops, cafes and hotels in the area continues to boost their recovery.

with 37km of trails and several toboggan runs. In summer there are marked hiking and mountain-biking trails.

Lake Mountain Alpine Resort (☎03-5957 7222; www.lakemountainresort.com.au; 1071 Lake Mountain Rd; ⌚8am-4.30pm Mon-Fri Oct-May, to 6.30pm Jun-Sep) has ski hire, a ski school, a cafe and undercover barbecue areas. **Marysville Ski Centre** (☎03-5963 3455, 0408 103 481; www.marysvilleski.com.au; 29 Murchison St; ⌚7.30am-6pm Mon-Fri, from 7am Sat & Sun Jun-Sep) hire skis, toboggans, clothing and car chains, while **Lake Mountain Ski Hire** (Map p144; ☎03-5963 3444; www.lakemountainskihire.com; 436 Maroondah Hwy, Narbethong) at the Black Spur Inn at Narbethong also rents equipment.

During the ski season the daily gate fee is $56 per car (up to 10 people). There are no fees outside snow season from mid-September to the end of May. There's no on-mountain accommodation; however Marysville is only 10km away. The **cafe** (☎03-5957 7253; Lake Mountain Alpine Resort; dishes $7-15; ⌚9am-4pm Mon-Fri Oct–mid-Jun, 9-5pm daily Jun-Oct) on top of the mountain is open year-round – but only from Friday to Monday in the summer. There's also a bistro that opens during the ski season.

Once the snow has melted, it's time for bushwalkers and cyclists to take over the mountain. There are a number of trails for hikers in the area, from boardwalks to a trail to the summit; further afield are trails in the Yarra Ranges National Park. There are also a number of guided walks held throughout the green season.

For mountain bikers there are 20km of single-track downhill trails, as well as extensive cross-country trails for all levels. Road cycling is also popular, with the 21km climb involving a 932m ascent. You can hire bikes (from $15) on the mountain at the cafe, or from the visitor centre in Marysville.

In summer there's also a 240m flying fox ($20) and tube runs on inflatable tubes ($10) for kids.

Getting There & Away

During the ski season the **Lake Mountain Snow Bus** (Country Touch Tours; ☎03-5963 3753, 0417 633 753; www.lakemountainsnowbus.com; 24 Murchison St, Marysville; ⌚Jun-Aug) runs a return service including gate entry fee from Marysville (adult/child $35/25), departing 9am and 10.30am on weekends, and 10.30am other days – provided there's enough snow. The bus returns from Lake Mountain at 1.30pm or 3pm; book at their office in Marysville.

Other times you'll need your own vehicle, or if you're fit as a fiddle you can tackle the gruelling uphill climb on a bike.

All up it's a two-hour drive from Melbourne.

THE SPA COUNTRY

Daylesford & Hepburn Springs

POP DAYLESFORD 2565, HEPBURN SPRINGS 459

A favourite boutique weekend getaway, Daylesford and Hepburn Springs form the 'spa centre of Victoria'. Set among the scenic hills, lakes and forests of the Central Highlands, it's a fabulous year-round destination where you can soak away your troubles and sip wine by the fireside.

Even if you don't indulge in a spa treatment, there are plenty of great walks, a fabulous foodie scene and remnants of an arty, alternative vibe. The local population is an interesting blend of New Agers and old-timers, and there's also a thriving gay and lesbian scene here.

The health-giving properties of the area's mineral springs were first claimed back in the 1870s, attracting droves of fashionable Melburnians. The well-preserved and restored buildings show the prosperity of these towns, as well as the lasting influence of the many Swiss-Italian miners who came to work the tunnel mines in the surrounding hills.

Sights

Pick up a copy of the mineral springs leaflet from the visitor centre for a listing of the 100-odd springs in the region, which details the mineral composition for each.

Good local walks incorporating various mineral spring pumps include **Sailors Falls**, **Tipperary Springs**, **Central Springs Reserve** and the **Hepburn Springs Reserve**; take a water bottle with you to taste-test the naturally carbonated water. The visitor centre (p155) has maps and walking guides.

Convent Gallery GALLERY
(☎03-5348 3211; http://conventgallery.com.au; 7 Daly St, Daylesford; $5; ⌚10am-4pm) This beautiful 19th-century convent on Wombat Hill has been brilliantly converted into an art gallery with soaring ceilings, grand arch-

Hepburn Springs

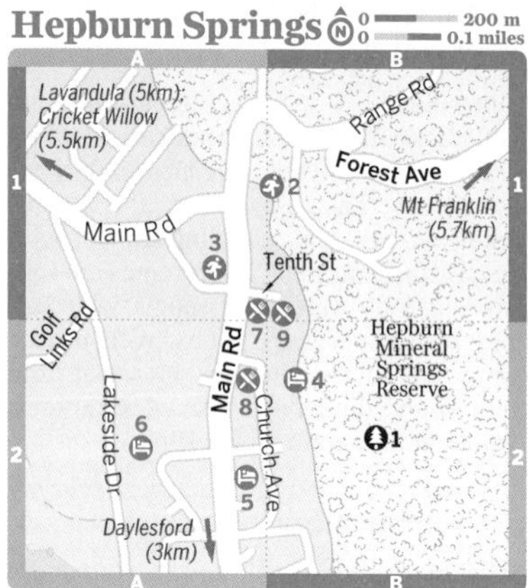

Hepburn Springs

Sights

1 Hepburn Mineral Springs Reserve B2

Activities, Courses & Tours

2 Hepburn Bathhouse & Spa B1
3 Mineral Spa at Peppers A1
Shizuka Ryokan .... (see 6)

Sleeping

4 Grande Hotel B2
5 Hepburn Springs Chalet A2
6 Shizuka Ryokan.....................................A2

Eating

7 Blue Bean Cafe..................................... A1
8 Frank and Connie's Kitchen A2
9 Surly Goat B1

Entertainment

Grande Hotel .... (see 4)

ways and magnificent gardens dotted with sculpture. Head up the path in the gardens behind the convent for sweeping views over the town. There's also an atrium cafe, cocktail bar and penthouse apartment (d including breakfast $295).

They run evening ghost tours here too (2½ hours, $49 including wine; book ahead).

Wombat Hill Botanic Gardens GARDENS
(Central Springs Rd, Daylesford; sunrise-sunset) Oak, pine and cypress trees fill these beautiful gardens, which have a picnic area and lookout tower with fine views of the countryside.

Activities

Day Spas

★Hepburn Bathhouse & Spa SPA
(Map p151; 03-5321 6000; www.hepburnbathhouse.com; Mineral Springs Reserve Rd, Hepburn Springs; 2hr bathhouse entry $25-44; 9am-6.30pm Sun-Thu, 8am-8pm Sat) Within the **Hepburn Mineral Springs Reserve** (Map p151), the main bathhouse is a sleek ultra-modern building where you can gaze out on the bush setting while soaking in the public pool or lazing on spa couches. The spa offers various treatments or a soak in a private mineral-springs pool in the original historic building (1895). Around the bathhouse are picnic areas, mineral spring pumps (bring an empty bottle to fill) and the historic **Pavilion** cafe.

Shizuka Ryokan SPA
(Map p151; 03-5348 2030; www.shizuka.com.au; 7 Lakeside Dr, Hepburn Springs; treatments from $130) Shiatsu massage and spa treatments with natural sea salts and seaweed extracts feature at this Japanese-style country spa retreat. The speciality here is its indulgent Geisha facial.

Mineral Spa at Peppers SPA
(Map p151; 03-5348 2100; www.mineralspa.com.au; 124 Main Rd, Springs Retreat, Hepburn Springs; 1hr from $65) A complex with indoor and outdoor mineral water spas and plunge pool. Also come for an exfoliation with Australian desert salts before an algae gel wrap, then move into the lavender-infused steam room or take a soft pack float.

Salus SPA
(03-5348 3329; www.lakehouse.com.au; 4 King St, Lake House, Daylesford) The pampering starts as you walk through a small rainforest to your exotic jasmine-flower bath in a cedar-lined tree house overlooking the lake.

Other Activities

Wombat Discovery Tours WILDLIFE WATCHING
(0484 792 212; www.wombatdiscoverytours.com.au; tours adult/child from $35/20) These highly recommended night tours are a wonderful opportunity to spot Australian wildlife in its natural habitat (as opposed to enclosures) in the Wombat State Forest. Here you're very likely to see wombats, kangaroos and wallabies, along with the occasional koala, echidna and glider. Trips are mostly Saturday nights, but check its website for the schedule. Rates include pickup from Daylesford.

Daylesford Spa Country Railway RAIL
(☎Sundays only 03-5348 3503; www.dscr.com.au; 18 Raglan St, Daylesford train station; return ticket adult/child/family to Musk $10/8/25, to Bullarto $15/13/35; ⏰10am-2.45pm Sun) This old rail-motor has popular rides to Musk and Bullarto and back every Sunday. It's a leisurely ride, but for extra sparkle go on the first Saturday of the month (at 5.30pm) when the **Silver Streak Food & Wine Train** (☎0421 780 100; www.dscr.com.au/silver-streak.php; adult/child $50/30) indulges you with drinks and finger food served on board.

Festivals & Events

ChillOut Festival LGBT
(www.chilloutfestival.com.au; ⏰mid-Mar) Held over the Labour Day weekend, this gay and lesbian pride festival is Daylesford's biggest annual event, attracting thousands of people for street parades, music and dance parties.

Sleeping

Daylesford

2 Dukes GUESTHOUSE $
(☎03-5348 4848; www.2dukesdaylesford.com; 2 Duke St, Daylesford; r with shared bathroom from $99;) Flying the flag for affordable accommodation in Daylesford is this well-run, former doctor's surgery turned guesthouse kitted out with vintage finds and original bright artworks. The five rooms each have their own personalities and share a bathroom (one room has an en-suite). Light breakfast is included and there's free wi-fi rounding out the best offer in town.

Jubilee Lake Holiday Park CAMPGROUND $
(☎03-5348 2186; www.jubileelake.com.au; 151 Jubilee Lake Rd, Daylesford; unpowered sites $18-30, powered sites $25-38, cabins $70-170;) Set in bushland on the edge of pretty Jubilee Lake, this friendly place is the best caravan park in the region. There's an open-air cinema in summer, paddle boat and canoe hire is available, and lower rates apply out of the summer high season.

Central Springs Inn MOTEL $$
(☎03-5348 3388; www.centralspringsinn.com.au; cnr Howe & Camp Sts, Daylesford; d from $130;) In a town full of pricey B&Bs, Central Springs offers more affordable motel-style lodging without skimping on character. Choose from large rooms in its 1875 heritage Provender building, or spa rooms in its newer section.

Lake House BOUTIQUE HOTEL $$$
(☎03-5348 3329; www.lakehouse.com.au; 4 King St, Daylesford; d incl half board from $610;) Overlooking Lake Daylesford, the famous Lake House is set in rambling gardens with bridges and waterfalls. Its 35 rooms are split into spacious waterfront rooms with balcony decks, and lodge rooms with private courtyards. Rates include breakfast and three-course dinner at its famed restaurant; two-night minimum on weekends.

Hepburn Springs

★**Hepburn Springs Chalet** HOTEL $$
(Map p151; ☎03-5348 2344; www.hepburnspringschalet.com.au; 78 Main Rd, Hepburn Springs; midweek/weekend r from $110/150;) If Don Draper was in town, this is where he'd drop his briefcase. Originally a 1920s guesthouse, the owners have retained the original features, complementing them with retro charm like deco mirrors and velvet lounges in the sitting areas and cocktail bar. Rooms are basic, but comfortable and cosy, and come with en-suites.

★**Grande Hotel** HERITAGE HOTEL $$$
(Map p151; ☎03-5348 1978; www.thegrandehotel.com.au; 1 Church Ave, Hepburn Springs; r incl half board $325-405) The recently restored historic Grande Hotel has been done up superbly with its boutique rooms delivering a quintessential Hepburn atmosphere. Room 5 is the pick with forest views and spa bath. Rates include breakfast and three-course dinner in its exquisite fine dining restaurant. It also has an elegant cocktail bar and a popular cabaret theatre (p155) with shows on Friday nights.

★**Clifftop at Hepburn** VILLA $$$
(☎1300 112 114; www.clifftopathepburn.com.au; 209-219 Main Rd; 2-bedroom apt from $350) The ultimate place to treat yourself in the area are these rustic-chic designer villas with wraparound windows overlooking the forest. Each two-bedroom villa features a suave decor of blonde woods, Danish furniture, ceramics, sun lounge, French wood-fire heaters and stand-alone stone bathtubs. Rooms have either a massage chair or arcade-game consoles, as well as personalised touches such as in-house dining.

Daylesford

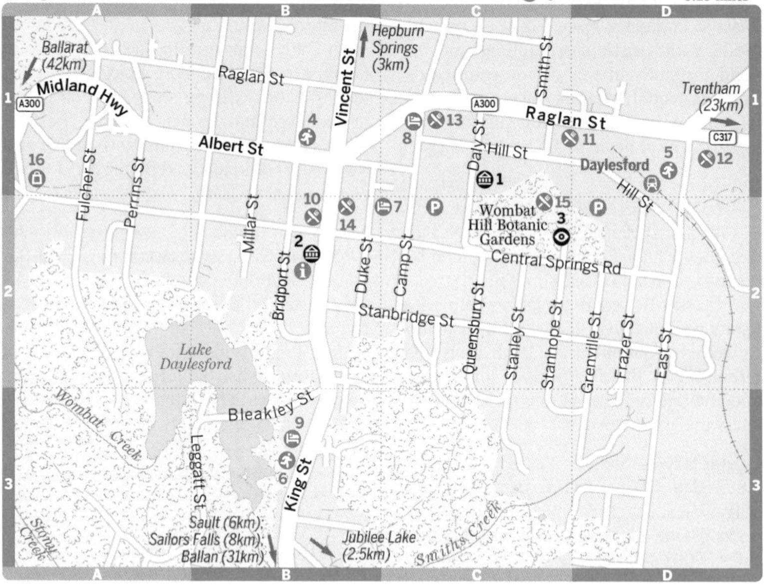

Daylesford

Sights
1 Convent Gallery C1
2 Daylesford Museum B2
3 Wombat Hill Botanic Gardens C2

Activities, Courses & Tours
4 Daylesford Day Spa B1
5 Daylesford Spa Country Railway D1
6 Salus B3
Silver Streak Food & Wine Train .... (see 5)

Sleeping
7 2 Dukes C2
8 Central Springs Inn C1
9 Lake House B3

Eating
10 Belvedere Social B2
11 Cliffy's Emporium C1
12 Farmers Arms D1
13 Kazuki's C1
Lake House .... (see 9)
14 Larder Daylesford B2
15 Wombat Hill House C2

Shopping
16 Mill Markets A1

Shizuka Ryokan GUESTHOUSE $$$
(Map p151; ☎03-5348 2030; www.shizuka.com.au; 7 Lakeside Dr, Hepburn Springs; d $230-350; 📶) Inspired by traditional places of renewal and rejuvenation in Japan, this traditional minimalist bush getaway has six rooms surrounding a serene Zen garden. Each room has tatami matting and plenty of green tea. Host and Japanophile Catherine cooks lovely traditional Japanese breakfasts and multicourse dinners (per person $75). Being a retreat, it's not a place for children.

Eating

Daylesford

Cliffy's Emporium DELI, CAFE $
(☎03-5348 3279; www.cliffysemporium.com.au; 30 Raglan St, Daylesford; mains $12-22; ⏰8am-4.30pm Sun-Fri, till late Sat; 📶) Behind the vine-covered verandah of this local institution is an old-world cafe perfect for breakfast, pies and baguettes, as well as local Malmsbury-roasted coffee. It's also a provedore crammed with preserves, meats and cheeses.

Farmers Arms PUB FOOD $$
(☎03-5348 2091; www.thefarmersarms.com.au; 1 East St, Daylesford; mains $22-42; ⏲noon-late) Modern and rustic surroundings and food meld tastefully in this classic country red-brick gastropub. There's a welcoming front bar and a beer garden for summer days, featuring local beers by Daylesford Brewery.

Belvedere Social MODERN AUSTRALIAN $$
(☎03-5348 2088; www.belvederesocial.com.au; 82 Vincent St, Daylesford; mains $25-39; ⏲3-11pm Wed, noon-1am Thu-Sat, noon-11pm Sun) The best thing to happen to Daylesford's main street in years, classy Belvedere Social is worth a look for its well-made cocktails and quality food. As well as its mains (rack of lamb, wagyu porterhouse etc), there's a heap of smaller bites and charcuterie options to go with its excellent wine list and original cocktails.

Larder Daylesford CAFE $$
(☎03-5348 4700; www.larderdaylesford.com.au; 57a Vincent St, Daylesford; mains $11-29; ⏲7.30am-3.30pm) One of Daylesford's most popular cafes is this smart space with exposed brick and gleaming wooden floorboards; it's divided into a main cafe and small next-door annex. Come for all-day breakfasts, homemade cakes and a good selection of teas and single-origin filter coffee.

Wombat Hill House CAFE $$
(☎03-4373 0099; www.wombathillhouse.com.au; Wombat Hill Botanic Gardens, Daylesford; mains $15-23; ⏲9am-4pm Sat-Mon, to 8.30pm Fri) Run by the folks from the Lake House this cutesy cafe in the Wombat Hill Botanic Gardens is a great spot to grab breakfast next to the fireplace or out in the patio garden. There's high tea on weekends from 2pm (per person $40), which includes a glass of sparkling. Also on offer are takeaway lunchboxes perfect for a picnic in the gardens.

★**Lake House** MODERN AUSTRALIAN $$$
(☎03-5348 3329; www.lakehouse.com.au; 4 King St, Daylesford; 2-4 course meals midweek/weekend $95/115; ⏲noon-2.30pm & 6-9pm; 📶) You can't talk about Daylesford without waxing on about the Lake House, long regarded as the town's top dining experience. It doesn't disappoint with stylish purple high-back furniture, picture windows showing off Lake Daylesford, a superb seasonal menu, an award-winning wine list and impressive service. If you can't decide, try the tasting menu ($155, or vegetarian $135). Book well ahead for weekends.

Kazuki's JAPANESE $$$
(☎03-5348 1218; www.kazukis.com.au; 1 Camp St, Daylesford; 3-/5-courses $80/110, 7-course tasting menu $140; ⏲6pm-late Thu-Mon, noon-2pm Sat & Sun) Kazuki's brings an unexpected twist to Daylesford's dining scene with its fusion of Japanese and French cuisine. The two-room restaurant, incorporating a wine and sake bar, is intimate, and there's an al-fresco courtyard at the side.

Sault MODERN AUSTRALIAN $$$
(☎03-5348 6555; www.sault.com.au; 2349 Ballan-Daylesford Rd, Daylesford; mains $36-43; ⏲6pm-late Wed & Thu, 11am-late Fri-Sun) Surrounded by lavender and a lake, and situated in a grand building about 7km south of Daylesford, stylish Sault has a reputation for serving innovative contemporary Australian dishes with a Spanish twist and a focus on local produce. Wednesday is 'locals' night' with a complimentary glass of wine served with mains.

Hepburn Springs & Around

Blue Bean Cafe CAFE $$
(Map p151; ☎03-5348 2297; www.facebook.com/bluebeanlovecafe; 115 Main Rd, Hepburn Springs; mains $15-25; ⏲8am-3pm Mon-Thu, to 9pm Fri-Sun) Taking over from the iconic Red Star Cafe is this equally cool, locally run spot. It does the best coffee in the region, featuring a weekly rotating single-origin coffee to go with tasty breakfasts and lunches. It also has an impressive craft beer selection with 25 varieties, as well as cocktails, local wines, live music on Fridays and a chilled-out courtyard.

Frank and Connie's Kitchen MODERN AUSTRALIAN $$
(Map p151; ☎03-5348 1156; www.frankandconnies.com.au; 97 Main Rd, Hepburn Springs; small/large plates from $14/25; ⏲6-9pm Wed & Thu, noon-2pm & 6pm-late Fri-Sun) Another example of Hepburn's re-emergence as a culinary destination is this endearing weatherboard cottage along the main road. Young owner-chef Calliopi Buck changes her menu weekly, which is all about shared plates of contemporary fare: think tacos with Chinese-style duck leg and pickled cucumber and slaw, lamb ribs with chimichurri, and a *Flintstones*-sized rib eye.

Surly Goat BISTRO $$$
(Map p151; ☎03-5348 4628; www.thesurlygoat.com.au; 3 Tenth St; mains $27-32; ⏲4pm-late Thu, noon-late Fri & Sat, to 5pm Sun) Just off the

WORTH A TRIP

MT FRANKLIN

Just 10km north of Daylesford, **Mt Franklin** is an extinct volcanic crater that you can drive straight into. Known to the Dja Dja Wurrung people as Lalgambook, it's a beautiful place with forest-covered walking trails that take you through lush vegetation, a picnic area and a summit lookout. Free short-term **camping** (www.parkweb.vic.gov.au) FREE is permitted in the crater (it's part of the Hepburn Regional Park).

Heading back towards Hepburn Springs, take the turn-off to **Shepherds Flat**, where there are two interesting spots. **Cricket Willow** (03-5476 4277; www.cricketwillow.com.au; 355 Hepburn-Newstead Rd, Shepherds Flat; museum adult/child $3/1.50, tours $6; 11am-3pm, call ahead) has been making their Jabaroo cricket bats for over a century using the willow grown on-site since 1902. Check out the immaculate cricket oval, tour the workshop, willow-tree nursery or sport memorabilia museum, or line up against the bowling machine ($25).

Further along, **Lavandula** (03-5476 4393; www.lavandula.com.au; 350 Hepburn-Newstead Rd; adult/child $4/1; 10.30am-5.30pm Sep-May, Sat & Sun Jun-Aug) is a lovely Swiss-Italian farm and stone cottage where you can meet the farm animals, check out the gardens and produce, wander between lavender bushes and enjoy lunch in the Ticinese grotto. There are free tours of the farm and cottage at noon, 2pm and 4pm.

main road in the heart of Hepburn Springs is this atmospheric, cosy inn with a social bar and open fire. As well as its interesting drinks menu, food is a highlight with a fine-dining restaurant doing the likes of tempura zucchini flower, chargrilled lamb shoulder and good ol' pavlova with passionfruit curd.

Drinking & Nightlife

Around Daylesford

Passing Clouds Winery WINERY
(03-5348 5550; www.passingclouds.com.au; 30 Roddas Lane, Musk; cellar door 10am-5pm daily, restaurant noon-3pm Fri-Mon) Undoubtedly one of the best wineries in the region, Passing Clouds is known for its cool climate pinots and chardonnays – several of which are featured at Melbourne's hottest restaurants. As well as tastings at the cellar door, its restaurant is also acclaimed with a menu of charcoal grilled meat mains, as well as charcuterie and cheese platters to accompany wine.

Daylesford Cider CIDER HOUSE
(03-5348 2275; www.daylesfordcider.com.au; 155 Dairyflat Rd, Musk; noon-4pm Wed-Fri, noon-5pm Sat & Sun) A 10-minute drive east of Daylesford is this wonderful cider house that produces English-style ciders from its 17 heritage-listed varieties of apples grown on its organic orchard. Go the tasting paddle ($10) to sample its seven different varieties, enjoyed in its scenic outdoor courtyard, a picnic on the grass or in its tavern by the fire.

Hepburn Springs & Around

★**Old Hepburn Hotel** PUB
(03-5348 2207; www.oldhepburnhotel.com.au; 236 Main Rd, Hepburn Springs; 4pm-midnight Mon & Tue, noon-midnight Wed & Thu, noon-1am Fri & Sat, noon-11pm Sun;) A country pub with both character and taste, the Old Hepburn makes for a great night out with live music on weekends (usually free). The pub food hits the spot, and it has a ripper beer garden and friendly locals. It's a bit out of town, but call ahead for free bus pickup and drop-off service from Hepburn.

Entertainment

★**Grande Hotel** CABARET
(Map p151; 03-5348 1978; www.thegrandehotel.com.au; 1 Church Ave, Hepburn Springs; tickets $10-30; Fri evenings) Since the demise of Hepburn's iconic Palais, the Grande has stepped in to fill a much needed-gap by opening its doors as a wonderful theatre hosting anything from cabaret and burlesque to sultry jazz. Shows are on Friday nights within its evocative basement space inside the historic old hotel which most folk combine with dinner and cocktails.

Shopping

Mill Markets MARKET
(03-5348 4332; www.millmarkets.com.au; 105 Central Springs Rd, Daylesford; 10am-6pm) You could just about fit a Boeing 747 in the enormous Mill Markets, housing a

DON'T MISS

HANGING ROCK

Made famous by the spooky Joan Lindsay novel (and subsequent film by Peter Weir) *Picnic at Hanging Rock*, about the disappearance of a group of 19th-century schoolgirls, **Hanging Rock** (☎03-5421 1469, 1800 244 711; www.visitmacedonranges.com; per vehicle $10 or per person $4; ⊙9am-5pm) is an ancient and captivating place. The volcanic rock formations are the sacred site of the traditional owners, the Wurundjeri people, but you're welcome to clamber up the rocks along the 20-minute path. Once also a hideout for bushrangers, many mysteries and legends surround it and an eerie energy is said to be felt by many who climb among the boulders. From the summit there are views of Mt Macedon and the surrounding countryside.

Hanging Rock is a 10-minute drive from the pleasant town of Woodend, worth a visit for its **Holgate Brewhouse** (☎03-5427 2510; www.holgatebrewhouse.com; 79 High St; ⊙noon-late). Woodend is easily reached from Melbourne by V/Line train ($8.80, one hour). There's no public transport to Hanging Rock, so if you don't have a car you'll need to arrange a taxi.

mind-boggling collection of furniture, collectables, antiques, books and retro fashions.

Information

TOURIST INFORMATION

Daylesford Visitor Centre (☎1800 454 891, 03-5321 6123; www.visitdaylesford.com; 98 Vincent St, Daylesford; ⊙9am-5pm) Within an old fire station, this excellent tourist centre has good information on the area and mineral springs. They also have a self-guided walking-tour map for Daylesford. There's a history **museum** (☎03-5348 1453; www.daylesfordhistory.com.au; 100 Vincent St, Daylesford; adult/child $4/1; ⊙1.30-4.30pm Sat & Sun) next door too.

Getting There & Away

Daylesford is 115km from Melbourne, a 1½-hour drive via the Calder Hwy; take the Woodend turnoff, from where it's a 35-minute drive.

Daily **V/Line** (☎1800 800 007; www.vline.com.au) train and coach services connect Melbourne by train to Woodend or Ballarat, then bus to Daylesford ($12.80, two to 2½ hours). The buses run from Bridport St opposite the fire station.

Local buses operate the 3km journey between Daylesford (from Bridport St) and Hepburn Springs ($2.40); it's a 10-minute journey.

MACEDON RANGES

A short distance off the Calder Fwy, less than an hour's drive north of Melbourne, the Macedon Ranges is a beautiful area of low mountains, native forest, excellent regional produce and wineries, often enveloped in cloud in winter, but great on a sunny day. The Macedon Ranges cover the towns of Gisborne, Mt Macedon, Woodend, Trentham, Lancefield, Romsey and Kyneton, and the legendary Hanging Rock.

The scenic drive up Mt Macedon, a 1010m-high extinct volcano, passes grand mansions and gardens, taking you to picnic areas, walking trails, sweeping lookouts and the huge memorial cross near the summit car park. There's a cafe and barbecue area at Cameron's Picnic Area.

There are some great wineries (www.macedonrangeswineries.com.au) in the area. **Wine Tours Victoria** (☎1800 946 386, 03-5428 8500; www.winetours.com.au; per person incl transport & lunch $175) can arrange tours.

Trentham

At an elevation of 700m, the small historic township of Trentham is noticeably cooler than the surrounding areas. It's worth a visit to stroll its quaint streetscape with some excellent new eateries and historic pubs, which have turned it into a mini Daylesford.

Sights & Activities

Trentham Falls WATERFALL

Just a short drive from Trentham is one of Victoria's highest single-drop waterfalls. Situated in the Wombat State Forest, the Coliban River cascades 32m over a sheer face of basalt rock.

Domino Trail WALKING

This walking trail follows the old Trentham railway through the Wombat State Forest, the habitat of the endangered powerful owl.

Trail maps are available from the tourist office (p157) at the old train station.

Sleeping

Wombat Discovery Farmstay FARMSTAY $
(☎0484 792 212; www.wombatdiscoverytours.com.au/farm-stay; per person incl food & activities $135) This property offers a wonderful opportunity to spend a night on a local farm, where you can meet the animals and be involved with daily affairs. Rates include meals prepared with homegrown produce, as well as pickup from Woodend station. Even if you're not staying, definitely sign up for its wildlife tours (p151).

Eating & Drinking

RedBeard Historic Bakery CAFE, BAKERY $
(☎03-5424 1002; www.redbeardbakery.com.au; Old Bakery Lane; sandwiches $9-15; ⏰8am-5pm Fri-Mon; 📶) Tucked down a lane off the main strip, RedBeard is owned by brothers with more than 25 years' baking experience, and is famous for its sourdough breads baked in a huge 19th-century wood-fired Scotch oven. They also do good breakfasts.

★Du Fermier CAFE $$$
(☎03-5424 1634; www.dufermier.com.au; 42 High St; set menu per person $66; ⏰noon-2.30pm Fri-Mon) Translating to 'from the farmhouse', celebrity chef Annie Smithers' Du Fermier focuses on rustic French provincial cooking with 90% of the produce sourced from her own garden.

Cosmopolitan PUB
(Cosmo; ☎03-5424 1516; www.thecosmopolitanhotel.com.au; cnr High St & Cosmo Rd; ⏰4-8pm Mon & Tue, noon-late Wed-Sun) Reopening in 2012 after burning down in 2005, the historic Cosmo is a Trentham institution where you can cosy up by the open fire with a local beer or cider under pressed-metal ceilings. In summer, the huge beer garden beckons. It's a great place for food too, with wood-fired pizzas, pub grub and more fine-dining options ($16-38).

Information

Trentham Visitor Centre (www.visittrentham.com.au; Victoria St, Trentham station; ⏰10am-4pm Sat & Sun) Only open on the weekend, this helpful little visitor centre is set up inside the old train station.

Getting There & Away

Trentham sits at the top of the Great Dividing Range, midway between Woodend and Daylesford, 97km from Melbourne.

Two to four buses run daily to Trentham from Woodend station ($4.20, 22 minutes) en route to Daylesford ($2.40, 23 minutes).

Great Ocean Road & Bellarine Peninsula

Includes ➡

Best Places to Eat

- ➡ Brae (p181)
- ➡ IGNI (p164)
- ➡ á la grecque (p178)
- ➡ Fen (p197)
- ➡ Chris's Beacon Point Restaurant (p183)
- ➡ Bespoke Harvest (p183)

Best Places to Sleep

- ➡ Great Ocean Ecolodge (p185)
- ➡ Beacon Point Ocean View Villas (p183)
- ➡ Vue Grand (p170)
- ➡ Cimarron B&B (p177)
- ➡ Bimbi Park (p185)

Why Go?

The Great Ocean Road (B100) is one of Australia's most famous road-touring routes. It takes travellers past world-class surfing breaks, through pockets of rainforest and calm seaside towns, and under koala-filled tree canopies. It shows off sheer limestone cliffs, dairy farms and heathlands, and gets you up close and personal with the crashing waves of the Southern Ocean.

Hunt out the isolated beaches and lighthouses in between the towns and the thick eucalyptus forests in the Otway hinterlands to really escape the crowds. Rather than heading straight to the Great Ocean Road, a fork in the road at Geelong can take you the long, leisurely way there, through the Bellarine Peninsula with visits to charming Queenscliff and wineries en route.

Day-tripping tourists from Melbourne rush in and out of the area in less than 12 hours but, in a perfect world, you'd spend at least a week here.

When to Go

Cape Otway

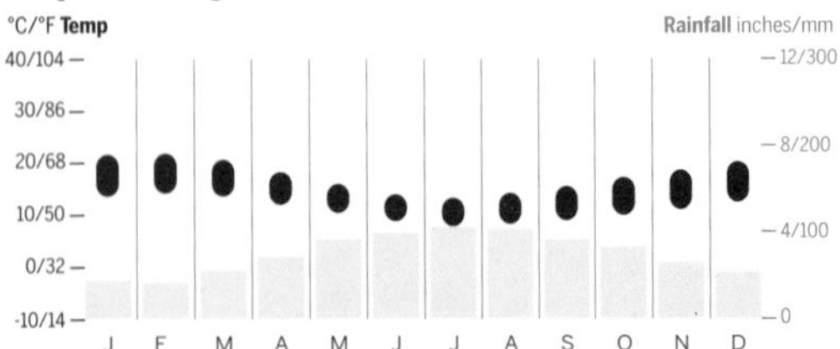

Mar Chill out to folk and roots tunes at the hugely popular Port Fairy Folk Festival.

Easter Head to Bells Beach during the Rip Curl Pro to witness spectacular surfing action.

Jul Visit coastal towns in mid-winter for bright seascapes, cosy cafes and whale watching.

GEELONG & BELLARINE PENINSULA

Geelong

POP 210,875

As Victoria's second-largest city, Geelong is a proud town with an interesting history and pockets of charm. While Melburnians love to deride their little cousin as a boring backwater, in reality few of the knockers have veered off its main thoroughfare enough to really know what makes the town tick. Geelong's new bypass means travellers can skip the city and head straight to the Great Ocean Road, but there are lots of reasons to make a stop here.

Geelong is centred around the sparkling Corio Bay waterfront and the city centre, where heritage buildings from the boom days of the gold-rush era and thriving wool industry have now been converted into swanky restaurants and bars. It's also a footy-mad town, passionate about its hometown AFL team, the Cats.

Sights & Activities

Geelong Waterfront WATERFRONT

(Map p162; Beach Rd) Geelong's sparkling revamped waterfront precinct is a great place to stroll, with plenty of restaurants set on scenic piers, plus historical landmarks, a 19th-century carousel, sculptures, grand homes, swimming areas, playgrounds and grassy sections ideal for picnics. In summer you can cool off at popular **Eastern Beach**, with an art-deco bathing pavilion complete with diving boards, sunbathing area and toddler pool. Jan Mitchell's 100-plus famous painted **Bay Walk Bollards** are scattered the length of the waterfront.

Geelong Waterfront Carousel HISTORIC SITE

(Map p162; 03-5224 1547; www.geelongaustralia.com.au/carousel; Geelong Waterfront; adult/child $4.90/4.40; 10.30am-5pm) A prominent feature along Geelong's waterfront is this ornate 19th-century hand-carved carousel, housed within a slick 21st-century glass pavilion.

Geelong Art Gallery GALLERY

(Map p162; 03-5229 3645; www.geelonggallery.org.au; 55 Little Malop St; 10am-5pm) FREE With over 6000 works in its collection, this excellent gallery has celebrated Australian paintings such as Eugene von Guérard's *View of Geelong* and Frederick McCubbin's 1890 *A Bush Burial*. Also exhibits contemporary works and has free tours on Sundays at 2pm.

National Wool Museum MUSEUM

(Map p162; 03-5272 4701; www.geelongaustralia.com.au/nwm; 26 Moorabool St; adult/child/family $9/5/30; 9.30am-5pm Mon-Fri, 10am-5pm Sat & Sun) More interesting than it may sound, this museum showcases the importance of the wool industry in shaping Geelong economically, socially and architecturally – many of the grand buildings in the area are former wool-store buildings, including the museum's 1872 bluestone building. There's a sock-making machine and a massive 1910 Axminster carpet loom that gets chugging at hourly intervals.

Powerhouse Geelong – City Precinct GALLERY

(Map p162; 0418 526 640; www.powerhouse-geelong.com; 20 Brougham St; 9.30am-5pm) FREE In addition to the **street art park** ($5; 10am-5pm) in the old power station in North Geelong are these galleries and studio spaces set within a 100-year-old brick wool storing house. Set above the **Brougham Street Markets** (03-5221 2490; www.facebook.com/broughamstreetmarkets; 10am-6pm), here everything is for sale and features the work of some 300 street artists from the area and beyond. Call ahead for street-art workshops (per hour $25).

Old Geelong Gaol HISTORIC BUILDING

(Map p162; 03-5221 8292; www.geelonggaol.org.au; cnr Myers & Swanston Sts; adult/child/family $10/5/22; 1-4pm Sat & Sun, daily school holidays) Built in 1849, HSM Prison Geelong may have closed its doors in 1991, but this old bluestone jail remains as terrifying as ever. You'll see its grim cells set over three levels, plus the shower block, watchtowers and gallows. Each exhibit is accompanied by audio, explaining anything from contraband of crude homemade weapons to former cellmates such as Chopper Read (cell 39). **Ghost tours** (Map p162; 1300 865 800; www.twistedhistory.net.au; adult/child $33/22) are also run here.

Boom Gallery GALLERY

(0417 555 101; www.boomgallery.com.au; 11 Rutland St, Newtown; 9am-4pm Mon-Sat) FREE Down an industrial street off Pakington St, Boom's warehouse space in an old wool mill shows contemporary works by Melbourne and local artists. It sells great design objects

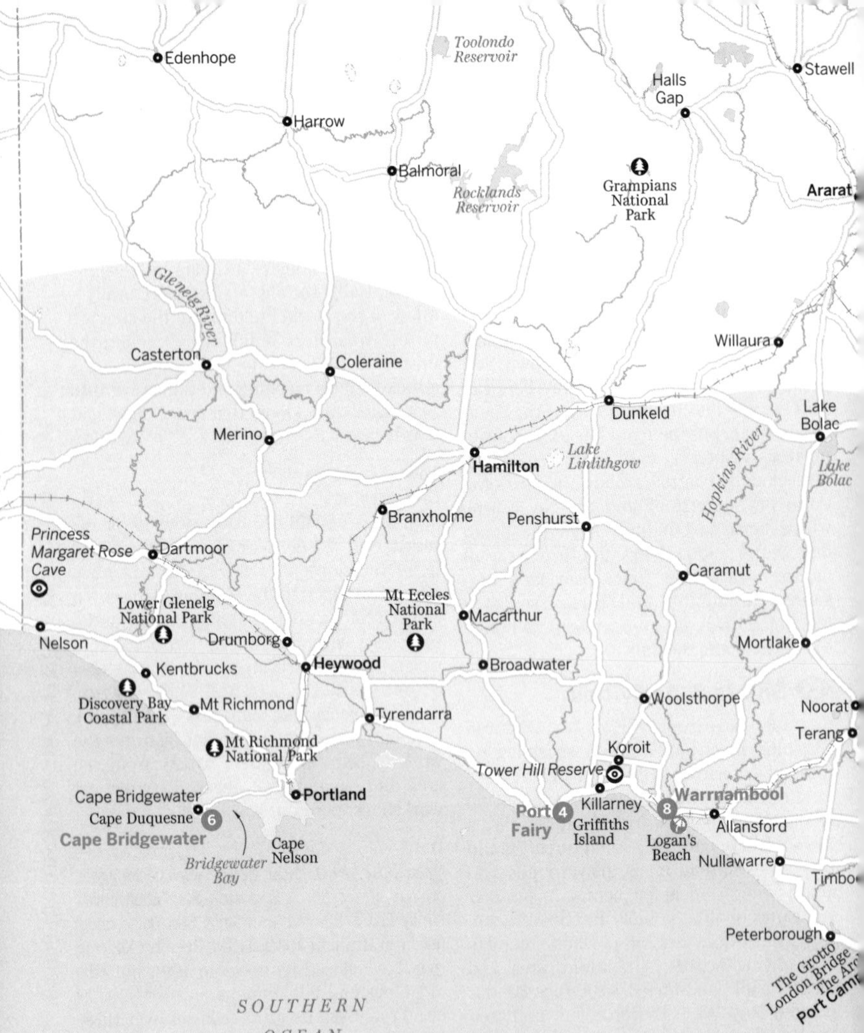

Great Ocean Road & Bellarine Peninsula Highlights

1. **Twelve Apostles** (p187) Being mesmerised by the outlook over these limestone pillars rising from the ocean.
2. **Cape Otway** (p184) Spying koalas as you head through the rainforest en route to the Cape Otway lighthouse.
3. **Lorne** (p178) Lapping up life in this relaxed resort town where the coast meets the bush.
4. **Port Fairy** (p194) Soaking up the maritime atmosphere in a heritage wharf town.
5. **Torquay** (p173) Shopping for surf gear before signing up to learn how to surf.

6 Cape Bridgewater (p199)
Hanging out on a 'secret' white powdery beach before checking out the seals.

7 Queenscliff (p168)
Strolling 19th-century streetscapes and tasting wines from Bellarine vineyards.

8 Warrnambool (p190)
Enjoying a romantic escape, looking for whales, and spotting wildlife at Tower Hill Reserve.

Geelong

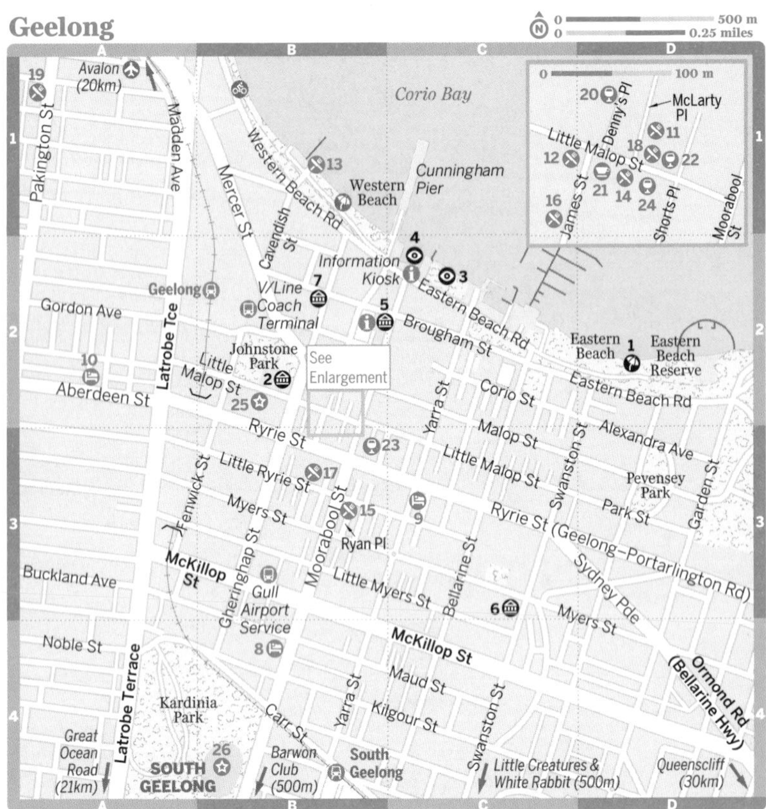

and jewellery, and the attached cafe does fantastic coffee and seasonal food.

Narana Aboriginal Cultural Centre CULTURAL CENTRE
(☎03-5241 5700; www.narana.com.au; 410 Torquay Rd, Grovedale; ⏲9am-5pm Mon-Fri, 10am-4pm Sat, cafe 8am-4pm Mon-Fri, to 3pm Sat, gallery Tue-Sat, by appointment Mon) FREE The Wathaurung people – the original inhabitants of Geelong – called the area Jillong, and this precinct in its outskirts offers a fascinating insight into their culture. There's a range of things going on: a **gallery** featuring Victoria's largest collection of indigenous art; a fusion cafe that offers contemporary dishes using indigenous ingredients; didgeridoo performances (or play it yourself); a boomerang-throwing gallery; and a native garden (by donation) which features emus, wallabies and koalas. Call ahead for daily tours.

City Walking Tours WALKING
(Map p162; ☎03-5244 7102; 26 Moorabool St, National Wool Museum Visitor Centre; 2hr tours $15) Volunteer-led city tours show Geelong's historic architecture and landmarks. Prices include tea and cake and two-for-one admission to the National Wool Museum (p159) and rides on the waterfront carousel (p159). Book one day in advance.

Festivals & Events

Toast to the Coast WINE
(www.toasttothecoast.com.au; tickets $45; ⏲early Nov) This wine festival, held on Melbourne Cup weekend, takes place at wineries from Geelong to the Bellarine. Shuttle service is an additional $30.

Avalon Airshow AIR SHOW
(www.airshow.com.au; Avalon Airport; ⏲Feb-Mar) Held in Avalon, 20km north of Geelong's city centre, this display of sky-bound might and

Geelong

Sights

1 Eastern Beach ... D2
2 Geelong Art Gallery ... B2
3 Geelong Waterfront ... C2
4 Geelong Waterfront Carousel ... C2
5 National Wool Museum ... B2
6 Old Geelong Gaol ... C3
7 Powerhouse Geelong – City Precinct .. B2

Activities, Courses & Tours

City Walking Tours ... (see 5)
Geelong Gaol Ghost Tours ... (see 6)

Sleeping

8 Devlin Apartments ... B4
9 Gatehouse on Ryrie ... C3
10 Irish Murphy's ... A2

Eating

11 Armageddon Cake Dessert Bar ... D1
12 Caruggi ... C1
13 Geelong Boat House ... B1
14 Hot Chicken Project ... D1
15 IGNI ... B3
16 James Street Bakery ... C1
17 Little Green Corner ... B3
18 Pistol Pete's Food n Blues ... D1
19 Tulip ... A1

Drinking & Nightlife

20 Blackman's Brewery ... D1
21 Cartel Coffee Roaster ... D1
22 Geelong Cellar Door ... D1
23 Union Street Wine ... B3
24 Workers Club Geelong ... D1

Entertainment

25 Geelong Performing Arts Centre ... B2
26 Kardinia Park ... B4

Shopping

Brougham Street Markets ... (see 7)

power happens every two years and attracts thousands of viewers.

Sleeping

Irish Murphy's HOSTEL $

(Map p162; ☎03-5221 4335; www.irishmurphys-geelong.com.au; 30 Aberdeen St, Geelong West; dm/s/d with shared bathroom $40/50/80, d with bathroom $60; P) Upstairs from an Irish pub, Geelong's only backpackers is a well-run affair with clean dorms, most of which only have two beds. Guests get 20% off meals in the lively pub downstairs, which also offers free haircuts on Thursdays if you buy a pint!

★ **Devlin Apartments** APARTMENT $$

(Map p162; ☎03-5222 1560; www.devlinapartments.com.au; 312 Moorabool St; r $160-500;) Geelong's most stylish offerings are these boutique apartments, housed in a 1926 heritage-listed building (the former Gordon Tech school). Each of the apartments has themed designs including 'New Yorker' loft-style apartments with arched windows; 'Modernist', furnished with Danish designer chairs; and 'Industrial', featuring wrought iron, rustic wood and tiled brick bathrooms. There are motel-style rooms too.

Gatehouse on Ryrie GUESTHOUSE $$

(Map p162; ☎0417 545 196; www.gatehouseonryrie.com.au; 83 Yarra St; d incl breakfast $110-130; P @) A prime location in the centre of town, this guesthouse is one of Geelong's best midrange choices. Built in 1897 it features gorgeous timber floorboards throughout, spacious rooms (most with shared facilities) and a communal kitchen and lounge area. Breakfast is in the glorious front room.

Eating

James Street Bakery CAFE $

(Map p162; ☎03-5221 3909; www.jamesstreetbakery.com.au; 10 James St; mains $12-20; 7am-4pm Mon-Fri, 8am-3pm Sat) Featuring an elegant interior of retro wood panels and light fittings, this popular cafe bakes its own sourdough and delicious cakes. They do great breakfasts too, such as chilli scrambled eggs with Manchego cheese on sourdough, and lunches such as Angus steak sandwiches with chipotle mayo.

Hot Chicken Project AMERICAN $

(Map p162; ☎03-5221 9831; 84a Little Malop St; mains from $16; noon-10pm) Slotting in perfectly along Little Malop is this cosy, welcoming diner specialising in authentic Nashville chicken. Choose from a menu of wings, tenders or dark meats – or hot fish or tofu – in a spectrum of heat levels peaking at 'Evil Chicken', served with a side of slaw or turnip greens.

Armageddon Cake Dessert Bar DESSERTS $

(Map p162; ☎0404 400 701; www.armageddoncakegeelong.wordpress.com; 7 McLarty Pl; from $10; 7-11pm Tue-Sat) It may sound like a bold idea to open up an alcohol-free dessert bar in the midst of Geelong's most happening entertainment district, but Armageddon continues to defy the odds to be one of Little Malop's most popular spots. Here it's all about slices of cake ($10), including a side of your choosing, or tasting platters ($20) to sample its full range.

Geelong Boat House FISH & CHIPS $

(Map p162; ☎03-5222 3642, 0427 319 019; www.geelongboathouse.com.au; Geelong Waterfront, Western Beach; fish & chips from $10; ⊙10am-8pm) Jutting out into the water, this fish-and-chip joint is built on top of a barge once used to dredge the Yarra River. Grab a chair on the deck or rooftop, or laze on one of its picnic blankets on the grassy banks. There's also a seafood restaurant in its attached boat shed.

Little Green Corner CAFE $$

(Map p162; ☎03-5273 0229; www.littlegreencorner.com.au; 42 Little Ryrie St; mains $13-20; ⊙7am-3.30pm Mon-Fri) Using fresh produce hand-picked from its kitchen garden or sourced from its family farm in nearby Waurn Ponds, the menu here is highly driven by what's seasonal and what's local. They also use foraged ingredients, and have started a community 'coffee for produce' initiative, where items grown in Geelong backyards are exchanged for a flat white – made using fresh biodynamic milk.

Caruggi ITALIAN $$

(Map p162; ☎03-5229 6426; www.caruggi.com.au; 66 Little Malop St; mains from $22; ⊙5.30-9pm Mon-Sat) Bringing a taste of fine dining to hipster Little Malop is this Ligurian-inspired trattoria. It hasn't missed a beat since relocating from its acclaimed restaurant in Anglesea to the 'big smoke' of Geelong. The signature regional dish is the *focaccia al formaggio di Recco* (cheese focaccia); however, most are here for the delectable pizzas.

Tulip MODERN AUSTRALIAN $$

(Map p162; ☎03-5229 6953; www.tuliprestaurant.com.au; 9/111 Pakington St, Geelong West; smaller/larger dishes from $18/22; ⊙noon-2.30pm Wed-Sat & 5.30-late Mon-Sat) One of only two hatted restaurants in Geelong, unassuming Tulip on 'Pako' St delivers a gastronomic experience with its mix of inventive small and large plates designed to share. Dishes may include native items such as kangaroo tartare with pepperberry oil, cured Spanish leg ham, whole lamb shoulder or poached ocean trout with grilled peas and mussels.

King of the Castle CAFE $$

(☎0418 227 366; www.kingofthecastlecafe.com.au; 24 Pakington St, Geelong West; mains $14-24; ⊙6.30am-3.30pm Mon-Sat, 7.30am-2.30pm Sun) Down the gritty end of Pako is this industrial-chic cafe with hanging pot plants and dangling light features. It does modern cafe cuisine such as matcha breakfast trifle; vegan fry-ups with scrambled tofu, facon and potato-quinoa hash; and meaty dishes such as pulled-lamb burgers.

Pistol Pete's Food n Blues AMERICAN $$

(Map p162; ☎03-5221 0287; www.pistolpetesfoodnblues.com.au; 93a Little Malop St; mains $17-24; ⊙noon-10pm Sun-Thu, to 12.30am Fri & Sat) A divey hang out serving up Cajun-style burgers, shrimp po'boys, southern-style fried chicken, gumbo, swamp fries and baloney sandwiches. Live music is also a feature with regular bluesy, Americana, twang bands to enjoy with US craft beers, Kentucky whiskeys and bourbons.

★IGNI MODERN AUSTRALIAN $$$

(Map p162; ☎03-5222 2266; www.restaurantigni.com; Ryan Pl; 5-/8-courses $100/150; ⊙6-10pm Thu & Sun, noon-2.30pm & 6-10pm Fri & Sat) Creating a buzz among food lovers across Melbourne is this latest venture by well-lauded chef (and local boy) Aaron Turner. The set tasting menus change on a whim, incorporating a mix of indigenous and European flavours from saltbush to oyster leaf, or marron to squab, using a wood-fired grill fuelled by ironbark and red gum.

Staff are exemplary, bringing a fine-dining experience without a hint of stuffiness. Foodies with an interest in watching the action can grab a stool to dine at the bar overlooking the open kitchen. Stick around for a Geelong-roasted coffee and complimentary freshly baked cakes.

For something more casual, check out its Hot Chicken Project (p163).

Drinking & Nightlife

★Cartel Coffee Roaster COFFEE

(Map p162; ☎03-5222 6115; www.coffeecartel.com.au; 1-80 Little Malop St; single-origin coffee $4.50; ⊙7am-5pm Mon-Thu, to 5.30pm Fri, to 2pm Sat, 9am-2pm Sun) A big player in Australia's third-wave coffee movement is this single-origin roaster run by a passionate owner who personally forges relations with farmers across Africa, Asia and Latin America. The result is well-sourced beans, expertly roasted and prepared in its smart space on happening Little Malop.

★ Little Creatures & White Rabbit BREWERY
(☎ Little Creatures 03-5202 4009, White Rabbit 03-5202 4050; www.littlecreatures.com.au; cnr Fyans & Swanston Sts; mains $16-28; ⏰ 11am-5pm Mon-Tue, 11am-9pm Wed-Fri, 8am-9pm Sat, 8am-5pm Sun; 📶) Sharing space within the historic red-brick wool mill complex are these two separate, well-respected breweries that have come together to create a giant playground for beer lovers. **Little Creatures** is the bigger operation, a vast indoor/outdoor vibrant space, while **White Rabbit**, relocated from Healesville in 2015, is the more boutique offering, with a chic set-up among its brewing equipment.

Union Street Wine WINE BAR
(Map p162; ☎ 03-5221 6291; 8 Union St; ⏰ 2-8pm Tue-Thu, to 11pm Fri & Sat, 5-11pm Sun) A wonderful find in Geelong's CBD is this cool little wine bar. Grab a stool at its elegant counter bar or large shared table to order a bottle of wine at retail price – plus $10 corkage – from a quality range hand-picked by the owners to go with a plate of cured meats.

Geelong Cellar Door WINE BAR
(Map p162; ☎ 03-5229 9568; www.geelongcellardoor.com.au; 97-99 Little Malop St; bottles of wine $22-250; ⏰ noon-11pm Tue-Sun) A wonderful spot to sample local wines is this tasteful wine bar on fashionable Little Malop. Of its wines, 99% come from Geelong, Bellarine, Moorabool and the Great Ocean Road. Come winter it's a cosy spot for a drink indoors by the fire; other times head to its brick courtyard, a space shared with neighbouring restaurants, which you're welcome to order from.

Workers Club Geelong BAR
(Map p162; ☎ 03-5222 8331; www.theworkersclubgeelong.com.au; 90-92 Little Malop St; mains $15-35; ⏰ noon-late Wed-Sun) Branching out from its inner-Melbourne venue in Fitzroy is this live music venue in a similar hipster locale. It does smoked meats – beef brisket, pulled pork, lamb ribs, jerk chicken – to accompany quality beers on tap. However, live music is its real staple, with a regular roster of indie bands throughout the week.

Blackman's Brewery BAR
(Map p162; www.blackmansbrewery.com.au; Denny's Pl; tasting paddles $16; ⏰ 4.30pm-late Tue-Sat, 3pm-late Sun) Following on from its success in Torquay (p174), Blackman's have opened up a taproom in Geelong's hipster enclave along Little Malop. It's in a space once used as the Country Fire Authority's stables, and offers its full range on tap, including a collaboration porter with Cartel (p164) coffee roaster from across the way.

☆ Entertainment

Barwon Club LIVE MUSIC
(☎ 03-5221 4584; www.barwonclub.com.au; 509 Moorabool St; ⏰ 11am-late) The Barwon has long been Geelong's premier live music venue, and has spawned the likes of Magic Dirt, Bored! and Warped, seminal bands in the 'Geetroit' rock scene. As well as catching local and international bands, it's a great pub for a beer.

Kardinia Park STADIUM
(Simonds Stadium; Map p162; ☎ 03-5224 9111; www.kardiniapark.vic.gov.au; 370 Moorabool St, South Geelong; tickets from $25) Recently renovated and fitted with light towers, this AFL stadium is sacred ground for locals as the home of their beloved team, the Cats, who play here in winter.

Geelong Performing Arts Centre THEATRE
(GPAC; Map p162; ☎ 03-5225 1200; www.gpac.org.au; 50 Little Malop St) Geelong's major arts venue uses three theatres and a variety of outdoor venues to show local amateur productions, as well as touring professional dance, musical and theatre shows.

Shopping

Geelong Vintage Market VINTAGE
(☎ 03-5277 1186; www.geelongvintagemarket.com.au; 287-301 Melbourne Rd, North Geelong; ⏰ 10am-6pm) The sprawling Geelong Vintage Market is set within a historic woollen mill complex, where you'll find several buildings full of antiques, collectables and vintage clothing. There's also a cool cafe here and a lot of potential for development.

ℹ Information

INTERNET ACCESS

Geelong Library (www.grlc.vic.gov.au; 51 Little Malop St; ⏰ 8.30am-5pm Mon-Fri; 📶) Geelong's modern new library is within a contemporary egg-shaped building with a good collection of books and 24-hour free wi-fi.

TOURIST INFORMATION

National Wool Museum Visitor Centre (Map p162; www.visitgreatoceanroad.org.au; 26

Moorabool St; ⌚9am-5pm; 📶) Geelong's main tourist information office has brochures on Geelong, the Bellarine Peninsula and the Otways, as well as free wi-fi. There's also a **visitor centre** (☎03-5283 1735; www.visitgreatoceanroad.org.au; Princes Hwy, Little River; ⌚9am-5pm) on Geelong Rd, at the service station near Little River, for those heading directly to the Great Ocean Road, and a small **kiosk** (Map p162; Geelong Waterfront; ⌚9am-5pm) on the waterfront.

Getting There & Away

AIR

Jetstar (p135) has services to/from **Avalon Airport** (p371), around a 20-minute drive from Geelong.

Avalon Airport Shuttle (p135) meets all flights at Avalon Airport and goes to Geelong (adult/child $22/15, 35 minutes) and along the Great Ocean Road, starting from Torquay ($50/25, one hour).

BUS

Gull Airport Service (Map p162; ☎03-5222 4966; www.gull.com.au; 45 McKillop St; ⌚office 9am-5pm Mon-Fri, 10am-noon Sat) Has 14 services a day between Geelong and Melbourne Airport (adult/child $32/20, 1¼ hours), departing from the city centre and Geelong station.

McHarry's Buslines (☎03-5223 2111; www.mcharrys.com.au) Runs frequent buses from Geelong station to Torquay and the Bellarine Peninsula ($3.20, 20 minutes).

BELLARINE WINERIES & PRODUCE

The Bellarine/Geelong area has over 50 wineries, and is a region well known for its cool-climate pinot noir, chardonnay and shiraz. It's also an area famous for its fantastic local produce, from goats-milk cheese and olives to mussels and blueberries. Combine a winery hop with the **Bellarine Taste Trail** (www.thebellarinetastetrail.com.au), and you've got yourself a fantastic day out.

If you don't have your own wheels, consider a winery tour with **For the Love of Grape** (☎0408 388 332; www.fortheloveofgrape.com.au; half-/full-day tours from Geelong $75/139, from Melbourne $85/149), or visit during **Toast to the Coast** (p162) festival in November.

Most listings here are open daily during summer and on weekends; other times call ahead. For a full list of wineries, check out www.winegeelong.com.au.

Scotchmans Hill (☎03-5251 3176; www.scotchmans.com.au; 190 Scotchmans Rd, Drysdale; ⌚10.30am-4.30pm) One of the Bellarine's first wineries remains one of its very best, producing a quality range of sauvignon blanc, pinot noir, chardonnay and cool-climate shiraz.

Jack Rabbit (☎03-5251 2223; www.jackrabbitvineyard.com.au; 85 McAdams Lane, Bellarine; ⌚noon-3pm daily, from 6pm Fri & Sat) Come to this boutique winery for stunning bay views enjoyed from its deck with a glass of its pinot and a bowl of mussels. There's also a well-regarded fine-dining restaurant that does creative dishes with local ingredients.

PIKNIK (☎03-5258 5155; www.piknik.com.au; 1195 Queenscliff Rd, Swan Bay; mains $14-28; ⌚7.30am-4pm Wed-Sun, daily in Jan) Fantastic breakfasts and lunches using local ingredients, plus great coffee and homemade ice cream.

Flying Brick Cider Co. (☎03-5250 6577; www.flyingbrickciderco.com.au; 1251-1269 Bellarine Hwy, Wallington; tasting paddles $13; ⌚bar 10am-5pm Sun-Thu, 10am-late Fri & Sat, restaurant noon-3pm Mon-Thu, noon-3 & 6-9pm Fri & Sat, noon-4pm Sun) A popular stop along the highway is this cider house that produces a range of quality apple and pear alcoholic ciders, enjoyed on its grassy outdoor area. Food is also a lure with gourmet sharing plates.

Basils Farm (☎03-5258 4280; www.basilsfarm.com.au; 43-53 Nye Rd, Swan Bay; ⌚10am-5pm Fri-Sun, daily in Jan) Enjoy a bottle of prosecco and a produce platter while enjoying fabulous views of Swan Bay at this picturesque boutique winery.

Banks Road (☎cellar door 03-5258 3777, restaurant 03-5245 7282; www.banksroad.com.au; 600 Banks Rd, Marcus Hill; ⌚11am-5pm Fri-Sun, or by appointment) Come for a glass of wine while looking out to open-air sculptures in a pastoral setting shared with an outstanding French restaurant.

The Whiskery (www.facebook.com/thewhiskery; 2120 Portarlington Rd, Bellarine) Aiming for a mid-2017 opening, this whisky and gin distillery is being set up by a local family who know

V/Line (Map p162; ☎1800 800 007; www.vline.com.au; Gordon Ave, Geelong Train Station) Buses run from Geelong station to Apollo Bay ($19, 2½ hours, three daily) via Torquay ($3.20, 25 minutes), Anglesea ($6.40, 45 minutes), Lorne ($11.60, 1½ hours) and Wye River ($14.40, two hours). On Monday, Wednesday and Friday a bus continues to Port Campbell ($33.20, five hours) and Warrnambool ($37.60, 6½ hours), which involves a change at Apollo Bay. The train is a much quicker and cheaper option for those heading direct to Warrnambool ($25.80, 2½ hours), though you'll miss out on the Great Ocean Road experience. Heading inland, there's a bus to Ballarat ($10.20, 1½ hours).

CAR

The 25km Geelong Ring Road runs from Corio to Waurn Ponds, bypassing Geelong entirely. To get to Geelong city, be careful not to miss the Princes Hwy (M1) from the left lanes.

TRAIN

V/Line trains run frequently from **Geelong station** (☎03-5226 6525; www.vline.com.au; Gordon Ave) to Melbourne's Southern Cross station (from $8.80, one hour). Trains also head from Geelong to Warrnambool ($25.80, 2½ hours, three daily).

their stuff. It's all produced on-site with a tasting room to sample the goods, to go with pizzas and platters.

Oakdene (☎03-5256 3886; www.oakdene.com.au; 255 Grubb Rd, Wallington; tastings $5, mains from $22; ⏰cellar door 10am-4pm, cafe noon-3pm & 5-7.30pm Wed-Sat, 9.30am-11pm Sat & Sun, restaurant 6.30pm-late Wed-Fri, noon-2pm Sat & Sun) Set in a quirky upside-down barn and surrounded by eclectic arty objects, this is a vineyard with a difference. They also do fine and casual dining.

Terindah Estate (☎03-5251 5536; www.terindahestate.com; 90 McAdams Lane, Bellarine; mains $26-38; ⏰10am-4pm) Another winery with incredible views, quality pinots and fine dining in its glasshouse shed.

McGlashan's Wallington Estate (☎03-5250 5760, 0409 016 840; www.mcglashans.com.au; 225 Swan Bay Rd, Wallington; ⏰11am-5pm Thu-Sun, daily mid-Dec–Jan) Unpretentious winery with tastings in a large barn decorated with motor memorabilia. It also brews its own ales and does wood-fired pizzas and delicious seafood platters featuring abalone.

Leura Park Estate (☎03-5253 3180; www.leuraparkestate.com.au; 1400 Portarlington Rd, Curlewis; ⏰10.30am-5pm Thu-Sun, daily in Jan) Tour the 60 hectares of vineyards on a Segway before sampling 'maritime climate' wines, produce platters and pizzas. Live music on Sundays.

Tuckerberry Hill (☎03-5251 3468; www.facebook.com/tuckerberryhill; 35 Becks Rd, Drysdale; ⏰9am-5pm Sat & Sun mid-Oct–May, daily in Jan) Pick your own berries or sample its blueberry muffins, milkshakes or soft-serve ice cream in the cafe.

Drysdale Cheeses (☎0437 816 374; www.drysdalecheeses.com; 2140 Portarlington Rd, Bellarine; ⏰1-4pm 1st Sun of the month) Taste award-winning goats-milk cheese and yogurts on the first Sunday of each month.

Manzanillo Olive Grove (☎03-5251 3621, 0438 513 621; www.manzanillogrove.com.au; 150 Whitcombes Rd, Drysdale; ⏰11am-4.30pm Sat & Sun) Dunk bread into samples of cold-pressed extra virgin and chilli-infused olive oils.

Little Mussel Cafe (☎03-5259 1377; www.advancemussel.com.au; 230-250 Queenscliff Rd, Portarlington; mains $16-28; ⏰10am-5pm Fri-Sun) The place to sample local mussels and oysters, served as chowder, in bowls of tomato and chilli, or on tasting plates. They also stock Bellarine Brewing Company's mussel stout.

Bellarine Smoked Fish Company (www.bellasmokedfish.com.au; 2230-2250 Portarlington Rd, Portarlington; ⏰11am-6pm) Adding variety to the day is this no-frills smoked-fish specialist, where you can pick up a smoked salmon or dip for home.

Bellarine Peninsula

Melburnians have been making the drive down the Princes Hwy (Geelong Rd) to the seaside villages along the Bellarine Peninsula for more than a century. It's known for its family and surf beaches, historic towns and its wonderful cool-climate wineries.

As well as linking up with the Great Ocean Road, it's just a short ferry trip from here over to the Mornington Peninsula.

Activities

Bellarine Rail Trail CYCLING

(www.railtrail.com/au/vic/bellarine) Following the route of the historical train line, this 32.5km bike path links South Geelong station with Queenscliff. It's a mostly flat sealed surface that, other than a few crossings, avoids riding on the main roads, passing through Drysdale en route to Queenscliff.

On Sundays you can bring your bike on-board the historic steam train (p170) at Drysdale or Queenscliff, if you're only wanting to do a section.

Information

Bellarine Visitor Information Centre (☎03-5250 6861, 1800 755 611; http://app.geelongbellarineovg.com; 1251 Bellarine Hwy, Wallington; ⊙9am-5pm) Located within the premises of **Flying Brick Cider Co.** (p166), this tourist information centre has a heap of brochures and ideas on what to do in the area.

Getting There & Away

BUS

McHarry's Buslines (p166) Connects Geelong with Barwon Heads (30 minutes), Ocean Grove (45 minutes), Portarlington (45 minutes), Point Lonsdale (55 minutes) and Queenscliff (one hour). A two-hour ticket costs $3.20, full day is $6.40; myki cards required.

CAR

From Melbourne, the Bellarine Peninsula is easily accessible via the Princess Fwy (M1) to Geelong; be sure not to take the Geelong bypass, and instead take the Geelong exit and follow the signs to the Bellarine Hwy (B110).

FERRY

Port Phillip Ferries (p372) A serious boon for the region is the introduction of a new ferry service linking Portarlington with Melbourne (one-way adult/child $13.50/6, 1½ hours). There are three departures per day from Portarlington to Melbourne's Docklands.

Queenscliff–Sorrento Ferry (p372) Runs between Queenscliff and Sorrento (40 minutes); till 7pm at peak times.

Queenscliff

POP 1418

Historic Queenscliff is a charming seaside town that mixes a salty maritime character with one of Victoria's most picturesque streetscapes. Many of its heritage-listed 19th-century buildings have been converted into hotels, restaurants and art galleries. It's a great base from which to explore the nearby wineries and beaches, along with several historical sites and museums in town. The views across the Port Phillip Heads and Bass Strait are glorious.

Sights

Fort Queenscliff HISTORIC SITE

(☎03-5258 1488; www.fortqueenscliff.com.au; cnr Gellibrand & King Sts; 90-min tours adult/child/family $12/6/30; ⊙11am, 1pm & 3pm daily school holidays, 11am Mon-Fri, 1pm & 3pm Sat & Sun nonpeak season) Queencliff's fort was first used as a coastal defence in 1882 to protect Melbourne from a feared Russian invasion. It remained a base until 1946, before being used as the Army Staff College until late 2012; today it functions as the defence archive centre. The 90-minute guided tours take in the military museum (not always accessible), the magazine, cells and its twin lighthouses. It's a defence area, so bring ID for entry. Cash only.

Queenscliff Gallery GALLERY

(☎03-5258 4927; www.qgw.com.au; 81 Hesse St; ⊙10am-5pm Wed-Mon) FREE A lovely space inside a historic stone church (c 1868), this interesting gallery exhibits works by contemporary Australian artists who work on paper. Lithograph is the main focus, and it's all for purchase.

Salt Gallery GALLERY

(☎03-5258 3988; www.salt-art.com.au; 33-35 Hesse St; ⊙10.30am-4pm Fri-Mon, daily in Jan) FREE Within a heritage building on the main street is this quality gallery with a focus on contemporary Australian artists.

Queenscliff Maritime Museum MUSEUM

(☎03-5258 3440; www.maritimequeenscliffe.org.au; 2 Wharf St; adult/child $8/5; ⊙10.30am-4.30pm) Home to the last lifeboat to serve the Rip, this recommended museum has displays on the pilot boat process, shipwrecks,

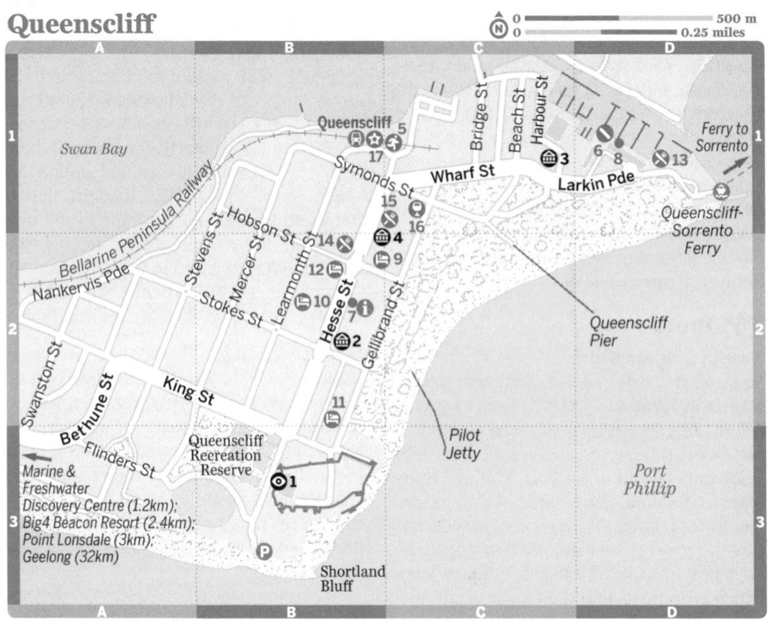

Queenscliff

Sights

1 Fort Queenscliff B3
2 Queenscliff Gallery B2
3 Queenscliff Maritime Museum C1
4 Salt Gallery B2

Activities, Courses & Tours

5 Bellarine Peninsula Railway C1
6 Dive Victoria D1
7 Queenscliff Heritage Walk B2
8 Sea-All Dolphin Swims D1
South Bay Eco Adventures .... (see 8)

Sleeping

9 Athelstane House B2
10 Queenscliff Dive Centre B2
11 Twomey's Cottage B2
12 Vue Grand B2

Eating

13 360 Q D1
14 Alchemy Woodfire Bakehouse B2
Athelstane House .... (see 9)
15 Shelter Shed C1
Vue Grand Dining Room .... (see 12)

Drinking & Nightlife

16 Queenscliff Brewhouse C1
Vue Street Bar .... (see 12)

Entertainment

17 Blues Train B1

lighthouses and steamships. Don't miss the historic 1895 boat shed with its paintings that served as a record of passing ships in the bay.

Activities

Dive Victoria DIVING
(Queenscliff Dive Centre; ☎03-5258 4188; www.divequeenscliff.com.au; Queenscliff Harbour; per dive with/without gear $140/65) Victoria's premier dive operator offers SSI dive courses and trips for all levels, from intro to technical. There are some 200 sites in the area, taking in rich marine life and shipwrecks from the past three centuries, and WWI submarines. Also does snorkel trips and dive lessons.

South Bay Eco Adventures ADVENTURE SPORTS
(☎03-5258 4019; www.southbayecoadventures.com; Wharf St East, Queenscliff Harbour; discovery tours adult/child $85/45) These tours get you where you want to go. Up-close encounters with Australian fur seals? Birdwatching on Mud Island? A trip out to a 19th-century island fortress? Sign up here.

Bellarine Peninsula Railway RAIL
(03-5258 2069; www.bellarinerailway.com.au; Queenscliff Train station; Drysdale return adult/child/family $30/20/70, Lakers Siding $15/12/40; departs to Drysdale 11am & 3pm Sun, to Lakes Siding 1.30pm Sun, plus Tue & Thu during school holidays) Run by a group of cheerful volunteer steam-train tragics, Bellarine's railway has beautiful heritage steam and diesel trains that ply the 1¾-hour return journey to Drysdale each Sunday, along with a trip to Lakers Siding (33 minutes return).

Tours

Sea-All Dolphin Swims WILDLIFE
(03-5258 3889; www.dolphinswims.com.au; Queenscliff Harbour; sightseeing tours adult/child $75/65, 3½hr snorkel $145/125; 8am & 1pm Oct-Apr) Offers sightseeing tours and swims with seals and dolphins in Port Phillip Heads Marine National Park. Seal sightings are guaranteed; dolphins aren't always seen, but there's a good chance. Snorkelling trips take in Pope's Eye (an unfinished military fort), which is home to abundant fish and an Australasian gannet breeding colony, before visiting a permanent Australian fur seal colony at Chinaman's Hat.

Queenscliff Heritage Walk WALKING
(03-5258 4843; incl afternoon tea $15; 2pm Sat) The visitor centre runs the 1¼-hour guided Queenscliff Heritage Walk at 2pm each Saturday (or by appointment), taking in the town's historic buildings.

Festivals & Events

Queenscliff Music Festival MUSIC
(03-5258 4816; www.qmf.net.au; last weekend Nov) One of the coast's best festivals features big-name Australian and international musos with a folksy, bluesy bent. Held late November.

Sleeping

Queenscliff Dive Centre HOSTEL $
(03-5258 4188; www.divevictoria.com.au; 37 Learmonth St; dm divers/nondivers $30/40, s/d $100/120;) While this hostel-style accommodation is primarily for divers, if there are rooms available it's a good option for budget travellers too. The modern shared kitchen and lounge facilities are bright and airy, while the simple rooms are out the back. It's BYO linen and towels ($15 to hire). It was built in 1864 when it was used as Cobb & Co horse stables.

Twomey's Cottage B&B $$
(0400 265 877; www.classiccottages.com.au; 13 St Andrews St; d $110-140) Just the place to soak up Queenscliff's historical atmosphere, this heritage fisher's cottage is fantastic value. Its claim to fame is as the residence of Fred Williams when he painted his Queenscliff series, plus renowned recitalist Keith Humble composed music here, so creative vibes abound.

★ **Vue Grand** HOTEL $$$
(03-5258 1544; www.vuegrand.com.au; 46 Hesse St; r incl breakfast $178-258;) One of Queenscliff's most elegant historic buildings, the Vue has everything from standard pub rooms to its modern turret suite (boasting 360-degree views) and bay-view rooms (with freestanding baths in the lounge).

Athelstane House BOUTIQUE HOTEL $$$
(03-5258 1024; www.athelstane.com.au; 4 Hobson St; r incl breakfast $180-310;) Dating back to 1860, double-storey Athelstane House is a beautifully kept historic building that's notable as Queenscliff's oldest guesthouse. Its rooms are spotless, and mix period touches with modern comforts such as corner spa baths, iPod docks and fast wi-fi. Its

YOU'VE GOT BUCKLEY'S CHANCE

As you tour this stretch of coast from the Bellarine Peninsula to the Great Ocean Road, give thought to the indigenous Wathaurung who inhabited the area from Geelong to Aireys Inlet.

One of the best insights into their lives is told through the remarkable story of William Buckley, an escaped convict who lived with the Wathaurung people for 32 years (1803-1835). They accepted this 'wild white man' as one of their own. He lived, hunted and camped with them through Point Lonsdale, Torquay, Point Addis, Anglesea and Aireys Inlet, all detailed in his autobiography *The Life and Adventures of William Buckley*.

His story lends its name to the colloquialism 'you've got Buckley's chance' – meaning you've got little to no chance – entrenched in the Australian vernacular as a tribute to Buckley's survival against the odds.

front lounge is a good place to hang out, with a vintage record player and a stack of vinyl.

Eating

Alchemy Woodfire Bakehouse BAKERY **$**
(☎0400 860 944; 36 Hesse St; croissants $3; ⏲9am-4pm) Using a wood-fired Scotch oven dating to 1905, this artisan bakery produces organic sourdough. They also make their own croissants and French pastries, as well as sandwiches and empanadas.

Shelter Shed CAFE **$$**
(☎03-5258 3604; www.sheltershedqueenscliff.com.au; 25 Hesse St; dishes $15-30; ⏲8am-3pm;) Within a wonderful light-filled space with a glowing fire in winter, and an inviting garden courtyard for sunny days, this is a great choice for breakfast or lunch. It's popular for the Asian eggs on jasmine rice with abalone sauce, and its prawn watercress roll with dill mayo. There's plenty of grilled seafood and meat dishes too.

360 Q INTERNATIONAL **$$**
(☎03-5257 4200; www.360q.com.au; 2 Wharf St; breakfast from $15, lunch from $18, dinner $26-39; ⏲8am-4pm daily, 6-9pm Fri & Sat) Undoubtedly one of Queenscliff's best restaurants, 360 Q features wonderful views overlooking the picturesque marina. It does an original breakfast menu and some light lunch options such as a Vietnamese pork bánh mì, while for dinner try its fragrant chilli-tomato Portarlington mussels with crusty bread.

Athelstane House MODERN AUSTRALIAN **$$$**
(☎03-5258 1024; www.athelstane.com.au; 4 Hobson St; breakfast $14-22, mains $30-38; ⏲8-10am & 6-8pm) Come for breakfast or dinner inside this lovely heritage home, or outside on the pretty garden deck. For dinner choose from a daily seasonal menu that may include chargrilled eye fillet or tempura battered fish. In the morning they do homemade oven-baked muesli as well as the usual hot breakfasts.

Vue Grand Dining Room MODERN AUSTRALIAN **$$$**
(☎03-5258 1544; www.vuegrand.com.au; 46 Hesse St; 2-/3-course meals $59/79, 5-course Bellarine tasting menu without/with wine or beers $95/149; ⏲6-9pm Wed-Sat) The grande dame of Queenscliff dining, Vue Grand's stately dining room serves up fabulous dishes such as lamb back strap with saffron, fennel, pomegranate and whipped feta, backed up by a splendid wine and beer menu. The Bellarine tasting menu has local-produce-heavy dishes matched with local wine or beers.

Drinking & Nightlife

Queenscliff Brewhouse PUB
(☎03-5258 1717; www.queenscliffbrewhouse.com.au; 2 Gellibrand St; ⏲11am-1am Mon-Sat, to 11pm Sun) Prickly Moses have set up their second brewhouse here in Queenscliff, branching out from their Otways base. Their full range is showcased on tap, as well as a selection of guest brewers, best enjoyed in the beer garden.

Vue Street Bar BAR
(☎03-5258 1544; www.vuegrand.com.au; 46 Hesse St; pizzas $18; ⏲noon-8pm Wed-Sat, to 3pm Sun) Sit and watch Queenscliff wander by, a craft beer in one hand and slice of pizza in the other. Terrific meals, great ambience. In summer head up to its rooftop bar for amazing views of town and the surrounding coast.

Entertainment

Blues Train LIVE MUSIC
(☎132 849; www.thebluestrain.com.au; Queenscliff train station; tickets incl dinner from $101.65; ⏲departures 6.30pm Fri & Sat) Get your foot tapping with train trips that feature blues and rootsy music and meals on a historic train departing Queenscliff station. Check the website for upcoming shows, which usually take place each week; it's popular so book well ahead.

Information

Queenscliff Visitor Centre (☎03-5258 4843; www.queenscliff.com.au; 55 Hesse St; ⏲9am-5pm;) Plenty of brochures on the area. Also sells the self-guided walking tour map *Queenscliff – A Living Heritage*. Wi-fi and internet access next door at the library.

Ocean Grove

POPULATION 12,555

Ocean Grove, 3km northeast of Barwon Heads and 12km west of Queenscliff, is the big smoke of the Bellarine Peninsula. Similarly to Torquay it's undergone a massive growth spurt over the past few decades, turning it from sleepy coastal town to sprawling residential suburb. It has the best stretch of beach along the Bellarine, popular with surfers, families and beach bums.

Eating

Piping Hot Chicken and Burger Grill AMERICAN $
(03-5255 1566; www.pipinghotchickenshop.com.au; 63a The Terrace; mains $7-15; 10am-4pm Sun-Thu, to 10pm Fri & Sat) Not your ordinary takeaway barbecue chook joint, the 'chicken shop' is straight outta Louisiana, with buffalo wings, pulled-pork rolls, slow-cooked brisket, Reuben sandwiches and chilli cheese fries (and yes, barbecue chicken) to go with a monthly roster of blues gigs. It has a cool retro interior minus any hipster pretension. They do great coffee, too.

Uncle Jack's CAFE $
(03-5256 3735; www.unclejackscafe.com.au; 82 The Terrace; breakfast $8-22, burgers $15; 7am-3pm;) Opened by three local mates, this cool corner cafe does a menu of buttermilk fried wings, awesome burgers, single-origin coffee and craft beer on tap.

Napona MODERN AUSTRALIAN $$
(03-5256 3153; www.napona.com.au; 24 Hodgson St; breakfast $8-20, lunch & dinner mains $18-39, 5-course degustation menu $75; 8am-4pm Sun-Tue, to late Wed-Sat, longer hrs in Jan) For what is Ocean Grove's best restaurant, Napona has an unlikely location off the main strip in a residential street. Its menu is big on local ingredients and items made from scratch. It does house-baked fruit sourdough for breakfast, homemade spaghetti with local seafood for lunch. For dinner, splurge on the five-course degustation menu.

Dunes CAFE $$
(03-5256 1944; www.dunescafe.com.au; Surf Beach Rd; breakfast from $9, mains $16-35; 6.30am-10pm) Enjoy Mod Oz classics with a beer or wine while gazing out to crashing waves at this surfside eatery.

Barwon Heads

POPULATION 3536

At the mouth of the broad Barwon River, Barwon Heads is a haven of sheltered beaches, tidal river flats and holidaymakers. It was made famous as the setting for *SeaChange*, a popular TV series, and, over a decade on, still trades on the kudos. In a case of life imitating TV, the original bridge linking Barwon Heads with Ocean Grove was controversially recently replaced with two modern bridges.

Feisty **Thirteenth Beach**, 2km west, is popular with surfers. There are short walks around the headland and the **Bluff** with panoramic sea vistas.

Sleeping

Barwon Heads Caravan Park CAMPGROUND $
(03-5254 1115; www.barwonheadscaravanpark.com.au; Ewing Blyth Dr; unpowered sites $30-48, powered sites $36-84, d cabins $115-160, d houses $190-295;) Overlooking the sea, this popular park contains cabins of varying levels of comfort – the best come with waterfront views, and there's the option to stay in Laura's house from *SeaChange* – as well as tea-tree-shaded sites. There's a seven-night minimum between 19 December and 30 January – a period which routinely gets booked well in advance.

Eating & Drinking

★**At the Heads** MODERN AUSTRALIAN $$
(03-5254 1277; www.attheheads.com.au; 1a Ewing Blyth Rd, aka Jetty Rd; breakfast $7-22, mains from $16; 9am-late) Directly overlooking the confluence of the river and ocean, this glassed-in weatherboard cafe-bar is right on the waterfront. Breakfast does the full circle from superfood smoothie bowls to dirty breakfast burgers, while mains are a mix of sharing plates and bar food. Expect the likes of Southern fried softshell crab burgers, seafood linguine and wagyu steaks.

Annie's Provedore CAFE $$
(03-5254 3233; www.anniesprovedore.com.au; 2/50 Hitchcock Ave; breakfast $10-20, mains $15-25; 6.30am-6pm Sun-Wed, to 9.30pm Thu-Sat) Run by Italian-Australian owner Annie is this delightfully cluttered temple to food, with shelves crammed full of quality goods. Peruse its drool-inducing display of hearty salads, homemade pies, Italian cured meats, cheeses and wines. Or order from its menu – including pizzas from Thursday to Sunday. Otherwise stop by for an *aperitivo*.

Hanoi Kitchen VIETNAMESE $$
(03-4202 0525; www.hanoikitchen.com.au; 37 Hitchcock Ave; mains $12-22; 11am-late Tue-Sat, 8.30am-3.30pm Sun) Run by husband and wife team Nick and Hong, this vibrant eatery on the main strip features authentic Vietnamese dishes. The menu includes all-day Asian cooked breakfasts, fragrant salads, hearty bowls of pho, bánh mì and roll-your-own rice-paper rolls.

GREAT OCEAN ROAD

Torquay

POP 17,105

In the 1960s and '70s Torquay was just another sleepy seaside town. Back then, surfing in Australia was a decidedly countercultural pursuit, its devotees crusty hippy dropouts living in clapped-out Kombis, smoking pot and making off with your daughters. These days it's become unabashedly mainstream and the town's proximity to world-famous Bells Beach, and status as home of two iconic surf brands – Rip Curl and Quiksilver, both initially wetsuit makers – ensures Torquay's place as the undisputed capital of the Australian surf industry. It's one of Australia's fastest growing towns, experiencing a population increase of 67% between 2001 and 2013 that these days makes it feel almost like an outer suburb of Geelong.

Sights & Activities

Torquay's beaches lure everyone from kids in floaties to backpacker surf-school pupils. **Fisherman's Beach**, protected from ocean swells, is the family favourite. Ringed by shady pines and sloping lawns, the **Front Beach** beckons lazy bums, while surf life-savers patrol the frothing **Back Beach** during summer. Famous surf beaches nearby include Jan Juc, Winki Pop and, of course, **Bells Beach**.

★Australian National Surfing Museum MUSEUM
(☎03-5261 4606; www.surfworld.com.au; 77 Beach Rd, Surf City Plaza; adult/child/family $12/8/25; ⊙9am-5pm) The perfect starting point for those embarking on a surfing safari is this well-curated museum that pays homage to Australian surfing. Here you'll see Simon Anderson's groundbreaking 1981 thruster, Mark Richard's awesome airbrushed board art collection and, most notably, Australia's Surfing Hall of Fame. It's full of great memorabilia (including Duke Kahanamoku's wooden longboard), videos and displays on surf culture through the 1960s to the '80s.

Surfing

Go Ride a Wave SURFING
(☎03-5261 3616, 1300 132 441; www.gorideawave.com.au; 1/15 Bell St; 2hr lessons from adult/child $69/59) Offers lessons for surfing, SUP and kayaking, and hires boards, too. They run camps along the Great Ocean Road and Bellarine Peninsula. Rates are cheaper with advance booking.

Torquay Surf Academy SURFING
(☎03-5261 2022; www.torquaysurf.com.au; 34a Bell St; 2hr group/private lessons $60/180) Offers surf lessons for groups or one-on-one. Also hires surfboards (from $25), SUPs (from $35), body-boards ($20) and wetsuits ($10), as well as bikes (from $20).

Sleeping

Bells Beach Backpackers HOSTEL $
(☎03-5261 4029; www.bellsbeachbackpackers.com.au; 51-53 Surfcoast Hwy; van s/d $20/24, dm/d from $32/80; @ 📶) On the main highway in Torquay (not Bells Beach) is this friendly backpackers, which does a great job of fitting into the fabric of this surf town. It has a casual, homely atmosphere with basic rooms that are clean and in good nick, and a large kitchen that 'van packers' can also use.

Torquay Foreshore Caravan Park CAMPGROUND $
(☎03-5261 2496; www.torquaycaravanpark.com.au; 35 Bell St; powered sites $37-89, d cabins $109-295, 2-bedroom units $190-395; 📶) Just behind the Back Beach is the largest camping ground on the Surf Coast. It has good facilities and premium-priced cabins with sea views. Wi-fi is in the camp kitchen only.

Beachside Accommodation APARTMENT $$
(☎0419 587 445; www.beachsideaccommodationtorquay.com.au; 24 Felix Cres; d $110-160; ❄ 📶) Only a five-minute stroll to the beach is this

> **GREAT OCEAN ROAD TOURS**
>
> **Go West Tours** (p187) Melbourne-based company offering full-day tours taking in Bells Beach, koalas in the Otways, the Twelve Apostles and around, returning back to Melbourne. Free wi-fi on bus.
>
> **Otway Discovery Tour** (p187) Very affordable Great Ocean Road tours. The two-day tours include Phillip Island, while the three-day version takes in the Grampians.
>
> **Ride Tours** (p187) Two-day, one-night minibus trips along the Great Ocean Road. Rates include dorm accommodation and meals.

relaxed residential-style accommodation owned by a German-English couple, where you'll get a private patio with BBQ and an Aussie backyard atmosphere.

Eating & Drinking

Bottle of Milk BURGERS $
(☎03-5264 8236; www.thebottleofmilk.com; 24 Bell St; burgers from $10; ⏰noon-9pm) Trading off the success of its **Lorne** (Map p179; ☎03-5289 2005; www.thebottleofmilk.com; 52 Mountjoy Pde; burgers $11-18; ⏰8am-8pm) branch, Bottle of Milk's winning formula of burgers, beaches and beers makes it rightfully popular. Inside is decked out with booth seating, polished floorboards and tiled walls, or head out to its beer garden with an open fireplace. Good coffee, too.

Cafe Moby CAFE $
(☎03-5261 2339; 41 The Esplanade; mains $12-18; ⏰6.30am-3pm; 📶👪) This old weatherboard house on the Esplanade harks back to a time when Torquay was simple, which is not to say its meals aren't modern: fill up on a pork belly burger, wood-fired pizza or honey-roasted lamb souvlaki. There's a whopping great playground out the back for kids, and a little bar out the front doing Forrest brewery beers.

★**Bomboras Kiosk** CAFE $$
(www.bomboras.com.au; 48 The Esplanade, Fisherman's Beach; meals $5-22; ⏰7.30am-5pm) Right on the sand, this is just the place for hungry beachgoers to recharge with homemade sausage rolls, cakes, salads, milkshakes or locally roasted coffee. During the summer they open the rooftop bar with local brews, ciders, DJs and prime ocean views.

Fisho's SEAFOOD $$
(☎0474 342 124; www.facebook.com/fishostorquay; 36 The Esplanade; mains from $19; ⏰noon-3pm & 5-8pm) Not your average fish and chip shop, instead this oceanfront joint does an original take on the classics such as tempura flake, zesty lime shark popcorn and sweet potato cakes. It's set up on the waterfront in an atmospheric weatherboard house with AstroTurf front seating, and local beers and cider on tap.

Ginger Monkey CAFE $$
(☎03-5264 8957; www.gingermonkeycafe.com; 4 Baines Cres; meals from $17; ⏰7am-4pm; 📶) This rustic-chic cafe does one of the best coffees in town using Proud Mary beans from Collingwood. For brekkie go the nasi goreng or mushroom ragout with poached egg, while there are burgers and the like for lunch, including a hand-pressed tofu burger for vegos. If you're around Friday, head out to the car park for its famous paella cook up.

Drinking & Nightlife

★**Blackman's Brewery** MICROBREWERY
(☎03-5261 5310; www.blackmansbrewery.com.au; 26 Bell St; ⏰noon-10pm Wed-Sun, daily in summer) One of Vic's best microbreweries is this brewpub where you can taste all eight of Blackman's beers, which are produced on-site. Go the tasting paddle ($16) to enjoy its range of IPAs, unfiltered lager, pale ale and porters by a roaring fire or in the AstroTurf beer garden. They've also got a smoker for BBQ meats, pizzas and platters. Swing by at 4pm for a free brewery tour.

Shopping

Rip Curl Surf Factory Outlet FASHION & ACCESSORIES
(Baines Seconds; 16 Baines Cres; ⏰9am-5.30pm) Rips Curl's shiny main outlet is in the Surf City Plaza, but head round the back to the industrial estate for Rip Curl's factory outlet, where you'll get 30% off the price of last season's clothing and wetsuits. A big-name global brand these days, Rip Curl was founded here in Torquay in 1969.

Information

Torquay Visitor Information Centre (www.greatoceanroad.org; Surf City Plaza, Beach Rd; ⏰9am-5pm) The well-resourced tourist office next to the Australian National Surfing Museum makes a good starting point along the Great Ocean Road to fine tune your itinerary. There's free wi-fi and internet available at the library next door.

Getting There & Away

Torquay is 15 minutes' drive south of Geelong on the B100.

Torquay to Anglesea

The Great Ocean Road officially begins on the stretch between Torquay and Anglesea. A slight detour takes you to famous **Bells Beach**, the powerful point break that is part of international surfing folklore; it has hosted Australia's premier surfing event, the Bells Classic, since 1973. (It was here too, in name only, that Keanu Reeves and Patrick Swayze had their ultimate showdown in the film *Point Break*.)

Around 3km away, on the outskirts of Torquay, is the surf town of **Jan Juc**, a local hang-out for surfers, with a mellow, sleepy vibe. Nine kilometres southwest of Torquay is the turn-off to spectacular **Point Addis**, a vast sweep of pristine clothing-optional beach that attracts surfers, nudists, hang-gliders and swimmers, as well as those embarking on the recommended Koorie Cultural Walk.

Activities

Koorie Cultural Walk WALKING

A highly recommended detour signposted off the Great Ocean Road is the fantastic Koorie Cultural Walk, a 2km trail that details how the indigenous Wathaurung people lived here for millennia. It's a lovely bushwalk through the Great Otway National Park, with echidnas and wallabies, and spectacular coastal outlooks of dramatic cliffs and pristine beaches, including the lovely **Addiscott Beach**.

It's part of the Surf Coast Walk, and the beach here stretches all the way to the clothing-optional beach at **Point Addis**.

In 1836 there was a community of some 700 people who resided in the immediate area, which tragically by 1853 was reduced to a mere 35 as a direct result of European settlement. At the car park at the top of the hill there's also a plaque on William Buckley (p170), an escaped convict who spent 32 years living with the local Wathaurung people from 1803.

Surf Coast Walk WALKING

(www.surfcoastwalk.com.au) This epic walks follows the scenic coastline for 30km from Torquay to Moggs Creek, just outside Aireys Inlet. The full route takes 11 hours, but otherwise it's divided into 12 distinct walks which cover a good variety of landscapes.

Festivals & Events

Rip Curl Pro SURFING

(www.aspworldtour.com; Easter) Since 1973, Bells has hosted the Rip Curl Pro every Easter long weekend. The world championship ASP tour event draws thousands to watch the world's best surfers carve up the big autumn swells, where waves have reached 5m during the contest! The Rip Curl Pro occasionally decamps to Johanna Beach, two hours west, when fickle Bells isn't working.

WINERY DETOURS

Wolseley Winery (0412 990 638; www.wolseleywines.com; 1790 Hendy Main Rd, Paraparap; 11am-5pm Wed-Sun) An inland treasure away from the beach is this atmospheric winery that's known for its Sunday live music sessions. Enjoy a glass on its deck overlooking the dam, along with wood-fired pizzas by the slice ($5).

Bellbrae Estate (03-5264 8480; www.bellbraeestate.com.au; 520 Great Ocean Rd, Bellbrae; 11am-5pm Sat & Sun, daily Oct-Mar) Stop by this winery cellar door to taste their medal-winning chardonnay and cool-climate reds. They also do cheeseboards and wine by the glass to enjoy on the picnic tables, and live music on weekends.

Brown Magpie (03-5266 2147; www.brownmagpiewines.com; 125 Larcombes Rd, Modewarre; 11am-4pm Sat & Sun Nov-Mar) One of the Geelong region's most respected wineries, Brown Magpie offers free tastings of its award-winning pinot noirs in a tin-shed cellar door overlooking bucolic rows of grapevines.

Anglesea

POPULATION 2653

Mix sheer orange cliffs falling into the ocean with hilly, tree-filled 'burbs and a population that booms in summer and you've got Anglesea, where sharing fish and chips with seagulls by the Anglesea River is a decades-long family tradition for many.

Activities

Main Beach is the ideal spot to learn to surf, while sheltered **Point Roadknight Beach** is good for families.

Anglesea Golf Club GOLF

(03-5263 1582; www.angleseagolfclub.com.au; Golf Links Rd; 20min kangroo tours adult/child $10/5, 9/18 holes from $25/45, club hire 9/18 holes $25/35; 10am-4pm Mon-Fri) Here you can watch kangaroos graze on the fairways on an organised tour, or, even better, pair your sightings with a round of golf. If you don't want to do a tour, you'll be able to spot kangaroos from the road.

WORTH A TRIP

GREAT OCEAN ROAD CHOCOLATERIE & ICE CREAMERY

A sure way to placate those backseat nags of 'are we there yet?' is this roadside **chocolaterie** (☎03-5263 1588; www.gorci.com.au; 1200 Great Ocean Rd, Bellbrae; ⊙9am-5pm), located 11km outside Anglesea. It's a massive site that makes all of its own truffles and chocolates (try its bush-tucker range), as well as 20 flavours of ice cream. There's an on-site cafe, and chocolate-making courses (from $40) most Saturdays; book online.

Go Ride a Wave SURFING
(☎03-5263 2111, 1300 132 441; www.gorideawave.com.au; 143b Great Ocean Rd; 2hr lessons adult/child from $69/59, 2hr board hire from $25; ⊙9am-5pm) Long-established surf school that runs lessons and hires out boards, SUPs and kayaks.

Sleeping

Anglesea Backpackers HOSTEL $
(☎03-5263 2664; www.angleseabackpackers.com; 40 Noble St; dm $30-35, d/f $115/150; @ 🛜) While most hostels like to cram 'em in, this simple, homely backpackers has just two dorm rooms and one double/triple, and is clean, bright and welcoming. In winter the fire glows warmly in the cosy living room. There are free bikes for guests and the owner can pick you up from town or as far away as Torquay.

Anglesea Beachfront Family Caravan Park CAMPGROUND $
(☎03-5263 1583; www.angleseabeachfront.com.au; 35 Cameron Rd; powered sites $38-86, d cabins $110-271; @ 🛜 ≋) Beach- and riverfront caravan park with a pool, wi-fi, two camp kitchens, a jumping pillow, an indoor spa and a games room. No, you probably won't get that book read.

Eating

Coffetti Gelato GELATO $
(☎0434 274 781; www.facebook.com/coffettigelato; Shop 4, 87-89 Great Ocean Rd, Anglesea Shopping Village; cups from $4; ⊙8am-6pm, to 9.30pm in summer) Run by an Italian-Aussie husband-wife team is this authentic gelateria doing a range of delicious homemade flavours as well as popsicles, granitas and Ugandan coffee. It's just outside the entrance of the supermarket.

Maids Pantry CAFE $
(☎03-5263 1420; 119 Great Ocean Rd; breakfasts & sandwiches from $8; ⊙7am-5pm) Across from the Anglesea River is this bright, rustic cafe that doubles as a provedore general store stocking a good selection of local produce. It has a wide selection of sandwiches, sliders, pies and brunch specials, and has garden seating round the back.

McGain's Cafe CAFE $
(☎03-5263 3841; www.mcgains.com.au; 1 Simmons Ct; dishes from $7; ⊙cafe 8.30am-3pm, shop to 5pm; 🛜) Snack among the foliage at this lovely sunlit cafe with an atrium nursery locale. The menu is largely organic using produce from their attached foodstore. As well as delicious breakfasts and lunches, it does great single-origin coffee roasted by Cartel in Geelong. It's left off the Great Ocean Road before you hit the Anglesea shops.

Captain Moonlite MODERN AUSTRALIAN $$
(☎03-5263 2454; www.captainmoonlite.com.au; 100 Great Ocean Rd; mains from $25; ⊙8am-10pm Fri-Sun, 8am-4pm Mon, 5-10pm Thu) Sharing space with the Anglesea Surf Life Saving Club – with unbeatable views over the beach – Captain Moonlite mixes unpretentious decor with a quality, highly seasonal menu, which it describes as 'coastal European'. Expect tasty breakfasts such as ocean trout and soft-boiled egg on rye, mezze-style plates and mains such as slow-roasted lamb and fresh seafood.

Drinking & Nightlife

Rusty Anchor Bar BAR
(www.amyc.club; Melba Pde, Point Roadknight; ⊙5-8pm daily 27 Dec–31 Jan, weekends Feb-Apr) Right on the beach at Point Roadknight is this tiny shack bar above the Anglesea Motor Yacht Club. It's popular with locals, and only opens for a few hours for sunset in the summer, and on weekends till Easter.

Information

Anglesea Visitor Information Centre (www.visitgreatoceanroad.org.au; Great Ocean Rd; ⊙9am-5pm; 🛜) Located at the lake, this information centre has a heap of brochures for the area, including walks in the surrounding national park.

Getting There & Away

Bus There are four to six daily V/Line buses to/from Geelong to Anglesea ($6.40, 45 minutes) on weekdays, and two departures on weekends.

Car The Geelong bypass has reduced the time it takes to drive from Melbourne to Anglesea to around 75 minutes.

Aireys Inlet & Around

POP 1071

Midway between Anglesea and Lorne, Aireys Inlet is an attractive coastal hamlet with a tight-knit community of locals and sea-changers, plus plenty of holidaymakers. It's home to a historic lighthouse which forms the backdrop to glorious stretches of beach, including **Fairhaven** and **Moggs Creek**. Ask at the Anglesea visitor centre for brochures on the great coastal walks around here.

Sights & Activities

The lovely 3.5km **Aireys Inlet Cliff Walk** begins at Painkalac Creek, rounds Split Point and makes its way to Sunnymead Beach. The Surf Coast Walk (p175) continues along the coast here – pick up a copy of *Walks of Lorne & Aireys Inlet* from visitor centres.

★Split Point Lighthouse LIGHTHOUSE
(1800 174 045, 03-5263 1133; www.splitpointlighthouse.com.au; Federal St; 45min tours adult/child/family $14/8/40; tours hourly 11am-2pm, summer holidays 10am-5pm) Scale the 136 steps to the top of the beautiful 'White Queen' lighthouse for sensational 360-degree views. Built in 1891, the 34m-high lighthouse is still operational (though now fully automated). During off-peak times a tour guide will accompany you to the top, whereas in summer it's run as a self-guided tour with staff on hand to answer questions.

Fairhaven Beach BEACH
This attractive wide expanse of surf is the longest beach along the Great Ocean Road, stretching for 10km from Split Point Lighthouse to Eastern View. Its only patrolled section is the surf life-saving club at Fairhaven.

Blazing Saddles HORSE RIDING
(0418 528 647, 03-5289 7322; www.blazingsaddlestrailrides.com; Lot 1 Bimbadeen Dr; per person 1¼hr bush rides from $50, 2½hr beach & bush rides $115) People come from around the world to hop on a Blazing Saddles horse and head along stunning Fairhaven Beach or into the bush.

Sleeping

Inlet Caravan Park CABIN $
(03-5289 6230; www.aicp.com.au; 19-25 Great Ocean Rd; powered sites $39, cabins d $105-280;) More cabin town than tent city, this neat park is close to the township's few shops.

★Cimarron B&B B&B $$
(03-5289 7044; www.cimarron.com.au; 105 Gilbert St; d $125-225;) Built in 1979 from local timbers and using only wooden pegs and shiplap joins, Cimarron is an idyllic getaway with views over Point Roadknight. The large lounge area has book-lined walls and a cosy fireplace, while upstairs are two unique, loft-style doubles with vaulted timber ceilings; otherwise there's a denlike apartment. Out back, it's all state park and wildlife. Two-night minimum stay. Gay friendly, but no kids.

Seahaven B&B $$
(03-5289 6408, 0408 599 678; seahavenbandb@iprimus.com.au; 62 Wybellenna Dr, Fairhaven; d incl breakfast $120-150;) Overlooking Painkalac Creek and the Aireys lighthouse is this wonderful self-contained bungalow that offers great value. Enjoy the views from your balcony, where you're often accompanied by king parrots and kookaburras, and look for kangaroos in the distance. It's equipped with air-con, wi-fi, a barbecue, a spa bath and cable TV, while for breakfast fresh homebaked bread and bacon to cook up are provided.

Pole House RENTAL HOUSE $$$
(03-5220 0200; www.greatoceanroadholidays.com.au; 60 Banool Rd, Fairhaven; from $470) One of the most iconic houses along the Great Ocean Road, the Pole House is a unique architectural piece that, as the name suggests, sits atop a pole, with extraordinary ocean views. Access to the house is via an external pedestrian bridge.

Eating & Drinking

Willows Tea House CAFE $
(03-5289 6830; 7 Federal St; scones $4, breakfast from $8; 9am-5pm;) Soak up Aireys' seafaring atmosphere at this teahouse set up within a historic weatherboard cottage a few steps from the lighthouse. Stop by for morning or afternoon tea to indulge in homemade scones with jam and cream, enjoyed in its cosy interior or at outdoor tables.

Truffles Cafe Deli CAFE $$
(03-5289 7402; www.trufflesrestaurant.com.au; 34 Great Ocean Rd; mains $15-35; 8am-4pm Wed, to 8pm Thu-Sun;) Long established Truffles does the lot – hearty breakfasts, homemade pies (go the beef rendang), pizza in the evenings, Southeast Asian curries, good vegetarian choices, homebaked

sourdough, regional wines, local beers, coffee, free wi-fi and a happy ambience. The attached restaurant serves its eponymous black truffle mushroom pasta.

Captain of Aireys PIZZA $$
(☎03-5297 4024; www.thecaptainofaireys.com.au; 81 Great Ocean Rd; pizzas $15-25; ⊙11am-8pm Thu-Sun, longer hours in summer) Named after a local seafaring character who resided in the area during the early 20th century is this popular pizzeria doing authentic Neapolitan-style wood-fired pizzas.

Fairhaven Surf Life Saving Club PUB FOOD $$
(www.fairhavenslsc.org; cnr Great Ocean Rd & Yarringa Rd; mains $18.50-31.50; ⊙from 4pm daily Jan, Fri-Sun Feb-Easter) The slickly renovated surf club runs a bar and bistro from January to Easter from its commanding dune location overlooking Fairhaven Beach; a glorious spot for sunset. The food is good too, a variation of parmas, steaks and vegetarian dishes that's a step above the usual pub versions.

★**á la grecque** GREEK $$$
(☎03-5289 6922; www.alagrecque.com.au; 60 Great Ocean Rd; mains $28-40; ⊙noon-3pm & 6-9.30pm Wed-Sun Aug-Dec, noon-3pm & 6-9.30pm daily Dec-Apr, closed May-Jul) Be whisked away to the Mediterranean at this outstanding modern Greek taverna. Mezze such as seared scallops or braised cuttlefish with apple, celery and a lime dressing, and mains such as grilled pork shoulder, are sensational. So is the wine list.

★**Aireys Pub** MICROBREWERY
(☎03-5289 6804; www.aireyspub.com.au; 45 Great Ocean Rd; pots from $5; ⊙11.30am-late; 📶) Established in 1904, this pub is a survivor, twice burning to the ground before closing its doors in 2011, only to be revived by a bunch of locals chipping in to save it. Now it's better than ever, with an on-site brewery, Rogue Wave, to go with its fantastic kitchen (mains $20 to $34), meat smoker, roaring fire, live music and sprawling beer garden.

Getting There & Away

Car From Melbourne count on around a 1¾-hour drive for the 123km trip to Aireys Inlet, and a bit longer if you're heading via Torquay (27km, 25 minutes).

Public Transport Departing from Geelong Station, V-Line has four to six daily buses (two on weekends) to Aireys Inlet ($8.80, one hour), which continue on to nearby stops at Fairhaven, Moggs Creek and Eastern View for the same fare.

Lorne

POP 1046

One of the Great Ocean Road's original resort towns, Lorne may be a tad overdeveloped these days but it still retains all the charms that have lured visitors here since the 19th century. Beyond its main strip it has an incredible natural beauty: tall old gum trees line its hilly streets, and Loutit Bay gleams irresistibly. It gets busy; in summer you'll be competing with day trippers for restaurant seats and lattes, but, thronged by tourists or not, it's a lovely place to hang out.

Sights & Activities

Kids will love the beachside swimming pool, trampolines and skate park. There are more than 50km of **bushwalking** tracks around Lorne, taking in lush forests and waterfalls. Pick up the *Lorne Walks & Waterfalls* brochure from the visitor centre. There are also seasonal tracks for 4WD enthusiasts and mountain bikers.

For bikes, surfboards and beach cricket sets, head to HAH (p180) on the foreshore.

★**Qdos Art Gallery** GALLERY
(Map p179; ☎03-5289 1989; www.qdosarts.com; 35 Allenvale Rd; ⊙9am-5pm Thu-Mon, daily Jan) FREE Amid the lush forest that backs on to Lorne, Qdos always has something interesting showing at its contemporary gallery, to go with its open-air sculpture garden. There's also a lovely little cafe doing wood-fired pizzas and *ryokan*-style accommodation (p180).

Great Ocean Road Story MUSEUM
(Map p179; 15 Mountjoy Pde; ⊙9am-5pm) FREE Set up inside the Lorne Visitor Centre is this permanent exhibition of displays, videos and books that offer an informative background to the interesting history of the Great Ocean Road's construction.

Erskine Falls WATERFALL
(Erskine Falls Access Rd) Head out of town to see this lovely waterfall. It's an easy walk to the viewing platform, or 250 (often slippery) steps down to its base, from where you can explore further or head back on up.

Festivals & Events

Falls Festival MUSIC
(www.fallsfestival.com; 2-/3-/4-day tickets $249/299/339; ⊙28 Dec–1 Jan) A four-day knees-up over New Year's on a farm just out of town, this stellar music festival attracts a top line-up of

Lorne

Lorne

Top Sights
1 Qdos Art Gallery ... A3

Sights
2 Great Ocean Road Story ... B1

Sleeping
3 Grand Pacific Hotel ... D4
4 Lorne Foreshore Caravan Park ... B1
Qdos ... (see 1)

Eating
5 Bottle of Milk ... B2
6 HAH ... C2
7 Ipsos ... B2
8 Lorne Beach Pavilion ... C2
9 Mexican Republic ... B2
10 Swing Bridge Cafe & Boathouse ... C1

Drinking & Nightlife
11 Lorne Hotel ... B3

international rock and indie groups. Past headliners include Iggy Pop, Kings of Leon and the Black Keys. Sells out fast (usually within an hour), and tickets include camping.

Pier to Pub Swim SPORTS
(www.lornesurfclub.com.au; participant entry from $70) This popular event in January inspires up to 4500 swimmers to splash 1.2km across Loutit Bay to the Lorne Hotel. It's a photo opportunity for local politicians and celebrities.

Sleeping

Big Hill Track CAMPGROUND $
(☎13 1963; www.parkweb.vic.gov.au; 1265 Deans Marsh-Lorne Rd, Benwerrin) A good option for backpackers with tents or a van is this free camping ground located 15km north of Lorne, along the road heading to Birregurra. You'll need to chance your luck, however, as there are no bookings, with the 12 sites filled on a first-come, first-served basis.

Lorne Foreshore Caravan Park CAMPGROUND $

(Map p179; ☎03-5289 1382; www.lornecaravanpark.com.au; 2 Great Ocean Rd; unpowered sites $28-55, powered sites $37-89, d cabins $97-189; 📶) Book at the Foreshore Caravan Park for all of Lorne's five caravan parks. Of the five, **Erskine River Caravan Park**, where the booking office is located, is the prettiest, though note there's no swimming in the river. It's on the left-hand side as you enter Lorne, just before the bridge. Book well ahead for peak-season stays. Wi-fi in reception only.

Grand Pacific Hotel HISTORIC HOTEL $$

(Map p179; ☎03-5289 1609; www.grandpacific.com.au; 268 Mountjoy Pde; d $115-155, apt from $180; ❄📶) An iconic Lorne landmark, harking back to 1875, the Grand Pacific has been restored with a sleek modern decor that retains some classic period features. The best rooms have balconies and stunning sea views looking out to the pier. Plainer rooms are boxy, but still top value, and there are self-contained apartments, too.

★**Qdos** RYOKAN $$$

(Map p179; ☎03-5289 1989; www.qdosarts.com; 35 Allenvale Rd; r incl breakfast from $300; 📶) The perfect choice for those seeking a romantic getaway or forest retreat, Qdos' luxury Zen tree houses are fitted with tatami mats, rice-paper screens and no TV. Two-night minimum; no kids.

Eating

HAH CAFE $

(Health and Hire; Map p179; ☎0437 759 469, 0406 453 131; www.hahlornebeach.com.au; 81 Mountjoy Pde; mains from $8; ⏰8.30am-5pm, longer hours in summer; 📶) Keep that beach body in check and head down to this health-conscious cafe with a prime location on the foreshore. Its menu is loaded with superfoods, protein balls, salads and leafy smoothies, as well as gourmet toasties and homebaked banana bread drizzled with Lorne honey.

Swing Bridge Cafe & Boathouse CAFE $

(Map p179; ☎0423 814 770; 30 Great Ocean Rd; meals $10-16; ⏰8am-2.30pm Fri-Mon, daily in summer) This tiny cafe overlooking the water at the historic swing bridge (c 1934) has an appealing retro beach vibe. It's the place for single-origin coffee, to go with its range of brioches filled with anything from pulled pork and beef brisket to jerk tofu with salsa verde. On summer evenings they do Argentinian-style charcoal barbecues or paella on the lawn.

Mexican Republic MEXICAN $

(Map p179; ☎03-5289 1686; www.mexicanrepubliclorne.com; 1a Grove Rd; tacos from $7; ⏰noon-9pm summer, noon-3pm & 5.30-9pm Sat & Sun winter) Bringing Melbourne's Mexican street-food craze to Lorne, this pop-up-style taqueria does authentic soft corn tortilla tacos, burritos with smoky chipotle mayo and imported Mexican beers.

★**Lorne Beach Pavilion** MODERN AUSTRALIAN $$

(Map p179; ☎03-5289 2882; www.lornebeachpavilion.com.au; 81 Mountjoy Pde; breakfast $9-23, mains $19-45; ⏰9am-5pm Mon-Thu, 9am-9pm Fri, 8am-9pm Sat & Sun) With its unbeatable location on the foreshore, life here is literally a beach, especially with a cold drink in hand. Cafe-style breakfasts and lunches hit the spot, while a more upmarket Modern Australian menu of seafood and rib-eye steaks is on for dinner. Come at happy hour for $7 pints, or otherwise swing by at sunset for a bottle of prosecco.

Ipsos GREEK $$

(Map p179; ☎03-5289 1883; www.ipsosrestaurant.com.au; 48 Mountjoy Pde; sharing plates $5-29; ⏰noon-3pm & 6-10pm Thu-Mon, longer hours in summer) From the same family that ran Kosta (a Lorne institution that's relocated to Aireys Inlet) comes this smart, casual taverna that's opened in the exact same location where it all started in 1974. Run by the sons, the menu comprises mainly Greek-influenced sharing plates, or you can go its signature slow-roasted lamb shoulder ($66 for two).

Drinking & Nightlife

Lorne Hotel PUB

(Map p179; ☎03-5289 1409; www.lornehotel.com.au; 176 Mountjoy Pde; ⏰11am-late) Since first opening its doors in 1876, this pub has been one of Lorne's best spots for a beer. Its AstroTurf outdoor rooftop deck, overlooking the main street and ocean, is the place to be come summer, with regular bands and DJs. Its bistro also gets views and is popular for its seafood platters.

Information

Lorne Visitor Centre (Map p179; ☎03-5289 1152, 1300 891 152; www.lovelorne.com.au; 15 Mountjoy Pde; ⏰9am-5pm; 📶) Stacks of information (including heaps of ideas for walks

WORTH A TRIP

BRAE & BIRREGURRA

Located only a 30-minute drive from Lorne is the picturesque town of Birregurra. Known affectionately as 'Birrie', it features an attractive historic 19th-century streetscape and is famous for the restaurant Brae.

Regarded as one of Australia's best restaurants, **Brae** (03-5236 2226; www.braerestaurant.com; 4285 Cape Otway Rd, Birregurra; 8-course tasting plates per person $190-220, plus matched wines $125; noon-3pm Fri-Mon & from 6pm Thu-Sat) was set up in 2012 by owner-chef Dan Hunter who mostly uses whatever is growing in its 12 hectares of organic gardens to create some delightful gastronomic concoctions, all masterfully presented, and with plenty of surprises. For good reason it's a regular on the list of the World's Best 100 restaurants. Reservations are essential, and need to be made well in advance. Brae's on-site boutique **eco-suites** (03-5236 2226; www.braerestaurant.com; 4285 Cape Otway Rd; r incl breakfast $615;) (only for dining guests) look out to pastoral views, with bathtubs, art painted on the walls, and turntables with a cool collection of vinyl.

Even if you don't have a reservation for Brae, the town is a worthwhile stop with a number of great spots to eat and drink, including **Birregurra Farm Foods & Providore** (The Meating Place; 03-5236 2611; www.birregurrafarmfoods.com.au; 43 Main St; pizzas $18-21; 10am-4pm Sun-Tue, 9.30am-5.30pm Wed-Fri, 9am-5pm Sat) and the **Royal Mail Hotel** (03-5236 2626; www.royalmailhotelbirregurra.com.au; 49 Main St; 2-11pm Tue, noon-11pm Wed-Fri, 11am-late Sat & Sun), and it makes for a nice drive through rainforest and pastoral surrounds. In the second weekend of October is the annual **Birregurra Festival** with live music and food.

in the area), helpful staff, fishing licences, bus tickets and accommodation referrals. Also has a gift shop, internet access, free wi-fi and a charger out the front for electric cars.

Getting There & Away

Bus V/Line buses pass through daily from Geelong ($11.60,1½ hours) en route to Apollo Bay ($5, from one hour).

Car If driving from Melbourne, allow just under two hours for the 143km journey.

Wye River

POPULATION 140

The Great Ocean Road snakes spectacularly around the cliff-side from Cumberland River before reaching this little town with big ideas. Nestled discreetly in the pretty (steep) hillsides are some modest holiday houses and a few grander steel-and-glass pole-frame structures built on the 'challenging' housing sites. Unfortunately, on Christmas Day in 2015, major bushfires destroyed some 116 homes in the area, and the entire town was evacuated; fortunately, no deaths were recorded.

Sleeping & Eating

Big4 Wye River Holiday Park CAMPGROUND $
(www.big4wyeriver.com.au; 25 Great Ocean Rd; unpowered sites $30-45, powered sites $38-50, cabins $120-185, houses $310-395;) Just back from the beach is this popular caravan park, which sprawls over 10 hectares. Featuring an Otways forest backdrop, its grassy sites are great for camping, and there's a range of comfortable units.

Wye River Foreshore Camping Reserve CAMPGROUND $
(03-5289 0412; sites $40; Nov-Apr) This camping ground offers powered beachside sites during summer.

★ **Wye Beach Hotel** PUB FOOD $$
(03-5289 0240; www.wyebeachhotel.com.au; 19 Great Ocean Rd; mains from $27; 11.30am-11pm;) Undoubtedly one of the best coastal pubs in Victoria, if not Australia – the ocean views just don't get much better than this. It has an unpretentious, local vibe and an all-regional craft-beer selection on tap – with brews from Forrest, Torquay and Aireys Inlet. There's pub food too, though it's a bit on the pricey side.

There are also comfortable motel-style double rooms ($130 to $160) with great views.

Wye General CAFE $$
(03-5289 0247; www.thewyegeneral.com; 35 Great Ocean Rd; mains $15-26; 8am-5pm Mon-Sat, to 4pm Sun) This well-loved general store does provisions and groceries; however it's most noteworthy for its smart indoor-outdoor cafe/bar. Polished concrete floors, tim-

ber features and a sophisticated retro ambience, it does old-fashioned cocktails, beer on tap and a menu of breakfasts, burgers and sourdough toasties made in-house.

Getting There & Away

Bus There are several buses a day here from Geelong ($14.40, two hours).

Car Wye River is located 159km from Melbourne, around a 2½-hour drive. It's positioned approximately halfway between Lorne and Apollo Bay on the Great Ocean Road.

Kennett River

Located 25km east of Apollo Bay is Kennett River, which has some great **koala spotting** just behind the caravan park. There are also **glow worms** that shine at night up the same stretch of Grey River Rd (take a torch).

The friendly bush **Kennett River Holiday Park** (☎03-5289 0272, 1300 664417; www.kennettriver.com; 1-13 Great Ocean Rd; unpowered sites $31-58, powered sites $37-68, d cabins from $115; 📶) is one of the best sites along the coast, equally popular with surfers, families, travellers and young couples. The beach-view cabins have amazing vistas. There are free electric barbecues and a camp kitchen for cooking. Keep an eye out for koalas, which are regularly spotted here.

Kennett River is located directly on the Great Ocean Road, 165km from Melbourne. It's a 30-minute drive to Lorne. From Geelong there are three buses a day ($16, two hours).

Apollo Bay

POP 1095

One of the larger towns along the Great Ocean Road, Apollo Bay has a tight-knit community of fisherfolk, artists, musicians and sea changers. Rolling hills provide a postcard backdrop to the town, while broad, white-sand beaches dominate the foreground. It's also an ideal base for exploring magical Cape Otway (p184) and Otway National Park. It has some of the best restaurants along the coast and several lively pubs, and is one of best towns on the Great Ocean Road for budget travellers with numerous hostels and ready transport access.

Sights & Activities

Mark's Walking Tours WALKING

(☎0417 983 985; www.greatoceanwalk.asn.au/markstours; tours $50) Take a walk around the area with local Mark Brack, son of the Cape Otway lighthouse keeper. He knows this stretch of coast, its history and its ghosts better than anyone around. Daily tours include shipwreck tours, historical tours, glow-worm tours and Great Ocean Walk treks. Minimum two people – prices drop the more people on the tour.

Apollo Bay Surf & Kayak ADVENTURE

(☎0405 495 909; www.apollobaysurfkayak.com.au; 157-159 Great Ocean Rd; 2hr kayak tours $70, 2hr surf lessons adult/child $65/60) Head out to an Australian fur seal colony in a double kayak. Tours (with full instructions for beginners) depart from Marengo Beach (to the south of the town centre). Also offers surf and SUP lessons, plus boards and mountain bikes (half-day $30) for hire.

Sleeping

YHA Eco Beach HOSTEL $

(☎03-5237 7899; www.yha.com.au; 5 Pascoe St; dm/d/f from $29/75/112; @📶) This multimillion-dollar, architect-designed hostel is an outstanding place to stay, with eco-credentials, great lounge areas, kitchens, a boules pit and rooftop terraces. Rooms are generic but spotless. It's a block behind the beach.

Surfside Backpacker HOSTEL $

(☎0419 322 595, 03-5237 7263; www.surfsidebackpacker.com; cnr Great Ocean Rd & Gambier St; dm from $28, d with shared/private bathroom $65/85; 📶) Right across from the beach, this fantastic, sprawling, old-school 1940s beach house will appeal to those looking for budget accommodation with a true Apollo Bay character. Run by the delightful owner Robyn, its homely lounge is full of couches, board games and huge windows looking out onto the ocean. It's a 15-minute walk from the bus stop.

Pisces Big4 Apollo Bay CAMPGROUND $

(☎03-5237 6749; www.piscespark.com.au; 311 Great Ocean Rd; unpowered/powered sites from $34/42, cabins from $99; 📶🏊) It's the unbeatable views from the oceanfront villas (from $190) that set this family-oriented park apart from the others.

DON'T MISS

FORREST

Tucked away in the hinterland of the Otways, a 30-minute drive from Apollo Bay, the former logging town of Forrest has emerged as one of the new tourist hotspots in the Otways.

Since the closure of the logging industry, it has reinvented itself as one of the best **mountain-biking** destinations in the state. Parks Victoria and the Department of Environment and Primary Industries (DEPI) have opened 16 cross-country trails (adding up to more than 50km) – ranging from beginner to highly advanced. Grab a trail map (www.rideforrest.com.au/trails) from the **Corner Store** (www.thecornerstoreforrest.com.au; cnr Blundy & Station Sts, Forrest; bike hire half-/full day $75/95; ⏲9am-4pm Mon-Thu, 8am-5pm Fri-Sun), which, in addition to renting out bikes, has a wealth of info, arranges tours, and stocks accessories, maps and repair kits. The town hosts the **Otway Odyssey Mountain Bike Marathon** (www.rapidascent.com.au; ⏲late Feb) in late February, and the **Forrest Festival** (www.forrestfestival.com.au; ⏲Dec) stage race in the first weekend of December.

Located 7km from Forrest is scenic **Lake Elizabeth**, famous for its population of platypuses and surreal scenery of dead trees jutting from its glassy water. **Otway Eco Tours** (☎0419 670 985; www.platypustours.net.au; adult/child $85/50) runs guided canoe trips at dusk and dawn to spot platypuses. There's also free camping here – BYO drinking water.

The town is also very well known for its microbrewery, the **Forrest Brewing Company** (☎03-5236 6170; www.forrestbrewing.com.au; 26 Grant St, Forrest; 6-beer tasting pallets $12, pots/pints from $5.50/10; ⏲9am-5pm Sun-Wed, to 11pm Thu-Sat, daily Dec-Jan), where you can sample eight different beers brewed on-site and dig into quality pub meals.

For food, **Bespoke Harvest** (☎03-5236 6446; www.bespokeharvest.com.au; 16 Grant St, Forrest; set menu $65; ⏲noon-2.30pm Fri-Mon, 6-8pm Fri & Sat) is bringing people into town with its highly seasonal, contemporary Med-inspired cuisine, most of which is sourced from its kitchen garden. The **Forrest General Store** (☎03-5236 6496; 33 Grant St, Forrest; dishes from $10; ⏲8am-5pm) is also worth popping into for a coffee, plus lovely homemade pies and chorizo sausage rolls.

There are plenty of B&Bs in town, but the best accommodation option is the wonderful **Forrest Guesthouse** (☎03-5236 6446; www.forrestaccommodation.com.au; 16 Grant St, Forrest; s/d incl breakfast $150/195; ❄📶), with comfortable, spacious rooms looking out to flower-filled garden. Otherwise **Wonky Stables Holiday Park** (☎03-5236 6275; www.wonkystables.com.au; 1 Station St; unpowered/powered sites $30/35, cabins d with shared/private bathroom from $65/105) has camping, pod vans, safari tents and en-suite cabins, along with a fully equipped camp kitchen for self-caterers. Further afield there's a free camping ground at **Stevensons Falls** (www.delwp.vic.gov.au; sites free), about 12km southwest of town, with 50 sites, drop toilets and fireplaces, but no showers.

★Beacon Point Ocean View Villas VILLA **$$$**
(☎03-5237 6218, 03-5237 6411; www.beaconpoint.com.au; 270 Skenes Creek Rd; r incl breakfast $200-350; ❄📶) With a commanding hill location among the trees, this wonderful collection of comfortable one- and two-bedroom villas is a luxurious yet affordable bush retreat. Most villas have sensational coast views, balcony and wood-fired heater. There's also a popular restaurant.

Eating

★Chris's Beacon Point Restaurant GREEK **$$$**
(☎03-5237 6411; www.chriss.com.au; 280 Skenes Creek Rd; mains from $34; ⏲6pm-late daily, plus noon-2pm Sat & Sun; 📶) Feast on memorable ocean views, deliciously fresh seafood and Greek-influenced dishes at Chris's hilltop fine-dining sanctuary among the treetops. Reservations recommended. You can also stay in its wonderful stilted villas. It's accessed via Skenes Creek.

La Bimba MODERN AUSTRALIAN **$$$**
(☎03-5237 7411; www.labimba.com.au; 125 Great Ocean Rd; mains $36-42; ⏲8.30am-3pm & 5.30-9.30pm Wed-Mon) This upstairs Mod Oz restaurant is worth the splurge. It's a warm, relaxed smart-casual restaurant with ocean views and a good wine list. Try the chilli Portarlington mussel hotpot, the local lamb or a kangaroo main.

Drinking & Nightlife

★**Great Ocean Road Brewhouse** MICROBREWERY

(☎03-5237 6240; www.greatoceanroadbrewhouse.com.au; 29 Great Ocean Rd; pots $5; ⏰pub 11am-11pm Mon-Thu, to 1am Fri & Sat, Tastes of the Region noon-8pm Mon-Thu, noon-9pm Fri, 10am-9pm Sat, 10am-8pm Sun) Set up by renowned Otways brewery Prickly Moses, this new taphouse pours an impressive range of ales. It's divided into two distinct entities: the front bar is more your classic pub and bistro with pool table; while through the back is their 'Taste of the Region' room, with 16 of their beers on tap to enjoy with local produce tasting platters.

Hello Coffee COFFEE

(☎0438 443 489; www.hellocoffee.com.au; 16 Oak Ave; ⏰7am-3pm Mon-Fri, 9am-2pm Sat; 📶) Set up by a couple of local mates in a backstreet industrial estate is this roaster-cafe that does the best coffee in the region. They roast single-origin beans from around the world on-site, served as V60 pourovers, Chemex, nitro cold brew or classic espresso. It has a cosy lounge-room set up, and does good breakfasts and smoked pulled-pork rolls etc.

Information

Great Ocean Road Visitor Centre (☎1300 689 297; www.visitapollobay.com; 100 Great Ocean Rd; ⏰9am-5pm; 📶) Modern and professional tourist office with a heap of info for the area, and an 'eco-centre' with displays. It has free wi-fi and can book bus tickets, too.

Getting There & Away

Car From Melbourne the fastest route is inland via the Geelong bypass that leads through to Birregurra and Forrest, a 200km drive. If taking the scenic route along the Great Ocean Road (highly recommended) count on a 4½-hour drive.

Bus Apollo Bay is easily reached by public transport from Melbourne ($27.20, 3½ hours) via train to Geelong and transferring to a connecting bus. There are three daily services during the week, and twice on weekends; stops include Torquay ($15.40, two hours), Anglesea ($11.20, 1¾ hours) and Lorne ($5, one hour), among others.

Cape Otway

Cape Otway is the second-most-southerly point of mainland Australia (after Wilsons Promontory) and one of the wettest parts of the state. This coastline is particularly beautiful, rugged and historically treacherous for passing ships. The turn-off for Lighthouse Rd, which leads 12km down to the lighthouse, is 21km from Apollo Bay. It's a beautiful forested road with towering trees, which are home to a sizeable population of koalas.

Sights

Cape Otway Lightstation LIGHTHOUSE

(☎03-5237 9240; www.lightstation.com; Lighthouse Rd; adult/child/family $19.50/7.50/49.50; ⏰9am-5pm) Cape Otway Lightstation is the oldest surviving lighthouse on mainland Australia and was built in 1848 by more than 40 stonemasons without mortar or cement. The **Telegraph Station** has fascinating displays on the 250km undersea telegraph cable link with Tasmania, laid in 1859. It's a sprawling complex with plenty to see, from Aboriginal cultural sites to WWII bunkers.

WALKING THE GREAT OCEAN ROAD

The superb multiday **Great Ocean Walk** (p185) starts at Apollo Bay and runs all the way to the Twelve Apostles. It takes you through changing landscapes along spectacular clifftops, deserted beaches and forested Otway National Park.

It's possible to start at one point and arrange a pickup at another (public transport options are few and far between). You can do shorter walks or the whole 104km trek over eight days. Designated camp sites are spread along the Great Ocean Walk catering for registered walkers only; bring cooking equipment and tents (no fires allowed). Otherwise there are plenty of comfortable accommodation options from luxury lodges to caravan parks. Check out the helpful FAQ page on the website for all the info.

Walk 91 (☎03-5237 1189; www.walk91.com.au; 157-159 Great Ocean Rd, Apollo Bay; 3 day/4 night guided walks per person $800) can arrange your itinerary, transport and equipment hire, and can shuttle your backpack to your destination.

WORTH A TRIP

OTWAY FLY DETOUR

Twenty kilometres inland from the logging town of **Lavers Hill** on the Colac Rd (C155) is the popular **Otway Fly** (☎1800 300 477, 03-5235 9200; www.otwayfly.com; 360 Phillips Track; treetop walks adult/child $25/15, zipline tours $120/85; ⏰9am-5pm, last entry 4pm). It's an elevated steel walkway suspended among the forest canopy, and includes a swaying lookout tower, 50m above the forest floor. Kids will enjoy the 'prehistoric path' loaded with dinosaurs, and everyone can test their bravery on the guided 2½-hour **zipline tour** – including a 120m run. You can also abseil down one of the giant trees.

Along the same road as the Fly is **Triplet Falls**, which passes a historic timber site and is worth the 900m hike. The **Beauchamp** and **Hopetoun Falls** are just past Beech Forest, down the Aire Valley Rd, and are also worth the trip.

On the corner just before the Fly, pop into **Otway NouriShed** (☎03-5235 9226; 3810 Colac-Lavers Hill Rd; mains $10-20; ⏰9am-5pm Wed-Mon), an old potato shed converted into a rustic cafe serving meals and fair-trade coffee. Further afield towards Colac, past Gellibrand, is the **Otway Estate** (☎03-5233 8400, brewery 03-5233 8515; www.otwayestate.com.au; 10-30 Hoveys Rd, Barongarook) brewery, which produces Prickly Moses beer plus cider and wine; call ahead to check they're open. They have accommodation in self-contained cottages from $200. As they now have a **taphouse** (p184) at Apollo Bay, it's not essential to make the trek all the way out here, but it's a nice drive.

Seven kilometres southwest of Lavers Hill is **Melba Gully** with a rainforest nature walk under a canopy of blackwoods, myrtle beeches and ferns; here also is the 300-year-old 'Big Tree', a messmate eucalyptus that sadly recently toppled over. The highlight here is after dark, however, when **glow worms** glimmer in the park.

Sleeping

★**Bimbi Park** CARAVAN PARK $
(☎03-5237 9246; www.bimbipark.com.au; 90 Manna Gum Dr; unpowered sites $20-40, powered sites $25-45, dm $20, cabins $100-145; 📶) 🍃 Down a dirt road 3km from the lighthouse is this character-filled caravan park with bush sites, cabins, dorms and old-school caravans. It's a fantastic option for families, and also for hikers on the **Great Ocean Walk** (www.greatoceanwalk.com.au). There's plenty of wildlife about, including koalas, plus horse rides (adult/child $65/55 per hour) and a rock-climbing wall. Good use of water-saving initiatives too.

Blanket Bay CAMPGROUND $
(☎13 19 63; www.parkweb.vic.gov.au; sites from $28.70) Blanket Bay is one of those 'secret' camping grounds that Melburnians love to lay claim to discovering. It's serene (depending on your neighbours) and the nearby beach is beautiful. It's not really a secret; in fact it's so popular during summer and Easter holidays that it regularly books out.

★**Great Ocean Ecolodge** LODGE $$$
(☎03-5237 9297; www.greatoceanecolodge.com; 635 Lighthouse Rd; r incl activities from $380; 🚭) 🍃 Reminiscent of a luxury African safari lodge, this mud-brick homestead stands in pastoral surrounds with plenty of wildlife. It's all solar-powered and rates go towards the on-site **Centre for Conservation Ecology** (www.conservationecologycentre.org). It also serves as an animal hospital for local fauna and has a captive tiger quoll breeding program, which you'll visit on its dusk wildlife walk with an ecologist.

Cape Otway Lightstation B&B $$$
(☎03-5237 9240; www.lightstation.com; Lighthouse Rd; d incl entry to lighthouse $240-450) There's a range of options at this romantic and historic windswept spot (p184). You can book out the whole Head Lightkeeper's House (sleeps 16), or the smaller Manager's House (sleeps two). Prices are halved if you stay a second night.

Cape Otway to Port Campbell National Park

After Cape Otway, the Great Ocean Road levels out and enters the fertile Horden Vale flats, returning briefly to the coast at tiny Glenaire. Six kilometres north of Glenaire, a 5km detour goes to the wild, thrashing and often massive surf of **Johanna Beach** (forget swimming). The world-famous Rip Curl Pro surfing competition relocates here when conditions at Bells Beach are flat. From here

THE SHIPWRECK COAST

In the era of sailing ships, Victoria's beautiful and rugged southwest coastline was one of the most treacherous on earth, due to hidden reefs and frequent heavy fog. Between the 1830s and 1930s, more than 200 ships were torn asunder along the so-called Shipwreck Coast between Cape Otway and Port Fairy. From the early 1850s to late 1880s, Victoria's gold rush and subsequent economic boom brought countless shiploads of prospectors and hopefuls from Europe, North America and China. After spending months at sea, many vessels (and lives) were lost on the 'home straight'.

The **lighthouses** along this coast – at Aireys Inlet, Cape Otway, Port Fairy and Warrnambool – are still operating and you'll find shipwreck museums, memorial plaques and anchors that tell the story of wrecks along this coast. The most famous is that of the iron-hulled clipper **Loch Ard**, which foundered off Mutton Bird Island (near Port Campbell) at 4am on the final night of its long voyage from England in 1878. Of 37 crew and 19 passengers on board, only two survived. Eva Carmichael, a nonswimmer, clung to wreckage and was washed into a gorge – since renamed **Loch Ard Gorge** – where apprentice officer Tom Pearce rescued her. Tom heroically climbed the sheer cliff and raised the alarm but no other survivors were found. Eva and Tom were both 19 years old, leading to speculation in the press about a romance, but nothing actually happened – they never saw each other again and Eva soon returned to Ireland (this time, perhaps not surprisingly, via steamship).

the road heads inland again up north to the historic logging township of **Lavers Hill**, a popular pit stop for travellers, with several cafes and pubs. The road meanders further onward to the Twelve Apostles through several relaxed towns, including the coastal hamlet of Princetown.

This stretch also forms a leg of the Great Ocean Walk, which runs from Apollo Bay to the Twelve Apostles; see www.greatoceanwalk.com.au for details.

Sleeping

Johanna Beach Camping Ground CAMPGROUND $

(☎13 19 63; www.parkweb.vic.gov.au; unpowered sites from $27.30) This Johanna camping ground is on a protected grassy area between the ocean and the rolling hills. The unpowered sites are for a maximum of six people.

There's an ablutions facility, but fires are banned, so you'll need to bring in your own gas cooker as well as drinking water. Take all your rubbish with you. Book well ahead online.

Pebble Point TENTED CAMP $$

(☎03-5243 3579; www.pebblepoint.com.au; 20 Old Coach Rd, Princetown; d $145-175;) Pebble Point's luxury camping makes you feel like you're on safari with its African-style ensuite tented rooms. They overlook a valley in a bush setting, yet are only a short drive from the Twelve Apostles.

Drinking & Nightlife

Otway Central Tavern PUB, CAFE

(☎03-5237 3251; 57 Great Ocean Rd, Lavers Hill; 8.30am-9pm) This rustic country roadhouse is divided into a pub at one end and a tourist-friendly cafe at the other. It uses its own beef and lamb produce, and brews its own Crowes Nest ale on tap. Go the lamb and rosemary pie, or a Sunday roast (winter) or a barbecue (summer) in the evenings from 5.30pm.

Getting There & Away

V/Line runs a coach service from Apollo Bay to Lavers Hill ($5, 40 minutes) and Princetown ($9.80, one hour 10 minutes) three times a week on Monday, Wednesday and Friday, en route to Warrnambool. However, once you're here you'll need a car to get around, hence it's pretty much essential to have your own vehicle – unless of course you're traversing this stretch on foot via the **Great Ocean Walk** (p185).

Port Campbell National Park

East of the Otways, the Great Ocean Road levels out and enters narrow, flat scrubby escarpment lands that fall away to sheer, 70m-high cliffs along the coast between Princetown and Peterborough – a distinct change of scene. This is Port Campbell National Park, home to the Twelve Apostles, and the most famous and most photographed stretch of the Great Ocean Road.

None of the beaches along this stretch are suitable for swimming because of strong currents and undertows.

Sights

★Twelve Apostles LANDMARK

(Great Ocean Rd) The most iconic sight and enduring image for most visitors to the Great Ocean Road, the Twelve Apostles provide a fitting climax to the journey. Jutting out from the ocean in spectacular fashion, these rocky stacks stand as if they've been abandoned to the ocean by the retreating headland. Today only seven 'apostles' can be seen from a network of viewing platforms connected by timber boardwalks around the clifftops.

There's pedestrian access to the viewing platforms from the car park at the Twelve Apostles Visitor Centre – more a kiosk and toilets than an info centre – via a tunnel beneath the Great Ocean Road.

The best time to visit is sunset, not only for optimum photographic opportunities and to beat the tour buses, but also to see **little penguins** returning ashore. Sightings vary, but generally they arrive 20 to 40 minutes after sunset. You'll need binoculars, which can be borrowed from the Port Campbell Visitor Centre (p189).

Gibson Steps BEACH

These 86 steps, hacked by hand into the cliffs by 19th-century landowner Hugh Gibson (and more recently replaced by concrete steps), lead down to wild Gibson Beach. You can walk along the beach, but be careful not to get stranded by high tides.

Information

Twelve Apostles Visitor Centre Kiosk
(10am-5pm Sun-Fri, to 5.30pm Sat) Based across the road from the iconic Twelve Apostles is this tourist information building with a kiosk, interpretative panels and toilets. To access the Twelve Apostles you'll need to park here, from where you can access the site via a tunnel that passes under the road.

Port Campbell

POPULATION 618

This small, laid-back coastal town was named after Scottish Captain Alexander Campbell, a whaler who took refuge here on trading voyages between Tasmania and Port Fairy. It's a friendly town with some nice little eateries and drinking spots, which make for an ideal place to debrief after visiting the Twelve Apostles. Its tiny bay has a lovely sandy beach, one of few safe places for swimming along this tempestuous stretch of coast.

Sleeping

Port Campbell Guesthouse Flashpackers GUESTHOUSE $

(0407 696 559; www.portcampbellguesthouse.com; 54 Lord St; s/d without bathroom $50/80, r with bathroom from $100;) A place for budget, independent-minded travellers who aren't into the whole hostel scene. Instead this homely guesthouse feels more like go-

TWELVE APOSTLES TRANSPORT & TOURS

Unless you're booked on a tour, having your own car is pretty much the only way to go in terms of exploring this area. The Apostles are located 15km from Port Campbell, with Loch Ard Gorge a little closer to town (around 12km).

Port Campbell Boat Charters (0428 986 366; www.portcampbellboatcharters.com.au; scenic tours/diving/fishing per person from $50/60/70) offers a unique way of viewing the Twelve Apostles, allowing you to see them from out on the water. Otherwise you can arrange a **scenic helicopter flight** (03-5598 8283; www.12apostleshelicopters.com.au; 15min flights $145) that'll take you over this dramatic stretch of coast.

From Port Campbell you can arrange a trip here with **Port Campbell Touring Company** (03-5598 6424, 0447 986 423; www.portcampbelltouring.com.au; half-day tours per person from $120, walks from $85). Otherwise the following tour operators make the trip here from Melbourne:

Go West Tours (03-9485 5290; www.gowest.com.au; tours $130)

Otway Discovery Tour (03-9629 5844; www.greatoceanroadtour.com.au; 1/2/3-day tours $109/289/380)

Ride Tours (1800 605 120, 0427 180 357; www.ridetours.com.au; tours $210)

ing around to a mate's place. Set up within a historic cottage are four cosy rooms, a comfy lounge and a country kitchen with filter coffee.

Port Campbell Hostel HOSTEL $
(☎03-5598 6305; www.portcampbellhostel.com.au; 18 Tregea St; dm/s/d/tr/q from $38/80/130/175/240; @📶) This modern purpose-built double-storey backpackers has rooms with western views, a huge shared kitchen and an even bigger lounge area. There's a range of clean mixed dorms and private rooms with en suites. It's a short stroll to the beach, and there are pizzas in the evenings ($10) and mountain-bike hire. Wi-fi only in the lounge area.

The opening of its new brewery Sow and Piglets (p189) is another reason to stay.

12 APOSTLES GOURMET TRAIL

Head inland to the Corangamite hinterland on the **12 Apostles Gourmet Trail** (www.12apostlesfoodartisans.com) to taste cheeses, chocolate, wine, single-malt whiskies, snails and ice cream, among other gourmet regional produce.

Start at Timboon, an ex-logging town 15km from Point Campbell, home to **Timboon Railway Shed Distillery** (☎03-5598 3555; www.timboondistillery.com.au; 1 Bailey St; meals from $19; ⏲10am-4.30pm; 📶), a historic railway shed converted into a vibrant cafe. Inspired by Timboon's illegal 19th-century whisky trade, here they produce single malts and spirits on-site. Watch the distillery process, sample a few whiskies and vodkas, and nab some keepsakes. The restaurant is big on local produce, and makes fantastic wood-fired pizzas. Across from here is **Timboon Fine Ice Cream** (☎0432 611 596; www.timboonfineicecream.com.au; 1a Barrett St; ice cream from $4; ⏲10am-5pm), set up in an architecturally designed building, selling seasonal flavours using local dairy produce. Keep an eye out for its 'Sundae School' where you can make up your own ice cream.

Up the road you can pick your own strawberries and blackberries at **Berry World** (☎03-5598 3240; www.berryworld.com.au; 24 Egan St; adult/child $6/4; ⏲10am-4.30pm Tue-Sun Nov-Apr) between November and April, or just stop by for a cup of strawberries and cream, a spot of high tea, or scones with cream and homemade jam.

Further along is **Timboon Cheesery** (☎03-5598 3322; www.timbooncheesery.com.au; 23 Ford & Fells Rd; ⏲11am-4pm) 🍃, a lovely garden cafe owned by Schulz Organic Dairy, a third generation of German cheesemakers, offering free tasting of its organics cheeses, as well as platters, wine and scones with cream. **Apostle Whey Cheese** (☎0437 894 337; www.apostlewheycheese.com.au; 9 Gallum Rd, Cooriemungle; ⏲10am-5pm) also offers tastings of delectable award-winning blue cheeses, bries and gumtree-smoked cheddar on its dairy farm. Midweek you can watch cheesemaking in action.

From here it's time for a change of scene with a visit to **Simpson Snails** (☎0427 589 872, 03-5219 5990; www.simpsonsnails.com.au; 399 Centre Rd, Simpson; half-dozen snails $12; ⏲10am-5pm, closed winter), an organic free-range snail farm where you can do a tour and a taste test – sampling them cooked in garlic, parsley butter or encased in a vol-au-vent. Note they close in winter when the snails hibernate.

The day wouldn't be complete without wine and chocolate. **Newtons Ridge Estate** (☎0407 878 213, 03-5598 7394; www.newtonsridgeestate.com.au; 1170 Cooriemungle Rd, Cooriemungle; ⏲11am-4pm Thu-Mon Sep-Dec & Feb-Apr, daily Jan) offers tastings of its pinot, cool-climate shiraz, rose and chardonnay at its cellar door, while **GORGE Chocolates** (☎0488 557 252; www.gorgechocolates.com.au; 1432 Princetown Rd, Cooriemungle; ⏲10am-5pm) is an essential stop for its handmade Belgian chocolates, with plenty of goodies and samples.

No doubt after this you're feeling a little bloated, so luckily the **Camperdown–Timboon Rail Trail** offers a 34km track for cyclists and walkers, following the historical railway line. You can hire mountain bikes from **Crater to Coast** (☎0438 407 777; www.cratertocoastbicyclehire.com.au; Bailey St; bike hire half-/full day $25/30, car tours per hour $50).

If you don't have your own wheels, you can take a tour of the area with **Timboon Taxi Service** (☎0438 407 777; www.timboonbikehireandtaxis.com) or **Port Campbell Touring Company** (p187).

Sea Foam Villas APARTMENT $$

(☎03-5598 6413; www.seafoamvillas.com.au; 14 Lord St; r $185-570) Located directly across from the water, Sea Foam undoubtedly has the best views in town. It's only really worth it, however, if you can snag one of the bay-view apartments which are large, comfortable and luxurious.

Port Campbell Holiday Park CAMPGROUND $$

(☎03-5598 6492, 1800 505 466; www.pchp.com.au; Morris St; powered sites $31-86, cabins $105-270; @ 📶) Offers sites for campers and vans, plus a range of comfortable cabins and villas that offer good value if you have a group; a two-minute walk to the beach and town.

Eating & Drinking

★**Forage on the Foreshore** CAFE $$

(☎03-5598 6202; 32 Cairns St; mains from $14; ⊙9am-5pm; 📶) In the old post office is this seafront cottage cafe with wooden floorboards, art on the walls, an open fireplace and a vintage record player spinning vinyl. There's an all-day breakfast menu, burgers and curries for lunch, and items featuring fresh crayfish and abalone.

12 Rocks Cafe Bar CAFE $$

(☎03-5598 6123; www.12rocksbeachbar.com.au; 19 Lord St; mains $18-30; ⊙9.30am-11pm) Watch flotsam wash up on the beach from this busy eatery, which has perfect beachfront views. Try a local Otways beer with a pasta or seafood main, or just duck in for a coffee or ice cream from nearby Timboon.

Sow and Piglets MICROBREWERY

(☎03-5598 6305; 18 Tregea St; ⊙noon-late) Just opening its doors at time of research is this new nanobrewery set up inside the Port Campbell Hostel (p188). Overseen by a German brewer, here they produce four beers on-site, all unfiltered and unpasteurised, including a Kölsch, IPA and inventive seasonals such as a strawberry yogurt stout, made using local ingredients.

Information

Port Campbell Visitor Centre (☎1300 137 255; www.visit12apostles.com.au; 26 Morris St; ⊙9am-5pm) Stacks of regional and accommodation information and interesting relics from various shipwrecks – the anchor from the *Loch Ard* is out the front. Offers free use of binoculars, stargazer telescopes, cameras, GPS equipment and scavenger hunts for kids.

Getting There & Away

V/Line (p167) buses leave Geelong on Monday, Wednesday and Friday and travel through to Port Campbell ($32, five hours), but you'll need to transfer to a different bus in Apollo Bay ($11.20, two hours 15 minutes), which leaves a few hours later. There's also a bus to Warrnambool ($7.60, one hour 20 minutes).

Port Campbell to Warrnambool

Don't for a moment think that the Twelve Apostles are the end point of the Great Ocean Road, particularly given there's a whole string of iconic rock stacks on the road heading westward of Port Campbell. Some are arguably more scenic than the apostles themselves.

The drive continues through acres and acres of farming land here, passing through some laid-back towns. **Timboon**, about 16km inland from Peterborough, is best known for being surrounded by a number of wonderful places to sample local produce on the 12 Apostles Gourmet Trail. Here you'll be able to sample single-malt whiskeys, local homemade ice cream and chocolate, and fine wine and cheese.

Sights & Activities

London Bridge LANDMARK

Just outside Port Campbell, en route to Peterborough, London Bridge has indeed fallen down. It was once a double-arched rock platform linked to the mainland, but in January 1990 the bridge collapsed leaving two terrified tourists marooned on the world's newest island – they were eventually rescued by helicopter. It remains a spectacular sight nevertheless. At dusk keep an eye out for penguins, who are often spotted on the beach.

Bay of Islands Coastal Park VIEWPOINT

Past Peterborough (12km west of Port Campbell), the lesser-visited **Bay of Martyrs** and **Bay of Islands** both have spectacular lookout points of rock stacks and sweeping views comparable to the Twelve Apostles. Both have fantastic coastal walks, and there's a great beach at **Crofts Bay**.

The Arch LANDMARK

Offshore from Point Hesse, the Arch is a rock formation worth stopping for. There's some good photo ops from the various viewing points looking down upon this intact bridgelike formation.

The Grotto VIEWPOINT
A scenic stopover heading west from Port Campbell is the Grotto, where steep stairs lead down to a hollowed-out cavelike formation where waves crash through. It's approximately halfway between Port Campbell and Peterborough, a short drive from London Bridge (p189).

Allansford Cheese World FACTORY
(www.cheeseworld.com.au; Great Ocean Rd, Allansford; ⏲9am-5pm Mon-Fri, 10am-4pm Sat & Sun) FREE On the outskirts of Warrnambool (12km east) in the dairy township of Allansford is the slightly tacky Cheese World. It's run by the Warrnambool Cheese & Butter factory, whose processing plant across the road has been in business since 1888. Here you can sample cheeses, visit its dairy farm museum (surprisingly worthwhile) and get one of its famous creamy milkshakes from the cafe.

Warrnambool

POPULATION 33,979

Once a whaling and sealing station, these days Warrnambool is booming as a major regional commercial and whale-watching centre. Overall it's an attractive city with heritage buildings, beaches, gardens and tree-lined streets; however, the major housing and commercial development around the fringes of the city looks much like city suburbs anywhere in Australia.

While it's the whales that Warrnambool is most famous for, it has some great art galleries and historical sights to visit. Plus its sizeable population of uni students gives the town some spark, and you'll find some cool bars and cafes about.

Sights & Activities

Sheltered **Lady Bay**, with fortifications at the breakwater at its western end, is the main swimming beach. **Logan's Beach** has the best surf and there are breaks at **Levy's Beach** and **Second Bay**.

For bike, surfboard, SUP and kayak rentals, get in touch with Warrnambool Beach Backpackers (p192).

★**Flagstaff Hill Maritime Village** HISTORIC SITE
(Map p191; ☎03-5559 4600; www.flagstaffhill.com; 89 Merri St; adult/child/family $18/8.50/48; ⏲9am-5pm, last entry 4pm) The world-class Flagstaff Hill precinct is of equal interest for its shipwreck museum, heritage-listed lighthouses and garrison as it is for its reproduction of a historical Victorian port town. It also has the nightly **Shipwrecked** (adult/child/family $26/14/67), an engaging 70-minute sound-and-laser show telling the story of the *Loch Ard*'s plunge. The village is modelled on a pioneer-era Australian coastal port, with ye olde shoppes such as blacksmiths, candle makers and shipbuilders. If you're lucky the **Maremma dogs** (☎03-5559 4600; www.warrnamboolpenguins.com.au; adult/child $16/10) will be around for you to meet.

★**Warrnambool Art Gallery** GALLERY
(WAG; Map p191; ☎03-5559 4949; www.thewag.com.au; 165 Timor St; ⏲10am-5pm Mon-Fri, noon-5pm Sat & Sun) FREE One of Australia's oldest art galleries (established in 1886), Warrnambool's collection of rotating permanent artworks showcases many prominent Australian painters. Its most famous piece is Eugene von Guérard's oil landscape *Tower Hill*, so detailed it was used by botanists as a historical record when regenerating the Tower Hill area to its original state. There's a contemporary component too, and several concurrent exhibitions on show.

Artery GALLERY
(Map p191; www.thefproject.org.au; 224 Timor St; ⏲10am-4pm Wed-Sun) Set up in a former funeral home by local art collective the F Project, this contemporary art gallery always has something interesting showing at its monthly exhibitions. There are also some cool street art murals outside. Its shop is another reason to visit, with some wonderful jewellery, accessories and artworks to pick up.

Reel Addiction WHALE WATCHING
(☎0468 964 150; www.boatcharterswarrnambool.com.au; whale-watching trips per person $65, half-day fishing per person from $180) Runs morning and afternoon trips to see the whales when they're in town – usually from June to September – or otherwise to see the seal colony on Lady Julia Percy Island. Fishing trips are also their speciality.

Port Fairy to Warrnambool Rail Trail CYCLING
Divided into three stages, this 38km cycling track follows the old railway line that links Warrnambool's breakwater to Port Fairy, via Koroit and Tower Hill.

Warrnambool

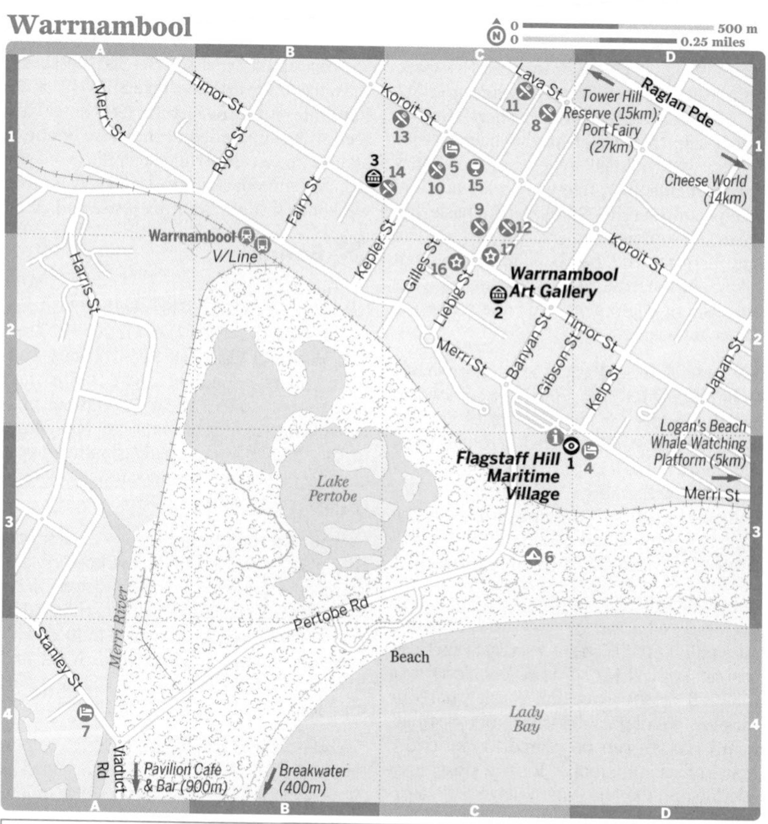

Warrnambool

Top Sights
1 Flagstaff Hill Maritime Village C3
2 Warrnambool Art Gallery C2

Sights
3 Artery B1

Sleeping
4 Flagstaff Hill Lighthouse Lodge D3
Garrison Camp .... (see 1)
5 Hotel Warrnambool C1
6 Surfside Holiday Park C3
7 Warrnambool Beach Backpackers A4

Eating
8 Brightbird Espresso C1
9 Fishtales Café C1
10 Graze Urban Cafe & Delicatessen C1
Hotel Warrnambool .... (see 5)
11 Kermond's Hamburgers C1
12 Pickled Pig C1
13 Rough Diamond C1
14 Standard Dave C1

Drinking & Nightlife
Dart & Marlin ....(see 14)
15 Lucy C1

Entertainment
16 Lighthouse Theatre C2
17 Loft C2

Sleeping

Garrison Camp CABIN $
(Map p191; 1800 556 111; www.flagstaffhill.com/accommodation; cabins with shared bathroom $50) Located within the Flagstaff Hill Maritime Village (p192) is this budget lodging in the Garrison Camp, a unique spot with replica 1870s Crimea-era British officer huts – small wooden A-frame bunk cabins. If you're around for longer they'll set up the bell tents (three-night minimum). It's BYO bedding or you can rent it for $15.

Warrnambool Beach Backpackers HOSTEL $
(Map p191; ☎03-5562 4874; www.beachbackpackers.com.au; 17 Stanley St; per person camping $12, dm $28-36, d $80-90; @) A short stroll to the beach, this hostel has all backpackers' needs, with a huge living area, a kitchsy Aussie-themed bar, free wi-fi, a kitchen and free pick-up service. Its rooms are basic, but clean. As well as campers, 'vanpackers' can stay here for $12 per person. It hires out bikes, surfboards, SUPs, wetsuits, kayaks and fishing equipment, plus offers free use of boogie boards.

Surfside Holiday Park CAMPGROUND $
(Map p191; ☎03-5559 4700; www.surfsidepark.com.au; Pertobe Rd; unpowered sites s/d/family from $29/34/40, powered sites s/d/family $31/38/48, cabins from $120-245; @) One of several Warrnambool caravan parks, this one offers good self-contained cabins, beach chalets, camping and caravan sites. It's well situated between the town and the beach.

Flagstaff Hill Lighthouse Lodge GUESTHOUSE $$
(Map p191; ☎1800 556 111; www.lighthouselodge.com.au; Flagstaff Hill; d/house incl dinner from $155/375;) Once the former harbour master's residence, this charming weatherboard cottage can be rented as the entire house or separate rooms. It has a grassy area overlooking the Maritime Village and coastline. The rate includes entry to Flagstaff Hill Maritime Village (p190), the Shipwrecked light show, dinner at Pippies restaurant and a bottle of wine, which makes it terrific value all up.

Hotel Warrnambool PUB $$
(Map p191; ☎03-5562 2377; www.hotelwarrnambool.com.au; cnr Koroit & Kepler Sts; d incl breakfast without/with bathroom from $110/140;) Renovations to this historic 1894 hotel have seen rooms upgraded to the more boutique end of the scale, while keeping a classic pub-accommodation feel. Don't stay here on weekends if you're wanting peace and quiet.

Eating

Brightbird Espresso CAFE $
(Map p191; ☎03-5562 5749; www.brightbird.com.au; 157 Liebig St; mains from $12-20; 7.30am-4pm Mon-Fri, 8.30am-2pm Sat) Polished concrete floors, dangling light bulbs and single-origin coffees brewed by tattooed baristas brings a slice of inner-city Melbourne to the 'bool. All-day breakfasts encompass creative dishes, vegetarian sausage rolls and egg-and-bacon rolls.

Kermond's Hamburgers BURGERS $
(Map p191; ☎03-5562 4854; www.facebook.com/kermondshamburgers; 151 Lava St; burgers $7.20-10; 9am-9.30pm) Not much has changed at this burger joint since it opened in 1949, with Laminex tables, wood-panelled walls and classic milkshakes served in stainless-steel tumblers. Its burgers are an institution.

Standard Dave PIZZA $$
(Map p191; ☎03-5562 8659; 218 Timor St; pizza $15-24; 5pm-late Tue-Sun, noon-2pm Fri) Standard Dave attracts a young indie crowd here for awesome pizzas, a drink and decent music. Its thin-crust pizzas use quality ingredients made from scratch or sourced locally. Be sure to head through next door to Dart & Marlin (p193).

HAVE A WHALE OF A TIME IN WARRNAMBOOL

In the 19th century Warrnambool's whale industry involved hunting them with harpoons, but these days they're a major tourist attraction, with crowds gathering to see them frolic offshore on their migration between May and September. Southern right whales (named thus due to being the 'right' whales to hunt) are the most common visitors, heading from Antarctica to these more temperate waters.

Although whales can be seen between Portland and Anglesea, undoubtedly the best place to see them is at Warrnambool's **Logan's Beach whale-watching platform** (Warrnambool Foreshore Promenade) – they use the waters here as a nursery. Sightings aren't guaranteed, but you've got a very good chance of spotting them breaching and slapping their tails about as they nurse their bubs in the waters. Call ahead to the **visitor centre** (p193) to check if the whales are about, or see www.visitwarrnambool.com.au or the Great Ocean Road Whales Facebook page for the latest sightings.

MEET THE MAREMMA: PENGUIN PROTECTORS

One of the more unique conservation efforts taking place in Australia, the Maremma Project has worked wonders in restoring Warrnambool's once fledgling penguin colony. In an unlikely pairing, Maremma dogs (pure bred, white sheepdogs from Italy) were introduced onto Middle Island in 2006 to protect the little penguins from predators, namely foxes which have decimated its population. In 1999 there were some 600 penguins living on Middle Island, yet numbers were reduced to as few as 10 in 2005 as sneaky foxes found a way to access the island at low tide. Remarkably, however, since the project was launched, not a single fox has been sighted, and the population has grown to around 200.

The Maremma have recently found fame as the subject of the popular 2015 film *Oddball*, a quirky Aussie film based on the true story of the dogs on the island and their owner, Swampy, a local chicken farmer.

You can meet the dogs on **Meet the Maremma Tours** (p190), where you can interact with the canines and learn about their role on the island, either on a trip to Middle Island (summer only) or other times at Flagstaff Hill Maritime Village; visit its website for the schedule.

Graze Urban Cafe & Delicatessen CAFE **$$**
(Map p191; ☎1300 105590; www.graze.net.au; 52a Kepler St; mains from $15; ⏰7am-4pm Mon-Fri, to 2.30pm Sat; 📶) A hipster-centric deli doing the likes of sourdough Reuben sandwiches and gourmet toasties filled with pulled pork, chipotle mayo and jalapeños. Breakfast features poached eggs with anything from kimchi to corn fritters, while coffee is from a Sydney-based roaster.

Pavilion Cafe & Bar CAFE **$$**
(☎03-5561 1551; www.pavilion.net.au; 50 Viaduct Rd; mains $20-25; ⏰8am-5pm; 📶) Sun streams into this industrial-feeling cafe right on the breakwater. Over breakfast, gaze out to the ocean through big glass windows or from out on the decking. Lunch is Mod Oz, with the likes of salt-and-pepper calamari washed down by a couple of pots of cold beer.

Hotel Warrnambool PUB FOOD **$$**
(Map p191; www.hotelwarrnambool.com.au; cnr Koroit & Kepler Sts; lunch mains $12-27, dinner $28-34; ⏰noon-late; 📶) One of Victoria's best coastal pubs, Hotel Warrnambool mixes pub charm with bohemian character and serves wood-fired pizzas, among other gastro-pub fare.

Fishtales Café CAFE **$$**
(Map p191; ☎03-5561 2957; www.fishtalescafe.com.au; 63 Liebig St; mains $13-25; ⏰6am-8.30pm; 📶✍) Upbeat, earthy and friendly, with a massive menu covering the globe. There are plenty of enticing breakfast options too, while its sunny courtyard is a nice spot for a glass of wine.

Rough Diamond CAFE **$$**
(Map p191; ☎03-5560 5707; www.roughdiamond-coffee.com.au; 203 Koroit St; ⏰7am-2pm Mon-Fri, 8am-2pm Sat) So cool that it rocks an ugly brick 1970s motel-style facade – done out with AstroTurf and hipster signage – it won't come as much surprise that Rough Diamond also does awesome single-origin coffee. Choose between African or Latin American beans for pourover coffees, and order from a menu featuring brioche buns, banana on sourdough, and Korean pulled-beef tacos.

Pickled Pig EUROPEAN **$$$**
(Map p191; ☎03-5561 3188; www.pickledpig.com.au; 78 Liebig St; dishes $17-37; ⏰6-10pm Tue-Sat) Warrnambool's place to dress up, the Pickled Pig is smart dining with linen-clad tables and chandeliers. The food is seasonal contemporary European cuisine, which is best showcased in the chef's six-course tasting menu (per person $85); bookings are advised.

Drinking & Nightlife

Lucy BAR
(Map p191; www.facebook.com/thelucybar; 2/167 Koroit St, Ozone Walk; cocktails from $12; ⏰3pm-late) A cool new dive bar tucked down a graffiti-splashed laneway. It's a tiny red-brick space, with a cassette deck for tunes and a drinks menu that specialises in local spirits produced by Victorian distilleries. They make a mean single-origin espresso Martini, and there are also gourmet jaffles, local wines, beers and ciders.

Dart & Marlin BAR

(Map p191; 216-218 Timor St; ⏲5-11pm Wed-Fri, 2-11pm Sat & Sun) One of the city's coolest drinking dens is this old-fashioned-style bar with plenty of character – from church pew booth-style seating, art-deco features and distressed walls, to a battered old piano that beckons to be played. Pull up a stool at its wooden bar to order from its quality selection.

☆ Entertainment

Lighthouse Theatre THEATRE

(Map p191; ☎03-5559 4999; www.lighthousetheatre.com.au; 185 Timor St; ⏲box office 9.30am-4.30pm Mon, Wed & Fri, 12.30-4.30pm Tue & Thu) A major venue for live productions, ballet and music, the Lighthouse Theatre is within a striking space that incorporates the original facade of the 1890 town hall building. Check its website for upcoming shows.

Loft LIVE MUSIC

(Map p191; ☎03-5561 0995; www.theloftbar.com.au; 58 Liebig St; ⏲5.30pm-1am Wed-Sun) Warrnambool's premier live music venue, hosting Aussie indie bands like You Am I, as well as DJs and local acts.

ℹ Information

INTERNET ACCESS

Warrnambool Library (☎03-5559 4990; www.warrnambool.vic.gov.au; 25 Liebig St; ⏲9.30am-5pm Mon & Tue, to 6pm Wed-Fri, 10am-noon Sat; 📶) Free internet and wi-fi access.

TOURIST INFORMATION

Warrnambool Visitor Centre (Map p191; ☎1800 637 725; www.visitwarrnambool.com.au; 89 Merri St; ⏲9am-5pm) For the latest on whale sightings, local tours and accommodation bookings, plus bike and walking trail maps.

ℹ Getting There & Away

BUS

There are three V/Line buses a day along the Great Ocean Road to Apollo Bay ($21, two hours), as well as five daily buses to Port Fairy ($4.60, 35 minutes) and three to Portland ($12.40, 1½ hours). There's also a bus to Halls Gap ($27.20, three hours) four days a week via Dunkeld ($18.20, two hours) en route to Ararat ($32, three hours 40 minutes). There's a coach to Melbourne too via Ballarat ($18.20, two hours 50 minutes) departing Warrnambool at 7.15am Monday to Friday. Buses are run by **Christian's Bus Co** (☎03-5562 9432, 1300 734 441; www.christiansbus.com.au).

CAR

Warrnambool is an hour's drive west of Port Campbell on the Great Ocean Road, and about a three-hour drive from Melbourne on the Princes Hwy (A1).

TRAIN

V/Line (Map p191; ☎1800 800 007, 03-5562 9432; www.vline.com.au; Merri St) trains run to Melbourne ($34.60, 3¼ hours, three or four daily) via Geelong ($24.80, 2½ hours).

Tower Hill Reserve

15km west of Warrnambool, Tower Hill is a vast caldera born in a volcanic eruption 35,000 years ago. Aboriginal artefacts unearthed in the volcanic ash show that Indigenous people lived in the area at the time, and today the Worn Gundidj Aboriginal Cooperative operates the **Tower Hill Natural History Centre** (☎03-5565 9202, 0448 509 522; www.worngundidj.org.au; walks adult/child $22.95/10.65; ⏲10am-4pm). The centre is housed within a UFO-like building designed by renowned Australian architect **Robin Boyd** in 1962.

Bushwalks led by Indigenous guides depart daily at 11am and 1pm, and include boomerang throwing and bush-tucker demonstrations. **Spotlighting night walks** (adult/child $28.95/14/65) are available too, with 24 hours' advance notice. The centre also sells handicrafts, artwork and accessories designed by the local Worn Gundidj community. As well as the guided walks, there are other excellent routes, including the steep 30-minute Peak Climb with spectacular 360-degree views.

Parks Victoria manages the park and it's one of the few places where you'll spot wild emus, kangaroos and koalas hanging out together. It's also home to over 200 species of bird, with its wetland habitat attracting both resident and migratory birds. After a century of deforestation and environmental degradation, a detailed 1855 painting of Tower Hill by Eugene von Guérard (now exhibited in the Warrnambool Art Gallery) was used to identify species for a replanting program; over 300,000 trees have been replanted since 1961.

Located 6km from Tower Hill Reserve in the town of Koroit is **Mickey Bourke's Koroit Hotel** (☎03-5565 8201; www.mickeybourkes.com.au; 101 Commercial Rd; ⏲meals noon-2pm & 6-8pm, pub open till late), one of the most atmospheric pubs in Victoria and well worth a detour. At the forefront of Koroit's Irish heritage, the historic hotel (c 1853) has an art-nouveau facade, ornate period features and, of course, Guinness on tap. The pub is located along the railway trail, so it's feasible to cycle here from Port Fairy or Warrnambool.

Port Fairy

POP 2835

Established as a whaling and sealing station in 1833, Port Fairy has retained its historic 19th-century maritime charm. Here it's all about heritage bluestone and sandstone buildings, whitewashed cottages, colourful fishing boats and wide, tree-lined streets. In 2012 it was voted the world's most liveable small community, and for most visitors, it's not hard to see why.

There's also a number of nice beaches, surfing, fishing and plenty of wildlife to see.

Sights

Wishart Galley GALLERY
(Map p196; ☎03-5568 2423; www.wishartgallery.com.au; 19 Sackville St; ⏰8am-4pm Wed-Fri, 10am-5pm Sat & Sun) FREE Port Fairy's best gallery was set up in a historic bank building by the former curator of the Warrnambool Art Gallery. The multiroom space exhibits contemporary work by local and national artists.

Wharf Area PORT
(Map p196) Back in the 1850s Port Fairy's port was one of the busiest in Australia, serving as the main departure point for ships heading to England loaded up with wool, gold and wheat. Today there's still plenty going on at this charming marina, from the luxury yachts to the weather-worn fishing boats moored here.

Battery Hill HISTORIC SITE
(Map p196) Located across the bridge from the picturesque harbour, Battery Hill is worthy of exploration, with cannons and fortifications positioned here in 1887 to protect the town from foreign warships. You'll also encounter resident black wallabies. It was originally used as a flagstaff, so the views are good.

Port Fairy History Centre MUSEUM
(Map p196; ☎03-5568 1266; www.historicalsociety.port-fairy.com; 30 Gipps St; adult/child/under 13yr $4/1/free; ⏰2-5pm Wed & Sat, 10.30am-12.30pm Sun) Housed in the old bluestone courthouse (complete with mannequins acting out a courtroom scene), this museum has shipping relics and old photos.

Activities

Pick up a range of maps and brochures at the visitor centre (p197) that will guide you through various aspects of the town's heritage. It also has maps for the popular Maritime & Shipwreck Heritage Walk, while architecture buffs will want to buy a copy of *Historic Buildings of Port Fairy*.

Go Surf SURFING
(☎0408 310 001; www.gosurf.com.au; 2hr lessons $40, board hire 2hr/1 day $25/50, SUP hire 2hr $35) Surf school, stand-up paddleboard tours ($50, two hours) and board rental. Visit its website for the schedule and bookings.

Mulloka Cruises Boat CRUISE
(Map p196; ☎0408 514 382; cruises adult/child $15/3) Runs half-hour cruises of the port, bay and Griffiths Island.

Festivals & Events

★**Port Fairy Folk Festival** MUSIC
(www.portfairyfolkfestival.com; tickets $250-300; ⏰Mar) Australia's premier folk-music festival is held on the Labour Day long weekend in March. It includes an excellent mix of international and national acts, while the streets are abuzz with buskers. Accommodation can book out a year in advance.

Sleeping

Much of Port Fairy's holiday accommodation is managed by agents, including **Port Fairy Accommodation Centre** (Map p196; ☎03-5568 3150; www.portfairyaccom.com.au; 2/54 Sackville St) and **Port Fairy Holiday Rentals** (Map p196; ☎03-5568 1066; www.lockettrealestate.com.au; 62 Sackville St). The visitor centre (p197) offers a free booking service.

Port Fairy YHA HOSTEL $
(Map p196; ☎03-5568 2468; www.portfairyhostel.com.au; 8 Cox St; dm $26-30, s/tw/d from $41.50/70/75; @📶) Easily the best budget option in town, in the rambling 1844 home of merchant William Rutledge, is this friendly, well-run hostel with a large kitchen, a pool table, free cable TV and peaceful gardens.

Gardens by East Beach Caravan Park CAMPGROUND $
(Map p196; ☎03-5568 1060; www.portfairycaravanparks.com; 111 Griffiths St; unpowered/powered sites from $38/43, cabins from $125; 📶) One of

Port Fairy

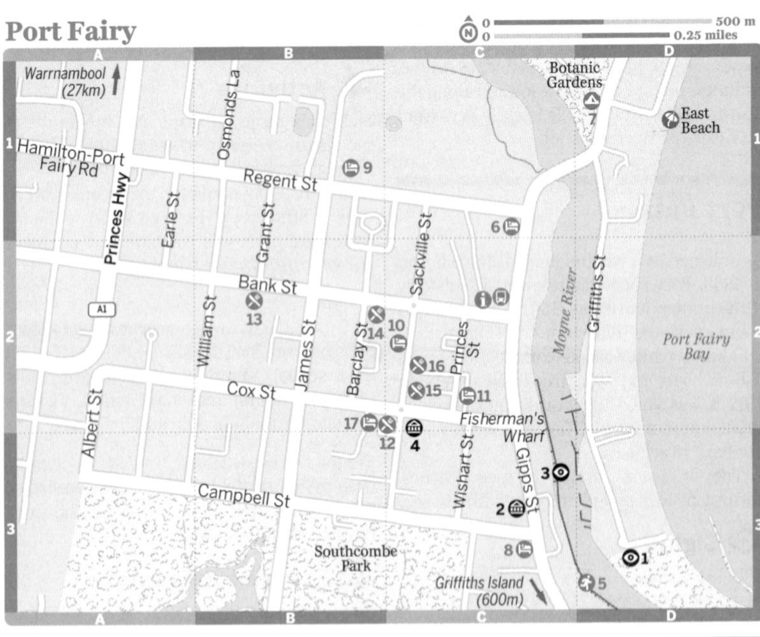

Port Fairy

Sights
- 1 Battery Hill ... D3
- 2 Port Fairy History Centre ... C3
- 3 Wharf Area ... C3
- 4 Wishart Galley ... C2

Activities, Courses & Tours
- 5 Mulloka Cruises Boat ... D3

Sleeping
- 6 Drift House ... C1
- 7 Gardens By East Beach Caravan Park ... D1
- 8 Merrijig Inn ... C3
- 9 Pelican Waters ... B1
- 10 Port Fairy Accommodation Centre ... C2
- Port Fairy Holiday Rentals ... (see 10)
- 11 Port Fairy YHA ... C2
- 12 Seacombe House ... B2

Eating
- 13 Blakes Restaurant ... B2
- 14 Cobb's Bakery ... B2
- 15 Coffin Sally ... C2
- 16 Farmer's Wife ... C2
- 17 Fen ... C2
- Merrijig Kitchen ... (see 8)

several local caravan parks, this place is next to the botanical gardens, 200m from East Beach and a short walk to the town centre. W-fi costs $3 for two hours.

Seacombe House GUESTHOUSE $$
(Map p196; ☎03-5568 1082; www.seacombe-house.com.au; 22 Sackville St; r without/with bathroom from $90/160, cottages $200; ❄📶) Built in 1847, historic Seacombe House has cosy (OK, tiny) rooms, but it offers all the atmosphere and romance you'd hope for from this seafaring town. Modern motel rooms are available in its rear wing. It's above the acclaimed Fen restaurant (p197).

Pelican Waters CABIN $$
(Map p196; ☎03-5568 1002; www.pelicanwater-sportfairy.com.au; 34 Regent St; cabins from $110; ❄) Why stay in a hotel when you can sleep in a train? This beautifully presented farm property has cabins as well as rooms in converted old-school Melbourne suburban trains with all the mod cons (DVDs, air-con, kitchens). Has alpacas and llamas, too.

Merrijig Inn HOTEL $$
(Map p196; ☎03-5568 2324; www.merrijiginn.com; 1 Campbell St; d from $120; 📶) At the heritage-listed Merrijig, one of Victoria's oldest inns, you can make your choice between the quaint

doll's house 'attic' rooms upstairs, and roomier, more comfortable rooms downstairs. There's a wonderful back lawn with veggie garden and silkie bantam chickens, plus comfy lounges with fireplaces throughout.

★Drift House BOUTIQUE HOTEL **$$$**
(Map p196; ☎0417 782 495, 03-5568 3309; www.drifthouse.com.au; 98 Gipps St; d from $375; ❄📶) An intriguing mix of 19th-century grandeur and 21st-century design, Drift House is a must for architecture lovers. Its grand frontage is the original 1860 double terrace, yet rooms open up to ultra-slick open-plan designs, decked out with boutique fittings. It's won a bunch of awards, and is undoubtedly *the* spot to treat yourself in town.

Eating

Farmer's Wife CAFE **$**
(Map p196; ☎03-5568 2843; www.facebook.com/farmerswifeportfairy; 47a Sackville St; mains $10-20; ⏲8am-2.30pm) Hidden down a walkway in a modern lot, Farmer's Wife doesn't need a heritage building to impress, and instead lets its food do the talking. Overseen by the chef previously from acclaimed Stag, the seasonal brunch menu features tempting items such as pork belly Benedict brioche, chilli fried eggs with pork quesadilla and salsa, and sourdough fruit toast.

Cobb's Bakery BAKERY **$**
(Map p196; ☎03-5568 1713; 25 Bank St; pies from $4.50; ⏲7am-5.30pm Mon-Fri, to 4.30pm Sat & Sun) Great selection of homemade pies, including seafood and gourmet varieties. It's also known for its French vanilla slice and homebaked breads.

★Coffin Sally PIZZA **$$**
(Map p196; www.coffinsally.com.au; 33 Sackville St; pizzas $13-20; ⏲4-11pm) This historic building was once used as a coffin makers; today it's well regarded for traditional thin-crust pizzas, cooked in an open kitchen and wolfed down on streetside stools or in the dimly lit dining nooks out back next to an open fire. Its bar is also a good spot for a drink.

Blakes Restaurant SEAFOOD **$$**
(Map p196; ☎03-5568 1287; www.facebook.com/blakesonbank; 57 Bank St; mains from $20; ⏲5.30-9.30pm Tue-Sun) One of Port Fairy's best places for seafood, the Irish-owned Blakes has a cosy atmosphere with a roaring fireplace inside a former horse stables. Most are here for the seafood platter (per person $50), which can be shared, but there's a good choice of local fish dishes too.

★Fen MODERN AUSTRALIAN **$$$**
(Map p196; ☎03-5568 3229; www.fenportfairy.com.au; 22 Sackville St; mains $39, 5-course degustation menu $110, tasting menu from $150; ⏲6-11pm Tue-Sat) One of coastal Vic's best restaurants, this husband-and-wife-run operation earned itself two chef's hats in 2017. Set up inside a heritage bluestone building, the decor is minimalist and relaxed, while the menu showcases seasonal local produce from southwestern Victoria. Expect local lamb, seafood and duck dishes, infused with indigenous flavours.

Merrijig Kitchen MODERN AUSTRALIAN **$$$**
(Map p196; ☎03-5568 2324; www.merrijiginn.com; 1 Campbell St; mains $28-38; ⏲6-9pm Thu-Mon; 📶) Here at Port Fairy's most atmospheric restaurant you can warm yourself by the open fire and enjoy superb dining with a menu that changes daily according to what's seasonal. It has a kitchen garden, cures meats, smokes fish and features an award-winning wine list. Delectable food with great service.

Drinking & Nightlife

Basalt Wines WINERY
(☎0429 682 251; www.basaltwines.com; 1131 Princes Hwy, Killarney; ⏲9am-4pm, open longer in summer; 📶) Just outside Port Fairy in Killarney is this family-run biodynamic winery that does free tastings in its tin shed, with a glass atrium to enjoy the views. They do tasty tapas dishes too, such as smoky lamb ribs, and abalone with wasabi mayo, as well as local cheeses, charcuterie and locally distilled gins, single malts and vermouths. Grab a Cuban cigar to round it out.

Information

Port Fairy Visitor Centre (Map p196; ☎03-5568 2682; www.portfairyaustralia.com.au; Bank St; ⏲9am-5pm; 📶) Provides spot-on tourist information, walking-tour brochures (20 cents), free wi-fi, V/Line tickets, tourism brochures and publications. There's also bike hire (half-/full day $15/25).

Getting There & Away

CAR

Port Fairy is 20 minutes' drive west of Warrnambool on the A1. If coming from Melbourne it's a 288km journey, with the most direct route being along the B140 highway from Geelong.

GREAT SOUTH WEST WALK

The 250km signposted loop that is the Great South West Walk begins and ends at Portland's visitor centre. It takes in some of the southwest's most stunning natural scenery: from the remote, blustery coast, through the river system of the Lower Glenelg National Park, and back through the hinterland to Portland. The whole loop would take at least 10 days, but it can be done in sections, and parts can be done as day walks or even a two-hour loop. Maps are available from visitor centres in **Portland** (p199) and **Nelson** (p201).

Visit www.greatsouthwestwalk.com for all information, FAQs and registration details.

TRAIN & BUS

Catch a train to Warrnambool, from where **V/Line** (Map p196; ☎1800 800 007; www.vline.com.au) run four to five buses a day to Port Fairy ($4.60, 35 minutes). The bus also heads to Tower Hill ($3.20) and Koroit ($3.20). There's also a bus from Port Fairy to Portland ($8.60, 55 minutes).

Portland

POPULATION 10,700

Portland's claim to fame is as Victoria's first European settlement, founded as a whaling and sealing base in the early 1800s. Despite its colonial history, attractive architecture and beaches, blue-collared Portland feels much more like a regional hub than a tourist town.

Though with that said, there's a lot on offer. The Great Southwest Walk is a big attraction, as are seafood and fishing, whale-watching in winter, plus some good surf breaks outside town.

Sights

Historic Waterfront WATERFRONT

(Cliff St) The grassy precinct overlooking the harbour has several heritage bluestone buildings. **Customs House** (1850) is still a working office, but you can ask to see its fascinating display of confiscated booty in the cellar, including a stuffed black bear among other random items. Also here is the 1845 **courthouse**, and the 1886 **Rocket Shed** with a display of ship rescue equipment.

History House MUSEUM

(☎03-5522 2266; Cliff St; adult/child $3/2; ⏲10am-noon & 1-4pm) Located in the former town hall (1863), this is an interesting museum detailing Portland's rich colonial and maritime history. There's also info on the drama-filled period St Mary MacKillop spent in Portland teaching in the 1860s.

Portland Maritime Discovery Centre MUSEUM

(☎1800 035 567; Lee Breakwater Rd; adult/child under 15yr $7.50/free; ⏲9am-5pm) Excellent displays on shipwrecks and Portland's whaling history, plus a sperm whale skeleton that washed ashore and an original 1858 wooden lifeboat. There's also a **cafe** (☎03-5521 7341; mains from $17; ⏲9.30am-4.30pm) here with one of the best views in town.

Portland Cable Tram LANDMARK

(☎03-5523 2831; http://portlandcabletrams.com.au; 2a Bentinck St; adult/child/family $17.50/7/40; ⏲departures 10am, 11.15am, 12.30pm, 1.45pm & 3pm, museum 9am-4pm) This restored 1886 cable tram (now diesel-powered) does five trips a day, plying a 7.4km circular route on a track laid in 2002 that links the **vintage-car museum** (☎03-5523 5795; cnr Glenelg & Percy Sts; adult/child/family $8/1/16; ⏲10am-4pm), **botanical gardens** (⏲sunrise-sunset), Maritime Discovery Centre and WWII memorial water tower. Hop on and off as you please. Also here is a tram museum, historical photographs, a rock exhibit and a toy train exhibit.

Activities

Whales often visit during winter; see www.whalemail.com.au for latest sightings.

The tourist office offers several self-guided walking-tour brochures, including a **heritage building tour** and one that traces the steps of Australia's only ordained saint, Mary MacKillop, from the time she spent here in Portland during the 1860s.

Sleeping

Hotel Bentinck HISTORIC HOTEL **$$**

(☎03-5523 2188; cnr Bentinck & Gawler Sts; motel s/d $70/90, hotel r incl breakfast $115-217; ❄📶) An attractive historic hotel (c 1856) on the main street, Bentinck's rooms offer local character, comfort and overall good value. Room 27 is the pick with water views, spa bath and chesterfield couches. There are also motel rooms around the back, which are generic, but get the job done if you're on a budget.

Annesley House BOUTIQUE HOTEL **$$**
(☎0429 852 235; www.annesleyhouse.com.au; 60 Julia St; r $200-280; ❄📶) This restored former doctor's mansion (c 1878) has six very different self-contained rooms, some featuring claw-foot baths and lovely views. All have a unique sense of style, and they come with complimentary port wine.

Clifftop Accommodation GUESTHOUSE **$$**
(☎03-5523 1126; www.portlandaccommodation.com.au; 13 Clifton Ct; d from $140; ❄📶) The panoramic ocean views from the balconies here are incredible. Three self-contained rooms are huge, with big brass beds, telescopes and a modern maritime feel.

Eating

Deegan Seafoods FISH & CHIPS **$**
(☎03-5523 4749; 106 Percy St; fish from $6; ⏲9am-6pm Mon-Fri) This fish and chip shop famously serves up the freshest fish in Victoria. Whether you go the flake or the calamari rings, you're in for a serious treat.

Mac's Hotel PUB FOOD **$**
(Bentinck Hotel; 41 Bentinck St; lunch $10; ⏲11am-1am) Portland's best pub for a cold beer and a feed is this historic hotel that's most popular for its $10 counter lunches. There's also its more upmarket Admelia's dining room, with historic charm and a good selection of schnitzels.

Clock by the Bay MODERN EUROPEAN **$$**
(1 Cliff St; breakfast $10-16, lunch $16-26, dinner $26-40; ⏲9am-11pm) Within the former post office (c 1882) is Portland's best restaurant for fine dining, known for its French-inspired cuisine, and dishes made with fish bought straight off the boat.

Cafe Bahloo CAFE **$$**
(www.cafebahloo.com.au; 85 Cliff St; mains $12-29; ⏲7.30am-3pm Tue-Thu, 7.30am-10pm Fri, 8am-late Sat, 8am-2pm Sun; 📶) Housed in the original bluestone watchkeeper's house, across from the harbour, vibrant and arty Bahloo serves all-day breakfasts, toasties, Mt Gambier–roasted single-origin coffees and juices, and has a well-stocked bar.

ℹ Information

Portland Visitor Centre (☎1800 035 567; www.visitportland.com.au; Lee Breakwater Rd; ⏲9am-5pm) In a modern building on the waterfront, this excellent information centre has a stack of suggestions for things to do and see.

ℹ Getting There & Away

Bus V/Line buses connect Portland with Port Fairy (from $8.60, 50 minutes) and Warrnambool (from $12.40, 1 hour 40 minutes) three times daily on weekdays, and once a day on weekends. Buses depart from Henty St.

Car Portland is a one-hour drive west of Port Fairy on the Princes Hwy (A1).

WORTH A TRIP

BUDJ BIM CULTURAL TOUR

Based in the town of Heywood, a 25-minute drive from Portland, **Budj Bim** (☎0458 999 315, 03-5527 0000, 03-5527-1699; www.budjbimtours.com; 12 Lindsay St, Heywood; tours from $40) Tours can arrange a tour to visit the nearby Mt Eccles-Budj Bim National Park and Tyrendarra indigenous protected area. It's the traditional homeland of the Gunditjmara people, most famous as the site of some of the oldest constructed aquaculture systems in the world. Note, however, that the team can be notoriously hard to contact, so you'll need to organise a visit well in advance – get in touch with Portland Visitor Centre for more info.

Otherwise you can drive here yourself to visit the habitat characterised by lava flow from the nearby Mt Eccles, a dormant volcano that is believed to have erupted 30,000 years ago. There's a boardwalk with info boards, but it's not overly detailed.

In mid-2016 it was announced that the area would receive an $8-million government upgrade in an effort that would likely see it become a Unesco World Heritage site.

Portland to South Australia

Cape Bridgewater

Home to one of Australia's finest stretches of white-sand surf beach, Cape Bridgewater makes for an essential 21km detour off the Portland–Nelson Rd. Its powdery white sands and turquoise waters resemble Queensland more than a remote Victorian beach. Though the beach is the main drawcard, there are also a number of walks featuring some dramatic scenery and an opportunity to swim with Australian fur seals, which makes this destination one of the coast's best-kept secrets.

Sights & Activities

While the stunning white sandy beach is the main attraction, the road here continues on to Cape Duquesne where walking tracks lead to a spectacular **blowhole** and the eerie **Petrified Forest** on the clifftop (the wind farm is a blight, but adds to its surreal feel). A longer two-hour return walk takes you to a **seal colony** where you can see dozens of fur seals sunning themselves on the rocks.

Tours

★ **Seals by Sea Tours** WILDLIFE
(03-5526 7247; www.sealsbyseatours.com.au; Bridgewater Rd; 45min tours adult/child $40/25, cage dives $60/30; Sep-May) With some 1000 Australian fur seals residing in the area, here you can either visit their colony on a boat cruise or strap on a mask and swim with them from the safety of a cage. If you're lucky you'll encounter other marine wildlife such as dolphins or whales.

Sleeping & Eating

Cape Bridgewater Coastal Camp HOSTEL, CAMPGROUND $
(0427 267 247, 03-5526 7247; www.capebridgewatercoastalcamp.com.au; Blowholes Rd; unpowered/powered sites $20/30, s/d/house from $25/100/150;) Sprawling Cape Bridgewater Coastal Camp has budget options with large dorms, self-contained rooms (linen $5), camping, a huge kitchen, wood-fired pizzas and a cinema in an old church (c 1870), all on a grassy property a short walk from the beach. Check it's not booked out by school groups first, though. It's owned by the same team who run the Seals by Sea Tours.

★ **Cape Bridgewater Seaview Lodge** B&B $$
(03-5526 7276; www.capebridgewaterseaviewlodge.com.au; 1636 Bridgewater Rd; budget s $40, s/d incl breakfast $110/140;) Overlooking the water is this wonderful double-storey house that was built as a replica of the original historic Bridgewater Hotel that burnt down here in 1927. As well as five cosy beach-house-style en-suite doubles – with use of the lounge, fire place, kitchen and dining areas – there are some budget rooms out the back. The owners can pick you up from Portland.

★ **Bridgewater Bay Cafe** CAFE $$
(03-5526 7155; www.bridgewaterbay.com.au; 1611 Bridgewater Rd; mains $16-22; 9am-5pm Sat-Thu, to 8pm Fri;) Plonked directly on the beach, views just don't get any better than this. Enjoy the outlook with homemade sausage rolls, fresh fish and chips, single-origin coffee, local craft beers and wine by the glass. There's free wi-fi too.

Nelson

POPULATION 311

Tiny Nelson is the last vestige of civilisation before the South Australian border – just a general store, a pub and a handful of accommodation places. It's a popular holiday and fishing spot at the mouth of the Glenelg River, which flows through Lower Glenelg National Park. It's pretty much the halfway mark between Melbourne and Adelaide, and likes to think of itself as the beginning of the Great Ocean Road. Note that Nelson uses South Australia's 08 telephone area code.

Activities

Fishing and boating along the Glenelg River are the main activities that bring folk into Nelson; bream and estuary perch are the main catches.

★ **Nelson Canoe Hire** CANOEING
(0409 104 798; www.nelsonboatandcanoehire.com.au; canoe hire per half-/full day $40/65, kayak hire per half-/full day $25/60) Exploring the 65km stretch of scenic river along Lower Glenelg National Park on a multiday canoe trip is one of Victoria's best hidden secrets. This outfit can rig you up for leisurely paddles or serious river-camping expeditions – three days including waterproof barrels. There's no office but they'll deliver you all the gear; BYO tent and supplies.

WORTH A TRIP

CAPE NELSON LIGHTHOUSE

Head up to the top of the still-operational **Cape Nelson Lighthouse** (0428 131 253; www.capenelsonlighthouse.com.au; adult/child/family $15/10/40; tours 11am & 2pm) (c 1884) for fantastic views overlooking the edge of the world. You'll also get shown around the premises while hearing tales of shipwrecks and the history of the area. The **accommodation** here is the perfect opportunity to indulge in that fantasy of living in a remote, windswept lighthouse keeper's cottage. While the historic cottages have been refitted with modern comforts, they retain their maritime charm. You can book one or two rooms, with your pick of a sunrise or sunset view.

There's a good choice of breakfast dishes, hearty mains and cakes, as well as coffee and wines at **Isabella's Cafe** (03-5523 5119; mains $15-20; 11am-4pm, closed Tue in winter), housed in what was once the stables for the lighthouse keeper's horses.

★**Nelson Boat Hire** BOATING
(0427 571 198, 08-8738 4048; www.nelsonboatandcanoehire.com.au; dinghies per 4hr $115, motorboat per hr $55, houseboats per night $410-480; Sep-Jul) Whether you head out for a few hours' fishing or hire a self-contained houseboat, cruising along the scenic waters of Lower Glenelg National Park will likely be the most relaxing time of your trip. The best bit is you don't need a boat licence. Houseboats, which sleep six, come with bathroom, fridge and kitchen, and have a two-night minimum hire period.

Nelson River Cruises CRUISE
(0448 887 1225, 08-8738 4191; www.glenelgrivercruises.com.au; cruises adult/child $32.50/10; Sep-Jun) These leisurely 3½-hour cruises head along the Glenelg River, departing Nelson at 1pm on Wednesday and Saturday, or daily during school holidays; check the website for the schedule. Tours include the impressive **Princess Margaret Rose Cave** (08-8738 4171; www.princessmargaretrosecave.com; Princess Margaret Rose Caves Rd, Mumbannar, Lower Glenelg National Park; adult/child/family $20/13/44; tours depart 10am, 11am, noon, 1.30pm, 2.30pm, 3.30pm & 4.30pm, reduced hours winter), with its gleaming underground formations; tickets for the cave cost extra.

Sleeping

There are nine camp sites between Nelson and Dartmoor along the Glenelg River, which are popular with canoeists but are also accessible by road, with ablutions and fireplaces (BYO firewood). **Forest Camp South** on the river is the nicest of these. Prearrange camping permits online; contact http://parkweb.vic.gov.au for more info.

Kywong Caravan Park CAMPGROUND $
(08-8738 4174; www.kywongcp.com; 92 North Nelson Rd; unpowered sites $23-28, powered sites $28-35, cabins d from $70;) Set 1km north of town, this 10 hectare park is next to the national park and Glenelg River, with plenty of wildlife (including bandicoots) and great birdwatching.

Nelson Cottage COTTAGE $
(08-8738 4161; www.nelsoncottage.com.au; cnr Kellett & Sturt Sts; s/d with shared bathroom & breakfast $70/90;) This 1882 cottage, once used as a police station, has old-fashioned rooms with clean shared amenities. The owners are keen travellers so call ahead first to check if they're around.

Drinking & Nightlife

★**Nelson Hotel** PUB
(08-8738 4011; www.nelsonhotel.com.au; Kellett St; 11am-late;) As real as outback pubs come, the Nelson Hotel (established in 1855) is an essential stop for a beer and a friendly yarn with locals. It's got a character-filled front bar, featuring a dusty stuffed pelican, and a bistro serving hearty meals (mains from $15).

There are basic rooms too, which, while in need of a refurb, are perfectly fine for the night (single/double with shared bathroom $45/65).

Information

Nelson Visitor Centre (08-8738 4051; www.nelsonvictoria.com.au; 10am-12.30pm & 1.30-5pm;) Good info on both sides of the border; particularly helpful for the parks and the Great South West Walk. Also has wi-fi. During summer they have longer opening hours, otherwise they leave tourist packages for visitors after hours.

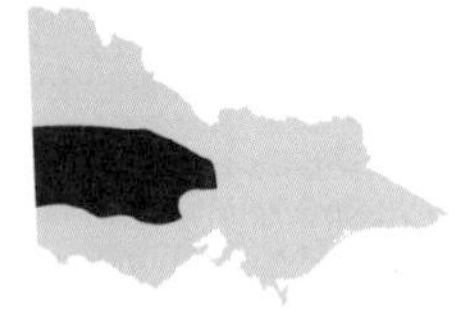

Goldfields & the Grampians

Includes ➜

Best Places to Eat

- Royal Mail Hotel (p230)
- Public Inn (p221)
- Mason's of Bendigo (p215)
- Mr Carsisi (p218)
- Catfish (p209)

Best Places to Sleep

- The Schaller Studio (p214)
- D'Altons Resort (p229)
- Little Desert Nature Lodge (p234)
- The Newnorthern (p221)
- Flop House (p217)

Why Go?

History, nature and culture combine spectacularly in Victoria's regional heart. For a brief time in the mid-19th century, more than a third of the world's gold came out of Victoria and, today, the spoils of all that precious metal can be seen in the grand regional cities of Bendigo and Ballarat, and the charming towns of Castlemaine, Kyneton and Maldon. This is a fantastic region for touring, with a range of contrasting landscapes, from pretty countryside and green forests, red earth and granite country, to farmland, orchards and wineries.

Further west, there's a different type of history to experience at Grampians National Park, one of Victoria's great natural wonders. Some 80% of Victoria's Aboriginal rock-art sites are found here, and the majestic ranges are an adventurer's paradise, lording it over the idyllic Wartook Valley and the towns of Halls Gap and Dunkeld.

When to Go

Ballarat

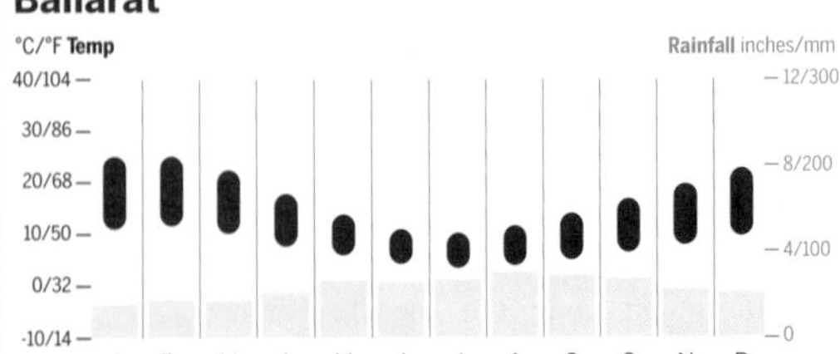

Easter Join the dragon procession at the Bendigo Easter Festival.

Mar–May Autumn colours, hiking and wine touring without the crowds.

Sep–Nov When the wildflowers bloom in Grampians National Park.

BALLARAT

POP 93,501

Ballarat was built on gold and it's easy to see the proceeds of those days in the grand Victorian-era architecture around the city centre. The single biggest attraction here is the fabulous, re-created gold-mining village at Sovereign Hill, but there's plenty more in this busy provincial city to keep you occupied, including grand gold-mining-era architecture, art galleries and microbreweries. Rug up if you visit in the winter months – Ballarat is renowned for being chilly.

History

The area around here was known to the local indigenous population as 'Ballarat', meaning 'resting place'. When gold was discovered here in August 1851, giving irresistible momentum to the central Victorian gold rush that had begun two months earlier in Clunes, thousands of diggers flooded in, forming a shanty town of tents and huts. Ballarat's alluvial goldfields were the tip of the golden iceberg, and when deep shaft mines were sunk they struck incredibly rich quartz reefs. In 1854 the Eureka Rebellion pitted miners against the government and put Ballarat at the forefront of miners' rights.

Sights

★Sovereign Hill HISTORIC SITE

(Map p206; 03-5337 1100; www.sovereignhill.com.au; Bradshaw St; adult/child/family $54/24.50/136; 10am-5pm, until 5.30pm during daylight saving) You'll need to set aside at least half a day to visit this fascinating re-creation of Ballarat's 1860s gold-mining township. The site was mined in the gold-rush era and much of the equipment is original, as is the mine shaft. Kids love panning for gold in the stream, watching the hourly gold pour and exploring the old-style lolly shop.

The main street here is a living history museum, with people performing their chores dressed in costumes of the time; check the schedule for daily parades and demonstrations. Sovereign Hill opens again at night for the impressive sound-and-light show, **Blood on the Southern Cross** (Map p206; 03-5337 1199; www.sovereignhill.com.au/sound-light-show; Bradshaw St, Sovereign Hill; show only adult/child/family $59.50/31.80/162, combined with Sovereign Hill ticket $113.50/56.30/298), a dramatic simulation of the Eureka Stockade battle. There are two shows nightly, but times vary so check in advance; bookings are essential. In July, its Winter Wonderlights (p208) festival is a blockbuster event.

Your ticket also gets you into the nearby **Gold Museum** (Map p206; 03-5337 1107; www.sovereignhill.com.au/gold-museum-ballarat; Bradshaw St; adult/child $12.90/6.80; 9.30am-5.30pm), which sits on a mullock heap from an old mine. There are imaginative, modern displays and samples from all the old mining areas, as well as gold nuggets, coins and a display on the Eureka Rebellion.

To get here from town, take bus 21 from Ballarat Station.

★Art Gallery of Ballarat GALLERY

(Map p206; 03-5320 5858; www.balgal.com; 40 Lydiard St Nth; 10am-5pm, tour 2pm) FREE Established in 1884 and moved to its current location in 1890, the Art Gallery of Ballarat is the oldest provincial gallery in Australia. The architectural gem houses a wonderful collection of early colonial paintings, combined with modern art, with works from noted Australian artists (including Tom Roberts, Sir Sidney Nolan, Russell Drysdale, Albert Tucker, Fred Williams and Howard Arkley) along with contemporary works. There are free guided tours at 2pm daily.

Museum of Australian Democracy at Eureka MUSEUM

(MADE; Map p206; 1800 287 113; www.made.org; 102 Stawell St; adult/child/family $12/8/35; 10.30am-3.30pm Mon-Fri, 9.30am-4.30pm Sat & Sun) Standing on the site of the Eureka Rebellion, this fine museum opened in May 2013 and has already established itself as one of Ballarat's top attractions. Taking the Eureka Rebellion as its starting point – pride of place goes to the preserved remnants of the original Eureka flag and multimedia displays that re-create the events of 1854 – the museum then broadens out to discuss democracy in Australia and beyond through a series of interactive exhibits.

Its Saltbush Kitchen (p208) cafe is worth eating at to sample indigenous flavours.

Botanic Gardens GARDENS

(Wendouree Pde; sunrise-sunset) FREE On the western side of the lake, Ballarat's beautiful and serene gardens were first planted in 1858. Stroll through the 40 hectares of immaculately maintained rose gardens, wide lawns and colourful conservatory. Visit the cottage of poet Adam Lindsay Gordon or walk along the Prime Ministers' Avenue, a

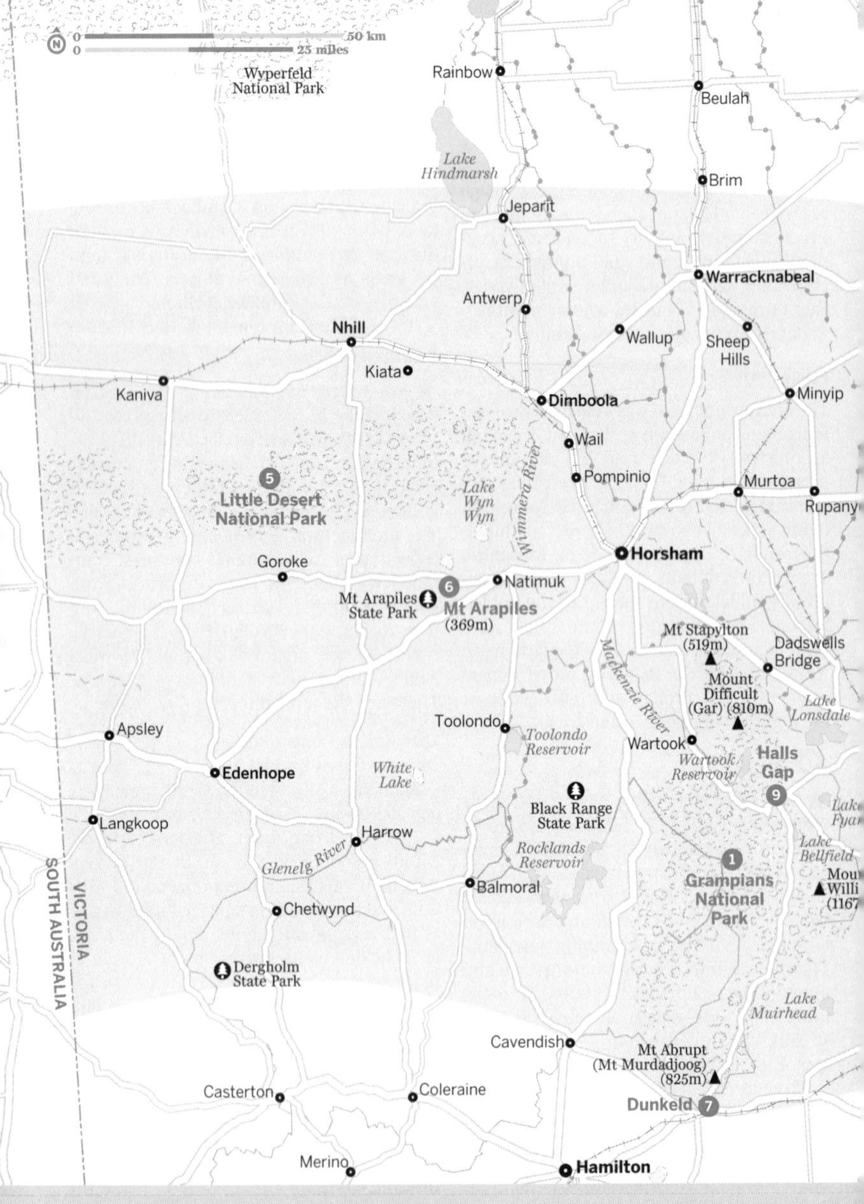

Goldfields & the Grampians Highlights

1 **Grampians National Park** (p225) Setting up camp and walking to waterfalls and stunning lookouts.

2 **Bendigo** (p211) Wandering historic streets lined with elegant architecture and fantastic restaurants.

3 **Sovereign Hill** (p203) Experiencing a real gold-rush town at Ballarat's famous child-friendly open-air museum.

4 **Castlemaine** (p218) Soaking up the atmosphere of this happening country town.

5 **Little Desert National Park** (p233) Camping under

the stars at this remote wilderness getaway.

6 **Mt Arapiles** (p232) Scaling the heights at Victoria's best rock-climbing destination.

7 **Dunkeld** (p230) Climbing Mt Sturgeon, then dining in style at the Royal Mail Hotel.

8 **Maldon** (p223) Revisiting the past along the postcard-pretty main street.

9 **Halls Gap** (p226) Discovering the traditional stories of Gariwerd at the Brambuk Cultural Centre.

Ballarat

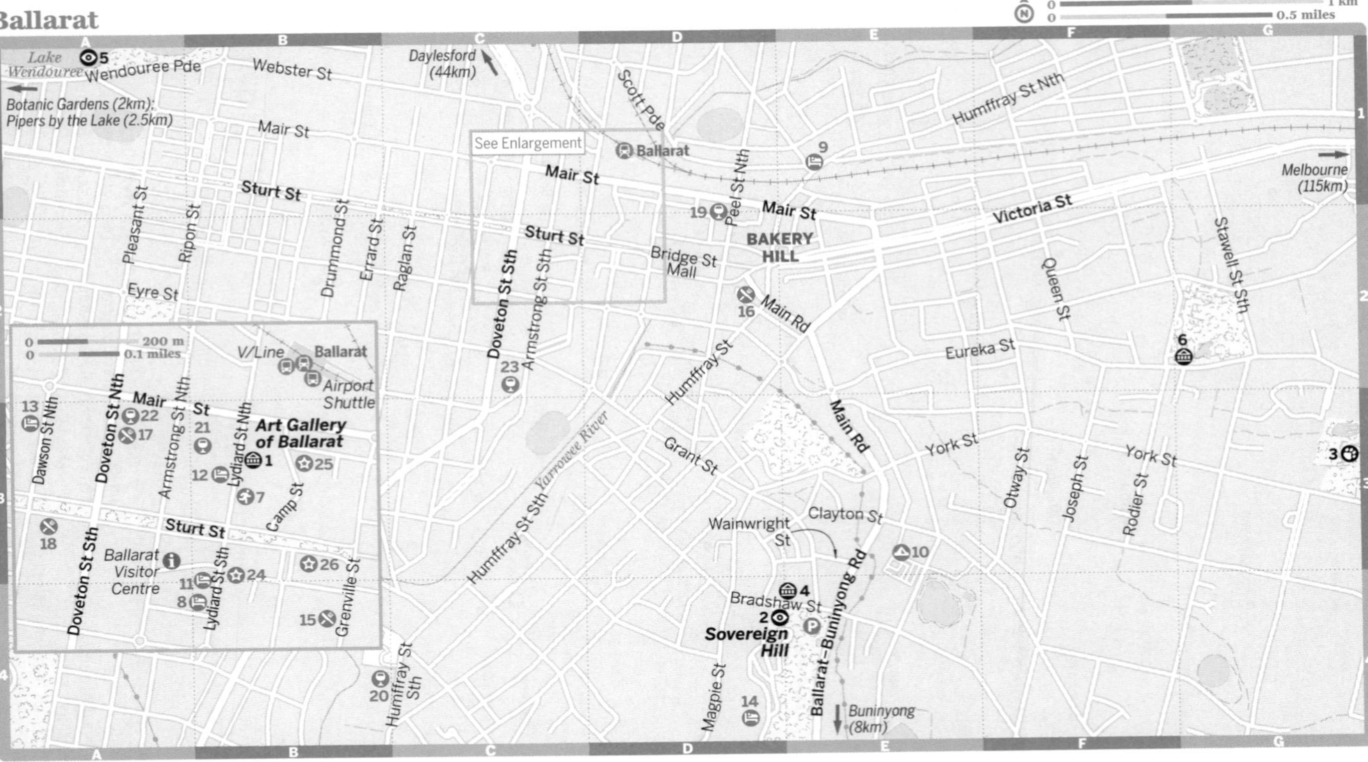

Lake Wendouree
5
Wendouree Pde
Botanic Gardens (2km); Pipers by the Lake (2.5km)
Webster St
Mair St
Sturt St
Pleasant St
Ripon St
Eyre St
Drummond St
Errard St
Raglan St
Daylesford (44km)
See Enlargement
Doveton St Sth
Armstrong St Sth
23
Scott Pde
Ballarat
Mair St
Sturt St
Bridge St Mall
Peel St Nth
19
9
Mair St
BAKERY HILL
16
Main Rd
Humffray St
Humffray St Nth
Victoria St
Melbourne (115km)
Stawell St Sth
Queen St
Eureka St
6
3
Main Rd
York St
Otway St
Joseph St
Rodier St
York St
Grant St
Yarrowee River
Humffray St Sth
Wainwright St
Clayton St
10
Ballarat–Buninyong Rd
4
Bradshaw St
2
Sovereign Hill
Magpie St
14
Buninyong (8km)
Humffray St Sth
20
0 200 m
0 0.1 miles
V/Line
Ballarat
Airport Shuttle
13
Dawson St Nth
Doveton St Nth
Mair St
22
17
Armstrong St Nth
21
Lydiard St Nth
Art Gallery of Ballarat
1
25
12
7
Camp St
18
Sturt St
Doveton St Sth
Ballarat Visitor Centre
11
8
Lydiard St Sth
24
26
Grenville St
15
0 1 km
0 0.5 miles

Ballarat

Top Sights

collection of bronze busts of all of Australia's prime ministers.

Ballarat Wildlife Park ZOO
(Map p206; ☎03-5333 5933; www.wildlifepark.com.au; cnr York & Fussell Sts; adult/child/family $33/18.50/90; ⊙9am-5pm, tour 11am) Ballarat's tranquil wildlife park is strong on native fauna: Tasmanian devils, cassowaries, dingoes, quokkas, snakes, eagles and crocs. There are also animals from nearby neighbouring countries such as tree kangaroos from PNG and a komodo dragon. There's a daily guided tour, as well animal encounters throughout the day – check the website for the schedule.

Lake Wendouree LAKE
(Map p206) Lake Wendouree, a large artificial lake used for the 1956 Olympics rowing events, is a natural focal point for the town. Old timber boat sheds spread along the shore, and a popular walking and cycling track encircles the lake. Alongside the lake are restaurants, the botanical gardens (p203) and a **tourist tramway** (☎03-5334 1580; www.btm.org.au; Gillies St North; rides adult/child $4/2; ⊙12.30-5pm Sat & Sun, daily during holidays).

Activities

If you've gold fever and want to head out prospecting you're free to chance your luck if you pick up a Miners Right licence – available online ($23.70 – valid for 10 years...). But unless you know what you're doing, sign up for a tour with Gold & Relics (p207).

Ballarat-Skipton Rail Trail CYCLING
(www.ballaratskiptonrailtrail.com) Running for 56km along a disused old 19th-century train line is this bike trail that goes from Ballarat right through to Skipton. The trail leads you through historic gold-mining towns and beautiful natural scenery and farmland. The website has great info as well as accommodation options.

Gold Shop OUTDOORS
(Map p206; ☎03-5333 4242; www.thegoldshop.com.au; 8a Lydiard St North; ⊙10am-5pm Mon & Wed-Fri, 10am-3pm Sat) Hopeful prospectors can pick up miners' rights and rent metal detectors at the Gold Shop in the historic Mining Exchange. It also has gold nuggets and jewellery for sale, and its owner Cornell is a wealth of knowledge on everything gold in the region.

Tours

Goldfields Bike Tours CYCLING
(☎0418 303 065; www.goldfieldsbiketours.com.au; 1845 Sturt St, Bell Tower Inn; per day bike rental $50, electric bike $80) As well as offering a number of wonderful bike tours in the region, this is the spot to pick up any number of bikes (including handy e-bikes) to tackle the Ballarat-Skipton Rail Trail (p207). Bikes are available for pick up from the Bell Tower Inn at the beginning of the trail, but you'll need to book ahead.

Gold & Relics OUTDOORS
(☎1300 882 199; www.goldandrelics.com.au; per person $247; ⊙8.30am-5.30pm) After hearing all the gold rush stories, it's time to hit the goldfields on a prospecting tour in search of awaiting riches. Here you'll learn the tricks of the trade, and hopefully find a few nuggets along the way.

Festivals & Events

White Night Ballarat CULTURAL
(www.whitenightballarat.com.au; ⊙7pm-7am Mar) FREE Ballarat is the latest city in the world to be blessed by this wonderful all-night arts festival. It features a packed program of performances, exhibitions and patterned projections over its historical streetscape.

Winter Wonderlights CHRISTMAS
(http://christmasinjuly.sovereignhill.com.au; Bradshaw St, Sovereign Hill; ⊙Jul) Debuting in 2016 was this wildly successful family festival held at Sovereign Hill celebrating Christmas in July. Expect carols, snowfalls and colourful light projections upon the old buildings.

Sleeping

Ballarat Backpackers Hostel HOSTEL $
(Eastern Hotel; Map p206; ☎0427 440 661; www.ballaratbackpackers.com.au; 81 Humffray St Nth; dm/s/d $35/40/70;) In the old Eastern Station Hotel (1862), this refurbished hostel is also a decent corner pub with occasional live music. Rooms are simple but decent value.

Big4 Ballarat Goldfields Holiday Park CAMPGROUND $
(Map p206; ☎1800 632 237, 03-5330 8000; www.ballaratgoldfields.com.au; 108 Clayton St; powered sites from $40, cabins $85-185; @) Only a 300m walk to Sovereign Hill (and 1.5km from town), this caravan park offers a good holiday atmosphere with a heap of play areas and activities for kids. There's a good mix of cabins, houses and en-suite camp sites. In winter there's an indoor pool and heated toilet floors.

Quest Ballarat APARTMENT $$
(Map p206; ☎03-5309 1200; www.questballarat.com.au; 7-11 Dawson St North; studio from $165, 1-/2-bed apt from $175/285;) Housed behind the facade of a stately red-brick building (the historic Loreto Girls College), are these large and modern apartments, with friendly, professional staff.

Sovereign Hill Hotel HISTORIC HOTEL $$
(Map p206; ☎03-5337 1159; www.sovereignhill.com.au/sovereign-hill-hotel; 39-41 Magpie St; r $175-195;) Formerly the Comfort Inn, is this handily located hotel, a stone's throw from Sovereign Hill itself, with bright, modern rooms. Ask about its accommodation-and-entertainment packages.

George Hotel HOTEL $$
(Map p206; ☎03-5333 4866; www.georgehotelballarat.com.au; 27 Lydiard St North; r from $175;) This grand old pub has seen bags of history since it was first built in 1852. It's right in the thick of things and the recently refurbished rooms are tasteful and comfortable, plus there's a good bar and restaurant. If you're thinking of staying here on a weekend, though, remember that the nightclub below is open till 5am.

Ansonia on Lydiard B&B $$
(Map p206; ☎03-5332 4678; www.theansoniaonlydiard.com.au; 32 Lydiard St South; r/apt from $160/185;) In a heritage building that was originally a bank, the Ansonia exudes calm with its minimalist design, polished floors, dark-wood furnishings and light-filled atrium. Stylish rooms have large-screen TVs and range from studio apartments for two to family suites.

Craig's Royal Hotel HOTEL $$$
(Map p206; ☎03-5331 1377; www.craigsroyal.com; 10 Lydiard St South; s/d from $230/280) The best of the grand old pubs was so named after it hosted visits by the Prince of Wales and Duke of Edinburgh, as well as literary royalty in Mark Twain. It's a wonderful Victorian-era building full of old-fashioned opulence – including a grand staircase and an elegant 1930s elevator – and the rooms have been beautifully refurbished with king beds, heritage furnishings and marble bathrooms.

Eating

Fika Coffee Brewers CAFE $
(Map p206; ☎0427 527 447; www.fikacoffeebrewers.com.au; 36a Doveton St North; dishes $8-20; ⊙7am-4pm Mon-Fri, 8am-3pm Sat) Ballarat's best cafe for food is this smart, urban-chic space with dangling light bulbs and wood-panelled walls. Here you can expect the likes of 'cacao pops' with almond milk and banana; peanut butter-and-tomato on sourdough; or pulled-pork bagels with cheddar and chilli. They don't roast their own beans, but its baristas know how to make a decent cuppa coffee.

THE EUREKA REBELLION

Life on the goldfields was a great leveller, erasing social distinctions as doctors, merchants, ex-convicts and labourers toiled side by side in the mud. But as the easily won gold began to run out, the diggers recognised the inequalities between themselves and the privileged few who held land and the government.

The limited size of claims and the inconvenience of licence hunts, coupled with police brutality and taxation without political representation, fired the unrest that led to the Eureka Rebellion.

In September 1854 Governor Hotham ordered the hated licence hunts to be carried out twice weekly. In the following October a miner was murdered near a Ballarat hotel after an argument with the owner, James Bentley. Bentley was found not guilty by a magistrate (and business associate), and a group of miners rioted and burned his hotel. Bentley was retried and found guilty, but the rioting miners were also jailed, which fuelled their distrust of authority.

Creating the Ballarat Reform League, the diggers called for the abolition of licence fees, a miner's right to vote and increased opportunities to purchase land.

On 29 November 1854 about 800 miners, led by Irishman Peter Lalor, burnt their licences at a mass meeting and built a stockade at Eureka, where they prepared to fight for their rights.

On 3 December the government ordered troopers to attack the stockade. There were only 150 diggers within the barricades at the time and the fight lasted only 20 minutes, leaving 30 miners and five troopers dead.

The short-lived rebellion was ultimately successful. The miners won the sympathy of Victorians and the government chose to acquit the leaders of the charge of high treason.

The licence fee was abolished. A miner's right, costing £1 a year, gave the right to search for gold and to fence in, cultivate and build a dwelling on a moderate-sized piece of land – and to vote. The rebel leader Peter Lalor became a member of parliament some years later.

Saltbush Kitchen AUSTRALIAN **$**

(Map p206; ☎1800 287 113; www.made.org/visit/saltbush-kitchen; 102 Stawell St South; mains from $12.50; ⏲10:30am-3.30pm Mon-Fri, 9.30am-4pm Sat & Sun) A rare opportunity to sample indigenous flavours is this cafe that's within the Museum of Australian Democracy at Eureka (p203). Its menu features contemporary everyday cafe fare infused with native ingredients such as mountain pepper, finger lime, saltbush, lemon myrtle and wattleseed. Also try their cocktails, including a white rum with roasted wattleseed.

★ **Catfish** THAI **$$**

(Map p206; ☎03-5331 5248; www.catfishthai.com.au; 42-44 Main Rd; mains $18-34; ⏲6pm-late Tue-Sat, noon-2pm Sun) Run by chef Damien Jones, Catfish is Ballarat's most acclaimed restaurant, featuring a salivating menu of contemporary yet authentic Thai dishes to share. They're probably the only hatted restaurant in Australia to do takeaway too, a recommended option if they're booked out.

L'Espresso ITALIAN **$$**

(Map p206; ☎03-5333 1789; www.facebook.com/lespressoballarat; 417 Sturt St; mains $13.50-20; ⏲7.30am-6pm Sat-Thu, to late Fri) A mainstay on Ballarat's cafe scene for over 30 years is this old-school European-style cafe that doubles as a cool record shop – choose from their fine taste of indie, jazz, blues and world vinyl while you wait for your espresso or Tuscan bean soup. Fabulous risotto and house-made pastas.

Pipers by the Lake CAFE **$$**

(☎03-5334 1811; www.pipersbythelake.com.au; 403 Wendouree Pde; mains $15-28; ⏲9am-4pm Mon-Fri, 8.30am-4.30pm Sat & Sun) The 1890 Lakeside Lodge was designed by WH Piper and today it's a lovely light-filled cafe with huge windows looking out over the lake and an al fresco courtyard. Dishes range from baked eggs and chorizo for breakfast, to pulled-lamb shoulder or battered whiting for lunch. Otherwise drop by for tea with scones and cream.

Ballarat Steakhouse STEAK $$

(Map p206; ☎03-5332 6777; www.ballaratsteakhouse.com.au; 10 Grenville St; steaks $24-36; ⊙noon-2.30pm Thu & Fri, 6-10pm daily) The best steaks in town can be found on the grill at this upmarket meat-lovers' paradise. As well as prime cuts, lamb chops and spare ribs, sauces include creamy garlic and Danish blue cheese.

Craig's Royal Hotel MODERN AUSTRALIAN $$$

(Map p206; ☎03-5331 1377; www.craigsroyal.com.au; 10 Lydiard St South; mains $20-45; ⊙7am-10pm; 📶) Even if you can't afford to stay here, you can experience some royal treatment dining in the Gallery Bistro, a sumptuous light-filled dining room serving European-inspired cuisine. Otherwise, come for a cocktail in the historic, wood-panelled Craig's Bar.

Drinking & Nightlife

★**Hop Temple** BEER HALL

(Map p206; ☎03-5317 7158; www.hoptemple.com.au; rear of 24-28 Armstrong St North; ⊙4-11pm Wed-Fri, noon-11pm Sat, noon-9pm Sun) Symbolic of the Rat's meteoric rise from bogan country town to cool happening city is this massive converted red-brick warehouse tucked down a laneway. There are 16 craft beers on tap (plus 200 kinds in the fridge), along with artisan cocktails, to go with a menu of buttermilk fried chicken po' boys, smoked BBQ meats and mac 'n' cheese.

★**Mitchell Harris** WINE BAR

(Map p206; ☎03-5331 8931; www.mitchellharris.com.au; 38 Doveton St North; ⊙11am-9pm Mon-Wed, to 11pm Thu-Sat, to 6pm Sun) A stylish wine bar without a hint of pretension is this attractive red-brick space set up by local winemakers Mitchell Harris. It not only showcases their own range, but wines from the entire Victorian Pyrenees. As well as tastings ($10 for four wines), there's wine by the glass to go with a menu of local produce.

Red Duck MICROBREWERY

(☎0407 526 540, 03-5332 0723; www.redduckbeer.com.au; 11A Michaels Dr, Alfredton; ⊙10am-4pm Mon-Fri) With a no frills cellar door (literally a table and few chairs at reception), here at Red Duck the priority is all about brewing quality beer – which they've been doing since 2005. They have a few on tap, and some 26 seasonal ales you can choose from the fridge. They've also just fired up their gin distillery, so keep an eye out for that.

The Mallow Hotel PUB

(Map p206; ☎03-5331 1073; www.themallow.com.au; 20 Skipton St; ⊙noon-6pm Wed-Sun) One of the first pubs in town to start serving decent beer, the Mallow remains a much cherished local. It has 12 beers and ciders on tap, featuring predominately Victorian microbreweries. Food is good too, from craft-beer-battered fish-and-chips and pulled pork spring rolls to its signature Mallow burger.

Athletic Club Brewery MICROBREWERY

(Map p206; ☎03-5332 7031; www.athleticclubbrewery.com.au; 47 Mair St; ⊙11am-late) One of Ballarat's best new spots for quality ales is this city microbrewery that does a great range of craft beers. Its taproom overlooks the brewing equipment, and the passionate owner-brewer is good for a chat. It shares space with a restaurant next door from where you can order food.

Cubby Haus Brewery BREWERY

(Map p206; ☎03-4343 1777; www.cubbyhausbrewing.com.au; 884 Humffray St South, Mt Pleasant; ⊙noon-8pm Fri-Sat, noon-5pm Sun, or by apt) In an industrial estate on the outskirts of town is this awesome little brewer that produces a number of session beers to enjoy at its homely little taproom with free popcorn. There's a record player with a stack of vinyl, and live music on Sundays.

Entertainment

★**Karova Lounge** LIVE MUSIC

(Map p206; ☎03-5332 9122; www.karovalounge.com; 15 Field St; ⊙9pm-late Wed-Sat) Ballarat's best original live-music venue showcases local and touring bands in a grungy, industrial style.

Suttons House of Music LIVE MUSIC

(Map p206; ☎03-5333 4393; www.suttonshouseofmusic.com.au; 31 Sturt St; ⊙10am-6pm Tue & Wed, 10am-late Thu-Sat, 9am-5pm Sun) A cool spot to catch live rockabilly, ska, blues and jazz bands on Friday and Saturday evenings. They also have a kitchen doing typical cafe- and pub-style meals.

Her Majesty's Theatre THEATRE

(Map p206; ☎03-5333 5888; www.hermaj.com; 17 Lydiard St South) Ballarat's main venue for the performing arts since 1875, 'Her Maj' is in a wonderful Victorian-era building and features theatre, live music, comedy and local productions. Check the website for a calendar of shows.

BALLARAT PASS

The three-attraction **Ballarat Pass** (www.visitballarat.com.au/ballarat-pass; adult 3/4-attraction pass $105/116, child $55/63, family $279/311) covers entry to Sovereign Hill, Kryal Castle and Ballarat Wildlife Park. The four-attraction pass adds in the Museum of Australian Democracy at Eureka. Buying the pass will save you around 10% off the normal entry price. The pass can be bought over the phone or at the Ballarat visitor centre.

Information

Ballarat Visitor Centre (Map p206; ☎1800 446 633, 03-5337 4337; www.visitballarat.com.au; 225 Sturt St, Town Hall; ⏲9am-5pm;) Inside the town hall is this modern and well-equipped info centre that sells the Ballarat Pass, stocks free self-guided walking maps and offers complimentary internet access.

Getting There & Away

Ballarat is 116km west from Melbourne (1½ hours), accessed via the Western Hwy.

Airport Shuttle Bus (Map p206; ☎03-5333 4181; www.airportshuttlebus.com.au; Ballarat Railway Station; ⏲office 8.30am-5.30pm Mon-Fri, 9am-1pm Sat) Goes direct from Melbourne Airport to Ballarat train station (adult/child $35/17, 1½ hours, 12 daily, seven on weekends).

Firefly (☎1300 730 740; www.fireflyexpress.com.au) Buses between Adelaide ($60, 8¾ hours, departs Adelaide 8.15pm) and Melbourne ($50, 1¾ hours), stopping in Ballarat if you ask the driver.

V/Line (Map p206; ☎1800 800 007; www.vline.com.au) Has frequent direct trains between Melbourne (Southern Cross Station) and Ballarat (from $14.42, 1½ hours, 28 daily) and at least three services from Geelong ($10.20, 1½ hours).

BENDIGO

POP 92,888

Bendigo is a city to watch. New hotels, a dynamic dining scene and a stunning reimagining of historic spaces have joined an already formidable array of attractions that range from gold-rush-era architecture and a fine art gallery to the Chinese dragons that awaken for the Easter Festival. Sitting as it does in the heart of goldfield and wine-growing country, the only question is why Bendigo has taken so long to take off.

History

The fantastically rich Bendigo Diggings covered more than 360 sq km after gold was discovered in nearby Ravenswood in 1851, and later Bendigo Creek. It's said the maids at the Shamrock Hotel mopped the floor every night to collect the gold dust brought in on the drinkers' boots. The arrival of thousands of Chinese miners in 1854 had a lasting effect on the town, despite the racial tensions that surfaced.

In the 1860s the scene changed again as independent miners were outclassed by the powerful mining companies with their heavy machinery. The companies poured money into the town and some 35 quartz reefs were found. The ground underneath Bendigo is still honeycombed with mine shafts and the gold is still around – Bendigo Mining successfully resumed operations at the Kangaroo Flat mine in 2008.

Sights

Pick up the multi-attraction **Bendigo Experience Pass** (adult/child/family $56.50/31.50/155) from the visitor centre (p217) if you plan on visiting a few sights.

The city's most impressive buildings are found in **Pall Mall**, while **View St** is a historic streetscape with some fine buildings, including the **Capital**, which houses the Bendigo Art Gallery.

★Golden Dragon Museum & Gardens MUSEUM
(Map p212; ☎03-5441 5044; www.goldendragonmuseum.org; 1-11 Bridge St; adult/child/family $11/6/28; ⏲9.30am-5pm Tue-Sun) Bendigo's Chinese heritage sets it apart from other goldfields towns, and this fantastic museum is the place to experience it. Walk through a huge wooden door into an awesome chamber filled with dragons and amazing Chinese heritage items and costumes. The highlight for many are the imperial dragons, including Old Loong (the oldest in the world) and the soon-to-be-retired Sun Loong (the longest in the world at over 100m); it's replacement, Dai Gum Loong, will be unveiled in 2018.

★Bendigo Talking Tram LANDMARK
(Map p212; ☎03-5442 2821; www.bendigotramways.com; 1 Tramways Ave; adult/child/family $17.50/11/51; ⏲10am-4pm) For an interesting tour of the city, hop aboard one of the re-

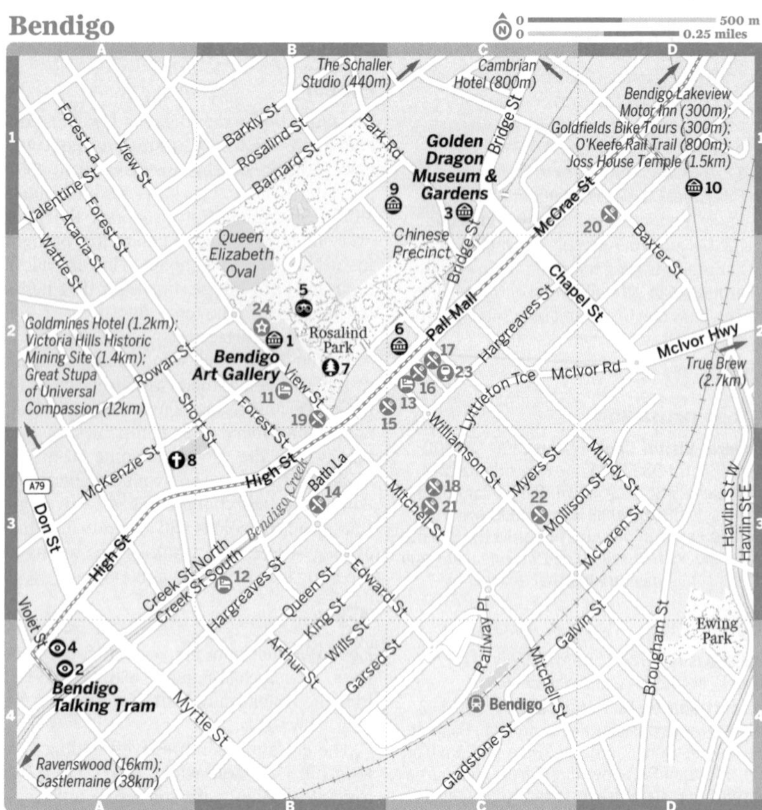

stored vintage 'talking' trams. The hop-on, hop-off trip runs from the Central Deborah Goldmine to the Tramways Depot (p214) every half-hour, making half-a-dozen stops, including at the Golden Dragon Museum and Lake Weeroona. Tickets are valid for two days.

★Bendigo Art Gallery GALLERY

(Map p212; ☎03-5434 6088; www.bendigoartgallery.com.au; 42 View St; free to $25; ⏲10am-5pm Tue-Sun, tour 2pm) One of Victoria's finest regional galleries (founded in 1887), the permanent collection here includes outstanding colonial and contemporary Australian art. It showcases works by the likes of Russell Drysdale, Arthur Boyd, Brett Whiteley and Fred Williams. Aim to visit at 2pm for free tours of the gallery. Its equally impressive temporary exhibitions are cutting edge and have been an important part of Bendigo's renaissance.

It has an art and design shop, while the **Gallery Cafe** overlooking Rosalind Park is a good spot for coffee or a light lunch.

Bendigo Pottery ARTS CENTRE

(☎03-5448 4404; www.bendigopottery.com.au; 146 Midland Hwy; ⏲9am-5pm) FREE Australia's oldest pottery works, the Bendigo Pottery was founded in 1857 and is classified by the National Trust. The historic kilns are still used; watch potters at work, admire the gorgeous ceramic pieces (all for sale) or throw a pot yourself (per 30 minutes $18, an extra $10 to glaze and post home). The attached **museum** (adult/child $8/4) tells the story of pottery through the ages. It's just over 4km north of the town centre.

Sacred Heart Cathedral CHURCH

(Map p212; cnr Wattle & High Sts) You can't miss the soaring steeple of this magnificent cathedral. Though construction began in the 19th century it was only completed in 2001

Bendigo

Top Sights
1 Bendigo Art Gallery B2
2 Bendigo Talking Tram A4
3 Golden Dragon Museum & Gardens C1

Sights
4 Central Deborah Goldmine A4
5 Lookout Tower B2
6 Post Office Gallery C2
7 Rosalind Park B2
8 Sacred Heart Cathedral A3
9 Sandhurst Gaol C1
10 Tramways Depot D1

Sleeping
11 Allawah Bendigo B2
12 Bendigo Backpackers B3
13 Shamrock Hotel C2

Eating
14 Brewhouse Coffee Roasters B3
15 Bunja Thai C2
16 Cantina Mexicana C2
17 El Gordo C2
GPO Bar & Grill .... (see 16)
18 Mason's of Bendigo C3
19 Mr Beebe's Eating House & Bar B2
20 Percy and Percy D1
21 Toi Shan C3
Wine Bank .... (see 11)
22 Woodhouse C3

Drinking & Nightlife
23 Dispensary Bar & Diner C2
Get Naked Espresso .... (see 21)
Handle Bar .... (see 21)

Entertainment
24 Capital B2
Ulumbarra Theatre .... (see 9)

with the installation of bells from Italy in the belfry. Inside, beneath the high-vaulted ceiling, there's a magnificently carved bishop's chair, some beautiful stained-glass windows, and wooden angels jutting out of the ceiling arches.

Victoria Hills Historic Mining Site HISTORIC SITE
(24-32 Happy Valley Rd) FREE Back in the day this sprawling site was the world's deepest gold mine. Today you can wander by its relics and open-cut mines that date to the 1850s, and climb up the poppet head for wonderful views. In 100 years of operation Victoria Hills yielded the equivalent of $8 billion in today's money.

At the entrance of the mine is a small memorial to the Black Saturday bushfires that ravaged this area in 2009.

After a visit here, pop in across the road for a beer at the historic Goldmines Hotel (p216).

Sandhurst Gaol HISTORIC BUILDING
(HM Prison Bendigo; Map p212; 1800 813 153; www.bendigotourism.com/tours/bendigo/sandhurst-gaol-tour; adult/child $15/10; tours 11am Tue & 2pm Sun) Originally opened in 1863, this Pentonville-designed prison (decommissioned in 2005) has recently been converted into the slick Ulumbarra Theatre (p216). To visit you'll need to sign up for its twice-weekly tours to see its very intact cells and learn of its notorious inmates and executions that took place here. Book online or through the visitor centre. Otherwise, if there's an evening show on you *should* be able to access the jail for a look around beforehand.

Great Stupa of Universal Compassion BUDDHIST SITE
(03-5446 7568; www.stupa.org.au; 25 Sandhurst Town Rd, Myers Flat; by donation; 9am-5pm Mon-Fri, 10.30am-5pm Sat & Sun) In Myers Flat, just beyond Bendigo's city limits, this Buddhist stupa, surrounded by gum trees, promises to be the largest stupa in the Western world (with its 50m base and a height of 50m). When completed it will house a massive Buddha statue (also the world's largest) carved from jade. It can be visited, though it was still to be completed at the time of research.

Central Deborah Goldmine HISTORIC SITE
(Map p212; 03-5443 8255; www.central-deborah.com; 76 Violet St; adult/child/family mine experience $30/16/83; 9.30am-5pm) For a very deep experience, descend into this 500m-deep mine with a geologist. The mine has been worked on 17 levels, and about 1 tonne of gold has been removed. After donning hard hats and lights, you're taken down the shaft to inspect the operations, complete with drilling demonstrations. The 'Mine Experience' tours are the main option with four tours a day that last about 75 minutes.

Other tours include the 2½-hour Underground Adventure (adult/child/family $85/52.50/245) and, for the claustrophobes, a self-guided surface tour ($15/7.50/40).

Rosalind Park PARK

(Map p212) In the city centre, this lovely green space is reminiscent of a London park with lawns, grand old trees, fernery, 19th-century statues and the fabulous **Cascades Fountain**, which was excavated after being buried for 120 years. Climb to the top of the poppet head **lookout tower** at the back of the Bendigo Art Gallery for sensational 360-degree views or wander through the **Conservatory Gardens**. You can download a walking tour map from Bendigo Tourism's website (www.bendigotourism.com).

Joss House Temple TEMPLE

(03-5443 8255; www.bendigojosshouse.com; Finn St; adult/child/family $6/4/18; 11am-4pm) Painted red, the traditional colour for strength, this is the only remaining practising joss house in central Victoria. It's 2km northwest of the centre.

Tramways Depot MUSEUM

(Map p212; 03-5442 2821; www.bendigotramways.com; 1 Tramways Rd; 10am-4pm) FREE The last stop on the Bendigo Talking Tram (p211) line is this depot workshop where you clamber aboard old trams and watch repairs and renovations. There's a self-guided tour map for a look around, as well as videos, displays and old photographs on the history of Bendigo Tramways. They're occasionally closed on weekends, so call ahead.

Activities

Goldfields Bike Tours CYCLING

(0418 303 065; www.goldfieldsbiketours.com.au; Bendigo Lakeview Motor Inn, 286 Napier St; per day bike rental $50, electric bikes $80, tours per person from $140) Pick up a bike from the Bendigo Lakeview Motor Inn, strategically located at the beginning of the highly recommended **O'Keefe Rail Trail** on Lake Weeroona. As well as recreational bicycles they hire electric bikes, which are a perfect way to explore the surrounding wineries. They offer a range of interesting themed tours, including a Bendigo to Ballarat trip.

O'Keefe Rail Trail CYCLING

(www.railtrails.org.au) Completed in 2015 is this rail trail bike path that follows a disused railway line for 49km from Lake Weeroona to Heathcote. There's a heap of wineries and eateries along the way; the Bendigo tourism website (www.bendigotourism.com) has a useful map. Bikes and tours can be arranged through Goldfields Bike Tours.

Festivals & Events

Vesak Festival of Light CULTURAL

(May) Held at the Great Stupa of Universal Compassion (p213) is this annual festival celebrating Buddha's birthday, culminating in a spectacular light show and fireworks display. During the day there are tours of the stupa, meditation classes and chanting by Tibetan monks, along with vegetarian food and multicultural performances.

Easter Festival CARNIVAL

(www.bendigoeasterfestival.org.au; Easter weekend) Bendigo's major festival, held in March or April, attracts thousands with its carnival atmosphere and colourful and noisy procession of Chinese dragons, led by Sun Loong, the world's longest imperial dragon.

Sleeping

Bendigo Backpackers HOSTEL $

(Map p212; 03-5443 7680; www.bendigobackpackers.com.au; 33 Creek St South; dm/d/f with shared bathroom $35/55/70;) This small and friendly hostel is in a homely weatherboard cottage with a handy central location. It has bright cheery rooms with all the usual amenities plus a few extras and a lovely courtyard.

★ **The Schaller Studio** BOUTIQUE HOTEL $$

(03-4433 6100; www.artserieshotels.com.au/schaller; cnr Bayne & Lucan Sts; d from $112; P) At the forefront of Bendigo's style makeover, the Schaller Studio is part of the classy Art Series hotel chain that has won plaudits in Melbourne. The hotel takes as its inspiration the studio of Australian artist Mark Schaller, with his signed works in all their colourful glory. Public areas are edgy and cool, while most of the rooms have an almost playful energy.

Its foyer doubles as a vibrant cafe and bar, and has a tiny gym too. They offer rental of its Smart car (per 24 hours $50) as well as bikes (per hour $5).

★ **Allawah Bendigo** APARTMENT $$

(Map p212; 03-5441 7003; www.allawahbendigo.com; 45 View St; r $125-210;) Allawah offers two lovely options in the heart of Bendigo's historic centre, both in former heritage bank buildings. The maisonette rooms at the rear of the stunning Wine Bank (p215) are the more affordable choice, while its more boutique Fountain Suites are across the road in a splendid 19th-century building. For both, check-in is at the Wine Bank.

Bendigo Lakeview Motor Inn MOTEL $$
(☎03-5445 5300; www.bendigolakeviewmotorinn.com.au; 286 Napier St; d from $140; ❄📶🏊) You've got Lake Weeroona across the road, spacious units around the central courtyard, shaded pool, piazza and Quills, a fine-dining restaurant with an excellent reputation. Big plans are in place to redevelop this motel into a four-storey 90-room hotel to maximise the lake views – so watch this space.

Shamrock Hotel HOTEL $$
(Map p212; ☎03-5443 0333; www.hotelshamrock.com.au; cnr Pall Mall & Williamson St; d incl breakfast $130-200, ste $200-285; ❄📶) One of Bendigo's historic icons, the Shamrock is a stunning Victorian building with stained glass, original paintings, fancy columns and a *Gone with the Wind*-style staircase. The refurbished upstairs rooms range from small standard rooms to spacious deluxe and spa suites.

There are daily tours here at 2pm. Upstairs is its **Yard Bird** restaurant doing southern fried US-diner food, while downstairs is its **Gold Dust** basement club.

Eating

Percy and Percy CAFE $
(Map p212; ☎03-5442 2997; www.facebook.com/percyandpercy; cnr Hargreaves & Baxter Sts; dishes $12.50-19; ⏲7am-4pm Mon-Fri, 8am-3pm Sat & Sun) An appealing space inside a former milk bar, this corner cafe does a mouthwatering array of rolls, gourmet pies and all-day breakfasts. It has a nice outdoor section too with picnic tables.

Brewhouse Coffee Roasters CAFE $
(Map p212; ☎03-5442 8224; www.brewhousecoffee.com.au; 402 Hargreaves St; mains $11-22; ⏲6am-5pm; 📶) One of Bendigo's best spots for coffee is this Melbourne-like warehouse space that sources its beans globally and roasts locally. Great breakfasts segue nicely into lunchtime pizzas, sandwiches and dishes such as soft-shell crab burgers or Guinness-braised lamb shanks.

Toi Shan CHINESE $
(Map p212; ☎03-5443 5811; www.toishan.com.au; 65 Mitchell St; mains $13-23, buffet $13-16; ⏲11.30am-9.30pm Sun-Thu, to 10.30pm Fri & Sat) Opening its doors in 1892, cheap and cheerful Toi Shan has been around since the gold rush – reportedly Australia's oldest Chinese restaurant. Fill up on an excellent-value lunchtime smorgasbord ($13). BYO booze.

★ **Mason's of Bendigo** MODERN AUSTRALIAN $$
(Map p212; ☎03-5443 3877; www.masonsofbendigo.com.au; 25 Queen St; small plates $10-18, large plates $28-36; ⏲noon-2.30pm & 6-8.30pm Tue-Sat) Casual yet sophisticated, the menu at hatted Mason's is dominated by local produce to create an agreeable mix of fine food and great atmosphere. Order a bunch of tasting plates such as duck spring rolls or gin-and-tonic cured salmon with yabbie tails to go with a larger shared dish such as its signature roast lamb loin with crispy belly and rolled shoulder.

There's a great wine and beer list as well as divine desserts.

El Gordo SPANISH $$
(Map p212; ☎0401 412 894, 0466 432 156; www.elgordobendigo.com; Shop 3/70 Chancery Lane; dishes $8-18; ⏲8am-4pm Tue-Sat, 6-10pm Fri & Sat) Hidden down a city laneway is this Spanish cafe doing authentic tapas such as patatas bravas as well as soft-shell crab *bocadillos* (baguette) with jalapenos and aioli. There's also a good menu of *raciones* and Western brunch items, to go with Spanish beers, sangria and Industry Beans (p115) coffee from Melbourne.

Wine Bank BISTRO $$
(Map p212; ☎03-5444 4655, 0409 804 032; www.winebankonview.com; 45 View St; breakfast $9-22, mains $25-44; ⏲8am-11pm Mon-Thu, 8am-1am Fri, 8.30am-1am Sat, 8.30am-4pm Sun) Wine bottles line the walls in this beautiful former bank building (1876), which serves as a wine shop and bar specialising in central Victorian wines, and an atmospheric Italian-style cafe serving breakfasts, tapas and platters.

They also hire out foldable bikes (per half-/full-day/24hr $25/35/45).

Mr Beebe's Eating House & Bar MODERN AUSTRALIAN $$
(Map p212; ☎03-5441 5557; www.mrbeebes.com.au; 17 View Point; small/large plates from $10/20, tasting menu 5/6 dishes $52/62; ⏲11am-11pm) Another eatery inside an elegant old bank building (like most restaurants in this area) is the casual-chic Mr Beebe's. It does a delicious range of inventive shared plates, but the chef's tasting plate is a good choice. Otherwise pop in for its tasty bar food with an awesome (and well-priced) choice of beers on tap and local wines by the glass.

Bunja Thai THAI $$

(Map p212; ☎03-5441 8566; www.bunjathai.com.au; 32 Pall Mall; lunch $10, mains $19-29; ⊙noon-2.30pm & 5.30-9.30pm) A palatial-like setting within a historical bank (c 1887), the regal interior of this Thai restaurant is stunning. The food is delicious with authentic curries and noodle dishes, along with the local Brookes beer on tap. Disappointingly, however, the service here is a big letdown. Its $10 lunchtime specials are a good option for takeaway in the park.

Cantina Mexicana MEXICAN $$

(Map p212; ☎03-5443 2788; www.cantinabendigo.com.au; 66 Pall Mall; tacos $6.90, dishes from $14.50; ⊙11am-late) A photogenic, urban space of exposed brick, booth seating and cool Day of the Dead projections, this new Mexican restaurant is doing soft-shell corn tacos pressed in house. They go beautifully with a fine selection of Mexican beers and tequilas.

GPO Bar & Grill MEDITERRANEAN $$

(Map p212; ☎03-5443 4343; www.gpobendigo.com.au; 60-64 Pall Mall; tapas from $11, pizzas from $18, mains $21-37; ⊙11.30am-late; 📶) Rated highly by locals, the food and atmosphere here is superb. Its porterhouse brioche rolls and Moroccan pulled-lamb pizzas are terrific lunch orders. The bar is a chilled place for a drink with an impressive wine and cocktail list.

Woodhouse STEAK $$$

(Map p212; ☎03-5443 8671; www.thewoodhouse.com.au; 101 Williamson St; pizza $20-25, mains $38-65; ⊙noon-2.30pm & 5.30pm-late Tue-Fri, noon-late Sat) In a warehouse-style space clad in warm brick tones, Woodhouse has some of the finest steaks you'll find anywhere in regional Victoria – all cooked on a red gum wood-fired grill. The Wagyu Tasting Plate ($68) is pricey but close to heaven for dedicated (and hungry) carnivores. Its $22 lunch special gets you pizza and a glass of wine or craft beer.

Drinking & Nightlife

★**Goldmines Hotel** PUB

(☎03-5442 2453; www.thegoldmineshotel.weebly.com; 49-57 Marong Rd; ⊙4-11pm Tue & Wed, noon-11pm Thu & Fri, 11am-11pm Sat & Sun) Just outside the CBD in the west of town is this old local watering hole in a grand old mansion (1857). It's famous for its leafy beer garden that keeps on going and going. It has a bunch of craft beers on tap, live blues bands in its wine cellar on Fridays, and a menu of pulled-pork tacos, po' boys and pub classics.

★**Dispensary Bar & Diner** BAR

(Map p212; ☎03-5444 5885; www.dispensarybendigo.com; 9 Chancery Lane; ⊙noon-late Tue-Fri, 8.30am-late Sat, 8.30am-5pm Sun) With its sneaky laneway location and intimate den-like space, the Dispensary is equal to any of Melbourne's hip city bars. They have a selection of 90 craft beers, 40 gins and 60 whiskies, along with quality cocktails. Food is of equal attraction, whether a plate of steamed buns or larger dishes such as Roast Aylesbury duck.

True Brew MICROBREWERY

(☎03-5442 9432; www.truebrewbendigo.com.au; 97 Beischer St, East Bendigo; ⊙11am-7pm Tue-Thu, 11am-late Fri, 9am-3pm Sat) Set up by two brothers in the east of town, True Brew does a range of 16 beers, including six on tap (tasting paddles $15). On Friday nights take its courtesy bus to catch its mystery act, along with street food.

Handle Bar BAR

(Map p212; ☎0417 477 825; www.facebook.com/handlebarbendigo; 73 Mitchell St; ⊙noon-11pm Thu-Sun) Hidden out the back of Get Naked Espresso (p216) cafe is this awesome little red-brick courtyard bar with decking, plants and a shack bar doing craft beers on tap. It's a chilled-out spot for a drink during the day, and can get lively in the evenings with regular live music and DJs.

Cambrian Hotel PUB

(☎03-5443 3363; www.cambrianhotel.com.au; 200 Arnold St, North Bendigo; ⊙3pm-late Tue & Wed, noon-late Thu-Sun) A must for lovers of craft beer, this laid-back country-style pub has eight Victorian microbreweries on tap. It has a casual backyard beer garden with retro couches and large projector screen. Its food is another reason to visit with 12-hour smoked meats and Caribbean-style curries.

Get Naked Espresso CAFE

(Map p212; ☎0411 950 044; www.getnakedespressobar.com; 73 Mitchell St; ⊙6.30am-2pm; 📶) A cool little city cafe bar, Get Naked Espresso is a great spot to hang out and taste quality Mt Beauty roasted coffee. They also have a second cafe across from the Bendigo Art Gallery. For booze head out back to its Handle Bar (p216).

Entertainment

Ulumbarra Theatre THEATRE

(Map p212; ☎03-5434 6100; www.ulumbarratheatre.com.au; 10 Gaol Rd) Opening up within the old Sandhurst Gaol (p213) is this new 951-seat theatre complex that has the largest stage in regional Australia. It hosts a varied schedule of concerts, dance and performances.

Capital THEATRE

(Map p212; ☎03-5434 6100; www.thecapital.com.au; 50 View St) The beautifully restored Capital is the main venue for the performing arts, with hundreds of performances and exhibitions each year.

Shopping

Miners Den SPORTS & OUTDOORS

(☎03-5448 4140; www.minersdenbendigo.com.au; 109 Watson St; ⊙8.30am-5pm Mon-Sat) One for budding prospectors hoping to find a nugget is this shop that specialises in quality detectors, pans, books and maps. It's 6km north of the city in an area called Jackass Flats.

Information

Bendigo Visitor Centre (Map p212; ☎1800 813 153, 03-5434 6060; www.bendigotourism.com; 51-67 Pall Mall; ⊙9am-5pm) In the historic former post office this helpful visitor centre can book tickets for sights and tours, provide accommodation referrals and has a bazillion brochures. Also here is the **Post Office Gallery** (Map p212; ☎03-5434 6179; www.bendigoartgallery.com.au; 51-67 Pall Mall; gold coin donation; ⊙9am-5pm).

Getting There & Away

Bendigo Airport Service (☎03-5444 3939; www.bendigoairportservice.com.au; adult one way/return $45/83, child $22/44; ⊙office 9am-5pm Mon-Fri) Runs direct between Melbourne's Tullamarine Airport and Bendigo train station. Bookings essential.

V/Line (☎1800 800 007; www.vline.com.au) Has frequent trains between Melbourne (Southern Cross Station) and Bendigo (from $21.84, two hours, around 20 daily) via Castlemaine ($4.80, 20 minutes) and Kyneton ($7.84, 40 minutes).

GOLDFIELDS TOWNS

As splendid as Ballarat and Bendigo are, you need to get out and explore the country towns and former gold-mining relics that make up central Victoria to really appreciate this part of the world. Touring the likes of Castlemaine, Kyneton, Maryborough and Maldon will give you a good understanding of the incredible growth and inevitable decline of the gold towns, but you'll also pass through gorgeous countryside and an increasingly flourishing (and trendy) wine and food region.

Kyneton

POP 6629

Kyneton, established a year before gold was discovered, was the main coach stop between Melbourne and Bendigo and the centre for the farmers who supplied the diggings with fresh produce. Today its historic Piper St is a destination in itself, as Melbourne foodies flock here on the weekends to sample its string of quality restaurants and cafes in a precinct lined with heritage buildings. The rest of Kyneton remains blue collar, with a built-up shopping area around Mollison and High Sts.

Sleeping

★**Flop House** ACCOMMODATION SERVICES $$

(☎0438 160 671; www.flophouse.com.au; 1/58-60 Piper St; d from $185-750; ❄ 📶) A boutique and personalised accommodation booking service, here at Flop House they've set up nine wonderful rustic cottages around town. Decked out with style and charm, choose between renovated weatherboards, riverside farmhouses or an open-plan Scandinavian-style studio. The hosts go to great lengths in offering tips for around town, as well as free bike rental.

Piper & Powlett B&B $$$

(☎0417 440 228; www.piperandpowlett.com.au; 63 Piper St; d weekday/weekend $230/280, additional adult $50; ❄) An opportunity to stay right in the thick of happening Piper St, this well-presented Californian bungalow has several bedrooms, a light-filled kitchen and lounge with fireplace.

Eating & Drinking

Kyneton's eat street is along historic Piper St, with its quarter-mile strip showcasing some of the region's best eateries and bars.

Dhaba at the Mill INDIAN $

(☎03-5422 6225; www.dhaba.com.au; 18 Piper St; mains $12-16; ⊙5-9pm Thu-Sat, noon-2.30pm & 5-9pm Sun; 🌶) Behind the heavy wooden doors at the old bluestone steam mill, you can tuck into authentic, affordable curries – classics such as butter chicken, palak paneer and lamb vindaloo. It's an appealing space decked out in retro Bollywood film posters and jars of spices.

La Bontà ITALIAN $$
(03-5422 3683; www.labonta.com.au; 12-14 Piper St; mains $16-34, 5-course set menu per person $74; noon-2.30pm & 6-10pm Tue-Sat) Slotting in nicely along epicurean Piper St is this contemporary Italian restaurant serving inventive dishes with authentic flavours. Expect to be wowed by the likes of *risotto asticino* (Moreton Bay bug poached in tomato butter on saffron risotto) or *gnocchi di zucca* (pumpkin gnocchi in burnt butter and sage with cider-braised duck), alongside a selection of mozzarellas and all-regional wine list.

Royal George MODERN AUSTRALIAN $$
(03-5422 1390; www.royalgeorge.com.au; 24 Piper St; pizzas $12, mains $22-35; noon-late Fri-Mon, 4-9.30pm Tue-Thu) The historic Royal George hotel has a wonderful relaxed country pub atmosphere, but with an added bonus of 16 craft beers on tap and awesome food. The menu is wide-ranging, from $12 prosciutto pizzas or a Kyneton Fried Chicken burger, to 12-hour roasted lamb shoulder with jus and roast veggies.

★ Source Dining MODERN AUSTRALIAN $$$
(03-5422 2039; www.sourcedining.com.au; 72 Piper St; mains $36-40; noon-2.30pm & 6-9pm Thu-Sat, noon-2.30pm Sun) One of central Victoria's best restaurants, this fine place has a menu that changes with the seasons and dish descriptions that read like a culinary short story about regional produce and carefully conceived taste combinations.

★ Mr Carsisi MIDDLE EASTERN $$$
(03-5422 3769; www.mrcarsisi.com; 37c Piper St; mezze $5-15.50, mains $32.50-38.50; 11.30am-late Fri-Tue) For the moment, Turkish tastes and Middle Eastern mezze dominate the menu at the well-regarded Mr Carsisi. It does a faultless job of combining foreign flavours with local produce – the honey-and-cardamom Milawa duck breast is typical of the genre. There are plans to overhaul its menu, however, so expect a possible shift in direction.

Major Tom's BAR
(03-5422 6395; www.majortoms.com.au; 57 Piper St; 5-11pm Tue-Fri, noon-late Sat & Sun) Bringing a bit of Castlemaine hipster cool to Piper St is this little bar with beers, burgers and live bands.

Information

Kyneton Visitor Centre (1800 244 711, 03-5422 6110; www.visitmacedonranges.com; 127 High St; 9am-5pm) On the southeastern entry to town, with a large selection of brochures, including self-guided town and nature walks, and scenic driving routes.

Getting There & Away

Kyneton is just off the Calder Hwy about 90km northwest of Melbourne.

V/Line (www.vline.com.au) Regular V/Line trains on the Bendigo line run here from Melbourne (from $11.62, 1¼ hours). The train station is 1km south of the town centre.

Castlemaine

POP 9730

At the heart of the central Victorian goldfields, Castlemaine is a picturesque historic town home to some stirring examples of late-19th-century architecture and gardens. A rewarding working-class town, in recent years it's seen an influx of Melburnians – known locally as 'latte sipping blow-ins' (LSBIs) – and is popular with artists and tree-changers bringing with them inner-city style, bars and live music venues.

History

After gold was discovered at Specimen Gully in 1851, the Mt Alexander Diggings attracted some 30,000 diggers and Castlemaine became the thriving marketplace for the goldfields. The town's importance waned as the surface gold was exhausted by the 1860s but, fortunately, the centre of town was well established by then and remains relatively intact.

Even after the gold rush subsided, Castlemaine has always had a reputation for industry and innovation – this was the birthplace of the Castlemaine XXXX beer-brewing company (now based in Queensland) and Castlemaine Rock, a hard-boiled sweet lovingly produced by the Barnes family since 1853.

Sights & Activities

Castlemaine has a number of interesting historic buildings, all dating from the mid- to late-19th century. They include the Roman basilica façade of the old **Castlemaine Market** (Map p220) (1862) on Mostyn St; the Theatre Royal (p222) (1856) on Hargreaves St; the post office (1894); and the original **courthouse building** (Map p220) built in 1851 on Goldsmith Cres.

★The Mill HISTORIC BUILDING
(Map p220; www.millcastlemaine.com.au; 1/9 Walker St) Originally the Castlemaine Woollen Mills (1875), this red-brick industrial complex has been developed into one of the town's coolest precincts. It's worth dropping in for a look around; a number of local businesses have set up since 2014, including a brewery, vintage stores, an artisan ice-cream shop, an Austrian-inspired coffee house and even a winery.

★Castlemaine Art Gallery & Historical Museum GALLERY
(Map p220; ☎03-5472 2292; www.castlemainegallery.com; 14 Lyttleton St; adult//child $10/free; ⏲10am-5pm Mon & Wed-Fri, noon-5pm Sat & Sun) A superb art deco building houses this gallery, which features colonial and contemporary Australian art, including works by well-known Australian artists such as Frederick McCubbin, Russell Drysdale, Fred Williams and Sir Sidney Nolan. There's a guided tour each Saturday at 2pm.The museum, in the basement, provides an insight into indigenous and colonial history, period costumes, porcelain, silverware and gold-mining relics.

Old Castlemaine Gaol MUSEUM
(Map p220; ☎03-5472 3749; www.oldcastlemainegaol.com.au; 36-48 Bowden St; adult/concession/child $20/15/free, self-guided tour $10; ⏲guided tours 2pm Fri, 10am & 2pm Sat & Sun, self-guided tours 9am-4pm daily) Built in 1861, the last prisoners moved out of the imposing Pentonville-style Old Castlemaine Gaol in 1990. Today you can take a guided tour of the old cells, gallows and watchtowers, and hear tales of executions and notable inmates. At other times you can do a self-guided tour ($10).

Castlemaine Farmers Market MARKET
(Map p220; ☎0490 366 243; www.castlemainefarmersmarket.org; Victory Park, Forest St; ⏲9am-1pm 1st Sun of month) Held on the first Sunday of the month in Victory Park is this market with stalls selling fresh produce, food and coffee. Combined with the **artists market** (Map p220; www.castlemaineartistsmarket.com.au; Forest St, Western Reserve; ⏲9am-2pm first Sun of month) across the road, it's the place to be if you're in town. Otherwise every other Saturday there's a more low-key market here.

Buda MUSEUM
(Map p220; ☎03-5472 1032; www.budacastlemaine.org; 42 Hunter St; adult/child/family $12/5/30; ⏲noon-5pm Wed-Sat, 10am-5pm Sun) Home to a Hungarian silversmith and his family for 120 years, Buda has permanent displays of the family's extensive art and craft collections, furnishings and personal belongings. There's an interesting mix of architectural styles: the original Indian-villa influence, and later Edwardian-style extensions dating from 1861.

Victorian Goldfields Railway RAIL
(Map p220; ☎03-5470 6658; www.vgr.com.au; adult/child return $45/20, first class $65/60) This historic steam train heads through the box-ironbark forests of Victoria's gold coun-

VICTORIA'S GOLD RUSH

When gold was discovered in New South Wales in May 1851, a reward was offered to anyone who could find gold within 300km of Melbourne, amid fears that Victoria would be left behind. They needn't have worried. By June a significant discovery was made at Clunes, 32km north of Ballarat, and prospectors flooded into central Victoria.

Over the next few months, fresh gold finds were made almost weekly around Victoria. Then in September 1851 the greatest gold discovery ever known was made at Moliagul, followed by others at Ballarat, Bendigo, Mt Alexander and many more. By the end of 1851 hopeful miners were coming from England, Ireland, Europe, China and the failing goldfields of California.

While the gold rush had its tragic side (including epidemics that swept through the camps), plus its share of rogues (including bushrangers who attacked the gold shipments), it ushered in a fantastic era of growth and prosperity for Victoria. Within 12 years the population had increased from 77,000 to 540,000. Mining companies invested heavily in the region, the development of roads and railways accelerated and huge shanty towns were replaced by Victoria's modern provincial cities, most notably Ballarat, Bendigo and Castlemaine, which reached the height of their splendour in the 1880s.

The world's largest alluvial nugget, the 72kg Welcome Stranger, was found in Moliagul in 1869, while the 27kg Hand of Faith (the largest nugget found with a metal detector) was found near Kingower in 1980.

Castlemaine

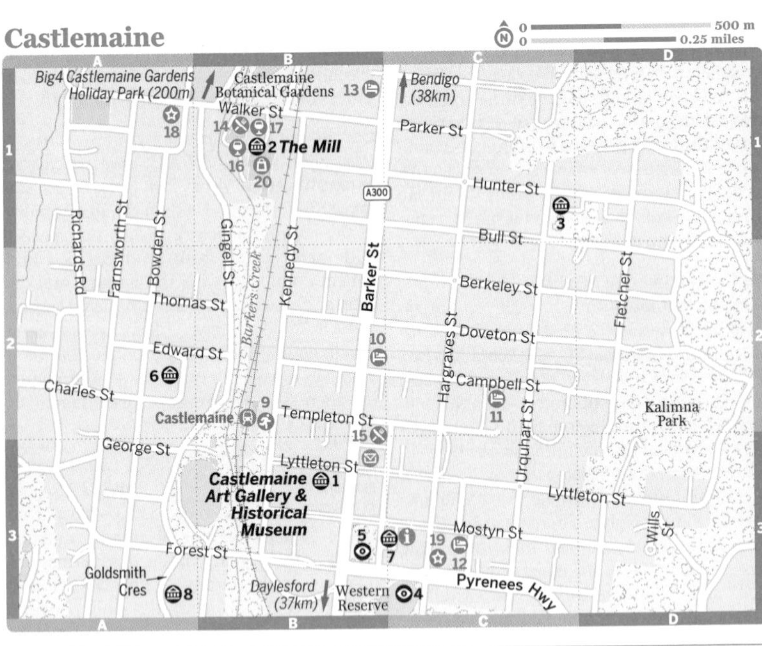

Castlemaine

Top Sights
- 1 Castlemaine Art Gallery & Historical Museum B3
- 2 The Mill B1

Sights
- 3 Buda C1
- 4 Castlemaine Artists' Market C3
- 5 Castlemaine Farmers Market B3
- 6 Old Castlemaine Gaol A2
- 7 Old Castlemaine Market C3
- 8 Old Courthouse A3

Activities, Courses & Tours
- 9 Victorian Goldfields Railway B2

Sleeping
- 10 Castlemaine Colonial Motel B2
- 11 Rembrandts Retreat C2
- 12 The Empyre C3
- 13 The Newnorthern B1

Eating
- Governor's Cafe .... (see 6)
- 14 Icecream Social B1
- Johhny Baker .... (see 13)
- 15 Public Inn B3

Drinking & Nightlife
- 16 Boomtown Wine B1
- 17 Castlemaine Brewing Co. B1

Entertainment
- 18 Bridge Hotel A1
- 19 Theatre Royal C3

Shopping
- 20 Platform No 5 .... B1

try, running between Castlemaine and Maldon up to three times a week.

Festivals & Events

Castlemaine State Festival ART
(www.castlemainefestival.com.au; Mar) One of Victoria's leading arts events, this 10-day festival features theatre, music, art and dance. Held in March in odd-numbered years.

Sleeping

Rembrandts Retreat B&B $
(Map p220; 03-5470 6724, 0418 534 490; www.rembrandtsretreat.wordpress.com; 40-42 Campbell St; r $75) At the back of a historic convent (c 1912) is this self-contained bungalow surrounded by a garden that's a great choice for artists, writers and art lovers. The main building is the family residence and studio of painter Brian Nunan.

Big4 Castlemaine Gardens Holiday Park CARAVAN PARK $
(☎03-5472 1125, 1300 472 762; www.big4.com.au; 1 Doran Ave; unpowered/powered sites from $38/40, cabins $105-155; ❄📶) Beautifully situated next to the botanical gardens and public swimming pool (adult/child $5/4), this leafy park has a camp kitchen, barbecues, recreation hut and a heap of stuff for kids.

★**The Newnorthern** BOUTIQUE HOTEL $$
(Map p220; ☎03-5472 3787; www.newnorthern.com.au; 359 Barker St; r with shared/private bathroom incl breakfast from $164/240; ❄📶) The old Northern Hotel (c 1870) has been beautifully restored and decorated by renowned furniture maker/artist Nicholas Dattner. Rooms are spacious, comfortable and feature art works, antiques and furniture. Though not all rooms are en suite, each room is allocated its own private bathroom. It has a lovely lounge and bar downstairs, where breakfast is served.

Castlemaine Colonial Motel MOTEL $$
(Map p220; ☎03-5472 4000; www.castlemaine-motel.com.au; 252 Barker St; r $142-195; ❄📶) Conveniently central and the best of Castlemaine's motels, the Colonial has a choice of high-ceilinged apartments in a beautifully converted school building (c 1852) or modern motel rooms, some with spa.

The Empyre HISTORIC HOTEL $$$
(Map p220; ☎03-5472 5166; www.empyre.com.au; 68 Mostyn St; d incl breakfast from $265; ❄📶) A beautifully restored 19th-century hotel done out in an elegant period style, and with a location perfect for the theatre and restaurants.

Eating

Johhny Baker BAKERY $
(Map p220; ☎03-5470 5695; www.johnnybaker.com.au; 359 Barker St; pies & pastries from $5; ⏲6.30am-4pm) Not your usual country bakery, here it's all about hand-rolled croissants baked with Belgian butter, among other mind-blowing sugary pastries. Its pies are equally as popular, with favourites including the vegetarian lentil-and-eggplant shepherd's pie, or minted lamb and pea, which you can wolf down on the milk crate seating out the front.

Icecream Social ICE CREAM $
(Map p220; ☎0468 729 743; www.icecreamsocial.com.au; 9 Walker St; from $3; ⏲noon-6pm Thu-Sun, daily in summer) A hole-in-the-wall artisan ice creamery doing seasonal 'one-off' flavours including gin garden, lemon lime & bitters or 'emo kid' with chocolate and black sesame.

Governor's Cafe CAFE $$
(Map p220; ☎03-5472 3749; www.oldcastlemaine-gaol.com.au; Old Castlemaine Gaol, 36-48 Bowden St; breakfast & lunch $8-22, dinner $20-38; ⏲8am-4pm Mon & Thu, 8am-11pm Fri & Sat, 8am-5pm Sun) A part of the Old Castlemaine Gaol (p219), the Governor's has a commanding hilltop location with sweeping views over town. It does local Malmsbury roasted coffee, brekky burritos, steak sandwiches and has an outdoor area with a shipping container bar. It's open for dinner on Friday and Saturdays doing dishes such as char grilled steaks and braised lamb shoulder.

★**Public Inn** MODERN AUSTRALIAN $$$
(Map p220; ☎03-5472 3568; www.publicinn.com.au; 26a Templeton St; 2-/3-course meal $55/69, cafe $15/26; ⏲restaurant 6-10pm daily, noon-3pm Sat & Sun, cafe 8am-10pm) A rustic facade of what was Castlemaine's former fire station opens to a slick yet casual restaurant and bar space with a 'barrel wall', where local wines are dispensed. Food is a set menu of highly seasonal, high-end contemporary fare.

Next door is its more casual **Cafe re-Public** with all-day breakfasts, pork-and-pinenut sausage hot dogs and veggie pakora burgers.

Drinking & Nightlife

Castlemaine Brewing Co. BREWERY
(Map p220; ☎0438 042 901, 0425 323 005; www.castlemainebrewing.com; 9 Walker St, The Mill; ⏲noon-6pm Tue & Wed, to 8pm Thu & Sun, to 10pm Fri & Sat) It's been a long time in between drinks, but finally Castlemaine has got a brewery back in town. It's a good one too, set up within the Mill complex, with 10 of its beers on tap and a bar looking on to its vats. There are pizzas and platters to go with its IPAs, pale, red and golden ales, ginger beer and cider.

Boomtown Wine WINERY
(Map p220; ☎0417 237 155, 0432 382 454; www.boomtownwine.com.au; 9 Walker St, The Mill; ⏲Mon-Thu by apt, 5-11pm Fri, noon-5pm Sat & Sun) Three winemaker mates have come together to use this shared space to produce their wines on site using locally grown grapes. It's within the Mill (p218) complex, and offers free tastings along with a small bar to enjoy a glass. Friday nights are the most social with live bands and food.

Entertainment

Bridge Hotel LIVE MUSIC
(Map p220; ☎03-5470 6426; www.facebook.com/thebridgecastlemaine; 21-23 Walker St; ⏲noon-late)

One of regional Victoria's best live-music venues, the Bridge books a solid lineup of rock 'n' roll and indie bands, such as King Gizzard and the Lizard Wizard, and a few internationals. They also do great burgers and have a killer beer garden.

Theatre Royal THEATER
(Map p220; ☎03-5472 1196; www.theatreroyal-castlemaine.com.au; 30 Hargreaves St; cinema tickets adult/child $15/10) A continually operating theatre since the 1850s, this is a fabulous entertainment venue – classic cinema (dine while watching a movie), touring live performers, a bar and a cafe. Check the program on the website.

Shopping

Platform No 5 HOMEWARES
(Map p220; ☎0417 870 767; www.platformno5.com; 9 Walker St, The Mill) Another reason to visit the historic woollen mill complex is this interesting shop featuring original industrial-style pieces created using recycled timber and old furniture sourced from former Soviet countries in Eastern Europe.

Information

Castlemaine Visitor Centre (Map p220; ☎03-5471 1795; www.maldoncastlemaine.com; 44 Mostyn St; ⏲9am-5pm) In the magnificent old Castlemaine Market is this handy tourist info office with a bunch of brochures, books, downloadable walking tours and bikes for rent (half-/full-day $20/30).

Getting There & Away

V/Line (www.vline.com.au) Trains run hourly between Melbourne and Castlemaine (from $15.96, 1½ hours) and continue on to Bendigo ($4.48, 30 minutes).

Bendigo Airport Service (☎03-5444 3939; www.bendigoairportservice.com.au; adult one-way/return $45/83, child $22/44) Runs direct between Melbourne's Tullamarine Airport and Castlemaine train station. Bookings essential.

Harcourt & Around Castlemaine

About 10km northwest of Castlemaine, the **Harcourt** region (bypassed by the new Calder Fwy) is known as Victoria's 'apple centre'. In recent years it has also developed as an excellent mini-wine centre, an extension of the Bendigo wine region for which the Castlemaine visitor centre (p222) can provide a map and a list of cellar doors.

The announcement of **Harcourt Mountain Bike Park** in Mount Alexander is a boon for the area, with 34km of trails scheduled to open early 2018.

Sleeping & Eating

The Scout Hall B&B $$
(☎03-5474 3172; www.thescouthall.com.au; 138 Victoria Rd, Harcourt; d midweek/weekend incl breakfast from $180/250; ❄📶) In 2007, the former Castlemaine Scout Hall (c 1908) was relocated to Harcourt to be converted into this stylish B&B. Its open-plan interior has high ceilings, gleaming floorboards, wood-fire heater and a stage that's now a TV lounge with bean bags. Other features are its mezzanine loft, modern kitchen (with supplied breakfast provisions) and outdoor deck.

Bress OSTERIA $$$
(☎03-5474 2262; www.bress.com.au; 3894 Calder Hwy; 3-course menu $60; ⏲cellar door 11am-5pm Fri-Sun, restaurant noon-2.30pm Sat & Sun Sep-May) Set over 18 acres is this cellar door that offers tastings of its French-style wines and ciders. It's most popular, however, for its al-fresco provincial-style lunches, featuring its signature wood-fire grilled chicken and seasonal items grown in the kitchen garden.

Drinking & Nightlife

Henry of Harcourt CIDER
(☎03-5474 2177; www.henrycider.com; 219 Reservoir Rd, Harcourt; ⏲10am-5pm) One for cider purists is this family orchard that grows 42 varieties of French and English heritage-listed apples. They produce 'real' dry ciders, with free tastings of its seven varieties, and you'll get to learn about the whole production process.

Harcourt Valley Vineyards WINERY
(☎03-5474 2223; www.harcourtvalley.com.au; 3339 Harmony Way, Harcourt; ⏲11am-6pm) As well as producing shiraz, riesling and chardonnay, Harcourt Valley does a ginger beer and their 'Sightings' American pale ale – named after numerous big cat sightings on the property.

Blackjack Wines WINE
(☎03-5474 2355; www.blackjackwines.net.au; Harmony Way; ⏲11am-5pm Sat & Sun) Drop by Blackjack's Wine cellar door to taste its range of reds, including award-winning shiraz and blends.

Getting There & Away

The main places of interest surrounding Castlemaine lie around 10km north of town along the Midland Hwy.

Castlemaine Bus Lines (03-5472 1455; www.castlemainebuslines.com.au) has three daily buses a week from Castlemaine to Harcourt.

Maldon

POP 1432

Like a pop-up folk museum, the whole of tiny Maldon is a well-preserved relic of the gold-rush era, with many fine buildings constructed from local stone. The population is significantly lower than the 20,000 who used to work the local goldfields, but this is still a living, working town – packed with tourists on weekends but reverting to its sleepy self during the week.

Sights & Activities

Evidence of those heady mining days can be seen around town – you can't miss the 24m-high **Beehive Chimney**, just east of Main St. A short trip south along High St reveals the remains of the **North British Mine**, where interpretive boards tell the story of what was once one of the world's richest mines.

Mt Tarrengower VIEWPOINT

Take the 3km drive up to Mt Tarrengower for panoramic views from the poppet-head lookout.

Carman's Tunnel HISTORIC SITE

(03-5475 2656; off Parkin's Reef Rd; adult/child $7.50/2.50; tours 1.30pm, 2.30pm & 3.30pm Sat & Sun, daily in school holidays) Carman's Tunnel is a 570m-long mine tunnel that was excavated in the 1880s and took two years to dig, yet produced only $300 worth of gold. For a hands-on experience, descend with a guide for a 45-minute candlelit tour.

Festivals & Events

Twilight Food & Wine Festival WINE, FOOD

(www.tasteofgold.com; Jan) Fine food, lanterns, live music and wine tasting along Maldon's main street in early January. Arrive by **steam train** (03-5470 6658; www.vgr.com.au; adult/child return $45/20, 1st class $65/60).

Maldon Folk Festival MUSIC

(www.maldonfolkfestival.com; 2-day ticket $150; Oct or Nov) Maldon's main event is a four-day festival attracting dozens of performers, who provide a wide variety of world music at venues around town and at the main stage at Mt Tarrengower Reserve.

Sleeping

Butts Reserve Camp Site CAMPGROUND $

(13 19 63; www.parkweb.vic.gov.au; Mt Tarrengower Rd) FREE A free camp site with toilets and picnic tables. From High St, head west along Franklin St and follow the signs to Mt Tarrengower.

Maldon Caravan Park CARAVAN PARK $

(03-5475 2344; www.maldoncaravanpark.com.au; 11 Hospital St; unpowered site $18-30, powered sites from $30-35, d cabins $70-140;) In town but backing up to the bush, this friendly park has a camp kitchen, barbecues and swimming pool next door. Call ahead for the free courtesy bus to the Kangaroo Hotel (p223).

Maldon's Eaglehawk MOTEL $

(03-5475 2750; www.maldoneaglehawk.com; 35 Reef St; r $105-125;) Beautiful heritage units here are set in delightful grounds with little alcoves overlooking the pool, barbecue nooks and vine-trimmed verandahs.

Eating & Drinking

Berryman's Café & Tearooms CAFE $

(03-5475 2904; 30 Main St; meals from $6-12; 8am-5pm) Disappear into this classic old-style tearoom for its Devonshire tea ($7.50), a slice of lemon tart, or enjoy a pie and light lunch on the footpath.

Miss Pritchard's Pantry CAFE $$

(03-5475 2282; www.facebook.com/misspritchardspantry; 31 High St; mains $17-26; 9am-4pm Wed-Sun, to 9pm Sat) This cute weatherboard-cottage cafe is run by a husband-wife team doing an eclectic daily changing menu of homemade comfort food and cakes. There are also local beers and wines to enjoy at its street-side tables or rear courtyard with hay bales for chairs.

Kangaroo Hotel PUB

(03-5475 2214; www.thekangaroohotel.com.au; cnr High & Fountain Sts; 3-10.30pm Mon & Tue, noon-late Wed-Sun) A pub since 1856, the Kangaroo is a Maldon institution and is still the go-to place for meals in its beer garden, a jug of beer on the street side tables, a lively pool table and music on weekends.

Information

Maldon Visitor Centre (03-5475 2569; www.maldoncastlemaine.com.au/maldon; 95

WORTH A TRIP

CLUNES

It was in Clunes, roughly halfway between Maryborough and Ballarat, that a find in June 1851 sparked the gold rush that would transform Victoria's fortunes. These days, the small town (population 1656) is a quintessential gold-mining relic, with gorgeous 19th-century porticoed buildings whose grandeur seems way out of proportion to the town's current size.

But Clunes has another, more modern claim to fame. The town hosts the annual **Clunes Booktown Festival** (www.clunesbooktown.com.au; May) in early May and is home to no fewer than (at last count) eight bookstores, most of which are a bibliophile's delight, with a focus on the secondhand trade. In 2012 it was awarded the status of Australia's first international book town. It will host the 2018 Biannual Conference of the International Organisation of Booktowns. For more info on literary events visit www.clunesbooktown.com.au.

Definitely more interesting than it sounds, the town's **bottle museum** is located within a beautiful historic school (c 1881) and knitting mill, and also the location of the **Clunes Visitor Centre** (03-5345 3896; www.visitclunes.com.au; 70 Bailey St; 11am-4pm Thu-Sun). It has a fascinating range of items, including bottles from the old Clunes Brewery and cordial factory, porcelain 19th-century wine bottles from Milawa and Rutherglen, and a small reproduction of a historic street.

For lunch, drop into the **Bread & Circus Provedore** (0412 223 554; 53 Fraser St; 8.30am-4.30pm Wed & Sun;) for its delectable homemade pastries and pies. Afterwards, stop in at the **Mount Beckworth Wines** (03-5343 4207; www.mountbeckworthwines.com.au; 48 Fraser St; Fri-Sun 11am-5pm) enoteca for tasting, or grab a glass of wine ($5) or a pale ale to enjoy on the picturesque street.

Located halfway between Ballarat and Daylesford, Clunes is approximately a 30-minute drive in either direction. It's 139km from Melbourne. The town is on the train line with two to three daily departures heading to Ballarat ($4.80, 30 minutes) and Melbourne ($20.40, 1½ to 2½ hours).

High St; 9am-5pm) Among the stacks of info, pick up the *Information Guide* and the *Historic Town Walk* brochure, which guides you past some of the town's most historic buildings. Also sells local books, and has internet access.

Getting There & Away

Maldon is 19km northwest of Castlemaine along the Bridgewater-Maldon Rd (C282).

Castlemaine Bus Lines (p223) runs three to four buses a day between Maldon and Castlemaine ($3.20, 20 minutes); the last bus back to Castlemaine is around 5pm.

Maryborough

POP 7174

Maryborough is part of central Victoria's 'Golden Triangle', where prospectors still turn up a nugget or two. The town's pride and joy is the magnificent railway station, and now that passenger trains are running here again from Melbourne, it's worth a day trip. It's a classic goldfields country town blissfully free of the gentrification undergone in neighbouring towns of Castlemaine and Kyneton.

Sights

Maryborough Railway Station HISTORIC BUILDING

(03-5461 4683; 38 Victoria St; 10am-5pm) FREE The town boasts plenty of impressive Victorian-era buildings, but Maryborough Railway Station leaves them all for dead. Built in 1892 the inordinately large station, complete with clock tower, was described by Mark Twain as 'a train station with a town attached'. Still very much operational, today it also houses the Railway Cafe & Tracks Bar (p225) and **Museum of Australian History and Art Gallery** (0477 589 692; 29 Station St; admission $6; 10am-4pm Thu-Sun).

Tours

★**Coiltek Gold Centre** TOURS

(03-5460 4700; www.thegoldcentre.com.au; 6 Drive-in Ct; tours per person $140; 8.30am-5pm Mon-Thu, 9am-4.30pm Fri & Sat, 9am-5pm Sun) If you're interested in finding your own gold nuggets, Coiltek Gold Centre offers full-day prospecting courses with state-of-the-art metal detectors. It also sells and hires out prospecting gear, booklets and maps.

Sleeping & Eating

Maryborough Caravan Park CARAVAN PARK $
(03-5460 4848; www.maryboroughcaravanpark.com.au; 7-9 Holyrood St; unpowered sites $26-31, powered sites $32-37, cabins $90-140;) Close to the town centre and nicely located beside Lake Victoria, the caravan park is well set up, with Maryborough's cheapest accommodation. It's set on 9 acres and is popular with families, with playgrounds, a footy oval and canoeing and fishing in the lake. Also has a camp kitchen for cooking.

Railway Cafe & Tracks Bar CAFE $$
(03-5461 1362; www.railwaycafe.com.au; Maryborough Railway Station, 29 Station St; cafe $12-22, restaurant $26-39; 10am-4pm Mon & Wed, 10am-10pm Thu-Sat, 9am-5pm Sun;) Inside Maryborough's grand railway station is this lovely space with polished floorboards and period furnishings. It's now used as a cafe, restaurant and bar, and there's also seating on the platform itself or in a white-tableclothed dining room. It has a gallery space exhibiting contemporary works, and hosts regular events and live music.

Information

Central Goldfields Visitor Centre (03-5460 4511; www.visitmaryborough.com.au; cnr Alma & Nolan Sts; 9am-5pm) Loads of helpful maps and friendly staff. Also has a life-size replica of the famous Welcome Stranger nugget, found not too far from here.

Getting There & Away

Maryborough is 169km northwest of Melbourne via the Calder and Pyrenees Fwys – just over a two-hour drive.

It's 69km southwest of Bendigo, and around 50km west of Castlemaine. Heading further west it's 136km to Halls Gap (1¾ hours).

By public transport, take the train from Melbourne's Southern Cross ($23, 2¼ hours), from where there's a number of connecting options via Ballarat or Castlemaine, either by awaiting bus or train.

THE GRAMPIANS

Rising up from the western Victorian plains, and acting as a haven for bushwalkers, rock climbers and nature lovers, the Grampians are one of the state's most outstanding natural and cultural features. The rich diversity of wildlife and flora, unique rock formations, Aboriginal rock art, spectacular viewpoints and an extensive network of trails and bush camp sites offers something for everyone. The local Indigenous Jardwadjali people called the mountains Gariwerd – in the local language *'gari'* means 'pointed mountain', while *'werd'* means 'shoulder'. Explorer Major Thomas Mitchell named the ranges the Grampians after the mountains in Scotland.

Grampians National Park (Gariwerd)

It's one thing to appreciate the Grampians' spectacular backdrop from afar – ie from Halls Gap with glass of wine in hand – but don't leave the region without getting out into the national park itself. With more than 150km of well-marked walking tracks, ranging from half-hour strolls to overnight treks through difficult terrain, there's something here to suit all levels. Along with scenic drives and adventure activities such as abseiling and rock climbing, there are many ways to experience the park.

In mid-January 2014, a series of bushfires swept through the Grampians region, with the northern region the hardest hit. Homes were lost around Wartook and Brimpaen, while large swathes of forest turned to ash in the areas around Mt Difficult. In spite of the fires, the Grampians remain very much open for business – check with the various visitors centres and Parks Victoria to see which, if any, trails are closed.

Orientation

The four greatest mountain ranges of the Grampians are the Mt Difficult Range in the north, Mt William Range in the east, Serra Range in the southeast and Victoria Range in the southwest. They spread from Ararat to the Wartook Valley and from Dunkeld almost to Horsham. Halls Gap, the main accommodation base and service town, lies in the Fyans Valley. The smaller Wonderland Range, close to Halls Gap, has some of the most splendid and accessible outlooks, such as those that go to the Pinnacles or Silverband Falls.

Sights & Activities

One of the most popular sights is spectacular **MacKenzie Falls**. From the car park the steep 600m path leads to the base of the falls and a large plunge pool (no swimming). Other popular places include: **Boroka Lookout**, with excellent views over Halls Gap and Lake Bellfield, and **Reed Lookout**, with its short walk to the **Balconies** and views over Lake Wartook.

Tours

Hangin' Out OUTDOORS

(☎0407 684 831; www.hanginout.com.au; 4hr/full-day rock climbing from $75/130) Rock-climbing specialists who will get you started with a four-hour introductory session and private guiding. Experienced guide Earl will get you onto the cliff faces, giving you a lively interpretation of the surrounding country as you go. His full-day adventure walk includes rock climbs and abseils – an exhilarating Grampians experience.

Grampians Mountain Adventure Company ADVENTURE

(GMAC; ☎0427 747 047; www.grampiansadventure.com.au; half-/full-day from $120/160) Specialises in rock climbing and abseiling adventures, and instruction from beginner to advanced.

Camping

Parks Victoria maintains **camp sites** (per vehicle or six people free-$28.70) throughout the park, with toilets, picnic tables and fireplaces (BYO water). Permits are required; you can register and pay at the office at the Brambuk Cultural Centre. Bush camping is permitted (no campfires); download the parks notes at www.parkweb.vic.gov.au for a listing of sites.

Information

Parks Victoria (Map p229; ☎03-5361 4000, 13 19 63; www.parkweb.vic.gov.au; 277 Grampians Tourist Rd, Brambuk Cultural Centre, Halls Gap) The Brambuk Cultural Centre at Halls Gap is the place for park maps and advice about where to go, where to camp and what you might see. They also issue camping permits and fishing permits required for fishing in local streams.

ROCK ART

Traditional Aboriginal owners have been occupying Gariwerd for more than 20,000 years and this is the most accessible place in Victoria to see Indigenous rock art. Sites include **Bunjil's Shelter**, near Stawell, one of Victoria's most sacred Indigenous sites, best seen on a guided tour from the Brambuk Cultural Centre (p228). Other rock-art sites in the west of the park are the **Manja Shelter**, reached from the Harrop Track car park, and the **Billimina Shelter**, near the Buandik camping ground. In the north is the **Ngamadjidj Shelter**, reached from the Stapylton camping ground.

These paintings, in protected rock overhangs, are mostly handprints, animal tracks and stick figures. They indicate the esteem in which these mountains are held by local Indigenous communities and should be treated with respect.

Halls Gap

POP 613

Nudging up against the craggy Wonderland Range, Halls Gap is a pretty little town – you might even say sleepy if you visit midweek in winter, but boy does it get busy during holidays. This is the main accommodation base and easiest access for the best of the Grampians. The single street through town has a neat little knot of shops, a supermarket, adventure-activity offices, restaurants and cafes.

There are plenty of kangaroos about its grassy surrounds, with the football oval being a particular favourite hangout. Emus are also often spotted.

Sights & Activities

★**Brambuk Cultural Centre** CULTURAL CENTRE

(Map p229; ☎03-5361 4000, 03-8427 2311; www.brambuk.com.au; 277 Grampians Rd; gold coin donation; ⏲9am-5pm) FREE Don't leave Halls Gap without missing the superb cultural centre at Brambuk, 2.5km south of town. Run by five Koori communities in conjunction with Parks Victoria, the centre offers insights into local culture and history through traditional stories, art, music, dance, weapons, tools and photographs.

The building itself is a striking design that combines timeless Aboriginal motifs with contemporary design and building materials. Its flowing orange roof represents the open wings of a cockatoo, as well as referencing the peaks of the Grampians.

The **Gariwerd Dreaming Theatre** (tickets adult/child/family $5/3/15) shows two 15-minutes films explaining Dreaming stories of Gariwerd and the creation story of Bunjil. The ceiling here represents the southern

The Grampians (Gariwerd)

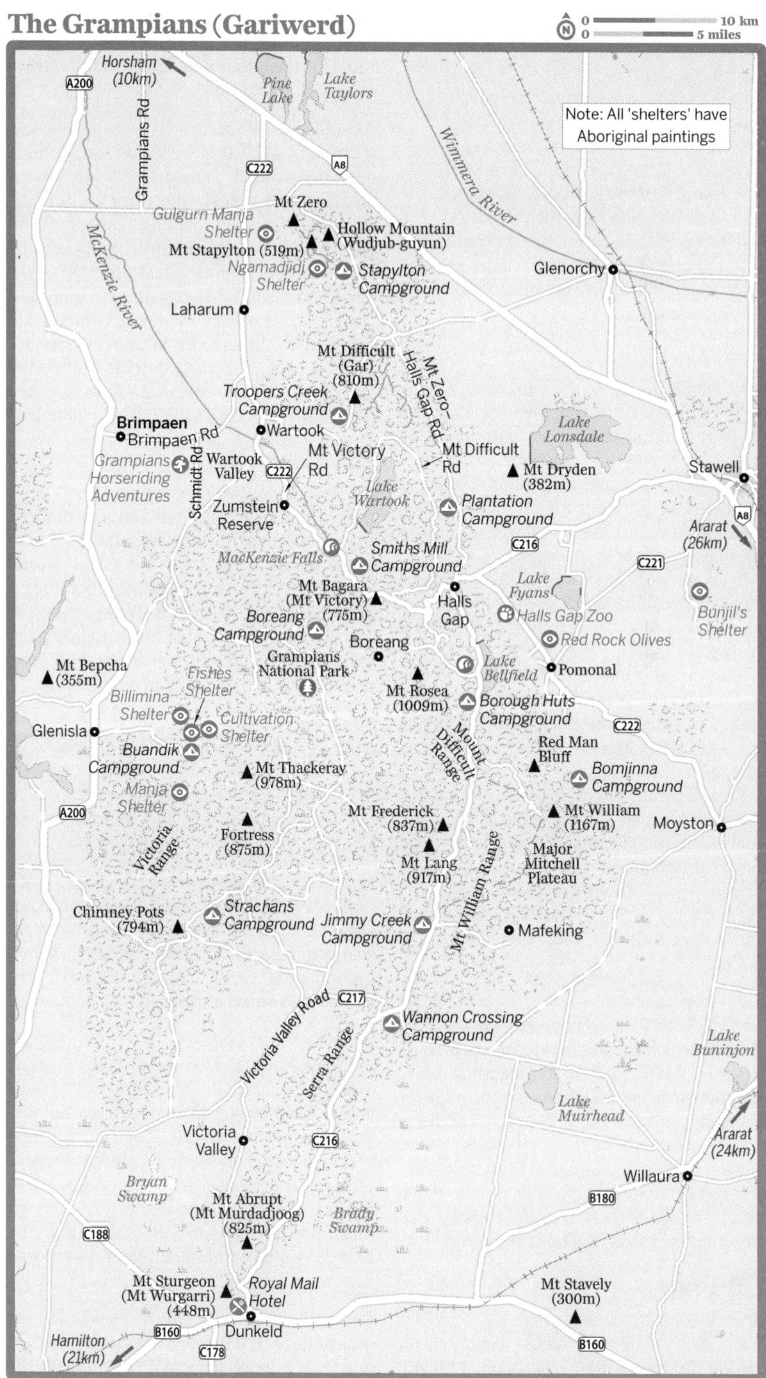

WALKS IN THE GRAMPIANS

All the walks start from the various car parks, picnic grounds and camping areas in the park. For longer walks, let someone know where you're going (preferably the Parks Victoria rangers).

If you're based in Halls Gap and have time for only one walk, the **Wonderland Loop** is a good choice, taking you through evocative landscapes and climaxing with stunning vistas of the **Pinnacles**.

right whale (totem of the Gunditjmara people). There's an art room where kids can try their hand at Indigenous painting ($15), classes on boomerang throwing and didgeridoo playing ($6), and holiday programs are organised. Planted outside are native plants used for food and medicine, where you can arrange a bush-tucker tour ($9).

Trips to visit nearby Aboriginal rock-art sites (adult/child $80/50) are offered as well, which takes in other significant sites along the way.

Also in the centre is an important section on indigenous political issues experienced during colonial times, including a sobering coverage of the massacres that took place in the region.

In a separate building – where you first enter the complex – are a souvenir shop and interesting educational displays covering the natural features and the history of the Grampians; staff can advise on walks and sell camping permits. The bush-tucker cafe (p229) has a lovely deck overlooking the gardens.

Halls Gap Zoo ZOO
(03-5356 4668; http://hallsgapzoo.com.au; 4061 Ararat–Halls Gap Rd; adult/child/family $28/14/70; 10am-5pm) Get up close to Australian native animals such as wallabies, dingoes, quolls, Tasmanian devils and wombats, in addition to exotic critters such as meerkats, spider monkeys, bison and tamarin. They have plenty of reptiles and birds too. This is a top-notch wildlife park with breeding and conservation programs and a natural bush setting.

Tours

★**Brambuk Cultural Centre** CULTURAL
(Map p229; 03-5356 4452; www.brambuk.com.au; Grampians Rd; 3/5hr tours $70/140) Rangers lead cultural and rock-art tours with numerous fascinating insights into local Indigenous culture. Bookings essential.

Absolute Outdoors ADVENTURE
(Map p229; 1300 526 258; www.absoluteoutdoors.com.au; 105 Grampians Rd; climbing & abseiling half-day $75) Offers rock climbing, abseiling, mountain biking, canoeing and guided nature walks. Its overnight camping trips (www.grampianspeaks.com.au) are also popular, and they can hire out tents and sleeping bags, as well as arrange water dropoffs. Stop by the shop for hiking boots, accessories and guidebooks on local bouldering and climbing sites. Mountain bike hire (per hour/half-/full-day $10/25/40) is available.

Sleeping

Halls Gap and the surrounding region has a huge range of accommodation – with more than 6000 beds, this is regional Victoria's most visited area after the Great Ocean Road, and tourists far outnumber locals. Whether you're camping, backpacking or looking for a motel or log cabin, there's plenty to choose from, but it still gets very busy in holiday periods – book ahead.

Tim's Place HOSTEL $
(Map p229; 03-5356 4288; www.timsplace.com.au; 44 Grampians Rd; dm/d from $30/70, apt from $120; @) Friendly, spotless eco backpackers with a homely feel and friendly owner; free mountain bikes and herb garden.

Halls Gap Caravan Park CAMPGROUND $
(Map p229; 03-5356 4251; www.hallsgapcaravanpark.com.au; 26 School Rd; unpowered/powered sites from $32/40, cabins $120-195;) Camping and cabins right in the town centre. Gets crowded at peak times.

Brambuk Backpackers HOSTEL $
(Map p229; 03-5356 4250, 03-5361 4000; www.brambuk.com.au; 332 Grampians Rd; dm/d/tr $30/75/90;) Across from the cultural centre, this friendly Aboriginal-owned and -run hostel gives you a calming sense of place with a relaxed feel and craggy views out of the lounge windows. All rooms, including dorms, have en suites and the lounge, dining room, kitchen and barbecue deck are all top-notch.

Grampians YHA Eco-Hostel HOSTEL $
(Map p229; 03-5356 4544; www.yha.com.au; cnr Grampians & Buckler Rds; dm/d/f from $31/95/110;

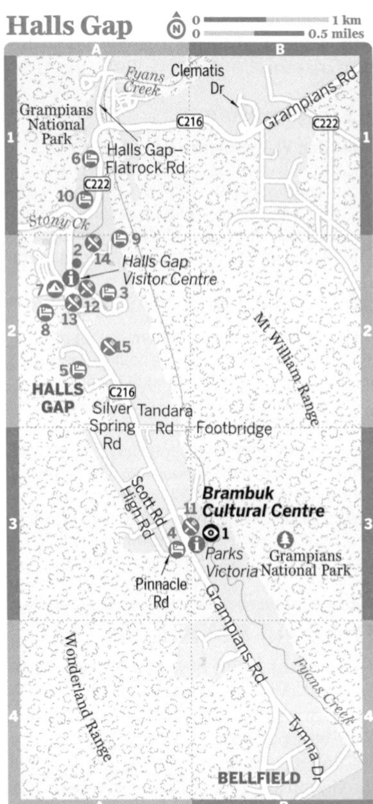

Halls Gap

Top Sights

1 Brambuk Cultural Centre B3

Activities, Courses & Tours

2 Absolute Outdoors A2
Brambuk Cultural Centre .... (see 1)

Sleeping

3 Aspect Villas A2
4 Brambuk Backpackers A3
5 D'Altons Resort A2
6 Grampians YHA Eco-Hostel A1
7 Halls Gap Caravan Park A2
8 Mountain Grand Guesthouse A2
9 Pinnacle Holiday Lodge A2
10 Tim's Place A1

Eating

11 Brambuk Bushfood Cafe A3
12 Harvest A2
13 Kookaburra Hotel A2
14 Livefast Lifestyle Cafe A2
15 Spirit of Punjab A2

@) This architecturally designed and ecofriendly hostel utilises solar power and rainwater tanks and makes the most of light and space. It's beautifully equipped with a spacious lounge, a *MasterChef*-quality kitchen and spotless rooms.

★ D'Altons Resort COTTAGE $$
(Map p229; 03-5356 4666; www.daltonsresort.com.au; 8 Glen St; studio/deluxe/family cottages from $110/125/160;) These delightful timber cottages, with cosy lounge chairs, cute verandahs and log fires, spread up the hill from the main road between the gums and kangaroos. They're immaculately kept and the friendly owners are a mine of local information. There's even a tennis court and a saltwater pool.

Pinnacle Holiday Lodge MOTEL $$
(Map p229; 03-5356 4249; www.pinnacleholiday.com.au; 21-45 Heath St; 1-/2-bedroom unit from $99/163, d with spa from $140;) Right in the centre of Halls Gap, this gorgeous property behind the Stony Creek shops has a spectacular mountainous backdrop and plenty of kangaroos. The spacious grounds have a bucolic feel with barbecue areas, an indoor pool and tennis courts. Modern self-contained units, two-bedroom family apartments and a swanky spa suite feature gas log fires.

Mountain Grand Guesthouse GUESTHOUSE $$
(Map p229; 03-5356 4232; www.mountaingrand.com.au; Grampians Rd; s/d incl breakfast $146/166;) This gracious, old-fashioned timber guesthouse prides itself on being a traditional old-fashioned lodge where you can take a pre-dinner port in one of the lounge areas and mingle with other guests. The rooms are still quaint but with a bright, fresh feel. The **Balconies Restaurant** here is well regarded.

Aspect Villas VILLA $$$
(Map p229; 03-5356 4457; www.aspectvillas.com.au; off Mackey's Peak Rd; d $520;) These two luxury villas are situated close to town, but seem a world away when you're reclining on your bed or by the log fire, taking in views of the Wonderland Range through floor-to-ceiling windows. They make the most of local building materials such as Grampians stone, and sit on a secluded property complete with its own lagoon.

Eating & Drinking

Brambuk Bushfood Cafe AUSTRALIAN $
(Map p229; ☎03-5361 4000; www.brambuk.com.au; Brambruk Cultural Centre, 277 Grampians Rd; mains $8.50-22; ⏲9am-4pm) Within the Brambuk Cultural Centre (p226) is this cafe that's a must for those who have yet to sample native Australia flavours such as wattleseed, lemon myrtle and bush tomato. Expect items such as saltbush lasagne, kangaroo pies, grilled emu and wattleseed damper. The bushfood platter ($22) is a good choice to sample a bit of everything.

Livefast Lifestyle Cafe CAFE $
(Map p229; ☎03-5356 4400; www.livefast.com.au; Shop 5, Stony Creek Stores; breakfast $8-17, lunch $15-19; ⏲7am-4pm Mon-Fri, to 5pm Sat & Sun; 📶) Halls Gap's best coffee and a sunny atmosphere are the hallmarks of this cafe. It does interesting breakfasts, including Spanish- and Japanese-influenced dishes, and fresh and tasty lunches such as Vietnamese tofu salad with noodles and rosemary beef burgers. Great selection of craft beers and Grampian wines.

Harvest CAFE $$
(Map p229; ☎03-5356 4782; www.harvesthg.com.au; 2 Heath St; day menu $9.80-16.50, dinner $22-32; ⏲8am-4pm Mon-Thu & Sun, to 10pm Fri & Sat) Utilising the rich bounty of produce in the region, Harvest's cafe menu specialises in locally grown food and wine. It does all-day gourmet breakfasts (Mexican baked eggs) and bites like sourdough steak sandwiches for lunch.

Spirit of Punjab INDIAN $$
(Map p229; ☎03-5356 4234; www.spiritofpunjabrestaurant.com; 161-163 Grampians Rd; mains $13.50-25; ⏲noon-2.30pm & 5-9pm) For a taste of the subcontinent in an Aussie bush setting head to this excellent Punjabi restaurant, which features some fairly bizarre folk sculpture out front. They do an array of dishes with authentic flavours, including a good tandoori selection.

Kookaburra Hotel MODERN AUSTRALIAN $$
(Map p229; ☎03-5356 4222; www.kookaburrahotel.com.au; 125-127 Grampians Rd; mains $18-36; ⏲6-9pm Tue-Fri, noon-3pm & 6-9pm Sat & Sun) This Halls Gap institution is famed for its excellent pub food, such as the sublime crispy-skin duck and Aussie dishes such as barramundi and kangaroo fillet (cooked rare or medium-rare only, as it should be). The wine list features mostly Grampians area wines, and there's beer on tap at the convivial bar.

Information

Halls Gap Visitor Centre (Map p229; ☎1800 065 599; www.visithallsgap.com.au; 117-119 Grampians Rd; ⏲9am-5pm; 📶) The staff here are helpful and can book tours, accommodation and activities. They also sell detailed maps ($3.50) and info on walks and drives in the park.

Getting There & Away

Halls Gap is located 254km from Melbourne along the Western Hwy (three hours), passing through Ballarat (142km) around the halfway mark. If coming from the Great Ocean Road it's 156km north of Port Fairy.

Halls Gap is well linked by public transport. V/Line connects it with Melbourne ($33.20, 3½ hours) and Ballarat ($17.20, two hours); connecting buses await at Ararat or Stawell stations. There's also a bus from Warrnambool ($28.20, three hours) on Tuesday, Friday and Sunday.

Dunkeld & Around

The southern point of access for the Grampians, **Dunkeld** (population 461) is a sleepy little town with a very big-name restaurant. The setting is superb, with Mt Abrupt and Mt Sturgeon rising up to the north, while the Grampians Tourist Rd to Halls Gap gives you a glorious passage into the park, with the cliffs and sky opening up as you pass between the Serra and Mt William Ranges. Fit hikers can walk to the summit of **Mt Abrupt** (6.5km, three hours return) and **Mt Sturgeon** (7km, three hours return) for panoramic views of the ranges. Both walks leave from signposted car parks off the Grampians Tourist Rd.

Sleeping

Royal Mail Hotel BOUTIQUE HOTEL $$$
(☎03-5577 2241; www.royalmail.com.au; 98 Parker St; r incl breakfast $295; ❄📶🏊) If you've come this far you might as well hang around post meal and stay at the Royal Mail's lovely rooms that look out to the Grampians. Rooms are comfortable and stylish, with a pool, native flora and a kitchen garden that you can tour with one of the chefs.

Eating

★**Royal Mail Hotel** MODERN AUSTRALIAN $$$
(☎03-5577 2241; www.royalmail.com.au; 98 Parker St; bistro $24-42, lunch $75-95, dinner $95-165;

FIRE BANS

Pay close attention to fire restrictions – apart from the damage you could do to yourself and the bush, you can be jailed for lighting any fire, including a fuel stove, on days of total fire ban. Check www.cfa.vic.gov.au for details of fire restrictions before heading out.

bar & bistro noon-3pm & 6-9pm, restaurant noon-2.30pm Thu-Sun & 6-10pm Wed-Sun) Dunkeld's main attraction is the showpiece restaurant at the Royal Mail – long regarded as one of the finest in the state. Continuously licensed since 1855, today the kitchen is overseen by chef Robin Wickens who's behind its daily changing menu of local seasonal produce. Its attached Parker St Project bistro is a more affordable option without skimping on quality.

A striking art deco building, inside is a smart but relaxed space with open fire and views out to the Grampians' Mt Sturgeon. Most of the menu is sourced from its farm and garden kitchen to create its highly seasonal menu with plenty of delightful surprises.

Information

Dunkeld Visitor Centre (1800 807 056, 03-5577 2558; www.visitgreaterhamilton.com.au; 55 Parker St) Has useful information about this small town south of the Grampians.

Getting There & Away

Dunkeld is 64km south of Halls Gap, so if you're coming specifically to eat at the Royal Mail you can theoretically make it as a return trip.

It's located 269km from Melbourne, a three-hour drive. If you're coming from the Great Ocean Road you can head through Warrnambool from where it's 100km to Dunkeld.

There are three buses to Dunkeld a week from Warrnambool ($19, two hours) which continue on through to Halls Gap.

Wartook Valley & the Northern Grampians

Wartook Valley runs along the Grampians' western foothills, giving a completely different perspective of the mountains. Heading to or from Horsham, this is the scenic alternative to the Western Hwy (A8). From Wartook, the sealed Roses Gap Rd and Mt Victoria Rd pass through the park, and there are lots of unsealed roads and tracks passing little creeks, waterfalls and idyllic picnic spots. Most of the tourist infrastructure was spared during the 2014 fires, but much of the land has turned from green to black and will take some time to recover.

NORTHWEST OF THE GRAMPIANS

Heading northwards from the Grampians, the terrain peters out as you enter Victoria's Wimmera region. It's an area characterised by flat and dry farm land, with the exception of Mt Arapiles, which rises dramatically like a mini Uluru and is a detour popular with rock climbers from around the world.

Also here is Horsham, a major regional hub with a fantastic art gallery, a few good cafes and botanical gardens, but little else.

Horsham

POP 15 894

The major town to the northwest of the Grampians and the capital of the Wimmera region, Horsham makes a convenient base for exploring the surrounding national parks and Mt Arapiles. The main shopping strip has postal and banking facilities, supermarkets and plenty of other shops and eateries.

Sights

★ **Horsham Regional Art Gallery** GALLERY
(03-5382 9575; www.horshamartgallery.com.au; 80 Wilson St; 10am-5pm Tue-Fri, 11am-4.30pm Sat, 1-4.30pm Sun) FREE Horsham's newly revamped gallery, within the historic art deco town hall, is a must for art lovers. Its downstairs space exhibits interesting contemporary shows, while upstairs has a permanent collection of photography featuring quality works by Bill Henson, Frank Hurley and Wolfgang Sievers. Also upstairs are paintings by Sir Sidney Nolan, John Bracks, Fred Williams and Brett Whiteley.

Eating

Nourish'd Eatery CAFE $
(0476 007 054; www.nourishdeatery.com.au; 34 Roberts Ave; dishes $12-18; 8am-3pm Mon-Fri, to 2pm Sat;) An unexpected find in northwest Victoria is this modern cafe with a menu loaded with antioxidants and superfoods. There's a focus on organic and local produce, with the owners personally visiting the farms they source from.

Information

Horsham & Grampians Visitors Centre (03-5382 1832; www.visithorsham.com.au; 20 O'Callaghan's Pde; 9am-5pm) Very helpful centre for information on Horsham and the surrounding area, including walking maps and art trails.

Getting There & Away

Horsham is 300km from Melbourne along the Western Hwy, passing through Ballarat en route. The Little Desert National Park (74km) is just over an hour's drive, while Halls Gap (73km) in the Grampians is just under a hour.

From Melbourne's Southern Cross Station there's a daily train-coach service to Horsham ($39, four hours) with a transfer in Ararat.

Mt Arapiles State Park

Mt Arapiles is Australia's premier rock-climbing destination. Topping out at 369m it's not the world's biggest mountain, but with more than 2000 routes to scale, it attracts salivating climbers from around the world. Popular climbs include the Bard Buttress, Tiger Wall and the Pharos. In the tiny nearby town of Natimuk, a community of avid climbers has set up to service visitors, and the town has also developed into something of a centre for artists.

Activities

Arapiles Climbing Guides CLIMBING
(03-5384 0376; www.arapiles.com.au; Natimuk) Climbing instruction and guiding around Mt Arapiles.

Natimuk Climbing Company CLIMBING
(0400 871 328, 03-5387 1329; www.climbco.com.au) Offers climbing, bouldering and abseiling instruction.

Arapiles Mountain Shop CLIMBING
(03-5387 1529, 0428 871 529; www.facebook.com/arapilesresoles; 67 Main St, Natimuk; 1-5.30pm Mon & Fri, 4.30-6pm Tue & Thu, 11am-5.30pm Sat, noon-5.30pm Sun) Sells and hires climbing equipment.

Sleeping

Most climbers camp at the foot of the mountain, but otherwise there's accommodation in nearby Natimuk.

Centenary Park Campground CAMPGROUND $
(13 19 63; www.parkweb.vic.gov.au; Centenary Park Rd, Mt Arapiles; camp sites per person $5.30) Most climbers head for this popular camping ground at the base of the mountain with three separate sites – the Lower Gums, the Pines and Upper Gums areas. There are toilets, communal fireplaces and picnic tables, but you'll need to bring your own drinking water and firewood.

National Hotel HOTEL $
(03-5387 1300; www.natimukhotel.com.au; 65 Main St, Natimuk; d $85; 11am-late Tue-Sat, 3pm-late Sun & Mon;) This place in Natimuk has tidy motel-style units at the back and pub rooms upstairs, plus good counter meals (lunch $13.50, dinner $19-30).

Duffholme Cabins CABIN $
(0421 442 050; 1859 Natimuk Frances Rd, Mitre; camping $10, d incl breakfast $100) A self-contained cottage and camp site (with toilets and shower) surrounded by wildlife and with views of Mt Arapiles. Ring to make arrangements (it's not staffed).

Eating

If you're camping there are fireplaces for cooking, but you'll need to bring your own fire wood. Given collecting wood in the park is prohibited, a gas cooker will make life much easier. Otherwise there's a cafe and pub at Natimuk. Horsham has the closest supermarket for shopping.

Natimuk Cafe CAFE $
(03-5387 1316; www.natimukcafe.com.au; 2 Jory St, Natimuk; dishes $10-17; 8.30am-10pm Fri & Sat, 8.30am-4.30pm Sun-Thurs) A lovely rustic little cafe with a menu of locally sourced, homemade goods, including big breakfasts, lasagnes and daily specials. It's a great hangout for climbers with a bunch of rock-climbing magazines and books.

Getting There & Away

Mt Arapiles is 37km west of Horsham and 12km west of Natimuk.

Wimmera Roadways (coach pickup 0428 861 160, office 08-8762 2962; www.wimmeraroadways.com.au) runs a bus service from Horsham to Mt Arapiles ($6, 30 minutes) from Monday to Friday passing through Natimuk ($4.80). It's essential to phone ahead to request Mt Arapiles as a stop. It leaves Mt Arapiles at 9.40am and Horsham at 2.40pm.

LITTLE DESERT NATIONAL PARK & AROUND

Heading into Mallee country in the heart of the Wimmera, this northwest corner of Victoria is noticeably drier and dustier with a more laid-back Aussie outback feel. The Little Desert National Park is the main attraction, with its unique expanse of wilderness ideal for camping. Along the way you'll pass through sleepy country towns that make for lovely stopovers, while further north is the **Silo Art Trail** (www.facebook.com/siloarttrail), that's fast becoming a tourist attraction as word gets out.

Dimboola

Located on the eastern edge of the Little Desert National Park, beside the Wimmera River, Dimboola is a classic country town made famous by Jack Hibberd's play *Dimboola*, and the subsequent 1979 John Duigan film of the same name about a country wedding. The national park entrance is about 4km south of town on a sealed road, but from then on it's gravel. There are numerous easily accessed walks around the flats area along the river.

Beside the Western Hwy, about 19km northwest of Dimboola, the **Pink Lake** is a colourful salt lake with a bright pink-purple hue.

Sights

Nolan Studio PUBLIC ART
(Lochiel St; 24hr) FREE Just next to the supermarket is this shopfront window displaying info and replica works by acclaimed Australian painter Sir Sidney Nolan, stationed in Dimboola during WWII.

Sleeping

Dimboola Riverside Caravan Park CAMPGROUND $
(03-5389 1416; www.riversideholidayparkdimboola.com.au; 2 Wimmera St; unpowered/powered sites $20/37, cabins from $68) Set among eucalypts and pine trees beside the Wimmera River.

Riverside Host Farm CABIN $
(03-5389 1550; 150 Riverside Rd; sites $25, cabins d $94;) This friendly hobby farm on a bend in the Wimmera River is a lovely place to stay, with cosy self-contained cabins, camp sites and a rustic open-sided camp kitchen lounge area with pot-belly stove. Hire canoes, or help out with farm activities.

Eating & Drinking

Good Paddock DELI
(03-5389 2079; 102 Lloyd St; 10am-5.30pm Mon-Fri, to noon Sat) A delightful little provedore stocking local gourmet produce such as olive oil and ice cream, as well as meats such as scotch fillet steaks. They do locally roasted coffee too.

Mason Clarke COFFEE
(03-5389 2070; www.masonclarke.com.au; 86 Lloyd St; 8am-1pm Sat & Sun) While they've scaled back from meals, you can still pop into this coffee roaster for a cuppa on weekends. They do jars of homemade preserves and milkshakes too.

Getting There & Away

Dimboola is 336km from Melbourne along the Western Hwy.

There's a bus here from Horsham ($4.80, 20 minutes), which continues on through to Nhill ($4.80, 25 minutes).

Little Desert National Park

While you shouldn't expect rolling sand dunes, this arid park does cover a huge 1320 sq km and is rich in flora and fauna that thrive in the dry environment. There are over 670 indigenous plant species here, and in spring and early summer the landscape is transformed into a colourful wonderland of wildflowers. The best-known resident is the Malleefowl, an

SILO ART TRAIL

Despite its out-of-the-way location in the heart of the Wimmera, this series of disused grain silos decorated in giant murals is fast gaining recognition as a tourist destination. The original was the **Brim Silos** (just south of Brim) 78km north of Horsham with its evocative, photogenic mural depicting local farmers. Its success has led to a 200km 'art trail' (www.facebook.com/siloarttrail), with similar epic works appearing on silos at **Patchewollock** and **Sheep Hills**, while more are commissioned for **Lascelles**, **Rosebery** and **Rupanyup**.

industrious bird that can be seen in an aviary at the Little Desert Nature Lodge.

The Nhill–Harrow Rd through the park is sealed and the road from Dimboola is gravel, but in the park the tracks are mostly sand and only suitable for 4WD vehicles or walking. Some are closed to 4WDs in the wet season (July to October).

Sleeping

★Little Desert Nature Lodge CAMPGROUND, RESORT **$**
(☎03-5391 5232; www.littledesertlodge.com.au; camp sites $35, bunkhouse d $56, motel r $130; ❄) On the northern edge of the desert, 16km south of Nhill, this well-equipped and friendly-run bush retreat is a superb base for exploring the park. With a spacious camping ground, bunkhouse and comfortable ensuite motel-style rooms there's something for everyone. A key attraction here is the tour of the Malleefowl aviary ($30), where you can see these rare birds in a breeding program.

It also does nightly guided tours to its sanctuary ($30) to observe the intriguing brush-tailed bettongs, as well as the Malleefowl, gliders and bush stone-curlews. A range of other tours is listed on their website.

The premise of the lodge is entirely conservation based, with its focus upon a long-term 're-wilding' project that aims to reintroduce locally extinct species such as bettongs and bandicoot into the wild. Its 120-hectare property is surrounded by a high-tech predator-proof fencing, where volunteers conduct regular surveys of local fauna and reptile species. Get in touch with **Conservation Volunteers Australia** (www.conservationvolunteers.com.au) if you want to help out.

Camping Grounds CAMPGROUND **$**
(☎13 19 63; www.parkweb.vic.gov.au; sites from $27.40) There are several camping grounds in the national park, with the most popular being in the eastern block at **Horseshoe Bend** and **Ackle Bend** – both on the Wimmera River south of Dimboola. They have toilets, picnic tables and fireplaces. Otherwise, there's free bush camping in the more remote central and western blocks where there are designated sites.

Information

Little Desert Park Office (☎13 19 63, 03-8427 2129; www.parkweb.vic.gov.au; Nursery Rd, Wail Nursery; ⏰9am-5pm Mon-Fri) Now that all info and bookings are online there's little reason to stop by here, but rangers can offer advice on camping inside the park.

Getting There & Away

The national park can be accessed from entry points at Dimboola, Nhill or from the south along the tarred road (C206) that passes through the centre of the park.

Public transport will only get you as far as Dimboola or Nhill, so basically you'll need your own vehicle to visit here. However, if you're staying at Little Desert Nature Lodge it may be possible to arrange a lift from Nhill.

Nhill

Nhill is the main base for the northern entrance to the Little Desert National Park and Kiata campground. It's a big town for this part of the world – the main industries here are wheat farming and producing ducks for Victorian restaurant tables. Nhill is an Aboriginal word meaning 'mist over the water' – check out the artificial **Lake Nhill** and surrounding wetlands to see if there's any water. It has a sizeable community of Karen refugees who have been settled here after spending decades in camps along the Thai-Burma border.

Nhill has some grand old pubs, cafes, motels and a caravan park, but your best bet for accommodation is to head down to Little Desert Nature Lodge near the national park entrance.

There are plenty of pubs in town doing counter meals, as well as takeaway and fast food restaurants and generic cafes. There's a decent supermarket for self-caterers heading into the Little Dessert National Park.

Hindmarsh Visitors Centre (☎03-5391 3086; www.wimmeramalleetourism.com.au; Victoria St; ⏰9am-5pm Mon-Fri) In Goldsworthy Park in the town centre, has plenty of information on the park and local sights and accommodation.

Nhill lies at approximately the halfway point between Melbourne (374km) and Adelaide (352km) on the Western Hwy.

From Horsham there's a V/Line bus to Nhill ($8.80, 45 minutes).

Mornington Peninsula & Phillip Island

Includes ➡

Best Places to Eat

- Ten Minutes by Tractor (p247)
- Captains of Rye (p240)
- The Epicurean (p245)
- Cape Kitchen (p251)
- Green Olive at Red Hill (p244)
- Red Hill Brewery (p245)

Best Places to Sleep

- Hotel Sorrento (p240)
- Island Accommodation YHA (p251)
- Glen Isla House (p251)
- Clifftop (p251)
- Royal Hotel (p237)

Why Go?

More a playground for locals than a lure for foreign travellers, Mornington Peninsula is a string of holiday communities that curls around Port Phillip Bay's eastern half. At the tip of the peninsula, a world of rugged ocean surf beaches, sublime links golf courses and coastal bushwalks opens up. Away from the coast, the peninsula's interior is a wine- and food-lover's paradise, with more than 50 cellar doors and some of Victoria's finest winery restaurants.

Away to the east, it's a short ferry ride to wild and isolated French Island and to Phillip Island, one of Victoria's premier attractions. Apart from the famous nightly parade of little penguins, Phillip Island is blessed with wonderful surf beaches, accessible wildlife and enough activities to keep you (and the kids) busy for a week.

When to Go

Phillip Island

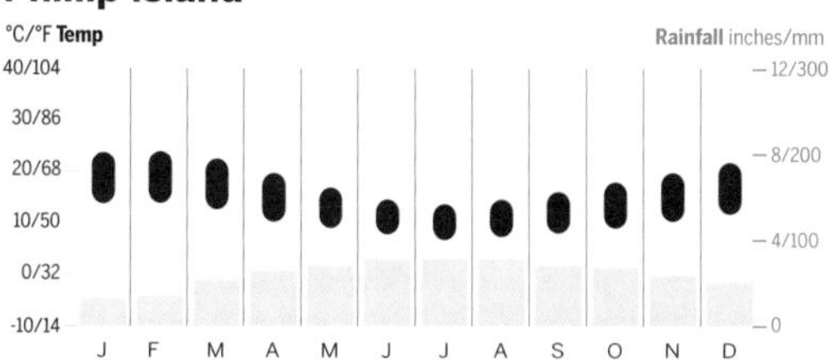

Jan–Feb Phillip Island is one of the closest summer playgrounds to Melbourne.

Nov–Dec The best time to view seals and penguins at Phillip Island.

Mar–May, Sep–Oct Hit the beaches and wineries, after the holiday crowds have departed.

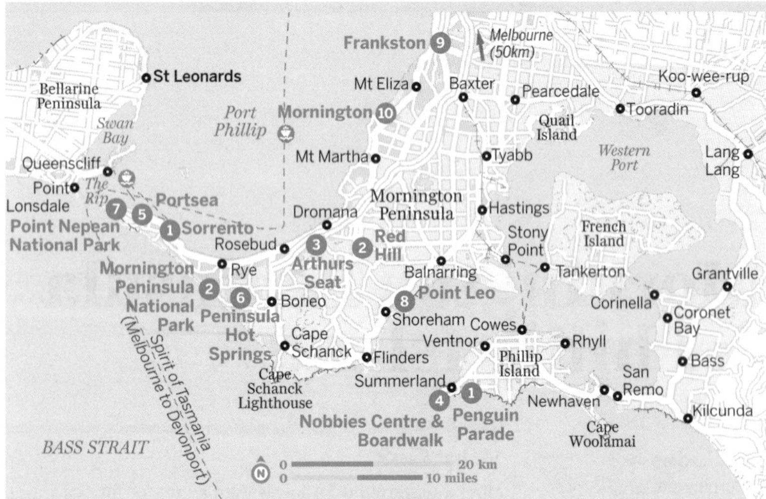

Mornington Peninsula & Phillip Island Highlights

1 **Penguin Parade** (p248) Settling in at dusk for this famous wildlife spectacle at Phillip Island.

2 **Red Hill** (p244) Treating yourself to a day of wine tasting, in between a long lunch and visits to cheesemakers.

3 **Arthurs Seat Eagle** (p239) Taking in soaring coastal views from the Arthurs Seat gondola.

4 **Nobbies Centre** (p248) Looking out to this spectacular viewpoint while learning about its waters at the Antarctic Journey centre.

5 **Sea Kayaking** (p241) Paddling out from Portsea to visit a seal colony, with regular dolphin encounters en route.

6 **Peninsula Hot Springs** (p239) Indulging in a long, relaxed soak at this mineral waters spa.

7 **Point Nepean National Park** (p242) Cycling out to the peninsula's tip and historic military fortress.

8 **Point Leo** (p244) Hanging out at this relaxed surf town while learning to catch a wave.

9 **Mornington Peninsula Regional Gallery** (p237) Being wowed by quality modern Australian art.

MORNINGTON PENINSULA

The Mornington Peninsula – the boot-shaped area of land between Port Phillip Bay and Western Port Bay – has been Melbourne's summer playground since the 1870s, when paddle steamers ran down to Portsea. Today, much of the interior farming land has been replaced by vineyards and orchards – foodies love the peninsula, where a winery lunch is a real highlight – but it still retains lovely stands of native bushland.

The calm 'front beaches' are on the Port Phillip Bay side, where families holiday at bayside towns from Mornington to Sorrento. The rugged ocean 'back beaches' face Bass Strait and are easily reached from Portsea, Sorrento and Rye; there are stunning walks along this coastal strip, part of the Mornington Peninsula National Park.

The bay heads are so close that it's just a short hop by ferry across from Sorrento to Queenscliff on the Bellarine Peninsula.

Information

Peninsula Visitor Information Centre (Map p238; ☎1800 804 009, 03-5987 3078; www.visitmorningtonpeninsula.org; 359b Nepean Hwy, Dromana; ⊙9am-5pm) The visitor information centre can book accommodation and tours, and stocks an abundance of brochures.

Getting There & Away

The fastest way to the Mornington Peninsula is via the tollway Eastlink (M3) and exit at the Mornington Peninsula Fwy (M11) via Peninsula Link. The Point Nepean Rd (B110) also feeds into the Mornington Peninsula Fwy (M11), the main peninsula access. Alternately, exit the Moorooduc Hwy to Mornington and take the coast road around Port Phillip Bay.

Frequent Metlink trains run from Melbourne to Frankston, Hastings and Stony Point.

Inter Island Ferries (Map p238; ☎03-9585 5730; www.interislandferries.com.au; adult/child/bicycle return $26/12/8) Runs between Stony Point and Cowes via French Island.

Queenscliff–Sorrento Car & Passenger Ferries (Map p238; ☎03-5257 4500; www.searoad.com.au; foot passenger one way adult/child $11/8, driver & car one way/return $64/118; ⏱hourly 7am-6pm, until 7pm Jan & long weekends) Sails between Sorrento and Queenscliff, enabling you to cross Port Phillip Bay by car or bicycle.

Ventura Bus Lines (☎03-9786 7088; www.venturabus.com.au) Offers public transport across the peninsula.

➡ 788 From Frankston to Portsea via Mornington, Dromana and Sorrento.

➡ 786 From Rye to St Andrews Beach.

➡ 787 From Dromana to Sorrento.

➡ 782 From Frankston train station to Flinders via Hastings and Balnarring.

Mornington

POP 22,421

Pretty Mornington, with its cute bathing boxes and swimming beaches, is the gateway to the peninsula's holiday coastal strip – just beyond the reaches of Melbourne's urban sprawl. These days it's known for its cosmopolitan cafes and heritage buildings.

Originally part of the lands of the Boonwurrung people, it was founded as a European township in 1854. The town thrived and by 1890 there were steamers and a daily train service from Melbourne – now sadly defunct.

Sights

★Mornington Peninsula Regional Gallery GALLERY
(MPRG; Map p238; ☎03-5975 4395; http://mprg.mornpen.vic.gov.au; Dunns Rd; adult/child $4/free; ⏱10am-5pm Tue-Sun) The outstanding Mornington Peninsula Regional Gallery has changing exhibitions and a permanent collection of modern and contemporary Australian prints and paintings, representing the likes of Boyd, Tucker and Whiteley. There are free guided tours at 3pm on Wednesday, Saturday and Sunday.

Beaches

Mothers Beach is the main swimming beach, while at **Fossil Beach**, where limestone was mined in the 1860s, there are remains of a lime-burning kiln. Fossils found here date back 25 million years! At Mills Beach you can see colourful and photogenic **bathing boxes**.

Sleeping

Morning Star Estate HISTORIC HOTEL $
(☎03-9787 7760; www.morningstarestate.com.au; 1 Sunnyside Rd, Mt Eliza; d from $120; 📶) Morning Star is a huge 1867 Victorian mansion on 38 acres that operates as a winery, restaurant and boutique hotel. Once owned by the Catholic Church, it was a home for delinquent boys. The many outbuildings, rose gardens and sweeping bay vistas make it a lovely place to wander around.

Royal Hotel HOTEL $$$
(☎03-5975 8555; www.theroyal.com.au; 770 The Esplanade; r incl breakfast $280-400; ❄📶) Classified by the National Trust, the Royal Hotel (c 1857) is tastefully renovated, offering authentic old-world accommodation in a range of rooms, most with bay views. The pick are the balcony suites with bathrooms and sea views – the best you'll get along the entire coast. All come with Apple TV, wi-fi and aircon. The bar and restaurant downstairs are also lovely with plenty of period charm.

Eating

Commonfolk Coffee CAFE $
(Map p238; ☎03-5902 2786; www.commonfolkcoffee.com.au; 16 Progress St; dishes $10-21; ⏱6.30am-5pm Mon-Fri, 8am-5pm Sat, 8am-4pm Sun; 📶) Another reason to veer down Mornington's industrial backstreets is this coffee roaster that specialises in beans mainly from Africa. It's a massive space with industrial-chic decor, that's buzzing with folk here for delicious breakfasts, organic sourdoughs and bagels. There's local beer on tap, and an attached studio space of artists in residence.

Coffee Traders CAFE $
(☎03-5977 1177; www.facebook.com/coffeetradersmornington; 3 Blake St; dishes $11-18; ⏱6am-6pm Mon-Sat, 7am-6pm Sun; 📶) A long-term fixture just off Mornington's cafe strip is this charming old favourite that's still going strong with friendly service, great coffee, tasty breakfasts and fresh sandwiches.

Mornington Peninsula

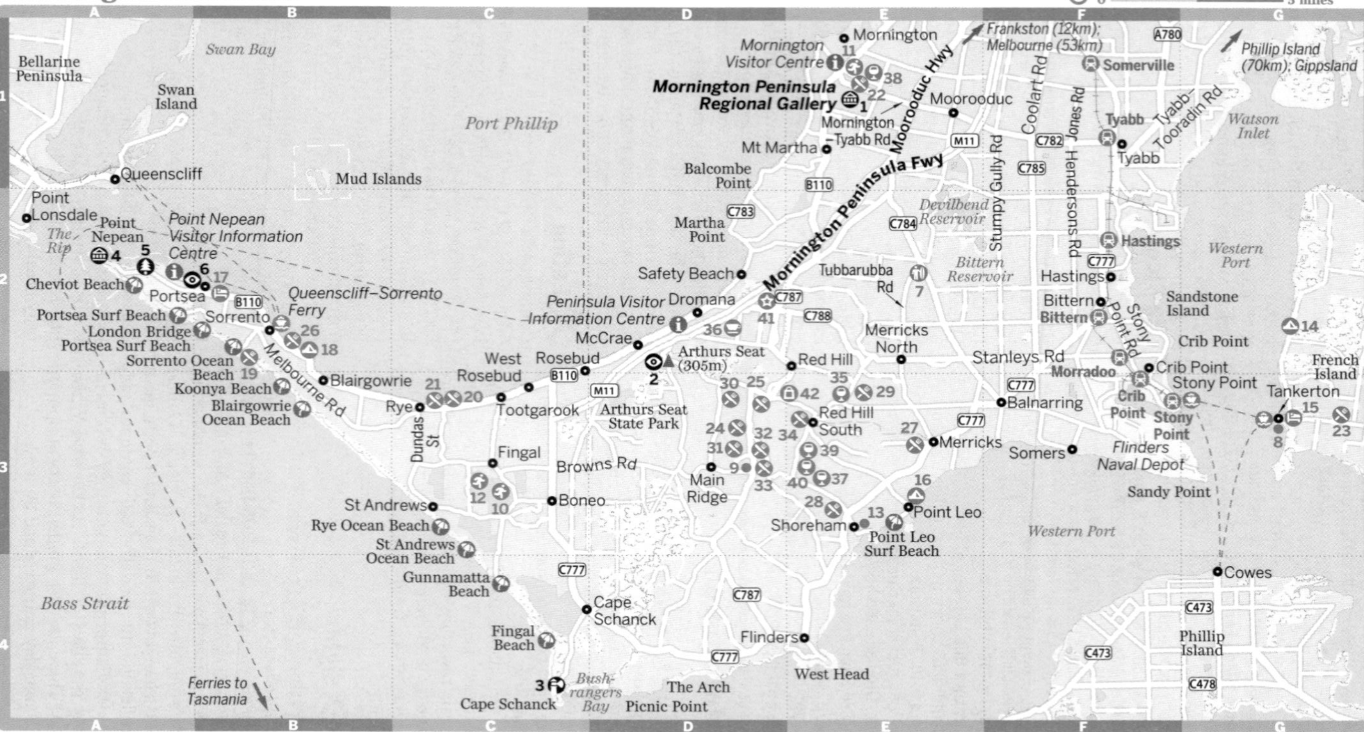

D.O.C ITALIAN $$

(☎03-5977 0988; www.docgroup.net; 22 Main St; mains $18-24; ⊙9.30am-late) As authentic as you're going to get outside Italy, this cafe and deli, with Italian staff, displays imported cheeses and meats and D.O.C (quality assured) wines. They do pizzas and handmade pastas to go with spritzes, negronis and Italian craft beers.

The Rocks SEAFOOD $$

(☎03-5973 5599; www.therocksmornington.com.au; 1 Schnapper Point Dr; mains $19-54; ⊙8am-10pm Wed-Sun, Mon & Tue noon-10pm) At the Mornington Yacht Club, this restaurant, with an open-sided deck overlooking the marina, is the perfect place for a drink, light meal or fine dining. The restaurant is strong on fresh seafood, with oysters done every which way.

Drinking & Nightlife

★Mornington Peninsula Brewery MICROBREWERY

(Map p238; ☎03-5976 3663; www.mpbrew.com.au; 72 Watt Rd; ⊙3-11pm Thu & Fri, noon-late Sat, noon-7pm Sun) In the middle of a commercial estate is this gem of a brewery with a taproom set up among its production space. They do four core beers and a few seasonals to enjoy in its slick industrial space or beer garden with wood-fired pizzas (from $14).

Information

Mornington Visitor Centre (Map p238; ☎03-5975 1644; www.visitmorningtonpeninsula.org; 320 Main St; ⊙9am-5pm) Has useful regional information and a Mornington walking-tour map. There's also a visitor centre at the **old courthouse** (cnr Main St & the Esplanade; ⊙11am-4pm).

Getting There & Away

Mornington is 71km from Melbourne; take the Peninsula Link/Mornington Peninsula Fwy (M11) and exit at Bungower Rd.

There are several buses that pass through Mornington from Frankston, however the best option is bus 781.

Mornington to Blairgowrie

From Mornington, the Esplanade heads south for the gorgeous scenic drive towards Sorrento, skirting the rocky Port Phillip Bay foreshore. Inland, the Nepean Hwy (B110) takes a less-scenic route and again becomes the Mornington Peninsula Fwy.

From **Dromana** take the steep hairpin-bend Arthurs Seat Rd inland up to the lookout at **Arthurs Seat** (called Wonga by the Boonwurrung people), which, at 305m, is the highest point on the Port Phillip Bay coast, with fine views across the bay. Its famous chairlift finally reopened in December 2016. Back in Dromana there's a relic of the 1960s, the National Trust–listed Dromana Drive-In (p240).

Sights & Activities

Arthurs Seat Eagle CABLE CAR

(Map p238; ☎03-5987 0600; www.aseagle.com.au; 795 Arthurs Seat Rd, Arthurs Seat; adult/child one-way $17.50/11, return $24/15; ⊙10am-8pm Dec-Apr, to 5pm May-Nov) After being out of action for 10 years, Arthurs Seat has got its iconic chairlift back. Featuring a sleek 21st-century makeover in a Swiss-built gondola, you can now enjoy the all-encompassing views that stretch as far as Melbourne's city skyline and Mt Macedon. While most opt for return tickets, the trek back down (45 minutes) is along a steep but scenic route through state forest.

Peninsula Hot Springs SPA

(Map p238; ☎03-5950 8777; www.peninsulahotsprings.com; Springs Lane, Fingal; bathhouse adult/child Tue-Thu $35/20, Fri-Mon $45/30; ⊙7.30am-10pm) There are lots of spas and massage centres popping up along the peninsula, but none better than Peninsula Hot Springs, a large and luxurious complex that utilises hot, mineral-rich waters pumped from deep underground. There's a huge menu of spa, private bathing and massage treatments available, or you can just relax in the bathhouse. It's about 7km inland from Rye, off Browns Rd.

★Moonah Links GOLF

(Map p238; ☎03-5988 2000; www.moonahlinks.com.au; 55 Peter Thomson Dr, Fingal; 18 holes $75-95) By far the most famous golf course along the peninsula is this Peter Thomson–designed pro 18-hole course that's hosted the Australian Open on numerous occasions. As well as its premier **Open Course**, there's also the less challenging **Legends Course** to suit all levels.

Sleeping

There's holiday accommodation all along the coast, and council-managed **foreshore camping** (☎03-5986 8286; www.mornpen.vic.gov.au; unpowered/powered sites $26/40, peak season $41/48; ⊙Oct-May) at Rosebud, Rye and Sorrento. These camping areas are close to the beach and are open from September to April – it's next to impossible to get a site during the Christmas and Easter holidays.

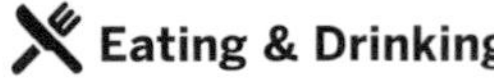

Eating & Drinking

Rye

Captains of Rye CAFE, BAR $

(Map p238; ☎03-5985 6025; www.facebook.com/captainsofrye; 2285 Point Nepean Rd; dishes $7.50-20; ⏲cafe 7.30am-3pm, bar 4-11pm Oct-Apr) One of the peninsula's best cafes is this rustic cafe-provedore doing excellent locally roasted coffee, pulled-pork rolls, crab burgers and Red Hill beers. There's an industrial back space too, and in the summer it has a cider bar and smoker for BBQ meats.

Baha MEXICAN $$

(Map p238; ☎03-5985 2077; www.bahatacos.com.au; 2203-2209 Pt Nepean Rd, Rye; dishes $14-25; ⏲taqueria from 1pm Fri-Sun, from 5pm Tue-Thu, restaurant 5pm-late daily) Doing its part to transform Rye from daggy suburb to hip beach town is this bohemian Mexican restaurant that also hosts regular live bands.

In the afternoons it has a caravan taqueria, and by night its vibrant space does awesome local craft and Mexican beers to go with soft corn tacos and shared mains. It gets a good mix of bands on weekends ($10 cover).

Dromana

★**Little Rebel** COFFEE

(Map p238; ☎0418 121 467; www.littlerebel.com.au; 22 Collins Rd, Dromana; ⏲8am-2pm Mon-Fri) Coffee aficionados will definitely want to make a detour to this micro-roastery tucked away down a random industrial estate in Dromana. All of its single-origin beans are sourced directly from farmers across Africa, Latin America and Asia. They do filter and machine coffee to go with Johnny Ripe (p245) donuts and jaffles. It's closed on weekends.

Entertainment

Dromana Drive-In CINEMA

(Map p238; ☎03-5987 2492, office 03-5931 0022; www.dromanadrivein.com.au; 133 Nepean Hwy; adult/child $17/11; ⏲7.30pm & 10pm Thu-Sun) At Dromana there's a relic of the 1960s when there were more than 330 drive-in cinemas across Australia. The National Trust–listed Dromana Drive-In is one of just a handful that remain.

Sorrento

POP 1448

Historic Sorrento is the standout town on the Mornington Peninsula for its beautiful limestone buildings, ocean and bay beaches, and buzzing seaside summer atmosphere. This was the site of Victoria's first official European settlement, established by an expedition of convicts, marines, civil officers and free settlers who arrived from England in 1803.

Sights & Activities

The calm bay beach is good for families and you can hire **paddle boards** on the foreshore. At low tide, the rock pool at the back beach is a safe spot for adults and children to swim and snorkel, and the surf beach is patrolled in summer. The 10-minute climb up to **Coppins Lookout** offers good views.

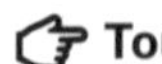

Tours

Moonraker Charters WILDLIFE

(☎03-5984 4211; www.moonrakercharters.com.au; Esplanade Rd; sightseeing from $45, dolphin & seal swimming from $135) Operates dolphin- and seal-swimming tours from Sorrento Pier.

Sleeping

Sorrento Foreshore Camping Ground CAMPGROUND $

(Map p238; ☎03-5950 1011; www.mornpen.vic.gov.au/activities/camping; Nepean Hwy; unpowered/powered sites $26/40, peak season $41/48; ⏲Oct-May) Hilly, bush-clad sites between the bay beach and the main road into Sorrento.

Hotel Sorrento HOTEL $$

(☎03-5984 8000; www.hotelsorrento.com.au; 5-15 Hotham Rd, Sorrento; r weekdays/weekends incl breakfast from $170/210; ❄📶) The legendary Hotel Sorrento trades on its famous name and has a swag of accommodation. Its lovely 'On the Hill' double and family apartments have airy living spaces, spacious bathrooms and private balconies. Its pub has fabulous water views and is a good spot for a drink.

Eating

All Smiles MODERN AUSTRALIAN $$

(Map p238; ☎03-5984 5551; www.allsmiles.com.au/mornington-peninsula; 250 Ocean Beach Rd; mains $22-26; ⏲9.30am-2.30pm Wed-Sun) Literally on the Sorrento back beach, the menu here is decent enough with pizza, fish and chips, and calamari salad, but it's really all about the view. The Sunday buffet breakfasts (adult/child $20/12) are a great way to treat yourself.

Acquolina Ristorante ITALIAN $$
(☎03-5984 0811; 26 Ocean Beach Rd; mains $25-38; ⏱6-10pm Wed-Mon Oct-Nov & Mar-May, daily in summer) Acquolina set the bar when it opened in Sorrento with its authentic northern-Italian fare. This is hearty, simple food – handmade pasta and ravioli dishes matched with wines sourced first-hand from Italy, grappa and homemade (utterly irresistible) tiramisu.

The Baths MODERN AUSTRALIAN $$
(☎03-5984 1500; www.thebaths.com.au; 3278 Point Nepean Rd; mains $26-42; ⏱11.30am-3pm & 5.30-9pm Mon-Sat) The waterfront deck of the former sea baths: the perfect spot for lunch or a romantic sunset dinner overlooking the jetty and the Queenscliff ferry. There are some good seafood choices among its menu of Modern Australian dishes, as well local beers and wines. It reopened in late 2016 after burning down the year prior.

Cakes & Ale Bistro FRENCH $$$
(☎03-5984 4995; www.cakes-and-ale.com.au; 100-102 Ocean Beach Rd; mains $29-45; ⏱noon-9pm Mon-Fri, 9am-9pm Sat & Sun) Offering some much needed class on Sorrento's main street is this smart restaurant doing seasonal produce sourced from around Victoria. Its attractive space is fitted out with plants, polished floors and distressed walls, and has a French-inspired menu of fisherman's pot pie, confit Milawa duck leg and roasted spatchcock. It does breakfasts on weekends, with quality coffee by Little Rebel (p240).

Loquat MODERN AUSTRALIAN $$$
(Map p238; ☎03-5984 4444; www.loquat.com.au; 3183 Point Nepean Rd; 2-/3-course meal $55/70, mains $28-35; ⏱6-9pm Thu-Sun) An in-crowd frequents this trendily converted cottage, but its staying power is due to excellent food – everything from prawn linguine to slow-cooked beef brisket and pork belly dishes.

Information

Sorrento Beach Visitors Centre (☎03 5984 1478; www.visitmorningtonpeninsula.org; cnr Ocean Beach Rd & George St; ⏱10am-4pm) The visitors centre is on the main drag in town, with a whopping selection of brochures and an after-hours info touch screen.

Getting There & Away

Sorrento is 109km from Melbourne, accessed along Eastlink (M3) and Mornington Peninsula Freeway (M11).

From Frankston station, bus 788 has regular trips during the day to Sorrento. Otherwise the **ferry** (p237) is a great way to get across to Queenscliff, from where you can explore the Bellarine Peninsula and Great Ocean Rd.

Portsea

POP 446

The last village on the peninsula, posh Portsea is a bit like Victoria's equivalent of the Hamptons, where many of Melbourne's wealthiest families have built seaside mansions.

As well as its adjoining Point Nepean National Park, of most interest for tourists are the dive shops here offering a number of tours – from wreck dives and snorkelling to sea kayak trips to visit seals and dolphins.

You can walk the Farnsworth Track (1.5km, 30 minutes) out to scenic **London Bridge**, a natural rock formation, and spot middens of the Boonwurrung people who once called this area home.

Another big lure is the iconic Portsea Hotel, with its fantastic beer garden overlooking the bay.

Activities

★**Bayplay** DIVING, WATER SPORTS
(Map p238; ☎03-5984 0888; www.bayplay.com.au; 3755 Pt Nepean Rd; dives $68-130) A must for anyone wanting to get out on the water is this dive operator that offers PADI courses as well as guided diving and snorkelling trips to see a heap of marine life. However, it's most popular for its **sea-kayaking tours** (adult/child $99/88), where you can regularly spot dolphins and seals. They also do stand-up paddleboard tours (two hours $75), sailing trips (from $99) and hire out kayaks.

For landlubbers they rent out bikes (per day $30), organise glamping and run tours to visit Fort Nepean (p242).

Dive Victoria DIVING, SNORKELLING
(Map p238; ☎03-5984 3155; www.divevictoria.com.au; 3770 Point Nepean Rd; 1/2 dives from $72/130) A well-established, reputable operator offering diving and snorkelling trips. Its website has excellent info on local dive sites, along with a schedule of its upcoming trips.

Sleeping

Portsea Hotel HOTEL $$

(Map p238; ☎03-5984 2213; www.portseahotel.com.au; 3746 Point Nepean Rd; s/d without bathroom from $75/145, s/d with bathroom from $135/180;) This 19th-century hotel and pub offers old-style accommodation (most rooms have shared bathroom) that increases in price based on sea views. Weekend rates are higher.

Drinking & Nightlife

Portsea Hotel PUB

Portsea's pulse is the sprawling, half-timber Portsea Hotel (c 1876), an enormous pub with a great lawn and terrace area looking out over the bay and historic pier. It's where the beautiful people come to be seen (especially come polo season), with regular events and DJs over summer. There's an excellent bistro (mains $24 to $27) and old-style accommodation.

Getting There & Away

Portsea is just under a two-hour drive from Melbourne (123km) via a combination of Eastlink (M3) and Mornington Peninsula (M11) Fwys.

By public transport, from Melbourne take the train to Frankston station from where you can transfer to bus 788 to Portsea – with around 10 trips a day via Dromana, Rye and Sorrento.

Point Nepean National Park

At the peninsula's western tip is the scenic **Point Nepean National Park** (Map p238; ☎13 19 63; www.parkweb.vic.gov.au; Point Nepean Rd; 8am-5pm), a historic site that played an important role as Australia's defence site from the 1880s to 1945. Remarkably, it was from here where the first Allied shots were fired in both WWI and WWII.

The national park is known for its stunning coastal scenery and features a number of lovely walks and cycling paths. A large section of the park is a former range area and still out of bounds due to unexploded ordnance.

You can visit its **Fort Nepean** (Map p238), as well at the fascinating historic **Quarantine Station precinct**. Dating from 1852, this complex was used to quarantine passengers right until 1979; today it's a museum with interesting displays detailing its history, along with some 50 heritage buildings to explore, including the **Hospital** and **Wash House**.

Police Point HISTORIC SITE

(Map p238) Before the entrance to the national park is Police Point, a heritage-listed site where quarantined patients could be visited while separated by a barrier preventing physical contact; all watched on closely by the police. There's also a good lookout point here.

Information

Point Nepean Visitor Information Centre (Map p238; ☎03-8427 2099; www.parkweb.vic.gov.au; Ochiltree Rd; 10am-5pm) Will give you the lowdown on the park, hires bikes for $30.10 per day, as well as self-guided walking maps and iPod audio tours ($13.90). From Portsea you can walk or cycle to the point (12km return), or take the shuttle bus (adult/child return $10/7.50), a hop-on, hop-off bus service that departs the visitor centre every 30 minutes from 10.30am to 4pm.

Getting There & Away

Point Nepean National Park is at the far western tip of the Mornington Peninsula, facing directly across from Queenscliff and 112km from Melbourne. It's located about 2km west of Portsea.

To get to the national park by public transport take bus 788 from Frankston to the end of the line at Portsea, from where it's a 1km walk to the visitor centre.

Mornington Peninsula National Park

Stretching from Portsea on the sliver of coastline to Cape Schanck and inland to the Greens Bush area, this national park showcases the peninsula's most beautiful and rugged ocean beaches. Along here are the cliffs, bluffs and crashing surf beaches of **Portsea**, **Sorrento**, **Blairgowrie**, **Rye**, **St Andrews**, **Gunnamatta** and **Cape Schanck**.

This is spectacular coastal scenery – well known to the surfers, hikers and fisherfolk who have their secret spots – and it's possible to walk all the way from Portsea to Cape Schanck (26km, eight hours).

Swimming and surfing is dangerous at these beaches: the undertow and rips can be severe, and drownings continue to occur. Swim only between the flags at Gunnamatta and Portsea during summer.

Sights & Activities

Cape Schanck Lighthouse LIGHTHOUSE

(Map p238; ☎0407 348 478; www.facebook.com/theladyofhistory; 420 Cape Schanck Rd; tours incl museum & lighthouse adult/child/family $13/7/38;

HAROLD HOLT

On a hot day in December 1967, Harold Holt (1908–67) disappeared in wild surf off Cheviot Beach, while serving as Australia's prime minister. Despite a three-week air and land search – the biggest in Australia's history – his body was never recovered. This, and the fact that it happened during the height of the Cold War, led to a raft of conspiracy theories.

It was suggested that the CIA had Holt murdered because he wanted to withdraw Australian troops from Vietnam. It was also alleged that various people and companies with vested interest had him bumped off because, with the covert activities of the Atomic Energy Commission (AEC) at Lucas Heights in Sydney, Australia was secretly emerging as a major nuclear energy supplier. Some said that Holt committed suicide because he was depressed and there was a leadership challenge emerging within the Liberal Party. The most colourful theory was that Holt was spying for the Chinese government, and that he climbed aboard a Chinese submarine waiting off Cheviot Beach and died in the mid-1980s, after living out his days with a lover in France.

The lack of a body meant that an inquest was never held, but in 1985 the Victorian Coroners Act was amended so that 'suspected deaths' had to be investigated. The inevitable 2005 coroner's inquest found he died by accidental drowning.

In the Point Nepean National Park there's a memorial 500m from Cheviot Hill, overlooking the stretch of water in which he went missing.

select weekends) Cape Schanck Lightstation (1859) is a photogenic working limestone lighthouse on the peninsula's remote southwest tip. It's part of a historic precinct that you can explore anytime from the outside; to go inside, however, you'll need to visit as part of a tour, held only on select weekends. Check the Facebook page for upcoming times. A cafe was on its way too, which will only be open weekends.

There are some lovely walks here. From the lightstation, descend the steps of the boardwalk that leads to the craggy cape for outstanding views. Longer walks include tracks to Bushrangers Bay, which can be approached from Cape Schanck or the Bushrangers Bay car park on Boneo Rd (C777) – 5km return.

Flinders

POP 860

Little Flinders, where the thrashing ocean beaches give way to Western Port Bay, has so far been largely spared the development of the Port Phillip Bay towns. It's a delightful little community and home to a busy fishing fleet, and more recent influx of boutiques, galleries and cafes. Surfers have been coming to Flinders for decades, drawn by oceanside breaks such as Gunnery, Big Left and Cyril's, and golfers know the clifftop Flinders Golf Club course as the most scenic and wind blown in Victoria.

Sleeping

Flinders Hotel HOTEL **$$$**
(03-5989 0201; www.flindershotel.com.au; cnr Cook & Wood Sts; r incl breakfast $250-300;) The historic (though recently modernised) Flinders Hotel has been a beacon on this sleepy street corner longer than anyone can remember. Attached is its boutique accommodation wing with contemporary en-suite rooms, which are by far the best in the region.

Eating

Flinders Sourdough BAKERY **$**
(0459 160 023; www.facebook.com/flinderssourdough; 58 Cook St; toasties from $9.50; 9am-4pm Fri-Sun) Tucked away off the main road is this artisan bakery that uses an old wood-fire Scotch oven to bake its organic sourdough. It's only open on weekends, when you can pick up a sourdough cheese-and-prosciutto toastie for lunch or grab a loaf to take home.

Village Cafe CAFE, BAR **$$**
(03-5989 0700; www.facebook.com/villagecafeflinders; 49 Cook St; breakfast $10-15, mains $15-32; 8am-4pm Thu-Tue, to 8.30pm Fri & Sat;) An inviting cafe inside an old weatherboard cottage, this family-run affair comes with polished floorboards and a cosy open fire. It features an eclectic menu of homemade items, including delicious cakes, sausage rolls, sandwiches and tasty mains; Fridays and Saturdays they open for dinner. During

summer there's a little courtyard with bar, and out front are tables overlooking the street.

The Deck MODERN AUSTRALIAN **$$**
(☎03-5989 0201; www.flindershotel.com.au/the-deck; Flinders Hotel, cnr Cook & Wood Sts; mains $28-34; ⊙noon-3pm & 5.30-9pm) Inside the Flinders Hotel this bistro does upmarket pub fare as well fancier items such as confit duck or 12-hour braised lamb. Alternatively, head into the front bar for counter meals.

Shopping

Mornington Peninsula Chocolates CHOCOLATE
(☎03-5989 0040; www.mpchocolates.com.au; 45 Cook St; ⊙10am-4pm Thu-Mon) Run by a couple who are passionate about making chocolate, stop by to peruse its drool-inducing range of delicious handmade pralines. Expect the likes of strawberry-and-pink peppercorn to dark chocolate lime delight.

Cook Street Collective GALLERY
(☎03-5989 1022; www.cookstreetcollective.com.au; 41 Cook St; ⊙10am-4pm) Set up by a group of local artists is this fantastic art gallery featuring contemporary paintings and lithographs, sculpture and hand-made jewellery. Everything's for sale.

Getting There & Away

Flinders is hidden away in the southeast corner of the peninsula, 100km from Melbourne. Take the Peninsula Link/Mornington Peninsula Fwy (M11), exiting on the Old Moorooduc Rd (C784), and from here follow the signs to the Frankston-Flinders Rd (C777) in to town.

Taking public transport, from Frankston train station bus 782 heads to Flinders via Hastings, Balnarring and Merricks.

Red Hill & Around

POP 731

The undulating hills of the peninsula's interior around Red Hill and Main Ridge are one of the region's undoubted highlights. The centre of the region's viticulture and wine-making industries, it's unsurprisingly a favourite destination for foodies. Full of trees and tumbling hills, you can spend a sublime afternoon hopping around the winery cellar doors, restaurants and producers of local delights.

Sights & Activities

Given most attractions of Red Hill lie inland, you can easily forget that the coast is just over that hill, where some lovely surf beaches await. Favourites include **Shoreham**, **Point Leo** and **Merricks**. Both East Coast (p244) and Salty Surf School (p244) offer lessons, while **Trigger Brothers** (Map p238; ☎03-5989 8402; www.triggerbros.com.au; 14 Point Leo Rd, Point Leo; surfboard rental incl wesuit per 1/2hr $35/60; ⊙9am-5pm) offers board rental.

East Coast Surf School SURFING
(Map p238; ☎0417 526 465; www.eastcoastsurfschool.net.au; 226 Balnarring Road, Merricks North; lessons per person $60) Offers surfing lessons along the Mornington Peninsula, from Point Leo to Portsea.

Tours

Horseback Winery Tours HORSE RIDING
(Map p238; ☎03-5989 6119; www.horseback.com.au; 356 Shands Rd, Main Ridge; per person 2-/3-hr tour $130/170; ⊙closed mid-Jul–Aug) A unique way to go wine hopping is by horseback, with these tours trotting by four or five of the area's finest wineries. Also offers lessons.

Salty Surf School SURFING
(Map p238; ☎0475 910 032; www.saltysurfschool.com; 10 Marine Pde, Shoreham; public/private surf lesson per 2hr from $60/160) A highly recommended choice for those wanting to learn to surf is this homegrown company offering lessons for all levels.

Sleeping

Point Leo Foreshore Reserve CAMPGROUND **$**
(Map p238; ☎03-5989 8333; www.pointleo.com; 1 Point Leo Ring Rd; unpowered site $30-37, powered sites $35-45) This sprawling campground on the foreshore of Point Leo is one of the peninsula's best kept secrets, with its mix of seasonal and year-round sites close to the beach. It's a great spot for surfers and those wanting to learn. There are free barbecues, and a camp kitchen planned for 2018. Online bookings only.

Eating

Green Olive at Red Hill MODERN AUSTRALIAN **$$**
(Map p238; ☎03-5989 2992; www.greenolive.com.au; 1180 Mornington-Flinders Rd, Main Ridge; tapas $12.95; ⊙9am-5pm; 📶) Set on a 27-acre farm is this family-run enterprise that revolves around its light-filled restaurant with lovely outdoor tables overlooking the pastoral

surrounds. Food is from the farm or locally sourced, with a menu of shared plates, wood-fired pizzas, homemade sausages and slow-cooked meats. They produce their own olive oil, wines and beers, among other homemade goods for purchase.

Merricks General Wine Store CAFE $$
(Map p238; ☎03-5989 8088; www.merricksgeneralstore.com.au; 3460 Frankston-Flinders Rd, Merricks; breakfast $10-20, meals $16-36; ⏲8.30am-5pm) Dating back to the 1920s is this iconic stop that's an attractive, sprawling space with wooden floorboards and open fire. The rustic bistro is renowned for using fresh, local produce; a cellar door showcases wines from the Elgee Park and Baillieu Vineyard wineries. There's also an art gallery exhibiting local contemporary works.

Johnny Ripe BAKERY $
(Map p238; ☎03-5989 2033; www.johnnyripe.com.au; 1/1016 Mornington-Flinders Rd, Red Hill; $3-7.50; ⏲8am-4pm Mon & Thu-Sat, to 3pm Sun) One for those in the know is this small artisan bakery, famous for its donuts, apple tarts and gourmet pies.

The Epicurean PIZZA $$
(Map p238; ☎03-5989 4000; www.theepicurean.com.au; 165 Shoreham Rd, Red Hill South; pizzas $20-32, mains $28-47; ⏲8.30am-9pm Wed-Sat, to 4pm Sun; 📶) Whether you're here for its inviting cafe or slick cavernous restaurant doing wood-fired pizzas, the popular Epicurean is a class act. The restaurant is the main attraction, within its striking atrium 'shed' (a former apple-packing house) with exposed sleepers, polished concrete floors and copper pendant lighting. As well as its Italian restaurant, there's a cellar room representing local wineries (tastings $9).

Red Hill Cheese CHEESE
(Map p238; ☎03-5989 2035; www.redhillcheese.com.au; 81 William Rd, Red Hill; ⏲11am-5pm Sat & Sun) If you're around on a weekend, stop in for cheese tastings at this picturesque cellar door surrounded by bush. They specialise in artisan cheeses made from sheep, goat and buffalo milk.

Sunny Ridge Strawberry Farm FOOD
(Map p238; ☎03-5989 4500; www.sunnyridge.com.au; cnr Shands & Mornington-Flinders Rds; adult/child $9/4; ⏲9am-5pm Nov-Apr, 11am-4pm Sat & Sun May-Oct) If all this booziness is too much, pick your own strawberries at Sunny Ridge Strawberry Farm. Admission includes 500g of strawberries (250g for kids) and there's a cafe serving all things strawberry – from wines to ice cream.

Drinking & Nightlife

★**Bass & Flinders** DISTILLERY
(Map p238; ☎0419 548 430, 03-5989 3154; www.bassandflindersdistillery.com; 232 Red Hill Rd, Red Hill; tasting flight $10, class per hr $140; ⏲11am-5pm Fri-Sun) Drop by this boutique distillery to taste its wonderful range of unique gins, from its shiraz grape gin and a truffle varietal to its 'Angry Ant' – distilled using indigenous Australian botanicals sourced from outback Western Australia and infused with bull-ant pheromone! They also offer gin master classes where you can make up your own batch from a choice of botanicals.

★**Red Hill Brewery** MICROBREWERY
(Map p238; ☎03-5989 2959; www.redhillbrewery.com.au; 88 Shoreham Rd, Red Hill South; ⏲11am-6pm Fri-Sun) Established in 2005, this popular microbrewery produces fantastic beers to sample by the pot, pint or tasting paddle ($12), accompanied by a plate of southern-style smoked BBQ (from $15) to enjoy on its deck.

Getting There & Away

Located in the approximate centre of the peninsula, Red Hill is 84km from Melbourne. Take the Mornington Peninsula Fwy (M11) and exit on to the Nepean Hwy towards Red Hill/Flinders region.

From Frankston, bus 782 passes through Merricks and Point Leo en route to Flinders.

FRENCH ISLAND

POP 110

Exposed, windswept and wonderfully isolated, French Island is two-thirds national park and it retains a real sense of tranquillity – you can only get here by passenger ferry, so it's virtually traffic-free, plus it's off the grid with no mains water or electricity! Here folk use tank water, generators or solar. The main attractions are bushwalking and cycling, taking in wetlands, checking out one of Australia's largest koala colonies and observing a huge variety of birds and wild orchids.

The island served as a penal settlement for prisoners serving out their final years from 1916. You can still visit the original prison farm, however the property was sold early 2017, so check to see if it's still open to tourists.

The French Island Community Association (www.frenchislandinfo.com) has good info on the island.

Sights & Activities

If you want to see the best of the island, especially if your time is limited, a tour is the way to go. Book ahead and arrange a pick up from Tankerton Jetty.

Cycling is the most popular way to get around, with bikes available from the general store. All roads on the island are unsealed and some are quite sandy. There are plenty of walks too. Pick up the Parks Victoria brochure at the Tankerton Jetty for a list of walks and cycling routes.

Bayview Chicory Kilns HISTORIC SITE
(☎03-5980 1241; www.frenchislandtours.com.au; Bayview Rd) FREE Located 10km from Tankerton is the Bayview Chicory Kilns, where fourth-generation local Lois will give you a tour of the historic kilns (by donation). She'll whip you up chicory coffee and Devonshire teas in her rustic cafe. Chicory (a coffee substitute) was the island's biggest industry from 1897 to 1963.

Tours

French Island Tours WALKING
(Map p238; ☎03-5980 1241, 0412 671 241; www.frenchislandtours.com.au; per person half-day $35, min 2 people) Fourth-generation islander Lois from the Chicory Kilns also runs half-day walking tours to see the island and koalas. Call ahead to pre-book. It's a minimum of two people, and prices include a morning or afternoon Devonshire tea. She'll meet you at the jetty.

Sleeping

There's a reasonable choice of options on the island, from camping and dorms to B&B rooms and en-suite cabins.

The McLeod Eco Farm, on the site of the historic prison, was sold early 2017, so keep an eye out for whether it will reopen as an accommodation option.

Fairhaven CAMPGROUND $
(Map p238; ☎03-5986 9100; www.parkweb.vic.gov.au) FREE On the western shore where the wetlands meet the ocean, this camping ground offers a real getaway experience with sites offering little more than a compost toilet. There are no bookings, so it's first here, first served. Bring along your own drinking water; take out all your own rubbish.

French Island Eco Inn B&B $
(Map p238; ☎03-5980 1234, 0438 497 715; innonfrench@gmail.com; 10 Tankerton Rd, Tankerton; per person camping $15, dm $39, cabins s/d $130/180) A short stroll from the ferry, this spot has knockout water views and is the best value for budget travellers with dorms, camping and well-priced cabins. They have electric bikes for rent from $40 per hour. Meals are also available including breakfasts, sandwiches and mains, and there's a bar too. Cash only.

French Island Glamping TENTED CAMP $$$
(☎0498 843 850; www.frenchislandglamping.com.au; 59 Barge Access Rd; tents d with shared bathroom from $230) Set on a 100-acre property are these yurt-style tents that look out to the bush and ocean. All are equipped with double beds and sound system, but share bathrooms. There's no restaurant, so you'll need to bring along your own food to cook at its fully equipped kitchen or fireplace. Also has bike hire for $25 per day.

Eating

Only a few of the accommodation places offer meals, so many people bring along supplies from the mainland to cook their food. The general store does burgers and the like, plus a few basic groceries such as milk, bread and canned goods, but there are no supermarkets.

French Island General Store CAFE $
(Map p238; ☎03-5980 1209; Lot 1, Tankerton Rd; ⏱8am-5pm Mon-Fri, 9am-5pm Sat & Sun; 📶) The only shop on the island is the French Island General Store, which does burgers, bacon-egg rolls, soups and the like, as well as basic groceries, supplies and bottles of local wines. It also rent bikes for $30 per day. It's located 2km from the jetty, about a 35-minute walk. On weekends there's a courtesy bus from the jetty if you're hiring a bike or dining here, and they also have accommodation for $170 which sleeps four. Free wi-fi too.

Getting There & Away

Ferry is the only way to get on to the island, with regular departures during the day from Stony Point (Mornington Peninsula) or Cowes (Phillip Island).

Inter Island Ferries (Map p238; ☎0408 553 136; www.interislandferries.com.au; return adult/child/bike $26/12/8) runs the service between Stony Point and Tankerton (10 minutes, at least six daily) from approximately 7am to 7pm; as well as three ferries a day between Cowes and Tankerton (for the same cost), departing in the morning, around midday and late afternoon. Check the website for the latest schedule. You can reach Stony Point directly from Frankston on a Metlink train.

The ferry docks at Tankerton; from there it's around 2km to the licensed French Island General Store to hire a bike ($25 per day). On weekends they offer a courtesy bus for those hiring bikes from the jetty.

Another option to get to the island is via the **French Island Barge Company** (☎ 0428 880 729; Corinella; car overnight/day $150/200, foot passenger return $20) which runs a barge from Corinella if you need your own car on the island. Its schedule departs in accordance with the tides.

PHILLIP ISLAND

POP 9406

Famous for the Penguin Parade and Motorcycle Grand Prix racing circuit, Phillip Island attracts a curious mix of surfers, petrolheads and international tourists making a beeline for those little penguins.

At its heart, Phillip Island is still a farming community, but nature has conspired to turn it into one of Victoria's most popular tourist destinations. Apart from the nightly waddling of the penguins, there's a large seal colony, abundant bird life and fauna. The rugged south coast has some fabulous surf beaches, a swag of family attractions and plenty of accommodation. Visit in winter, though, and you'll find a very quiet place where the local population of farmers, surfers and hippies go about their business.

The Boonwurrung people are the traditional inhabitants of the island, though what they'd have made of coachloads of Penguin Parade tourists and biker gangs making their way over the San Remo bridge is anyone's guess.

Orientation

Cowes runs along the island's north coast, while Rhyll, 7km to the east, occupies a promontory that juts out from the island's northeast corner. Cape

MORNINGTON PENINSULA WINERIES

Most of the peninsula's wineries are in the hills between Red Hill and Merricks, and most have excellent cafes or restaurants attached. Several companies offer winery tours – ask at the **visitor centre** (p236). For an overview, check out **Mornington Peninsula Wineries & Region** (www.mpva.com.au). Wineries to consider include the following:

Montalto (Map p238; ☎ 03-5989 8412; www.montalto.com.au; 33 Shoreham Rd, Red Hill South; ⏰ cellar door & cafe 11am-5pm, restaurant noon-3pm, 6.30-11pm Fri & Sat) One of the Peninsula's best winery restaurants, renowned for its pinot noir and chardonnay. There's also the piazza and garden cafe for casual dining, as well as a beguiling sculpture garden.

Pier 10 (Map p238; ☎ 03-5989 8849; www.pier10wine.com.au; 10 Shoreham Rd; mains $16-37; ⏰ cellar door 11am-5pm, restaurant noon-2.30pm Thu-Sun, 6pm-late Fri & Sat) This scenic, boutique winery is within a converted tin shed that houses both its cellar door and bistro restaurant.

Port Phillip Estate (Map p238; ☎ 03-5989 4444; www.portphillipestate.com.au; 263 Red Hill Rd, Red Hill South; 2-/3-course meal from $68/85, cellar door mains $15-22; ⏰ cellar door 11am-5pm, restaurant noon-3pm Wed-Sun, 6.30-9pm Fri & Sat) A stunning winery inside a building that resembles a Bond villain's lair. It has one of the peninsula's best restaurants with stunning views, a gastronomic menu or lighter meals, and wine tastings ($5).

Red Hill Estate (Map p238; ☎ 03-5931 0177; www.redhillestate.com.au; 53 Shoreham Rd, Red Hill South; ⏰ cellar door 11am-5pm, restaurant noon-5pm, 6-9pm Sat) Sample maritime cool climate pinots and chardonnays or dine at the renowned Max's Restaurant, which in 2017 was about to undergo major redevelopment.

Ten Minutes By Tractor (Map p238; ☎ 03-5989 6080; www.tenminutesbytractor.com.au; 1333 Mornington-Flinders Rd, Main Ridge; 5-/8-course tasting menu $114/144, 2-/3-course meal $69/92; ⏰ cellar door 11am-5pm, restaurant noon-3pm Wed-Sun, 6.30-9pm Thu-Sat) This is one of regional Victoria's best restaurants and you won't find a better wine list on the Peninsula. The unusual name comes from the three vineyards, which are each 10 minutes apart by tractor.

Woolamai, 14km southeast of Cowes, is a long finger of land that extends out into the ocean from the island's far southeast, south of Newhaven.

Sights

★Nobbies Centre & Boardwalk VIEWPOINT
(Map p249; ☎03-5951 2800; Summerlands) FREE At the island's southwestern tip is this dramatic viewpoint for the **Nobbies** offshore rock formations. Here the gigantic cafe and souvenir shop known as the **Nobbies Centre** has incredible ocean vistas and the multimedia Antarctic Journey. In front of the centre, a **boardwalk** winds down to vantage points of the formations, as well the blow hole, and beyond to the Seal Rocks – inhabited by Australia's largest fur-seal colony. There are coin-operated binoculars, but bring your own if you have them.

On the drive here you'll pass by memorable landscapes of windswept grassy plateau and rugged coastal scenery. The area is a protected wildlife reserve, where penguins come to nest nightly (look for their purpose-built burrows); however, everyone is required to leave the site one hour before sunset. There's an abundance of wildlife on the roads, particularly Cape Barren geese, so take care driving – usually they won't budge.

★Penguin Parade WILDLIFE RESERVE
(Map p249; ☎03-5951 2800; www.penguins.org.au; 1019 Ventnor Rd, Summerland Beach; admission from adult/child/family $25.10/12.50/62.70, underground viewing $60/30/150; ⌚9.30am-dusk, penguins arrive at sunset) The Penguin Parade attracts more than half-a-million visitors annually to see the little penguins *(Eudyptula minor)*, the world's smallest, and probably cutest of their kind. The main penguin complex includes concrete amphitheatres that hold up to 3800 spectators who come to see the little fellas just after sunset as they waddle from the sea to their land-based nests. There's also an underground viewing section, premium seats and VIP platforms for those wanting prime views; come summer book well in advance.

Penguin numbers swell after breeding in summer, with as many as 32,000 arriving on a given night, but they're in residence year round. After the parade, hang around the boardwalks for a closer view as the stragglers search for their burrows and mates. Bring warm clothing, and take note there's strictly no photography or videoing. Be sure to arrive an hour beforehand – check the website for their ETA.

There are a variety of specialised tours where you can be accompanied by rangers to explain the behaviour of penguins, tours with night-vision goggles, behind-the-scenes tours and highly recommended Aboriginal heritage guided walks ($60) that conclude with premium penguin viewing. There's also a cafe and an interpretive centre at the complex, where you can spy penguins nesting during the day; it's free entry until 4pm. A new building was being constructed in 2017, which will further improve facilities.

Antarctic Journey OBSERVATORY, THEATRE
(Map p249; ☎03-5951 2800; www.penguins.org.au/attractions/recreational-areas/the-nobbies; 1320 Ventnor Rd, Nobbies Centre, Summerlands; adult/child/family $18/9/45; ⌚9am-5pm) On the southwest tip of the island is this cutting-edge multimedia exhibition space that spotlights the shared waters between here and Antarctica. Its interactive displays are highly informative, with cool augmented reality features. It's located in the Nobbies Centre a five-minute drive from the Penguin Parade, so aim to visit in mid afternoon if you're seeing the penguins.

Churchill Island FARM
(Map p249; ☎03-5951 2800; www.penguins.org.au; Phillip Island Rd, Newhaven; adult/child/family $12.50/6.25/31.25; ⌚10am-5pm Mon-Fri, from 9am Sat & Sun) Connected to Phillip Island by a bridge near Newhaven, Churchill Island is a delightful working farm where Victoria's first crops were planted. Its historic homestead and garden is surrounded by paddocks of grazing highland cattle and looks out to fabulous ocean views. There are several pleasant walking tracks looping around the island. Time your visit for farm activity demonstrations, including sheep shearing, cow milking and watching working sheep dogs in action.

Phillip Island Chocolate Factory FACTORY
(Map p249; ☎03-5956 6600; www.phillipisland-chocolatefactory.com.au; 930 Phillip Island Rd; tours adult/child/family $17/11/50; ⌚9am-6pm) Like Willy Wonka's, Panny's place is full of fquirky surprises. As well as free samples of handmade Belgian-style chocolate, there's a walk-through tour of the chocolate-making process, including a remarkable gallery of chocolate sculptures, from Michelangelo's *David* to an entire model village! Naturally, you can buy chocolate penguins, but most of the chocolate is prepackaged.

Phillip Island

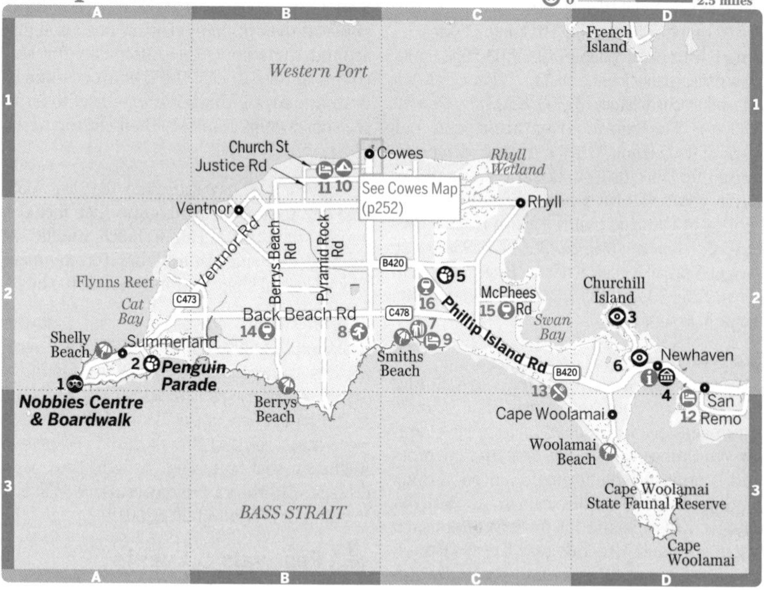

0 5 km
0 2.5 miles
Western Port
French Island
Church St
Justice Rd
Cowes
Rhyll Wetland
See Cowes Map (p252)
Ventnor
Rhyll
Ventnor Rd
Berrys Beach Rd
Pyramid Rock Rd
B420
Flynns Reef
C473
Cat Bay
Back Beach Rd
C478
Phillip Island Rd
McPhees Rd
Swan Bay
Churchill Island
Shelly Beach
Summerland
Penguin Parade
Smiths Beach
Newhaven
Nobbies Centre & Boardwalk
Berrys Beach
B420
Cape Woolamai
San Remo
Woolamai Beach
Cape Woolamai State Faunal Reserve
BASS STRAIT
Cape Woolamai

Phillip Island

Top Sights
1 Nobbies Centre & Boardwalk A2
2 Penguin Parade A2

Sights
Antarctic Journey .... (see 1)
3 Churchill Island D2
History of Motorsport Museum ..... (see 8)
4 Islantis Surf Experience D2
5 Koala Conservation Centre C2
6 Phillip Island Chocolate Factory D2

Activities, Courses & Tours
Grand Prix Guided Circuit Tours .... (see 8)
7 Island Surfboards C2
Phillip Island Circuit Go Karts .... (see 8)
8 Phillip Island Grand Prix Circuit B2
Rip Curl Phillip Island .... (see 4)

Sleeping
Apartments at Glen Isla .... (see 11)
9 Clifftop C2
10 Cowes Caravan Park B1
11 Glen Isla House B1
Island Accommodation YHA .... (see 4)
12 Westernport Hotel D3

Eating
BEANd .... (see 12)
13 Cape Kitchen C2

Drinking & Nightlife
14 Phillip Island Winery B2
15 Purple Hen Winery C2
16 Rusty Water Brewery C2

Koala Conservation Centre ZOO
(Map p249; ☎03-5951 2800; www.penguins.org.au; 1810 Phillip Island Rd, Cowes; adult/child/family $12.50/6.25/31.25; ⏲10am-5pm, extended hrs in summer) While in the wild there are only 20 to 30 of these furry marsupials left on the island, here at the Koala Conservation Centre you're guaranteed to see them. Whether from the treetop boardwalks or trails along the ground, you'll spot them chewing on eucalyptus leaves or dozing away – they sleep about 20 hours a day!

Activities

Phillip Island Grand Prix Circuit ADVENTURE SPORTS
(Map p249; ☎03-5952 9400; Back Beach Rd) Even when the motorbikes aren't racing, petrolheads love the Grand Prix Motor Racing Circuit. The visitor centre runs **guided circuit tours** (Map p249; ☎03-5952 9400;

www.phillipislandcircuit.com.au; Back Beach Rd; 1hr tour adult/child/family $25/15/60; ⏲tours 2pm), or check out the **History of Motorsport Museum** (Map p249; ☎03-5952 9400; www.phillipislandcircuit.com.au; Back Beach Rd; adult/child/family $17.50/8.50/42; ⏲9am-5.30pm). The more adventurous can cut laps of the track with a racing driver in hotted-up V8s ($360; bookings essential). Drive yourself in a go-kart around a scale replica of the track with **Phillip Island Circuit Go Karts** (Map p249; ☎03-5952 9400; www.phillipislandcircuit.com.au; Back Beach Rd; per 10-/20-/30-min $35/60/80; ⏲9am-5.30pm, longer hr in summer).

Surfing

Excellent surf beaches bring day-tripping board riders from Melbourne. The island's south-side ocean beaches include spectacular **Woolamai**, which has rips and currents and is only suitable for experienced surfers. Beginners and families can go to **Smiths Beach**, where Island Surfboards offers surfing lessons and hires out gear. **Berrys Beach** also has a beautiful wave and is usually quieter than Woolamai or Smiths. Around the Nobbies, Cat Bay and Flynns Reef will often be calm when the wind is blowing onshore at the Woolamai and Smiths areas.

Rip Curl Phillip Island SURFING
(Map p249; ☎03-5956 7553; 10-12 Phillip Island Tourist Rd; ⏲9am-5pm) As well selling surf apparel and running a surf **museum** (Map p249; ☎03-5956 7553; www.theislantissurfexperience.com.au; 10-12 Phillip Island Rd, Big Wave Complex, Newhaven; adult/child $4.50/2.50; ⏲9am-5pm), they also rent out boards (per hour/day $12.50/40) and wetsuits.

Island Surfboards SURFING
(Map p252; ☎03-5952 2578; www.islandsurfboards.com.au; 147 Thompson Ave, Cowes; lessons from $70, board hire per hr/day $12.50/40; ⏲9am-5pm Mon-Sat, to 3pm Sun) The Cowes branch of this local **surf shop** (Map p249; ☎03-5952 3443; www.islandsurfboards.com.au; 225 Smiths Beach Rd, Smiths Beach; lessons from $70, surfboard hire per hr/day $12.50/40; ⏲9am-5pm) rents out boards and has a surf school.

Tours

Wild Ocean Eco Boat WILDLIFE WATCHING
(☎03-5951 2800; www.penguins.org.au; Cowes or Rhyll Jetty; per person adult/child/family Adventure Tour $85/65/235, Island Discovery $130/75/345, Shearwater Sunset $65/49/179; ⏲Adventure Tour 3pm, Island Discovery 11am Dec-Apr, Shearwater Sunset 7.15-8.30pm Nov-Apr) These boat tours give you the option of visiting various sights around the island: the Australian fur seal colony at Seal Rocks; the scenic coastline of dramatic rock formations; or sunset tours to see shearwaters return to their clifftop nests.

Go West TOURS
(☎03-9485 5290; www.gowest.com.au; tour $135) One-day tour from Melbourne that includes entry to the Penguin Parade, lunch, wildlife encounters and wine-tasting. It has iPod commentary in several languages and wi-fi on the bus.

Wildlife Coast Cruises BOATING
(Map p252; ☎1300 763 739, 03-5952 3501; www.wildlifecoastcruises.com.au; 11/13 the Esplanade, Cowes; seal watching adult/child/family $78/52/215; ⏲2pm Fri-Wed Sep-Jul, plus 11am & 4.30pm in summer & school holidays) Runs a variety of cruises including seal watching, twilight and cape cruises; also runs a full-day cruise to Wilsons Promontory (adult/child $250/195).

Festivals & Events

Australian Motorcycle Grand Prix SPORTS
(☎1800 100 030; www.motogp.com.au) The island's biggest event is the Australian Motorcycle Grand Prix, one of the most scenic circuits on the MotoGP international calendar. Its three days of action are usually held in October, when the the island's population jumps from 8000 people to over 150,000.

Sleeping

Most of the accommodation is in and around Cowes, although there are a few places in Rhyll and Newhaven. There are B&Bs and caravan parks scattered around the island. During big motor-racing events, Christmas, Easter and school holidays, rates are sky high and you'll need to book way in advance.

Phillip Island Glamping TENTED CAMP **$$**
(☎0404 258 205; www.phillipislandglamping.com.au; d tent hire weekday/weekend from $120/140) A different kind of arrangement to the norm, here you book your camp site (choosing from any of the island's campgrounds), and the staff sets up your bell tent. It'll be ready to go upon your arrival, equipped with mattress, bedding, towels, heater, digital radio, table and chairs, esky and full cooking utensils. Once you're done, they'll clean it all up again – lazy camping at its best.

Cowes

Cowes Caravan Park CARAVAN PARK $
(Map p249; ☎03-5952 2211; www.cowescaravanpark.com.au; 164 Church St, Cowes; campsites from $40, cabins from $90-130;) The place for beach-side camping is this park that offers a range of campsites and en-suite cabins – the better ones have air-con and beach views. It's 1km from Cowes.

Westernport Hotel PUB $
(Map p249; ☎03-5678 5205; www.thewesternport.com.au; 161 Marine Pde, San Remo; d with shared/private bathroom $55/80;) At the San Remo bridge leading into Phillip Island, these no-frills pubs rooms are a good budget option for those not into the whole backpacker scene. Rooms can get a bit noisy, but given you're above a pub, what did you expect? The Westernport itself is a nice spot for a drink, with friendly staff, live music and good food. Rates go up a bit in summer.

Apartments at Glen Isla APARTMENT $$
(Map p249; ☎03-5952 2822; www.apartmentsatglenisla.com.au; 234 Church St; d $140-170;) Only a short stroll to the beach are these suburban self-contained apartments featuring all the amenities you need. The highlight is its classic Aussie backyard lined with palms, small pool, spa and, of course, a barbie – a scene that's straight off the set of *Neighbours*.

★**Clifftop** BOUTIQUE HOTEL $$$
(Map p249; ☎03-5952 1033; www.clifftop.com.au; 1 Marlin St, Smiths Beach; d $235-290;) It's hard to imagine a better location for your island stay than perched above Smiths Beach. Of the seven luxurious suites here, the top four have ocean views and private balconies, while the downstairs rooms open onto gardens – all have fluffy beds and slick contemporary decor.

★**Glen Isla House** BOUTIQUE HOTEL $$$
(Map p249; ☎03-5952 1882; www.glenisla.com; 230 Church St, Cowes; d/ste from $255/355;) This brilliant boutique hotel is one of the best addresses on the island. Ensconced in a renovated 1870 homestead and outbuildings, Glen Isla is all about understated, old-world luxury with modern touches such as huge plasma TVs. It has 2 acres of lovely gardens and is only a five-minute walk to the beach. No children under 12.

Newhaven

★**Island Accommodation YHA** HOSTEL $
(Map p249; ☎03-5956 6123; www.theislandaccommodation.com.au; 10-12 Phillip Island Rd, Newhaven; dm $27-50, d $99-155;) This large purpose-built backpackers has huge identical living areas on each floor, complete with table tennis, PlayStations and cosy fireplaces for winter. Its rooftop deck has terrific views and its eco-credentials are excellent. Cheapest dorms sleep 12 and doubles are motel-standard. They have bike hire (per day $20), with the cycle path out front leading all the way to Cowes.

Eating

Cowes

BEANd CAFE $
(Map p249; ☎0407 717 588; www.beand.com.au; 157 Marine Pde, Shop 4; breakfast $8-15; ⏲7am-4pm Thu-Tue) At the bridge heading into Phillip Island is this micro-coffee roaster that does a top-notch brew, using single-origin beans sourced from around Africa, Asia and Latin America. It's a vibrant, friendly little cafe, with all its coffee roasted onsite and prepared as pour overs, aeropress and espresso. All-day breakfasts and burgers for lunch.

Madcowes CAFE, DELI $
(Map p252; ☎03-5952 2560; www.madcowescafe.com.au; 17 the Esplanade, Cowes; mains $9-18; ⏲6.30am-3pm) This stylish cafe-foodstore looks out to the main beach and cooks up some of the heartiest breakfasts and light lunches on the island. Its quinoa bowl makes for a healthy start to the day, while its deluxe breakfast roll (filled with bacon, fried egg, cheese and a hash brown) is the perfect hangover cure. For lunch it does roast beef sandwiches, tempura squid and local wines.

Fig & Olive at Cowes MODERN AUSTRALIAN $$
(Map p252; ☎03-5952 2655; www.figandolive.com.au; 115 Thompson Ave, Cowes; mains $20-42; ⏲noon-2pm & 5-9.30pm Tue-Sat) One of Cowe's smartest restaurants has an eclectic menu strong on grilled seafood and meats, but is best known for its wood-fired pizzas.

Newhaven

Cape Kitchen MODERN AUSTRALIAN $$
(Map p249; ☎03-5956 7200; www.thecapekitchen.com.au; 1215 Phillip Island Rd, Newhaven; breakfast from $19, lunch $27-48; ⏲8.30am-4.30pm Fri-

Mon) Grab a window seat to take in all-encompassing ocean vistas while enjoying delicious breakfasts such as house-smoked salmon with scrambled eggs and sourdough. For lunch there's the likes of charcoal trout, red-curry Gippsland mussels or a roasted South Gippsland lamb shoulder to share.

Drinking & Nightlife

Rusty Water Brewery MICROBREWERY
(Map p249; ☎03-5952 1666; www.rustywaterbrewery.com.au; 1821 Phillip Island Rd; ⏲noon-late) The island's best spot for a cold one is this microbrewery with seven of its own ales on tap – which is all brewed off site. The usual range of IPAs, pale and golden ales are on offer, plus a few seasonals to go with its menu of upmarket pub fare. It's on the main road just across from the koala sanctuary.

Purple Hen Winery WINERY
(Map p249; ☎03-5956 9244; www.purplehenwines.com.au; 96 McPhees Rd, Rhyll; ⏲11am-5.30pm Thu-Mon, daily Dec-Easter) Try the signature pinot noir and chardonnay at the cellar door of this scenic winery with views over Western Port Bay (tastings $5).

Phillip Island Winery WINERY
(Map p249; ☎03-5956 8465; www.phillipislandwines.com.au; 414 Berrys Beach Rd; ⏲noon-6pm weekends, daily in school holidays) Sample excellent estate wines and share platters of cheese, terrine, smoked salmon, trout fillets and pâté ($15-38) among scenic surrounds.

Information

Phillip Island Visitor Information Centre (Map p249; ☎1300 366 422; www.visitphillipisland.com; 895 Phillip Island Tourist Rd, Newhaven; ⏲9am-5pm, to 6pm school holidays; 📶) The main visitor centre on the island has a wall of brochures and maps. It sells tickets to the penguin parade, and sight packages that bring healthy discounts. It also offers a super-helpful accommodation booking service and has free wi-fi.

Cowes Visitor Information Centre (Map p252; ☎1300 366 422; www.visitphillipisland.com; cnr Thompson & Church Sts, Cowes; ⏲9am-5pm) An alternative to the info centre in Newhaven.

Getting There & Away

About 140km from Melbourne by car, Phillip Island can only be accessed by crossing the bridge between San Remo and Newhaven. From Melbourne take the Monash Fwy (M1) and exit at Pakenham, joining the South Gippsland Hwy at Koo Wee Rup.

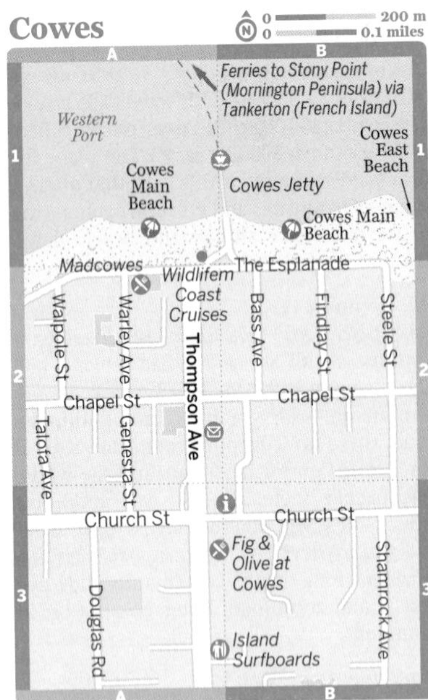

If you're on foot or bicycle, you can get here by ferry from Stony Point to Cowes.

Once on the island it's easy and quick to get around by car or bike – it's just a 15-minute drive from Cowes to the Penguin Parade or Grand Prix circuit.

By public transport you'll need to get a combination of train and bus to Phillip Island. V/Line runs around eight trips a day from Melbourne's Southern Cross Station to Cowes via Koo Wee Rup ($14.40, 2½ hours) or a longer journey via Dandenong (3½ hours).

Inter Island Ferries (Map p252; www.interislandferries.com.au; Cowes Jetty; one-way adult/child $13/6; ⏲departures 8.30am-8.15pm Mon-Thu, to 5.30pm Sat & Sun) Runs between Stony Point on the Mornington Peninsula and Cowes via French Island (45 minutes). There are three sailings Saturday to Thursday, and four on Fridays.

Getting Around

Hire bicycles from **Island Accommodation YHA** (p251) or an electric bike from **Island E Bike Hire** (☎0457 281 965; www.islandebikehire.com.au; per 1hr/day $20/60).

A bus runs between San Remo to Cowes about seven times a day, via Newhaven, Cape Woolamai and Smiths Beach.

Wilsons Promontory & Gippsland

Includes ➜

Best Places to Eat

- Koonwarra Store (p257)
- Nautica (p268)
- Pier 70 (p267)
- Lucy's (p277)
- Wildfish (p263)
- Tinamba Hotel (p266)

Best Places to Sleep

- Lighthouse Keepers' Cottages (p261)
- Wilderness Retreat – Tidal River (p261)
- Limosa Rise (p262)
- Adobe Abodes (p276)
- Tin Chalet (p273)
- Rodondo (p263)

Why Go?

The Great Ocean Road may get the crowds, but Gippsland hides all the secrets. Gippsland is one region where it pays to avoid the cities – the towns along the Princes Hwy are barely worth a traveller's glance. But beyond the highway are some of the state's most absorbing, unspoiled and beautiful wilderness areas and beaches.

Along the coast there's Wilsons Promontory National Park, a fabulous destination for hikers and sightseers alike. This is only the start when it comes to stirring beaches. Epic Ninety Mile Beach yields to Cape Conran Coastal Park and Croajingolong National Park. Put them together and it's one of the wildest, most beautiful coastlines on Earth.

Inland, the Buchan Caves are a must-see attraction, while the national parks at Snowy River and Errinundra are as deeply forested, remote and pristine as any in the country.

When to Go

Point Hicks

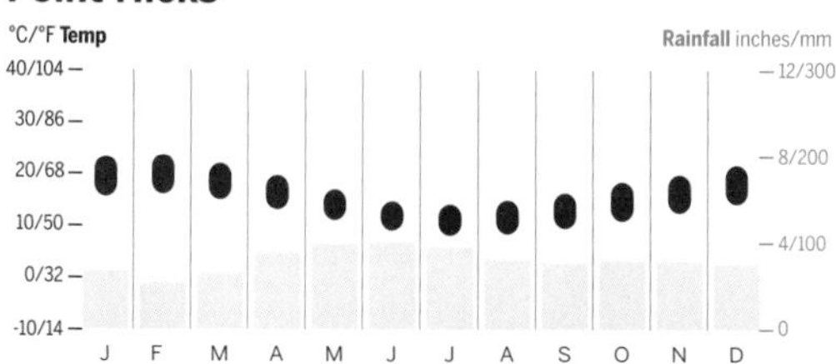

Feb–Mar Revel in long days of sunshine without the holiday crowds.

Sep–Nov Spring is the time for wild flowers and wildlife, as well as bushwalking.

Dec–Jan It gets busy, but there's no better time to hit the oceans and lakes than summer!

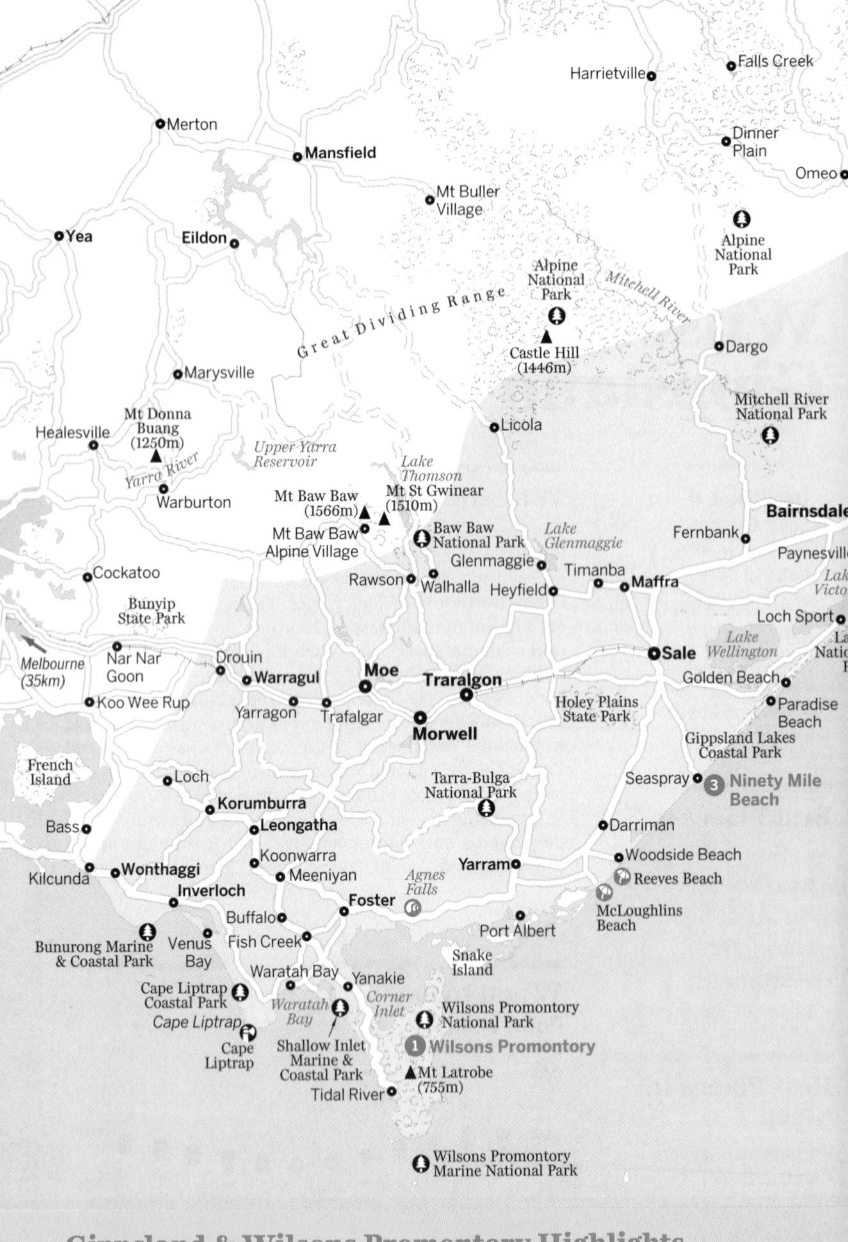

Gippsland & Wilsons Promontory Highlights

1. **Wilsons Promontory** (p258) Hiking from Tidal River to Sealers Cove, past remote lighthouses, in this national park.
2. **East Gippsland Rail Trail** (p274) Saddling up for Gippsland's longest cycle path.
3. **Ninety Mile Beach** (p266) Camping in the dunes and fishing from the beach at this legendary beach.
4. **Snowy River National Park** (p271) Hiking deep into the forest or driving remote tracks in this beautiful region.
5. **Buchan** (p271) Exploring

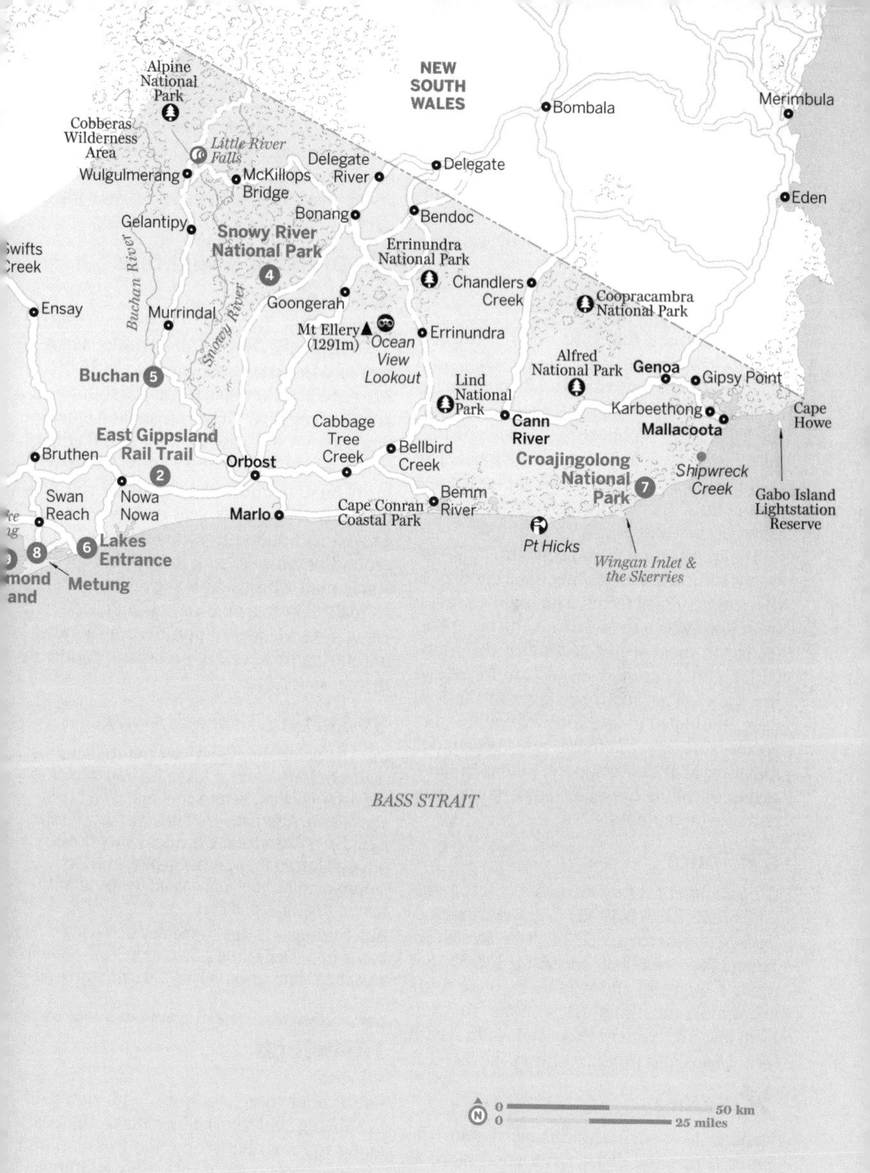

ancient limestone caves at the foot of the Snowy Mountains.

6 **Lakes Entrance** (p268) Taking an afternoon winery cruise then feasting on a seafood dinner.

7 **Croajingolong National Park** (p277) Finding your quiet corner of the world in this humbling wilderness area.

8 **Metung** (p267) Cruising the waters of the Lakes District from this tranquil marina village.

9 **Raymond Island** (p267) Looking for koalas in this little-known spot.

SOUTH GIPPSLAND

South Gippsland has plenty of gems along the coast between Melbourne and Wilsons Promontory – Venus Bay, Cape Liptrap Coastal Park and Waratah Bay are all worth exploring. Inland among the farming communities are some great drives through the Strzelecki Ranges and trendy villages such as Koonwarra.

Sights & Activities

Great Southern Rail Trail OUTDOORS
(www.railtrails.org.au) This 74km cycling and walking path follows the old rail line from Leongatha to Port Welshpool, passing through the villages of Koonwarra, Meeniyan, Buffalo, Fish Creek, Toora and Welshpool. The trail meanders through farmland with a few gentle hills, trestle bridges and occasional views of the coast and Wilsons Prom.

The first section from Leongatha to Koonwarra is through the rolling open country of the region's dairy farms. The middle section from Koonwarra to Meeniyan and on to Foster is the most scenic section of the route, with plenty of bridges, eucalyptus forest and fine views. The final few stages of the trail were completed in late 2016, extending from Foster through to Toora and Welshpool, finishing at Port Welshpool, taking in landscapes of rolling hills, bushland, dairy farms and coastal outlooks.

Tours

Gippsland Food Adventures FOOD & DRINK
(☎03-5663 2386, 0419 153 377; www.gippslandfoodadventures.com.au; 1720 Buffalo–Waratah Rd, Tarwin Lower; farm tours adult/child $55/35) Set up by a husband-and-wife team, these tours encompass anything from visits to their farm and area winery to coastal walks – with local Gippsland produce always the focus.

Eating

Famous as a dairy-producing region, the South Gippsland district is a good place to sample local produce. Check out the **Southern Gippsland Foodmap** (www.southerngippslandfoodmap.com.au) for ideas of where you can visit cheesemakers, wineries, gastropubs, cafes and provedores.

Prom Country Cheese CHEESE $
(☎03-5657 3338; www.promcountrycheese.com.au; 275 Andersons Inlet Rd, Moyarra; plates from $10; ⏰10am-5pm Sat & Sun, daily school holidays) Get among Gippsland's rolling green countryside, famed for its dairy products, and pay a visit to this family-run farm producing award-winning soft cheeses. Grab a tasting plate ($10) to sample eight of its cheeses, or the ploughman's platter that showcases local produce. Here you can watch the cheesemakers at work, or head out and play with the lambs.

Drinking & Nightlife

★**Loch Brewery & Distillery** BREWERY, DISTILLERY
(☎0423 812 172, 0414 590 474; www.lochbrewery.com.au; 44 Victoria Road, Loch; half/pint $6/10, gin & tonic $10; ⏰11am-4pm Fri-Sun) A shining example of regional Victoria's rise as a epicurean destination is this brewery and distillery inside an old 19th-century bank. Set up by a husband-and-wife team in 2014, Loch produces traditional UK real cask ales on-site, as well as London dry gins using 12 hand-ground botanicals, and, its primary focus, a single malt whisky – due for release in 2018.

You can grab a pint (or half) of ale poured using a wooden hand pump from the weekly rotating cask, or grab a tasting paddle of three ales for $10.

Getting There & Away

Car The South Gippsland Hwy (A440) links the region to Melbourne; it takes 2½ hours to drive to Foster (174km) before continuing on to Wilsons Prom. Alternatively if driving from Phillip Island you'll head along the Bass Hwy (B460) through Kilcunda, Wonthaggi and Inverloch before winding your way inland to link up with the South Gippsland Hwy.

Bus The region is well connected by V/Line buses from Melbourne's Southern Cross station, as well as local buses linking the smaller towns.

Inverloch

POP 4960

Calm inlet beaches, surf, and outstanding diving and snorkelling make the coast along the road between Cape Paterson and Inverloch a popular destination. You'll wonder what all of the fuss is about if you pass through in winter, but stay for a few days in summer and you'll come to appreciate Inverloch's charms, not least among which is its unpretentious vibe.

Sleeping

Big 4 Inverloch Holiday Park CABIN $
(☎1800 468 375, 03-5674 1447; www.inverlochholidaypark.com.au; 2 Cuttriss St; powered sites from

$50, 2-bedroom cabins from $140;) The reliable Big 4 chain offers spacious powered sites for vans, and a range of multibedroom cabins catering to families and groups. There's a heap of ways to keep busy, including an indoor pool, an adventure playground, tennis, ping pong and basketball.

If you're wanting a more basic setup, head to its **foreshore** (03-5674 1236; www.inverlochforeshorecamping.com.au; cnr Esplanade & Cuttriss St; unpowered sites $38-65, powered sites $43-75) camping ground for unpowered sites.

Inverloch Views RENTAL HOUSE **$$$**
(0407 100 070; www.inverlochviews.com; 9 Scarborough St; house $450;) A sleek, architect-designed house with a resort ambience and handily adjacent to the park, beach and shops. It has four bedrooms (the master room features a spa), so it's well set up for groups, as well as several lounges and a rooftop deck with ocean views. It's Gippsland's only purpose-built wheelchair accessible accommodation, and includes a lift among other features. Two-night minimum stay.

Eating

★ **Tomo's Japanese Inverloch** JAPANESE **$$**
(03-5674 3444; www.tomos-japanese.com; 23 A'Beckett St; sushi from $2.50, mains $17-36; noon-2pm & 6-8pm Wed-Sun, daily Dec-Feb) Modern Japanese cuisine prepared to perfection. Start with tender sushi or sashimi, and don't miss the gyoza (dumplings) or tempura tiger prawns. They have Sapporo on tap and a good range of Japanese whiskies. Cash only.

Vela Nine CAFE **$$**
(03-5674 1188; velanine.com.au; 9 A'Beckett St; mains $14-19; 8am-5pm Sun-Thu, to 8pm Fri & Sat;) New owners have transformed this tapas bar into a smart cafe-bar that does excellent coffee, cooked breakfasts, steak sandwiches and homemade pies. On Friday and Saturday nights they do a modern Australian dinner.

Information

Bunurong Environment Centre & Shop (03-5674 3738; www.sgcs.org.au; cnr Esplanade & Ramsey Blvd; 10am-4pm Fri-Mon, daily in school holidays) An excellent selection of books and an abundance of brochures on environmental and sustainable-living topics – from beachcombing to dinosaur fossils. Also here is the Shell Museum ($2) with more than 6000 shells.

Inverloch Visitor Centre (1300 762 433; www.visitbasscoast.com; 39 A'Beckett St; 9am-5pm) Helpful staff, brochures and free accommodation bookings. There's free wi-fi at the library next door.

Getting There & Away

Car From Melbourne (148km), follow the signs to Phillip Island and Wonthaggi. The route via Leongatha, 27km northeast of Inverloch, is less picturesque but slightly quicker.

Public Transport V/Line (www.vline.com.au) trains depart daily from Melbourne's Flinders St and Southern Cross Stations for Dandenong, connecting with buses to Inverloch ($19, 3½ hours). A quicker option (2½ hours) is the V/Line coach with a change at gloriously named Koo Wee Rup.

Koonwarra

POP 385

Tucked away in rolling dairy country along the South Gippsland Hwy is this tiny township that's built itself a reputation as something of a niche foodie destination. It has a cooking school, renowned farmers market and produce store, plus wineries nearby. There's plenty of wildlife about in the surrounding bush.

Courses

Milly & Romeo's Artisan Bakery & Cooking School COOKING
(03-5664 2211; www.millyandromeos.com.au; 1 Koala Dr; adult/child from $100/50; 9am-4pm Thu-Sun, longer hrs in summer) Victoria's first organic-certified cooking school offers short courses in making cakes, bread, traditional pastries, French classics and pasta, as well as cooking classes for kids. They also have a bakery selling their baked goods, made using local ingredients.

Sleeping & Eating

The Wine Farm B&B **$$**
(03-5664 3204; www.thewinefarm.com.au; 370 Koonwarra–Inverloch Rd; d $150;) Set on a 15-acre family-run boutique winery is this three-bedroom self-contained weatherboard cottage that's excellent value for couples and groups ($25 per extra person). It's a must for wine-lovers; South African vintner Neil Hawkins impresses with his range of 10 cool-climate varieties. Tastings at the cellar door can be arranged.

★ **Koonwarra Store** CAFE **$$**
(03-5664 2285; www.koonwarrastore.com.au; 2 Koonwarra–Inverloch Rd; mains $12-26; 8.30am-4pm;) Local produce and wines are on sale in this renovated timber building. It's

also a renowned cafe that serves simple food with flair, priding itself on using organic, low-impact suppliers and products – go the Koonie burger with all-Gippsland ingredients. Soak up the ambience in the wooded interior, or relax at a table in the gardens with local ice cream, regional wines and a cheese paddle.

Getting There & Away

Car By road the town is 32km southwest of Korumburra and 21km northeast of Inverloch.

Bus V/Line runs buses between Melbourne's Southern Cross station and Koonwarra ($17.20, 2½ hours) three to four times a day.

Fish Creek

POP 791

Travellers in the know have been stopping for a bite to eat at Fish Creek on their way to the coast or the Prom for years. These days it has developed into a little bohemian artists community with craft shops, galleries, studios, bookshops and some great cafes. The Great Southern Rail Trail (p256) passes through too.

Sights

Celia Rosser Gallery GALLERY

(03-5683 2628, 0455 777 334; www.celiarossergallery.com.au; Promontory Rd; 10am-4pm Fri-Sun) FREE A bright art space featuring the works of renowned botanical artist Celia Rosser who's most famous for her banksia watercolours. The *Banksia rosserae* was named after her; Queen Victoria is the only other woman to have a banksia in her name.

Sleeping & Eating

Fish Creek Hotel PUB $

(03-5683 2404; www.fishcreekhotel.com.au; 1 Old Waratah Rd; mains $16-30, d with shared/private bathroom $85/100; noon-2pm & 6-9pm) The striking art deco Fish Creek Hotel, universally known as the Fishy Pub, is not only an essential stop for a beer or bistro meal, but also serves as a handy base for trips into Wilsons Prom. There's a choice of upstairs comfortable pub rooms (no TV or kettle) with shared bathrooms, and self-contained motel accommodation at the back.

Drinking & Nightlife

Waratah Hills Vineyard WINERY

(03-5683 2441; www.waratahhills.com.au; 20 Cottmans Rd; 11am-4pm Fri-Sun, daily Jan) A five-minute drive out of Fish Creek on the road to the Prom, this attractive winery offers free tastings at its cellar door in a converted tractor shed. Grab a glass of its award-winning pinot or chardonnay and a cheese plate, and enjoy views of the Hoddle Ranges from its Adirondack chairs.

Getting There & Away

Car Follow the signs off the South Gippsland Hwy at Foster (13km) or Meeniyan (28km). It's 24km (20 minutes) from the Wilsons Promontory entrance gate.

Public Transport There are four direct daily buses from Melbourne's Southern Cross station ($20.40, 2¾ hours). It's also along the Korumburra–Foster bus line, with at least three departures daily.

WILSONS PROMONTORY NATIONAL PARK

If you like wilderness bushwalking, stunning coastal scenery and secluded white-sand beaches, you'll absolutely love this place. The Prom, as it's affectionately known, is one of the most popular national parks in Australia. Hardly surprising, given its accessibility from Melbourne, its network of more than 80km of walking tracks, its swimming and surf beaches and the abundant wildlife. The southernmost part of mainland Australia, the Prom once formed part of a land bridge that allowed people to walk to Tasmania.

Tidal River, 30km from the park entrance, is the hub, although there's no fuel to be had here. It's home to the Parks Victoria office, a general store, a cafe and accommodation. The wildlife around Tidal River is incredibly tame, but to prevent disease do not feed the animals or birds.

LOCAL MARKETS

Food is an increasingly important part of the traveller experience in Gippsland. It's always worth checking the dates of the farmers and other markets in the small towns across the region.

- Koonwarra – 1st Sat of the month
- Korumburra – 2nd Sat of the month
- Foster – 3rd Sat of the month
- Mirboo North – last Sat of the month
- Inverloch – last Sun of the month

Wilsons Promontory National Park

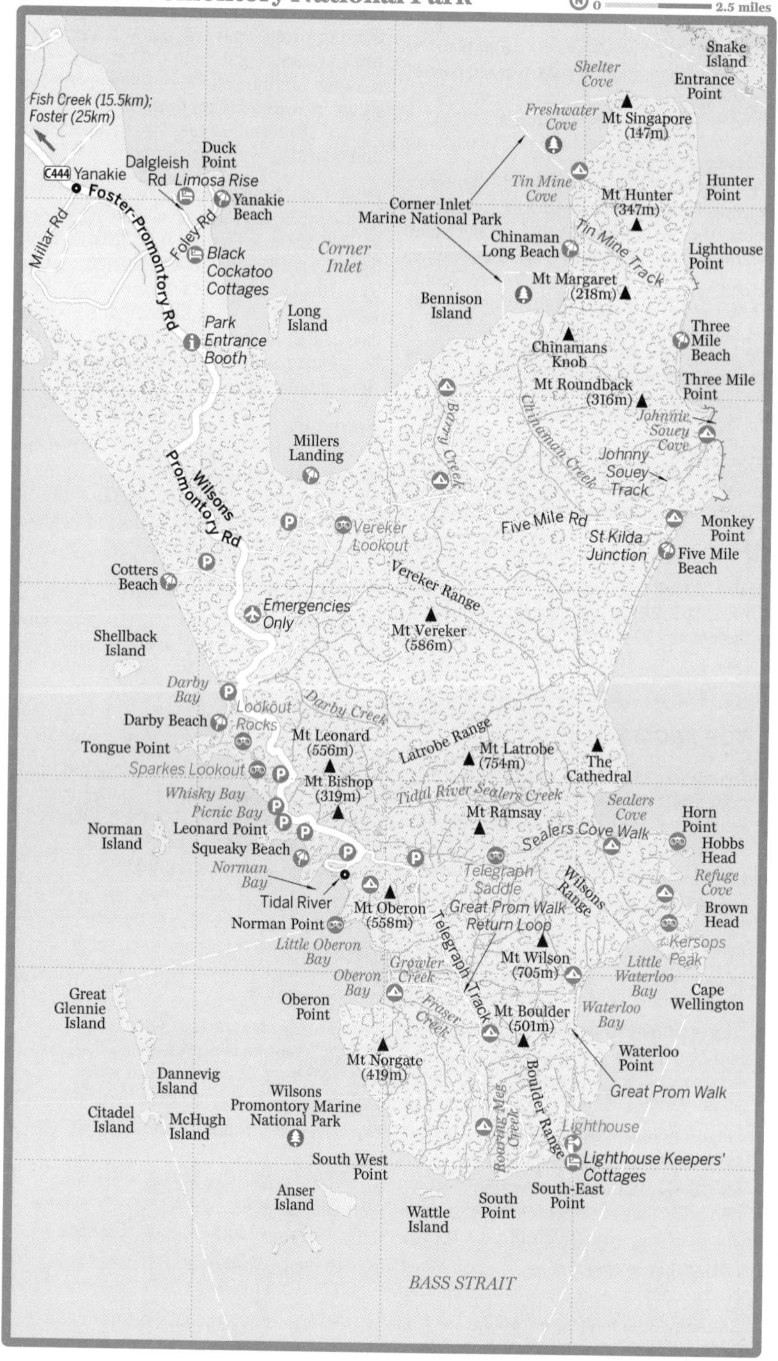

0 — 5 km
0 — 2.5 miles

Snake Island
Shelter Cove
Entrance Point
Freshwater Cove
Mt Singapore (147m)
Tin Mine Cove
Mt Hunter (347m)
Hunter Point
Corner Inlet Marine National Park
Chinaman Long Beach
Tin Mine Track
Lighthouse Point
Mt Margaret (218m)
Corner Inlet
Bennison Island
Long Island
Three Mile Beach
Chinamans Knob
Mt Roundback (316m)
Three Mile Point
Johnnie Souey Cove
Johnny Souey Track
Chinaman Creek
Barry Creek
Millers Landing
Fish Creek (15.5km); Foster (25km)
C444 Yanakie
Dalgleish Rd
Duck Point
Limosa Rise
Yanakie Beach
Foster-Promontory Rd
Millar Rd
Foley Rd
Black Cockatoo Cottages
Park Entrance Booth
Wilsons Promontory Rd
Vereker Lookout
Five Mile Rd
St Kilda Junction
Monkey Point
Five Mile Beach
Cotters Beach
Vereker Range
Emergencies Only
Mt Vereker (586m)
Shellback Island
Darby Bay
Lookout Rocks
Darby Creek
Darby Beach
Tongue Point
Mt Leonard (556m)
Latrobe Range
Mt Latrobe (754m)
The Cathedral
Sparkes Lookout
Mt Bishop (319m)
Tidal River
Sealers Creek
Whisky Bay
Picnic Bay
Sealers Cove
Horn Point
Norman Island
Leonard Point
Mt Ramsay
Sealers Cove Walk
Hobbs Head
Squeaky Beach
Norman Bay
Telegraph Saddle
Wilsons Range
Refuge Cove
Tidal River
Mt Oberon (558m)
Great Prom Walk Return Loop
Brown Head
Norman Point
Telegraph Track
Kersops Peak
Little Oberon Bay
Mt Wilson (705m)
Little Waterloo Bay
Growler Creek
Oberon Bay
Cape Wellington
Great Glennie Island
Oberon Point
Fraser Creek
Mt Boulder (501m)
Waterloo Bay
Waterloo Point
Mt Norgate (419m)
Boulder Range
Great Prom Walk
Dannevig Island
Wilsons Promontory Marine National Park
Citadel Island
McHugh Island
Roaring Meg Creek
Lighthouse
Lighthouse Keepers' Cottages
South West Point
Anser Island
South-East Point
South Point
Wattle Island
BASS STRAIT

Sights

Norman Beach BEACH

(Tidal River) The Prom's most popular beach is this beautiful stretch of golden sand, perfect for swimming and surfing, conveniently located at Tidal River campground.

Wilsons Promontory Lighthouse LIGHTHOUSE

(Wilsons Promontory National Park) Close to being the southernmost tip of mainland Australia, this 19m granite lighthouse dates back to 1859. It's only accessibly on foot, a six-hour walk (18.3km) from Telegraph Saddle car park, hence most stay overnight at the Lighthouse Keepers' Cottages (p261), or Roaring Meg campsite, 5.2km away.

Wilsons Promontory Marine National Park NATIONAL PARK

The offshore version of Wilsons Prom National Park. It's Victoria's largest marine protected area and popular with divers.

Activities

Foster Kayak & Outdoor OUTDOORS

(☎0475 473 211; www.facebook.com/fosterkayakandoutdoor; 50 Main St, Foster; bike hire half/full day $35/70) Run by a Kiwi outdoor enthusiast, this adventure company hires out bikes for those wanting to tackle the Great Southern Rail Trail (p256) (and surrounding mountain-bike trails). They also offer a range of innovative outdoor activities, where you can do anything from learning to free dive and kayak-fish to handplane bodysurfing.

Prom Country Scenic Flights SCENIC FLIGHTS

(☎0488 555 123; www.promcountryflights.com.au; 3680 Meeniyan Promontory Rd, Yanakie; 45-min flights adult/child under 10yr $210/100; ⏲9am-5pm) Head to the skies for spectacular Prom views with these 45-minute flights over the coast, lighthouse and bushland. They're based just past the Yanakie General Store on the road into the park.

Swimming

Swimming is safe at the gorgeous beaches at Norman Bay (Tidal River) and around the headland at Squeaky Beach – the ultrafine quartz sand here really does squeak beneath your feet!

Tours

First Track Adventures ADVENTURE

(☎03-5634 2761; www.firsttrack.com.au; ⏲Dec & Jan) In the summer months this

TOP PROM WALKS

During school holidays and on weekends from Christmas to Easter, a free shuttle bus operates between the Tidal River visitor car park and the Telegraph Saddle car park – a nice way to start the Great Prom Walk. They run every 30 minutes from 8.30am to 5.45pm, with a break for lunch at 1pm. For the overnight walks you'll need to arrange a hiking permit beforehand, as well as payment for campsites and or other accommodation.

Great Prom Walk The most popular long-distance hike is a moderate 45km circuit across to Sealers Cove from Tidal River, down to Refuge Cove, Waterloo Bay and the lighthouse, returning to Tidal River via Oberon Bay. Allow three days and coordinate your walk with tide times, as creek crossings can be hazardous. It's possible to visit or stay at the lighthouse (p261) by prior arrangement with the parks office.

Sealers Cove Walk The best overnight hike, this two-day walk starts at Telegraph Saddle and heads down Telegraph Track to stay overnight at beautiful Little Waterloo Bay (12km, 4½ hours). The next day, walk on to Sealers Cove via Refuge Cove and return to Telegraph Saddle (24km, 7½ hours).

Lilly Pilly Gully Nature Walk An easy 5km (two-hour) walk through heathland and eucalyptus forests, with lots of wildlife.

Mt Oberon Summit Starting from the Mt Oberon car park, this moderate-to-hard 7km (2½-hour) walk is an ideal introduction to the Prom with panoramic views from the summit. The free Mt Oberon shuttle bus can take you to the Telegraph Saddle car park and back.

Little Oberon Bay An easy-to-moderate 8km (three-hour) walk over sand dunes covered in coastal tea trees with beautiful views over Little Oberon Bay.

Squeaky Beach Nature Walk An easy 5km return stroll through coastal tea trees and banksias to a sensational white-sand beach.

Yarragon-based company organises customised bushwalking, canoeing and abseiling trips to the Prom for individuals and groups. Prices vary according to group size and activity.

Sleeping

Nothing beats a night at the Prom. The main accommodation base is Tidal River, and there are remote bush camp sites in the north and south sections of the park. The helpful visitor centre (p262) at Tidal River books all park accommodation, including permits for camping away from Tidal River.

Otherwise there are B&Bs, hostels and pub accommodation outside the park that can be used for day trips into the park.

There are 11 bush-camping (outstation) areas around the Prom. All are only accessible via overnight hikes, which you'll need to obtain a permit for before setting out. For details of campsites on the southern and northern hikes visit www.parkweb.vic.gov.au. For bookings in towns around the Prom, such as Yanakie, Foster and Fish Creek, try www.promcountry.com.au.

Tidal River

Situated on Norman Bay and a short walk to a stunning beach, Tidal River is incredibly popular. Book accommodation online well in advance through Parks Victoria (p262), especially for weekends and holidays.

Of Tidal River's 484 camp sites, only 20 are powered sites – so you'll need to book well in advance to secure these. For the Christmas school holiday period there's a ballot for sites (apply online by 30 June through Parks Victoria).

There are also wooden huts with bunks and kitchenettes, comfortable self-contained units and spacious safari-style tented camping with en-suite bathrooms.

★ **Lighthouse Keepers' Cottages** COTTAGE $$$
(☎13 19 63, 03-5680 9555; www.parkweb.vic.gov.au; Wilsons Promontory National Park; d cottages $352-391, 12-bed cottages per person $127-141) These isolated, heritage-listed 1850s cottages, attached to a working light station on a pimple of land that juts out into the wild ocean, are a real getaway. Relax after the 19km hike (around six hours) from Tidal River and watch ships or whales passing by. The cottages have thick granite walls and shared facilities, including a fully equipped kitchen.

Park Campsites – Tidal River CAMPGROUND $
(☎03-8427 2122, 13 1963; www.parkweb.vic.gov.au; Tidal River, Wilsons Promontory National Park; unpowered/powered sites $56.10/62.50) Camp sites sprawled across the precinct and along the foreshore within close assess to the beach. A maximum of eight campers are allowed at each site. There's access to hot showers, flush toilets, a dish-washing area, rubbish disposal points and gas barbecues. No camp fires permitted.

Park Cabins – Tidal River CABIN $$
(☎13 1963, 03-8427 2122; www.parkstay.vic.gov.au; Tidal River, Wilsons Promontory National Park; 6-bed cabins from $234.50) These spacious and private self-contained cabins with fully equipped kitchen (but no TV) sleep up to six people. They have large, sliding-glass doors and a deck, and overlook the bush or river.

Wilderness Retreat – Tidal River TENTED CAMP $$$
(www.wildernessretreats.com.au; Tidal River, Wilsons Promontory National Park; d $318.50, extra person $26.20) Nestled in bushland at Tidal River, these large safari tents, each have their own deck, bathroom, queen-sized beds, fridge and heating, and there's a communal tent kitchen. Tents sleep up to four people and are pretty cool. It's like being on an African safari with a kookaburra soundtrack.

Park Huts – Tidal River HUT $$
(☎03-8427 2122, 13 1963; www.parkstay.vic.gov.au; Tidal River, Wilsons Promontory National Park; 4-/6 bed huts from $100.53/153.20) If you're travelling tent-free, these cosy wooden huts are a decent option, with bunks, minibar, kitchenette and cooking utensils, but no bathrooms. Bring your own linen, pillows and towels.

Yanakie & Foster

The tiny settlement of Yanakie offers the closest accommodation – from cabins and camping to luxury cottages – outside the park boundaries. Foster, the nearest main town, has a backpackers and several motels.

Top of the Prom at Promview Farm COTTAGE $$
(☎03-5687 1232, 0407 804 055; 4295 Meeniyan Promontory Rd, Yanakie; d $140-155, per extra person $20; Wi-Fi) Only 200m from the park entrance, this two-bedroom dairy cottage is the closest private accommodation to the Prom. It has a

kitchen, wi-fi, a DVD player and views over the paddocks; BYO linen and towel.

★**Limosa Rise** COTTAGE $$$
(☎03-5687 1135; www.limosarise.com.au; 40 Dalgleish Rd, Yanakie; d $295-400; ❄📶) The views are stupendous from these luxury, self-contained cottages near the Prom entrance. The three tastefully appointed cottages (a studio, one bedroom and two bedroom) are fitted with wood-fire heaters, and full-length glass windows to take complete advantage of sweeping views across Corner Inlet, farmland and the Prom's mountains. Two-night minimum.

Black Cockatoo Cottages COTTAGE $$
(☎03-5687 1306; www.blackcockatoo.com; 60 Foley Rd, Yanakie; d $150-250, 6-person houses $295-450) You can take in glorious views of the national park without leaving your very comfortable bed in these private, stylish, timber cottages. There are three modern cottages painted in a cool 'yellow-tailed black cockatoo' colour scheme, as well a 1970s-style brown-brick three-bedroom house.

Eating

The **General Store** (☎03-5680 8520; Tidal River; mains $5-24; ⏰9am-5pm Mon-Fri, to 6pm Sat, to 4pm Sun) in Tidal River stocks grocery items (but no alcohol), some camping equipment and a cafe. If you're hiking, or here for a while, it's cheaper to stock up in Foster. There's also a general store in Yanakie which is handy for food supplies, cold beer and Gippsland wines.

Information

Prom Country Visitor Information Centre (cnr McDonald & Main St, Foster; ⏰9am-5pm) Helpful info for those heading into Wilsons Prom, as well as ideas for the surrounding region.

Tidal River Visitors Centre (☎03-5680 9555, 03-8427 2122, 13 19 63; www.parkweb.vic.gov.au; ⏰8.30am-4.30pm, to 4pm in winter) The helpful visitor centre at Tidal River books all park accommodation (including permits for camping away from Tidal River), and offers info for all hiking options in the area.

Getting There & Away

Car Tidal River lies approximately 224km southeast of Melbourne. There is no fuel here; the closest petrol station is at Yanakie.

Public Transport There's no direct public transport between Melbourne and the Prom. The closest towns accessible by V/Line buses are Fish Creek ($20.40, 2¾ hours) and Foster ($23, three hours, four daily) via Dandenong and Koo Wee Rup.

EAST OF THE PROM

Heading eastwards into Gippsland from Wilsons Prom takes you past green dairy farms en route to a string of sleepy coastal hamlets and charming historic towns. Port Albert sees the most tourist traffic with its beach, fresh fish and seafaring atmosphere. Yarram (one hour's drive from Wilsons Prom) is one of Gippsland's most picturesque towns, distinguished by grand colonial-era architecture. There's also some scenic bushland, swimming holes and waterfalls, including Agnes Falls, a 15-minute drive from Toora.

For cyclists the **Great Southern Rail Trail** has recently been extended east of Foster to conclude at Port Welshpool.

Port Albert

POP 247

This little old fishing village, 111km by road northeast of Tidal River, is developing a reputation as a worthwhile stopover for boating, fishing and sampling the local seafood. The town proudly pronounces itself Gippsland's first established port, and the many historic timber buildings in the main street dating from the busy 1850s each bear a brass plaque, detailing their age and previous use.

Sights & Activities

Gippsland Regional Maritime Museum MUSEUM
(☎03-5183 2520; Tarraville Rd; adult/child $6/1; ⏰10.30am-4pm daily Sep-May, Sat & Sun Jun-Aug or by appointment) In the old Bank of Victoria (1861) is this interesting museum that will give you an insight into the highlights of Port Albert's maritime history, with stories of shipwrecks, the town's whaling and sealing days, and local Aboriginal legends.

Port Albert Boat Hire BOATING
(☎0447 527 222; Slip Jetty; kayaks per hr $15, pedal boats per 30min $25, motor boat per 2/5/8hr $80/150/200; ⏰call for bookings) Here you can hire boats and canoes from the Slip Jetty for cruising around the sheltered waters of the Nooramunga Marine & Coastal Park. No boat licence required. Fishing rods and equipment are included in boat rental.

Sleeping

There's a caravan park at Seabank, about 6km northwest of Port Albert, and there are a few B&Bs in town.

Rodondo B&B $
(☎0429 333 303, 03-5183 2688; www.portalbert-accommodation.com.au; 74 Tarraville Rd; r from $100) The contemporary blends seamlessly with the historic in this renovated 1871 home. The rooms have a homely but luxurious feel, and the friendly hospitality adds to the satisfaction of staying here. There's also a cosy, self-contained cabin in the former wash house.

Port Albert Motel MOTEL $
(☎03-5183 2435; www.portalbertmotel.com.au; 35-37 Wharf St; s/d $80/100, extra person $15; ❄📶) The last vestige of the historic Port Albert Hotel, which burnt down in 2013, are these pub rooms, which have since been refurbished into motel-style accommodation. It's well placed for the water and restaurants, and, ironically, next door to the new pub. Rooms are comfortable, spacious and sleep up to four.

Eating

★**Port Albert Wharf** FISH & CHIPS $
(☎03-5183 2002; 40 Wharf St; fish from $7, minimum chips $2.70; ⏰11am-7.30pm Sun-Thu, to 8pm Fri & Sat) If there's one reason to visit Port Albert, it's to drop in for a bit of flake from this renowned fish and chippery on the jetty. Lightly battered, white and tender flesh, perfectly presented and as fresh as you'd expect from a town built on fishing.

★**Wildfish** SEAFOOD $$
(☎03-5183 2002; www.wildfish.restaurant; 40 Wharf St; mains $17-32; ⏰noon-2pm Mon, noon-2pm & 6-8pm Thu-Sun) With a sublime harbourside location and the freshest local seafood, Wildfish is earning a well-deserved reputation for serving good food. By day it does crumbed burgers with slaw and aioli, and chilli and lime calamari; by night the menu turns to thoughtful seafood dishes such as macadamia-crusted duckfish and seafood spaghetti with white-wine butter sauce.

Customs House Inn PUB FOOD $$
(☎03-5183 2566; 39 Wharf St; mains $15; ⏰10.30am-11pm) With Port Albert's historic pub burning down in 2013, the next door Customs House Inn has stepped up to take over duties as PA's local watering hole. And a fine job it's doing, with several local beers on tap including its own house-brewed Customs House lager. There's good food, including fish and chips, and roasts.

Getting There & Away

Car Take the South Gippsland Hwy and follow the signs to Port Albert along the Yarram–Port Albert Rd.

Bus The closest public transport from Melbourne is the V-Line bus service to Yarram, located12km north of Port Albert.

WEST GIPPSLAND

Walhalla

POP 12

Tiny Walhalla lies hidden high in the green hills and forests at the foot of Baw Baw National Park. It's a postcard-pretty collection of sepia-toned period cottages and other timber buildings (some original, but mostly reconstructed). The setting is gorgeous, strung out along a deep, forested valley with Stringers Creek running through the centre of the township.

Gold was discovered here on 26 December 1862, although the first find was not registered until January 1863, which is when the gold rush really began. In its gold-mining heyday, Walhalla's population was 5000, today it's just 12!

Like all great ghost towns, the dead that are buried in the stunningly sited cemetery vastly outnumber the living.

Sights

The historical sights, including museums and a gold mine, are the main attraction in town. There's also a walk to extraordinary

GETTING OFF THE GRID

Despite being one of the first towns in Australia to get electric street lighting, albeit briefly in 1884, Walhalla was also the last mainland town in Australia to be connected to the electricity grid – in 1998! Despite that, there's still no street lighting. Nor is there TV reception, mains water (bring bottled water), mobile coverage or an internet network, so it's just the place for that digital detox. There's also no ATM or petrol either, in case you were wondering.

AUSTRALIAN ALPS WALKING TRACK

One of Australia's best and most challenging walks, the Australian Alps Walking Track begins in Walhalla and ends close to Canberra. This 655km epic traverses the valleys and ridge lines of Victoria's High Country, and en route to Tharwa in the ACT it climbs to the summit of Mt Bogong, Mt Kosciuszko and Bimberi Peak, the highest points in Victoria, New South Wales and the ACT respectively. Making the full trek is a serious undertaking that requires good navigational skills and high levels of fitness and self-sufficiency. If you're planning on making the trek, which takes up to eight weeks to complete, track down a copy of *Australian Alps Walking Track* by John and Monica Chapman.

Walhalla Cemetery (20 minutes return), where the gravestones cling to the steep valley wall. Their inscriptions tell a sombre, yet fascinating, story of the town's history.

Post & Telegraph Office Museum MUSEUM
(☎0400 276 004; www.walhallaboard.org.au; Main Rd; gold coin donation; ⏲10am-4pm Sat & Sun) The last of Walhalla's original, unrenovated buildings is the old post office on the main road. Dating to 1886, it has been preserved as a museum open on weekends; literally nothing seems changed once you walk through its doors.

Walhalla Historical Museum MUSEUM
(☎03-5165 6250; www.victoriancollections.net.au/organisations/walhalla-museum#collection-records; 41 Main Rd; gold coin donation; ⏲10am-4pm) In a restored historic building along the main street, Walhalla Historical Museum displays artefacts from its bygone era, as well as acting as an information centre, souvenir shop and post office.

Long Tunnel Extended Gold Mine MINE
(☎03-5165 6259; www.walhallaboard.org.au; off Walhalla-Beardmore Rd; adult/child/family $20/15/50; ⏲tours 1.30pm daily, plus noon & 3pm Sat, Sun & holidays) Relive the mining past with guided tours exploring Cohens Reef, once one of Australia's top reef-gold producers. Almost 14 tonnes of gold came out of this mine.

Activities

Walhalla Goldfields Railway RAIL
(☎03-5165 6280; www.walhallarail.com; adult/child/family return $20/15/50; ⏲from Walhalla station 11am & 1pm, from Thomson Station 11.40am & 1.40pm Wed, Sat, Sun & public holidays) A star attraction is the scenic Walhalla Goldfields Railway, which offers a 20-minute ride between Walhalla and Thomson Stations (on the main road, 3.5km before Walhalla). The train snakes along Stringers Creek Gorge, passing lovely, forested gorge country and crossing a number of trestle bridges. There are daily departures during school holidays.

Tours

Walhalla Ghost Tours TOURS
(☎03-5165 6250; www.walhallaghosttour.info; adult/child/family $25/20/75; ⏲7.30pm Sat, 8.30pm during daylight saving) Locals lead rather spooky ghost tours through this real-life ghost town on Saturday nights. Book through the Walhalla Historical Museum.

Sleeping

North Gardens Campground CAMPGROUND $
(sites free) You can camp for free at North Gardens, with 20 unpowered sites with flush toilets and barbecues (but no showers) at the north end of the village. There's no bookings, so it's first come first served.

Windsor House B&B $$
(☎03-5165 6237; www.windsorhouse.com.au; off Walhalla Rd; d $170, ste $175-215) The five rooms and suites in this beautifully restored two-storey 1878 home are fittingly old fashioned and ghost free. No children under 12.

Walhalla Star Hotel HISTORIC HOTEL $$
(☎03-5165 6262; www.starhotel.com.au; Main Rd; d incl breakfast $189-249; ❄@☜) The rebuilt historic Star offers stylish boutique accommodation with king-sized beds and simple but sophisticated designer decor, making good use of local materials such as corrugated-iron water tanks. Guests can dine at the upmarket house restaurant; others need to reserve in advance.

Eating

Greyhorse Cafe CAFE $
(☎03-5165 6262; Main Rd, Walhalla Star Hotel; dishes from $5; ⏲10am-2pm) Attached to the Star Hotel, this cafe serves breakfasts, pies, toasted sandwiches, coffee and cake.

Walhalla General Store & Miner's Cafe CAFE $

(☎03-5165 6227; Main Rd; mains $14; ⏲10am-4pm Tue-Fri, 9am-5pm Sat & Sun) In a replica historical building on the main road, this cafe does burgers, flathead tails, steak sangas, beers and wine, and, most importantly bottled water – handy given there's no drinkable tap water in Walhalla. It's also a general store stocking bread, milk, newspapers etc.

Information

There's tourist information at the **Walhalla Historical Museum** (p264), and ww.walhalla.org.au is another helpful resource.

Getting There & Away

Walhalla lies approximately 180km east of Melbourne. There's no public transport. By road, the town can be reached along a lovely, winding forest drive from Moe or Traralgon. If coming down the summit from Mt Baw Baw it's around an hour's drive for the slow, twisting 48km journey.

LAKES DISTRICT

The Gippsland Lakes form the largest inland waterway system in Australia, with the three main interconnecting lakes – Wellington, King and Victoria – stretching from Sale to beyond Lakes Entrance. The lakes are actually saltwater lagoons, separated from the ocean by the Gippsland Lakes Coastal Park and the narrow coastal strip of sand dunes known as Ninety Mile Beach. Apart from the beach and taking to the water, the highlights here involve hanging out at the pretty seaside communities.

Sale

Sights & Activities

Gippsland Art Gallery ART GALLERY

(☎03-5142 3500; www.gippslandartgallery.com; 68 Foster St, Civic Centre; ⏲10am-5pm Mon-Fri, to 4pm Sat & Sun) FREE Sale's gallery exhibits works by both local and nationally renowned artists, as well as touring exhibitions. They are preparing to move into a new space in late 2017, which will have more of a focus on landscapes, plus a dedicated gallery showcasing the works of Dutch-born Australian textile artist, Annemieke Mein.

Sale Wetlands Walk WALKING

The Sale Wetlands Walk (4km, 1½ hours) is a pleasant wander around Lake Gutheridge (immediately east of where the Princes Hwy does a dogleg in the centre of Sale) and its adjoining wetlands. It incorporates an Indigenous Art Trail commemorating the importance of the wetlands to the local Kurnai community.

Tours

Port of Sale Heritage Cruises BOATING

(☎0400 933 112; www.saleheritagecruises.com.au; 1½hr cruises adult/child under 15yr $20/15; ⏲10am & 2pm) Explore Sale's scenic waterways on the *Rubeena*, a 1911 heritage boat that's older than the *Titanic* and the longest continuously running vessel in Australia. Along the way you'll learn about Indigenous and local history, see plenty of birdlife and often koalas. The trip concludes at the historic swing bridge (c 1883), the oldest of its kind in Australia.

Eating

Criterion Hotel PUB FOOD $$

(☎03-5143 3320; www.crihotel.com.au; 90 Macalister St; mains $26-33; ⏲11am-late) It's pubs like this that make travelling in country Victoria so great. Originally built in 1865, the Criterion was restored in 2013 and is one of Sale's best spots for a meal. Here they keep things local, with dishes such as pale-ale battered Lakes Entrance shark and their signature parma with Maffra cheese and double-smoked Gippsland ham.

It's a good spot for a drink too, including $2 pots and wine at happy hour on Friday and Saturday (5pm to 6pm). The rooms here are also recommended.

Red Catt CAFE $$

(☎03-5143 1911; 192 Raymond St; breakfast $12-15, mains $15-25; ⏲8am-5pm Mon-Thu, to 10pm Fri & Sat) Along Sale's main strip is this cafe, often packed with folk who've come for the excellent coffee and mains such as salt-and-Sichuan-pepper squid, Korean fried chicken and pulled-pork tacos. They're open for dinner Fridays and Saturdays, and it's a good spot for a drink too.

Information

Wellington Visitor Information Centre (☎03-5144 1108; www.tourismwellington.com.au; 8 Foster St; ⏲9am-5pm; 📶) A ton of brochures, wi-fi access and a free accommodation-booking service. From late 2017 they will be relocating to a new address at the Civic Centre, sharing space with the new **Gippsland Art Gallery** (p265) and library.

Maffra

POP 5112

Maffra is a sizeable but relaxed country town with a picturesque main street lined with 19th-century buildings. It's popular with cyclists tackling the Gippsland Plains Rail Trail, which runs 67km from Traralgon to Stratford, as well as foreign backpackers here to work in the region.

It's 20km from Sale and a short drive to Tinamba, where there's a renowned restaurant.

Sleeping

Cambrai Hostel HOSTEL $
(☎03-5147 1600; www.maffra.net.au/hostel; 117 Johnson St; dm per night/week $35/175, s/d $75/80) One of the few true backpackers in Gippsland is this relaxed 'worker's' hostel that attracts primarily international travellers who are here to fruit pick etc. It's in a 120-year-old building that was once a doctor's residence, with a licensed bar, an open fire and a pool table in the cosy lounge, a self-catering kitchen and cheerful, well lived-in rooms.

Its front garden bar is a great place to chill and hosts regular events. The owners can sometimes arrange work in the region, however the business is up for sale as of 2017 – so be sure to call ahead.

Happy Days INN $$
(☎0428 451 484, 03-5145 1751; www.happydaysaccommodation.com; 6a Tinamba-Seaton Rd, Tinamba; d $140; ❄️📶🏊) A 10-minute drive away from Maffra in Tinamba, Happy Days is on a 5-acre property and is popular with those here for the Tinamba Hotel, or as a stop on the Gippsland Plains Rail Trail. Though its decor is straight out of 1987 – thick carpet, blonde-wood panel walls and a kitschy indoor pool in the foyer – the rooms are comfortable and have lovely views.

Eating

★ **Tinamba Hotel** MODERN AUSTRALIAN $$
(☎03-5145 1484; www.tinambahotel.com.au; 4-6 Tinamba Seaton Rd, Tinamba; 2-/3-course lunch incl drink $30/39.50, dinner mains $35-39; ⏲noon-2pm & 6-8pm Wed-Sat, noon-2pm Sun) In the small township of Tinamba, 10km west of Maffra, is this classy restaurant that's well known for its delectable menu using local, seasonal produce. Its dining room with piano and Chesterfield couches is in keeping with the lavishly presented cuisine centred around slow-cooked meats, Gippsland steaks and local seafood, accompanied by great local wines.

> WORTH A TRIP
>
> **KROWATHUNKOOLONG KEEPING PLACE**
>
> **Krowathunkoolong Keeping Place** (☎03-5152 1891, 03-5150 0737; www.batalukculturaltrail.com.au; 37-53 Dalmahoy St; adult/child $3.50/2.50; ⏲9am-5pm Mon-Fri) is a stirring and insightful Koorie cultural exhibition space that explores Kurnai life from the Dreaming until after European settlement. The exhibition traces the Kurnai clan from their Dreaming ancestors, Borun the pelican and his wife Tuk the musk duck, and covers life at Lake Tyers Mission, east of Lakes Entrance, now a trust privately owned by Aboriginal shareholders. The massacres of the Kurnai from 1839 to 1849 are also detailed.

Getting There & Away

Car Maffra is located 19km north of Sale, with the fastest route being via the Maffra–Sale Rd (C492).

Public Transport There's a V/Line train-bus service from Melbourne ($28.20, 3½ hours) four times a day.

Ninety Mile Beach

To paraphrase the immortal words of Crocodile Dundee...that's not a beach, *this* is a beach. Isolated Ninety Mile Beach is a narrow strip of sand backed by dunes, featuring lagoons and stretching unbroken for more or less 90 miles (150km) from near McLoughlins Beach to the channel at Lakes Entrance. The area is great for surf fishing, camping and long beach walks, though the crashing surf can be dangerous for swimming, except where patrolled at Seaspray, Woodside Beach and Lakes Entrance.

The main access road to Ninety Mile Beach is the South Gippsland Hwy from Sale or Foster, turning off to Seaspray, Golden Beach and Loch Sport.

Paynesville & Raymond Island

POP 3776

Paynesville is a relaxed little lake town where life is all about the water, fishing and boating; some residents have their luxury boats moored right outside their house on purpose-built canals.

A good reason to detour here is to take the ferry on one of it's regular, five-minute hops across to Raymond Island for some **koala spotting**. There's a large colony of koalas here, mostly relocated from Phillip Island in the 1950s.

Activities

Bulls Cruisers BOATING

(☎03-5156 1200; www.bullscruisers.com.au; 54 Slip Rd; boat hire from $120, cruiser 2-nights from $910; ⏱8am-4.30pm) The perfect way to enjoy the lakes is to hire a boat and get out on the water yourself. Grab a fishing boat for the day, or hire a cruiser (equipped with air-con cabins, beds, kitchens and bathrooms, and sleeping from six to 12 people) for a night or two. You don't need a boat licence to operate any of the boats, so you have no excuses.

PS Curlip CRUISE

(☎0433 416 445; www.paddlesteamercurlip.com.au; adult/child/family $25/15/60; ⏱10.30am Sat & Sun, longer hours Dec & Jan) Relocated from Marlo is this 19th-century paddle streamer refitted with a 21st-century eco, solar-powered makeover. A not-for-profit community project, it was still being rebuilt as of 2017; keep an eye on the website for updates on its upcoming trips along the Mitchell River and surrounding Ramsar-listed wetlands.

Sleeping

Gippsland Lakes Escapes ACCOMMODATION SERVICES $$

(☎03-5156 0432; www.gippslandlakesescapes.com.au; 87 The Esplanade) Offers a good range of house rentals for both Paynesville and Raymond Island, and also books Point Hicks Lighthouse (p278) further afield.

Mariners Cove MOTEL $$

(☎03-5156 7444; www.marinerscoveresort.com; 2-8 Victoria St; s/d from $125/135, apt $200-225; ❄📶) These bright, sunny waterside motel-style units open directly on to the picturesque canal, and are well located near the Raymond Island ferry.

Eating

★ **Pier 70** SEAFOOD $$

(☎03-5156 1199; www.pier70.com.au; 70 The Esplanade; breakfast $6-22, mains $16-38; ⏱9am-10pm Wed-Mon) With a sublime location right on the marina, this breezy and luxurious cafe has an outdoor deck on which to enjoy a 'breakfast jar', or a Wagyu beef burger with twice-cooked beer-battered chips for lunch. At night it's more fine dining, with fantastic seafood dishes and Gippsland porterhouse steaks.

Getting There & Away

Car Paynesville is 16km south of Bairnsdale along the C604 – watch for signs to the turn-off along the Princes Hwy in the centre of Bairnsdale.

Public Transport V-Line coaches travel twice daily between Bairnsdale and Paynesville ($6.40, 30 to 45 minutes), connecting with onward, Melbourne-bound trains.

Metung

POP 1222

Curling around Bancroft Bay, little Metung is one of the prettiest towns in the Lakes District. Besotted locals call it the Gippsland Riviera, and with its absolute waterfront location and unhurried village charm, it's hard to argue.

WORTH A TRIP

RAYMOND ISLAND

For one of the best places in Victoria to see koalas, drop down off the Princes Hwy to the relaxed lakeside town of Paynesville. Agreeable in its own right, Paynesville is the departure point for a five-minute ferry crossing to Raymond Island. There's a large colony of koalas here, mostly relocated from Phillip Island in the 1950s. Kangaroos and echidnas are also regularly spotted.

The flat-bottom car-and-passenger ferry operates every 20 minutes from 6.40am to midnight and is free for pedestrians and cyclists. Cars cost $12 and motorcycles $5.

Sights & Activities

Riviera Nautic BOATING

(☎03-5156 2243; www.rivieranautic.com.au; 185 Metung Rd; 2½hr tours adult/child/under 6yr $45/20/free, boat hire per 2hr/day $85/175, yachts & cruisers for 3 days from $1065; ⊙tours 2.30pm Tue, Thu, Sat) Getting out on the water is easy in Metung, with Riviera Nautic hiring out boats and yachts for cruising, fishing and sailing on the Gippsland Lakes. There are also sightseeing cruises three times a week, with regular sightings of seals and dolphins. The liveaboard boats and motorised yachts offer a unique form of accommodation, and good value if you have a group. No boat licence required.

Sleeping

McMillans of Metung RESORT $$

(☎03-5156 2283; www.mcmillansofmetung.com.au; 155 Metung Rd; cottages/villas from $110/160;) This swish lakeside resort has won stacks of tourism awards for its complex of English country-style cottages set in 3 hectares of manicured gardens, as well its modern villas, private marina and spa centre.

Moorings at Metung APARTMENT $$$

(☎03-5156 2750; www.themoorings.com.au; 44 Metung Rd; apt $160-390;) At the end of the road in Metung, and with water views to either Lake King or Bancroft Bay, this contemporary complex has a range of apartments from spacious studios to two-bedroom, split-level town houses. The complex has a tennis court, indoor and outdoor pools, a spa and a marina. Outside peak season it's good value.

Eating

★**Nautica** MODERN AUSTRALIAN $$

(☎03-5156 2345; www.facebook.com/nauticametung; 50 Metung Rd; breakfasts from $10, mains from $19; ⊙8am-2pm & 6pm-late Wed-Sat, 8am-3pm Sun) A classy affair with smart polished wooden floorboards, open fire and views out to the water, Nautica is one not to miss in Metung. Start the day by treating yourself to a breakfast brioche roll filled with double bacon and Swiss cheese, while for lunch go the panko calamari or oysters. Dinner is anything from slow-cooked lamb shoulder to crispy-skin barramundi.

Its attached fish and chip shop is also worth popping by – enjoy on its patch of grass overlooking the lake.

★**Metung Hotel** PUB FOOD $$

(☎03-5156 2206; www.metunghotel.com.au; 1 Kurnai Ave; mains $25-40; ⊙kitchen noon-2pm & 6-8pm, pub 11am-late;) You can't beat the location overlooking Metung Wharf, and the big windows and outdoor timber decking make the most of the water views. The bistro serves top-notch pub food with a focus on fresh local seafood. The hotel also has the cheapest rooms in town ($85).

Bancroft Bites CAFE $$

(☎03-5156 2854; www.bancroftbites.com.au; 2/57 Metung Rd; breakfast $7.50-17.50, mains $12-26; ⊙8am-3pm, & dinner in summer) A seriously good cafe with great coffee, Bancroft does build-your-own brekkies and hearty lunches including its popular seafood hotpot with sourdough.

Information

Metung Visitor Centre (☎03-5156 2969; www.metungtourism.com.au; 3/50 Metung Rd; ⊙9am-5pm) Accommodation-booking and boat-hire services. Also has a gift shop with local produce.

Getting There & Away

Metung lies south of the Princes Hwy along the C606; the turn-off is signposted at Swan Reach. The nearest major towns are Bairnsdale (28km) and Lakes Entrance (24km). The nearest inter-city rail services are at Bairnsdale.

Lakes Entrance

POP 4569

With the shallow Cunninghame Arm waterway separating the town from the crashing ocean beaches, Lakes Entrance basks in an undeniably pretty location. In holiday season it's a packed-out tourist town with a graceless strip of motels, caravan parks, minigolf courses and souvenir shops lining The Esplanade. Still, the bobbing fishing boats, fresh seafood, endless beaches and cruises out to Metung and Wyanga Park Winery should win you over.

Sights & Activities

Venture Out ADVENTURE SPORTS

(☎0427 731 441; www.ventureout.com.au; 347 The Esplanade; bike hire per hr/day $18/50, SUPs & kayaks per 2hr $25, tours from $45; ⊙10am-5pm, or call for bookings) Rents out bicycles, sea kayaks and stand-up paddleboards (SUPs), as well as running mountain-biking tours on single tracks through the surrounding forest.

Mako Fishing Charters FISHING
(☎0412 699 394, 0421 340 764; www.makofishingcharters.com; 3½hr tours adult/child $100/80) A father and son team running offshore fishing trips through the Entrance on a 15m boat, where you'll catch snapper, flathead and gummy sharks. Tours run from 3½ hours to all day. Bring your own beer, and you'll need to arrange your own fishing licence.

Sea Safari CRUISE
(☎0458 511 438; www.lakes-explorer.com.au; Post Office Jetty; 1¼hr cruises adult/child/family $15/10/40) These safaris aboard the *Lakes Explorer* have a focus on research and ecology, identifying and counting seabirds, testing water for salinity levels and learning about marine life.

Tours

Lonsdale Eco Cruises CRUISE
(☎0413 666 638; www.lonsdalecruises.com.au; Cunningham Quay; 3hr cruises adult/child/family $50/25/120; ⏲1pm Thu-Tue) Scenic cruises out to Metung and Lake King on a former Queenscliff–Sorrento passenger ferry, with common dolphin sightings.

Peels Lake Cruises CRUISE
(☎03-5155 1246, 0409 946 292; www.peelscruises.com.au; Post Office Jetty; 4hr Metung lunch cruises adult/child $55/16, 2½hr cruises adult/child $45/22.50; ⏲11am Tue-Sun, 2pm Tue-Thu & Sat) This long-running operator has daily lunch cruises aboard the *Stormbird* to Metung and 2½-hour cruises on the *Thunderbird*.

Sleeping

Eastern Beach Tourist Park CARAVAN PARK $
(☎03-5155 1581, 1800 761 762; www.easternbeach.com.au; 42 Eastern Beach Rd; unpowered sites $28-50, powered sites $35-69, cabins $118-285; @) Most caravan parks in Lakes pack 'em in, but this one has space, grassy sites and a great location away from the hubbub of town in a bush setting back from Eastern Beach. A walking track takes you into town (30 minutes). New facilities are excellent, including a camp kitchen, barbecues and a kids' playground. Sells beers at reception, too.

Bellevue on the Lakes HOTEL $$
(☎03-5155 3055; www.bellevuelakes.com; 201 The Esplanade; d from $189, 2-bedroom apt from $249;) Right in the heart of the Esplanade, Bellevue has neatly furnished rooms in earthy tones, most with water views. For extra luxury, go for the spacious spa suites or two-bedroom self-contained apartments.

Goat & Goose B&B $$
(☎03-5155 3079; www.goatandgoose.com; 27b McCrae St; d from $120-200) Bass Strait views are maximised at this wonderfully unusual, multistorey, timber pole–framed house, with quaint rooms featuring spas.

Kalimna Woods COTTAGE $$
(☎03-5155 1957; www.kalimnawoods.com.au; Kalimna Jetty Rd; d $130-160;) Retreat 2km from the town centre to Kalimna Woods, set in a large rainforest-and-bush garden, complete with friendly resident possums and birds. These self-contained country-style cottages (some with spas) have wood-burning fireplaces and are spacious, private and cosy.

Eating

★**Ferryman's Seafood Cafe** SEAFOOD $$
(☎03-5155 3000; www.ferrymans.com.au; Middle Harbour, The Esplanade; mains lunch $18-24, dinner $21-45; ⏲10am-late) It's hard to beat the ambience of dining on the deck of this floating cafe-restaurant (an old Paynesville to Raymond Island passenger ferry), which will fill you to the gills with fish and seafood dishes. The fisherman's basket for lunch and seafood platter for dinner are popular orders. Downstairs you can buy fresh seafood, including prawns and crayfish.

Sparrows Nest CAFE $$
(www.facebook.com/sparrowsnestlakesentrance; 581 The Esplanade; meals $11-21; ⏲7.30am-4pm;) Bringing a bit of urban style to Lakes Entrance is this cool spot doing single-origin coffees and house-made crumpets spread with Raymond Island honeycomb-butter speckled with bacon bits for breakfast. Lunches are good too, with the likes of pulled-pork baguettes and craft beer by Sailors Grave Brewing (p274) in Marlo.

Floating Dragon CHINESE $$$
(☎03-5155 1400; www.floatingdragon.com.au; 160 The Esplanade, Western Boat Harbour; mains $26-39; ⏲6pm-late) This floating restaurant on the harbour dishes up high-end Cantonese cuisine with soothing views through the floor-to-ceiling windows. Chilli-pepper salt calamari, half-roasted duck and pork belly are favourites.

Lakes Entrance

Miriam's Restaurant STEAK, SEAFOOD $$$
(☎03-5155 3999; www.miriamsrestaurant.com.au; cnr The Esplanade & Bulmer St; mains $29-59; ⏲noon-late) The upstairs dining room at Miriam's overlooks The Esplanade, and the Gippsland steaks, local seafood dishes and casual cocktail-bar atmosphere are excellent. Try its epic 'Greek fisherman's plate' – 500g of local seafood for $59. It offers a good choice of local wines and craft beer too.

Information

Lakes Entrance Visitor Centre (☎1800 637 060, 03-5155 1966; www.discovereastgippsland.com.au; cnr Princes Hwy & Marine Pde; ⏲9am-5pm; 📶) Free accommodation- and tour-booking services. Also check out www.lakesentrance.com.

Getting There & Away

Lakes Entrance lies 314km from Melbourne along the Princes Hwy.

V/Line (☎1800 800 007; www.vline.com.au) runs a train-bus service from Melbourne to Lakes Entrance via Bairnsdale ($39.80, 4½ hours, three daily).

EAST GIPPSLAND & THE WILDERNESS COAST

Beyond Lakes Entrance stretches a wilderness area of spectacular coastal national parks and old-growth forest. Much of this region has never been cleared for agriculture and it contains some of the most remote and pristine national parks in the state, making logging in these ancient forests a hot issue.

Buchan

POP 385

The sleepy town of Buchan, in the foothills of the Snowy Mountains, is famous for the spectacular and intricate limestone cave system at the Buchan Caves Reserve, open to visitors for almost a century. Underground rivers cutting through ancient limestone rock formed the caves and caverns, and they provided shelter for Aboriginal people as far back as 18,000 years ago.

Buchan has huge potential as an outdoor adventure destination, with some 600 caves in the area – however only five remain open to the public. There are also swimming holes, mountain-biking trails, bushwalks and white-water rafting; see www.buchan.vic.au for more info.

Sights

★**Buchan Caves** CAVE
(☎13 19 63; www.parks.vic.gov.au; tours adult/child/family $22/12.90/60.90, 2 caves $33/19.10/90.90; ⏲tours 10am, 11.15am, 1pm, 2.15pm & 3.30pm, hours vary seasonally) Since it was unveiled to Melburnians as a blockbuster sight in the early 1900s, the Buchan Caves has been dazzling visitors with its fantasy world of glistening calcite formations. Parks Victoria runs guided cave tours daily, alternating between **Royal** and **Fairy Caves**. They're both impressive: Royal has more colour, a higher chamber and dripping candle-like formations; Fairy has more delicate decorations and potential fairy sightings.

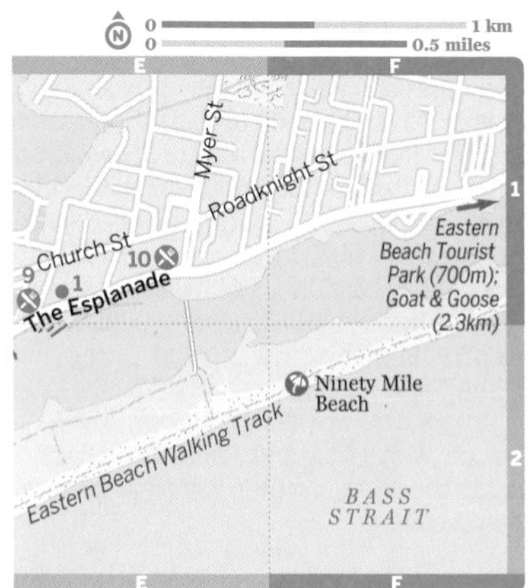

Lakes Entrance

Activities, Courses & Tours
1 Lonsdale Eco Cruises E1
2 Mako Fishing Charters D2
3 Peels Lake Cruises D2
Sea Safari .... (see 3)
4 Venture Out D2

Sleeping
5 Bellevue on the Lakes D2
6 Kalimna Woods A1

Eating
7 Ferryman's Seafood Cafe D2
8 Floating Dragon D2
9 Miriam's Restaurant E1
10 Sparrows Nest E1

The rangers also offer hard-hat guided tours to the less-developed **Federal Cave** or **Murrindal** Cave during the high season.

The reserve itself is a pretty spot with shaded picnic areas, walking tracks and grazing kangaroos. Invigoration is guaranteed when taking a dip in the icy rock pool.

Sleeping

Buchan Caves Motel LODGE **$$**
(☎03-5155 9419; www.buchanmotel.com.au; 67 Main Rd; d $130, tr & q $150) Enjoy views of the bucolic countryside from your balcony at this comfortable hilltop lodge with modern rooms featuring boutique touches. The friendly, young, enthusiastic owners are a wealth of knowledge on the area and have grand plans to capitalise on Buchan's tourism potential.

Buchan Caves Reserve CAMPGROUND **$$**
(☎13 19 63; www.parks.vic.gov.au; unpowered/powered sites from $46/51, d cabins from $90, wilderness retreats d $191;) You can stay right by the caves at this serene Parks Victoria camping ground edged by state forest. Though its campsites are exorbitantly priced, there are a couple of decent-value cabins, plus safari-style tents providing a 'luxury' wilderness experience, with comfortable queen-sized bed and air-conditioning. In summer there's a freshwater pool.

Drinking & Nightlife

Buchan Caves Hotel PUB
(☎03-5155 9203; www.facebook.com/buchancaveshotel; 49 Main Rd; ⊙11am-late) Rising from the ashes, the 125-year-old Buchan pub is back in business after burning to the ground in 2014. It came about via the world's first crowd-funding campaign to build a pub, with funds raised from around the globe. It reopened its doors in December 2016. Be sure to celebrate its return by stopping in for a chicken parma and a cold frothy.

Getting There & Away

Buchan is an easy drive 56km north of Lakes Entrance. **Dyson's** (☎03-5152 1711) runs a bus service on Wednesday and Friday from Bairnsdale to Buchan ($16, two hours). It meets the train at Bairnsdale. At other times you'll need your own transport.

Snowy River National Park

Northeast of Buchan, this is one of Victoria's most isolated and spectacular national parks, dominated by deep gorges carved through limestone and sandstone by the Snowy River on its route from the Snowy Mountains in NSW to its mouth at Marlo. The entire park is a smorgasbord of unspoiled, superb bush and mountain scenery. It covers more than 950 sq km and includes a huge diversity of vegetation, ranging from alpine woodlands and eucalyptus forests to rainforests.

Walking and **canoeing** are the most popular activities, but you need to be well prepared for both – conditions can be harsh and subject to sudden change.

The classic canoe or raft trip down the Snowy River from McKillops Bridge to a pull-out point near Buchan takes at least four days and offers superb scenery: rugged gorges, raging rapids, tranquil sections and excellent camping spots on broad sandbars.

The hilly and difficult Silver Mine Walking Track (15km, six hours) also starts at the eastern end of McKillops Bridge.

Tours

Snowy River Expeditions ADVENTURE
(☎03-5155 0220; www.karoondapark.com; Karoonda Park; tours per day $110-275) Snowy River Expeditions is a well-established company operating out of Karoonda Park, running adventure tours including one-, two- or four-day rafting trips on the Snowy. Half- or full-day abseiling, caving and horse-riding trips are also available. Costs include transport, meals and camping gear.

Sleeping

All of the camp sites in the Snowy River park are free, with six basic but scenic setups around the park. You'll find bush camping at Balley Hooley, McKillops Bridge, Raymond Creek Falls, Waratah Flat, Jackson's Crossing and Hicks camp sites. Hikers are also permitted to pitch a tent, providing you're 30m from a river or creek.

McKillops Bridge CAMPGROUND $
(☎13 19 63; www.parkweb.vic.gov.au; camp sites free) The most popular of the free camping grounds in the area is this beautiful spot along the Snowy River. Sites have nonflush toilets and fireplaces. It's a popular launching site for canoeists, and a range of hikes start out from here.

Karoonda Park FARMSTAY $
(☎03-5155 0220; www.karoondapark.com; 3558 Gelantipy Rd; dm/s/d/tr $35/50/70/90;) Just south of Gelantipy, 40km north of Buchan on the road to Snowy River National Park, is this 1800-acre cattle-and-sheep property with comfortable backpacker and cabin digs. Meals are available with prior notice, and there's a kitchen for self-caterers. They can also arrange activities such as abseiling, horse riding, wild caving and white-water rafting.

To get here by public transport, there's a bus on Wednesday and Friday from Bairnsdale – the driver can drop you off at the farm upon request.

Getting There & Away

The two main access roads to the park are the Buchan-Jindabyne Rd from Buchan, and the Bonang Rd north from Orbost. These roads are joined by McKillops Rd (also known as Deddick Valley Rd), which runs across the northern border of the park. Various minor access roads and scenic routes run into and alongside the park from these three main roads. The 43km Deddick Trail, which runs through the middle of the park, is only suitable for 4WDs.

Dyson's (☎03-5155 0356) operates a bus service from Bairnsdale to Gelantipy (via Buchan) on Wednesday and Friday ($21.80, 2¾ hours), which can drop folks off at **Karoonda Park**.

Errinundra National Park

Errinundra National Park contains Victoria's largest cool-temperate rainforest and is one of east Gippsland's most outstanding natural areas. The gorgeous

SAVING EAST GIPPSLAND'S FORESTS

A former logging town, the tiny township of **Goongerah** on the northwest boundary of Errinundra National Park now serves as a stronghold for environmentalists, conservationists, activists, self-sufficient eco-farmers and people who live off-grid. A number of local conservation groups are based here campaigning to save East Gippsland forests and endangered species such as the potoroo, spot-tailed quoll, greater glider, powerful owl and Orbost spiny crayfish.

The **Goongerah Environment Centre** (GECO; ☎0414 199 645, 03-5154 0174; www.geco.org.au; 7203 Bonang Rd) may be of interest to travellers: every three months they arrange 'citizen science' survey camps where volunteers can assist with the counting of endangered species residing in potential logging areas. Volunteers either camp at the free Goongerah camping ground or stay at the centre itself (vegetarian meals are provided for $5). Keep an eye on its website for upcoming events.

Environment East Gippsland (☎03-5154 0145; www.eastgippsland.net.au; Goongerah) is another group in Goongerah open to visitors; you can book accommodation at their **Tin Chalet** (p273) eco-cottage which couldn't look more Australian.

EAST GIPPSLAND RAIL TRAIL

The **East Gippsland Rail Trail** (www.eastgippslandrailtrail.com.au) is a 94km walking/cycling path along the former railway line between Bairnsdale and Orbost, passing through Bruthen and Nowa Nowa, and close to a number of other small communities. On a bike the trail can comfortably be done in two days, but allow longer to explore the countryside and perhaps detour on the Gippsland Lakes Discovery Trail to Lakes Entrance.

The East Gippsland Rail Trail passes through undulating farmland, temperate rainforest, the Colquhoun Forest and some impressive timber bridges. Arty Nowa Nowa is a real biking community, with a mountain bike park and trails leading off the main rail trail. There are plans to extend the trail from Orbost down to Marlo along the Snowy River.

For those without their own bike, **Snowy River Cycling** (p274) offers self-guided tours with a map and bike ($40), plus luggage transport ($15); return transport is $50. They also run guided cycle adventures.

forests surrounding the park are a constant battleground between loggers and environmentalists.

The national park covers an area of 256 sq km and has three granite outcrops that extend into the cloud, resulting in high rainfall, deep, fertile soils and a network of creeks and rivers that flow north, south and east. The park has several climatic zones – some areas of the park are quite dry, while its peaks regularly receive snow. This is a rich habitat for native birds and animals, which include many rare and endangered species such as the potoroo.

Nestled by the edge of the national park is tiny **Goongerah** (population 50), a thriving community for conservationists.

Sights & Activities

You can explore the park with a combination of scenic drives and short- and medium-length walks. **Mt Ellery** has spectacular views; **Errinundra Saddle** has a rainforest boardwalk; and from **Ocean View Lookout** there are stunning views down the Goolengook River as far as the town of Bemm River. The park also has **mountain plum pines**, some of which are more than 400 years old and easily accessible from Goonmirk Rocks Rd.

Sleeping

Tin Chalet COTTAGE $
(☎03-5154 0145; Goongerah; houses $90) A genuine rustic getaway is this solar-powered, double-storey cottage constructed from corrugated iron. It features a charming interior with wood-fire stove, reclaimed timber and plenty of character. By the river and surrounded by forest, it's set on an organic farm and orchard run by Jill Redwood, a well-known environmentalist who set up Environment East Gippsland (p272).

Goongerah Camp Site CAMPGROUND $
(free) The most accessible of the free camping grounds on the park's edges is Goongerah, a 1½ hour's drive north of Orbost. It's within a state forest on the edge of the park, set along the Brodribb River, from which you are able to drink.

Frosty Hollow Camp Site CAMPGROUND $
(☎13 19 63; www.parkweb.vic.gov.au; sites free) This is the only camping area within the national park, with basic sites (nonflush toilets, no fireplaces) along the eastern side. The only way to reach the campsite is along unsealed tracks into the park off the Bonang Rd north of Goongerah.

Getting There & Away

Errinundra National Park lies approximately 490km east of Melbourne. The main access roads to the park are Bonang Rd from Orbost and Errinundra Rd from Club Terrace. Bonang Rd passes along the western side of the park, while Errinundra Rd passes through the centre. Roads within the park are all unsealed, but are 2WD accessible. Road conditions are variable. Expect seasonal closures between June and November, though roads can deteriorate quickly at any time of year after rain and are often closed or impassable after floods (check Parks Victoria in Orbost or Bendoc first). Also watch out for logging trucks when driving.

Orbost

POP 2493

Servicing the surrounding farming and forest areas, Orbost is a relaxed country town that's gaining popularity as the start (or end) point of the East Gippsland Rail Trail. While few people spend the night here it's a good stopover for a meal (or to check out the microbrewery) for those en route to the mountains or the beach.

Sights & Activities

Snowy River Cycling CYCLING
(☎0428 556 088; www.snowyrivercycling.com.au; 7 Forest Rd; per day $40) A specialist in Gippsland's rail trails, particularly the **East Gippsland Rail Trail** (p273) that passes through Orbost, this bike operator arranges tours and mountain-bike hire. It shares space with the Sailors Grave brewery.

Eating & Drinking

Morganics CAFE $
(☎03-5154 2188; 36a Nicholson St; dishes from $5; ⏰9.30am-5.30pm Mon-Sat) A hangout for Gippsland greenies is this earthy cafe and organic grocer that also hosts live gigs. Good coffee, toasted sandwiches and cheese-and-vegetarian pies.

★**Sailors Grave Brewing** MICROBREWERY
(☎0466 331 936; www.sailorsgravebrewing.com; 7 Forest Rd; ⏰by appointment) Set up in an old butter factory, this microbrewery is notable for its inventive brews – from a Gose produced using local seaweed to a whisky sour Berliner Weisse. Other core beers include IPA and southern right ale. While it plans to open a taproom in the future, for the moment you'll need to call ahead to sample its range.

Information

Orbost Visitor Information Centre (☎03-5154 2424; 39 Nicholson St; ⏰9am-5pm) is in the historic 1872 Slab Hut relocated from Buchan. It has an open fire and books on local history for sale.

Getting There & Away

Car Most travellers fly through as the Princes Hwy passes just south of the town. The Bonang Rd heads north towards the Snowy River and Errinundra National Parks, and Marlo Rd follows the Snowy River south to Marlo and continues along the coast to Cape Conran Coastal Park.

Bicycle Orbost is the start or finishing point of the **East Gippsland Rail Trail** (p273).

Bus There are three buses a day from Bairnsdale ($19, one hour 40 minutes).

Cape Conran Coastal Park

This blissfully undeveloped part of the coast is one of Gippsland's most beautiful corners, with long stretches of remote white-sand beaches. The 19km coastal route from Marlo to Cape Conran is particularly pretty, bordered by banksia trees, grass plains, sand dunes and the ocean.

Activities

Cape Conran is a fabulous spot for walking. One favourite is the nature trail that meets up with the East Cape Boardwalk, where signage gives you a glimpse into how Indigenous peoples lived in this area. Following an indigenous theme, take the West Cape Rd off Cape Conran Rd to **Salmon Rocks**, where there's an Aboriginal **shell midden** dated at more than 10,000 years old.

For some relaxed swimming, canoeing and fishing, head to the Yerrung River, which shadows the coast east of the cape and can be reached along Yerrung River Rd. There's good surfing at West Cape Beach, extending northwest from the cape and accessible from West Cape Rd. For qualified divers, Marlo-based **Cross Diving Services** (☎03-5154 8554, 0407 362 960; www.crossdiving.com.au; 20 Ricardo Dr; ⏰shore dives with/without equipment hire $80/15, boat dives $100/150, 4-day open course $550) offers dives on most weekends.

Sleeping

Parks Victoria has three excellent privately managed accommodation options in Cape Conran Coastal Park – offering camping, cabins and safari-style tented camping, which are all privately managed.

Banksia Bluff Camping Area CAMPGROUND $
(☎03-5154 8438; www.conran.net.au; Marlo-Conran Rd; unpowered sites $35.90-39.90) Run by Parks Victoria, this excellent privately managed camping ground is right by the foreshore. Its generous sites are surrounded by banksia woodlands offering shade and privacy. It has flush toilets, cold showers and a few fireplaces, but you'll need to bring drinking water. A ballot is held for using sites over the Christmas period.

Cape Conran Wilderness Retreat TENTED CAMP $$
(☎03-5154 8438; www.conran.net.au; d $191.20) Nestled in the bush by the sand dunes, these stylish safari tents are a great option, offering

all the simplicity of camping, but with comfortable beds and a deck outside your flywire door. Two-night minimum stay on weekends.

Cape Conran Coastal Park Cabins CABIN $$
(☎03-5154 8438; www.conran.net.au; cabins $171.70-237.20) These self-contained cabins, which can sleep up to eight people, are surrounded by bush and just 200m from the beach. Built from local timbers, the cabins are like oversized cubby houses, with lofty mezzanines for sleeping.

West Cape Cabins CABIN $$
(☎03-5154 8296; www.westcapecabins.com; 1547 Cape Conran Rd; d $195-255) Crafted from locally grown or recycled wood, these self-contained cabins a few kilometres from the park are works of art. The timbers are all labelled with their species, and even the queen-sized bed bases are made from tree trunks. The outdoor spa baths add to the joy. The larger cottage sleeps eight. It's a 15-minute walk through coastal bush to an isolated beach.

Getting There & Away

Cape Conran Coastal Park lies south of the Princes Hwy, 405km from Melbourne. The well-signposted turn-off from the highway lies just east of the small settlement of Cabbage Tree. The park is around 15km south of the turn-off along Cabbage Tree–Conran Rd.

Mallacoota

POPULATION 1032

One of Gippsland's, and indeed Victoria's, little gems, Mallacoota is the state's most easterly town, snuggled on the vast Mallacoota Inlet and surrounded by the tumbling hills and beachside dunes of beautiful Croajingolong National Park. Those prepared to come this far are treated to long, empty, ocean-surf beaches, tidal estuaries and swimming, fishing and boating on the inlet.

It's a good place for wildlife too with plentiful kangaroos, as well as koalas and echidnas.

Sights & Activities

The calm estuarine waters of Mallacoota Inlet have more than 300km of shoreline – hiring a boat is the best way to explore, and there are plenty of great walks along the water's edge.

For good surf, head to Bastion Point or Tip Beach. Get in touch with Surf Shack for board rental and surf classes. There's swimmable surf and some sheltered water at Betka Beach, which is patrolled during Christmas school holidays. There are also good swimming spots along the beaches of the foreshore reserve, at Bastion Point (patrolled by a surf life-saving club) and at Quarry Beach.

Gabo Island ISLAND
On Gabo Island, 14km offshore from Mallacoota, the windswept 154-hectare **Gabo Island Lightstation Reserve** is home to seabirds and one of the world's largest colonies of little penguins, far outnumbering those on Phillip Island. Whales, dolphins and fur seals are regularly sighted offshore. The island has an operating **lighthouse**, built in 1862 and the tallest in the southern hemisphere – you can stay in the old keepers' cottages (p276) here.

Transport out here however is an issue, with boat access often restricted due to bad weather; Wilderness Coast Ocean Charters (p276) and Gabo Island Escapes (p276) are your best bet.

While there no longer direct flights offered to Gabo Island from Mallacoota, **Merimbula Air Services** (☎02-6495 1074; www.mairserv.com.au) can arrange a drop-off and pickup service, but unless you have a group, it certainly ain't cheap (four seater one-way $775).

Mallacoota Equipment Hire ADVENTURE SPORTS
(☎0488 329 611; www.mallacootahire.com.au; Buckland Dr, Mallacoota Foreshore Caravan Park; per hr/day bike hire from $10/40, kayaks $15/75; ⏰9am-5pm) Hires bikes, kayaks and fishing gear, and has plenty of ideas for trails and itineraries. Can deliver bikes to where you're staying.

Mallacoota Hire Boats BOATING
(☎0438 447 558; www.mallacootahireboats.com; 10 Buckland Dr; motorboats per 2/8hr $70/160, kayaks 1/2 people per 2hr $30/50) Hires out kayaks, motorboats, pedal boats and fishing equipment. No boat licence required; cash only. They're based out of Mallacoota Foreshore Holiday Park (p276).

Tours

★**Wilderness Coast Ocean Charters** BOATING
(☎0417 398 068, 03-5158 0701) Runs trips to Gabo Island (p275) – $60, 30 minutes, minimum six people – for a five-hour tour, which can include a tour of the lighthouse

for $10. They also run occasional trips down the coast to view the seal colony off Wingan Inlet if there's enough demand.

Gabo Island Escapes BOATING
(☎0437 221 694, 03-5158 0605; per person $100) Runs boat trips to Gabo Island (p275) for around $100 a head (minimum six people) including lighthouse tours.

Surf Shack SURFING
(☎03-5158 0909; www.surfshack.com.au; 41 Maurice Ave; surf lessons per person $60, rental per half/full day surfboard $25/35, SUP $35/50; ⏲9am-5pm) Runs surf lessons at nearby Bastion Point or Cape Conran, normally on Tuesday and Thursday (or by appointment); minimum three people. Otherwise they hire out surfboards, SUPs and wetsuits (per half/full day $15/20).

MV Loch-Ard CRUISE
(☎0438 580 708; www.mallacootacruises.com; Main Wharf, 1 Buckland Dr; adult/child 2hr cruises $30/15) Runs several inlet cruises, including wildlife spotting and a twilight cruise on the MV *Loch-Ard*, a 1910 heritage passenger boat.

Sleeping

Shady Gully Caravan Park CARAVAN PARK $
(☎03-5158 0362; www.mallacootacaravanpark.com; 95 Mallacoota-Genoa Rd; unpowered/powered sites from $23/28, cabins with shared/private bathroom from $60/80;) Run by friendly management, this bush caravan park is full of kangaroos and birdlife. There's a good variety of campsites and cabins, including uniquely designed cylindrical units made of corrugated iron and kitted out with all the mod cons. I

Mallacoota Foreshore Holiday Park CARAVAN PARK $
(☎03-5158 0300; cnr Allan Dr & Maurice Ave; unpowered sites $16.60-33, powered sites $23.70-53;) Curling around the waterfront, the grassy sites here morph into one of Victoria's most sociable and scenic caravan parks, with sublime views of the inlet and its resident population of black swans and pelicans. No cabins, but the best of Mallacoota's many parks for campers. Reception is across the road in the same building as the visitor information centre.

★**Adobe Abodes** APARTMENT $$
(☎0499 777 968; www.adobeabodes.com.au; 17-19 Karbeethong Ave; d $95-145, extra person $15) These unique mud-brick self-contained units in Karbeethong are something special. With an emphasis on recycling and eco-friendliness, the flats have solar hot water and guests are encouraged to compost their kitchen scraps. The array of whimsical apartments are comfortable and well equipped, and come with welcome baskets of wine and chocolate, and wonderful views- They promote themselves proudly as a wi-fi free zone.

★**Karbeethong Lodge** GUESTHOUSE $$
(☎03-5158 0411; www.karbeethonglodge.com.au; 16 Schnapper Point Dr; r incl breakfast $100-150) It's hard not to be overcome by a sense of serenity as you rest on the broad verandahs of this early 1900s timber guesthouse, which give uninterrupted views over Mallacoota Inlet and the expansive gardens. The large guest lounge and dining room have an open fire and period furnishings, there's a mammoth kitchen and the pastel-toned bedrooms are small but tastefully decorated.

Gabo Island Lighthouse COTTAGE $$
(☎03-8427 2123, Parks Victoria 13 19 63; www.parkweb.vic.gov.au; up to 8 people $323.70-359.70) For a truly wild experience head out to stay at this remote lighthouse. Accommodation is available in the historic three-bedroom assistant lighthouse keeper's residence. There's a two-night minimum stay and a ballot for use during the Christmas and Easter holidays; take note there's no refunds if you're unable to reach the island (or get stranded there) during inclement weather.

Mallacoota Wilderness Houseboats HOUSEBOAT $$$
(☎0409 924 016; www.mallacootawildernesshouseboats.com.au; Karbeethong Jetty; 4 nights midweek from $800, weekly from $1250) These six-berth houseboats are not as luxurious as the ones you'll find on the Murray, but they are the perfect way to explore Mallacoota's waterways, and they are economical for a group or family. They're fully self-contained with kitchen, fridge and hot-water showers. There's a $500 deposit from which fuel costs are deducted upon return. No boat licence required.

Eating & Drinking

Croajingolong Cafe CAFE $
(☎03-5158 0098; Shop 3, 14 Allan Dr; mains $10-19; ⏲8am-4pm Tue-Sun) Overlooking the inlet, this cafe has a vintage nautical theme and an outdoor terrace with views over the water; the

OFF THE BEATEN TRACK

GIPPSLAND OFF-ROAD TOURS

Most of the Snowy River and Errinundra National Parks are inaccessible with a 2WD, and sections of Croajingolong are only open to a limited numbers of walkers. An easier way to see these beautiful wilderness areas is with an organised tour.

An ecotourism award winner, **Gippsland High Country Tours** (☎03-5157 5556; www.gippslandhighcountrytours.com.au) is an East Gippsland–based company running easy, moderate and challenging five- to seven-day hikes in Errinundra, Snowy River and Croajingolong National Parks. The Croajingolong trips include three nights' accommodation in the Point Hicks Lighthouse (p278). There's also a five-day birdwatching tour in Snowy River country.

Snowy River Expeditions (p272) is an established company running adventure tours including rafting trips. abseiling or caving trips.

place to spread out the newspaper over coffee, toasted sandwiches or an all-day breakfast.

★**Lucy's** ASIAN $$
(☎03-5158 0666; 64 Maurice Ave; mains $8-28; ⏲8am-8pm) Lucy's is popular for delicious and great-value homemade rice noodles with chicken, prawn or abalone, as well as dumplings stuffed with ingredients from the garden. It's also good for breakfast.

Mallacoota Hotel PUB
(☎03-5158 0455; www.mallacootahotel.com.au; 51-55 Maurice Ave; ⏲noon-10pm) The local pub is a popular spot for a drink with a cosy indoor bar and a wonderful outdoor beer garden full of palm trees. Its bistro serves hearty meals (mains $20 to $40) from its varied menu, with reliable favourites being the chicken parma, Gippsland steak and pale ale fish and chips. Bands play regularly in summer.

There's motel pub accommodation (single/double from $100/110) here too.

ℹ Information

Mallacoota Visitor Centre (☎03-5158 0800, 03-5158 0116, 0408 315 615; www.visitmallacoota.com.au; cnr Allan Dr & Maurice Ave; ⏲9am-5pm; 📶) On the main strip across from the water is this extremely helpful tourist centre with a ton of info on the area and its walking trails, and a handy booklet on local sights ($1). Has wi-fi and internet access too.

ℹ Getting There & Away

Mallacoota is 23km southeast of Genoa (on the Princes Hwy), which is 492km from Melbourne. Take the train to Bairnsdale (3¾ hours), then the V/Line bus to Genoa ($51.80, 3½ hours, one daily). The Mallacoota–Genoa bus meets the V/Line coach on Monday, Thursday and Friday, plus Sunday during school holidays, and runs to Mallacoota ($3.20, 30 minutes).

Croajingolong National Park

Croajingolong is one of Australia's finest coastal wilderness national parks, recognised by its listing as a World Biosphere Reserve by Unesco (one of 14 in Australia). The park covers 875 sq km, stretching for about 100km from the town of Bemm River to the NSW border. Magnificent, unspoiled beaches, inlets, estuaries and forests make it an ideal park for camping, walking, swimming and surfing. The five inlets, **Sydenham**, **Tamboon**, **Mueller**, **Wingan** and **Mallacoota** (the largest and most accessible), are popular canoeing and fishing spots.

Two sections of the park have been declared wilderness areas (which means no vehicles, access to a limited number of walkers only and permits required): the **Cape Howe Wilderness Area**, between Mallacoota Inlet and the NSW border, and the **Sandpatch Wilderness Area**, between Wingan Inlet and Shipwreck Creek.

👁 Sights & Activities

Point Hicks was the first part of Australia to be spotted by Captain Cook and the *Endeavour* crew in 1770, and was named after Lieutenant Zachary Hicks. There's a lighthouse (p278) here and accommodation in the old cottages (p278). You can still see remains of the SS *Saros,* which ran ashore in 1937, on a short walk from the lighthouse.

Croajingolong is a birdwatcher's paradise, with more than 300 recorded species (including glossy black cockatoos and the rare ground parrot), while the inland waterways are home to myriad waterbirds, such as the delicate azure kingfisher and the magnificent sea eagle. There are also many small mammals here, including possums, bandicoots and gliders, as well as some huge goannas.

Park vegetation ranges from typical coastal landscapes to thick eucalyptus forests, with areas of warm-temperate rainforest. The heathland areas are filled with impressive displays of orchids and wild flowers in the spring.

The **Wilderness Coast Walk** runs for 100km between the eastern shores of Sydenham Inlet and Wonboyn in the Nadgee Nature Reserve, across the border in New South Wales. You can walk shorter sections of the trail; Thurra River is a good starting point, making for an easy-to-medium hike (59km, five days) to Mallacoota.

Point Hicks Lighthouse LIGHTHOUSE
(☎10am-3pm Mon-Fri 03-5158 4268; www.pointhicks.com.au; Lighthouse Track, Tamboon; adult/child/family $7/4/20; ⏲tours 1pm, Fri-Sun) Climb to the top of this remote 1890 lighthouse for fantastic views and interesting stories, including one about the ghost of Kristofferson, a former lighthouse keeper. Note there's no vehicle access to the lighthouse, so it's a 2.2km walk to get here from the car park.

Sleeping

Mueller Inlet CAMPGROUND $
(☎03-5158 4268; www.pointhicks.com.au; unpowered sites from $25) The calm waters here are fantastic for kayaking and swimming, and the camp sites are only a few metres from the water. It has eight sites, three of them walk-in, but no fireplaces. There's no vegetation to provide privacy, but outside Christmas and Easter holidays it's usually quiet. Bookings are made through Point Hicks Lighthouse (p278).

Thurra River CAMPGROUND $
(☎03-5158 4268; www.pointhicks.com.au; unpowered sites from $25) This is the largest of the park's camping grounds, with 46 well-designed sites stretched along the foreshore from the river towards the lighthouse. Most of the sites are separated by bush, and there are communal fireplaces and pit toilets. Bookings are made through Point Hicks Lighthouse. (p278)

Shipwreck Creek CAMPGROUND $
(☎13 19 63; www.parkweb.vic.gov.au; unpowered sites from $26.50) Only 15km from Mallacoota, this is a beautiful camping ground set in forest above a sandy beach. It's a small area with just five sites, drop toilets and fireplaces (BYO wood) and there are lots of short walks to do here. Bookings through Parks Victoria.

Wingan Inlet CAMPGROUND $
(☎13 19 63; www.parkweb.vic.gov.au; unpowered sites from $25.80) This serene and secluded camping ground has 24 sites among superb sandy beaches and great walks. The Wingan River Walk (5km, 2½ hours return) through rainforest has great waterholes for swimming. Bookings though Parks Victoria (p278).

Point Hicks Lighthouse COTTAGE $$
(☎03-5156 0432; www.pointhicks.com.au; bungalows $120-150, cottages $360-550) This remote lighthouse has two comfortable, heritage-listed cottages and one double bungalow, which originally housed the assistant lighthouse keepers. The cottages sleep six people, and have sensational ocean views and wood-burning fireplaces. Bring along your own bedding and towels, or you can hire it for $15 per person. To get here you'll need to walk 2.2km from the car park.

Getting There & Away

Croajingolong National Park lies 492km east of Melbourne. Unsealed access roads of varying quality lead south off Princes Hwy and into the park from various points between Cann River and the NSW border. Among these are tracks leading to camping grounds at Wingan Inlet, Mueller Inlet, Thurra River and Shipwreck Creek.

Apart from Mallacoota Rd, all of the access roads are unsealed and can be very rough in winter, so check road conditions with Parks Victoria in **Cann River** (☎13 19 63, 03-5158 6351; www.parkweb.vic.gov.au; Cann River) or **Mallacoota** (☎13 19 63, 03-8427 2123; www.parkweb.vic.gov.au; Mallacoota) before venturing on, especially during or after rain.

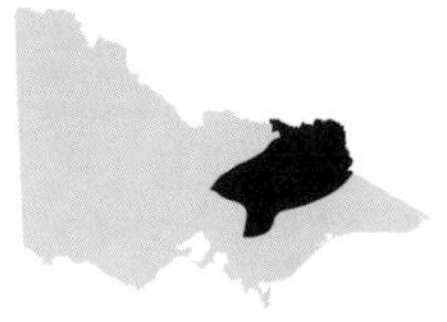

The High Country

Includes ➡

Best Places to Eat

- Provenance (p291)
- Harrietville Snowline Hotel (p303)
- Tani (p298)
- Parker Pies (p295)
- Patricia's Table (p288)

Best Places to Sleep

- Freeman on Ford (p290)
- Odd Frog (p298)
- Dreamers (p300)
- Shady Brook Cottages (p303)
- Spring Spur (p300)

Why Go?

With its enticing mix of history, adventure and culinary temptations, Victoria's High Country is a wonderful place to spend some time. The Great Dividing Range – Australia's eastern mountain spine – curls around eastern Victoria from the Snowy Mountains to the Grampians, peaking in the spectacular High Country. These are Victoria's Alps – a mountain playground attracting skiers and snowboarders in winter and bushwalkers and mountain bikers in summer. Here the mountain air is clear and invigorating, winter snowfalls at the resorts of Mt Buller, Mt Hotham and Falls Creek are fairly reliable, and the scenery is spectacular.

Away from the mountain tops, there are activities aplenty and Bright is one of the loveliest gateway towns in the state. Throw in historic towns such as Beechworth, the wineries of King Valley and Rutherglen, and the gourmet food offerings of Milawa and you'll find plenty of reasons to linger.

When to Go

Mt Hotham

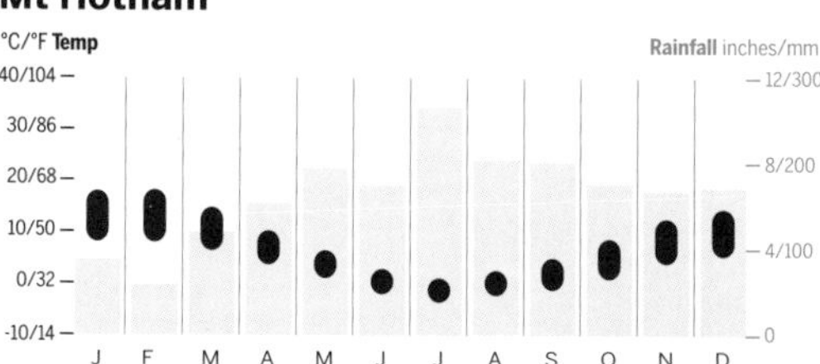

Apr–May Best time for glorious autumn colours around Bright and Omeo.

Jul–Aug Hit the snowy mountain slopes for the peak ski season.

Dec–Feb The green season for mountain biking, horse riding and wine touring.

The High Country Highlights

1 **Murray to Mountains Rail Trail** (p297) Cycling Victoria's second-longest bike path with winery stops aplenty.

2 **Beechworth** (p289) Visiting Ned Kelly's cell, then sampling the brews at Bridge Road Brewers in this picturesque historic town.

3 **Milawa** (p288) Hitting the gourmet trail, and tasting wine, gin, cheese, mustard and olives in this fertile region.

4 **Falls Creek** (p300) Skiing the piste at fashionable Falls in winter, and zipping downhill on mountain bikes in summer.

5 **Bright** (p297) Enjoying the vibrant colours of the autumn and spring festivals in this charming town.

6 **Rutherglen** (p293) Spending a day or two sampling big, bold reds in one of Victoria's best wine regions.

7 **Kiewa Valley** (p300) Making like *The Man from Snowy River* and going horse riding on the high plains.

8 **Omeo** (p306) Driving along the Great Alpine Rd to isolated, historic picturesque towns like Omeo.

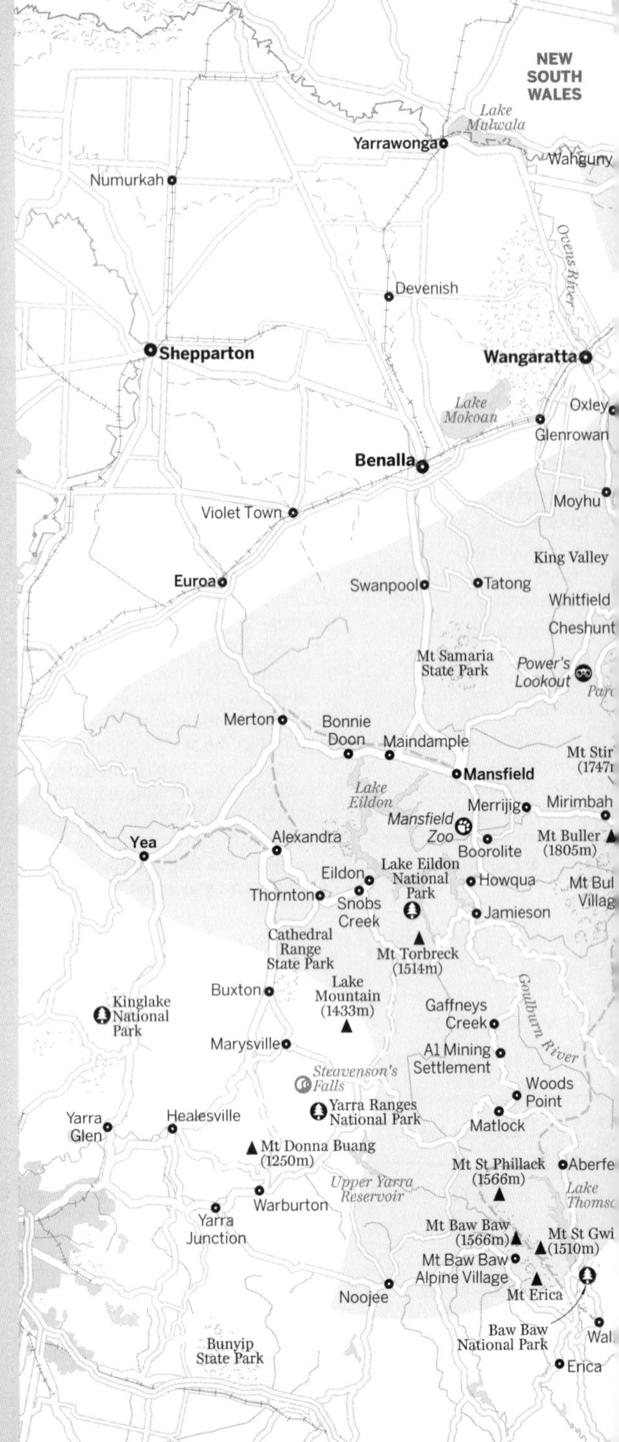

0
50 km
0
25 miles
Walwa
Pine Mountain (1062m)
Burrowa-Pine Mountain National Park
Murray River
Rutherglen
Albury
Talgarno
Bellbridge
Tintaldra
hiltern
Wodonga
Granya
Mt Burrowa (1300m)
Towong
Tallangatta
Bullioh
Colac Colac
Stanley State Forest
Red Bluff
Corryong
Berringama
Khancoban
Yackandandah
2 Beechworth
Everton
Stanley
Murray River
NEW SOUTH WALES
Milawa
Tallandoon
Mitta Mitta River
horouly
Gapsted
Eskdale
Dartmouth
Myrtleford
Ovens
Mitta Mitta
Murray to Mountains Rail Trail
Lake Dartmouth
Mt Buffalo National Park
1
Kiewa Valley
Tawonga
Park Entrance Station
Porepunkah
7
Mt Bogong (1986m)
Dingo Dell
5 Bright
Mt Beauty
The Horn (1723m)
Cresta Valley
Wandiligong
Bogong
4 Falls Creek
Harrietville
Mt Feathertop (1922m)
Glen Valley
bonga teau
Hotham Heights
Anglers Rest
Benambra
Alpine National Park
Mt Hotham (1868m)
Dinner Plain
Mt Hotham Airport
raig's lut
t Dividing Range
8 Omeo
Mt Howitt (1742m)
Wonnangatta River
Road Closed in Winter
Victoria Falls Camping Area
Alpine National Park
Swifts Creek
Buchan River
Dargo River
Ensay
Dargo
Buchan
Licola
Mitchell River National Park
Bruthen
Nowa Nowa
Mitchell River
Bairnsdale
Lake Tyers
Metung
Heyfield
Maffra
Stratford
Paynesville
Lakes Entrance
BASS STRAIT

Mt Baw Baw

Most known for its ski resort, Mt Baw Baw and its encompassing national park is the southernmost region of Victoria's High Country. It's Victoria's smallest (and also cheapest and closest to Melbourne) downhill-skiing resort and is a relaxed option for both beginners and families.

An offshoot of the Great Dividing Range, the Baw Baw Plateau and the forested valleys of the Thomson and Aberfeldy Rivers are also wonderful places for bushwalking, with marked tracks through subalpine vegetation, ranging from open eucalypt stands to wet gullies and tall forests on the plateau.

The highest points are **Mt St Phillack** (1566m) and **Mt Baw Baw** (1564m). The higher sections of the park are snow-covered in winter, when everyone heads for Baw Baw Village ski resort and the **Mt St Gwinear** cross-country skiing area.

Activities

Winter Activities

The downhill-skiing and snowboarding area is set over 35 hectares with a vertical drop of 140m and seven ski lifts. Lift tickets per adult/child/family for weekdays cost $53/38/135 (weekends $80/45/200). If you're on a budget, Wednesdays are $35 for everyone.

Its gentle slopes are a very good choice for beginners and families. On Saturdays there's also night skiing from 6pm to 8pm.

Mt Baw Baw Ski Hire (03-5165 1120; www.bawbawskihire.com.au; 26 Currawong Rd; 8.30am-5.30pm Mon-Fri, 8am-5.30pm Sat & Sun mid-Jun–Sep) rents out equipment.

Baw Baw is also a base for **cross-country skiing**, with 10km of trails, including one that connects to the Mt St Gwinear trails on the southern edge of the plateau.

As well as ski runs there are designated snow-play areas comprising toboggan parks and sections to build snowmen. There are also more novel opportunities such as **dog sleds** (0488 040 308; www.howlinghuskys.com.au; sled tours 2 people from $175, 1hr snow pup tours adult/child $75/50; Jul & Aug) piloted by Siberian huskies, snowmobile safaris and snow-groomer tours in the evenings. In winter the day car park costs $56 per vehicle.

Summer Activities

While not as big as other mountain resorts, **mountain biking** is increasing in popularity on Mt Baw Baw with a number of cross-country and downhill trails. You can rent a cross-country mountain bike from **Baw Baw Sports & Outdoors** (1800 106 078, 0418 434 829; www.bawbawsports.com; Mt Baw Baw Alpine Resort, 7 Currawong Rd; $20/50 per hr/day; 7am-7pm daily winter, 9am-4pm Sat & Sun green season).

Sleeping & Eating

Alpine Backpackers HOTEL $

(03-5165 1136; Currawong Rd; dm from $40, d summer/winter from $98/175, tr from $110/250) Superb value, the Alpine offers year-round backpacker and motel 'flashpacker'-style accommodation. In winter the downstairs Alpine Hotel is *the* place to hang while local bands belt out rock covers until 2am. In winter there's a two-night minimum; BYO bedding.

Kelly's Lodge B&B $$

(03-5165 1129, 0409 557 158; www.kellyslodge.com.au; 11 Frosti Lane; 4-bed r summer/winter from $120/370) Long-running and super-friendly Kelly's, with comfortable rooms and a cosy lounge, is in the centre of everything on the mountain. The ski-in cafe is a Baw Baw favourite, with pizzas and lamb shanks.

Village Central CAFE $$

(03-5165 1123; 32 Currawong Rd; mains $16.50-28; 10.30am-late daily winter, 10am-5pm Fri & Mon, 10.30am-late Sat & Sun summer;) This cafe-restaurant specialises in local produce and has good valley views.

Information

Mt Baw Baw Alpine Resort Management Board (03-5165 1136; www.mountbawbaw.com.au; 8.30am-7.30pm Sat-Thu, to 9pm Fri ski season, 9am-5pm rest of year) Offers general tourist information and an accommodation booking service. Its website is an invaluable resource for activities and updates on trails.

Getting There & Away

The main access road to Baw Baw Village, located about 120km east of Melbourne, is the windy Baw Baw Tourist Rd via Noojee, reached off the Princes Hwy at Drouin. An alternative back route from the Latrobe Valley is the unsealed, but all-season, South Face Rd from Rawson, north of Moe. Either way, the last 5km up to Baw Baw Village is probably the steepest road in the country – low gear all the way. The closest petrol station is at Neerim Junction.

In winter, **Mountain Top Experience** (03-5134 6876; www.mountaintopexperience.com; one way $50, same-day return $60; Jun-Sep) offers a daily bus service from Moe train station.

It meets train arrivals from Melbourne at 9.18am Monday to Saturday, and 9.48am Sunday.

To get to Moe take the V/Line train from Melbourne ($16, two hours).

Lake Eildon & Around

Surrounding most of its namesake lake, **Lake Eildon National Park** is the low-lying southern gateway to the High Country, covering over 270 sq km and providing superb opportunities for walking and camping.

Originally called Sugarloaf Reserve, Lake Eildon was created as a massive reservoir for irrigation and hydroelectric schemes. It was constructed between 1915 and 1929 and flooded the town of Darlingford and surrounding farm homesteads. After years of drought, recent rains have brought the lake back to near capacity. Behind the dam wall, the 'pondage' (outflow from the dam) spreads below Eildon township, a little one-pub town and a popular recreation and holiday base.

On the northern arm of the lake is **Bonnie Doon**, a popular weekend getaway, which reached icon status as the nondescript spot where the Kerrigan family enjoyed 'serenity' in the satirical 1997 Australian film *The Castle*.

Activities

Goulburn Valley Fly-Fishing Centre FISHING
(☎03-5773 2513; www.goulburnvlyflyfishing.com.au; 1270 Goulburn Valley Way, Thornton; introductory/4hr fishing $75/280) If you're looking for specialist tuition and guided fishing trips, either on private waterways or local rivers, this is the place to go. Passionate owners. The four-hour tuition is the recommended option if you want to actually catch a fish.

Eildon Trout Farm FISHING
(☎03-5773 2377; www.eildontroutfarm.com.au; 460 Back Eildon Rd; entry/fishing $3/3; ⏲9am-5pm) Catching trout or salmon is guaranteed at this farm located on the back road between Thornton and Eildon. There are five ponds to choose from and you can either bring your own gear or rent some ($3). You can keep what you catch and take it home for dinner (or barbecue it on the spot). There's also catch-and-release fly-fishing.

Rubicon Valley Horse Riding HORSE RIDING
(☎03-5773 2292; www.rubiconhorseriding.com.au; 90 Rubicon Rd, Rubicon; introductory/2hr/half-day/full-day rides $55/80/120/210) This company caters for all levels, including children, and the setting is lovely. Full-day trips include lunch.

Sleeping

Lake Eildon is best known as a place to rent a houseboat and spend a few days on the water. Expect to pay anywhere from $2000 to $5000 a week.

It's also a beautiful place for bush camping, with several lakeside national park camp sites ($26 to $52.60), which must be booked online at www.parkweb.vic.gov.au.

Eildon

POP 733

The little one-pub town of Eildon, which sits on the edge of the pondage, is a popular recreation and holiday base, built in the 1950s to house Eildon Dam project workers. Unless you're here to rent a houseboat, there's not much else to keep you entertained.

Activities

Lake Eildon and the rivers that feed into it are popular for fishing, but you don't have to be a dedicated angler to have fun here. You can drive up to and across the dam's massive retaining wall to a lookout point, with sensational views over the lake, town and houseboat building yards. There are quiet walking and cycling trails along the shores that give easy access to the best fishing spots.

Sleeping

There are a few places to stay in Eildon and on the back road to Thornton, but the best accommodation is on board a houseboat (p284) on Lake Eildon – they build 'em in Eildon. For a full list of options, see www.lakeeildon.com.

Blue Gums Caravan Park CAMPGROUND $
(☎03-5774 2567; www.bluegums.com.au; 746 Back Eildon Rd; dm $31, unpowered/powered site from $28/36, cabins $122-159; ❄📶🏊) On the banks of the Goulburn River about 5km southwest of Eildon, this is a fabulous family caravan park with two swimming pools, a playground, manicured lawns for camping and slick self-contained cabins.

Eildon Lake Motel MOTEL $
(☎03-5774 2800; www.eildonlakemotel.com.au; 2 Girdwood Pde; s/d/tr $100/110/125; ❄) A block back from the Goulburn River, this motel has spacious if fairly standard brick-walled rooms.

★ **Eildon Houseboat Hire** HOUSEBOAT $$$
(☎0437 944 162; www.eildonhouseboathire.com.au; 190 Sugarloaf Rd; per 4 days winter/summer from $2100/2800) If the Murray River is too far, or

you want more room to manoeuvre, Lake Eildon is the next best place in Victoria to stay on a houseboat. Here you can hire a luxurious 10- or 12-berth houseboat. Book well ahead for holiday periods. No boat licence required.

★ **Lake Eildon Marina & Houseboat Hire** HOUSEBOAT $$$
(03-5774 2107; www.houseboatholidays.com.au; 190 Sugarloaf Rd; 12-bed houseboat low/high season per week $2800/3800) Ten or 12-berth houseboats, but you'll need to book months in advance during the high season.

Information

Eildon Visitor Information Centre (03-5774 2909; www.lakeeildon.com; Main St; 10am-2pm) Friendly staff run this small office opposite the shopping centre.

Getting There & Away

Eildon, 139km northeast of Melbourne, is best reached via the Maroondah Hwy.

From Melbourne, bus 684 departs from Southern Cross station to Eildon ($19, three hours) several times a day via Healesville and Marysville.

Jamieson

POP 384

From Eildon, a sealed and scenic back road skirts the southern edge of the national park to Jamieson, a charming little town where the Goulburn and Jamieson Rivers join Lake Eildon. Jamieson was established as a supply town for gold miners in the 1850s and a number of interesting historical buildings remain.

Sleeping

Jamieson has a lovely **caravan park** (03-5777 0567; www.jamiesoncaravanpark.com.au; 6 Grey St; unpowered/powered site $30/35, cabin from $120;) on the river, plus B&Bs and motel-style rooms in the pub; for full listings, visit www.jamieson.org.au/hotel-motels.

There's good bush camping along the Jamieson and Goulburn Rivers but you must be self-sufficient and camp at least 20m from the water – take the Jamieson-Licola Rd east or the Woods Point Rd to the south.

Drinking & Nightlife

Wrong Side Brewing MICROBREWERY
(0405 487 261; www.wrongsidebrewing.com.au; 5953 Eildon-Jamieson Rd; 8am-4.30pm) Taking over the Jamieson Brewery, Wrong Side had just started brewing in early 2017. Its range includes a raspberry pale ale and American pale ale, both of which can be enjoyed in its 3-acre beer garden by the river. A taproom and restaurant were on the way. It's 3km north of Jamieson along the road to Eildon.

Getting There & Away

It's around a three-hour drive from Melbourne to Jamieson via the Maroondah Hwy, from where there are two options. You can keep heading north through Yea before looping around the north of Lake Eildon via Mansfield, or take the more scenic route through Healesville on to Eildon, from where it's a twisting, winding road.

There's only one bus a week to/from Mansfield on Thursday.

Mansfield

POP 4360

Mansfield is the gateway to Victoria's largest snowfields at Mt Buller, but also an exciting all-seasons destination in its own right. There's plenty to do here in *The Man from Snowy River* country, with horse riding and mountain biking popular in summer, and a buzzing atmosphere in winter when the snow bunnies hit town.

Sights

Mansfield Zoo ZOO
(03-5777 3576; www.mansfieldzoo.com.au; 1064 Mansfield Woods Point Rd; adult/child $15/13.50; 10am-5.30pm, to 6.30pm or sunset summer) Located 10km south of Mansfield is this surprisingly good wildlife park with lots of native fauna and some exotics, including lions, which are fed at 1.30pm. You can sleep in the paddocks in a tent or swag (adult/child $65/45, including zoo entry for two days) and wake to the dawn wildlife chorus.

Mansfield Cemetery CEMETERY
The three Mansfield police officers killed at Stringybark Creek by Ned Kelly and his gang in 1878 rest in Mansfield Cemetery.

Activities

All Terrain Cycles MOUNTAIN BIKING
(03-5775 2724; www.allterraincycles.com.au; 58 High St; bicycle hire per half/full day $30/40) Hires out hybrid bicycles and equipment, as well as info on trails in the local area. Also runs guided tours and transfers for the **Great Victorian Rail Trail** (www.greatvictorianrailtrail.com.au).

CRAIG'S HUT

Cattlemen built huts throughout the High Country from the 1850s onwards, but the most iconic is Craig's Hut, built in 1981 for the film *The Man from Snowy River*. It was converted from a film set into a visitor centre 10 years later, then rebuilt in 2003. In 2006 it burned down in bushfires, before being rebuilt (again) in 2007. It's on Mt Stirling in the Alpine National Park about 53km east of Mansfield. The last 1.2km is accessible only by walking or 4WD, but it's worth it for the breathtaking views.

Watson's Mountain Country Trail Rides HORSE RIDING
(☎03-5777 3552; www.watsonstrailrides.com.au; 296 Three Chain Rd, Booroolite; 1hr/2hr/full-day ride $50/90/175) A peaceful property where children can learn with pony rides or short trail rides, or take off on overnight catered rides. One of the highlights is the view from Kate Cameron's Peak, looking down the steep run featured in *The Man from Snowy River*.

High Country Horses HORSE RIDING
(☎03-5777 5590; www.highcountryhorses.com.au; 10 McCormacks Rd, Merrijig; 2hr/half-day/full-day ride $100/130/300, overnight from $640; ⏲Oct-May) Based at Merrijig on the way to Mt Buller, High Country Horses offers everything from a short trot to overnight treks to Craig's Hut (p285), Howqua River and Mt Stirling.

Sleeping

Delatite Hotel PUB $
(www.thedelatitehotel.com.au; 95 High St; r $100-110, s/d with shared bathroom $80/90; 📶) Run by a friendly owner who also runs the Mansfield Regional Produce Store (p285), this country hotel on the main road has pub accommodation upstairs. Rooms are basic, but they're spacious and adequate for those on a budget. Downstairs has an atmospheric bistro with local beers – go for the Mansfield pale ale.

Mansfield Travellers Lodge HOSTEL, MOTEL $
(☎03-5775 1800; www.mansfieldtravellerslodge.com.au; 116 High St; s & dm from $40, r/f from $120/180; ❄📶) Located close to the centre of town, this long-time favourite for backpackers and families is run by the enthusiastic owner, Jed. The spacious dorms, in a restored heritage building, are often booked as private singles, while the motel section features spotless one- and two-bedroom units.

Highton Manor B&B $$
(☎03-5775 2700; www.hightonmanor.com.au; 140 Highton Lane; d stable/tower $130/365; ❄🏊) Built in 1896 for Francis Highett, who sang with Dame Nellie Melba, this stately two-storey manor has style and romance but doesn't take itself too seriously. There's group accommodation in the shared room, modern rooms in the converted stables and lavish period rooms in the main house. If you want the royal treatment, choose the tower room, which includes breakfast.

Eating & Drinking

★**Mansfield Coffee Merchant** CAFE $$
(☎03-5779 1703; www.mansfieldcoffeemerchant.com.au; 23 Highett St; mains $14-19; ⏲6.30am-4pm) This roaster setup within a cavernous, slick space is the place for coffee lovers. It also does contemporary fare such as brekky burgers, tempura-prawn rolls and smoked-lamb ribs. All of its single-origin beans are roasted on site, and prepared as siphon, V60 pour overs or machine coffee.

Mansfield Regional Produce Store CAFE $$
(☎03-5779 1404; www.theproducestore.com.au; 68 High St; mains $12-24; ⏲9am-5pm Sat-Thu, to 9pm Fri) Wildly popular with folk for breakfast and brunch is this rustic store-cafe with mismatched furniture that stocks an array of local produce and wine. The ever-changing menu offers full breakfasts, locally made sourdough baguettes and coffee.

Bos Taurus STEAK $$$
(☎03-5775 1144; www.bostaurus.com.au; 13-15 High St; mains from $35; ⏲2.30-9.30pm Mon-Fri, from 11.30am Sat & Sun) A must for carnivores is this steakhouse specialising in premium pasture-fed chargrilled Angus fillets cut to size. The upper deck is a wonderful spot to enjoy a drink and a meal when the sun's out.

Social Bandit Brewing Co MICROBREWERY
(☎03-5775 3281; www.facebook.com/socialbanditbrewing; 223 Mt Buller Rd; pizzas from $18; ⏲11am-9pm Thu-Sun) In a commercial estate on Mansfield's outskirts, this boutique brewery is on the road to Mt Buller. It has taps to sample the numerous beers produced on site, including American and Australian pale ales, accompanied by pizzas and pretzels. Grab a few bottles to enjoy up on the mountain.

Information

Mansfield & Mt Buller High Country Visitor Centre (1800 039 049; www.mansfieldmt-buller.com.au; 173 High St; 9am-5pm) In a modern building next to the town's original railway station, the visitor centre books accommodation for the region and sells lift tickets.

Getting There & Away

Mansfield is 209km northeast of Melbourne, but allow at least 2½ hours if you're driving; take the Tallarook or Euroa exits from the Hume Hwy.

V/Line (1800 800 007; www.vline.com.au) coaches run between Melbourne's Southern Cross station and Mansfield ($28.20, three hours) at least once daily, with more frequent departures during the ski season.

Mt Buller

Victoria's largest and busiest ski resort is also the closest major resort to Melbourne, so it buzzes all winter long. It's also developing into a popular summer destination for mountain bikers and hikers, with a range of cross-country and downhill trails. The downhill-skiing area covers 180 hectares, with a vertical drop of 400m.

Sights & Activities

Buller is a well-developed resort with a vibrant village atmosphere and quality snow sports in the white season. While things are quiet in summer, on weekends some life returns to the mountain when cyclists descend en masse.

Riding the slopes is, of course, what Mt Buller is really all about. It features world-class runs for downhill skiers and snowboarders, and is suitable for all levels. For non-skiers there's tobogganing, snow-tubing, excellent snowshoeing and dog-sled runs. Even during periods of low snowfall, the snow-making machines kick in to ensure skiing all season long. In winter there's night skiing on Wednesday and Saturday.

There are plenty of outlets spread across Mansfield and Mt Buller that rent ski and other equipment – check out www.mtbuller.com.au for a full list of options.

National Alpine Museum of Australia MUSEUM
(NAMA; 03-5777 6077; www.nama.org.au; Level 1, Community Centre, Summit Rd; by donation; 1-4pm daily winter, noon-3pm Sat & Sun summer or by app) This small museum highlights the fascinating history of this area, covering Indigenous and colonial history to fashion on the slopes.

Australian Sleddog Tours DOG SLEDDING
(03-5159 1626, 0418 230 982; www.sleddogtours.com.au; Corn Hill Rd; per person/family $165/500; mid-Jun–Sep) During the snow season hop aboard for a sled-dog tour with a team of rescued Siberian huskies. If there's no snow, you can do a tour on grass on Fritz-Dyck carts (providing the temperature isn't over 15°C). Otherwise you can visit the dogs year-round ($20) at their base in Cobungra, near Mt Hotham.

Sleeping

There are over 7000 beds on the mountain. Rates vary throughout the ski season, with cheaper rates midweek. A handful of places are open year-round. **Mt Buller Alpine Reservations** (03-5777 6633; www.mtbullerreservations.com.au) books accommodation; there's generally a two-night minimum stay on weekends.

Buller Backpackers HOSTEL $
(1800 810 200; www.bullerbackpackers.com.au; Village Sq; dm $55-90; Jun-Sep) Only open during the ski season is this busy backpackers that's one of Bulla's best budget choices. Dorms are the only option here, all with en suite. While there's nowhere to hang out and no cooking facilities, it's right in the heart of the village with prime access to eateries and the chairlift.

Hotel Enzian CHALET $$$
(03-5777 6996; www.enzian.com.au; 69 Chamois Rd; r from $230-390;) Enzian has a good range of lodge rooms and apartments (sleeping up to 10) with all the facilities, alpine charm and an in-house restaurant and bar. Breakfast is included for the rooms, but not the apartments that have cooking facilities.

Mt Buller Chalet CHALET $$$
(03-5777 6566, 1800 810 200; www.mtbullerchalet.com.au; 5 Summit Rd; d incl breakfast $283-760; Jun-Oct;) With a central location, the Chalet offers a sweet range of suites, a library with billiards table, well-regarded eateries, an impressive sports centre and a heated pool. It only opens during the ski season.

Eating & Drinking

Black Cockatoo MODERN AUSTRALIAN **$$**
(☎03-5777 6566; www.blackcockatoo.net.au; Mt Buller Chalet Hotel, 207 Summit Rd; small plates $6-24, large plates $22-65, tasting menu $90; ⏲7-11am & 6-9pm June-Sep) Only open in winter, Black Cockatoo is the best restaurant on the mountain doing shared plates in its architecturally designed space. Expect dishes like Flinders Island saltgrass lamb shoulder, prawn toast *okonomiyaki* and smoked local rainbow trout.

Cattleman's Café CAFE, BISTRO **$$**
(☎03-5777 7970; Village Centre; mains $8-19; ⏲8am-9pm June-Sep) Open only during the ski season, Cattleman's Café is at the base of the Blue Bullet chairlift and is one of the best spots for breakfast, coffee or a bistro meal of steak, burgers or fish and chips.

Kooroora Hotel PUB
(☎03-5777 6050; www.facebook.com/thekooroorahotel; Village Sq, 3-5 The Avenue; ⏲10am-3am June-Sep) Rocks hard and late during the ski season. There's live music on Wednesday night and most weekends. Serves good bistro meals.

Information

Mt Buller Resort Management Board (☎03-5777 6077; www.mtbuller.com.au; Community Centre, Summit Rd; ⏲8.30am-5pm Mon-Fri, 10am-4pm Sat & Sun) Also runs an information office in the village square clock tower during winter.

Getting There & Away

Mansfield–Mt Buller Buslines (☎03-5775 2606; www.mmbl.com.au; 137 High St, Mansfield) runs a winter bus service from Mansfield (adult/child return $66/45).

In winter there are numerous shuttles from Melbourne; visit www.mtbuller.com.au for details

V/Line operates at least one daily bus between Melbourne and Mansfield ($28.20, three hours), but has no connecting service to Mt Buller; however, there's a shuttle (from $15) from the **Mirimbah Store** (☎03-5777 5529; www.mirimbah.com.au; per ride $15, daily $40; ⏲8am-4pm Thu-Sun Sep-May, daily winter), at the foot of the mountain, daily in January and weekends from February to the end of April.

King Valley

From Melbourne, turning east off the Hume Hwy near Wangaratta and onto the Snow Rd brings you to the King Valley, a prosperous cool-climate wine region and an important gourmet-food area. The valley extends south along the King River, through the tiny towns of Moyhu, Whitfield and Cheshunt, with a sprinkling of 20 or so wineries noted for Italian varietals and cool-climate wines such as sangiovese, barbera, prosecco and pinot grigio. The area used to be a tobacco-growing region until legislation closed down the industry, at which time many farmers turned to wine instead. Check out www.winesofthekingvalley.com.au.

Sleeping

There are a number of cottage B&Bs in the region, including rooms at several of the wineries and the Mountain View Hotel (p287); see www.visitkingvalley.com.au for full listings. There's also **camping** (3741 Wangaratta-Whitfield Rd, Edi Cutting) FREE at designated sites along the King River.

Eating

Food is a huge lure to the region, with a number of great restaurants and wineries using local produce. Here you'll find several Italian eateries, a gastropub and a dairy producing naturally cultured items. In mid-November the region's produce is showcased during **La Dolce Vita Wine & Food Festival** (www.winesofthekingvalley.com.au/events/la-dolce-vita; ⏲Nov).

★ **King Valley Dairy** DELI **$**
(☎1300 319 766, 03-5727 9329; www.kingvalleydairy.com.au; 107 Moyhu-Meadow Creek Rd, Moyhu; ⏲10am-4pm) The old Butter Factory in Myrtleford has moved to Moyhu in the King Valley to produce its naturally cultured dairy products. Its deli sells things like buttermilk ricotta, gourmet-flavoured butters and other local produce, so you can put together a hamper to enjoy on the farm or by the river.

Mountain View Hotel PUB FOOD **$$**
(☎03-5729 8270; www.mvhotel.com.au; 4 King Valley Rd, Whitfield; mains $20-38, 5-/7-course degustation $95/115; ⏲pub bistro 11am-late daily, restaurant noon-3pm & 6-10pm Wed-Sat, noon-3pm Sun) Smarter than your average country pub, this gastropub is definitely worth a look for its craft beers, quality menu and stellar beer garden. It has a few ales by local King River Brewing (p288), and items such as twice-cooked Milawa chicken, dry-aged Angus steaks, parmas and Bavarian-style dishes. There's also a fine-dining section doing a degustation menu paired with local wines.

Drinking & Nightlife

King River Brewing MICROBREWERY
(www.kingriverbrewing.com.au; 4515 Wangaratta-Whitfield Rd; 12.30-6pm Sat & Sun) On an old tobacco farm just north of Whitfield is this small brewery with its taphouse set inside a tobacco kiln. It has six beers on tap, doing an IPA, altbier and sour porter among others, as well as wood-fired pretzels using butter from King Valley Dairy (p287).

Chrismont WINERY
(03-5729 8220; www.chrismont.com.au; 251 Upper King River Rd; mains $28-38; 10am-5pm) This Italian-centric winery within a modern, architecturally designed space with magnificent views offers free tastings of its Italian varietals including prosecco, arneis and sagrantino. Its popular restaurant specialises in family recipes from Sicily and northern Italy, and the modern guesthouse among the vines is one of the nicest in the region.

Dal Zotto Estate WINERY
(03-5729 8321; www.dalzotto.com.au; 4861 Wangaratta-Whitfield Rd, Whitfield; cellar door 10am-5pm, restaurant noon-3pm Thu-Sun, plus 6-10pm Fri) Dal Zotto Estate is one of the best wineries in the area, known especially for its prosecco. It also has an excellent trattoria serving north Italian cuisine, including handmade pasta and antipasto using local produce.

Getting There & Away

The King Valley lies on the Mansfield–Whitfield Rd (C521) and is accessed from Melbourne (274km, three hours) via the Hume Hwy (M31).

From Wangaratta there are two buses a day to Whitfield ($3.20, 45 minutes) Monday to Friday, via Moyhu.

Milawa Gourmet Region

The Milawa/Oxley gourmet region (www.milawagourmet.com.au) is the place to indulge your taste buds. As well as wine tasting, you can sample cheese, olives, mustards and marinades, or dine in some of the region's best restaurants.

Eating

★ **Milawa Cheese Company** CHEESE $
(03-5727 3589; www.milawacheese.com.au; 17 Factory Lane, Milawa; 9am-5pm, meals 9.30am-3pm) From humble origins, the Milawa Cheese Company now produces a mouth-watering array of cheeses to sample or buy. It excels at soft farmhouse brie (from goat or cow) and pungent washed-rind cheeses. There's a bakery here and an excellent restaurant doing a variety of house-baked pizzas and sourdough toasties using Milawa cheese. It's 2km north of Milawa.

★ **Patricia's Table** MODERN AUSTRALIAN $$$
(03-5720 5540; www.brownbrothers.com.au/visit-us/victoria/eat; 239 Milawa-Bobinawarrah Rd, Milawa; 2-course meal & wine pairing $67; noon-3pm) Break up your travels with a long lunch at this fine-dining restaurant at the picturesque Brown Brothers (p288) winery. Regarded as one of the region's very best, expect beautifully presented, contemporary dishes featuring the likes of blackened barramundi and grilled honey-glazed pork paired with earthy seasonal flavours. All the set-course combinations are accompanied with wines, which makes this hatted restaurant excellent value.

Drinking & Nightlife

Hurdle Creek Still DISTILLERY
(0427 331 145, 0411 156 773; www.hurdlecreekstill.com.au; 216 Whorouly-Bobinawarrah Rd, Bobinawarrah; 10am-5pm Sat & Sun, by app Mon-Fri) This rural, small-scale, family-run distillery produces all its gins from a tin shed; drop by for tastings and pick up a bottle.

Brown Brothers WINERY
(03-5720 5500; www.brownbrothers.com.au; 239 Milawa-Bobinawarrah Rd, Milawa; cellar door 9am-5pm, 1hr tour 11am & 2pm Fri, 11am Sat & Sun) The region's best-known winery, Brown Brothers vineyard's first vintage was in 1889 and it has remained in the hands of the same family ever since. As well as the tasting room, there's the superb Patricia's Table (p288) and Epi.Curious restaurants, a gorgeous garden, kids' play equipment, and picnic and barbecue facilities.

Shopping

Walkabout Apiaries FOOD
(03-5727 3468; www.walkaboutapiaries.com.au; 1531 Snow Rd, Milawa; 9am-5pm) Stop by to sample a range of honey, cordial and mead; also sells beeswax candles.

Milawa Mustard FOOD
(03-5727 3202; www.milawamustards.com.au; 1597 Snow Rd, Milawa; 10am-4.30pm) Along the main street of Milawa, Milawa Mustard offers tastings of its handmade seeded mustards, herbed vinegars and preserves.

Getting There & Away

Milawa lies along the Snow Rd, between Wangaratta and Myrtleford. There's no public transport through the region.

Beechworth

POP 3700

Beechworth's historic honey-coloured granite buildings and wonderful gourmet offerings make it one of northeast Victoria's most enjoyable towns. It's also listed by the National Trust as one of Victoria's two 'notable' towns (the other is Maldon), and you'll soon see why.

Sights

★ Burke Museum MUSEUM

(☎03-5728 8067; www.burkemuseum.com.au; 28 Loch St; adult/child/family incl entry to Ned Kelly vault $8/5/16; ⏲10am-5pm) Dating to 1857 when it was the Beechworth Athenaeum, this is one of Australia's oldest museums. It was renamed in 1861 in tribute to the famous explorer Robert O'Hara Burke – police superintendent at Beechworth from 1854 to 1858 – following the ill-fated Burke and Wills expedition. It shows gold-rush relics and an arcade of shopfronts preserved as they were over 140 years ago. Highlights include a taxidermy thylacine (Tasmanian tiger), Charles Dickens' writing desk, Burke's pistol and 'trench art' bullets from WWI.

The ticket here includes entry to the excellent Ned Kelly Vault.

Ned Kelly Vault MUSEUM

(☎03-5728 8067; www.burkemuseum.com.au; 101 Ford St; ⏲11am-4pm) Within the original subtreasury building (c 1858) where gold was stored, is this exhibition space dedicated to Australia's most infamous bushranger, Ned Kelly. There's detailed info on the Kelly story, as well as one of his original death masks, an original Sir Sidney Nolan painting, rare photographs and an early manuscript of Peter Carey's *True History of the Kelly Gang*. There's also an exhibit on the iconic bulletproof suits, and a mask you can wear for a photo op.

Also on display are the original masks used in the films starring Heath Ledger and Mick Jagger.

Old Beechworth Gaol HISTORIC BUILDING

(www.oldbeechworthgaol.com.au; cnr Ford & Williams Sts; adult/child/family $15/10/40; ⏲tours 11.45am Thu-Mon) In late 2016 a consortium of locals banded together to buy the historic 1860 Beechworth prison in order to save it from being developed. Join its 'Rogues, Rat Bags and Mongrel Dogs' tours, held most days during the week to hear tales of its most infamous inmates – namely Ned Kelly, his family and sympathisers; in more recent times Carl Williams spent time in here. You'll get to visit the cells and gallows where eight prisoners were executed.

> **COMBINED TICKET**
>
> If you're going to visit more than a couple of Beechworth's museums, it's worth buying the combined **Golden Ticket** (adult/child/family $25/15/50), which can be bought online or in person through the **visitor centre** (p291). It covers entry over four consecutive days to most of the major sights and includes two guided tours.

Beechworth Courthouse HISTORIC BUILDING

(☎03-5728 8067; www.burkemuseum.com.au; 94 Ford St; adult/child/family $8/5/16; ⏲9.30am-5pm) The Beechworth Courthouse is notable for Ned Kelly's first court appearance; see the cell where Ned was held in the basement behind the Shire Hall. There are stories of other notable trials, and an interactive jury room where you can hand down a verdict. Entry here is included in the Golden Ticket (p290).

Beechworth Asylum HISTORIC SITE

(Albert Rd) One for those into dark tourism is this creepy, old 'lunatic' asylum, decommissioned in 1995, which sits on Mayday Hill overlooking town. While a lot of the buildings have been redeveloped into hotels and residential properties (and a proposed artists' studio is on the cards), a lot remains abandoned and downright spooky. You can't access inside any of the buildings, unless you sign up with Asylum Ghost Tours (p290), which operates historic tours by day and ghost tours by night.

Activities

As well as strolling the historic shopfronts there's plenty here to keep you busy, from cycling and abseiling to kayaking. Panning for gold is another unique activity that you can do independently or with a **tour** (☎0419 280 614; www.beechworthtouristguides.com; tours from $95); you need a licence, available from the visitor centre (p291).

Beechworth Honey Experience FOOD

(☎03-5728 1433; www.beechworthhoney.com.au; 31 Ford St; electric bike per half/full day $35/55, bicycle $25/40; ⊙9am-5.30pm) FREE Beechworth Honey's passionate owners, a fourth-generation family of honey producers, take you into the world of bees with regular guided tours, a live hive, highly educational displays and honey tastings. Visit its **Beechworth Honey Discovery** (☎03-5728 1433; www.beechworthhoney.com.au/beechworth-honey-discovery; 87 Ford St; ⊙9am-5.30pm) FREE centre down the road for more food, cooking demos, a bee garden and tastings. It also hires out electric bikes and bicycles.

Tours

Walking Tours TOURS

(adult/child/family $10/7.50/25; ⊙10.15am & 1.15pm) Daily guided walking tours leave from the visitor centre (p291) and feature lots of gossip and interesting details. The Gold Rush tour starts at 10.15am, the Ned Kelly–themed tour at 1.15pm. The good-value Golden Ticket (p290) includes both walking tours in the price.

Asylum Ghost Tours TOURS

(☎0473 376 848; www.asylumghosttours.com; Mayday Hills Village; tours adult/child $35/20) Beechworth's most creepy outing is a trip up to the town's former asylum (p289) with plenty of eerie tales of murder and mayhem. Visit during the day for a history tour or at night for ghost tours (kids under eight years not permitted). There are also photography tours (from $45), paranormal investigations ($50), horror film nights ($15) and sleepovers.

Festivals & Events

Beechworth Music Festival MUSIC

(www.beechworthmusicfestival.com; Madman's Gully Amphitheatre; tickets $85, child under 14yr free; ⊙late Jan) Held in the farmland surrounding the former asylum (p289) is this popular two-day indie music festival with a varied line-up of local bands. Free camping with admission.

Sleeping

Tanswell's Commercial Hotel PUB $

(☎03-5728 1480; www.tanswellshotelbeechworth.com.au; 50 Ford St; s/d with shared bathroom $60/82, apt $135;) In a town where accommodation ain't cheap, this historic main-street pub is here to save the day with its no-frills rooms that are perfectly placed for exploring Beechworth. It's worth staying for its beautifully restored downstairs bar (p291) and restaurant.

Lake Sambell Caravan Park CARAVAN PARK $

(☎03-5728 1421; www.caravanparkbeechworth.com.au; 20 Peach Dr; unpowered/powered sites from $24/32, cabins with/without bathroom $95/75;) This shady park next to Lake Sambell has great facilities, including a camp kitchen, playground, mountain-bike hire (half/full day $22/33) and canoe/kayak hire (from $45). Sunsets reflected in the lake are spectacular.

Old Priory GUESTHOUSE $$

(☎03-5728 1024; www.oldpriory.com.au; 8 Priory Lane; dm/s/d $50/70/100, cottages s $90, d $150-170, q $200;) This historic convent dating to 1904 is a spooky but charming old place. It's often used by school groups, but it's the best budget choice in Beechworth, with lovely gardens and a range of rooms, including beautifully renovated miners' cottages.

★ **Freeman on Ford** B&B $$$

(☎03-5728 2371; www.freemanonford.com.au; 97 Ford St; s/d incl breakfast from $250/275;) In the 1876 Oriental Bank, this sumptuous but homely place offers five-star Victorian luxury in six beautifully renovated rooms, right in the heart of town. The owner, Heidi, will make you feel very special.

Eating

Project Forty Nine ITALIAN $

(☎03-5728 1599; www.projectfortynine.com.au; 46-48 Ford St; dishes $9-25; ⊙9am-5pm Wed-Mon, to 9pm Fri) Opened by the former sommelier of Melbourne's acclaimed Vue de Monde is this popular husband-and-wife-operated Italian deli/wine bar. It does a casual menu of cured meats, antipasti and a pasta to go with Italian wine by the glass, as well as its own locally produced chardonnay.

Beechworth Bakery BAKERY $

(☎1300 233 784; www.beechworthbakery.com.au; 27 Camp St; pies from $5; ⊙6am-7pm) This popular place is the original in a well-known, statewide bakery chain. It's great for pies and pastries, cakes and sandwiches. Its signature pie is the Ned Kelly, topped with an egg and bacon, but the veggie cauliflower pie is also a winner.

Blynzz Coffee Roasters CAFE $$

(☎0423 589 962; www.coffeeroastersbeechworth.com.au; 43 Ford St; mains from $15; ⊙8.30am-2pm Thu-Sun) This inner-city-chic micro-roastery cafe on Beechworth's main strip has polished concrete floors and designer fittings along with great breakfasts and brunches. However, it's best known for its coffee, roasting all of its single-origin beans on site, with awaiting hessian sacks of green beans stacked at the back.

★ Provenance MODERN AUSTRALIAN **$$$**
(☎03-5728 1786; www.theprovenance.com.au; 86 Ford St; 2-/3-course meals $68/88, degustation menu without/with matching wines $115/180; ⏲6.30-9pm Wed-Sun) In an 1856 bank building, Provenance has elegant but contemporary fine dining. Under the guidance of acclaimed local chef Michael Ryan, the innovative menu features modern Australian fare with Japanese influences, such as smoked wallaby tartare with umeboshi, egg yolk and miso sauce. If you can't decide, go for the degustation menu. Its wine list is highly renowned, too. Bookings essential.

Drinking & Nightlife

★ Bridge Road Brewers MICROBREWERY
(☎03-5728 2703; www.bridgeroadbrewers.com.au; Old Coach House Brewers Lane, 50 Ford St; pizza $15.50-22; ⏲11am-10pm) Hiding behind Tanswell's Commercial Hotel (p291), Beechworth's gem of a microbrewery produces some excellent beer (taste 10 for $15), with nine of them on tap. It goes beautifully with freshly baked pretzels, gourmet house-made pizzas, burgers etc. There's a brewery tour each Saturday at 11am ($15), which includes tastings. It also offers free bike hire!

Tanswell's Commercial Hotel PUB
(☎03-5728 1480; www.tanswellshotelbeechworth.com.au; 50 Ford St; mains $24-34; ⏲10.30am-late) A gold-rush-era pub dating to 1856, the imposing Tanswell's Hotel is very much a fixture along Beechworth's picturesque main street. Its front bar is done out elegantly with gleaming polished wood, black-and-white checkered tiles and a roaring fire, resembling an English pub more than an Aussie country hotel. There's also a fine-dining restaurant, live music, a billiards room and accommodation (p290).

Information

Beechworth Visitor Centre (☎1300 366 321; www.beechworthonline.com.au; 103 Ford St; ⏲9am-5pm) Information and an accommodation and activity booking service in the town hall.

Getting There & Away

Beechworth is just off the Great Alpine Rd, 36km east of Wangaratta and 280km northeast of Melbourne.

V/Line runs a train/bus service between Melbourne and Beechworth ($36, 3½ hours, three daily), with a change at Wangaratta. There are direct buses from Wangaratta ($5, 35 minutes, five daily) and Bright ($4.80, 50 minutes, two daily).

Yackandandah

POP 950

An old gold-mining town nestled in beautiful hills and valleys east of Beechworth, 'Yack', as it's universally known, is original enough to be classified by the National Trust. Essentially a one-street town – bookended by two pubs, the Bottom Pub (p292) and the Top Pub (p291) – its historic streetscape is one of the most charming you'll find in country Australia.

Sights

Yackandandah Museum MUSEUM
(☎02-6027 0627; www.yackandandahmuseum.wordpress.com; 21 High St; gold coin donation; ⏲11am-4pm Wed-Sun, daily school holidays) In a former bank building, this interesting museum has changing historical exhibitions on Yackandandah. Out the back is an original 1850s cottage that's furnished in period style and includes a unique outdoor 'double dunny' (toilet). There's also a good selection of themed walking-tour maps in its gift shop.

Tours

Karrs Reef Goldmine Tour TOURS
(☎0408 975 991; adult/child $25/20; ⏲10am, 1pm & 4pm Sat & Sun or by app) Don a hard hat and descend into the original tunnels of this gold mine that dates to 1857. On the 1½-hour guided tour you'll learn all about the mine's history. Bookings can be made through the visitor centre (p292).

Eating & Drinking

★ Star Hotel PUB FOOD **$$**
(☎02-6027 1493; www.facebook.com/starhotelyack; 30 High St; mains $17-21; ⏲11am-late) Known locally as the 'Top Pub', this 1863 hotel does all the classic counter meals, but of more interest is its American-style BBQ using a red-gum smoker. It's also the place for craft beer, being the official home of Yack's very own Two Pot Brewing.

Saint Monday CAFE $$
(02-6027 1202; www.saintmondaycafe.com.au; 26 High St; mains $15-26; 8am-4pm Wed-Sun;) Deconstructed sushi and vegan doughnuts are definitely items you once couldn't order in Yackandandah, but those days are gone since the arrival of this lovely little cafe with art on the walls. The kitchen uses locally sourced ingredients to create delicious vegetarian and ethical cuisine.

Yackandandah Hotel PUB
(02-6027 1210; www.yackandandahhotel.com.au; 1 High St; s/d/tr $50/70/90; 11am-late) Dating back to 1867, the 'Bottom Pub' is your quintessential country hotel with cold beer and pub grub, including its signature double schnitzel burger. There are budget rooms upstairs from $50 a night.

Shopping

★**Kirby's Flat Pottery** CERAMICS
(02-6027 1416; www.johndermer.com.au; 225 Kirby's Flat Rd; 10.30am-5pm Sat & Sun or by app) The studio-cum-gallery-cum-shop of internationally renowned potter John Dermer, Kirby's Flat Pottery is a great place to pick up affordable, original pieces, or just browse the gallery with its stunning collection of salt-glazed ceramics. It's set in a lovely garden retreat 4km south of Yackandandah.

Information

Yackandandah Visitor Centre (02-6027 1988; www.exploreyackandandah.com.au; 37 High St; 9am-5pm) Stocks a good selection of brochures, walking tours and accommodation for Yack and beyond. Also sells mining licences for those who fancy prospecting for gold.

Getting There & Away

Yackandandah is 307km northeast of Melbourne. Take the Hume Hwy to the Great Alpine Rd exit north of Wangaratta then follow the signs to Beechworth. From here it's a further 22km to Yackandandah.

On weekdays there are daily buses to/from Beechworth ($2.40) en route to Albury-Wodonga.

Chiltern

POP 1640

Like an old-time movie set, tiny Chiltern is one of Victoria's most historic and charming colonial townships. Its two main streets are lined with 19th-century buildings, antique shops and a couple of pubs – authentic enough that the town has been used as a film set for period films, including the early Walt Disney classic *Ride a Wild Pony*. Originally called Black Dog Creek, it was established in 1851 and prospered when gold was discovered here in 1859.

Sights

Pick up a copy of the Chiltern Touring Guide from the Chiltern Visitor Centre (p293) – it guides you around 20 historic sites scattered about the town.

Chiltern Athenaeum MUSEUM
(03-5726 1280; www.chilternathenaeum.com.au; 57 Conness St; adult/child $2/free; 10am-3pm Tue-Fri, to 4pm Sat & Sun) Housed in the former historic town hall and library (1866) is this fantastic museum loaded with fascinating exhibits of yesteryear and local stories. Highlights include a gold-rush-era library, exquisite 19th-century gum-leaf paintings by Alfred William Eustace, a WWI horse saddle from the Battle of Beersheba and mementos from former primer minister John McEwen.

It's volunteer run, so opening hours can be sporadic.

Chiltern-Mt Pilot National Park NATIONAL PARK
(Chiltern Box-Ironbark National Park; 13 19 63; www.parks.vic.gov.au) This important national park protects some of Victoria's last stands of Box-Ironbark forest in a patchwork of protected areas around the town. This is also one of the last Victorian refuges for the endangered Regent's Honeyeater, along with more than 200 other bird species. The Chiltern Visitor Centre (p293) has maps, a park information sheet, a brochure entitled *Bird Trails of Chiltern*, and information on the best places to see the Regent's Honeyeater.

To immerse yourself in the Ironbarks, consider the 8.5km **Whitebox Walking Track**, which completes a circuit in the area of the park south of Chiltern; ask at the visitor centre for directions.

Lake View House HISTORIC BUILDING
(03-5726 1590, 03-9656 9889; www.nationaltrust.org.au/places/lake-view-house; 18-22 Victoria St; adult/child $2/1; 11am-2pm Wed, 10am-1pm Sat, 1-4pm Sun) This was the home of local author Ethel Florence Richardson (better known by her pen name Henry Handel Richardson), who wrote about life here in the book *Ultima Thule* (1929). Overlooking Lake Anderson, the house was built in 1870 and today is owned by the National Trust.

Eating

★Hub 62 CAFE $
(☎03-5726 1207; www.hub62cafe.wixsite.com/cafe-gallery; 62 Main St; mains $10-19; ⏲8am-4pm Mon & Wed-Fri, 7.30am-4pm Sat & Sun;) In the historic former Masonic Hall is this relaxed and vibrant, art-filled cafe that offers a distinct contemporary point of difference from the rest of ye olde town. As well as the best coffee in town, you can grab modern-style breakfasts and lunches.

Vine Chiltern PUB FOOD $$
(☎0475 044 866; www.facebook.com/thevinechiltern; cnr Main & Conness Sts; mains $14-28; ⏲5.30-9pm Wed & Thu, 5.30pm-late Fri & Sat, noon-4pm Sun) A pub way back in 1867, the Vine has brought this historic watering hole back to life with a menu of regional craft beers and wines to go with pizzas and burgers. It's named after the massive grapevine (the largest in Australia, possibly the world) in the courtyard next door, viewed from the alleyway.

Information

Chiltern Visitor Centre (☎03-5726 1611; www.chilternvic.com; 30 Main St; ⏲10am-4pm) Chiltern's helpful tourist office has information on the town and surrounding area, with useful tips on everything from birdwatching to gold prospecting.

Getting There & Away

Chiltern is 290km northeast of Melbourne and lies just off the Hume Hwy (M31).

Up to three **V/Line** (☎1800 800 007; www.vline.com.au) train services run daily from Melbourne's Southern Cross station to Chiltern ($36, 3¼ hours).

Rutherglen & Around

POP 2479

Rutherglen combines some marvellous gold-rush-era buildings (gold was discovered here in 1860) with northern Victoria's most celebrated winemaking tradition. The town itself has all the essential ingredients that merit a stopover, among them a great pie shop, antique dealers and classic country pubs to go with its changing face since the arrival of a swish new microbrewery and wine bar. It all adds up to an engaging destination in its own right and a good base for exploring the Murray River's Victorian hinterland.

Sights & Activities

An extension of the Murray to Mountains Rail Trail (p297) passes through Rutherglen and Wahgunyah and leads to some of the wineries. You can hire bicycles (half/full day $35/50), as well as tandem bikes (half/full day $50/85), from the Rutherglen Visitor Information Centre (p295), which also has bicycle and walking trail maps of the area.

Big Wine Bottle LANDMARK
(45 Campbell St) In line with Australia's fine tradition of kitschy oversized monuments (the Big Prawn, Big Pineapple, Big Koala etc), Rutherglen has the Big Wine Bottle. It stands at 36m tall and is actually a historic brown-brick water tower (c 1900).

Rutherglen Wine Experience WINERY
(☎1800 622 871; www.rutherglenvic.com; 57 Main St; ⏲9am-5pm) FREE Set up inside the visitor information centre (p295) is the centrepiece for the region's wine industry. Here you'll get an overview of the local wineries and a map of the area, as well as free tastings of various fortified wines and locally made cordials.

Tours

Behind the Scenes TOURS
(☎1800 622 871; www.rutherglenvic.com/behind-the-scenes-tours; ⏲2pm Mon, Wed & Thu, 11am Fri-Sun) FREE A few local wineries offer fantastic, free 'Behind the Scenes' winery tours that take you into the world of the wine-making process. Advance bookings are essential. Check the website to match your day with a winery, but it's best to pre-book through the visitor centre (p295).

Festivals & Events

★Tastes of Rutherglen FOOD & DRINK
(www.tastesofrutherglen.com.au; tickets $20, shuttle bus $27; ⏲Mar) A weekend of indulgence, this massive celebration of food and wine is held at dozens of vineyards and restaurants. There's a hop-on, hop-off shuttle bus linking the wineries.

★Winery Walkabout Weekend WINE, MUSIC
(www.winerywalkabout.com.au; ⏲Jun) Australia's original wine festival, this huge events attracts 25,000 revellers to town for a weekend of merriment including music, barrel racing, food vans and probably some wine.

RUTHERGLEN REDS

Rutherglen's wineries produce superb fortifieds (port, muscat and tokay) and some potent durifs and shirazes – among the biggest, baddest and strongest reds. Many wineries date back to the 1860s, and are still run by fifth- or sixth-generation winemakers.

All Saints (02-6035 2222, 1800 021 621; www.allsaintswine.com.au; All Saints Rd, Wahgunyah; 9am-5.30pm Mon-Sat, 10am-5.30pm Sun) With its aristocratic gardens and heritage-listed 19th-century castle, All Saints (established 1865) is a classy affair, which extends from its cheese-tasting room and cellar door to its fine-dining restaurant.

Buller Wines (02-6032 9660; www.buller.com.au; 2804 Federation Way; 9am-5pm Mon-Fri, 10am-5pm Sat & Sun) Making fine shiraz since 1921; keep an eye out for its new restaurant.

Rutherglen Estates (02-6032 7999; www.rutherglenestates.com.au; Tuileries, 13-35 Drummond St; 10am-5.30pm) Closest winery to town with shiraz, grenache and table red and white wines.

Stanton & Killeen Wines (02-6032 9457; www.stantonandkilleenwines.com.au; 440 Jacks Rd; 9am-5pm Mon-Fri, 10am-5pm Sat & Sun) This century-old winery is known for its durif-shiraz blend, rosé and vintage ports.

Warrabilla Wines (02-6035 7242; www.warrabillawines.com.au; 6152 Murray Valley Hwy; 10am-5pm) Run by a sixth-generation winemaker, this is one for those who like their reds big, brash and full of oak.

Morris (02-6026 7303; www.morriswines.com.au; 154 Mia Mia Rd; 9am-5pm Mon-Sat, 10am-5pm Sun) Rutherglen's oldest winery (1859) with a dusty cellar door designed by esteemed architect Robin Boyd, looking out to wine barrels and the dirt production floor.

Pfeiffer (02-6033 2805; www.pfeifferwinesrutherglen.com.au; 167 Distillery Rd, Wahgunyah; 9am-5pm Mon-Sat, 10am-5pm Sun) This atmospheric cellar door known for its gamay is run by a father-daughter winemaker team. It's on a river teeming with turtles and the occasional platypus.

Chambers Rosewood (02-6032 8641; www.chambersrosewood.com.au; Barkly St; 9am-5pm Mon-Sat, 10am-5pm Sun) One of Rutherglen's originals, this ramshackle tin-shed cellar door's wine tasting is all self-serve.

Cofield Wines (02-6033 3798; www.cofieldwines.com.au; Distillery Rd, Wahgunyah; 9am-5pm Mon-Sat, 10am-5pm Sun) Stop by to sample Champagne-style sparkling wines, produced using a traditional method.

St Leonard's Vineyard (02-6035 2222; www.stleonardswine.com.au; 201 St Leonards Rd, Wahgunyah; 10am-5pm Thu-Sun) Head through its dark (and kinda spooky) barrel room to enter a modern light-filled cellar door with grassy outdoors area and lagoon. Good food too.

Sleeping

Rutherglen

Victoria Hotel HOTEL $
(02-6032 8610; www.victoriahotelrutherglen.com.au; 90 Main St; s/d without bathroom from $50/90, d with bathroom from $120, f from $200;) A step up from your usual pub accommodation, this beautiful National Trust–classified pub is full of history, great bistro food and lovely guest rooms. Best pick are the spruced-up en-suite rooms overlooking Main St. At $50 a night it's a great spot for budget travellers.

★ **Amberesque** B&B $$
(02-6032 7000; www.amberesque.com.au; 80 Main St; d from $180;) Named after host Amber, who, along with her husband, has set up this wonderful B&B in a historic bank in the heart of town. Upstairs rooms are lovely, with king-sized beds and spa baths, and a patio overlooking the garden. The highlight is the beautiful downstairs space where you can enjoy a lavish personalised breakfast, complimentary port and welcome cheese-and-wine platter.

Tuileries BOUTIQUE HOTEL $$
(02-6032 9033; www.tuileriesrutherglen.com.au; 13 Drummond St; d $199, incl dinner $299;

) Looking out to the vineyards, all rooms at this luxurious place are individually decorated in bright contemporary tones. There's a guest lounge, tennis court, pool and fine-dining **restaurant** (lunch mains $16.50-19, dinner $31.50-40; noon-2pm & 6.30-9pm) and cafe. Located next to Rutherglen Estates (p294); rates include breakfast.

Carlyle House B&B $$
(02-6032 8444; www.carlylehouse.com.au; 147 High St; r $160-195;) Four traditional suites and modern garden apartments are beautifully presented in this lovingly restored home (c 1896), with lovely hosts Anthony and Sharyn. A choice of cafe-style cooked breakfasts is included in the rate.

Wahgunyah

Grapevine Glamping TENTED CAMP $$$
(02-6033 3798; www.cofieldwines.com.au/glamping.aspx; Cofield Wines, Distillery Rd, Wahgunyah; d from $260) Here at Cofield winery you can sleep among the vines in a luxury bell tent equipped with a king-sized bed. Rates include a bottle of wine, breakfast hamper, $50 winery voucher, stargazing kit, fishing gear and other features to ensure a lovely stay.

Eating

Rutherglen

★**Parker Pies** BAKERY $
(02-6032 9605; www.parkerpies.com.au; 86-88 Main St; pies $5-9; 8.30am-5pm) If you think a pie is just a pie, this award-winning local institution might change your mind. Try the gourmet pastries – emu, venison, crocodile, buffalo or the lovely Jolly Jumbuck (a lamb pastry with rosemary and mint).

★**Taste @ Rutherglen** MODERN AUSTRALIAN $$$
(03-5728 1480; www.taste-at-rutherglen.com; 121b Main St; breakfast mains $7-20, mains $36-40, 5-/7-course degustation $80/100; 8-11am & 6-11pm Wed-Sun) Taste @ Rutherglen is the town's go-to place for fine dining, coffee and breakfast, while its attached brewpub is *the* spot for beer. Its evening menu offers options such as confit-duck spring rolls to go with hickory-smoked eye fillets, or there's a degustation menu with paired wines. For breakfast the Rutherglen pork sausage and poached egg on sourdough is a winner.

Wahgunyah

Pickled Sisters Café MODERN EUROPEAN $$
(02-6033 2377; www.pickledsisters.com.au; Cofield Wines, Distillery Rd, Wahgunyah; mains $12-33; 10am-3pm Mon & Wed-Fri, 9am-4pm Sat & Sun) Attached to the Cofield (p294) winery, this popular little eatery does some interesting dishes such as honey-and-muscat-glazed confit duck, and twice-baked Milawa goats-milk cheese soufflé, along with various platters to go with wine. There's also the opportunity to spend the night in a luxury tent (p295).

★**Terrace Restaurant** MODERN EUROPEAN $$$
(02-6035 2209; www.allsaintswine.com.au/terrace-restaurant; All Saints Estate, All Saints Rd, Wahgunyah; 2-/3-course meal $60/80; noon-3pm Wed-Fri & Sun, noon-3pm & 6-11pm Sat) One of the region's best restaurants, this classy bistro serves inventive and modern seasonal European cuisine, overlooking the stately grounds of All Saints (p294) wine estate.

Drinking & Nightlife

★**Thousand Pound** WINE BAR
(02-6035 2222; www.thousandpound.com.au; 82 Main St; mains from $24; 5pm-late Fri-Sun) If ever there was a place suited to a wine bar, it's Rutherglen's picturesque main street. Grab a stool at the bar, by the window or on the communal table to select from 140 local and international family-owned wineries. Its food is also a highlight with charcoal-grilled steaks, seafood and tapas dishes.

★**Rutherglen Brewery** MICROBREWERY
(02-6032 9765; www.rutherglenbrewery.com; 121b Main St; 11am-2.30pm & 5.30-10pm Wed-Sat) An awesome new addition to town is this nanobrewery that knocks up quality crafted ales from its back shed. It produces nine beers, with usually five on tap, along with a cider to go with a menu of smoked BBQ meats and pizzas. Plans are in place to start up a distillery and speakeasy bar next door, which will no doubt be another hit.

Information

Rutherglen Visitor Information Centre
(1800 622 871; 57 Main St; 9am-5pm) In the same complex as the Rutherglen Wine Experience; has good info on accommodation, wineries and sights. Also rents bikes and has wi-fi access.

Getting There & Away

Rutherglen is 295km northeast of Melbourne. To get there by car, take the Hume Hwy (M31) and turn off at Chiltern.

V/Line (1800 800 007; www.vline.com.au) has a train and coach service between Melbourne and Rutherglen ($36, 3½ hours, eight weekly), with a change at Wangaratta. During festivals, bus transport to wineries can be organised through the **visitor centre** (p295).

The Murray to Mountains Rail Trail (p297) has an extension to Rutherglen, which means you can get here and around by bike.

Mt Buffalo National Park

Beautiful Mt Buffalo is an easily accessible year-round destination – in winter it's a tiny, family friendly ski resort with gentle runs, and in summer it's a great spot for bushwalking, mountain biking and rock climbing. Unlike the bigger ski resorts, there are no fees for visiting Mt Buffalo. You'll find granite outcrops, lookouts, streams, waterfalls, wildflowers and wildlife here.

It was named in 1824 by the explorers Hume and Hovell on their trek from Sydney to Port Phillip – they thought its bulky shape resembled a buffalo – and declared a national park in 1898.

Sights & Activities

The **Big Walk**, an 11km, five-hour ascent of the mountain, starts from Eurobin Creek picnic area, north of Porepunkah, and finishes at the Gorge day visitor area. A road leads to just below the summit of the Horn (1723m), the highest point on the massif. Nearby **Lake Catani** is good for swimming, canoeing and camping. There are 14km of groomed cross-country ski trails starting out from the Cresta Valley car park, as well as a tobogganing area. In summer Mt Buffalo is a hang-gliding paradise, and the near-vertical walls of the Gorge provide some of Australia's most challenging rock climbing and abseiling – get in touch with Adventure Guides Australia.

Mt Buffalo Olives FARM
(03-5756 2143; www.mtbuffaloolives.com.au; 307 Mt Buffalo Rd, Porepunkah; 11am-5pm Fri-Mon, daily school holidays) On the road up to Mt Buffalo from Porepunkah, this working olive grove has tastings and sales of olives, olive oils and other locally farmed products. It also has a lovely place to stay (Sunday to Thursday $195, Friday and Saturday $235, two-night minimum stay).

★ **Adventure Guides Australia** OUTDOORS
(0419 280 614; www.adventureguidesaustralia.com) Set up by the extremely knowledgeable David Chitty (a former SAS officer), this established operator offers abseiling (beginner/adventure $90/110), including on the 300m multi-pitch North Wall. It also offers caving with glow-worms through an underground river system (from $120); check its website for scheduled trips. It hires out kayaks for Lake Catani and runs a cross-country snow-shoeing ski school in winter.

Sleeping

Lake Catani Campground CAMPGROUND $
(13 19 63; www.parkweb.vic.gov.au; per site from $46.10; Nov-Apr) A popular summer camping ground on the lake shore, with 59 sites, flush toilets and showers. During winter there are also a few free camp sites available, but only non-flush toilet facilities. Book through Parks Victoria.

★ **Kilns** B&B $$$
(0400 733 170, 0408 553 332; www.kilnhouse.com.au; Cavedons Lane, Porepunkah; d from $300;) Hidden away on an old tobacco farm in Porepunkah are these boutique luxury cottages converted from old tobacco kiln houses. Making for a unique stay, the architecturally designed self-contained houses feature stylish furniture, polished concrete floors and a wood-fire with views to Mt Buffalo. Each has a bicycle so you can pedal to the wineries. Minimum two-night stay.

Eating & Drinking

★ **Feathertop Winery** WINERY
(03-5756 2356; www.feathertopwinery.com.au; 6619 Great Alpine Rd, Porepunkah; cellar door & cafe 10am-5pm daily, restaurant noon-3pm Fri-Mon) This winery-cafe-restaurant in Porepunkah, only 10km from Bright, is an essential stop along the Murray to Mountains Rail Trail (p297). Its cellar door offers tastings of prosecco, pinot gris and shiraz, all grown on site, or you can enjoy a glass on the terrace. The cafe does homemade sausage rolls and sourdough baguettes, while the attached provedore can make up picnic hampers.

Porepunkah Pub PUB
(03-5756 2111; www.porepunkahpub.com.au; 13 Nicholson St, Porepunkah; mains from $15; noon-late daily, kitchen Thu-Sun) The 'Punka Pub' has recently undergone a slick makeover (while retaining respect for its 100-year history),

and these days it's all about craft beers, cocktails on tap and wine sourced exclusively from the immediate area. It does great food using local produce and also offers boutique, well-priced rooms ($140).

Getting There & Away

The main access road is out of Porepunkah, between Myrtleford and Bright, from where it's around a one-hour drive to the summit. Porepunkah is 10km from Bright, and is on the Murray to Mountains Rail Trail (p297).

Bright

POP 2165

Famous for its glorious autumn colours, Bright is a popular year-round destination in the foothills of the alps and a gateway to Mt Hotham and Falls Creek. Skiers make a beeline through Bright in winter, but it's a lovely base for exploring the Alpine National Park, paragliding, fishing and kayaking on local rivers, bushwalking and exploring the region's wineries. It's a big cycling destination, too, with the **Murray to Mountains Rail Trail**, as well as single track mountain-bike and alpine road trails. Plentiful accommodation and some sophisticated restaurants and cafes complete the rather-appealing picture.

Sights & Activities

Bright is a base for all sorts of adventure activities, including fly-fishing, hiking, cycling and paragliding.

The **Murray to Mountains Rail Trail** between Bright and Wangaratta starts (or ends) behind the old train station. Bikes, tandems and baby trailers can be rented from **Cyclepath** (Map p297; ☎03-5750 1442; www.cyclepath.com.au; 74 Gavan St; recreational bikes per hour/half-/full day from $25/30/38, mountain/road bikes per day from $50/75; ⊙9am-5.30pm Mon-Fri, 9am-5pm Sat & Sun) or **Bright Electric Bikes** (Map p297; ☎03-5755 1309; www.brightelectricbikes.com.au; 2 Delany Ave; electric bike rental per hour/half-/full day $22/45/65, bicycle from $15/25/35; ⊙9am-6pm daily Sep-May, 9am-6pm Fri-Sun Jun-Aug). The **Mystic MTB Park** (www.alpinecommunityplantation.com.au/mystic) is getting rave reviews from mountain-bikers. On weekends you can organise shuttles through **Blue Dirt Mountain Biking** (☎0409 161 903; www.bluedirt.com.au/village-bike-cafe; Slalom car park, Bogong High Plains Rd; bike rental per day $50-90, shuttle service 1-/2 days $50/90; ⊙Sat & Sun Nov-May, daily Jan) for $50 per day.

Courses

★**Patrizia Simone Country Cooking School** COOKING
(Map p297; ☎03-5755 2266; www.simonesbright.com.au; 98 Gavan St; per person $180) One of northeastern Victoria's most celebrated chefs, Patrizia Simone runs fabulous four-hour cooking classes centred around Italian (especially Umbrian) cooking techniques using local ingredients. Her signature class is the 'Umbrian Experience', which touches on some of the recipes from Patrizia's cookbook, *My Umbrian Kitchen*.

Festivals & Events

Brighter Days MUSIC
(www.brighterdays.org.au; ⊙Mar) One for petrol heads and music lovers is this popular car and motorbike festival that's gotten bigger each year since its inauguration in 2013 (in which time it's raised almost a million dollars for children's charities). Gets well-known Aussie bands for a free line-up over the Labour Day long weekend.

Sleeping

Alpine Hotel Bright PUB $
(Map p297; ☎03-5755 1366; www.alpinehotelbright.com.au; 7-9 Anderson St; r $80-140) At the rear of this historic 1864 pub are refurbished motel-style rooms that offer excellent value for what's otherwise a pricey town accommodation-wise.

Coach House Inn MOTEL $
(Map p297; ☎1800 813 992; www.coachhousebright.com.au; 100 Gavan St; s/d from $85/105; ❄🛜🏊) This central place has simple but super-value rooms and self-contained units sleeping two to six people. There's a high-season surcharge.

Bright Holiday Park CARAVAN PARK $
(Map p297; ☎1800 706 685, 03-5755 1141; www.brightholidaypark.com.au; Cherry Lane; unpowered sites $33-50, powered sites $35-60, cabins $130-284; ❄🛜🏊) Straddling pretty Morses Creek, this lovely park is five minutes' walk to the shops. The riverside spa cabins are very nice and feature pay TV channels. It's a great spot for families with a pool, minigolf and playground.

★**Odd Frog** BOUTIQUE HOTEL $$
(☎0418 362 791; www.theoddfrog.com; 3 McFadyens Lane; d $150-195, q $250; ❄) 🌿

Bright

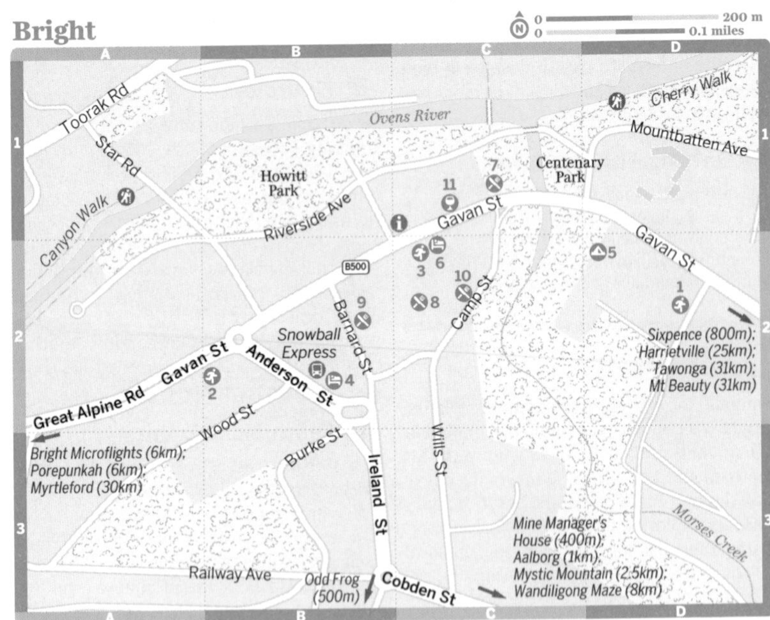

Bright

Activities, Courses & Tours
1 Bright Electric Bikes D2
2 Cyclepath B2
3 Patrizia Simone Country Cooking School C2

Sleeping
4 Alpine Hotel Bright B2
5 Bright Holiday Park D2
6 Coach House Inn C2

Eating
7 Ginger Baker C1
8 Tani C2
9 Thirteen Steps B2
10 Tomahawks C2

Drinking & Nightlife
11 Bright Brewery C1

Designed and built by the architect/interior-designer owners, these contemporary, ecofriendly studios feature light, breezy spaces and fabulous outdoor decks with a telescope for star gazing. The design features clever use of the hilly site with sculptural steel-frame foundations and flying balconies.

Aalborg APARTMENT $$
(☎0401 357 329; www.aalborgbright.com.au; 6 Orchard Ct; r $220-250; ❄📶) Clean-lined Scandinavian design with plenty of pine-and-white furnishings dominates this gorgeous place. Every fitting is perfectly chosen and abundant glass opens out onto sweeping bush views. There's a minimum two-night stay.

Eating

★ Tani MODERN AUSTRALIAN $$$
(Map p297; ☎03-5750 1304; www.tanieatdrink.com.au; 100 Gavan St; 2-/3-/6-course meal $50/60/88; ⏲6-10pm Wed-Sun) Another notch in the belt for regional Victoria's food scene, smart-rustic Tani offers understated class with its menu of local modern Australian food with plenty of indigenous and Asian twists. Its drinks list is an all-regional selection, and there's a distillery all set up to make gins on site from mid-2017.

Ginger Baker CAFE $
(Map p297; ☎03-5755 2300; www.gingerbaker.com.au; 127 Gavan St; mains $8-20; ⏲8am-3pm Sun-Thu, to 9pm Fri & Sat; 📶) This rightfully popular cafe within a cute rustic weatherboard cottage

opens up to an expansive garden with seating overlooking the river. Locally roasted coffee from Sixpence (p299) goes well with tasty hot breakfasts, while Bridge Road (p291) brewery beers on tap complement mains such as buttermilk-fried chicken with aioli, prawn linguine or Mt Beauty lamb cutlets.

Tomahawks CAFE $$
(Map p297; ☎03-5750 1113; 15 Camp St; mains $16; ⏰noon-11pm Wed-Fri, 9am-11pm Sat & Sun) A cool new kid in town, Tomahawks does a menu of urban fare from Korean sticky fried chicken and Old Bay spiced squid with charcoal mayo to a wagyu cheeseburger with habanero mustard, maple bacon and pickles. Also has a well-stocked bar, craft beers and single-origin coffees roasted in Mansfield.

Thirteen Steps MODERN AUSTRALIAN $$
(Map p297; ☎03-5750 1313; www.thirteensteps.com.au; 14 Barnard St; dishes $17-39; ⏰6-11pm Thu-Mon) Take 13 steps down to this atmospheric underground wine cellar and bistro where diners cram in to feast on local-produce plates or dishes ranging from modern Asian to American-style spare ribs.

Drinking

★**Bright Brewery** BREWERY
(Map p297; ☎03-5755 1301; www.brightbrewery.com.au; 121 Gavan St; ⏰11am-10pm; 📶) This boutique brewery produces a quality range of beers (sample six for $12) and beer-friendly food such as pizzas, Angus beef burgers and mezze boards. There's a guided tour and tasting on Monday, Friday and Saturday at 3pm ($18) and live blues on Sunday, or you can learn to be a brewer for a day ($360) – see the website for course dates.

Sixpence COFFEE
(☎0412 728 420; www.sixpencecoffee.com.au; 35 Churchill Ave; ⏰7.30am-2.30pm Mon-Fri) In an industrial estate a short drive from Bright's main strip is this micro-roastery that will excite coffee enthusiasts who love their Ethiopian beans. It's all roasted on site by Luke (formerly from Padre Coffee in East Brunswick, Melbourne) to be enjoyed on the garden tables, along with panini and fresh croissants. Sourdough bread is also baked, available most days.

Information

Alpine Visitor Information Centre (Map p297; ☎03-5755 0584, 1800 111 885; www.brightvictoria.com.au; 119 Gavan St; ⏰9am-5pm; 📶) Has a busy accommodation booking service, along with useful brochures, wi-fi access and attached cafe.

Getting There & Away

Bright is 310km northeast of Melbourne, around a 3½-hour journey that's mostly via the Hume Hwy (M31).

V/Line (☎1800 800 007; www.vline.com.au) runs train/coach services from Melbourne ($37.60, 4½ hours, two daily) with a change at Wangaratta.

O'Connells Omeo Bus Service (☎0428 591 377; www.omeobus.com.au; Day Ave) has a handy year-round service three times a week that heads from Bright to Harrietville ($4.20, 15 minutes) and Mt Hotham ($5, one hour) en route to Omeo ($12.80, two hours).

During winter the **Snowball Express** (Map p297; ☎1300 656 546; www.snowballexpress.com.au) operates from Bright to Mt Hotham (adult/child return $52/44, 1½ hours).

Mt Beauty & the Kiewa Valley

Huddled at the foot of Victoria's highest mountain, Mt Bogong (1986m), Mt Beauty and its twin villages of Tawonga and Tawonga South are the gateways to Falls Creek ski resort. It's reached by a steep and winding road from Bright, with some lovely alpine views.

Sights & Activities

The 2km **Tree Fern Walk** and the longer **Peppermint Walk** both start from **Mountain Creek Picnic Area**, on Mountain Creek Rd, off the Kiewa Valley Hwy (C531). Located about 1km south of Bogong Village (towards Falls Creek), the 1.5km return **Fainter Falls Walk** takes you to a pretty cascade. For information on longer walks in the area, visit the Mt Beauty Visitor Centre (p300).

Kiewa Valley Historical Museum MUSEUM
(☎03-5755 0596; www.kiewavalleyhs.wixsite.com/kvhs-museum; 31 Bogong High Plains Rd; gold coin donation; ⏰9am-5pm) FREE Within the Mt Beauty Visitor Centre (p300) is this interesting little museum that covers the history of the Kiewa Valley and Bogong High Plains, from Indigenous groups through to the colonial highland cattlemen. There's a replica of an old mountain hut, a historical background on skiing in the region and info on the **Bogong Power Station** (Map p302; ☎03-5754 3318; Bogong High Plains Rd; ⏰10.30am-2.30pm Sun) FREE.

Bogong Horseback Adventures HORSE RIDING

(Map p302; ☎03-5754 4849; www.bogonghorse.com.au; 52 Fredas Lane, off Mountain Creek Rd, Tawonga; 2/4hr ride $95/120, full day with lunch $250) Horse riders can experience this beautiful area on horseback on either short two-hour jaunts, day-long trips with a delicious lunch, or week-long pack-horse camping trips to remote alpine regions over Mt Bogong. It's 12km northwest of Tawonga, and includes the delightful Spring Spur (p300) homestay.

Big Hill MTB Park MOUNTAIN BIKING

One of Victoria's first single-track mountain-bike trails, this downhill path will have you flying through scenic alpine forest. While it's more suited to experienced riders, its maze of trails has something for all levels.

Sleeping

★ **Spring Spur** HOMESTAY $

(Map p302; ☎03-5754 4849; www.springspurstay.com.au; 52 Fredas Lane, off Mountain Creek Rd, Tawonga; per person from $90;) A wonderful place to soak up the High Country atmosphere is this family-run farm on a property known for its horseback tours (p300). The well-designed, modern rooms (minimum two-night stay) have private verandahs looking out to Mt Feathertop and the Kiewa Valley. Meals are a highlight (set lunch or dinner $30).

Mt Beauty Holiday Centre CARAVAN PARK $

(☎03-5754 4396; www.holidaycentre.com.au; 222-226 Kiewa Valley Hwy; unpowered/powered sites from $32/38, cabins & yurts $85-160;) This family caravan park close to Mt Beauty town centre has river frontage, games and an interesting range of cabins, including hexagonal 'yurts'.

★ **Dreamers** APARTMENT $$$

(☎03-5754 1222; www.dreamersmtbeauty.com.au; 218 Kiewa Valley Hwy, Mt Beauty; d $190-590;) Each of Dreamer's stunning self-contained eco apartments offers something special and architecturally unique. Sunken lounges, open fireplaces, loft bedrooms and balcony spas are just some of the highlights. Great views and a pretty lagoon complete a dreamily romantic five-star experience.

Eating & Drinking

★ **Å Skafferi** SWEDISH $$

(☎03-5754 4544; www.skafferi.com.au; 84 Bogong High Plains Rd, Mt Beauty; mains $16-23; ⊙8am-4pm Thu-Mon) This cool Swedish pantry and foodstore is a fabulous place to stop. Try the grilled Milawa cheese sandwiches for breakfast and the Swedish meatballs or the sampler of herring and *knäckebröd* (crispbread) for lunch.

Roi's Diner Restaurant ITALIAN $$$

(☎03-5754 4495; 177 Kiewa Valley Hwy; mains from $30; ⊙6.30-9.30pm Thu-Sun) It's hard to believe this unassuming timber shack on the highway 5km from Mt Beauty is an award-winning restaurant, specialising in exceptional modern northern Italian cuisine. Expect great risotto, eye fillet carpaccio, its signature roasted pork chops, homemade or imported pasta and handmade ice cream.

Sweetwater Brewing Company MICROBREWERY

(☎03-5754 1881; www.sweetwaterbrewing.com.au; 211 Kiewa Valley Hwy; ⊙1-7pm Fri, to 6pm Sat & Sun) This highway microbrewery in Mt Beauty utilises the fresh mountain water of the Kiewa River for its range of beers brewed on site – including a pale, golden, summer, IPA, wheat and porter. To sample its range, grab a tasting paddle, served on a cool, mini ski paddle.

Information

Mt Beauty Visitor Centre (☎03-5755 0596, 1800 111 885; www.visitmountbeauty.com.au; 31 Bogong High Plains Rd; ⊙9am-5pm) Has an accommodation booking service, and advice on local walks and mountain-bike trails. Its website is also a wealth of info. It also has the interesting Kiewa Valley Historical Museum and a lookout deck.

Getting There & Away

V/Line (☎1800 800 007; www.vline.com.au) operates a train/bus service from Melbourne to Mt Beauty ($42.60, 5½ hours) on Monday, Wednesday and Friday, via Wangaratta and Bright.

In winter, **Falls Creek Coach Service** (☎03-5754 4024; www.fallscreekcoachservice.com.au) operates daily direct buses from Melbourne to Mt Beauty (one way/return $85/134) and Falls Creek (one way/return $53/106) from 30 June to 17 September; prices include resort entry to Falls Creek. In early June and late September, there are less frequent services.

Falls Creek

ELEV 1780M

Victoria's glitzy, fashion-conscious resort, Falls Creek combines a picturesque alpine setting with impressive skiing and infamous après-ski entertainment. It offers some of

Alpine National Park – Bogong Region

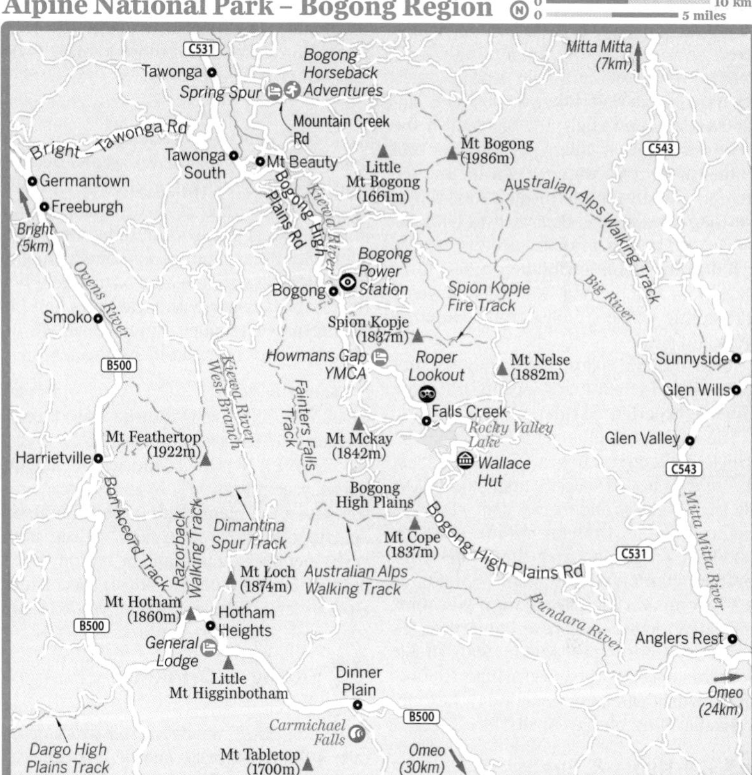

the best downhill skiing, snowboarding and cross-country skiing in Victoria, and plenty of snow activities for non-skiers. Summer is also a good time to visit, with scenic hiking and a fast-emerging mountain-biking scene attracting outdoor enthusiasts in droves.

Sights

Roper Lookout VIEWPOINT

(Map p302) A 5km return walk from Falls Creek through snow gums will lead you to this viewpoint (1706m) overlooking the Kiewa Valley; otherwise you can drive to the car park from where it's a 1.5km walk.

Activities

Winter Activities

Skiing at Falls Creek is spread over two areas – the **Village Bowl** and **Sun Valley** – with 19 lifts, a vertical drop of 267m and Australia's longest beginners' run at **Wombat's Ramble** (2.2km). Falls is also the free-ride snowboard capital, with four parks. Night skiing ($20) on Wombat's Ramble operates Wednesday and Saturday evening from 6pm to 9pm. The lift pass is also valid at Mt Hotham.

Cross-country skiing is also popular – Falls Creek is the training base for Australia's national team – with 65km of groomed trails. There's a network of snowshoeing trails too.

There's also plenty to do without a lift pass, with a number of snow activities in the Village Bowl for those who just want to play around, as well as Victoria's biggest snow-tube park (from $23), snowmobiles for kids and toboggan slopes. On Thursday evenings at 8pm in July and August there's a night show of pro skiers and snowboarders performing tricks, followed by a fireworks show. There are also fat bikes to rent (per day $50) from Falls Creek Hotel, with designated trails.

Summer Activities

Mountain biking is a big attraction in the green season, with the **Falls Creek MTB Park** (www.fallscreek.com.au/mtb; approximately Oct–mid-Jun) offering 40km of downhill single-track and flow trails; the highlight is the **Flowtown Trail**, a 10km pure gravity trail among snow gums with a 500m summit descent. It's mostly for intermediate-level riders, but there are sections dedicated to both advanced and beginner riders.

Blue Dirt Mountain Biking (p298) hires bikes from $50 a day; it also offers a weekend shuttle service (daily during January), tours and a cafe.

Road cycling is also very popular, but with steep, high-altitude ascents it's more suited to experienced riders.

The best local hiking trails include the walk to **Wallace Hut** (Map p302), built in 1889, and said to be the oldest cattleman's hut in the High Country, and **Rocky Valley Lake**.

The Falls to Hotham Alpine Crossing (p306), a 37km hike over three days with camping platforms (per night $31.60), is fast becoming a big attraction; if you want to do an abridged version, in January there's a shuttle service (per person $60) to Mt Hotham to begin the return hike to Falls Creek, which can be done in a day. It's only accessible November to April.

Festivals & Events

Falls Creek Dragon Boat Regatta CULTURAL
(www.fallscreek.com.au/events/falls-creek-dragon-boat-regatta; late Jan) Held on the Rocky Valley Lake (1600m), this is, not surprisingly, the highest dragon boat race in Australia. It's held late January over the Australia Day weekend and involves a number of festivities.

Sleeping

Most lodges in Falls Creek stipulate a minimum two-night stay, particularly on weekends. Rates skyrocket during the snow season, so budget travellers can consider using Mt Beauty as an alternative base, however, you should be able to find a dorm room for around $60.

Howmans Gap YMCA HOSTEL $
(Map p302; 03-5758 3228; www.camps.ymca.org.au/locate/howmans-gap.html; 2587 Bogong High Plains Rd; dm/s/d incl full board with shared bathroom $78/133/166; Jun-Sep;) Only open to guests during winter, this YMCA lodge is a good budget option for those wanting to come to the snow. The room rates include three meals a day, which makes it a reasonable deal. It also manages the Falls Creek Nordic Centre for those wanting to do cross-country skiing.

Diana Alpine Lodge LODGE $
(03-5758 3214; www.dianalodge.com; 6 Falls Creek Rd; per person incl breakfast $80-110;) One of the better-value choices in Falls Creek, Diana's has a mix of simple but homely rooms set over multiple levels with a classic alpine ambience. Lounge rooms have fireplaces, there's a tiny sauna and hot tub, and a cafe-bar with local beers and Mt Beauty–roasted coffee. Enquire about its glamping trips over summer.

QT Falls Creek RESORT $$$
(03-5732 8000; www.qthotelsandresorts.com/falls-creek; 17 Bogong High Plains Rd; 1-bedroom apt $225-1025;) One of the few hotels that opens year-round, QT is a large-scale resort along the main road. Its self-contained apartments are modern and stylish, with wi-fi, pay TV, kitchen and a balcony with outdoor hot tub looking out to spectacular alpine views. Within the complex is a day spa, a pub and two restaurants.

Eating & Drinking

Milch Café CAFE $$
(03-5758 3407; www.fvfallscreek.com.au/milchcafe; 4 Schuss St; mains from $20; 8am-late;) A vibrant, art-filled cafe run by a friendly owner, Milch does a good menu of breakfast rolls, house-baked breads and slow-cooked meats. Its bar is lined with a dangerous selection of schnapps bottles, and the coffee is specially roasted and best enjoyed on the AstroTurf terrace. It closes for a few months during the green season, so call ahead.

Huski MODERN AUSTRALIAN $$
(03-5758 3863; www.huski.com.au/dining; 3 Sitzmark St; breakfast & lunch $10-25, dinner $21-44; 10am-2.30pm & 5pm-late Thu-Sat, 10am-3pm Sun, daily winter) Falls Creek's best all-year restaurant, Huski does interesting breakfasts and lunches using local produce such as venison burgers on brioche buns, or Milawa fruit toast with Beechworth honey, ricotta, banana and berries. In the evening it serves up fusion sharing plates.

Feathertop MODERN AUSTRALIAN $$
(03-5758 3232; www.feathertoplodge.com.au; 14 Parallel St; mains $17-35; 4pm-late) This inviting winter-only restaurant at the Feathertop Lodge features leather chesterfield

couches, private alcoves and mood lighting. The food ranges from tapas to contemporary Australian cooking.

Summit Ridge MODERN AUSTRALIAN $$$
(☎03-5758 3800; www.summitridge.com.au/resturant; 8 Schuss St; mains from $36; ⏰6-10pm mid-Jun–late Sep) One of the best restaurants for fine dining on the mountain, Summit Ridge does a menu of alpine-inspired modern Australian dishes using local produce, such as wild-boar terrine, scotch fillet with truffle mash and wild mushrooms, and Milawa cheese platters.

Man Hotel PUB
(☎03-5758 3362; www.themanfallscreek.com; 20 Slalom St; ⏰4pm-late Jun-Sep) 'The Man' has been around forever, and is the heart of Falls' nightlife. It's only open in winter, when it fires up as a club, cocktail bar and live-music venue featuring popular Aussie bands. Good pub dinners and pizzas are available.

Information

For all the latest prices, packages and online tickets, visit www.fallscreek.com.au. Ski season daily resort entry is $49.50 per car, or $25 after 1pm and free after 4pm; however, it's cheaper to buy tickets online. One-day lift tickets per adult/child cost from $125/70. Combined adult lift-and-lesson packages cost from $195.

Falls Creek Resort Management (☎03-5758 1202; www.fallscreek.com.au; 1 Slalom St; ⏰9am-5pm Mon-Fri Nov-Jun, daily winter) Offers excellent information, as well as pamphlets on trails for skiing, hiking and mountain biking. Its website is useful too.

Activities Hotline (☎1800 204 424) Also handy for info on mountain activities.

Getting There & Away

Falls Creek is 375km from Melbourne, around a 4½-hour drive. The Hume Hwy (M31) to Wangaratta is the fastest route before heading through Milawa, Myrtleford, Bright and Mt Beauty. If coming from Gippsland way, note that the road to Omeo is only open when there's no snow – generally November (or December) to June.

During winter the **Falls Creek Coach Service** (☎03-5754 4024; www.fallscreekcoachservice.com.au) operates daily between Falls Creek and Melbourne (one way/return from $53/134) and also runs services to and from Albury and Mt Beauty. There's a reduced service in early June and late September.

Falls Bus (☎1300 781 221; www.fallsbus.com.au; 📶) also offers a service from Melbourne to Falls Creek (one way from $69, six hours) in winter.

If you've got camping gear you can hike here from Mt Hotham along the **Falls to Hotham Alpine Crossing** (p306) trail.

Getting Around

No vehicles are permitted into the Falls Creek Village during winter, so you'll have to walk (or better, ski) between your lodge and the car park, however, for families an Accommodation Transfer Service – an over-snow taxi service – operates between the car parks and the lodges ($32 return) from 7am to midnight daily (to 2am Friday, to 1am Saturday and Sunday). Car parking for day visitors is at the base of the village, next to the ski lifts.

Harrietville

POP 402

Harrietville is a pretty little town nestled on the Ovens River below Mt Feathertop. It has a great community with a fantastic pub and cafes. It's the last stop before the start of the winding road up to Mt Hotham. During ski season a bus shuttles between the town and Mt Hotham, making it a good choice for slightly cheaper off-mountain accommodation.

Sleeping & Eating

★ **Shady Brook Cottages** COTTAGE $$
(☎0438 050 475, 03-5759 2741; www.shadybrook.com.au; 20 Mountain View Walk; d from $140; ❄@) Set over 14 acres, a magnificent garden envelopes this lovely, peaceful group of self-contained country-style cottages. Two come with a spa and all have balconies.

Avalon House LODGE $$
(☎03-5759 2503, 0411 164 158; www.avalonhouse.com.au; 196 Great Alpine Rd; d $130-150; 📶) This friendly UK-owned lodge in a historic building is a good option for skiers and snowboarders looking for more affordable accommodation off Mt Hotham. It has a range of cosy rooms and a drying room for ski gear. Its atmospheric garden cafe specialises in wood-fired pizzas on Thursday to Sunday evenings.

★ **Harrietville Snowline Hotel** PUB FOOD $$
(☎03-5759 2524; www.snowlinehotel.com.au; 237 Great Alpine Rd; mains $20-36; ⏰noon-late; 📶) A welcome sight if you've taken the hair-raising drive down from Mt Hotham, this 100-year-old pub succeeds in mixing historical character with a cool, modern fit-out. It has a smoker to cook up Southern BBQ dishes, as well as venison burgers and Harrietville trout. It also offers inexpensive

off-mountain accommodation in comfortable motel rooms (doubles from $110).

Getting There & Away

Harrietville is at the base of Mt Hotham on its northern side, around a 30-minute drive along the Great Alpine Rd. Continuing north 20km from here will take you to Bright.

The **Omeo Bus Service** (p305) has three services a week that stop in Harrietville en route to Bright or Omeo via Mt Hotham.

During winter the **Snowball Express** (☎1300 656 546; www.snowballexpress.com.au; one way/return from $70/120; ski season) heads to Harrietville from Melbourne en route to Mt Hotham.

Mt Hotham & Dinner Plain

ELEV 1868M

Activities

Winter

The conjoined-twin ski resort towns of Mt Hotham and Dinner Plain together provide the quintessential alpine experience, offering quality skiing mixed with a charming atmosphere. Serious hikers, skiers and snowboarders make tracks for Mt Hotham, which has some of the best and most challenging downhill runs in the country. Over at Dinner Plain, 10km from Hotham village and linked by a shuttle, there are excellent cross-country trails around the village, including the Hotham–Dinner Plain Ski Trail.

With snowboarding and downhill and Nordic skiing, Mt Hotham and Dinner Plain resorts are a giant outdoor adventure playground come winter.

Mt Hotham is home to 320 hectares of downhill runs, with a vertical drop of 428m. About 80% of the ski trails are intermediate or advanced black diamond runs. Beginners hit the Big D, which is open for night skiing every Wednesday and Saturday in winter. Dinner Plain has excellent cross-country trails around the village, including the Hotham–Dinner Plain Ski Trail.

At least six operators offer ski and other equipment hire; the visitor centres have full lists of outlets, or visit www.mthotham.com.au.

Summer

Outside the ski season there are plenty of other interesting pursuits such as hiking, mountain-biking and even indoor skiing. Since the arrival of **Hotham365** (☎03-5759 3550; www.mthotham.com.au; Slatey Shed, Great Alpine Rd; per person 30min $15; 5-7pm daily Jun-Sep, by booking Mon-Fri summer, office 8.30am-4.30pm), skiing is no longer a winter-only activity on Mt Hotham, with two indoor ski slopes on synthetic grass on a conveyor belt adjustable for beginner to advanced levels.

From November to May, Hotham and Dinner Plain boast some stunning alpine trails for hiking, including the epic Falls to Hotham Alpine Crossing trail (p306) – a two-night/three-day trek to Falls Creek.

Mountain biking is also a newish activity that will likely become a big lure with the completion of the new MTB park. **DP Riders** (☎0439 559 010, 0409 538 935; www.dpriders.com.au; bike hire per day $25; Nov-Jun) hires bikes from $25 a day. There's also a tube park ($15pp) on grassy slopes at Dinner Plain.

Another great summer activity are guided 4WD tours run by **Great Alpine Adventures** (☎0488 040 308; www.highcountryadventure.com.au; 3hr tours per person from $110; Nov-Mar); these visit wild brumbies and historic mountain huts.

See www.mthotham.com.au for a comprehensive list of summer activities on the mountain.

★Howling Husky Sled Dog Tours DOG SLEDDING

(☎0488 040 308; www.howlinghuskys.com.au; tandem rides per double from $160, 1hr dog walks adult/child $75/50) Offering a unique experience are these dog-sled tours where you'll glide through snow with a team of energetic Siberian huskies. From 15-minute jaunts to three-hour 'full moon tours' under the stars to one-hour snowshoe walks with the dogs, there's something for everyone. Even when it's not snowing you can hitch a ride with the huskies on four-wheel carts (two people $80).

Sleeping

While the bulk of lodges only operate during the ski season, a few stay open year-round. For a comprehensive list, get in touch with accommodation booking services such as **Dinner Plain Accommodation** (☎1800 444 066, 03-5159 6696; www.accommdinnerplain.com.au; 19 Big Muster Dr, Dinner Plain), **Dinner Plain Central Reservations** (☎1800 670 019, 03-5159 6451; www.dinnerplain.com; 6 Big Muster Dr, Dinner Plain) and **Mt Hotham Accommodation Service** (☎1800 657 547; www.mthothamaccommodation.com.au). During the ski season, accommodation places generally stipulate a minimum two-night stay.

★General Lodge LODGE $$$
(Map p302; ☎03-5759 3523; www.thegeneral.com.au; Great Alpine Rd, Mt Hotham; studio/1-/2-bedroom apt from $195/205/295;) Attached to the General (p305) pub are these modern and stylish fully self-contained apartments with lounge, gas fireplaces and kitchen, and fantastic views from the balcony. Note prices double in winter, when there's a two-night minimum stay.

Arlberg Resort APARTMENT $$$
(☎03-5759 3618; www.arlberghotham.com.au; 1 Great Alpine Rd, Mt Hotham; 2 nights $460-920; mid-Jun–mid-Sep;) One of the largest resorts on the mountain, the Arlberg has a large range of apartments and motel-style rooms, plus restaurants, bars (including a brewery), ski hire and a heated pool. Ski season only.

Eating & Drinking

Mt Hotham

★Stone's Throw PUB FOOD $$
(☎03-5159 6324; www.hotelhighplains.com; Hotel High Plains, 185 Big Muster Dr, Dinner Plain; mains $19-28; 5pm-late) One of the best restaurants on the mountain, Stone's Throw specialises in produce from regional Victoria. The menu is seasonal, but expect the likes of peri peri Milawa chicken, Blizzard-beer-battered fish and chips and excellent gourmet wood-fired pizzas. It's located within the Hotel High Plains pub, which has local beers on tap, an open fire and accommodation (rooms $140) over summer.

★The General PUB FOOD $$
(☎03-5759 3523; www.thegeneral.com.au; Great Alpine Rd, Mt Hotham; meals $15-24; 9.30am-late Mon-Sat, to 4pm Sun, open late Sun winter;) The ever-reliable 'Genny' is a popular watering hole with some good local beers and amazing views from its outdoor deck. There's a menu of pizzas, burgers and pub classics, plus good breakfasts and wi-fi. There's an attached grocery store selling fresh cheeses, meats and alcohol, while the accommodation (p305) here is also first-class.

Dinner Plain

★Blizzard Brewing Co MICROBREWERY
(☎0447 847 029; www.blizzardbrewing.com; 5 Cattle Pen Dr, Dinner Plain; 2-8pm Fri & Sat, to 6pm Sun Sep-May, noon-late daily Jun-Aug) An unexpected find in the outskirts of Dinner Plain alpine village is this awesome little brewery that produces all of its American-style craft beers on site. The warehouse setup has a taphouse pouring all of its range of core and seasonal ales, with the option of tasting paddles. There are no meals, but there is a menu of beer snacks and platters.

Information

The ski-season admission fee is $46 per car per day, and $15 for bus passengers (this may be included in your fare). Lift tickets (peak) per adult/student/child cost $120/100/58. Passes are cheaper in September and there are packages that include gear hire and lessons. Lift tickets also cover Falls Creek.

Dinner Plain Visitor Centre (☎03-5755 0555; www.visitdinnerplain.com; Big Muster Dr, Dinner Plain; 10am-5pm Mon-Fri, 9am-5pm daily winter) In the Dinner Plain Alpine Village is this centre for chalet bookings, trail maps and general info. Its website is an excellent source of information too.

Mt Hotham Alpine Resort Management Board (☎03-5759 3550; www.mthotham.com.au; Great Alpine Rd, Mt Hotham; 8am-4.30pm Mon-Fri, 7am-6pm daily winter) At the village administration centre, this visitor centre has a range of brochures with maps for short, eco, heritage and village walks. Also has an app with stop-off points for driving in the area.

Mt Hotham Central Guest Services (☎03-5759 4470) Can assist with general tourist info on the mountain, from ski lessons to bus timetables.

Getting There & Away

Mt Hotham is 360km northeast of Melbourne. By car take the Hume Hwy to Wangaratta, then follow the Great Alpine Rd to Mt Hotham. Alternatively, you can take the Princes Hwy to Omeo, before continuing on the Great Alpine Rd to Hotham via Dinner Plain.

In winter all vehicles must carry diamond-patterned snow chains, to be fitted at the designated fitting bays. During ski season all vehicles will need to purchase a resort pass (per day $46); if you're just passing through you're only permitted to stay for 30 minutes. The winding drive down to Harrietville is on a knife's edge so take it easy if there's snow on the road.

During the ski season, both **Hotham Bus** (☎1300 781 221; www.hothambus.com.au; one way/return from $50/114; 24 Jun–11 Sep;) and **Snowball Express** (p304) run buses here from Melbourne.

Omeo Bus Service (☎0428 591 377; www.omeobus.com.au) has three buses a week connecting Mt Hotham and Dinner Plain with Bright ($6.40, two hours) and Omeo ($5 to $6.40, one hour); check its website for the schedule.

For hikers, there's the **Falls to Hotham Alpine Crossing** (www.parkweb.vic.gov.au; ⌚ Nov-Apr), a two-night/three-day 37km trek that links Hotham with Falls Creek.

Getting Around

In winter a shuttle service operates between Dinner Plain and Mt Hotham (return ticket adult/child $15/10) every 30 minutes between 7am and 5.30pm; cash only.

There's also a free shuttle in the evenings for patrons that connects the General (p305) in Hotham with Hotel High Plains (p305).

In Mt Hotham itself a free shuttle runs frequently around the resort from 6.45am to 2am.

Omeo

POP 487

High in the hills, historic Omeo is a pretty town reached after the winding drive up from the coast or down from the mountains. It was a booming gold-mining town back in the day, with a population of nearly 10,000; today many of the grand buildings remain, yet its streets are ultra sleepy.

It's the southern access route to Mt Hotham and Falls Creek and the main town on the eastern section of the Great Alpine Rd. The road is sometimes snowbound in winter, so always check conditions before heading this way.

Sights & Activities

Omeo Historical Park & Museum MUSEUM
(☎03-5159 1515; www.omeo.org.au/park; Day Ave; adult/child $4/1; ⌚10am-2pm) Back in the day, Omeo was one of Victoria's most lawless goldfield towns, and here you can visit the site where troublemakers were dealt with. Guided tours take you through the original 1861 courthouse and the 'new' courthouse built in 1893, both of which have historical displays and photographs. Also here is the original log jail, a rather grim wooden cell dating from 1858, and remarkably used until 1981.

Sleeping & Eating

Snug as a Bug Motel MOTEL $
(☎03-5159 1311, 0427 591 311; www.motelomeo.com.au; 188 Day Ave; s/d $120/130; ❄📶) Living up to its name, this quaint choice along the main strip has a range of rooms in lovely country-style historic buildings, with decor to match. Options include family motel rooms, the main guesthouse and a cute self-contained cottage.

Omeo Caravan Park CARAVAN PARK $
(☎03-5159 1351; www.omeocaravanpark.com.au; Old Omeo Hwy; unpowered/powered sites $15/35, d cabins with shared/private bathroom $70/110; ❄📶) In a pretty valley alongside Livingstone Creek about 2km from town, this park has spacious, grassy sites.

Golden Age Hotel HOTEL $
(☎03-5159 1344; www.goldenageomeo.com.au; Day Ave; s/d with shared bathroom $50/80, with private bathroom from $110/130; ⌚kitchen noon-2.30pm & 6-8.30pm) This beautiful art deco corner pub (c 1854) dominates Omeo's main street. Upstairs has simple but elegant pub rooms, all with cooked breakfast, some with en suite and spa – the best rooms open onto the balcony. The welcoming restaurant (mains $25) serves plates piled high with steaks, salads and gourmet pizzas.

Homestead House Cafe CAFE $
(☎03-5159 1511; 190 Day Ave; dishes from $12.50; ⌚8.30am-4pm) This smart and cheery little cafe on the main road does good coffee, roast-lamb rolls, wonderful homemade cakes and a daily changing menu of seasonal food.

Information

Omeo Visitor Information Centre (☎03-5159 1455; www.omeoregion.com.au; 179 Day Ave; ⌚8.30am-5pm Mon-Fri, 10am-2pm Sat & Sun; 📶) Friendly visitor centre in the library with info on a bunch of walking trails in the area.

Getting There & Away

Located 400km from Melbourne, Omeo is the gateway town to Mt Hotham (57km, 50 minutes) via Dinner Plain en route to Bright (108km, two hours) along the Great Alpine Rd. The road is open year-round but you'll need to attach car-tyre chains during the winter months. There's also a road to Falls Creek (C543), but it's only open during the warmer months (usually late November to May).

Omeo Bus Lines (☎0427 017 732; http://dysongroup.com.au/public-transport/regional; Day Ave) has a service to Omeo Monday to Friday from Bairnsdale ($16, two hours).

To get to the mountains, **O'Connells Omeo Bus Service** (p299) runs a year-round 'Alps Link' service to Dinner Plain ($5, 45 minutes), Mt Hotham ($6.40, one hour) and Bright ($12.80, two hours) three times a week.

The Murray River & Around

Includes ➡

Best Places to Eat

- ➡ Stefano's Restaurant (p313)
- ➡ Spoons Riverside Café (p316)
- ➡ Shebani's (p322)
- ➡ Fish in a Flash (p322)
- ➡ Brass Monkey (p313)

Best Places to Sleep

- ➡ Houseboat in Echuca (p322)
- ➡ Mildura Grand (p312)
- ➡ Adelphi Boutique Apartments (p321)
- ➡ Indulge Apartments (p313)
- ➡ Cock 'n Bull Boutique Hotel (p322)

Why Go?

The mighty Murray River is Australia's longest and most important inland waterway, and arrayed along its banks are some of Victoria's most historic and captivating towns. The region is a stirring place of wineries and orchards, bush camping, balmy weather and river red gum forests. The Murray changes character constantly along its 2400km route. History looms large in towns such as Echuca; food and wine dominate proceedings around Mildura; and national parks enclose soulful desert expanses in the far northwest. It's a world of picturesque river beaches, of paddle steamers that were once the lifeblood of Victoria's inland settlements, and of unending horizons that serve as a precursor to the true outback not far away. It's an intriguing, if relatively far-flung mix, that enables you to follow in the footsteps of some of Australia's earliest explorers who travelled along the river.

When to Go

Mildura

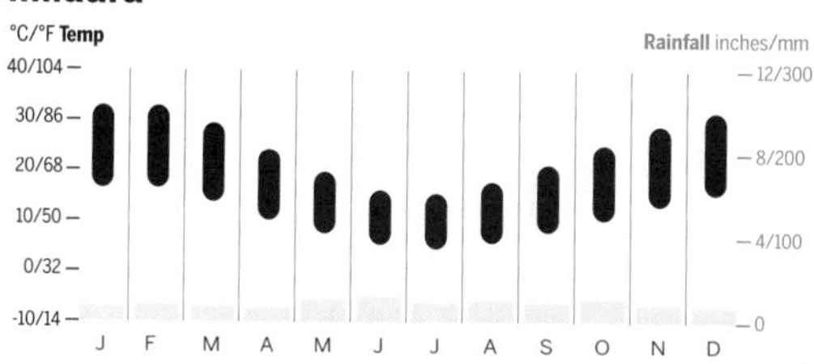

Year-round The Murray region, especially Mildura, enjoys year-round sunshine.

Sep–Nov Spring sees some of the best local festivals, without the heat.

Feb & Mar A good time for camping by the river after the holiday crowds have left.

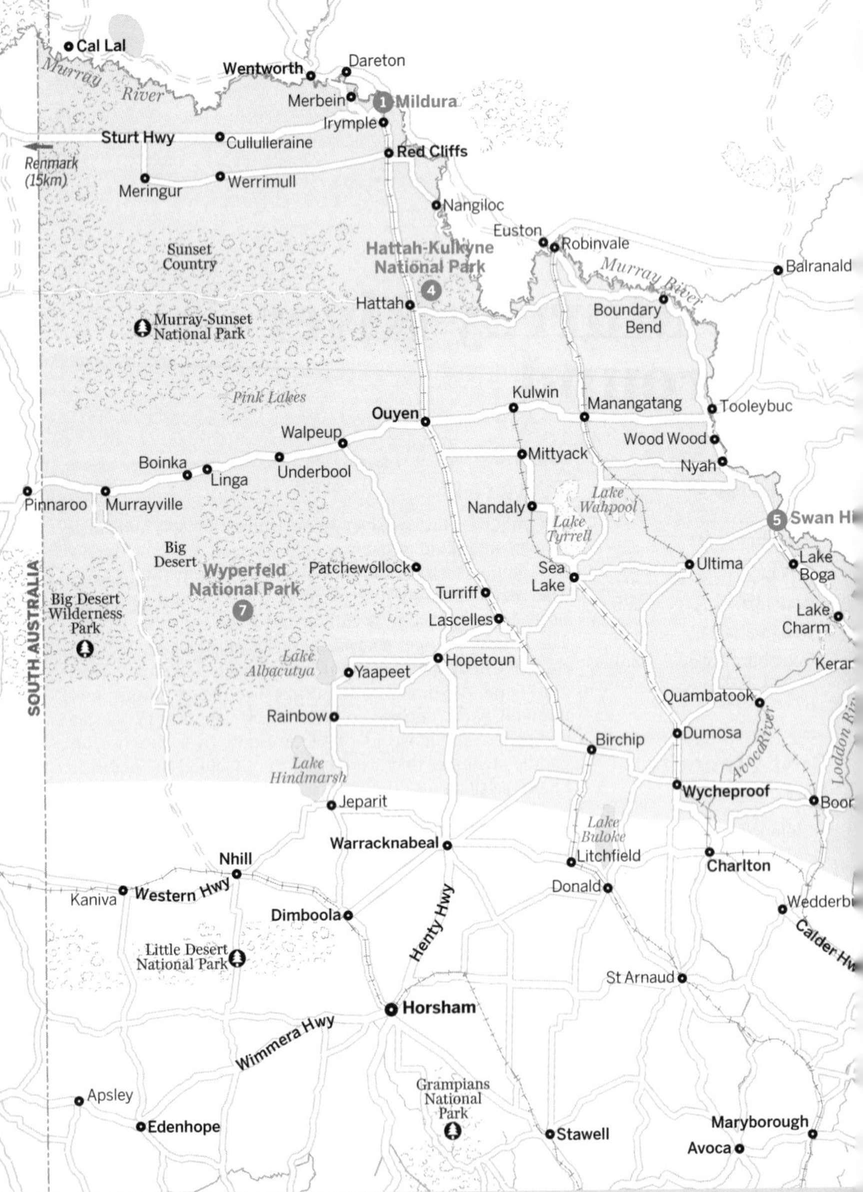

The Murray River & Around Highlights

1 **Mildura** (p310) Relaxing on a houseboat and dining out on 'Feast Street' in the sunny town.

2 **Echuca** (p317) Riding an original paddle steamer down the Murray for lunch at a winery in Echuca.

3 **Port of Echuca** (p317) Exploring the town's past in its discovery centre, old wharf area and historic Murray Esplanade.

4 **Hattah-Kulkyne National Park** (p327) Spotting the many species of waterbird at this beautiful park.

5 **Swan Hill** (p315) Taking the kids on a trip back in time at the Pioneer Settlement.

6 **Barmah National Park** (p323) Enjoying a boat ride amid the park's river red gums.

7 **Wyperfeld National Park** (p328) Disappearing in this remote spot to experience the vastness of the Mallee.

Mildura

POP 51,800

Sunny, sultry Mildura is something of an oasis amid some very dry country, a modern town with its roots firmly in the grand old pastoralist era. Its other calling cards include art deco buildings and some of the best dining in provincial Victoria. The hinterland, too, is worth exploring, from the nearby wilderness national parks to the Murray River, where activities include fishing, swimming, canoeing, waterskiing, houseboating, taking a paddle-steamer cruise or playing on riverside golf courses. The weather here is very much blue sky – you can expect warm, sunny days even in midwinter.

Sights

★Rio Vista & Mildura Arts Centre HISTORIC BUILDING

(Map p311; ☎03-5018 8330; www.milduraarts centre.com.au; 199 Cureton Ave; ⏲10am-5pm) FREE The grand homestead of William B Chaffey (a Mildura founder), historic Queen Anne–style Rio Vista has been beautifully preserved and restored. Each room has a series of historical displays depicting colonial life in the 19th century, with period furnishings, costumes, photos and a collection of letters and memorabilia. The Mildura Arts Centre, in the same complex, combines a modern-art gallery with changing exhibitions and a theatre showing cutting-edge productions (thanks to its involvement on the regional performance circuit).

Apex Beach BEACH

This popular swimming and picnic spot is about 3km northwest of the centre, with a sandy river beach on the Murray. There's a good walking and cycling track from here to the Old Mildura Homestead.

Old Psyche Bend Pump Station HISTORIC SITE

(☎03-5024 5637; Kings Billabong; adult/family $3/8; ⏲1-4pm Tue & Thu, 10.30am-noon Sun) This station is where William B Chaffey, set up his system in 1891 to supply irrigation and drainage. The modern pumps are electric now and have been placed a bit further up the river. You can walk around the old centrifugal pumps and Chaffey's triple-expansion steam-engine pump.

Old Mildura Homestead HISTORIC SITE

(Cureton Ave; by donation; ⏲9am-6pm) Along the river, near the historic Rio Vista & Mildura Arts Centre, this cottage was the first home of William B Chaffey. The heritage park here contains a few other historic log buildings, and picnic and barbecue facilities.

Chateau Mildura WINERY, MUSEUM

(☎03-5024 5901; www.facebook.com/chateau mildurawinery; 191 Belar Ave; museum adult/child $5/free; ⏲10am-4pm) Established in 1888 and still producing table wines, Chateau Mildura is part vineyard and part museum, with wine tastings and historical displays.

Activities

Paddle-steamer cruises depart from Mildura Wharf, with most going through a lock – you'll be able to see the gates opening and the water levels changing.

Sunraysia Cellar Door WINE

(Map p311; ☎03-5021 0794; www.sunraysiacella rdoor.com.au; 125 Lime Ave; ⏲9am-5pm Mon-Fri, 11am-5pm Sat & Sun) Sunraysia Cellar Door has free tastings and sales for around 250 local wines from 22 different wineries from the Murray–Darling region, as well as a handful of local craft beers and plenty of local edible products for purchase.

Tours

A standout tour is to the extraordinary and ancient natural formations of Mungo National Park (in New South Wales). Several operators run tours from Mildura, focusing on the park's culture, its 45,000 years of history and its wildlife.

★Harry Nanya Tours CULTURAL

(☎03-5027 2076; www.harrynanyatours.com.au; tours adult/child $180/110) Indigenous Australian guide Graham Clarke keeps you enchanted with stories of the Dreaming and his deep knowledge and understanding of the Mungo region. In summer (November to March) a spectacular sunset tour is offered. Minimum two people; Graham will pick up from central accommodation in Mildura.

Wild Side Outdoors ADVENTURE

(☎03-5024 3721, 0428 242 852; www.wildside outdoors.com.au; Canoes/kayaks/mountain bikes $35/25/25 per hr) For more than 20 years this ecofriendly outfit has offered a range of activities, including a sunset kayaking tour

Mildura

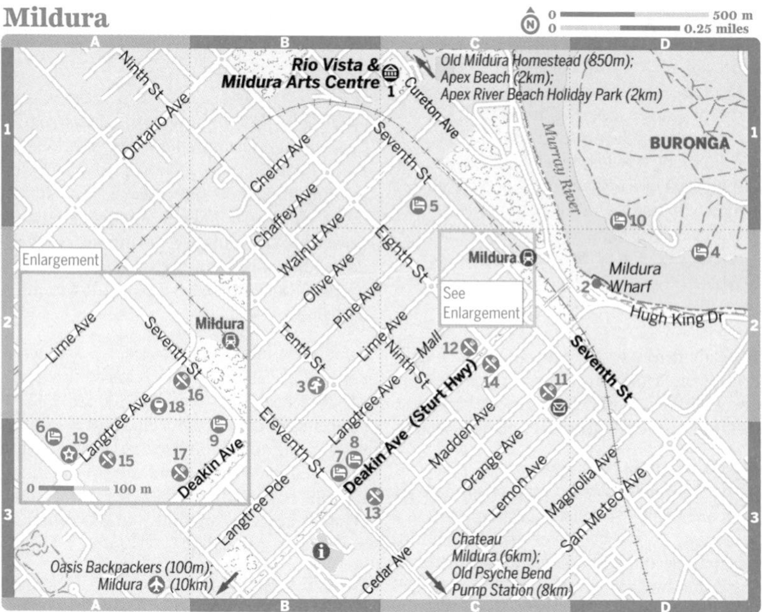

Mildura

Top Sights
1 Rio Vista & Mildura Arts Centre C1

Activities, Courses & Tours
2 PS Melbourne D2
PV Rothbury .... (see 2)
3 Sunraysia Cellar Door B2

Sleeping
4 Acacia Houseboats D2
5 Couples Retreats Mildura C1
6 Indulge Apartments A3
7 Kar-Rama Motor Inn B3
8 Mid City Motel B3
9 Mildura Grand B3
10 Mildura Houseboats D1

Eating
11 Black Stump C2
12 Blk.Mlk C2
13 Brass Monkey B3
14 Cider Tree C2
Pizza Café at the Grand .... (see 16)
15 Restaurant Rendezvous A3
16 Spanish Grill A2
17 Stefano's Cafe A3
Stefano's Restaurant .... (see 9)

Drinking & Nightlife
18 Mildura Brewery A2

Entertainment
19 Sandbar A3

at Kings Billabong ($120 for two people). Handily for independent travellers, they will support three-day river trips, supplying maps, gear and transport (from $450 for two people). Will deliver and collect gear too.

PS Melbourne BOATING
(Map p311; 03-5023 2200; www.paddlesteamers.com.au; 2hr cruises adult/child $30/14; 10.50am & 1.50pm Sun-Thu) One of the original paddle steamers (built in 1925), and the only one still driven by steam power. Watch the operator stoke the original boiler with wood.

Mungo National Park Tours TOURS
(0408 147 330, 1800 797 530; www.murraytrek.com.au; day/sunset tours $145/175) Small-group day and sunset tours to Mungo National Park led by the experienced Trevor Hancock. Minimum two people.

PV Rothbury BOATING
(Map p311; 03-5023 2200; www.paddlesteamers.com.au; cruises adult/child winery $70/35, dinner $70/35, lunch $35/17) Although it was built in 1881, *PV Rothbury* has a diesel engine and is one of the fastest paddle boats.

MILDURA HOUSEBOATS

Staying on a houseboat is bliss. The Mildura region has more than a dozen companies that rent houseboats, ranging from two- to 12-berth and from modest to luxurious. Most have a minimum hire of three days, and prices increase dramatically in summer and during school holidays. Most operators are located just across from Mildura Wharf in Buronga.

It heads through the lock on its twice-daily cruises on Fridays and Saturdays at 10.50am and 1.50pm, and also runs winery, lunch and dinner cruises on Tuesdays and Thursdays.

Moontongue Eco-Adventures KAYAKING
(0427 898 317; www.moontongue.com.au; kayak tours $35-65) A sunset kayaking trip is a great way to see the river and its wildlife. Local guide Ian will tell you about the landscape and birdlife as you work those muscles in the magnificent, peaceful surroundings of Gol Gol Creek and the Murray. Note: operates by appointment only.

Festivals & Events

Mildura Country Music Festival MUSIC
(www.milduracountrymusic.com.au; Sep & Oct) Ten days of free concerts in late September and/or early October.

Mildura Show AGRICULTURAL
(www.mildurashow.org.au; Oct) One of the largest agricultural shows in rural Victoria; held mid-October.

Sleeping

Mid City Motel MOTEL $
(Map p311; 03-5023 0317; www.midcityplantationmotel.com.au; 145 Deakin Ave; s/d from $75/90;) Rooms may be dated – the brick walls and brown carpets will beam you back into the 1970s – but this is one of Mildura's best-value options in terms of price. Some slightly more modern 'deluxe' rooms are available for around $20 more per person. Microwaves and toasters are useful touches and the owners are helpful.

Kar-Rama Motor Inn MOTEL $
(Map p311; 03-5023 4221; www.karramamotorinn.com.au; 153 Deakin Ave; s/d $78/83;) Highly affordable and central motel just south of the main strip, with plain but tidy rooms and a pool.

Apex RiverBeach Holiday Park CARAVAN PARK $
(03-5023 6879; www.apexriverbeach.com.au; Cureton Ave; unpowered/powered sites $39/41, cabins from $95;) Thanks to a fantastic location on sandy Apex Beach, just outside town, this bush park is always popular – prices are 25% higher during school holidays. There are campfires, a bush kitchen, a barbecue area, a boat ramp, good swimming and a cafe.

Acacia Holiday Apartments APARTMENT $
(03-5023 3855; www.acaciaapartments.com.au; 761 Fifteenth St; d cabins $100-125, 1-/2-/3-bedroom apt from $120/140/210;) Southwest of the centre on the Calder Hwy, these large self-contained units are an excellent, if more rustic alternative, to a drab motel. What it lacks in proximity to the centre, it makes up for in value.

Oasis Backpackers HOSTEL $
(03-5022 8200, 0401 344 251; www.milduraoasisbackpackers.com.au; 230-232 Deakin Ave; dm/d per week $165/175; @) Mildura is a big destination for travellers looking for fruit-picking work, so most of the city's half-a-dozen hostels cater to them only. Oasis is the best-equipped backpacker hostel, with a great pool and patio bar area, ultramodern kitchen and free internet. The owners can organise plenty of seasonal work. Minimum one-week stay.

★**Mildura Grand** HOTEL $$
(Map p311; 03-5023 0511, 1800 034 228; www.milduragrand.com.au; Seventh St; s/d from $85/130;) The standard rooms at the Grand aren't the most luxurious in town, but staying at this landmark hotel – Mildura's top address – gives you the feeling of being part of something special. Although cheaper rooms in the original wing are comfortable, go for one of the stylish suites with private spa.

Acacia Houseboats HOUSEBOAT $$
(Map p311; 0417 537 316, 1800 085 500; www.murrayriver.com.au/acacia-houseboats-949/fleet; 3 nights from $525) Has five houseboats, ranging from four to 12 berths, with everything supplied, except food and drink.

Indulge Apartments APARTMENT $$
(Map p311; 1300 539 559; www.indulgeapartments.com.au; 146a Eighth St; studios from $165, 1-/2-bedroom apt from $185/285;) These

smart contemporary apartments in the centre of town could be Mildura's best, with polished floors, plenty of space and excellent facilities. It has four apartment complexes around town. It services a mainly corporate crowd during the week, so offers all the mod cons. Rates can fluctuate.

Couples Retreats Mildura APARTMENT $$
(Map p311; ☎0419 840 451; www.couplesretreats mildura.com.au; 16 Olive Ave; d from $155; ❄📶) Local Pam runs two cottages and a modern apartment. Lemon Cottage is a flashback to the 1950s with lots of chrome and a working jukebox. Pammy's Palace, a converted miners cottage, has a more traditional, country-style interior. The modern apartment for couples has a king-sized bed with the bedhead made from a converted barn door. Eclectic and centrally located.

Mildura Houseboats HOUSEBOAT $$
(Map p311; ☎1800 800 842, 03-5024 7770; www.mildurahouseboats.com.au; 2- to 6-berth for 7 nights $1850-2000) Choose from a fleet of around 15 houseboats sleeping two to 12 people. Gourmet and golf packages also offered.

Eating

Mildura's cafe and restaurant precinct runs along Langtree Ave (otherwise known as 'Feast Street') and around the block dominated by the Grand Hotel. Italian restaurateur (and raconteur) Stefano de Pieri perhaps single-handedly stamped the town on the foodie map back in the 1980s, and others have jumped on board over the decades.

★**Black Stump** MODERN AUSTRALIAN $$
(Map p311; www.theblackstump.com.au; 110-114 Eighth St; mains $20-36; ⏲Tue-Sat) A hark back to its days as the Mildura Settlers Club, the Black Stump is one of the quirkiest and refreshingly different places to eat. To start with, it cleverly incorporates the historic building through its decor – vintage blue chairs, memorabilia and photos – while the kitchen, run by local chef Jim McDougall, serves Australian bistro meals with international influences.

The bistro adjoins a large bar, so after dining you can drink the night away to a live band or three.

★**Stefano's Cafe** CAFE $$
(Map p311; ☎03-5021 3627; 27 Deakin Ave; meals $14-22; ⏲7am-3pm Mon-Sat, 8am-noon Sun) Fresh bread, Calabrese eggs, pastries and, of course, good coffee – this casual daytime cafe and bakery keeps things fresh and simple. It's also a gourmet grocery store selling foodstuffs and wines. Great egg breakfasts set off the day and there's seating outdoors.

★**Brass Monkey** MODERN AUSTRALIAN $$$
(Map p311; ☎03-5021 4769; www.facebook.com/brassmonkeymildura; 32 Carter Lane; share plates $10-20; ⏲6-11pm Tue-Thu, noon-3pm & 6-11pm Fri-Sun) Don't be put off by its location, south of the centre and overlooking a car park: Brass Monkey epitomises 'hidden gem'. It's cosy, buzzy and fun, with a hipster edge. A large communal table reflects a philosophy of share plates, and it delivers on the food front: fresh, refined street cuisine, creative ideas and wonderful presentation.

★**Stefano's Restaurant** ITALIAN $$$
(Map p311; ☎03-5023 0511; www.stefano.com.au; Quality Hotel Mildura Grand, Seventh St; 5-course dinner set menu $97; ⏲7-11pm Tue-Sat) Stefano de Pieri was a celebrity chef before the term was invented. The charismatic Italian-Australian introduced fresh and simple farm-to-plate cuisine to households via his popular TV program and at this delightful restaurant. It's an intimate, candlelit experience and very popular – book well in advance. After a brief break from the helm, he is back.

Blk.Mlk CAFE $
(Map p311; ☎03-5023 1811; www.facebook.com/blk.mlk.specialty.coffee; 51 Deakin Ave; mains $10-20; ⏲7am-3pm) The deconstructed name might be a little pretentious (black milk, get it?) but the coffee and food are anything but. If you're like us, you'll find yourself sitting for a coffee and an hour later you will have polished off the likes of banana bread (served with edible flowers) or a pork belly salad. A great choice for gourmands and java hounds.

Cider Tree PUB FOOD $$
(Map p311; http://thecidertree.com.au; 56 Deakin Ave; mains $20-28; ⏲noon-late Mon-Sat) A no-nonsense ale house and kitchen that does hefty brews (there are 18 different ciders and beers on tap, plus plenty more in bottles) and hearty meals. It packs them in for specials, such as the Thursday Pot and Parmy night (a pot of beer with every parmigiana dish; $19.50).

Restaurant Rendezvous INTERNATIONAL $$
(Map p311; ☎03-5023 1571; www.rendezvousmildura.com.au; 34 Langtree Ave; mains $20-40; ⏲7am-

WINERIES AROUND MILDURA

Mildura is one of Australia's most prolific wine-producing areas. If you plan on touring the region's wineries, pick up a copy of the *Mildura Wines* brochure from the **visitor information centre** (Map p311; ☎1800 039 043, 03-5018 8380; www.visitmildura.com.au; cnr Deakin Ave & 12th St; ⏲9am-5.30pm Mon-Fri, to 5pm Sat & Sun), or visit www.mildurawines.com.au.

If you can't make it out to the wineries themselves, the in-town **Sunraysia Cellar Door** (p310) has free tastings and sales of around 250 local wines from 22 different wineries, as well as a handful of local craft beers.

4pm & 6pm-late Mon-Fri, 7am-2pm & 6pm-late Sat, 7am-2pm Sun) The warm, casual atmosphere of this long-running place on 'Feast Street' is almost swallowed up by the Grand Hotel and its bevvy of eateries. But it holds its own with well-prepared, Mediterranean-style seafood, grills, pasta, crepes and unusual specials.

Spanish Grill STEAK **$$$**
(Map p311; ☎03-5021 2377; www.stefano.com.au/the-spanish-grill; cnr Langtree Ave & Seventh St; mains $26-48; ⏲6-10pm Tue-Sat) In the Grand Hotel, this eatery re-opened late in 2016 under the stewardship of renowned local foodie Stefano de Pieri. Judging by his last results, it should be good, especially as the meat is sourced locally, and is cooked over gum and mallee-root coals.

Pizza Café at the Grand PIZZA **$$**
(Map p311; ☎03-5022 2223; www.pizzacafe.com.au; 18 Langtree Ave; pizza & pasta $16-22; ⏲11am-11pm Mon-Sat, 11.30am-late Sun) For simple and inexpensive family dining, with all the atmosphere of the Grand Hotel dining strip, Pizza Café is perfect. The wood-fired pizzas hit the spot and there's a supporting cast of salads, pasta and chicken dishes.

Drinking & Nightlife

★**Mildura Brewery** BREWERY
(Map p311; ☎03-5022 2988; www.mildurabrewery.com.au; 20 Langtree Ave; ⏲noon-late) Set in the former Astor cinema, this is Mildura's trendiest drinking hole, and part of chef and restaurateur Stefano de Piera's stable. Shiny stainless-steel vats, pipes and brewing equipment make a great backdrop to the stylish lounge, and the beers brewed here – Honey Wheat and Mallee Bull among them – are superb. Good food, too (mains $24 to $36).

☆ Entertainment

Sandbar LIVE MUSIC
(Map p311; ☎03-5021 2181; www.thesandbar.com.au; cnr Langtree Ave & Eighth St; ⏲noon-late Tue-Sun) On a balmy evening locals flock to the fabulous beer garden at the back of this lounge bar in a classic art deco building. Local, national, original and mainstream bands play in the front bar regularly, or you can take to the stage yourself at the Wednesday karaoke session.

Information

Mildura Visitor Information & Booking Centre (p312) Free service for booking accommodation, with interesting displays, local produce, a cafe, a library, and very helpful staff who book tours and activities.

Getting There & Away

Mildura is 542km northwest of Melbourne along the Calder Hwy (A79).

AIR

Victoria's busiest regional airport, **Mildura Airport** (p371) is about 10km west of the town centre off the Sturt Hwy. Mildura–Melbourne flights are served by **Qantas** (☎13 13 13; www.qantas.com.au) and **Virgin Australia** (☎13 67 89; www.virginaustralia.com). **Regional Express Airlines** (Rex; ☎13 17 13; www.regionalexpress.com.au) has flights to/from Melbourne, Sydney, Adelaide and Broken Hill.

BUS & TRAIN

V/Line (☎1800 800 007; www.vline.com.au) Combination train/coach services operate from the train station on Seventh St. There are no direct passenger trains to/from Mildura; change from V/Line trains to coaches at Ballarat, Bendigo or Swan Hill. Services ply the Mildura–Melbourne route ($50, seven to 10 hours, three to four daily).

NSW Trainlink (☎13 22 32; www.nswtrainlink.info) A coach/train combination covers the Mildura–Sydney route, with a coach to Cootamundra then Southern Express train to Sydney ($110, 13½ hours, once daily).

WORTH A TRIP

GUNBOWER NATIONAL PARK

Said to be the largest inland island in the world, superb Gunbower Island is formed between the Murray River and Gunbower Creek. In 2010 Parks Victoria created the 88 sq km Gunbower National Park (previously a state forest) to protect its beautiful river red gum forests. In addition to the majestic red gums, which have been extensively logged for timber since the 1870s, the park is home to abundant animals and birdlife. You might see kangaroos, possums, goannas, turtles and snakes, and more than 200 species of bird have been recorded here.

This is one of the great spots for free camping along the Murray River. A network of 'river tracks' crisscross the island and lead to more than 100 numbered bush-camping spots by the river bank (Victorian side only).

Roads are dirt and a bit rough, but passable to conventional vehicles when it's dry – after heavy rains, though, it's 4WD-only. The main access points to the island are from Cohuna in the north and tiny Gunbower in the south.

Getting Around

A paddle-steamer cruise here is a must. Mildura Paddlesteamers runs the three main vessels that paddle along: PS Melbourne (p311), PV Rothbury (p311) and **PV Mundoo** (the latter is for groups and weddings only). Check which services pass through the locks. You can enjoy sunset or even meal cruises.

Swan Hill & Around

POP 9890

Swan Hill is a sleepy river town without the tourist hype of nearby Mildura and Echuca, but with some appeal nonetheless. The riverside Pioneer Settlement is one of the best open-air museums in Victoria. What the town lacks in accommodation options (it's mainly ho-hum motels), it makes up for with its restaurants and cafes. While you wouldn't cross the state to come here, it makes a bearable stopover as you meander along the Murray.

Sights & Activities

Swan Hill Lift Bridge BRIDGE

(McCallum St) This wonderful bridge was built in 1896 to span the Murray River at McCallum St (Victoria)/Moulamein Rd (NSW), which had originally been navigated by a punt. The middle span of the bridge was crank-lifted by hand (one bridge cylinder alone weighed more than 4 tonnes) to allow river traffic to pass. These days, the traffic alternates directions as the bridge has only width for one car.

Riverside Park PARK

(Monash Dr; ⏲24hr) The riverside park on the banks of the Murray River is a great place for a leisurely stroll or picnic, and has ponds, fountains and beautiful native trees, plus outdoor gym equipment.

Pioneer Settlement MUSEUM

(☎03-5036 2410; www.pioneersettlement.com.au; Monash Dr, Horseshoe Bend; adult/child/family $30/22/82; ⏲9.30am-4pm) Swan Hill's main tourist attraction is a fun re-creation of a riverside port town of the paddle-steamer era (1830 to 1930). The settlement's displays include the restored PS *Gem*, one of Australia's largest riverboats; a great collection of old carriages and buggies; an old-time photographic parlour; a lolly shop; a school classroom; and the fascinating Kaiser Stereoscope.

The paddle steamer PS *Pyap* makes short cruises along the Murray. Every night at dusk the multi-media laser show **Heartbeat of the Murray** is beamed onto a water screen, and tells the story of the Murray River and its creation. There are combined packages for a cruise, show and settlement visit.

Swan Hill Regional Art Gallery GALLERY

(☎03-5036 2430; http://gallery.swanhill.vic.gov.au; Monash Dr, Horseshoe Bend; by donation; ⏲10am-5pm Tue-Fri, to 4pm Sat & Sun) This gallery has a permanent collection of more than 300 pieces, focusing on the works of contemporary and local artists. It's known for its collection of naive art. Located opposite Pioneer Settlement.

Burke & Wills Tree LANDMARK
(Curlewis St) This enormous Moreton Bay fig tree was planted to commemorate the explorers Burke and Wills as they passed through Swan Hill on their ill-fated journey. It's located on, what is these days, the nondescript Curlewis St.

Murray Downs Golf & Country Club GOLF
(☎03-5033 1422; www.murraydownsgolf.com.au; Murray Downs Dr; 9/18 holes $30/50, club hire $25) Itching for a round? One of the Murray's superb public-resort golf courses, Murray Downs is 5km east of Swan Hill in NSW, but is regarded as a Swan Hill club.

Tours

PS Pyap CRUISE
(☎03-5036 2410; www.pioneersettlement.com.au; adult/child/family $23.50/16/63; ⏲cruises 2.30pm daily, plus 10.30am weekends & school holidays) This old paddle steamer makes short cruises along the Murray.

Festivals & Events

Swan Hill Racing Carnival SPORTS
(Swan Hill Racecourse; ⏲Jun) The three-day racing carnival over the Queen's Birthday weekend in June is the main event of the year. Events culminate with the Swan Hill Cup on the Sunday.

Swan Hill Food & Wine Festival FOOD & DRINK
(www.swanhillfoodandwine.com.au; ⏲Mar) Foodies will love this March festival, which celebrates local producers. The quality is high. Dates change each year.

Sleeping

Riverside Caravan Park CARAVAN PARK $
(☎03-5032 1494, 1800 101 012; www.big4.com.au; 1 Monash Dr; unpowered/powered sites from $37/41, cabins $122-295) On the banks of the Murray, close to Pioneer Settlement, this park enjoys a fabulous central, and pretty location. It has a good range of cabins, some right on the river edge. Note: prices soar by more than 50% in holiday periods.

Comfort Inn Campbell MOTEL $$
(☎03-5032 4427; www.comfortinncampbell.com; 396 Campbell St; d from $135; P ᯤ ≋) As far as regular Aussie country motels go, this one is not much different, although the rooms are clean, many are spacious and there are a couple of different pricing options. Unfortunately, breakfast is extra, but facilities include fridges and kettles, so at least you can start the day with a cuppa.

Travellers Rest Motor Inn MOTEL $$
(☎03-5032 9644; www.bestwestern.com.au/travellersrest; 110 Curlewis St; d from $133; ❄ ᯤ ≋) Sitting in the 'shade' of the tree dedicated to explorers Burke and Wills, but on a rather exposed main road, this inn has basic rooms that are nevertheless spacious and comfortable, with the usual motel accompaniments. There's an outdoor pool.

Eating

Java Spice THAI $
(☎03-5033 0015; 24 McRae St; mains $13-14; ⏲11.30am-2.30am Mon-Fri) The takeaway branch of Swan Hill's much-loved Thai restaurant (p317).

Jilarty Gelato Bar ICE CREAM $
(☎03-5033 0042; 233 Campbell St; ⏲8am-5pm Mon-Sat, 10am-4pm Sun) Gelati on a hot summer's day? Unbeatable. This little cafe specialises in Italian-style gelati with local fruit flavours, along with great coffee and Spanish churros (fried dough dusted in sugar).

★ **Spoons Riverside Café** MODERN AUSTRALIAN $$
(☎03-5032 2601; www.spoonsriverside.com.au; 125 Monash Dr, Horseshoe Bend; lunch mains $12-25, dinner $28-39; ⏲8am-5pm Sun-Wed, to 11pm Thu-Sat) The riverside location alone is enough to lure you to this licensed cafe, which offers a big timber deck overlooking the Marraboor River and the Pioneer Settlement. As well as a cafe serving light lunches and innovative dinners (in which fresh local ingredients take centre stage), Spoons Riverside has a provedore selling fresh produce and gourmet hampers.

Boo's Place Café & Provedore CAFE $$
(☎03-5032 4127; www.facebook.com/boosplacecafeandprovedore; 12 McCrae St; mains $11-18; ⏲8am-5pm Mon-Fri, 8am-4pmSat , 8am-3pm Sun) Handily located next to the visitor information centre, this fabulous spot has the town's best coffee. Cuisine follows a paddock-to-plate ethos, and there are local veggies and oranges for sale. Fabulously healthy breakfasts are on the menu. Don't miss the eggs benedict or the smoothie bowl, a mix of seasonal fruits with peanut butter, shredded coconut and honey.

Java Spice THAI $$
(☎03-5033 0511; www.javaspice.com.au; 17 Beveridge St; mains $21-32; ⏱6pm-late Tue-Sun; ☑) Dining under open-sided thatched and teak-wood huts in a tropical garden, you'll think you've been transported to Southeast Asia. The authentic cuisine is predominantly Thai, with some Malaysian and Indonesian influences mixed in. It's the go-to place for locals and is the 'old one but the good one' on the foodie block. There's a takeaway branch in the town centre (p316).

Tellers Café, Bar & Restaurant BISTRO $$
(☎03-5033 1383; 223 Campbell St; mains $14-28; ⏱11.30am-2.30pm & 5.30pm-late Mon-Sat) Named 'Tellers' because of its location inside an old bank, what this place lacks on the decor front – black and dark – it makes up for with bistro-style meals comprising all-local produce. The food is prepared well. Very well. It's worth handing over the cash for the likes of Asian pork belly, Greek lamb rack and lemon myrtle kangaroo.

☆ Entertainment

Heartbeat of the Murray THEATRE
(www.pioneersettlement.com.au; adult/child/family $22/15/59) Every night at dusk this 360-degree laser, light and water show recreates the creation of the Murray River from prehistoric times to the present day.

Information

Swan Hill Region Information Centre
(☎1800 625 373, 03-5032 3033; www.visitswanhill.com.au; cnr McCrae & Curlewis Sts; ⏱9am-5pm) Helpful maps and brochures on the region.

Getting There & Away

Swan Hill is 338km northwest of Melbourne, travelling via Bendigo and Kerang. It sits on the Murray Valley Hwy (B400), 218km from Mildura and 156km from Echuca.

V/Line (☎1800 800 007; www.vline.com.au) trains run from Melbourne to Swan Hill ($40.20, four hours, three to four daily), and to Bendigo where you can change to coach for Swan Hill.

Daily V/line coaches run to Mildura ($29.60, 2½ to three hours) and Echuca ($18.20, three hours).

Around Swan Hill

The Swan Hill region doesn't compare with nearby Mildura in terms of grape production but there are a few good wineries, including **Andrew Peace Wines** (4077 Murray Valley Hwy, Piangil; ⏱9am-5pm Mon-Fri, noon-4pm Sat), which has cellar-door sales and tastings.

Just 16km southeast of Swan Hill, **Lake Boga** is an interesting little town – especially now that its namesake lake is full of water again. Flying boats were repaired and tested at Lake Boga during WWII, and the famous Catalina flying boat *A24-30* is on display at the **Flying Boat Museum** (☎03-5037 2850; www.flyingboat.org.au; Catalina Park; adult/child/family $15/8/30; ⏱9am-4pm). Inside you'll find lots of displays and photographs.

A patchwork of lakes, including **Kangaroo Lake** and **Lake Charm**, are popular water-sports destinations. Birdwatchers shouldn't miss the **Middle Lake Ibis Rookery**, 6km north of Kerang, where you can spot straw-necked and white ibis from a bird hide.

Sights

Olson Game Birds FARM
(☎03-5030 2648; www.gamebirds.com.au; 2167 Chillingollah Rd; adult/child/family $10/5/25; ⏱10am-4pm) Here's one for the kids: get a map and drive out to Olson Game Birds, a pheasant farm where game birds are bred and reared. Native birds are also on display and peacocks wander around looking gorgeous. Take a picnic or ring ahead if you'd like lunch.

Sleeping

★ **Burrabliss B&B** B&B $$
(☎03-5037 2527; www.burrabliss.com.au; 169 Lakeside Dr, Lake Boga; d $180, villa $300) This fabulous B&B is set in a lovely garden near Lake Boga, 10 minutes' drive from Swan Hill. A 'double' is in fact an entirely self-contained unit, with microwave and fridge. The ultrafriendly hosts provide a full home-cooked breakfast using their own produce. You can birdwatch in the wetlands, or walk by the lake.

Echuca & Around

POP 14,000

One of the loveliest towns in rural Victoria, Echuca is the state's paddle-steamer capital and a classic Murray River town, bursting with history, nostalgia and, of course, riverboats. The Aboriginal name translates as 'meeting of the waters', as it's here that three great rivers meet: the Goulburn, the Campaspe and the Murray.

Echuca

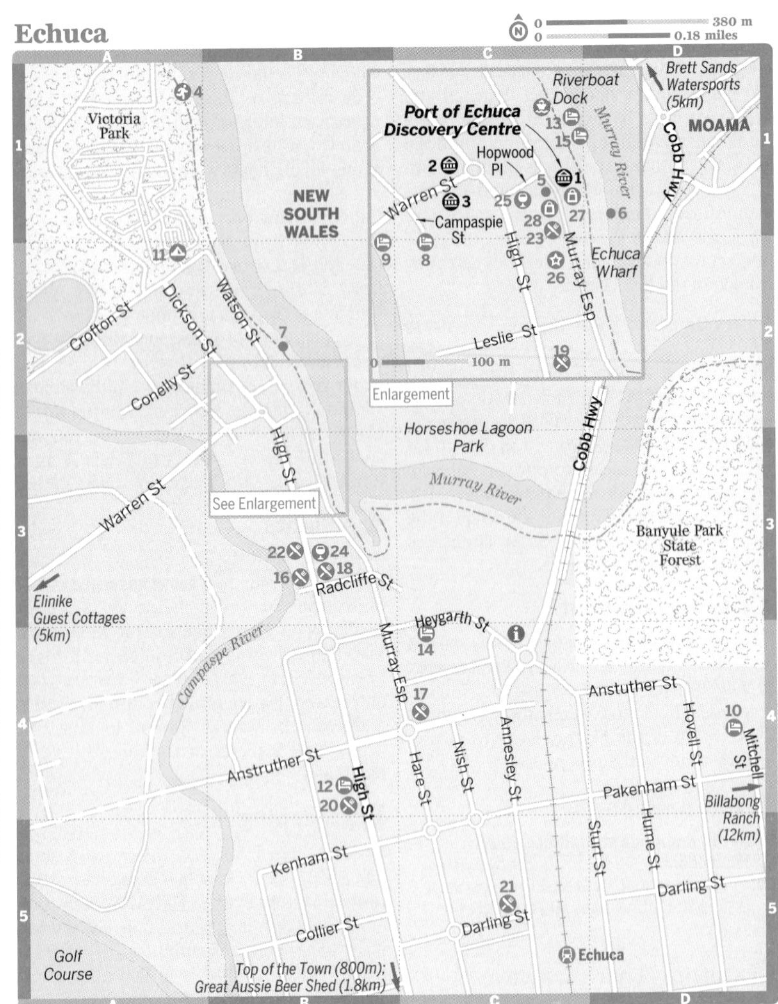

In the 1800s Echuca was an important crossing point between NSW and Victoria, and the ensuing river trade and transport ensured its success.

The highlight of Echuca is unquestionably its historic port area and the rivers themselves, best enjoyed on a riverboat cruise or a sunset stroll as cockatoos and corellas screech overhead.

History

For thousands of years, Indigenous Australians – the Bangerang people – inhabited a wide area, including where Echuca now sits. In 1853 ex-convict Henry Hopwood arrived and settled on the banks of the Murray. He converted some rough sheds into an inn and a store, then established punt and ferry crossings over the Murray and Campaspe Rivers; with his monopoly on transport and the gold rush in full swing, he profited handsomely. At the peak of the riverboat era there were more than 100 paddle steamers carting wool, timber and other goods between Echuca and the outback sheep stations.

It was too good to last though: the Melbourne–Echuca railway line opened in 1864,

Echuca

and within a decade the boom years of the riverboat trade had ended.

Sights

Ask at the visitor centre (p323) for the *Heritage Walk Echuca* brochure, which outlines a self-guided walking itinerary taking in the town centre's historic buildings.

Echuca's star attraction is the historic Port of Echuca. Everything is original, so you're exploring living history as you walk along the pedestrian-only Murray Esplanade, which you can wander for free.

★Port of Echuca Discovery Centre MUSEUM
(Map p318; ☎03-5481 0500; www.portofechuca.org.au; 74 Murray Esplanade; adult/child/family $14/8/45; ⏲9am-5pm) At the northern end of Murray Esplanade, the stunning Port of Echuca Discovery Centre is your gateway to the Echuca wharf area. It presents excellent displays (some of them interactive) on the port's history, the paddle steamers and the riverboat trade. Informative and fun free guided tours set out from the discovery centre twice daily (11.30am and 1.30pm).

Great Aussie Beer Shed MUSEUM
(☎03-5480 6904; www.greataussiebeershed.com.au; 377 Mary Ann Rd; adult/child/family $14/5/30; ⏲9.30am-5pm Sat, Sun & holidays) This is a wall-to-wall shrine of more than 17,000 beer cans in a huge shed. It's the result of 30 years of collecting – one can dates back to Federation (1901). Guided tours will take you through the history of beer. Very Aussie.

National Holden Museum MUSEUM
(Map p318; ☎03-5480 2033; www.holdenmuseum.com.au; 7 Warren St; adult/child/family $9.50/3.50/22.50; ⏲9am-5pm) Car buffs should check out this museum dedicated to Australia's four-wheeled icon, with more than 40 beautifully restored Holdens, from FJ to Monaro. There's also racing footage and memorabilia.

Echuca Historical Museum MUSEUM
(Map p318; ☎03-5480 1325; www.echucahistoricalsociety.org.au; 1 Dickson St; adult/child $5/1; ⏲11am-3pm) This historical museum is located in the old police station, which has been classified by the National Trust. It has a collection of local history items, charts and photos from the riverboat era and early records. Also runs informative historic town walks on request ($12 per person).

Activities

River Country Adventours CANOEING
(☎0428 585 227; www.adventours.com.au; half-/full-day safaris $65/100) For organised canoe safaris on the Goulburn River, this Kyabram-based team is the expert in this part of the world. It offers canoe and camping

PADDLE-STEAMER CRUISES

A paddle-steamer cruise is almost obligatory. Six boats – wood-fired, steam-driven (one is electric diesel) with interesting commentary – offer trips operating at various times. Privately owned Murray River Paddle Steamers runs PS Canberra (p320), PS Emmylou (p320) and PS Pride of the Murray (p320); Echuca Paddlesteamers runs PS Alexander Arbuthnot (p320), PS Pevensey (p320) and PS Adelaide (p320).

Buy tickets to any of these from the Port of Echuca Discovery Centre (p319), Echuca Moama visitor information centre (p323) or along Murray Esplanade. Note Murray River Paddle Steamers sells tickets only to the boats it runs. Your decision might be based on the boat's size, history and timetables – you can't really go wrong. Check timetables for lunch, dinner, twilight and sunset cruises.

safaris around the Barmah and Goulburn regions, as well as on the Murray.

Brett Sands Watersports WATER SPORTS
(☎03-5482 1851; www.brettsands.com; Merool Lane, Moama; half/full day $160/260) Several operators offer waterskiing trips and classes, but this outfit will teach you skills behind a boat for skis as well as wakeboard, kneeboard or barefoot. It also hires out gear.

Echuca Boat & Canoe Hire BOATING
(Map p318; ☎03-5480 6208; www.echucaboatcanoehire.com; Victoria Park Boat Ramp) Hires out motor boats (one/two hours $50/75), 'barbie boats' with on-board BBQs (10 people from $120/180), kayaks ($20/30) and canoes ($20/30). Multiday, self-guided 'campanoeing' trips, where you can arrange to be dropped upstream and canoe back, are also available.

☞ Tours

PS Adelaide CRUISE
(Map p318; ☎03-5482 4248; www.echucapaddlesteamers.net.au; adult/child/family $25/11/66) PS *Adelaide* is believed to be the oldest wooden-hulled paddle steamer still cruising any river in the world (it celebrated its 150th year in 2016). The steamer started life as a wool-carrying and then a logging boat. *Adelaide* departs from the wharf but is not available all the time; it can hold around 50 people.

Murray River Paddle Steamers CRUISE
(Map p318; www.murrayriverpaddlesteamers.com.au; 57 Murray Esplanade; ⏲9am-5pm) This private company runs three of Echuca's six paddle steamers: PS *Canberra*, PS *Emmylou* and PS *Pride of the Murray*. Each runs to a different timetable. You can buy tickets at the ticket office on Murray Esplanade.

PS Alexander Arbuthnot CRUISE
(Map p318; ☎03-5482 4248; www.echucapaddlesteamers.net.au; adult/child/family $25/11/66) One-hour cruises are offered aboard this 1923-built steamer, with less-regular two-hour twilight trips and 2½-hour dinner cruises. Seats around 46.

PS Pevensey CRUISE
(Map p318; ☎03-5482 4248, 1300 942 737; www.echucapaddlesteamers.net.au; adult/child/family $25/11/66) One of the oldest paddle steamers (1911) still running, the PS *Pevensey* offers one-hour cruises up to five times daily.

PS Canberra CRUISE
(Map p318; ☎03-5482 5244; www.murrayriverpaddlesteamers.com.au; adult/child/family $36/21/95) One-hour cruises aboard this lovely old steamer that was built in 1912 and restored in 2003. Four departures daily.

PS Pride of the Murray CRUISE
(Map p318; ☎03-5482 5244; www.murrayriverpaddlesteamers.com.au;adult/child/family $36/21/95) One-hour cruises.

PS Emmylou CRUISE
(Map p318; ☎03-5482 5244; www.murrayriverpaddlesteamers.com.au; cruises 1hr adult/child/family $28.50/18/78, 2hr $36/21/95) One of the most impressive and prettiest boats in Echuca, the *Emmylou* was built for the 1982 TV miniseries *All the Rivers Run* but is driven by an original, 105-year-old steam engine. Offers two one-hour cruises and one two-hour cruise daily, plus lunch, dinner and overnight cruises. The three-hour dinner cruise costs $110 per adult.

Echuca Moama Wine Tours WINE
(☎0407 735 743; www.echucamoamawinetours.com.au; tours from $110; ⏲Tue-Sun) Tours include the historic port, a cruise along the Murray on a paddle steamer and local wineries.

Festivals & Events

Check the online event calendar at www.echucamoama.com.

Echuca Steam Rally CARNIVAL
(www.echucasteamrally.com.au; day pass adult/child $20/5; Jun) Classic and historic vehicles and steam engines powered by all imaginable methods. Takes place on the Queen's Birthday weekend in June.

Riverboats Music Festival MUSIC
(www.riverboatsmusic.com.au; Feb) Music, food and wine by the Murray in late February. Recent performers include Paul Kelly, the Hoodoo Gurus, Missy Higgins and You Am I.

Sleeping

High Street Motel MOTEL $
(Map p318; 03-5482 1013; www.highstreetmotelechuca.com.au; 439 High St; d $120;) The current owners have done a good job at this motel makeover. Rooms are simple and as neat as a pin, and prices are fair for what you get. The decent mattresses will guarantee good slumber, and toasters and microwaves are handy for self-caterers. It's walking distance to Echuca's centre and good cafes. Very friendly owners.

Christies Beach Camping CAMPGROUND $
About 5km east of town, Christies Beach is a free camping area on the banks of the Murray. There are pit toilets, but bring water and firewood.

Echuca Gardens GUESTHOUSE $
(Map p318; 0419 881 054; www.echucagardens.com; 103 Mitchell St; wagons $80-160, guesthouse r $120-200;) Run by inveterate traveller Kym, this spot has some novel sleeping arrangements – two cosy 'gypsy wagons' that come complete with bathroom and kitchenette; a guesthouse (part of the owner's home, with private entry); or his entire home, which has a smart bathroom, a country kitchen and a TV room. The complex is surrounded by a pleasant garden with ponds, statues and fruit trees.

Echuca Holiday Park CAMPGROUND $
(Map p318; 03-5482 2157; www.echucacaravanpark.com.au; 51 Crofton St; unpowered/powered sites from $27/33, cabins $90-115;) Beside the river just a short walk from town, this park is cramped but the facilities are good, with modern timber camp kitchens and shady river red gums. Rates increase dramatically during school holidays and over Easter.

Adelphi Boutique Apartments APARTMENT $$
(Map p318; 03-5482 5575; www.adelphiapartments.com.au; 25 Campaspe St; 1-/2-bedroom apt from $185/360;) This semi-luxurious riverside accommodation, a block back from the main street, is a good choice, especially if you're willing to pay a little more for those apartments with a terrace overlooking the Campaspe River.

Quest Echuca APARTMENT $$
(Map p318; 03-5481 3900; www.questechuca.com.au; 25-29 Heygarth St; studio $159, 1-/2-bedroom apt from $189/319;) Stylish, modern, business-like apartments a block back from the Murray River and the main street make this a fine choice if the usual doily-and-lace Echuca aesthetic is not your thing.

Elinike Guest Cottages COTTAGE $$
(03-5480 6311; www.elinike.com.au; 209 Latham Rd; d $190-210;) These rustic but romantic little self-contained cottages are set in rambling gardens on the Murray River around 5km northwest of town. They blend

COMBINED TICKETS

Echuca's attractions can be grouped together in a series of combination tickets that can save you both time and money.

Heritage Package (adult/concession/child/family $55/49/26/171) Sold at the Port of Echuca Discovery Centre (p319) only, it includes admission to the discovery centre, the National Holden Museum (p319), the Great Aussie Beer Shed (p319), the Echuca Historical Museum (p319) and a one-hour paddle-steamer cruise.

Discovery Centre & One-Hour Cruise Package (adult/concession/child/family $35.20/30.25/17/100) Includes all-day access to the historic port area (guided tours offered at 11.30am and 1.30pm) and a one-hour cruise aboard any of the paddle steamers, except the *PS Emmylou*.

Wharf to Winery Package (per person $75) Paddle-steamer cruise to Morrisons Winery, two-course lunch and wine tasting.

old-world style with modern conveniences such as double spas. The lilac cottage has a glass-roofed garden room.

★**Cock 'n Bull Boutique Hotel** BOUTIQUE HOTEL **$$$**
(Map p318; 03-5480 6988; www.cocknbullechuca.com; 17-21 Warren St; s/d from $150/250;) These luxury apartments add a touch of class to Echuca's central motel-style options. The building's older section (once a bustling pub from the 1870s) looks out over the Campaspe River while a newer, modern section is at the rear. All apartments differ in mood and design, and all are tasteful.

Murray River Houseboats HOUSEBOAT **$$$**
(Map p318; 03-5480 2343; www.murrayriverhouseboats.com.au; Riverboat Dock; 2-7 bed houseboats per week $1550-2720) Six houseboats in the fleet, including the stunning four-bedroom *Indulgence*.

Rich River Houseboats HOUSEBOAT **$$$**
(Map p318; 03-5480 2444; www.richriverhouseboats.com.au; Riverboat Dock; per week $2500-$5200) These six beautiful boats are floating palaces. They cater mainly to larger groups, but bedding configurations can be altered to suit both couples and families.

Eating

★**Fish in a Flash** FISH & CHIPS **$**
(Map p318; 03-5480 0824; 602 High St; fish & chips from $9.90; 9am-8pm) Consistently ranked among the best fish-and-chip places in Victoria (the owner, Paul, has been frying for 27 years), Fish in a Flash does occasional river fish as well as the usual suspects, all dipped in the owner's secret batter. Great for a riverside picnic.

Top of the Town FISH & CHIPS **$**
(03-5482 4600; cnr High & Service Sts; fish & chips $12; 10am-8pm) This claims to be the best fish-and-chip shop in the state. It has a good range including river fish (redfin, yellowbelly), crays and oysters.

Cafe 3564 Wine Bar CAFE **$**
(Map p318; 03-5482 3564; www.facebook.com/cafe3564; 252 Hare St; mains $10-20; 7am-4.30pm, to 10pm Fri) Inhabiting the old Echuca post office, this smart contemporary cafe does fabulous coffee, light lunches, sweets and excellent wines, most of them local. Friday night brings tapas and a 5.30pm happy hour.

★**Shebani's** MEDITERRANEAN **$$**
(Map p318; 03-5480 7075; 535 High St; mains $17.50-20; 7.30am-4pm) Eating here is like taking a culinary tour of the Mediterranean – Greek, Lebanese and even North African dishes all get a run with subtle flavours. The decor effortlessly brings together Mediterranean tile work, Moroccan lamps and a fresh Aussie-cafe style. Great coffee, too.

Johnny & Lyle CAFE **$$**
(Map p318; 03-5480 3133; www.facebook.com/johnnyandlyle; 433 High St; mains $12-25; 6am-2pm) This ticks the right boxes in terms of colour: not only the cups (an array of bright hues) but the lovely courtyard and the vibrant dishes – blueberry pancakes ($16.50), brekky burgers ($14) and fabulous lunch dishes including pulled lamb with pumpkin hummus ($19) and steak sandwiches ($20). An excellent option and worth the slightly extra hike a few blocks south of the centre.

Black Pudding CAFE **$$**
(Map p318; 03-5482 2244; www.blackpuddingechuca.com.au; 525a High St; mains breakfast $7-18, lunch $18-35; 7am-3pm) Owned by two local brothers (who are often at the coffee machine), this place turns out a good brew, plus fabulous light lunches. Plates are not overly complicated – BLT (bacon, lettuce and tomato, plus avocado, cheddar and basil mayo) or French toast – but what they do, they do well.

Star Hotel BISTRO **$$**
(Map p318; 03-5480 1181; www.starhotelechuca.com.au; 45 Murray Esplanade; pizzas $20-24, mains $20-32; 11am-late) The historic 'Star Bar' is one of the liveliest places in town for a meal or a drink, especially on weekends when there's live music. Full cooked breakfasts and a reasonably priced lunch of calamari or chicken parma can be enjoyed on the front deck right beside the port. The wood-fired pizzas are easily the best in town.

Offers a kids' menu, too (mains $10). The High St entrance opens to a more upmarket wine bar, although it's all part of the same premises.

Ceres EUROPEAN **$$$**
(Map p318; 03-5482 5599; www.ceresechuca.com.au; 554 High St; lunch $13-16, dinner $24-41; 10am-late Mon-Fri, 9am-late Sat & Sun) In a beautifully converted 1881 brick flour mill, Ceres (named after the Roman goddess of agriculture) is forever reinventing itself; at

the time of research new owners were at the helm. The jury's still out, but it's a relaxed place for lunch, with all-day coffee, and in the evenings the downstairs restaurant focuses on Italian cuisine and modern Australian dishes.

Head upstairs to the wine bar and tapas joint for an entirely different ambience with leather couches and chandeliers.

Mill INTERNATIONAL **$$$**
(Map p318; ☎03-5480 1619; www.themillechuca.com; 2-8 Nish St; share plates $11-26, mains $36-44; ⊙noon-late Fri-Sun, 4pm-late Tue-Thu) This ambitious project – the transformation of a former flour mill (built in 1881) into a gathering space for locals – seems to have worked. The architectural melange of rustic and industrial-chic results in fun hangouts, including a buzzing bar and a sun-filled lounge-cum-restaurant. For nosh? Modern Australian dishes are especially substantial, with prices to match. For grog? Good drinks list.

Drinking & Nightlife

Bordello Wine Bar WINE BAR
(Map p318; ☎03-5480 6902; www.rivergalleryinn.com.au; 578 High St; ⊙8.30-11pm) An ideal spot for fine local wines, with a fabulous range of 50-plus world beers and Saturday-night live music. It attracts the over-30s crowd (read: despite the music, you can have a conversation).

Henry's Bridge Hotel PUB
(Map p318; ☎03-5480 1000; 1 Hopwood Pl; ⊙8am-3.30pm Mon & Tue, to 11pm Wed-Sun) Formerly known as the Bridge Hotel, this historic spot and Echuca's oldest pub was built in 1859 by town-founder Harry Hopwood. At the time of research it was being renovated. Its new image is intended to be a family oriented cafe-restaurant-pub serving burgers, fish and chips, steaks and other pub-style meals. Should be worth checking out.

Entertainment

Sharp's Magic Movie House & Penny Arcade CINEMA
(Map p318; ☎03-5482 2361; 43 Murray Esplanade; per person $7; ⊙9am-5pm) This place has authentic penny-arcade machines (the $7 entry gives you 7 pennies) and fudge tasting (a smidgen for free). The movie house shows old movies such as Buster Keaton, The Three Stooges or Laurel and Hardy classics.

Shopping

St Anne's FOOD & DRINKS
(Map p318; ☎03-5480 6955; www.stanneswinery.com.au; 53 Murray Esplanade; ⊙9am-5pm Mon-Sat, 10am-5pm Sun) Offers free tastings of local wines. Taste the range of fortified wines, aged in 100-year-old spirit barrels.

Port of Echuca Woodturners ARTS & CRAFTS
(Map p318; Murray Esplanade; ⊙9am-4pm) At Port of Echuca craftspeople turn out and sell beautiful red-gum products made with traditional equipment.

Information

Echuca Moama Visitor Information Centre (Map p318; ☎1800 804 446; www.echucamoama.com; 2 Heygarth St; ⊙9am-5pm;) In the old pump station; has helpful staff, brochures and offers booking services for accommodation and paddle steamers. Be sure to grab *Heritage Walk Echuca*, which points out historic buildings and sites.

Getting There & Away

Echuca lies 222km north of Melbourne. Take the Hume Fwy (M31) then the well-signposted turn-off to the B75, which passes through Heathcote and Rochester en route to Echuca.

V/Line (☎1800 800 007; www.vline.com.au) runs combined train and coach services between Melbourne and Echuca ($27.20, three to 3½ hours, regular departures) with a change at Bendigo, Shepparton or Murchison.

Around Echuca

Barmah National Park

About 40km northeast of Echuca, via the Cobb Hwy in NSW, Barmah is a significant wetlands area of the Murray River floodplain. It's the largest remaining red-gum forest in Australia and one of few places in Victoria to see the superb parrot. The forest's swampy understorey usually floods, creating a wonderful breeding area for many species of fish and bird. Several walks, covering 1.5km to 5km, loop through the park.

The park entry is about 6km north of the tiny town of Barmah (take the turn at the pub).

Activities

★Kingfisher Cruises CRUISE
(☎03-5855 2855; www.kingfishercruises.com.au; 2hr cruises adult/child/family $37/21/100; ⊙10.30am Mon, Wed, Thu, Sat & Sun) From the day-use area, Kingfisher Cruises takes you out in a flat-bottomed boat for an informative cruise. Your captain points out bird and mammal species along the way. Call ahead for departure times and bookings.

Sleeping

You can camp for free in the park, either in isolated spots or populated sandy beaches, or at the Barmah Lakes camping ground.

There's absolutely nothing available in the park, unless you fancy yourself as Crocodile Dundee and want to try your DIY survival skills. In short, stock up in a larger regional centre before you come. Tiny Barmah has essentials.

Barmah Lakes Camping CAMPGROUND
(www.parkstay.vic.gov.au; free) The bushy Barmah Lakes camping ground has tables, barbecue areas and pit toilets. It's a remote experience and out of holiday times you're likely to have it to yourself. Beware falling branches from the river red gum trees.

A convenient park entry for two-wheel drive vehicles and caravans is via Moira Lakes Rd, about 6km north of Barmah township. There are another 11 major entrance gates, all accessible from the Barmah–Picola Rd and the Murray Valley Hwy. You'll need your own transport.

Yarrawonga

POP 7100

Arrayed along the southern shores of Lake Mulwala, which was created when the Murray River was dammed for irrigation back in 1939, Yarrawonga is beloved by boaters, waterskiers, golfers and retirees. It also enjoys more sunshine hours than anywhere else in Victoria. Such positives make up for a lack of old-world character and its atmosphere as a fairly run-of-the-mill provincial Victorian town. It's an OK option to pass through, but you could do better if you're wanting a base.

Pick up the brochure *Farm Gate Trail*, a useful guide to the region's local producers.

Sights & Activities

Byramine Homestead Brewery & Ciderhouse HISTORIC BUILDING
(☎03-5748 4321; www.byraminehomestead.com.au; 1436 Murray Valley Hwy; adult/child/family $5/2.50/15; ⊙10am-4pm Sat-Thu) When Elizabeth Hume's husband was killed by bushrangers, she moved here (in 1842) and built a safe haven that saw her become the first permanent European settler in the area. The rooms are furnished, though it's a little run down these days. One of the home-

FISHING ON THE MURRAY

The Murray River is great for fishing, from its upper reaches where anglers cast flies in search of trout and salmon to its slow-moving, deep-water sections hiding perch (yellow-belly), redfin, bream and the dreaded European carp. The introduced carp has long been a problem in the Murray–Darling system, where it breeds intensively (think infestation), muddies the waters and generally upsets the riverine ecology. Carp is a declared pest, so it's illegal to release the fish back into the water once caught. And don't bother eating them – they taste like mud.

The big prize is the elusive Murray cod, Australia's largest freshwater fish and a native in these waters. The Murray cod is a long-lived fish – the biggest and oldest can weigh upwards of 100kg – and there are plenty of tales of the ones that got away. The cod is carnivorous and can be caught by using yabbies, grubs, river shrimp, small fish or trolling with a lure. Unfortunately, current numbers of cod are low. At the time of research, anything under 55cm must be released back into the water; the bag limit is one.

To fish in Victorian waters you need a recreational fishing licence ($10 per three days or $35 per year), available from many shops along the Murray or from the **Department of Economic Development, Jobs, Transport & Resources** (DEDJTR; ☎13 61 86; http://agriculture.vic.gov.au/fisheries/recreational-fishing/fishing-licence).

stead's rooms has an octagon shape (ask about its interesting history).

The on-site cider-house serves ciders, beers and light lunches. It's located 14km west of town. Guided tours at 11am daily.

Yarrawonga Mulwala Golf Club Resort GOLF
(☎03-5744 1911; www.yarragolf.com.au; Gulai Rd, Mulwala; 9/18 holes $28/45) Across the water in Mulwala, NSW, is Australia's largest public golf course, with one nine-hole and two 18-hole courses, all beautifully manicured. There's also good resort accommodation, a bar and a bistro.

Action Bike & Ski KAYAKING, CYCLING
(☎03-5744 3522; www.actionbikeski.com.au; 19 Hume St; ⏰9am-5pm Mon-Fri, to 1pm Sat year-round, plus Sun Jan) Hires out kayaks ($50 per day) and bikes ($20 per day). To really discover the lake and river, take one of the half-day guided kayak tours ($120), available with 48-hours notice (minimum five people).

Tours

Paradise Queen CRUISE
(☎0418 508 616; www.paradisequeen.com; cruises $15-50) Paradise Queen can take you cruising along the lake and the Murray River, pointing out historic spots and birdlife. There are 1½-hour sunrise breakfast cruises ($26), barbecue cruises ($30) and scenic cruises ($15) at noon, as well as dinner cruises during summer ($45 to $50).

Sleeping & Eating

Murray Valley Resort RESORT $$
(☎03-5744 1844; www.murrayvalleyresort.com.au; Murray Valley Hwy; s/d from $140/170, ste $190/230, apt from $290; ❄🏊) This place is a good reflection of the town itself – the modern, motel-style rooms don't have much character but the facilities (a gym, indoor and outdoor pools, tennis courts, billiard tables and spas) lift the standard.

Souleiado Sourdough CAFE $
(☎03-5744 3587; www.souleiadosourdough.com.au; 39 Belmore St; snacks $7-12) This small spot on the main street brings hipster flavour to Yarrawonga for your coffee hit. The fresh-roasted beans hail from nearby Albury, and you can stock up on loaves of sourdough bread (the owner grew up around bakers and all things baking). Good snacks, too, such as gourmet bagels.

Lake Cafe & Deck CAFE $$
(☎03-5743 3069; 1 Irvine Pde; mains $13-28; ⏰9am-4pm) Located in front of the visitor information centre and overlooking the lake, this modest spot serves up some big flavours, especially with its cakes (don't miss the lemon meringue cheesecake). Those with more savoury palates will enjoy the likes of Thai chicken burgers ($18) and smoked trout bruschetta ($20).

Criterion Hotel/Deck One PUB FOOD $$
(☎03-5744 3839; 1 Belmore St; mains $15-32; ⏰11am-9pm) The beer deck here takes up as much real estate as the entire Criterion Hotel of which it's a part. Shady umbrellas, good views of the lake and a kids playground. Good pub food is complemented with pizzas and pasta.

Shopping

Rich Glen Olive Oil FOOD
(☎03-5743 3776; www.richglenoliveoil.com; 734 Murray Valley Hwy; ⏰9am-4pm) This beautiful family-owned estate is based at an olive grove and devotes itself to all things olive. It sells more than 150 products – from oils and dressings to male grooming products – all made using the estate's own produce. The shop is housed in a historic home surrounded by a cottage garden. The on-site cafe serves excellent light lunches and cakes.

Information

Yarrawonga Mulwala Visitor Information Centre (☎1800 062 260, 03-5744 1989; www.yarrawongamulwala.com.au; 1 Irvine Pde; ⏰9am-5pm) Right beside the Mulwala Bridge and with a cafe overlooking the lake; book accommodation and tours here.

Getting There & Away

Yarrawonga is 283km northeast of Melbourne. By car, take the Hume Fwy (M31) and then head north from Benalla or Wangaratta.

V/Line (☎1800 800 007; www.vline.com.au) train and coach services run between Melbourne and Yarrawonga ($32, four hours, two to three daily), with a change to a coach at Benalla.

Wodonga

POP 35,000

The border town of Wodonga is separated from its NSW twin, Albury, by the Murray River. Although a busy little place with a lake formed off Wodonga Creek, most of the attractions and the best of the accommodation are on the NSW side.

Sights

Bonegilla Migrant Experience HISTORIC SITE
(☎02-6020 6912; www.bonegilla.org.au; 82 Bonegilla Rd; by donation; ⏰10am-4pm) FREE For 24 years from the end of WWII, Bonegilla, 10km east of Wodonga, was Australia's first migrant reception centre, providing accommodation for some 320,000 migrants from more than 30 countries. You can visit some of the preserved buildings of Block 19, the only remaining block, and follow the lives and experiences of individuals represented in photos and historical references.

Army Museum Bandiana MUSEUM
(☎02-6055 2525; Anderson Rd, South Bandiana; adult/child/family $5/2/10; ⏰10am-3pm Tue, Thu & Sat) The Army Museum Bandiana displays a variety of war weaponry, items from missions, and documents. The old cars are magnificent. There are Buick and Holden staff cars, Chevrolet and Dodge trucks, carriages and motorbikes. It's located on an army base, so visits require 24-hours advance notice for a security check.

Activities

There are signed trails for the many walking and cycling trails around Gateway Island, along the Murray River and the beautiful wetlands of **Sumsion Gardens**. Wodonga is also the start of the High Country Rail Trail, a cycling and walking path that skirts around the southern end of Lake Hume to Tallangatta.

High Country Rail Trail CYCLING
(☎03-6023 2425; www.highcountryrailtrail.org.au) Slip into your Lycra or don your hiking boots to hike or ride this 30km trail along the foreshore of Lake Hume from Wodonga to Tallangatta (the walking section continues further east to Shelley). You can get your cultural fixes at Bandiana and Bonegilla en route and your nature fill along the bird-filled shoreline.

Eating & Drinking

Cafe Grove CAFE $
(☎02-6024 5655; www.facebook.com/cafegrovewodonga; 198a High St; mains $12-20; ⏰6.30am-5.30pm Mon-Fri, 7am-4pm Sat) Located in one of only eight surviving art deco buildings in Wodonga, this trendy spot, housed in a former city office, is popular for its all-day breakfasts. On Friday evenings it puts on live entertainment and tapas.

Junction Place INTERNATIONAL $$
(Station Building, 46 Elgin Blvd; mains $8-25) Wodonga's former railway station has been transformed into a trendy foodie hub; excellent options line the old platform. Grab a brew at **Bean Station** (7am-4pm) before heading for craft beer at the **Goods Shed Craft Beer Cafe** (Wed-Sun 11am-late). Formal evening meals are served at **Miss Amelie** (Tues-Thurs & Sat 6pm-11pm, Frid noon-11pm).

Coffee Mamma CAFE
(☎02-6056 7511; www.coffeemamma.com.au; 190 High St; ⏰6.30am-2.30pm Mon-Fri, 8am-noon Sat) The town's best coffee can be enjoyed here.

Information

Wodonga Visitor Information Centre (☎1300 796 222; www.visitalburywodonga.com; 69-73 Hovell St; ⏰9am-5pm) Good info about attractions both local and further afield in Victoria and NSW, and an accommodation booking service.

Getting There & Away

Wodonga is 323km northeast of Melbourne along the Hume Fwy (M31). **V/Line** (☎1800 800 007; www.vline.com.au) train services ply the route ($36.20, four hours, three to four daily).

The Way North

Heading north to the Murray River from Melbourne opens up some unexpected regions of Victoria – vast desert national parks, sleepy rural towns and the fertile food bowl of the Goulburn Valley to name a few. The main routes north are the Hume Fwy to Wodonga (which continues on to Sydney), the Sunraysia Hwy through the Mallee to Mildura, the Northern Hwy to Echuca and the Goulburn Valley Hwy through Shepparton.

THE MALLEEFOWL

The rare Malleefowl is one of Australia's most fascinating birds. When mature they are about the size of a small turkey, with their wings and backs patterned in black, white and brown, which helps with camouflage in the mallee scrub. They can fly short distances if necessary. Until the establishment of the Mallee's national parks, the Malleefowl was threatened with extinction.

The life cycle of the Malleefowl is an amazing story of survival and adaptation. The male bird spends up to 11 months preparing a mound for the eggs. First he digs a hole, or opens up an old mound, fills it with leaves, bark and twigs, and covers the lot with sand to create the main egg chamber. When the mound has been saturated by rain so that the organic material starts to decompose, he covers it all with more sand – by now it can be up to 1m high and 5m in diameter – and tests the core temperature daily by sticking his beak inside. Once the temperature is stable at 33°C, he lets the female know that she can start laying her eggs.

The female lays between 15 and 20 eggs, which hatch at various stages over spring and summer. The male continues to check the mound temperature daily, and if it varies from 33°C he adjusts it by covering the mound or removing sand.

After hatching, the chicks dig their way up to the surface, can run within a few hours and fly on their first day out. However, the mortality rate is very high. The parents don't recognise or help their own young and, while an average pair of Malleefowl will produce around 90 chicks in their lifetimes, only a few will survive to reproduce.

Your best chances of seeing a Malleefowl are at dusk or dawn, either along the Ouyen–Patchewollock Rd (check along the roadsides), the Old Calder Hwy south of Hattah-Kulkyne National Park, or the Honeymoon Track (inside Hattah-Kulkyne National Park).

The Mallee

Occupying the vast northwestern corner of Victoria, the Mallee appears as a flat horizon and endless, undulating, twisted mallee scrub and desert. The attractions – other than the sheer solitude – are the semi-arid wilderness areas, including Wyperfeld National Park and Big Desert Wilderness Park. Collectively these parks cover more than 750,000 hectares, and are notable for their abundance of native plants, spring wildflowers and birds. Nature lovers might delight in it, but much of it is inaccessible to all but experienced 4WD enthusiasts. Visiting this, the Victorian outback, is best avoided in the hot summer months.

The main route through the Mallee is the Sunraysia Hwy (B220), via the towns of Birchip and Ouyen, but if you want to explore the region's national parks, turn off to the historic farming towns of **Jeparit** (birthplace of Sir Robert Menzies and the jumping-off point for Lake Hindmarsh), **Rainbow**, **Yaapeet** and **Hopetoun**.

Hattah-Kulkyne National Park

The vegetation of the beautiful and diverse Hattah-Kulkyne National Park ranges from dry, sandy mallee-scrub country to fertile riverside areas lined with red gum, black box, wattle and bottlebrush.

The **Hattah Lakes** system fills when the Murray River floods, which is great for waterbirds. The hollow trees are perfect for nesting, and more than 200 species of birds have been recorded in the area. Native animals include nocturnal desert types and wetland species, such as the burrowing frog, which digs itself into the ground and waits until there's enough water to start breeding. Reptiles here include the mountain devil, inspiration for the Australian saying, 'Flat out like a lizard drinking,' because it draws water into its mouth by lying flat on the ground.

Sleeping

You can camp at Lake Hattah and Lake Mournpall. Free camping is also possible anywhere along the Murray River frontage. Take your own provisions, including water as it's limited (the lake water is undrinkable).

MALLEE SCRUB

A mallee is a hardy eucalypt with multiple slender trunks. Its roots are twisted, gnarled, dense chunks of wood, famous for their slow-burning qualities and much sought after by woodturners. Mallee gums are canny desert survivors – root systems of over a thousand years old are not uncommon – and are part of a diverse and rich biosystem that includes waterbirds, fish in the huge (but unreliable) lakes, kangaroos and other marsupials, emus, and the many edible plants that thrive in this environment.

When the railway line from Melbourne to Mildura was completed in 1902, much of the region was divided into small blocks for farming. The first European settlers had terrible problems trying to clear the land. They used a method called mullenising (crushing the scrub with heavy red-gum rollers pulled by teams of bullocks, then burning and ploughing the land), but after rain, the tough old mallee roots regenerated and flourished. Farmers also had to deal with rabbit and mouse plagues, sand drifts and long droughts. Today the Mallee is a productive sheep-grazing and grain-growing district, with more exotic crops, such as lentils, also appearing.

Lake Hattah Campsite CAMPGROUND $
(www.parks.vic.gov.au; per site $28.70) At the time of research this camp site was closed due to flooding. This can occur from season to season, so check with Parks Victoria. When it's functioning, it has non-flush toilets, fireplaces and picnic tables.

Information

Hattah-Kulkyne National Park Visitor Centre (☎13 19 63; www.parks.vic.gov.au) A cool building with posters, tables and chairs. Ring the ranger to find out if the tracks are passable. It's located 74km southeast of Mildura off Robinvale Rd.

Getting There & Away

The main access road is from Hattah, 70km south of Mildura on the Calder Hwy. There are two nature drives, the Hattah and the Kulkyne, and a network of old camel tracks that are great for cycling, although you'll need thorn-proof tubes. Tell the rangers where you're going, and carry plenty of water, a compass and a map.

Wyperfeld National Park

We'll be frank, Wyperfeld National Park isn't for everyone. The main features of this vast park are river red gum, mallee scrub, dry lake beds and sand plains. While that's a bit desolate for some, there are nevertheless some attractive aspects. The park is covered with a carpet of native wildflowers in spring, and it's a birdwatchers's paradise, with more than 200 species of bird. The park also has a network of walking and cycling tracks.

A sealed road from the southern park entrance near Yaapeet leads to the visitor centre at Wonga Campground, which has pit toilets, picnic tables and fireplaces. Casuarina Campground, in the north, is reached via a gravel road off the Patchewollock–Baring Rd. Take all your supplies (and delights) with you, including water.

Wyperfeld can be accessed via the Western Hwy at Dimboola (for southern sections of the park), via the Sunraysia Hwy at Speed, via the Henty Hwy at Hopetoun or via the Mallee Hwy at Underbool.

Up the Hume

The multi-lane Hume Fwy (M31) neatly bypasses every town on its way north from Melbourne to the Victorian–NSW border. This used to be a track leading to Sydney, with bullock wagons piled with wheat waiting for those ahead to make the next river crossing. Even 45 years ago, heading north was a jostle of sedans, caravans and trucks on a narrow, potholed road. The towns along, or just off, the Hume Fwy are generally genuine little country towns whose distinguishing features are their colonial-style pubs and local bakeries .

Seymour

The rural town of Seymour is best known for industry and agriculture, and has an informative **visitor information centre** (☎03-5799 0233; 47 Emily St; ⏰9am-5pm).

For those interested in all things rail, **Seymour Railway Heritage Centre** (www.srhc.org.au; Victoria St) has a fantastic collection of heritage Victoria Railway locomotives and carriages, and offers occasional rail tours.

Sixteen kilometres northeast of Seymour, **Fowles Wine Cellar Door Café** (☎03-5796 2150; www.fowleswine.com; cnr Hume Fwy & Lambing Gully Rd, Avenel; mains $15-29; ⏲9am-5pm; P 👪) serves up some full and fresh wines, and is worth the stop for its decent cafe, with views to the Strathbogie Ranges.

Benalla

Benalla is a very pretty town just off the Hume Fwy. An hour or so will suffice to take in its sights.

Benalla Visitor Centre (☎03-5762 1749; www.enjoybenalla.com.au; Mair St; ⏲9am-5pm), by the lake, shares a home with the **Costume & Kelly Museum** (☎03-5762 1749; www.enjoybenalla.com.au; Mair St; adult/child $5/$1; ⏲9am-4pm), which has interesting costume exhibits, a display on local war hero Sir Edward 'Weary' Dunlop and Ned Kelly's sash. **Benalla Art Gallery** (☎03-5760 2619; www.benallaartgallery.com; Bridge St; ⏲10am-5pm Mon-Wed) FREE has a collection of Australian art, including paintings from the Heidelberg School, and a cafe that spreads onto a deck overlooking the lake. Nearby is the moving Weary Dunlop Memorial. A recent community initiative has created some fabulous street art on many of the local buildings, resulting in the annual **Wall to Wall Street Art Festival** (www.benallastreetart.com.au).

The **Winton Wetlands** (⏲24hr), 23km northeast of Benalla, is the largest wetlands restoration project in the Southern Hemisphere.

Benalla is conveniently located west of the Hume Fwy, 212km north of Melbourne. It is serviced by V/Line trains ($26, 2½ hours). On some services you must change at Seymour.

Glenrowan

Ned Kelly's legendary bushranging exploits came to their bloody end in Glenrowan in 1880. The story of Kelly and his gang has become an industry in this one-street town; you can't drive through Glenrowan without being confronted by the legend and the accompanying memorabilia, including a 2m armour-clad statue. The main sites of his capture are signposted, so pick up a walking map and follow the trail.

Ned Kelly's Last Stand (☎03-5766 2367; www.glenrowantouristcentre.com.au; 41 Gladstone St; adult/child/family $28/20/92; ⏲10am-4pm, shows every 30min) is an animated theatre where Kelly's story is told by a cast of animatronic characters, and culminates in a smoky shoot-out and Kelly's hanging (it may be too scary for young children). It's at the Glenrowan Tourist Centre.

Kate's Cottage (☎03-5766 2448; www.katescottageglenrowan.com.au; 35 Gladstone St; adult/child $6/1; ⏲9am-5.30pm) is a museum of sorts, with Kelly-related memorabilia and artefacts gathered from all over the district, plus a replica of the Kelly home.

Wangaratta

POP 18,400

Wangaratta (or 'Wang' to the locals) is a busy but attractive commercial centre situated along the Hume Fwy. It's the turn-off for the ski fields along the Great Alpine Rd and for the Rutherglen wine region. The name means 'resting place of the cormorants'.

The town sits neatly at the junction of the Ovens and King Rivers. The first buildings, in the 1840s, were based around a punt service that operated until 1855. What you see today is a modern provincial town with only faint echoes of that past. A recent river refurbishment has revived the waterfront with the town's best eateries and a pretty view of the river.

Sights & Activities

Wangaratta Cemetery CEMETERY

(Mason St; ⏲24hr) South of town lies the grave of Dan 'Mad Dog' Morgan, a notorious bushranger. It contains most of Morgan's remains – after he was fatally shot at nearby Peechelba Station in April 1865, his head was taken to Melbourne for a study of the criminal mind (his scrotum was supposedly fashioned into a tobacco pouch).

Pick up the brochure entitled *Wangaratta Cemetery – Self-Guided Tour* from the visitor centre.

Bullawah Cultural Trail WALKING

(www.culturewangaratta.com; ⏲24hr) This cultural trail provides a creative insight into the local Indigenous Australians, the Pangerang (Bangerang). Around 15 stations, each with indigenous sculptures and symbols, along with explanatory panels, line the 2km or so route along the Ovens River. The route crosses two suspension bridges; the trails' name comes from 'bulla', meaning 'two' and 'wah' meaning 'water', to represent the crossings.

Murray to the Mountains Rail Trail CYCLING

(www.murraytomountains.com.au) Wangaratta is the start of the Murray to Mountains

THE KELLY GANG

Bushranger and outlaw he may have been, but Ned Kelly is probably Australia's best-known folk hero. His life and death have been embraced as part of the national culture – from Sir Sidney Nolan's famous paintings to Peter Carey's Man Booker Prize–winning novel *True History of the Kelly Gang*. Ned himself has become a symbol of the Australian rebel character.

Born in 1855, Ned was first arrested in Benalla when he was 14 and spent the next 10 years in and out of jail. In 1877 he was once more being escorted to the Benalla court when he escaped and hid in a saddle-and-bootmaker's shop on Arundel St. It was here he told police trooper Thomas Lonigan that if ever he shot a man, it would be Lonigan – which he duly did a year later.

In 1878 a warrant was issued for his arrest for stealing horses, so he and his brother Dan went into hiding. Their mother and two friends were arrested, sentenced and imprisoned for aiding and abetting. The Kelly family had long felt persecuted by the authorities, and the jailing of Mrs Kelly was the last straw.

Ned and Dan were joined in their hideout in the Wombat Ranges, near Mansfield, by Steve Hart and Joe Byrne. Four policemen (Kennedy, Lonigan, Scanlon and McIntyre) came looking for them, and, in a shoot-out at Stringybark Creek, Ned killed Kennedy, Lonigan and Scanlon. McIntyre escaped to Mansfield and raised the alarm.

The government put up a £500 reward for any of the gang members, dead or alive. In December 1878 the gang held up the National Bank at Euroa, and got away with £2000. Then, in February 1879, they took over the police station at Jerilderie, locked the two policemen in the cells, and robbed the Bank of New South Wales wearing the policemen's uniforms. By this time the reward was £2000 a head.

On 27 June 1880, the gang held 60 people captive in a hotel at Glenrowan. A train-load of police and trackers was sent from Melbourne. Ned's plan to destroy the train was foiled when a schoolteacher warned the police. Surrounded, the gang holed up in the hotel and returned fire for hours, wearing heavy armour made from ploughshares. Ned was shot in the legs and captured, and Dan Kelly, Joe Byrne and Steve Hart, along with several of their hostages, were killed.

Ned Kelly was brought to Melbourne and tried, and then hanged on 11 November 1880. He met his end bravely; his last words are famously quoted as, 'Such is life.' His death mask, armour and the gallows on which he died are on display in the **Old Melbourne Gaol** (p60).

Rail Trail, which runs east via Beechworth to Bright and links Wangaratta with Rutherglen and Wahgunyah. Ask at the visitor information centre for information on local bike hire, although most who tackle the trail bring their own.

Festivals & Events

Wangaratta Jazz & Blues MUSIC
(03-5722 8199; http://wangarattajazz.com; late Oct or early Nov) The town's main claim to fame is the almost-world-famous Wangaratta Jazz & Blues Festival, which attracts jazz players and buffs from around Australia and the world over a weekend in late October or early November (it's always the weekend before the Melbourne Cup).

Wangaratta Sports Carnival SPORTS
(late Jan) An athletics meeting featuring the Wangaratta Gift, one of Victoria's more prestigious regional foot races.

Sleeping

Central Wangaratta Motel MOTEL $
(03-5721 2188; www.centralwangarattamotel.com.au; 11-13 Ely St; s $85, d $95-100, f $120) Neat, central, simple, clean and friendly. Plus a great location.

Painters Island Caravan Park CAMPGROUND $
(03-5721 3380; www.paintersislandcaravanpark.com.au; Pinkerton Cres; unpowered/powered sites from $30/34, cabins $95-165;) Set on 20 hectares along the banks of the Ovens River, and yet close to the town centre, this

impressive park has a playground, a camp kitchen and a good range of cabins with ensuite bathrooms.

Quality Hotel Gateway Wangaratta HOTEL $$
(☎03-5721 8399; www.wangarattagateway.com.au; 29-37 Ryley St; d/f from $175/210; ❄ 📶 🏊) On the main road into town, this upmarket hotel has a clean-lined look, excellent facilities (including a gym and a heated outdoor pool) and an attention to detail that elevates it above other options scattered around the town.

Hermitage Motor Inn MOTEL $$
(☎03-5721 7444; www.hermitagemotorinn.com.au; 7 Cusack St; d $140-170, f from $165; ❄ 📶 🏊) Close to the town centre, the Hermitage is one of Wang's better motels, with spacious rooms, contemporary decor and a pool.

Eating & Drinking

The town's cafe scene occupies Murphy St, Faithfull St and Reid St, and there are a couple of good restaurants in town. The most pleasant place to eat is along the riverfront.

★Cafe the Prevue CAFE $$
(☎03-5721 2092; www.cafetheprevue.com.au; 66-68 Faithfull St; mains $14-20; ⏲8am-4pm) This fabulous spot, whose large windows and terrace afford views over the Ovens River, is *the* spot to visit. Local friends, businesspeople and families flock here for the fabulous all-day breakfasts, from 'goat's toast' to house-made granola mix, plus great lunches. It's bright, light and contemporary, and serves Wang's best coffee.

Cafe Dérailleur CAFE $$
(☎03-5722 9589; www.cafederailleur.com.au; 38 Norton St; mains $14.50-19.50; ⏲7am-3.30pm Mon-Fri, to 2.30pm Sat, 8am-2.30pm Sun) So named because it was originally built to service the train line before the age of the dining car, this small corner cafe opposite the train station is off the rails in every sense. It's a hipster throwback to the 1950s and '60s, with laminate tables and lots of retro metal table legs, tea cosies and 'nana chic'.

Rinaldo's Casa Cucina ITALIAN $$
(☎03-5721 8800; www.rinaldos.com.au; 8-10 Tone Rd; mains $19-33) At the time of research, this popular eatery was moving premises to the waterfront along Faithfull St. Judging from last reports, its Northern Italian kitchen and seasonal menu will be worth checking out.

Vine Hotel PUB FOOD $$
(☎03-5721 2605; www.thevinehotel.net.au; 27 Detour Rd; mains $15-30; ⏲11am-10pm) Ned Kelly and his gang once hung out at this atmospheric pub; these days you're less likely to get shot and the food is better. Wednesday is schnitzel night ($14), while Thursday is steak night ($17). Head underground to the small 'museum' in the very dusty underground cellars. The Vine is about 3km north of town, on the road to Eldorado.

Buffalo Brewery BREWERY
(☎03-5726 9215; www.facebook.com/BoorhamanPubBuffaloBrewery; 1519 Boorhaman Rd, Boorhaman; ⏲noon-8pm Sun-Thu, to midnight Fri & Sat) At the Boorhaman Hotel, about 15km northwest of Wangaratta, this country pub-brewery produces five award-winning beers, including a wheat beer and a dark ale.

Information

Wangaratta Visitor Information Centre
(☎1800 801 065, 03-5721 5711; www.visitwangaratta.com.au; 100 Murphy St; ⏲9am-5pm) has displays, internet access, and videos depicting local rail trails and snippets from the annual Wangaratta Jazz Festival. Ned Kelly devotees can pick up the useful *Ned Kelly: Touring Route* brochure outlining various Kelly sites in the area.

Getting There & Away

Wangaratta lies 252km northeast of Melbourne along the Hume Fwy (M31).

V/Line (p373) train and coach services operate at least five times daily between Wangaratta and Melbourne's Southern Cross station ($27, 1½ to three hours).

Goulburn Valley

One of Victoria's major inland rivers, the Goulburn is an important irrigation source that makes intensive agriculture possible. Once a complex of rivers, creeks and billabongs, it has been tamed by dams, levees and channels, although you can still find many pockets of riverine ecology.

The Goulburn Valley is Victoria's 'food bowl', an important centre for fruit, dairy, food processing and some of Australia's oldest and best wineries. To get here, leave the Hume Fwy after Seymour and head north on its little-sibling road, the Goulburn Valley Hwy.

Shepparton

POP 49,000

Laid-back 'Shepp' is the capital of the Goulburn Valley, where the Goulburn and Broken Rivers meet. Drive through here on a rainy Monday afternoon and you're unlikely to be tempted to stop. But Victoria Park Lake is pleasant for a picnic and a stroll, and the small **Shepparton Art Museum** (SAM; 03-5832 9861; www.sheppartonartmuseum.com.au; 70 Welsford St; 10am-4pm) FREE has one of the best collection of ceramics in Australia as well as some excellent exhibitions.

As the heart of a rich farming and fruit-growing region (the giant SPC cannery is here), it's popular with travellers looking for fruit-picking work.

Fryers Street Food Store (03-5822 4660; http://thetellercollective.squarespace.com/fryersstreet-food-store; 53 Fryers St; mains $7-18; 7am-6pm Mon-Wed, to 9pm Thu & Fri, 8am-9pm Sat, to 5pm Sun) is a casual provedore-cum-cafe that's convenient for breakfast and lunch, plus reasonable coffee. Otherwise stop by **Collective** (03-5822 4660; www.thetellercollective.com; 53-55 Fryers St; mains $26-38; noon-3pm Wed-Sat; 6-9.30pm Tue-Sat), Shepparton's trendier eatery.

Shepparton is on the **V/Line** (1800 800 007; www.vline.com.au) train and coach route and has good links north to Wodonga, south to Melbourne and west to Echuca.

Nagambie

POP 1550

In the Goulburn Valley just west of the Hume Fwy, Nagambie inhabits the shores of pretty Lake Nagambie. It's a popular centre for water sports and skydiving. The surrounding area is known for its horse studs. Superstar horse Black Caviar was born here, and a life-sized bronze statue pays homage to him at Jacobson's Lookout on Lake Nagambie.

Activities

★Tahbilk Winery WINE

(03-5794 2555; www.tahbilk.com.au; 254 O'Neils Rd, Tahbilk; 9am-5pm Mon-Fri, 10am-5pm Sat & Sun) Just south of town, off THE Goulburn Valley Hwy, Tahbilk Winery is one of Victoria's best-known wineries. This fifth-generation, family-owned property features the oldest root stock grapes in Australia (1860). Pop down to the original cellars and wander through various parts of the property, set within beautiful bushland, before sitting on the deck of the Tahbilk Café (p332) that overlooks the Goulburn River.

Tahbilk features a wetlands and wildlife reserve, with 4km of track through a natural area that's rich in bird life.

Mitchelton Wines WINE

(03-5736 2222; www.mitchelton.com.au; 470 Mitchellstown Rd; 10am-5pm) Mitchelton Wines is set in a lovely location on the Goulburn River, 13km southwest of Nagambie. Its contemporary buildings and distinctive airport-style tower make for an interesting visit. Free cellar-door tastings are daily between 10am and 5pm. Its smart restaurant serves contemporary Australian fare with flair (mains $24 to $42; lunch from Thursday to Sunday).

Skydive Nagambie SKYDIVING

(1800 266 500, 03-5794 1466; www.skydive-nagambie.com; 12 Olivers Rd, Bailiestone; tandem dives per person $299-399) Offers tandem dives and a variety of other packages, including intensive nine-day courses.

Eating

★Tahbilk Café CAFE $$

(254 O'Neils Rd, Tahbilk; mains $18-36; 11am-4pm Thu-Mon) With a passionate chef at its helm, Tahbilk Café uses seasonal, organic and biodynamic produce from local suppliers to whip up the likes of 14-hour slow-roast lamb shoulder and house-cured and chargrilled silverside. A seat on the deck overlooking the Goulburn River, with eucalyptus trees and the wetlands beyond, equals Victoria-style heaven.

Information

Staff at the **Nagambie Lakes visitor information centre** (03-5794 1471; www.nagambie-lakestourism.com.au; 317 High St; 10am-4pm) are passionate about the lake, the town and the region.

Getting There & Away

Nagambie is served by **V/Line** (1800 800 007; www.vline.com.au) train services. These link south to Melbourne ($16, two hours, four daily), and to all main points north to Wodonga and west to Echuca (with a change in Shepparton or Murchison; $11.20; two to 2½ hours, three daily).

Understand Melbourne & Victoria

Melbourne & Victoria Today

Melbourne may be a great place to live (and to visit), but maintaining its place as one of the front runners in world and national liveability involves confronting major issues of rising costs, urban planning, social inequality, lack of affordable housing, increases in crime, and environmental sustainability. But Victoria is about more than just Melbourne, and regional Victorians have a different take on how those important questions should be answered in the future.

Best on Film

The Castle (1997) Cult-comedy classic set in a working-class Melbourne suburb.
Romulus, My Father (2007) Moving father-and-son story set in central Victoria; based on the memoir by Raimond Gaita.
Picnic at Hanging Rock (1975) Sensual, haunting film based on the classic novel by Joan Lindsay.
Dogs in Space (1986) Chaotic chronicle of the city's punk past.
Animal Kingdom (2010) Menacing, moody crime-family thriller.
Red Hill (2010) Western/cop-thriller genre mash-up, set in breathtaking East Gippsland.

Best in Print

True History of the Kelly Gang (Peter Carey; 2000) Man Booker Prize–winningl novel on the notorious bushranger.
The Slap (Christos Tsiolkas; 2008) An incident at a backyard BBQ in suburban Melbourne divides a group of friends.
Monkey Grip (Helen Garner; 1982) Drugs, relationships, music and share houses in inner-city Fitzroy.
The Ballroom: The Melbourne Punk & Post-Punk Scene (Dolores San Miguel; 2011) Memoir of St Kilda's late-'70s punk scene at the infamous Crystal Ballroom.

The Most Liveable City?

Melbourne consistently ranks as one of the world's most liveable cities. In 2016, Melbourne basked in the title of the World's Most Liveable City for the sixth year in a row, according to the prestigious *Economist* Intelligence Unit. What makes Melbourne so good?

Melbourne always ranks highly for infrastructure and safety, and although the state hasn't been immune to the global financial crisis, Victoria has consistently recorded growth rates that are the envy of the industrialised world.

The city does have some chinks in its armour. Melbourne weather can be glorious, but it can also be wet, windy and changeable at a moment's notice. The current Labor government is facing tough challenges around the increase in crime and drug problems, which threaten the high-safety ranking, while the ever-increasing number of homeless people are left wondering just how this 'most liveable city' claim can really be true. Then there's the spiralling cost of living. Salaries have largely kept pace, but everything from restaurant meals to hotel rooms have soared in recent years, while home ownership has become an unattainable dream for many. To see what we mean, stop by a real-estate auction and watch the prices skyrocket out of control.

Urban & Regional Sprawl

Urban planning stands at the centre of public debate in Melbourne, not least because Melbourne's population is expected to almost double to 10 million by 2050. All around its outer limits, new suburbs appear, often before transport infrastructure and other essential services are in place. With inner Melbourne already out of reach for many home buyers and renters, these questions grow in importance every year.

In the city's heart, it's no less complicated. A decade ago, the shift to higher-density living saw the rise of the Docklands precinct and inner-city apartment complexes. Success, however, has been partial at best. A lack of after-hours life and a failure to develop the necessary services for those who remain in the centre after the sun sets continue to plague area development.

Due to the rising real-estate costs, many Melburnians are choosing to leave the city altogether for a sea change to coastal areas or a tree change to commutable regional towns such as Geelong, Ballarat and Castlemaine, where they can get more value for money and a change in lifestyle while still being able to work in Melbourne. This also brings its own set of issues and demands on infrastructure and services.

The sprawl is not only evident in Melbourne and its suburbs. Drive through popular country and coastal towns and you'll see new estates being developed across the state. Once-sleepy coastal towns such as Point Lonsdale, or country towns such as Bright, are ever-expanding, with brand-new estates pushing the town boundaries out further.

City-Rural Divide

Country Victoria is so much more than a venue for a food lover's passions or a tree changer's escape. It's also a pillar of the state's economy and the place where many of the state's most pressing environmental issues are being confronted.

Victoria is Australia's most cleared state, with the highest number of threatened species. This includes the state fauna emblem, the Leadbeater's possum, which is critically endangered due to the devastation of the Black Saturday bushfires in 2009 and the impact of logging. A proposal to convert a state park into a national park called the Great Forest National Park, on the fringe of Melbourne, has been in discussion for several years. The current Andrews government seems to be distancing itself from the proposal over warnings and concerns about the impact on the forestry industry and potential job losses, while predominantly city-based environmentalists claim it could be a step toward turning the region into an ecotourism centre and work to protect the threatened species. Then there are the water-shortage issues affecting farmers throughout the state.

In country Victoria, these issues are very often seen primarily in terms of farmers' rights and important sources of employment for vulnerable communities. In the cities, they're environmental issues of wider global significance.

POPULATION: **6.07 MILLION**

AREA OF VICTORIA: **227,416 SQ KM**

AREA OF GREATER MELBOURNE: **9990 SQ KM**

PERCENTAGE OF POPULATION BORN OVERSEAS: **36.7%**

if Australia were 100 people

79 would speak English at home
3 would speak Chinese at home
2 would speak Italian at home
1 would speak Vietnamese at home
1 would speak Greek at home
14 would speak another language at home

belief systems

(% of population)

2 Muslim
1 Hindu
12 Other

population per sq km

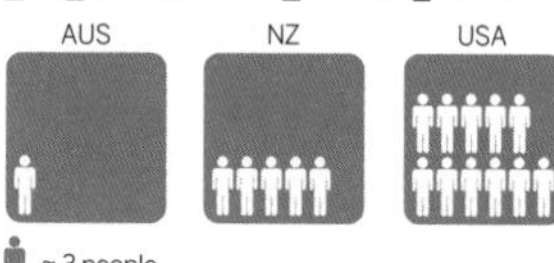

≈ 3 people

History

Victoria's history is one of Australia's more picaresque tales. It begins with geological upheaval and flourishing Indigenous cultures, but the unravelling of the latter that followed the European discovery of Australia in 1770 is a story of profound tragedy. The fraught and stop-start settlement of the state finally took hold with the discovery of gold in the mid-19th century – a find that thrust Victoria into the modern era, laying the foundations for the state's democracy, prosperity and multicultural make-up.

Estimates suggest that before Europeans arrived, Victoria's Aboriginal population was between 60,000 and 100,000. By the late 1840s it had dropped to 15,000, due to a combination of widespread killings by white colonisers and introduced disease and alcohol; by 1860 scarcely 2000 Aboriginal people survived.

Creation Stories

A mere 120 million years ago, Australia broke away from the vast supercontinent known as Gondwana, followed 40 million years later by another epic geological event – the separation of Australia from Antarctica. In prehistoric times, far lower sea levels exposed a land bridge between what is now Tasmania and Victoria. It was not until 10,000 years ago, with the rising sea levels that accompanied the end of the last ice age, that Victoria took on its current form as the southernmost extent of the Australian mainland.

Victoria's human history begins somewhat later: the earliest records of Australia's Indigenous people inhabiting the land date back around 52,000 years. At the time they hunted the giant marsupials that then roamed Victoria and Australia, among them a species of wombat the size of a rhinoceros and possibly even a giant, metre-long platypus.

The oral history of Indigenous Australians has its own version of Victoria's prehistory. For the Wurundjeri people, who lived in the catchment of the Yarra River where Melbourne is today, the land and the people were created in the Dreaming by the spirit Bunjil – 'the great one, old head-man, eagle hawk' – who continues to watch over all from Tharangalk-bek, the home of the spirits in the sky.

Indigenous Victoria

Victoria's Indigenous peoples lived in 38 different dialect groups that spoke 10 separate languages. These groups, some matrilineal, others patrilineal, were further divided into clans and sub-clans, each with its

TIMELINE

80 million years ago

The Australian continent breaks away from Antarctica to form its own land mass.

50,000 BC

The first humans colonise southeastern Australia. The people of the Kulin Nation live in the catchment of the Yarra River, and various other tribes, speaking 38 dialects among them, are spread throughout Victoria.

1770

Lieutenant Zachary Hicks becomes the first European to lay eyes on the eastern Australian shoreline. Captain Cook will later name the spot in far-east Gippsland 'Point Hicks'.

own complex system of customs and laws, and each claiming custodianship of a distinct area of land. Despite this, the British considered the continent to be *terra nullius* – 'a land belonging to no one'.

The Wurundjeri were a tribe of the Woiwurrung, one of five distinct language groups belonging to southern Victoria's Kulin Nation. They often traded and celebrated with their coastal counterparts, the Boonwurrung, among the towering red gums, tea trees and ferns at the river's edge, as well as with other Kulin clans from the north and west.

As the flood-prone rivers and creeks broke their banks in winter, bark shelters were built north in the ranges. Possums were hunted for their meat and skinned to make calf-length cloaks. During summer, camps were made along the Yarra and Maribyrnong Rivers and Merri Creek. Food – game, grubs, seafood, native greens and roots – was plentiful. Wurundjeri men and women were compelled to marry out of the tribe, requiring complex forms of diplomacy. Ceremonies and bouts of ritual combat were frequent.

Indigenous Victoria

- *Koorie Heritage Trust (Melbourne)*
- *Bunjilaka Aboriginal Cultural Centre (Melbourne Museum)*
- *Birrarung Marr (Melbourne)*
- *Brambuk Cultural Centre (Halls Gap)*
- *Harry Nanya Tours (Mildura)*
- *Tower Hill Natural History Centre (Warrnambool)*
- *Krowathunkoolong Keeping Place (Bairnsdale)*
- *Cape Conran Coastal Park*
- *Bullawah Cultural Trail (Wangaratta)*

Colonial Arrivals

Close to sunrise on 19 April 1770, Lieutenant Zachary Hicks, on watch duty on board the *Endeavour*, spied a series of low sand hills. He immediately called his commander, James Cook. Although they didn't know at the time whether it was an island or part of the mainland, it would later prove to be the first European sighting of Australia's east coast (although Dutch seamen had been intermittently exploring the west coast for more than a century). Point Cook is now part of Croajingolong National Park, between Cape Conran Coastal Park and Mallacoota. In 1788 the first colony was established at Sydney Cove in New South Wales.

The first European settlement in Victoria in 1803 didn't have an auspicious start. With a missed mail-ship communiqué and a notoriously supercilious British government calling the shots, Surveyor-General Charles Grimes' recommendation – that the best place to found a southern settlement would be by the banks of the 'Freshwater River' (aka the Yarra) – went unheeded. The alternative, Sorrento, on what is now the Mornington Peninsula, was an unmitigated disaster from the beginning – as Lieutenant David Collins pointed out to his superiors, you can't survive long without drinkable water. The colony moved to Van Diemen's Land (Tasmania), but one extremely tenacious convict escapee, William Buckley, was left behind; he was still on the lam when John Batman turned up a few decades later.

After the failed Sorrento colony, it was 20-odd years before explorers made their way overland to Port Phillip, and another decade before a settlement was founded on the southwest coast at Portland. Around the same time, in the early 1830s, the Surveyor-General of NSW, Major

1803

Victoria's first European settlement is at Sorrento. It is an unmitigated disaster, with no fresh water to be found; the settlers abandon the site after six months and relocate to Van Diemen's Land (Tasmania).

1834

Portland pioneer Edward Henty, his family and a flock of sheep arrive from Van Diemen's Land, marking the first permanent European settlement in the region that will become Victoria.

1835

John Batman meets with a group of local Aboriginal people and trades a casket of blankets, mirrors, scissors, handkerchiefs and other assorted curios for around 2400 sq km of land.

1837

The military surveyor Robert Hoddle draws up plans for the city of Melbourne, laying out a geometric grid of broad streets in a rectangular pattern on the northern side of the Yarra River.

Thomas Mitchell, crossed the Murray River (then called the Hume) near Swan Hill and travelled southwest. He was delighted to find the rich volcanic plains of the Western District. His glowing reports of such fertile country included him dubbing the area 'Australia Felix' (fortunate Australia) and encouraged pastoralists to venture into the area with large flocks of sheep and herds of cattle.

It was not until 1835, when Australian-born entrepreneur John Batman sailed from Van Diemen's Land to arrive in what we now know as Victoria, that the process of settling the area began in earnest. He would later write of travelling through 'beautiful land...rather sandy, but the sand black and rich, covered with kangaroo grass about ten inches high and as green as a field of wheat'. He noted stone dams for catching fish built across creeks, trees that bore the deep scars of bark harvesting and women bearing wooden water containers and woven bags holding stone tools. However, the Indigenous people's profound spiritual relationship with the land and intimate knowledge of story, ceremony and season would be irrevocably damaged within a few short years.

As European settlement fanned out through Victoria, and the city of Melbourne transformed from pastoral outpost to a heaving, gold-flushed metropolis in scarcely 30 years, the cumulative effects of dispossession, alcohol and increasing acts of organised violence and numerous massacres resulted in a shocking decline in Victoria's Indigenous population. From the earliest days the colonial authorities evicted Aboriginal people from their traditional homes. By the early 1860s the Board for the Protection of Aborigines had begun to gather together surviving Aboriginal people in reserves run by Christian missionaries at Ebenezer, Framlingham, Lake Condah, Lake Tyers, Ramahyuck and Coranderrk. These reserves developed into self-sufficient farming communities and gave their residents a measure of 'independence' (along with twice-daily prayers and new boots at Christmas), but at the same time inflicted irreversible damage.

By 1840, when the young Queen Victoria took the throne, Melbourne had 10,000 (occasionally upstanding) citizens and was looking decidedly like a city.

The Birth of Melbourne

'Modern' Melbourne's story begins in the 1830s. John Batman, an ambitious grazier from Van Diemen's Land, sailed into Port Phillip Bay in mid-1835 with an illegal contract of sale. (Britain's colonial claims of *terra nullius* relied on the fiction that the original inhabitants did not own the land on which they lived and hence could not sell it.) He sought out some tribal elders and on a tributary of the Yarra – it's been speculated that it was Merri Creek, in today's Northcote – found some 'fine-looking' men, with whom he exchanged blankets, scissors, mirrors and handkerchiefs for more than 2400 sq km of land surrounding Port Phillip.

1841

One of the largest of many organised massacres of the Indigenous population occurs at Warrigal Creek, Gippsland, as part of the colonisers' push to expand white territory.

1851

Victoria separates from the colony of New South Wales. Gold is discovered in central Victoria and the world's richest gold rush is on.

1854

Gold miners rebel over unfair licences, raising the Southern Cross flag at the Eureka Stockade. Brutally suppressed by soldiers and police, their actions enter into Australia's nation-building mythology.

1858

The Melbourne Football Club is formed. Australian Rules Football's first recorded match takes place between Scotch College and Melbourne Grammar School.

Despite the fact that the Aboriginal people from Sydney who were accompanying Batman couldn't speak a word of the local language and vice versa, Batman brokered the deal and signatures were gathered from the 'local chiefs' (all suspiciously called Jika-Jika and with remarkably similar penmanship). He noted a low, rocky falls several miles up the Yarra, where the Queens Bridge is today. Upstream fresh water made it a perfect place for, as Batman described it, 'a village'. Batman then returned to Van Diemen's Land to ramp up the Port Phillip Association.

It's at this point that the historical narrative becomes as turbid as the Yarra itself. Before Batman could get back to his new settlement of Bearbrass (along with 'Yarra', another cocksure misappropriation of the local dialect), John Pascoe Fawkner, a Launceston publican and childhood veteran of the failed Sorrento colony, got wind of the spectacular opportunity at hand. He promptly sent off a small contingent of settlers aboard the schooner *Enterprize*, who, upon arrival, started building huts and establishing a garden. On Batman's return there were words, and later furious bidding wars over allotments of land. Historians regard the two in various ways, but Fawkner's foremost place in Victoria's story was sealed by the fact he outlived the syphilitic Batman by several decades. Despite the bickering, hubris and greed of the founders, the settlement grew quickly – around a year later, almost 200 brave souls (and some tens of thousands of sheep) had thrown their lot in with the new colony.

Various kings, queens and assorted contemporary bigwigs (including Governor Bourke himself) got the nod in the naming of Melbourne's streets. More recent honoraries have extended to laneways for musicians: AC/DC, Chrissie Amphlett and Rowland S Howard.

New South Wales wasn't happy. Governor Bourke dispatched Captain William Lonsdale south in 1836, quashing any notion of ownership by the Port Phillip Association. Surveyors were sent for and the task of drawing up plans for a city began. Robert Hoddle, the surveyor in charge, arrived with the governor in March 1837, and was horrified by the lack of order, both of his unruly staff – who had absconded upriver to get drunk or shoot kangaroos one too many times – and the antipodean topography itself. For Hoddle it was all about straight lines, and his grid, demarcated by the Yarra and what was once a 'hillock' where Southern Cross Station now lies, is Melbourne's defining feature. Land sales commenced almost immediately, and so the surveying continued, but with little romantic notion of exploration or discovery. It was, by all accounts, a real-estate feeding frenzy. The British were well served by their *terra nullius* concept, as returns on investment were fabulous. The rouseabout 'Bearbrass' was upgraded to the rather more distinguished 'Melbourne', after the serving British prime minister.

During these years, the earliest provincial towns were also established along Victoria's coast, around the original settlement of Portland to the southwest and Port Albert to the southeast. Early inland towns rose up around self-sufficient communities of sheep stations, which at this stage

1859

Thomas Austin releases rabbits onto his property at Winchelsea, west of Melbourne, beginning a rabbit infestation that will spread across the southern part of Australia and continue to this day.

1880

The International Exhibition is held at the Royal Exhibition Building in Melbourne's Carlton Gardens. Over a million visitors come to see the fruits of the Empire.

1883–85

The railway line linking Sydney and Melbourne opens in 1883, followed two years later by Melbourne's first cable-tram service, running from the city centre to Richmond.

1884

HV McKay's invention of the Sunshine stripper harvester in Ballarat makes leaps and bounds in the efficient harvest of cereal crops, putting Australia on the map as a leading exporter of grain.

were still the main source of Victoria's fast-increasing fortunes. That, however, was soon to change.

Golden Years

In 1840 a local landowner described the fledgling city of Melbourne as 'a goldfield without the gold'. Indeed, with a steady stream of immigrants and confidence-building prosperity, there had been growing calls for separation from convict-ridden, rowdy New South Wales. By the end of 1850, the newly minted colony of Victoria had got its wish to go it alone. This quickly seemed like a cruel stroke of fate as gold was discovered near Bathurst in NSW in early 1851, sparking a mass exodus. Pastoral riches or not, there was every chance that without a viable labour force (many had already succumbed to the siren call of California) the colony would wither and die.

Melbourne jewellers had for some time been doing a clandestine trade with shepherds who came to town with small gold nuggets secreted in their kerchiefs. Wary of the consequences of a gold rush on civic order, but with few other options, the city's leading men declared that gold must indeed be found. As was the Victorian way, a committee was formed and a reward was offered. Slim pickings were discovered in the Pyrenees and Warrandyte, before a cluey Californian veteran looked north to Clunes. Just over a ridge, in what was to become Ballarat, was the proverbial pot at the end of the rainbow. It wasn't long before miners were hauling 27kg of the magic mineral into Geelong at a time, and the rush was well and truly on.

The news spread around the world and brought hopefuls from Britain, Ireland, China, Germany, Italy, the US and the Caribbean. By August 1852, 15,000 new arrivals were disembarking in Melbourne each month. Crews jumped ship and hotfooted it to the diggings, stranding ships at anchor. Chaos reigned. Everyone needed a place to stay, even if only for a night or two, and when there was no room at the inn, stables were let for exorbitant amounts. Wives and children were often dumped in town while husbands continued on to the diggings. Governor La Trobe despaired of his grand civic vision, as shanties and eventually a complete tent village sprung up. Canvas Town, on the south side of the Yarra, housed over 8000 people.

Chinese migrants founded Melbourne's Chinatown in Little Bourke St in 1851, making it the longest continuous Chinese settlement in any Western country.

Catherine Spence, a journalist and social reformer, visited Melbourne at the height of the hysteria and primly observed that 'this convulsion has unfixed everything. Religion is neglected, education despised…everyone is engrossed with the simple object of making money in a very short time.' The 567,000kg of gold found between 1851 and 1860 represented a third of the world's total. That said, relatively few diggers struck it lucky. The licensing system favoured large holdings, policing was harsh and

1901

Australia's collection of colonies become a nation. The Federation's first parliament is held at the Royal Exhibition Building; parliament will sit in Melbourne for the next 27 years.

1923

Vegemite, a savoury sandwich spread and Australia's most enduring culinary quirk, is invented in Melbourne, using autolysis to break down yeast cells from waste provided by Carlton & United Breweries.

1925

The first Australian-built Ford Model Ts roll off an improvised production line in a disused wool store in Geelong.

1928

Australia's first set of traffic lights begin operation at the junction of Collins and Swanston Sts in Melbourne.

scratching out a living proved so difficult for many that dissent became as common as hope had been a few years before.

For some, 1852 was indeed a golden year, but by 1854, simmering tensions had exploded in Ballarat.

Growing Inequalities

As the easily won gold began to run out, Victorian diggers despaired of ever striking it rich, and the inequality between themselves and the privileged few who held the land that they worked stoked a fire of dissent.

Men joined together in teams and worked cold, wet, deep shafts. Every miner, whether or not gold was found, had to pay a licence fee of 30 shillings a month. This was collected by policemen who had the power to chain those who couldn't pay to a tree, often leaving them there until their case was heard.

In September 1854, Governor Hotham ordered that the hated licence hunts be carried out twice a week. A month later a miner was murdered near the Ballarat Hotel after an argument with the owner, James Bentley. When Bentley was found not guilty by a magistrate (who happened to be his business associate), miners rioted and burned the hotel down. Though Bentley was retried and found guilty, the rioting miners were also jailed, which enraged the miners.

Gold Rush Sights

Sovereign Hill (Ballarat)

Victoria Hills Historic Mining Site (Bendigo)

Clunes

Walhalla

Maldon

Beechworth

NED KELLY

Victorian bushranger Ned Kelly (1854–80) became a national legend when he and his gang donned homemade armour in an attempt to deflect the bullets of several dozen members of the constabulary. Kelly's story, set among the hills, valleys and plains of northeastern Victoria, has a Robin Hood–like quality, as well as the whiff of an Irish rebel song.

Kelly's passionate, articulate letters, handed to hostages while he was robbing banks, paint a vivid picture of what he believed to be a harsh injustice of his time, as well as his lyrical intelligence. These, as well as his ability to evade capture for so long, led to public outrage when he was sentenced to death and finally hanged at the Old Melbourne Gaol in 1880.

The enduring popularity of the Kelly legend is evident in the mass of historical and fictional accounts that continue to be written to this day. His life has also inspired a long string of films, from the world's first feature film, *The Story of the Kelly Gang* (1906), to two more recent versions, both simply called *Ned Kelly,* with the first starring Mick Jagger (1970) and the second, the late Heath Ledger (2003). A series of paintings by Sidney Nolan featuring Kelly in his armour are among Australia's most recognisable artworks. In 2001 Australian novelist Peter Carey won the Man Booker Prize for his *True History of the Kelly Gang*.

1930

A plucky young chestnut gelding called Phar Lap wins the Melbourne Cup. His winning streak endears him to the nation and he remains one of the most popular exhibits in the Melbourne Museum.

1953

The first Italian Gaggia espresso machine is imported to Melbourne. Soon University Cafe in Carlton, Pellegrini's in the city and Don Camillo in North Melbourne are serving the city's first cappuccinos.

1956

Melbourne hosts the summer Olympic Games. Despite this mark of sporting bonhomie, the event is marked with political unrest due to the Suez crisis and the Soviet invasion of Hungary.

1964

The Beatles visit Melbourne, staying in the since-demolished Southern Cross Hotel on Bourke St and creating city-wide 'youthquake' hysteria.

The Ballarat Reform League was born. They called for the abolition of licence fees and for democratic reform, including the miners' rights to vote (universal suffrage was yet to exist) and greater opportunity to purchase land. This was to lead into the Eureka Stockade (p209).

Boom & Crash

Gold brought undreamed-of riches and a seemingly endless supply of labour to Victoria. Melbourne became 'Marvellous Melbourne', one of the world's most beautiful Victorian-era cities, known for its elegance – as well as its extravagance. Grand expressions of its confidence include the University of Melbourne, Parliament House, the State Library and the Victorian Mint. Magnificent public parks and gardens were planted both in the city and in towns across the state. By the 1880s Melbourne had become Australia's financial, industrial and cultural hub. The 'Paris of the Antipodes' claim was invoked: the city was flush with stylish arcades, and grand homes were decorated with ornate iron balconies. The city spread eastwards and northwards over the surrounding flat grasslands and southwards along Port Phillip Bay. A public transport system of cable trams and railways spread into the growing suburbs.

More than 90% of Australia's $100 million gold haul in the 1850s was found in Victoria.

Regional cities, especially those servicing the goldfields, such as Ballarat, Bendigo and Beechworth, also reaped the rewards of sudden prosperity, leaving a legacy of magnificent Victorian architecture throughout the state. 'Selection Acts' enabled many settlers and frustrated miners to take up small farm lots (selections). Although a seemingly reformist, democratic move, these farms were often too small to forge a real living from and life in the bush proved tough. Grinding poverty and the heavy hand of the law led to some settlers turning to bushranging (rural armed robberies of money or livestock), variously considered a life of crime and/or an act of subversion against British rule, depending on which side of the economic and religious divide you were on.

The Welcome Stranger, discovered in 1869 a few centimetres under the ground in the central Victorian town of Moliagul, was, at 72kg, the largest alluvial gold nugget ever found. At the time of its unearthing there were no scales capable of weighing a nugget of its size.

In 1880 (and again in 1888) Melbourne hosted an International Exhibition, pulling well over a million visitors. The Royal Exhibition Building was constructed for this event; Melbourne's soaring paean to Empire and the industrial revolution is one of the few 19th-century exhibition spaces of its kind still standing.

This flamboyant boast to the world was, however, to be Marvellous Melbourne's swansong. In 1889, after years of unsustainable speculation, the property market collapsed and the decades that followed were marked by severe economic depression.

A Difficult Half-Century

Despite the symbolic honour of becoming the new nation's temporary capital in 1901, Melbourne's fortunes didn't really rally until after WWI,

1967

Prime Minister Harold Holt disappears while swimming at Cheviot Beach near Portsea on the Mornington Peninsula; his body is never recovered.

1970

Melbourne's West Gate Bridge collapses during construction, killing 35 workers. The impact and explosion that follows is heard over 20km away. Melbourne's Tullamarine Airport opens in the same year.

1977

The Centenary Test, commemorating the first cricket Test match between Australia and England, is played at the MCG. Amazingly, Australia triumphs by the same margin as the original: 45 runs.

1982–84

The Victorian Arts Centre, built to the design of Roy Grounds, opens in stages at the site now known as Southbank after a construction period of 11 years.

and by then its 'first city' status had been long lost to Sydney. When WWI broke out, large numbers of young men from throughout Victoria fought in the trenches of Europe and the Middle East, with enormous losses.

There was a renewed spirit of expansion and construction in Victoria in the 1920s, but this came to a grinding halt with another economic disaster, the Great Depression (in 1931 almost a third of breadwinners were unemployed). When war broke out once again in 1939, Melbourne became the heart of the nation's wartime efforts, and later the centre for US operations in the Pacific. It was boom time again, though no time for celebration.

While the state's Victorian heritage did not fare well during the post-war construction boom – when Melbourne hosted the Olympic Games in 1956, hectares of historic buildings were bulldozed with abandon; this continued apace during the new boom days of the 1980s as well – significant parts of the city and many goldfield towns still echo with Victorian ambition and aspiration.

Kelly Gang Haunts

Glenrowan

Warby Range State Park

Beechworth

Old Melbourne Gaol

Melbourne's Multicultural Midcentury

In 1901 one of the first things the newly created Australian government did was to pass legislation with the express wish to protect its security and assert its sense of identity as a member of the British Empire. The so-called White Australia policy restricted the entry of non-Europeans, and was followed a couple of years later by the Commonwealth Naturalisation Act, which excluded all non-Europeans from attaining citizenship, and limited both citizens' and non-citizens' ability to bring even immediate family to Australia. This subsequent piece of legislation was particularly devastating to Victoria's Chinese community, who maintained strong family and business ties with China. Victoria's early history of diversity came to an abrupt end.

Although the state's loyalties and most of its legal and cultural ties to Britain remained firm, the 1920s did herald change, as small Italian and Greek communities settled in both the city and the state's agricultural heartland, part of a renewed spirit of expansion and construction at the

MULTICULTURAL STATE

Victoria's multicultural past continues to diversify. Around 28% of Victorians were born overseas and Melbourne is home to people from close to 200 countries. Together they speak 233 languages and dialects, and adhere to 116 religions. The largest group of foreign-born residents comes from the UK, more than double that of any other country. The other main source countries are New Zealand, China, India, Philippines, Vietnam and Italy.

1988

The Australian Tennis Open moves from Kooyong to the hard-court venues of Melbourne Park. Attendance jumps by 90%, to well over 250,000 spectators.

2002

Federation Sq opens – a year late for the centenary of federation – amid controversy about its final design and cost ($440 million), but to public praise.

2004

Michael Long, a former AFL player of Aboriginal decent, walks from Melbourne to Canberra to speak to the Prime Minister and raise awareness of the plight of Indigenous Australians. His walk is known as The Long Walk.

2006

Melbourne hosts the Commonwealth Games, the largest sporting event ever to be held in the city – in numbers of teams, athletes and events it eclipses the 1956 Olympics.

time. They set about establishing food production companies, cafes, restaurants, fish-and-chip shops, delis and grocers, and the efforts of these small business pioneers were to prove an inspiration for a new generation of migrants in the 1940s and '50s.

During Melbourne's years as the capital, the city's population of just over 500,000 people was the largest in Australia, and in the British Empire it was second in size only to London.

Close to a million non-British immigrants arrived in Australia during the 20 years after WWII – at first Jewish refugees from Eastern and Central Europe then larger numbers from Italy, Greece, the Netherlands, Yugoslavia, Turkey and Lebanon. With the demise of the blatantly racist White Australia policy in early 1973, many migrants from Southeast Asia also settled in Victoria. These postwar migrants also embraced the opportunity to set up small businesses, adding a vibrancy and character to their new neighbourhoods, such as Carlton, Collingwood, Richmond, Brunswick and Footscray. Melbourne's cultural life was transformed by these communities, and diversity gradually became an accepted, and treasured, way of life.

Political & Social Machinations

Victoria's historical reputation as something of a conservative counterpoint to the more radical politics of racy Sydney was born as far back as the 19th century, when the money that flooded the state during the gold-rush years established Victoria as one of the wealthiest places in Australia. Family dynasties grew up and the powerful families that controlled the business and political levers of the state made Melbourne one of the most powerful cities in the country – hence its choice as the nation's temporary capital from 1901. By the middle of the 20th century, Melbourne was a conservative city, the seat of the state's old-money families and still Australia's economic capital. This history is reflected in the fact that conservative political forces – the Liberal Party, usually in coalition with the predominantly rural National Party – held power in Victoria from 1955 to 1982.

But things were changing. During the early 1970s, a burgeoning counterculture's experiments with radical theatre, drugs and rock 'n' roll rang out through the Melbourne suburb of Carlton. By the later years of that decade, Melbourne's reputation as a prim 'establishment' city was further challenged by the emergence of a frantically subversive art, music, film and fashion scene that launched bands like the Birthday Party onto the world stage. During the real-estate boom of the 1980s, a wave of glamorous shops, nightclubs and restaurants made way for Melbourne's emergence as Australia's capital of cool. Changes to the licensing laws in the 1990s saw a huge growth of small bars, cafes and venues – and the birth of the laneway phenomenon.

These changes were reflected in the political arena. The left-centre Labor Party governed for 10 years from 1982, and it was during this

2009
Victoria records its hottest temperatures on record. The Black Saturday bushfires that follow leave 173 people dead, more than 2000 homes destroyed and 4500 sq km burned out.

2010
The conservative Liberal–National Party coalition returns to power in the Victorian state parliament, after 11 years in the political wilderness.

2011
Victoria is devastated by the worst 'flood events' in its recorded history, with the central and northern parts of the state, including the towns of Horsham, Shepparton and Swan Hill, worst hit.

2014
The Labor Party is voted back in after one term for the conservative Liberal–National Party coalition.

period that Victoria's reputation as a seat for progressive politics and as a centre for the arts was born. In 1992, Liberal Party premier Jeff Kennett won a landslide victory in statewide elections. Although from the conservative side of politics, Mr Kennett pursued a quite radical agenda, modernising many government institutions but alienating large sections of the community (particularly when it came to school reforms) in the process. An unexpected victory for the Labor Party in 1999 ushered in a decade of left-of-centre rule – a significant part of its success was its surprisingly good electoral results in regional Victoria. A twist came in December 2010, when a Liberal–National Party coalition came to government. It lasted just one term with the Labor Party being voted back in in 2014 with Daniel Andrews as premier. The next election will be held in 2018.

2015

Bushfires roar through parts of the Great Ocean Road on Christmas morning, destroying more than 100 homes between Wye River and Separation Creek.

2016

Freak weather conditions prompted thunderstorm asthma in Melbourne in November claiming the lives of nine people and sending 8500 people to hospital emergency departments in Melbourne and Geelong.

2016

A new law in Victoria allows Koorie people to protect and control the use of their culture and heritage by nominating for protection particular elements with significant spiritual and cultural connection to knowledge.

2017

The first Australian Women's AFL League launches with a massive audience turning up for the first match and thousands of spectators turned away due to a packed-out venue.

Food & Wine

Victoria's food scene is one of almost limitless choice, with a constant flow of new ideas and tastes. Melbourne has an exuberant culinary culture and a talent for innovation and adaptation – and a constantly evolving scene where new cafes, bars and restaurants open on a weekly basis. Regional Victoria has firmly cemented itself as an epicurean hot spot where local produce is celebrated, and food lovers are making special trips to dine at some of the country's best restaurants.

From Fine Dining to Small Plates

At the top of the city's food chain, fine dining thrives. While many Melbourne chefs experiment widely, mixing and matching techniques and ingredients, you'll rarely find chefs doing fusion for fusion's sake. There's too much respect for providence and context. You'll instead find menus that rove across regions and riff on influences. Modern Australian cuisine is a search to find a nation's own unique food and is hard to define. Some chefs and restaurants, such as Shannon Bennett at Vue de Monde, Ben Shewry at Attica and Fitzroy's Charcoal Lane, incorporate native ingredients, while other chefs incorporate both modern Mediterranean and Asian ideas and flavours to greater or lesser degrees: Andrew McConnell at Fitzroy's Cutler & Co and the city centre's Cumulus Inc manage to create a particularly thoughtful version of this style.

There's a long tradition of posh Italian dining in the city and it's often exemplary, with chefs such as Guy Grossi at Grossi Florentino. Mediterranean is also done with high-end flair and a modern sensibility by chefs such as Frank Camorra at MoVida and George Calombaris at Press Club and Gazi.

Over the past few years the city has been taken over by a growing fleet of Mexican restaurants ranging from upmarket chic to cheap and cheerful, many of them great-tasting and authentic. Mamasita is one of the long-standing originals and is still one of the best. The other dining trend popping up around town is the advent of food from the USA, ranging from Southern-style cooking to diner and deli fare at places such as Belles Hot Chicken in Fitzroy.

Regional Victoria also has several 'destination' restaurants. Some fit the stereotype of hearty country fare while others, such as acclaimed chef Dan Hunter's award-winning Brae at Birregurra (in the Otway Ranges), surprise with sophistication and creativity. Newcomer IGNI in Geelong was awarded Victoria's best regional restaurant in *The Age Good Food Guide* awards for 2017, thanks to chef Aaron Turner's creative flair with foraged local ingredients.

Given that there's always so much to try, city dwellers love to eat out often, rather than saving up restaurants for celebratory nights out. Melbourne really comes into its own for a casual, grazing style of dining. Small and large plates override the rigid three-course chronology, but an informal menu and more modest price tag doesn't mean high-quality produce or attention to detail are sacrificed.

In a similar manner, bar food is no longer seen as a mere consort to booze, but something that makes for an equal marriage of tastes and experiences. This kind of 'smart casual' eating out is an easy way to join the locals, and also a great way to sample widely without the price shock of fine dining. Pub grub is also a big part of Melbourne's eating-out repertoire, and ranges from a number of upmarket gastropub restaurants to basic counter-meal service, with nostalgic dishes such as bangers and mash (sausage and mashed potatoes), steaks, parmas (chicken parmigiana), roasts and curries.

There's no shortage of informal food that's cooked with love and is great value for money. Cafes often serve heartier dishes at lunchtime, and casual venues with wine licences are not uncommon. Look for authentic dishes from a smattering of cuisines from across the globe. A steaming bowl of *pho* (Vietnamese soup), a square of spanakopita (spinach and feta pie), a teriyaki salmon *maki* (hand roll) or a provolone and prosciutto *piadina* (Italian flatbread) will probably leave you change from $10 – and without doubt about Melbourne's status as a great food city.

Top Regional Gourmet Towns

- *Kyneton*
- *Milawa*
- *Red Hill*
- *Beechworth*
- *Mildura*
- *Birregurra*

Dishing Up Diversity

Take 140 cultures, mix and let simmer for a few decades. While the recipe might not be quite that simple, Victoria's culinary habits are truly multicultural. Many Melburnians have grown up with at least one other culinary heritage besides the rather grim Anglo-Australian fare of the mid-20th century – plus they're generally also inveterate travellers, which makes for a city of adventurous, if often highly critical, palates.

'Modern Australian' cooking is a loose term that describes a mix of British, European, Asian and Middle Eastern techniques and ingredients, with a seasonal, fresh-produce-driven philosophy similar to Californian cuisine. There's a base of borrowed traditions, yes, but its style and attitude is unique. The Melbourne manifestation (and the state's culinary offerings in general) tends more towards European and Mediterranean tastes, rather than Sydney's firmly Pacific Rim take on the cuisine. This is both a product of the city's very non-tropical climate – with four distinct seasons and strongly demarcated seasonal crops – and also the strong impact that Melbourne's Italian, Greek, Eastern European and Middle Eastern communities had on the city from the 1950s on. But that's not to say you won't find wonderful Asian cooking and a host of varied Asian influences as the city continues to absorb and reinvent these traditions, too.

Melbourne has long been a diverse city, but apart from the long-standing influence of the Chinese community through numerous restaurants

THE GHOSTS OF DINNERS PAST

The site of Melbourne was known for its edible delights long before John Batman set eyes on the natural falls of the Yarra. The Wurundjeri thrived because of the area's incredible bounty: the wetlands that spread south of the Yarra were teeming with life, and the river itself brimmed with fish, eels and shellfish. Depending on the season, Indigenous 'Melburnians' would have eaten roast kangaroo, waterfowl, fish and eel, as well as greens, grubs, yam daisies and a sweet cordial concocted from banksia blossoms.

The first Europeans didn't stop to notice the veritable native feast they had stumbled upon, but instead quickly went about planting European crops and tending large flocks of sheep. Although many new arrivals were astounded by the ready supply of fresh food – especially the Irish, who were escaping the famine of the 1840s – the early settlers dined mainly on mutton, bread and butter, tea, beer and rum (though it's hard to imagine that those familiar with the gentle art of poaching didn't help themselves to ducks and geese).

and importing businesses, tastes didn't really begin to shift from the Anglo-Celtic basics until the postwar period. As well as importing the goods they couldn't do without, such as olive oil, the city's southern and eastern European migrants set to producing coffee, bread, cheeses and smallgoods, which gradually found their way from specialist delis into mainstream supermarkets. These communities also helped shape the agricultural traditions of the state, bringing new crops and production methods to a land that often resembled the parts of the Mediterranean they had left behind. The Vietnamese, Lebanese and Turkish migrants that followed in the 1970s also had a lasting impact on the way Victorians eat. Many of the state's culinary leading lights and rising stars are the children or grandchildren of these first-generation migrants (or are migrants themselves): Guy Grossi, Greg Malouf, Karen Martini, Con Christopoulos, George Calombaris, Joseph Abboud, Shane Delia, Rosa Mitchell and Pietro Porcu, to name just a few.

While Victoria's eating habits have absorbed and incorporated a range of cuisines, creating something new in the process, many of the original inspirations are represented in kitchens across the city, and are constantly joined by those catering to its newest arrivals. Melbourne's ethnic restaurants, once clustered in tight community hubs, now flourish all over the city, though there are still loosely dedicated zones. Richmond's Victoria St is packed with Vietnamese restaurants and provedores, while the western suburb of Footscray draws those looking for the most authentic Vietnamese, Laotian and Cambodian food, as well as great East African and Indian restaurants.

Lygon St in Carlton has long been home to simple red-sauce Italian cooking – with notable innovators such as D.O.C – and its coffee and Italian delis are excellent. Chinatown, in the city centre, is home to Flower Drum, one of Australia's most renowned restaurants of any culinary persuasion, and there are places doing regional cuisines such as Sichuan- and Beijing-style dumplings up every other laneway. You'll find Japanese *izakayas* and Korean restaurants here, too. Just to the north, Lonsdale St has a handful of Greek taverns and bars. The northern suburbs of Brunswick and East Brunswick have a number of wonderful Middle Eastern bakers and grocers as well as cafes and restaurants. A large international student population has seen many Indian, Malaysian and Indonesian places spring up in the city and around the various university campuses, serving inexpensive and fabulously authentic dishes.

VEGETARIAN AND VEGAN

Vegetarians and vegans will have no trouble finding restaurants that cater specifically to them in Melbourne, particularly in neighbourhoods such as Fitzroy and St Kilda, and around Victoria.

There will also be at least a couple of dishes on most restaurant menus that will please, and few restaurateurs will look askance at special requests. Many fine-dining restaurants (Vue de Monde, Cutler & Co, Attica etc) offer vegetarian degustation tasting menus, and with advance warning these can usually be made dairy-free.

Most Asian and Indian restaurants will have large meatless menus, but with Chinese, Vietnamese and Thai cooking you'll need to be clear that you don't want the common additives of oyster or fish sauce. Casual Japanese places also have many vegetarian options, though similarly you'll need to ask if they can prepare your dish with *dashi* (stock) that hasn't been made with bonito fish (ask if they have mushroom or seaweed *dashi* instead).

Eating Local

Over the last decade, the organic and local food movement has gone from strength to strength in Victoria. Shopping at weekly markets and small grocers is a lifestyle choice that's embraced by many, and the Slow Food movement has a strong presence statewide – news and events can be found at www.slowfoodaustralia.com.au – as well as a monthly market at the Abbotsford Convent in Melbourne on the fourth Saturday of each month.

Queen Victoria Market in Melbourne's city centre, and its suburban counterparts in South Melbourne and Prahran, are beloved by locals for their fresh fruit, vegetables, meat and fish, and their groaning deli counters, not to mention a catch up with friends. There's also a weekly rota of inner-city farmers markets (see www.mfm.com.au) at Collingwood Children's Farm and South Melbourne's Gasworks, which bring local artisan producers and fresh, often organic, produce to town. They make for a pleasant Saturday morning coffee spot and food-related stroll.

A huge number of outer suburbs and regional towns also hold community markets, selling local produce as well as crafts and secondhand goods; a comprehensive list can be found at the Australian Farmers Market Association (www.farmersmarkets.org.au). The monthly markets at Red Hill, on the Mornington Peninsula, and St Andrews (www.standrewsmarket.com.au), around 40 minutes' drive north of Melbourne, are veterans of the scene and incredibly popular. Both are held in atmospheric, bush-ringed settings – the bellbird soundtrack is complimentary, no purchase required.

Food tourism is big news right throughout Victoria, with much of the action centred on wine-growing districts such as the Mornington and Bellarine Peninsulas and the Yarra Valley. Around the Great Ocean Road you'll find the gastronomic towns of Timboon and Birregurra, while the Goldfields-area spa towns of Kyneton, Trentham, Daylesford and Castlemaine are home to ever-increasing numbers of provedores and cafes offering local produce. The Milawa Gourmet Region – the first area to be given such a title in Australia – is unsurprisingly one of the state's richest; the foodie trail here also takes in the surrounding towns of Oxley and Beechworth. Out along the Murray, Mildura is also a destination for its produce and restaurants.

Cellar Door Dining

- *Max's at Red Hill Estate, Mornington Peninsula*
- *La Baracca at T'Gallant, Mornington Peninsula*
- *Jack Rabbit Winery, Bellarine Peninsula*
- *Passing Clouds Winery, Musk, Spa Country*
- *Terrace at All Saints, Rutherglen*
- *ezard @ Levantine Hill, Yarra Valley*
- *Patricia's Table at Brown Brothers, Milawa*

Victorian Vino

Bacchus appears to have smiled upon the state of Victoria. Its small size belies the variety of its climates, which makes for a splendidly diverse wine scene, with around 900 vineyards spread over 21 growing regions. Melbourne itself is surrounded by five of these – the Yarra Valley, Mornington Peninsula, Macedon Ranges, Geelong and Sunbury – all with distinct climates and soils. Wine-region weekends away and grape-grazing festivals are popular with Victorians, and with many of the regions close to favourite beach resorts or ski fields, they also provide a gourmet backdrop to seasonal holidays. Whether it's for confidently working your way through a Melbourne wine list or for creating a cellar-door itinerary, understanding what's what only makes the tasting sweeter.

Beginning at Melbourne's suburban fringe, the Yarra Valley is a patchwork of vines, and it's here that you'll find the glamorous big boys of the industry, Chateau Yering and Domain Chandon. These glistening temples to the grape absorb the tour-bus bustle surprisingly well, with a rota of produce markets and entertainment, as well as striking architecture, making up for the high traffic. The area still has its share of rustic tin sheds where it's just you and the winemaker, if that's more your style. Fruity, unwooded pinot noirs, peachy chardonnays and crisp sparklings are the darlings here, but there's also plenty of experimentation with other grapes.

A little further afield in Melbourne's southeast is the rarefied rusticity of the Mornington Peninsula. The hills and valleys of this favourite beach destination hide an embarrassment of small-scale viticulture riches – there's literally a winemaker around every bend (not to mention symbiotic cellar door, restaurant, gourmet provedore and shop selling French plimsolls). Mornington vignerons are a tenacious, innovative lot who coax the most out of the volcanic soil and capricious, often chilly, maritime climate to produce beautiful, early ripening pinot noir, subtle, honeyed chardonnay, pinot gris and fragrant Italian varietals such as arneis and pinot grigio, possibly Australia's best. The vineyards of the Bellarine Peninsula, on the opposite coast, have gained a following of their own, and their delicate maritime-climate aromatic whites are getting a lot of attention.

Best Victorian Varietals

- *Chardonnay*
- *Viognier*
- *Marsanne*
- *Pinot noir*
- *Shiraz*
- *Gamay*
- *Durif*
- *Tokay*

In Victoria's northeast, wine has been continuously produced since the thirsty days of the gold rush, with Brown Brothers making both fortified and table wines right through the 20th century. Northern Italian farmers also made a big contribution to this region's development. They noted similarities in the landscape and introduced grapes from their home regions that took to the local terroir. Today, the gloriously diverse geography, climate and soil, from the flats around Milawa to the high country of Beechworth and the cool, wet King Valley see a huge variety of wines produced. Rieslings, sauvignon blancs and sparklings (including an Italian-styled prosecco) shine in the King Valley, along with the complex, tightly structured chardonnay and spicy shiraz of Beechworth and Milawa's fortifieds, cabernet merlots, sangiovese, nebbiolos and pinot grigios. To the west of here, Rutherglen is also a pioneer, well known for its fortifieds and unctuous stickies. Big – well, absolutely huge – durif reds do well here too, but it's the long-cellared muscats and tokays (aka liquid Christmas pudding) that keep the faithful coming back.

Other less-visited regions include the Pyrenees, known for its French-influenced sparklings and, somewhat surprisingly, its absolutely Aussie big, ripe reds; Macedon, which produces crisp, cold-climate sparklings and minerally European-style chardonnays, rieslings and sauvignon blancs; the Goulburn Valley's Ngambie and Shepparton, for marsannes, viogniers and Rhône Valley reds, some of which are grown from original vines imported from France in the 1850s; and the Grampians for reds, such as cabernet and dolcetto, as well as an unforgettable sparkling shiraz.

Fashion & Shopping

Melbourne's reputation as a shopping mecca is utterly justified. Passionate retailers roam widely in search of the world's best goods as well as showcasing abundant local design talent. Fashion plays a huge part in Melbourne's self-image. Whether strictly suited or ultra glam, casual, creative or subversive, Melburnians of both sexes love to look good. And despite the stereotype, not everything's black.

City Style

Ask any Melbourne fashionista their favourite time of year and they'll invariably say it's winter – and usually for the fashion opportunities that crisp, cold days deliver. While Melbourne designers do produce swimwear (Gorman, Zoe Elizabeth and We Are Handsome's retro offerings are local favourites), it's during the autumn–winter season of the fashion cycle that the city comes into its own. Temperatures only have to drop a few degrees for boots and jackets to emerge, and unpredictable summers see many a cardigan or lightweight scarf thrown into the mix.

There's no shortage of places to shop. City laneways and Victorian shopping streets have long provided reasonably priced rental spaces that encourage creativity rather than conformity in shop owners; their vision contributes much to the city's eclectic identity and character. Yes, the chains and big global designers are all well represented, and there are suburban malls aplenty (including Chadstone, known as Chaddy, one of the largest in the southern hemisphere and Victoria's oldest; www.chadstoneshopping.com.au), but the city and surrounds offer a host of alternatives.

Buoyed by a culture of small shops and an adventurous-minded public, young designers flourish. Rather than adhering to the established studio's hierarchies, many start their own labels straight out of design school, giving the scene an amazing energy and vitality.

Made in Melbourne

Douglas & Hope

Aesop

Spacecraft

Alice Euphemia

Tomorrow Never Knows

Vintage style has long flourished in Melbourne, both in the retailing and the wearing of vintage pieces and in a general sensibility that pays heed to retro cuts and traditional tailoring. Vintage devotees should head to the city's arcades, and look for shops in Prahran, Windsor, Fitzroy, Collingwood, Brunswick and Northcote.

Melbourne Black

One constant in Melbourne fashion is colour, or lack of it. You'll not go long without hearing mention of 'Melbourne black', and it's true that inky shades are worn not just during the cold months but right through the hottest days of summer. Perhaps it's because black somehow suits the soft light and often grey days, or maybe it's the subliminal influence of the city's moody bluestone. Some muse that it's the long-lingering fallout of the explosive 1980s post-punk scene or southern European immigration. The fact remains that black clothes sell far better here than in any other city in the country. In Melbourne, black is always the new black.

Local Talent

Melbourne's designers are known for their tailoring, luxury fabrics, innovation and blending of global elements, all underscored with a fuss-free Australian sensibility.

Those to watch out for include the evergreen Scanlan Theodore for smart, lyrical elegance; Toni Matičevski and Martin Grant for demi-couture and dark reworkings of the classics; Nixi Killick, Ess Hoshika, Dhini and Munk for conceptual, deconstructed pieces; Anna Thomas and Vixen for the luxuriously grown up; Gwendolynne Burkin for vintage-inspired bridal fashion; Gorman, Arabella Ramsay, Búl and Obüs for hipster chic with a delightfully feminine twist; Yeojin Bae, Alpha60, Kloke and Claude Maus for clever, urban pieces; and, finally, scene stalwarts Bettina Liano for straight-ahead glamour and Alannah Hill for the original girly-girl layers.

For flattering and form-fitting jeans, you can't go past Nobody Denim. Christine Barro is Melbourne's queen of accessories. Millinery is also a speciality, due to the local fondness for racing carnivals, with names such as Richard Nylon, Melissa Jackson and Louise Macdonald.

Discount factory outlets can be found aplenty in Bridge Rd, Richmond; the lower end of Smith St, Collingwood; or at South Wharf, but savvy Melbourne fashionistas prefer designer-specific sample sales, discovered via word of mouth or mailing lists – check out Missy Confidential (www.missyconfidential.com.au).

Craft & Design

Melbourne's penchant for small-scale design goes one further with a bubbling subculture that sells through markets and online. Craft Victoria is the grand old (if eternally cool) dame of the scene, with a commitment to showing and selling handcrafted work at the highest levels of skill. **Thread Den** (www.threadden.com), in Fitzroy, combines a craft, DIY and vintage ethos with classes augmenting its retail offerings. The Nicholas Building, at the corner of Swanston St and Flinders Lane, is the city's most concentrated artisan hub, with small shops and much-coveted studios and workshops.

Melbourne's unpredictable weather hasn't deterred its entrepreneurial spirit, with many markets held in all-weather venues. The twice-yearly Melbourne Design Market (www.melbournedesignmarket.com.au) is huge, attracting around 10,000 visitors. It showcases 'design-led' stallholders and has a rigorous selection process that keeps quality high. Fitzroy's Rose Street Market (www.rosestmarket.com.au) is as much about the social buzz as the highly individual vendors.

WHERE TO SHOP

The city has national and international chains spread out over Bourke, Swanston and Collins Sts, as well as the city malls of Melbourne Central and QV. Smaller retailers and design workshops inhabit the laneways as well as the vertical villages of Curtin House and the Nicholas Building. Flinders Lane and the arcades and laneways that feed into it are particularly blessed. A strip of Little Collins heading east from Swanston is dedicated to sartorially savvy gentlemen, while the length of leafy Collins St is lined with luxury retailers.

Chapel St, South Yarra, has all the chains and classic Australian names, as well as some edgier designers once you hit Prahran. Up the hill, head to Hawksburn Village or High St, Armadale, for fashion-forward labels, super-stylish children's clothes and homewares. You'll find streetwear in Greville St, Prahran, and in Windsor; the latter is also good for vintage shopping.

In the north, Lygon St, Carlton, has some great small shops specialising in European tailoring and local talent. Brunswick St, Fitzroy, has streetwear and vintage shops, and pulses with the energy of young designers. Gertrude St, Fitzroy, mixes vintage with many of the city's most sought-after innovators, as well as some up-and-coming menswear names, art-supply shops and vintage furniture.

The Arts

Long regarded as the culture capital of Australia, Melbourne has always been a city for artists and art lovers. Its thriving live-music scene, strong community of street artists, and passion for literature, theatre and visual arts all provide a vibrant, creative backdrop fundamental to the fabric of the city. Art in Melbourne is highly accessible, in terms of the number of its art spaces and its appeal to a broad audience.

Visual Arts

Melbourne's visual-arts scene thrives and grows in myriad places: tucked away in basement galleries, exhibited in edgy spaces, stencilled on unmarked laneway walls, flaunted in world-class museums and sneaking up on you in parks and gardens.

Flinders Lane has the densest concentration of commercial galleries in Australia, with many more dotted throughout the city and inner suburbs. *Art Almanac* (www.art-almanac.com.au) has comprehensive listings, with good regional coverage as well.

Painting

Melbourne's visual-arts culture began in the traditions of the Kulin people, and ancestral design inspires contemporary Indigenous artists to this day. The late-19th-century artwork of Wurundjeri elder William Barak depicts ceremonial gatherings; several of his works are displayed in the Ian Potter Centre: NGV Australia. Prominent contemporary Koorie artists in Victoria include Vicki Couzens, Esther Kirby, Mandy Nicholson and Trevor 'Turbo' Brown, who paint upon a mix of traditional artefacts, possum-skin cloaks and emu eggs, as well as canvas (note: there are no dots in Indigenous Victorian art). In Melbourne, the Koorie Heritage Trust and Melbourne Museum's Bunjilaka Aboriginal Centre both provide an intimate picture of Victorian Aboriginal culture.

Early Europeans who visited the fledgling colony of Melbourne presented a very different experience of Australia. The Vienna-born Eugene von Guérard is one of Australia's most well-known colonial artists from the 1850s; his vast works include panoramic landscapes of early Geelong, the Otway Ranges, Gippsland and the Western District region, all depicted as colonial jewels with bucolic pastures and abundant forests.

In the late 19th century a new generation of Australian-born artists emerged, forming the Heidelberg School (aka the Australian Impressionists). Artists Tom Roberts, Arthur Streeton and Frederick McCubbin are fondly remembered for defining a more 'Australian' vision of the landscape and depicting the harshness in the beauty of the Victorian bush. They also created a heroic national iconography, ranging from the shearing of sheep to visions of a wide brown land.

The early- to mid-20th century saw the rise to prominence of a number of modernist painters, including internationally acclaimed Melbourne artists Sidney Nolan, John Brack, Charles Blackman, Fred Williams and Russell Drysdale. Heide, the Melbourne home of arts patrons John and Sunday Reed, played a pivotal role in the development of Australian modernism; Nolan's famous Ned Kelly series is said to have been painted at the Reeds' dining-room table. The Reeds nurtured an artistic community that included Nolan, Albert Tucker, Arthur Boyd, Joy Hester, John Perceval and Danila Vassilieff, who used styles incorporating elements of surrealism and expressionism. Their property has since been turned into the Heide Museum of Modern Art, which has an impressive collection of modern and contemporary Australian art exhibited in three galleries and scattered throughout the tranquil gardens.

Other well-known Melbourne painters of the 20th century include French expatriate Mirka Mora (b 1928), known for her colourful, bohemian paintings; she and her art-dealer husband Georges (founder of Tolarno Galleries) were hugely influential on Melbourne's art and cultural scenes. The late Howard Arkley (1955–99) is as Melbourne as they come: his airbrush technique produced fluorescent pieces that pay homage to suburbia, and he produced a well-known portrait of Melbourne musician Nick Cave.

Regional Galleries

Bendigo Art Gallery (p212)

Art Gallery of Ballarat (p203)

Mornington Peninsula Regional Gallery (p237)

TarraWarra Museum of Art (p141), Yarra Valley

Geelong Art Gallery (p159)

Contemporary Art

Between the commercial, public and artist-run galleries, there is much to discover in Melbourne's contemporary arts scene. A good place to tap in is Gertrude Contemporary Art Space, which hosts exhibitions by emerging artists and fosters innovative and challenging new works. The Australian Centre for Contemporary Art (ACCA) also hosts cutting-edge exhibitions as well as developing large-scale projects with Australian and international artists. The Australian Centre for the Moving Image (ACMI) exhibits film and multimedia works by contemporary artists, and the Centre for Contemporary Photography has a strong photo- and film-based program.

Street Art

With its growing reputation for street art, Melbourne's urban landscape is a beacon for visitors from all around the world. Dozens of laneway walls provide an outdoor canvas for paste-up, mural and stencil art.

Local street artists of note include ghostpatrol, miso, Tai Snaith and Ha-Ha (the latter for *his* iconic Ned Kelly images – move aside, Sidney Nolan). Many of these locals are represented in the documentaries *Rash* (2005) and *Children of the Iron Snake* (2013), which get behind the scenes of Melbourne's street-art phenomenon.

Melbourne's scene was helped by the legacy of renowned international street artists such as Keith Haring (1958–1990), the New York graffiti artist who visited in 1984. He was commissioned to paint large-scale murals at NGV International and what was then the Collingwood Technical School on Johnston St; the latter work still exists today (visible next door to the Tote music club).

The city's street-art scene received further recognition through Banksy, who stencilled extensively during a visit in 2003. While several of his works remain, many have disappeared (some accidentally painted over by unsuspecting workers). Other prominent international artists to contribute work to Melbourne's streets include Blek le Rat (France), Shepard Fairey (USA) and Invader (France).

Street-Art Sites

Hosier/Rutledge Lane

Caledonian Lane

Blender Lane

Union Lane

Croft Lane

Literature

It may seem at first glance that in Melbourne words and stories are relegated to the wings while sport and socialising take centre stage, but scratch the surface and you'll find that the city's home to writers of all descriptions, independent booksellers, a prosperous publishing industry, and a thriving culture of reading and discourse on the written word. Melbourne nourishes literary types with its tempestuous weather, rich range of cultures and identities, wine bars and moody architecture.

Melbourne's wordy reputation was formally recognised with its designation as a Unesco City of Literature (in 2008) and the birth of the Wheeler Centre, Australia's first centre for 'Books, Writing and Ideas'. Located within a wing of the State Library of Victoria, it's home to several literary organisations and hosts a rich roster of talks and events designed to get Melburnians thinking.

Literary publishing companies Black Inc, Scribe and Text are based in Melbourne, and the city produces a host of magazines, journals and websites that highlight literature and intellectual life, including the *Australian Book Review*, *Meanjin*, Black Inc's series of 'Best' anthologies and the *Quarterly Essay*, and the short-fiction collection *Sleepers Almanac*. The City Library in Flinders Lane has an entire section dedicated to books on Melbourne.

Has there been a great Victorian novel? Melbourne has certainly provided a variety of memorable backdrops for literary works, from the 19th-century cult crime fiction of *The Mystery of a Hansom Cab* (Fergus Hume; 1886) to Peter Temple's *The Broken Shore* (2005), which is also partly based in western Victoria. Christos Tsiolkas' *The Slap* (2008) is set in the backyards of the inner north, where post-war migrant families settled in Melbourne. AS Patrić won the Miles Franklin Award for his unsettling *Black Rock White City* (2015), about a Bosnian Serb refugee working in a Melbourne hospital. Helen Garner's *Monkey Grip* takes readers on a journey through drugs, love and music in urban Melbourne in the 1970s, while *Utopian Man* by Lisa Lang tells the story of the late-19th-century days of 'Marvellous Melbourne' and EW Cole's Book Arcade. Peter Carey's *True History of the Kelly Gang*, set in the central Victorian haunts of Australia's most famous bushrangers, won both the Man Booker and the Commonwealth Writers' Prize when it was published in 2001; despite Victoria's largely urban, multicultural population, it just may be a novel with a historical – even mythological – bush setting that can claim the 'great' title.

On the non-fiction front, Jill and Jeff Sparrow's *Radical Melbourne* (2001) looks at Melbourne's counter-culture and its secret history. Germaine Greer, another radical Melburnian, is best known for her work *The Female Eunuch* (1971), an international bestseller hailed for its contribution to feminism.

Notable books on Indigenous culture include *When the Wattle Blooms* (Shirley W Wiencke; 1984), about William Barak, a notable Wurundjeri elder; *Aboriginal Melbourne: The Lost Land of the Kulin People* (1994) by Gary Presland; and *The Melbourne Dreaming: A Guide to the Aboriginal Places of Melbourne* (1997) by Meyer Eidelson. *The Life and Adventures of William Buckley* (John Morgan; 1852) – a fascinating account of escaped convict William Buckley and the 32 years he spent living with the Wathaurung people – still offers one of the best insights into precolonial Kulin life.

Bookish Melbourne

- *State Library of Victoria (city centre)*
- *Wheeler Centre (city centre)*
- *Readings (city centre, Carlton, St Kilda)*
- *Hill of Content (city centre)*
- *Melbourne Writers Festival (August–September)*

Music

Melbourne's cultural identity has involved music since it produced two of the most fascinating talents of the early 20th century. Opera diva Dame Nellie Melba was an international star who lived overseas for many years

DOCUMENTING MELBOURNE PUNK

The following provide a great overview of Melbourne's punk scene:

➡ *We're Living on Dog Food* (2009) Doco directed by Richard Lowenstein.

➡ *Dogs in Space* (1986) Feature film also by Richard Lowenstein, starring INXS' Michael Hutchence.

➡ *The Ballroom: The Melbourne Punk & Post Punk Scene* (2011) Fantastic memoir by Dolores San Miguel recalling St Kilda's colourful punk history at the Crystal Ballroom.

but retained a sentimental attachment to her home town (hence her stage name). Percy Grainger, whose innovative compositions and performances prefigured many forms of 20th-century music, was born and brought up in Melbourne. Grainger's eccentric genius extended beyond music to the design of clothing and objects; he was also known for his transgressive sex life. His life story is all on display at the Percy Grainger Museum in Parkville.

Melbourne's live-music scene exploded in the mid-1960s with a band called the Loved Ones, who broke the imitative mould of American 1950s rock 'n' roll. The early 1970s saw groups such as AC/DC, Skyhooks and Daddy Cool capture the experience of ordinary Melbourne life in their lyrics for the first time. They provided a harder-edged counterpoint to Melbourne's other international pop-music success stories up to that point: the Seekers, Air Supply, Olivia Newton-John and the Little River Band.

By the end of the 1970s punk had descended; Melbourne's grey weather and grimy backstreets had a natural synergy with the genre, providing a more arty, post-punk sound. Nick Cave's Boys Next Door (which evolved into the Birthday Party) and the so-called 'Little Bands' shrieked their way through gigs at St Kilda's Crystal Ballroom, a venue whose dilapidated splendour was straight out of central casting. Bands and performers that grew out of (and beyond) this scene included the Models and Dead Can Dance.

In the 1980s, Kiwi Neil Finn called time on Split Enz and moved to Melbourne, hooking up with locals Paul Hester and Nick Seymour to form Crowded House. The '80s pub-rock scene also gave birth to Paul Kelly, Hunters and Collectors, and Australian Crawl, while the '90s and 2000s punk/grunge era saw the likes of the Dirty Three, Jet and Magic Dirt carry the torch passed on from their late-'70s predecessors.

Melbourne's biggest international artists of the moment include Nick Cave, Kylie Minogue, Gotye, the Temper Trap and Courtney Barnett. Other acts making waves within the Australian pond include Chet Faker (aka Nick Murphy), Big Scary, Meg Mac, Vance Joy, Tash Sultana, the Drones, and King Gizzard and the Lizard Wizard.

LIVE-MUSIC VENUES

Melbourne's live-music scene has had a rough run of late; residents moving into new apartment buildings near established venues have certainly had their voices heard, and as a result some clubs have been forced to close, or reduce the volume. The Tote in Collingwood was an apparent victim of new liquor-licensing laws requiring even small venues to have a security presence; when it closed, Melbourne's music lovers weren't happy. Around 20,000 people rallied in Melbourne's city centre, resulting in the future of live-music venues becoming an issue in the 2010 state election. SLAM (Save Live Australia's Music), an advocate action group, successfully lobbied for numerous law changes. There was a happy ending: the Tote got new owners and the music there continues, while other venues were granted seven-day 3am licences.

Despite the liquor-licence issues and noise complaints, Melbourne is still the live-music capital of Australia, drawing musicians from around the country. Some of the city's favourite pubs and drinking dens double as band venues: the best spots to catch a beer and a gig include the Northcote Social Club, Richmond's Corner Hotel, and Cherry and the Ding Dong Lounge in the city.

Though it prides itself on being a city dedicated to smaller, independent live-music spaces, Melbourne also has its fair share of major stadiums and arenas, which host a large number of international touring acts each year – pickings are particularly rich during the summer festival season. You'll find big-name acts selling out venues like Rod Laver Arena, Festival Hall, Sidney Myer Music Bowl and the Forum.

The city also has a healthy club and dance-music scene. The mega-clubs of the '80s gave way to a more fluid dance-party culture revolving around techno and other electronic styles. The 'doof' was born: these festivals, often held in bushland settings over several days, peaked in the late '90s, though they still have their devotees. Legendary laneway club Honkytonks took its musical responsibility very seriously, nurturing local DJ talent (and a generation of club kids) through the early years of this century. Since its demise, other venues have sprung up to fill the gap. Local electronic/synth-pop artists who have crossed into the mainstream include Cut Copy, the Avalanches and DJ Digital Primate.

Australian hip-hop is well represented in Victoria, with locals such as Illy, True Live and DJ Peril. Hip-hop has also proven enormously popular with young Aboriginal and Islander musicians (*All You Mob* is an excellent compilation CD of Indigenous artists). Other modern Indigenous musicians, such as Archie Roach, create unique styles by incorporating traditional instruments into modern rock and folk formats. There's nothing traditional about the music of Dan Sultan, an alternative rocker of Aboriginal heritage whose 2014 album *Blackbird* was certified gold.

Beat (www.beat.com.au) and *FasterLouder* (www.fasterlouder.com.au) have weekly, all-genre gig guides; Mess+Noise (www.messandnoise.com) is a great forum for local indie/rock news and happenings.

Jazz also has a dedicated local audience and a large number of respected musicians who are known for improvising, as well as crossing genres into world and experimental electronica. The heart of the scene is the long-running Bennetts Lane, an archetypal down-an-alley jazz club if ever there was one. Its Sunday sessions are legendary, and the venue draws a local crowd that knows its hard bop from its bebop. International and local talent also pull respectable numbers for gigs at the Melbourne International Jazz Festival.

A century after Nellie Melba was made a dame, classical music still has a strong presence in Melbourne. The Melbourne Symphony Orchestra, based at the Arts Centre's Hamer Hall, performs works drawn from across the classical spectrum, from the popular to challenging contemporary composition. The all-acoustic Melbourne Recital Centre hosts around 250 concerts a year.

Cinema & Television

Although Sydney might be considered the centre of the Australian film industry, new production facilities at Docklands, slightly lower costs for film production and generous government subsidies have seen Melbourne wield its movie-making muscle. And Melbourne does look gorgeous on the big screen. Film-makers tend to eschew the stately and urbane and highlight the city's complexity, from the winsomely suburban to the melancholic and gritty.

Film culture is nurtured in Victoria through local funding projects, tertiary education and exhibition. Funding for features, documentaries, shorts, digital media and game content is provided by Film Victoria (www.film.vic.gov.au), which also provides mentoring schemes. Federation Sq has consolidated a big part of Melbourne's screen culture, housing the Australian Centre for the Moving Image (ACMI) and the Special Broadcasting Service (SBS) television channel.

The prominence of film in Melbourne is evident in the number of film festivals the city hosts. Apart from the main Melbourne International Film Festival (www.melbournefilmfestival.com.au), there's everything from the Melbourne Underground Film Festival (www.muff.com.au) to shorts at the St Kilda Film Festival (www.stkildafilmfestival.com.au). Other film-festival genres include foreign made, seniors, hip-hop, queer and documentary.

Some well-known Australian films shot in Melbourne and regional Victoria include *Mad Max*, *Picnic at Hanging Rock*, *Chopper*,

Romper Stomper, *Animal Kingdom* and *The Man from Snowy River*, while international films include *Lion*, *Where the Wild Things Are*, *Ghost Rider*, *Jackie Chan's First Strike* and *Salaam Namaste*.

There's an enduring affection for police-drama and comedy shows on Australian TV, and many of these have emanated from Melbourne. The barely fictionalised organised-crime series *Underbelly* didn't initially make it to air in the city in which it was set – not because of its nudity but because a court decided that its plot lines could prejudice concurrent court proceedings. Other made-in-Melbourne TV series to hit the small screen include *Prisoner*, *The Secret Life of Us*, *Rush*, *Offspring* and *Miss Fisher's Murder Mysteries*, all shot in various parts of town, such as Fitzroy, Collingwood and the city's western waterfront. Beloved local comedy includes *Kath & Kim*, a hilarious spoof of nouveau-riche suburban habits – very much in the mould of Melbourne's favourite aunty, Dame Edna Everage from Moonee Ponds (among Barry Humphries' alter egos). And, of course, there's the never-ending froth of soap opera *Neighbours*. In regional Victoria, TV drama *Sea Change* was filmed on location at Barwon Heads on the Bellarine Peninsula.

Melbourne is a 'must-see' destination for many British travellers primarily because it's home to the TV program *Neighbours*. Pin Oak Ct in Vermont South is the suburban street that has been the show's legendary 'Ramsay St' for more than 20 years.

Theatre

Melbourne's longstanding theatrical heritage is evident in the city's legacy of Victorian-era theatres, such as the Princess and Athenæum. While the blockbusters pack out these grand dames, Melbourne's theatre scene encompasses a wide spectrum of genres.

Melbourne's most high-profile professional theatre company, the Melbourne Theatre Company (MTC; www.mtc.com.au), is Australia's oldest, and it stages up to a dozen performances year-round at both the Arts Centre and its own purpose-built theatre located nearby. Expect works by Australians such as David Williamson, locals Hannie Rayson and Joanna Murray-Smith, and well-known international playwrights.

The Malthouse Theatre (www.malthousetheatre.com.au) is dedicated to performing contemporary Australian works and nurturing emerging writers, and it's known for staging works of relevance, audacity and artistic daring.

Victoria also has thriving progressive fringe-theatre companies, including Wodonga's HotHouse, Black Lung, Mutation Theatre and Hayloft, which stage residencies in traditional theatre settings as well as popping up in unusual places.

Humble in size, Carlton's La Mama (www.lamama.com.au) has a huge place in the city's theatre scene. Founded in 1967, it is, as its name might suggest, the mother of independent theatre in Melbourne, and helped forge the careers of David Williamson, Jack Hibberd, Barry Dickins and Graeme Blundell.

Dance

The Australian Ballet (www.australianballet.com.au) is the national ballet company and considered one of the finest in the world. It performs regularly at Melbourne's Arts Centre, with a program of classical and modern ballets.

Victoria's flagship contemporary dance company, Chunky Move (www.chunkymove.com.au), is a tidy package of bold – often confronting – choreography, pop-culture concepts, technically brilliant dancers, sleek design and smart marketing. The artistic director and choreographer who founded the company in 1995, Gideon Obarzanek, moved on in 2012, and was succeeded by acclaimed Dutch choreographer Anouk van Dijk.

Kage (www.kage.com.au) is a modern dance company producing innovative, challenging, humorous and highly entertaining performances.

The company is a partnership between Kate Denborough and Gerard Van Dyck, who met while studying for a bachelor of dance at the Victorian College of the Arts.

Melbourne is also home to a few other acclaimed contemporary choreographers. Lucy Guerin has a small, eponymous company that has attracted high praise from *New Yorker* magazine's Joan Acocella. Shelley Lasica locates her work in non-theatre spaces, collaborating with visual artists and architects; her works blur the line between dance and performance art.

Architecture & Design

For a planned city, and a relatively youthful one, Melbourne's streetscapes are richly textured. Long considered one of the world's most lovely Victorian-era cities, Melbourne captures the confident spirit of that age, with exuberantly embellished Second Empire institutions and hulking former factories that would do Manchester proud. Flinders St station and the original Queen Victoria Hospital (now part of the QV shopping centre) commemorate the Federation era, when a new Australian identity was being fashioned from the fetching combination of red brick and ornate wood.

Look down Swanston St from Lonsdale St and you'll catch a glimpse of a mini-Manhattan – Melbourne's between-the-wars optimism is captured in its string of stunning (if somewhat stunted) art deco skyscrapers, such as the Manchester Unity Building. Walter Burley Griffin worked in the city at this time too, creating the ornate, organic Newman College at the University of Melbourne and a mesmerising ode to the metropolitan, the Capitol Theatre, now a part-time cinema and university lecture hall.

By mid-century, modernist architects sought new ways to connect with the local landscape as well as honour the movement's internationalist roots; the most prominent, Roy Grounds, designed the Arts Centre and the original NGV Australia on St Kilda Rd. Others include Robin Boyd, Kevin Borland and Alistair Knox, but their work is mostly residential so is rarely open to the public. You can, however, visit a beautiful Boyd building any time: Jimmy Watson's Wine Bar in Carlton. Melbourne also had its own mid-century furniture-design stars, Grant and Mary Featherston; their iconic Contour chair of 1951 is highly prized by collectors, as are their 1970s modular sofas.

The 1990s saw a flurry of public building works: Melbourne's architects fell in love with technology and designed with unorthodox shapes, vibrant colours, tactile surfaces and sleek structural features. Denton Corker Marshall's Melbourne Museum, Melbourne Exhibition & Convention Centre, Bolte Bridge, and CityLink sound tunnel are emblematic of this period. Federation Sq, one of the last of these major projects, continues to polarise opinion. Despite its detractors, its cobbled, inscribed piazza has become the city's chosen site for celebration and protest, surely the best compliment a populace can pay to an architect. Ashton Raggatt McDougall's Melbourne Recital Centre is a recent architectural prize winner, with an interior that is, according to Melbourne University's Philip Goad, 'like a beautiful violin'.

Melbourne's architectural energy today most often comes not from the monumental but from what goes on in between the new and the old, the towering and the tiny. It's also literally about energy: sustainable practice, in the inner city at least, has become all but de rigueur. Mid-careerists such as Six Degrees, Elenberg Fraser and Kerstin Thompson create witty, inventive and challenging buildings and interiors that see raw or reimagined spaces spring to life.

Sport

Cynics snicker that sport is the sum of Victoria's culture, although they're hard to hear above all that cheering, theme-song singing and applause. Victorians do take the shared spectacle of the playing field very seriously. It's undeniably the state's most dominant expression of common beliefs and behaviour, and brings people together from across all backgrounds.

Australian Rules Football (AFL)

The largest crowd at the MCG for an AFL game was 121,696 (the 1970 Grand Final). For the cricket, 91,112 attended the 2013 Ashes Test (a world record for any cricket match). The largest crowd *ever* at the MCG – 130,000 – was for US evangelist Billy Graham in 1959. These days capacity is just over 100,000.

Underneath the cultured chat and designer threads of your typical Melburnian, you'll find a heart that truly belongs to one thing: the footy. Understanding the basics of AFL is definitely a way to get a local engaged in conversation, especially during the winter season. Melbourne is the national centre for the sport, and the Melbourne-based Australian Football League (www.afl.com.au) administers the national competition.

During the footy season (March to September), the vast majority of Victorians become obsessed. They enter tipping competitions at work, discuss hamstring injuries and suspensions over the water cooler, and devour huge chunks of the daily newspapers devoted to mighty victories, devastating losses and the latest gossip (on and off the field).

The MCG, affectionately referred to as the 'G', has been the home of Australian football since 1859 and its atmosphere is unforgettable. The AFL now has teams in every mainland state, but nine of its 18 clubs are still based in Melbourne, along with regional Geelong. All Melbourne teams play their home games at either the MCG or Etihad Stadium, and matches between two local teams ensure a loud, parochial crowd. Barracking has its own lexicon and is often a one-sided 'conversation' with the umpire. One thing is certain: fans always know better. Once disparagingly referred to as 'white maggots' because of their lily-white uniforms, umpires are now decked out in bright orange and yellow-green, so players can spot them in the thick of the game. (With the colour switch, they are now simply called 'maggots'.)

After the final siren blows, and the winning club's theme song is played (usually several times over), it's off to the pub. Supporters of opposing teams often celebrate and commiserate together. Despite the deep tribal feelings and passionate expression of belonging that AFL engenders, violence is almost unheard of before, during or after games.

In early 2017 the inaugural AFL women's league was launched, with traditional rivals Carlton and Collingwood fittingly matched for the showcase game held at Princes Park to a lock-out crowd.

Cricket

Cricket is Victoria's summer love and it's the game that truly unites the state with the rest of Australia. It has a stronghold in Victoria, given the hallowed ground of the MCG and Cricket Australia's base in Melbourne. Spending a day at the Boxing Day Test at 'the G', which attracts crowds of 80,000-plus, is a must-do-before-you-die rite of devotion for cricket fans from around the world – for many sport-mad Melburnians, it's a bigger deal than Christmas itself. Warm days, cricket's leisurely pace and gangs of supporters who've travelled from far and wide often make for great spectator theatrics. A schedule of one-day internationals, T20 games (both the national Big Bash League and international matches) and the Sheffield Shield keep fans happy throughout the rest of the season.

In February 2017 Geelong was added to the list of venues to host international cricket, with the inaugural Australia versus Sri Lanka T20 match played at Kardinia Park.

Sporting Highlights

AFL at the MCG

Boxing Day Cricket Test, MCG

Bells Beach Surf Classic

Australian Open

Australian Grand Prix

Stawell Gift

Melbourne Cup

Tennis

The last two weeks of January is tennis time in Melbourne, when the city hosts the Australian Open (www.australianopen.com) championships. The world's best come to compete at Melbourne Park in the year's first of the big four Grand Slam tournaments. With daily attendance figures breaking world records – well over 500,000 people come through the turnstiles over the two weeks – a carnival atmosphere prevails. Visitors come from around the world to attend, but it's also a favourite with locals, who make the most of summer holiday leave or amble over after work. While the entertainment and a few glasses of sparkling wine in the sun are a big part of the draw, there's a hushed respect during matches on centre court. The most disruptive element is usually the elements themselves – the chance of at least one 40°C scorcher of a day is high. If you can't make it to the event itself, grab a deckchair at Federation Sq to watch a match on the big outdoor screen.

Soccer & Rugby

What many visitors know as 'football' in their home countries is referred to as 'soccer' in Australia, despite the Football Federation's official assertion of the football tag. Considering all the competition, the game's rise in Melbourne has been spectacular. A new A-League national competition was formed in 2005, running from October to May, and with it came a large supporter base and a higher profile for the game. Australia's solid performance in the 2006 FIFA World Cup also contributed to its new-found popularity, as does its status as the 'world game'. The city's original team, the Melbourne Victory (www.melbournevictory.com.au), was joined in the competition by the Melbourne City FC (www.melbournecityfc.com.au; originally known as Melbourne Heart) in the 2010–11 season. Soccer's amazingly vocal supporters (including a British-style cheer squad) make for some atmospheric play.

Melbourne Storm (www.melbournestorm.com.au), the first and only Victorian team in the National Rugby League (NRL), enjoyed spectacular success over the last decade, winning the premiership twice. It's actually

AUSTRALIAN GRAND PRIX

These are the kind of figures that make petrol-heads swoon: 300km/h, 950bhp and 19,000rpm. The Australian Grand Prix is held at Albert Park's 5.3km street circuit, which winds around the normally tranquil park's lake and is known for its smooth, fast surface. The buzz, both on the streets and in your ears, takes over Melbourne for four days in March, attracting 110,000 spectators for race day. Since 2009 it's been a twilight race, starting at 5pm (mainly for the benefit of TV audiences in the European time zones). Visit www.grandprix.com.au for event and ticketing details.

While the first official Australian Grand Prix F1 event was held at Albert Park in 1996 (after Melbourne controversially pinched the race from Adelaide), the lake track was used for grand-prix racing during the 1950s, seeing the likes of legends Jack Brabham and Stirling Moss battle it out. Today, with the retirement of Mark Webber, the nation's attention turns to Aussie young gun Daniel Ricciardo, who drives with the Red Bull Racing team.

won four titles, but sadly for Victorian league fans, it was stripped of its 2007 and 2009 titles for salary-cap breaches.

Rugby union is also growing in popularity, with the Melbourne Rebels joining the Super Rugby (Super 18) competition in 2011. Union draws large, often sellout, crowds to international Tests at Docklands Stadium, which recorded its highest sporting attendance – 56,605 – during a tour for the Wallabies (the national team).

Melbourne's new purpose-built rectangular stadium, AAMI Park, on the site of Olympic Park Stadium, has a capacity of 30,000, showing the state's continued commitment to embracing 'other' football codes in the future – hosting A-League matches, NRL and Super Rugby matches.

Horse Racing

The roses are in bloom, the city's aflutter, and the nerves of milliners, fashion retailers, dry cleaners, beauty therapists and caterers are beyond frayed. It's Spring Carnival time in Melbourne.

The 3.2km Melbourne Cup has been run on the first Tuesday of November at Flemington Racecourse since 1861. Watched by 700 million people in more than 170 countries, the Cup brings the whole of Australia to a standstill for its three-or-so minutes, and most Victorians have the day off as a public holiday. Once-a-year gamblers organise Cup syndicates with friends, and gather to watch the race from pubs, clubs, TAB betting shops and backyard barbecues. Punters, partiers, celebrities and the fashion-conscious pack the grandstands, car parks, lawns and marquees of Flemington.

The Cup's social whirl gets even headier at Derby Day and Oaks Day, which are considered more glamorous events than the Cup itself, while serious racegoers also bet their way through the Cox Plate, the Caulfield Cup, the Dalgety and the Mackinnon Stakes.

Survival Guide

Directory A–Z

Accommodation

Accommodation across the state ranges from boutique hotels and resorts to camping, caravan parks and motels. Book months in advance during summer-holiday season (from mid-December to the end of January) and during major events.

Hotels Everything from high-end boutique hotels to budget chains and pub accommodation.

Motels Popular with travellers looking for central, no-frills self-contained accommodation.

Camping & Caravan parks Plenty of options around Victoria, with outstanding national park camping grounds.

B&Bs & Guesthouses Could be a grand historic home, restored miners' cottage or beachside bungalow.

Hostels Most of Victoria's backpacker hostels are in Melbourne and the most popular regional centres such as Halls Gap, and along the Great Ocean Road.

B&Bs & Guesthouses

This segment of the accommodation market generally means staying in someone's home or in a purpose-built addition to a home, but increasingly B&Bs are self-contained cottages. It could be a grand historic home, secluded farmhouse, restored miners' cottage or a beachside bungalow. In the English tradition, a big cooked breakfast is part of the deal. Rates are usually midrange (from $130 to $250 for a double), but can be much higher depending on the location and level of luxury.

In many places a minimum two-night stay is required, and not only during peak periods – this is almost always the case on weekends, especially in places such as Daylesford.

Bookings can be made directly with the properties or online at these sites:

- Bed & Breakfast (www.bedandbreakfast.com.au)
- Great Places to Stay (www.greatplacestostay.com.au)

Camping & Caravanning

Victoria has some outstanding national park camping grounds and privately run caravan parks to choose from. The only place that camping or caravanning isn't viable is central Melbourne.

At commercial caravan parks, expect to pay at least $25 to $35 for an unpowered/powered site for two people, and from $90 to $180 for a cabin or unit, depending on the size and facilities. These rates will almost certainly double or even triple at coastal areas and popular holiday spots during school holidays. Parks Victoria (www.parkweb.vic.gov.au) camping grounds range from free to $28, and you can usually have up to six people and one vehicle per site. These should be booked in advance, but often a ranger will come in and collect your money. For the most popular sites, such as Wilsons Prom and Cape Otway, a ballot is held for sites over the Christmas and Easter holiday periods. Free camping is available in many places, including along the Murray and Goulburn rivers and in the High Country – check with Parks Victoria. There are also a couple of free campgrounds scattered around the Otway Ranges.

BOOK YOUR STAY ONLINE

For more accommodation reviews by Lonely Planet authors, check out http://lonelyplanet.com/hotels/. You'll find independent reviews, as well as recommendations on the best places to stay. Best of all, you can book online.

Hostels

There are eight YHA hostels (www.yha.com.au) in the state, and quite a few more independent backpackers. Expect to pay $25 to $35 for a dorm bed and from $75 for a private double.

Pubs, Hotels & Motels

Motels are the most common type of accommodation around the state and popular with travellers looking for central, no-frills, familiar accommodation. Motels usually have studios and family apartments from $100 to $200, with TV, en-suite bathroom, airconditioning, tea- and coffee-making facilities and usually a pool and barbecue area.

In Melbourne and large provincial centres, hotels are usually aimed at business and luxury travellers – centrally located, with business centres and restaurants attached. For a standard double room in a top-end hotel, expect to pay upwards of $250, midrange around $150 to $180 and for budget, doubles from $95.

In country towns, a hotel refers to the local pub, which may have furnished rooms upstairs, usually with shared facilities down the hall, though increasingly more towns are offering boutique pub accommodation with modern decor and a couple of options of private en-suites. Pubs are often a good budget option, with rooms just under $100, and you're sure to rub shoulders with a few locals down in the bar. Expect some noise when staying on a Friday or Saturday night in the majority of places.

Houseboat

One of the great ways to stay in Victoria is on a houseboat. They range from basic two-bedroom boats with a small kitchen and the simplicity of a rural cabin to luxurious 12-berth craft with deck spa and all modcons. They're especially popular in Mildura, Echuca, Eildon, Mallacoota and around Nelson and the Lower Glenelg National Park.

Apartments & Holiday Rentals

Most common along the coast and at ski resorts, and popular spots such as the Grampians and Murray River, holiday accommodation is generally self-contained, with a kitchen, one or two bedrooms and parking. Holiday houses along the coast are usually just that – an entire house that you can rent for a week or longer and is ideal for families or groups.

- Home Away (www.homeaway.com.au)
- Holiday Great Ocean Road (www.holidaygor.com.au)
- Holiday Shacks (www.holidayshacks.com.au)
- Stayz (www.stayz.com.au)

SLEEPING PRICE RANGES

Price ranges for accommodation in our reviews are rated with a $ symbol, indicating the price of a standard double room.

$ less than $130

$$ $150–250

$$$ more than $250

Customs Regulations

- **What to declare at customs** Cash amounts of more than $10,000, foodstuffs, goods of animal or vegetable origin, including wooden products and

LIGHTHOUSE STAYS

Lighthouse keepers in days of old notoriously endured a lonely, tough existence, but these days you can get a taste of what their lives must have been like...and do so in relative comfort. Of Victoria's 20-plus lighthouses, 10 are managed by Parks Victoria (www.parkweb.vic.gov.au), and you can stay in the refurbished keeper's cottages at five of them. Some, such as Point Hicks and Gabo Island, are remote, while Cape Otway and Cape Schanck are easily accessible to families.

Cape Schanck (☎0407 348 478; www.facebook.com/theladyofhistory; 420 Cape Schanck Rd; tours incl museum & lighthouse adult/child/family $13/7/38; ⊙select weekends)

Cape Otway (☎03-5237 9240; www.lightstation.com; Lighthouse Rd; d incl entry to lighthouse $240-450)

Gabo Island (☎03-8427 2123, Parks Victoria 13 19 63; www.parkweb.vic.gov.au; up to 8 people $323.70-359.70)

Point Hicks (☎03-5156 0432; www.pointhicks.com.au; bungalows $120-150, cottages $360-550)

Wilsons Promontory (☎13 19 63, 03-5680 9555; www.parkweb.vic.gov.au; Wilsons Promontory National Park; d cottages $352-391, 12-bed cottages per person $127-141)

medicines. All drugs and weapons are prohibited. Failure to declare quarantine items can mean an on-the-spot fine or prosecution.

➡ **Duty-free allowance** Travellers over 18 have a duty-free quota of 2.25L of alcohol, 50 cigarettes or 50g of tobacco, and dutiable goods up to the value of $900 (or $450 for those under 18).

➡ **State restrictions** There are also restrictions on taking fruit, vegetables, plants or flowers across state borders. There is a particularly strict fruit-fly exclusion zone, which takes in an area along Victoria's northeast border, stretching into NSW and SA. For full details refer to the Customs and Quarantine section of the Australian Government website (www.australia.gov.au).

Electricity

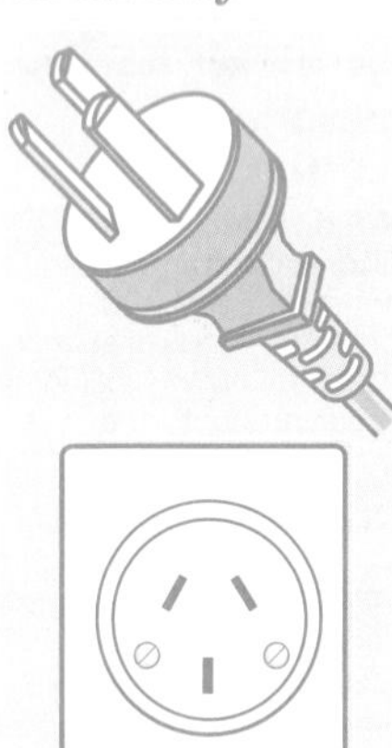

Type I
230V/50Hz

Etiquette

There's not too much to worry about in terms of etiquette in laid-back Victoria, though a few pointers won't go astray.

My Shout When in groups at a pub or bar, Victorians generally like to take it in turns to buy a round of drinks..

BBQs If invited to a BBQ, bring something to drink and some burgers or sausages (snags) or a salad.

LGBTQI Travellers

Homosexuality is legal and the age of consent is 17. The straight community's attitude towards gays and lesbians is, on the whole, open-minded and accepting.

The gay scene in Victoria is squarely based in Melbourne, where there are exclusive venues and accommodation options. Around the state, places such as Daylesford and Hepburn Springs, Phillip Island and the Mornington Peninsula have a strong gay presence and accommodation catering for gays and lesbians. Melbourne's **Midsumma Festival** (www.midsumma.org.au; ⏲Jan-Feb) in January is the state's biggest LBGQTIA+ festival and incorporates the annual pride march. Daylesford's **ChillOut Festival** (www.chilloutfestival.com.au; ⏲mid-Mar) in March is the biggest gay and lesbian event in regional Victoria.

Health

Few travellers to Victoria will experience anything worse than a hangover, but if you do fall ill the standard of hospitals and health care is high.

Before You Go

HEALTH INSURANCE

While the standard of health care in Australia is high and is not overly expensive by international standards, travel insurance should be considered essential for international travellers. Make sure you have appropriate coverage if you plan on doing any 'dangerous' activities such as skiing, rock climbing, diving or motorcycling.

RECOMMENDED VACCINATIONS

Proof of yellow-fever vaccination is required only from travellers entering Australia within six days of having stayed overnight or longer in a yellow-fever-infected country. No specific vaccinations are required to travel in Victoria.

In Victoria

AVAILABILITY & COST OF HEALTH CARE

Australia's Medicare system (www.medicareaustralia.gov.au) covers Australian residents for some health-care costs and emergency care, with reciprocity for citizens of New Zealand, Belgium, UK, Netherlands, Sweden, Finland, Italy, Malta and Ireland. Melbourne and the major provincial centres have high-quality hospitals.

Animal Bites & Stings

FLIES & MOSQUITOES

For four to six months of the year, you'll have to cope with those two banes of the Australian outdoors: the fly and the mosquito (mozzie). Flies aren't too bad in the city but they start getting out of hand in the country, and the further out you go, the more numerous and persistent they seem to be. Widely available repellents such as Aerogard and Rid may help to deter the little bastards, but don't count on it. For something stronger, try the Bushman's DEET-based repellent.

Mozzies are a problem in summer, particularly for campers near water. Try to keep your arms and legs covered as soon as the sun goes down and use insect repellent liberally. Mosquito-borne illnesses are becoming more prevalent throughout the state. Ross River virus is transmitted through mosquitoes and cases have been reported throughout the state and recently in Melbourne metropolitan areas. It can cause influenza-like symptoms with fever and joint pain. Apply a DEET-based repellent and try to avoid getting bitten, particularly at dawn and dusk.

Bairnsdale ulcer (or Buruli ulcer) is a rare flesh-eating bacteria that has seen a spike in reported cases in recent years, mostly in the Bellarine Peninsula and Mornington Peninsula areas. While it's not known exactly what causes it, it's believed it may be carried by mosquitoes. The ulcer starts as a small sore and, if left untreated, can become a large lesion requiring surgery.

SNAKES & SPIDERS

Bushwalkers should be aware that snakes and spiders, some venomous, are quite common in the Victorian bush, but the risk of getting bitten is very low. Snakes are usually quite timid in nature, and in most instances will move away if disturbed. Wear boots and socks to cover the ankles when walking in summer.

If bitten, a pressure bandage and immobilisation is the best course of action while awaiting medical care. All snake bites can be treated with antivenom. Spiders to watch out for include the redback and white-tail varieties.

TICKS & LEECHES

The common bush tick (found in the forest and scrub country all along Australia's east coast) can be dangerous if left lodged in the skin, as the toxin excreted by the tick can cause partial paralysis and, in theory, death, although this is extremely rare. Check your body for lumps every night if you're walking in tick-infested areas. Remove the tick by dousing it with methylated spirits or kerosene and levering it out, making sure you remove it intact.

Leeches are common, but while they will suck your blood, they are not dangerous and are easily removed by the application of salt or heat.

SUNBURN & SKIN CANCER

Australia has one of the highest rates of skin cancer in the world. Don't be fooled by Victoria's variable weather and cloudy days – UV exposure here is as dangerous as anywhere in the country. If you're going out in the summer sun, particularly at the beach, use 50-plus water-resistant sunscreen and wear a hat, sunglasses and shirt as much as possible.

Insurance

A good policy covering theft, loss and medical problems is essential. Make sure your policy fully covers activities you're likely to participate in, as some may exclude certain 'risky' ones.

Worldwide travel insurance is available at www.lonelyplanet.com/travel-insurance. You can buy, extend and claim online anytime – even if you're already on the road.

Internet Access

Wi-fi access is increasingly common throughout the state. In Melbourne, free wi-fi is available at central city spots such as Federation Sq, Flinders Street Station, Crown Casino and the State Library. Most hotels, caravan parks and cafes in Melbourne and Victoria offer wi-fi, and in regional Victoria you'll find free internet access at the local library and sometimes at the tourist office.

Legal Matters

Most travellers won't have any contact with the Victorian police or any other part of the legal system. Those who do are likely to do so while driving. There is a significant police presence on Victoria's roads, and they have the power to stop your car and ask to see your licence (you're required by law to carry it), to check your vehicle for roadworthiness, and also to insist that you take a breath test for alcohol. The blood alcohol limit is 0.05%.

If you are arrested, it's your right to telephone a friend, relative or lawyer before any formal questioning begins.

Money

ATMs can be found in most towns, and credit cards are widely accepted.

ATMs & Eftpos

Most bank branches have 24-hour ATMs and will accept debit cards linked to international network systems such as Cirrus, Maestro, Visa and MasterCard. Most banks charge a fee (around $2 or 3%) for the privilege of using their ATM if you don't have an account with them.

Almost all retail outlets have Eftpos, which allows you to pay for purchases electronically without a fee.

Currency

The Australian dollar is made up of 100 cents. There are 5¢, 10¢, 20¢, 50¢, $1 and $2 coins, and $5, $10, $20, $50 and $100 notes.

Exchange Rates

Canada	C$1	A$0.98
Europe	€1	A$1.38
Japan	¥100	A$1.15
New Zealand	NZ$1	A$0.93
UK	£1	A$1.61
US	US$1	A$1.30

For current exchange rates see www.xe.com

Money Changers

Change foreign currency at most larger banks or foreign-exchange booths in the city and at Melbourne Airport's international terminal. Most large hotels will also change currency (or travellers cheques) for guests, but the rate might not be as good as from other outlets.

Tipping

Tipping isn't obligatory in Australia and you'll rarely be made to feel uncomfortable if you don't do so. That said, tips are always appreciated, especially where the service has been notable, in which case 5% to 10% is ample in restaurants. For hotel porters, $5 should suffice. Tipping is less common in regional or country towns in Victoria, although a little rounding up never goes astray.

Post

Australia Post (☎13 76 78; www.auspost.com.au) Visit the website for up-to-date postage rates and the location of post offices. Stamps can be purchased at post offices, newsagents and some small grocery or general stores.

Public Holidays

Victoria observes the following 10 public holidays:

New Year's Day 1 January

Australia Day 26 January

Labour Day First or second Monday in March

Easter Good Friday and Easter Monday in March/April

Anzac Day 25 April

Queen's Birthday Second Monday in June

AFL Grand Final Day Friday preceding the final in September or October

Melbourne Cup Day First Tuesday in November

Christmas Day 25 December

Boxing Day 26 December

PRACTICALITIES

Newspapers

The Age (www.theage.com.au) is Melbourne's broadsheet, covering local, national and international news. *The Herald Sun* (www.heraldsun.com.au) is a big-selling tabloid strong on sport, especially AFL.

Radio

The Australian Broadcasting Commission (www.abc.net.au) is the national TV and radio broadcaster; tune into 774AM in case of emergencies. Melbourne's Triple R (102.7FM, www.rrr.org.au) is Australia's largest community radio station and a great place to hear local bands.

TV

Nartional TV stations ABC and SBS, and commercial networks Seven, Nine and Ten all have more than one digital channel.

Smoking

Banned in certain public places, including restaurants, pubs, cafes, around schools, childcare centres and hospitals, patrolled beaches, near kids' play equipment in parks, and on train- and tram-station platforms. As of August 2017, smoking will also be banned at all outdoor dining areas.

Safe Travel

Victoria is a relatively safe place to travel, but there are a few things to take note of, particularly in summer with the threat of bushfires, sharks, snakes and sun (p367).

There are occasional reports of alcohol-fuelled violence in some parts of Melbourne's city centre late on weekend nights – particularly in King St and along Swanston St close to Flinders Street Station.

The VicEmergency website (https://emergency.vic.gov.au), hotline (☎1800 226 226) and app provide the latest information and alerts on incidents, including shark sightings and bushfires.

Environmental Hazards

BUSHFIRES & EXPOSURE

Bushfires happen every year in Victoria. In hot, dry and windy weather, be extremely careful with any naked flame – cigarette butts thrown out of car windows have started many fires. On a 'total fire ban' day it's forbidden even to use a camping stove in the open. Locals will not be amused if they catch you breaking this particular law; they'll happily turn you in to the authorities, and the penalties are severe.

Bushwalkers should seek local advice before setting out – be careful, or delay your trip, if a total fire ban is in place. If you're out in the bush and you see smoke, even a long way off, take it seriously – bushfires move very quickly and change direction with the wind. Go to the nearest open space, downhill if possible. A forested ridge is the most dangerous place to be.

More bushwalkers actually die of cold than in bushfires. Even in summer, temperatures can drop below freezing at night in the mountains and Victorian weather is notoriously changeable. Exposure in even moderately cool temperatures can sometimes result in hypothermia. Always take suitable spare clothing and adequate water and carbohydrates.

SAFE SWIMMING

Popular Victorian beaches are patrolled by surf lifesavers in summer, with safe areas marked off by a pair of red and yellow flags. Always swim between the flags.

Victoria's ocean beaches often have treach

erous waves and rips. Even if you're a competent swimmer, you should exercise extreme caution and avoid the water altogether in high surf. If you happen to get caught in a rip when swimming and are being taken out to sea, try not to panic. Raise one arm until you have been spotted, and then swim parallel to the shore – *don't* try to swim back against the rip.

A number of people are also paralysed every year in rivers, lakes and off piers by diving into shallow water and hitting a sandbar or submerged log; always check the depth of the water before you leap.

TAP WATER

Tap water is safe to drink throughout the state.

Telephone

- Area code: ☎03
- Country code: ☎61
- International access code (for dialling overseas): ☎0011
- Many businesses have either a toll-free number (starting with 1800) or a number (beginning with ☎1300 or ☎13) that is charged at local call rates; these numbers can't be dialled from outside Australia.
- A variety of phonecards can be bought from newsagents and post offices.

Mobile Phones

All Australian mobile-phone numbers have four-digit prefixes beginning with ☎04. Australia's digital network is compatible with GSM 900 and 1800 handsets. Quad-based US phones will also work. Local SIM cards are readily available.

Time

Victoria (along with Tasmania, NSW and Queensland) keeps Eastern Standard Time, which is 10 hours ahead of GMT/UTC. That means that when it's noon in Melbourne, it's 9pm the previous day in New York, 2am in London and 11am in Tokyo.

Daylight-saving time, when clocks are put forward an hour, is between the first Sunday in October and the first Sunday in April.

Toilets

Public toilets are common in Melbourne and you'll find toilet blocks in a lot of regional towns and at many beaches across the state.

Refer to the very handy **National Public Toilet Map** (https://toiletmap.gov.au) to find public-toilet locations.

Tourist Information

Regional centres throughout the state will usually have a visitor centre or tourist information booth in a central location. Also refer to **Visit Victoria** (www.visitvictoria.com/Information/Visitor-information-centres) for a list of tourist offices.

Travellers with Disabilities

Many of the attractions in Melbourne and regional Victoria are accessible to wheelchairs. Trains and newer trams have low steps to accommodate wheelchairs and people with limited mobility. Many car parks in the city have convenient spaces allocated for disabled drivers. All pedestrian crossings feature sound cues and accessible buttons.

Resources

Visit Victoria For more information, check out the Accessible Victoria page at www.visitvictoria.com.

Lonely Planet Download Lonely Planet's free Accessible Travel guide from http://lptravel.to/AccessibleTravel.

Visas

All visitors to Australia must have a valid passport and visa (New Zealanders receive a 'special category' visa on arrival). Tourist visas are free and valid for three months. The easiest way to obtain a visa is to apply for an Electronic Travel Authority (ETA), which can be done online (www.eta.immi.gov.au) for a service fee of $20 or through your travel agent.

Women Travellers

Victoria is generally a safe place for women travellers, although the usual sensible precautions apply. It's best to avoid walking alone late at night, especially when no one else is around. Alcohol-fuelled violence is becoming more common in Melbourne's city centre. The same applies to rural towns, where there are often a lot of unlit, semi-deserted streets. Lone women should also be wary of staying in basic pub accommodation unless it looks safe and well managed.

Sadly, like many other places, Aussie male culture does sometimes manifest itself in sexist bravado, and sexual harassment isn't uncommon, especially when alcohol is involved.

The following organisations offer advice and services for women:

Royal Women's Hospital Health Information Service (☎03-8345 2000; www.thewomens.org.au; 20 Flemington Rd, Parkville)

Royal Women's Hospital Sexual Assault Unit (☎03-9635 3610; www.thewomens.org.au/patients-visitors/clinics-and-services/violence-sexual-assault/sexual-assault-response-service; 20 Flemington Rd, Parkville)

Transport

GETTING THERE & AWAY

Air

You can fly into Melbourne from most international hubs and from all major cities and tourist destinations in Australia. Not all international flights are direct and you may need to change planes and terminals in Sydney.

Airports & Airlines

Melbourne Airport (MEL; ☎03-9297 1600; www.melbourneairport.com.au; Departure Rd, Tullamarine) Often referred to as Tullamarine, it's around 25km northwest of the city centre. All international and domestic terminals are within the same complex. There are no direct train or tram services linking it with the city, but airport shuttle buses meet flights and taxis descend like flies.

Avalon Airport (☎03-5227 9100; www.avalonairport.com.au; 80 Beach Rd, Lara) Around 55km southwest of the city centre on the way to Geelong. At the time of writing, only Jetstar flights to/from Sydney, Adelaide, Gold Coast and Hobart use the airport. SkyBus operates an airport shuttle, meeting all flights and picking up or dropping off at Southern Cross Station ($22/42 one way/return). The trip takes around 40 to 50 minutes.

Essendon Airport (MEB; ☎03-9948 9400; www.essendonairport.com.au; 7 English St, Essendon Fields; 🚌59) Tiny **Sharp Airlines** (☎1300 556 694; www.sharpairlines.com) flies to Flinders Island, King Island, Portland and Warrnambool from Essendon Airport, 10km northwest of the city centre.

Mildura Airport (☎03-5055 0500; www.milduraairport.com.au; Alan Mathews Dr) Scheduled flights to/from Melbourne, Adelaide, Sydney and Broken Hill.

Land

Bus

Firefly (☎1300 730 740; www.fireflyexpress.com.au) Operates day and overnight buses between Melbourne's Southern Cross Station and Adelaide (from $60, 11 to 13 hours) and Sydney (from $65, 12 hours).

Greyhound (☎1300 473 946; www.greyhound.com.au) Interstate buses between Melbourne's Southern Cross Station and Sydney (from $120, 12 hours), and Canberra (from $58, eight hours).

Train

Great Southern Rail (☎13 21 47; www.gsr.com.au) Operates the Overland service between Melbourne and Adelaide ($69

CLIMATE CHANGE & TRAVEL

Every form of transport that relies on carbon-based fuel generates CO_2, the main cause of human-induced climate change. Modern travel is dependent on aeroplanes, which might use less fuel per kilometre per person than most cars but travel much greater distances. The altitude at which aircraft emit gases (including CO_2) and particles also contributes to their climate change impact. Many websites offer 'carbon calculators' that allow people to estimate the carbon emissions generated by their journey and, for those who wish to do so, to offset the impact of the greenhouse gases emitted with contributions to portfolios of climate-friendly initiatives throughout the world. Lonely Planet offsets the carbon footprint of all staff and author travel.

to $149, 10 hours, two trips per week), departing Melbourne at 8.05am and Adelaide at 7.45am.

Sea

Spirit of Tasmania (☎1800 634 906, 03-6419 9320; www.spiritoftasmania.com.au; Station Pier, Port Melbourne; adult/car 1 way from $99/188) is a vehicle and passenger ferry sailing nightly to Devonport on Tasmania's northern coast from Station Pier in Port Melbourne, with additional day sailings during peak periods. The crossing takes around 10 hours. A wide variety of seasonal fares are available, from basic seats ($99) to private en suite cabins. Vehicles can be taken across from $188 one way.

GETTING AROUND

Air

Because of the state's compact size, scheduled internal flights are limited and often ludicrously expensive, with the notable exception of Mildura, which is serviced by **QantasLink** (☎13 13 13; www.qantas.com). **Regional Express** (REX; ☎13 17 13; www.rex.com.au) flies to Albury and Mildura.

Bicycle

Without the vast distances of other mainland states, Victoria is perfect for cycling (p37), whether road touring or mountain biking.

Bicycles are carried for free on the Queenscliff–Sorrento ferry and all V/Line regional train services, provided you check in 30 minutes before departure – but be aware if buying a train-coach combination ticket that V/Line bus services do not carry bicycles. The system of rail trails (disused train lines adapted as cycling paths) is growing in country Victoria, and provides scenic, hassle-free cycling. Some routes connect with V/Line train stations. See www.railtrails.com.au for details.

Bikes can be hired in Melbourne and most towns in regional Victoria, particularly any town where there are well-established cycling paths. Typical hire costs $25 to $50 a day, depending on the quality of the bike. Melbourne also has a popular **bike share program** (☎1300 711 590; www.melbournebikeshare.com.au; subscription day/week $3/8) with pick-up and drop-off points around the inner city.

Boat

Scheduled boat services include the regular daily **car and passenger ferries** (Map p169; ☎03-5257 4500; www.searoad.com.au; 1 Wharf St East, Queenscliff; one-way foot passenger adult/child $11/8, car incl driver $64, bicycle free; ⏲hourly 7am-6pm) between Queenscliff and Sorrento and the **Inter Island Ferries** (Map p238; ☎03-9585 5730; www.interislandferries.com.au; adult/child/bicycle return $26/12/8) from Stony Point on the Mornington Peninsula to French Island and Cowes, Phillip Island. In late 2016 a new **ferry service** (☎03-9514 8959; www.portphillipferries.com.au; Portarlington Pier, Portarlington) between Portarlington on the Bellarine

VICTORIAN RAIL TRAILS

Rail trails are a great way to see parts of regional Victoria by bike, and more trails are being developed as funding becomes available. Some of the best:

TRAIL	START/FINISH	LENGTH
Murray to Mountains	Wangaratta/Bright	116km
East Gippsland	Bairnsdale/Newmerella (near Orbost)	94km
Great Southern	Leongatha/Port Welshpool	74km
High Country	Wodonga/Old Tallangatta	59km
Lilydale to Warburton	Lilydale/Warburton	40km
Bellarine Peninsula	South Geelong/Queenscliff	32.5km
Bass Coast	Wonthaggi/Anderson	23km
O'Keefe	Bendigo/Heathcote	50km
Gippsland Lakes	Colquhoun/Lakes Entrance	17km
Camperdown to Timboon	Camperdown/Timboon	40km
Ballarat–Skipton	Ballarat/Skipton	56km
Port Fairy–Warrnambool	Port Fairy/Warrnambool	37km

Peninsula and Melbourne's Docklands was introduced.

Charter boats and cruises can get you around on the water in the Gippsland Lakes and Murray region.

Bus

Victoria's regional **V/Line** (☎1800 800 007; www.vline.com.au) bus network offers both a relatively cheap and reliable service, though it can require planning if you intend to do more than straightforward city-to-city trips. The buses basically supplement the train services, so you'll often find yourself on a train and bus combination, changing services en route. For getting between smaller country towns, a bus may well be the only public transport option and it may not even run daily. In some regions, private transport companies run bus services that often connect with V/Line trains and buses.

Car & Motorcycle

Victoria has some fantastic touring routes for cars and motorcycles, and a lack of public transport in many places outside the metropolitan area means your own vehicle is often the best way to go. You'll find Uber operates in Melbourne and in some of the main towns, such as Geelong.

VicRoads (☎13 11 71; www.vicroads.vic.gov.au) supplies parking permits for disabled drivers.

Driving

Foreign driving licences are valid as long as they are in English or accompanied by a translation. If in doubt, pick up an International Drivers Licence from your home country's automobile association.

Driving is on the left-hand side of the road. The speed limit in residential areas is 50km/h, rising to 70km/h or 80km/h on some main roads and dropping to 40km/h in specially designated areas such as school zones. On highways the speed limit is generally 100km/h, while on some sections of freeway it's 110km/h.

Wearing seat belts is compulsory, and children up to seven years of age must be belted into an approved safety seat. Motorcyclists must wear crash helmets at all times. The police strictly enforce Victoria's blood-alcohol limit of 0.05% with random breath testing (and drug testing) of drivers.

Toll Roads

Melbourne's **CityLink** (☎13 26 29; www.citylink.com.au) tollway road system connects the Monash, West Gate and Tullamarine freeways.

A CityLink 24-hour pass costs $17.19 and is valid for 24 hours from your first entry through a tollway. A weekend pass is also $17.19. The easiest way to buy a pass is with a credit card online or by telephoning CityLink.

If you accidentally find yourself on the CityLink toll road (and it's very easy to do), don't panic – there's a three-day grace period in which you can arrange payment.

EastLink (☎13 54 65; www.eastlink.com.au), which connects the Eastern, Monash and Frankston freeways, charges $6.04 for a single-trip pass. To use CityLink and EastLink, you can start a 30-day Melbourne Pass ($5.50 start-up), which will automatically accumulate your tolls and fees.

Automobile Associations

The **RACV** (☎13 72 28; www.racv.com.au) provides emergency breakdown service, literature, maps and accommodation service. Annual basic roadside assistance membership starts at $134.

MELBOURNE'S TRAMS

Melbourne's tram network is the largest in the world (topping that of St Petersburg), with around 250km of double track, 450 trams in the fleet and more than 1700 tram stops. Trams, from the 50-year-old W-class trams to modern level-access models, operate along 24 routes and carry more than 203 million passengers a year.

TOP TOURING ROUTES

Great Ocean Road Torquay to Warrnambool

Great Alpine Highway Wangaratta to Bairnsdale

Eildon–Jamieson Rd Eildon to Jamieson

Grand Ridge Rd Warragul to Korumburra

Bogong High Plains Rd Mt Beauty to Omeo

Grampians Tourist Rd Halls Gap to Dunkeld; Halls Gap to Wartook

Around the Bay Melbourne roundtrip via Sorrento, Queenscliff and Geelong

Yarra Ranges Healesville to Marysville and Warburton

Wilderness Coast Orbost to Mallacoota via Marlo and Cann River

Goldfields Touring Castlemaine, Maldon, Maryborough, Dunolly, Bendigo

REGIONAL TRAIN LINES	MAIN STATIONS
Geelong	Melbourne, Geelong, Colac, Warrnambool
Bendigo	Melbourne, Kyneton, Castlemaine, Bendigo, Swan Hill, Echuca
Ballarat	Melbourne, Ballarat, Ararat, Maryborough
Gippsland	Melbourne, Traralgon, Sale, Bairnsdale
Seymour	Melbourne, Seymour, Wangaratta, Albury

Car Hire

The following car-hire companies are represented at the airport, at city locations in Melbourne and in major regional centres:

Avis (☎03-8855 5333; www.avis.com.au)

Budget (☎1300 362 848; www.budget.com.au)

Europcar (☎1300 13 13 90; www.europcar.com.au)

Hertz (☎13 30 39; www.hertz.com.au)

Thrifty (☎1300 367 227; www.thrifty.com.au)

Campervans

The following companies have offices in Melbourne and a range of van sizes:

Aussie Campervans (☎03-9317 4991; www.aussiecampervans.com)

Britz Australia (☎1300 738 087; www.britz.com.au)

Jucy (☎1800 150 850; www.jucy.com.au)

Travellers Autobarn (☎1800 674 374; www.travellers-autobarn.com.au)

Train

V/Line (☎1800 800 007; www.vline.com.au) runs a network of trains around the state, most emanating out of Melbourne's Southern Cross Station. It's a comfortable and efficient way to travel, but the rail network is limited to a handful of main lines, so you will often need to rely on train-bus combinations (conveniently also operated by V/Line).

Tours

Adventure Tours Australia (☎03-8102 7800; www.adventuretours.com.au) Backpacker-style bus tours between Melbourne and Adelaide, and Melbourne and Sydney, via the coast roads, plus a whole range of single- and multi-day tours.

Autopia Tours (☎03-9393 1333; www.autopiatours.com.au) Small-group tours to the Grampians, Great Ocean Road, Yarra Valley and snowfields, lasting one to three days.

Bunyip Tours (Map p56; ☎03-9629 5866; www.bunyiptours.com; 570 Flinders St; tours from $59) Tours to the Great Ocean Road, Phillip Island, Mornington Peninsula and Wilsons Promontory, along with surprisingly popular tours to the set of long-running Aussie soap *Neighbours*.

Echidna Walkabout (☎03-9646 8249; www.echidnawalkabout.com.au) Runs lengthy multi-day nature eco-trips featuring bushwalking and wildlife spotting, heading all over Australia.

Go West (☎03-9485 5290; www.gowest.com.au) Day tours to the Great Ocean Road and Phillip Island with commentary provided on iPods in several languages.

Groovy Grape (☎1800 059 490; www.groovygrape.com.au) Backpacker-style minibus with tours between Adelaide and Melbourne via the Great Ocean Road and the Grampians.

Steamrail Victoria (☎03-9397 1953; www.steamrail.com.au) For steam-train devotees, and those who are looking for an unusual day out, this not-for-profit organisation puts old trains back on the tracks for jaunts to various country destinations around the state.

Wildlife Tours (☎03-9393 1300; www.wildlifetours.com.au) One- to three-day trips to the Grampians and Phillip Island, and Melbourne to Adelaide via the Great Ocean Road.

TRAIN FARES

Sample one-way V/Line off-peak fares from Melbourne:

DESTINATION	FARE ($)	DURATION (HR)
Bairnsdale	36	3½
Ballarat	14.42	1½
Bendigo	21.84	2
Castlemaine	15.96	1½
Echuca	28.20	3½
Geelong	8.82	1
Seymour	10	1¼
Swan Hill	42	4¼
Warrnambool	36	3½

Behind the Scenes

SEND US YOUR FEEDBACK

We love to hear from travellers – your comments keep us on our toes and help make our books better. Our well-travelled team reads every word on what you loved or loathed about this book. Although we cannot reply individually to your submissions, we always guarantee that your feedback goes straight to the appropriate authors, in time for the next edition. Each person who sends us information is thanked in the next edition – the most useful submissions are rewarded with a selection of digital PDF chapters.

Visit **lonelyplanet.com/contact** to submit your updates and suggestions or to ask for help. Our award-winning website also features inspirational travel stories, news and discussions.

Note: We may edit, reproduce and incorporate your comments in Lonely Planet products such as guidebooks, websites and digital products, so let us know if you don't want your comments reproduced or your name acknowledged. For a copy of our privacy policy visit lonelyplanet.com/privacy.

OUR READERS

Many thanks to the travellers who used the last edition and wrote to us with helpful hints, useful advice and interesting anecdotes:
Ben Chudoschnik, Jonathan Sise, Nicolas Granger

WRITER THANKS

Kate Morgan

Big thanks to Destination Editor Tasmin Waby for the opportunity to basically eat and drink my way around Melbourne's best neighbourhoods! Thank you to Caro Cooper for suggestions and being a drinking partner on occasion, and to my partner, Trent, for all your help and support.

Kate Armstrong

Particular thanks to Jacqui Loftus-Hills, Visit Victoria; Wendy Jones, Goulburn River Valley Tourism; Sue Couttie, Tourism Northeast; Marie Glasson, Greater Shepparton City Council; Fran Martin, Echuca Visitor Information Centre. Finally, to my dear friends Sue Mulligan, Lou Bull and Emmo – with thanks.

Cristian Bonetto

First and foremost, an epic thank you to Drew Westbrook for his hospitality and generosity. Sincere thanks also to Craig Bradbery, Tim Crabtree, Amy Ratcliffe, Leanne Layfield, Terese Finegan, Michael Flocke, Simon Betteridge, Annabel Sullivan, Garry Judd and the many locals who offered insight and insider knowledge along the way. At Lonely Planet, a huge thanks to Tasmin Waby for her support and encouragement.

Peter Dragicevich

Researching this guidebook was an absolute pleasure, especially because of the wonderful company that I had on the road. Special thanks go to Braith Bamkin, Peter van Gaalen, Marg Toohey and Jo Stafford for all their practical assistance in Melbourne, and to David Mills and Barry Sawtell for the Canberra Morrissey safari. And cheers to all my eating and drinking buddies along the way, especially Errol Hunt, Kim Shearman, Cristian Bonetto and Maryanne Netto.

Trent Holden

First up a massive thanks to Tasmin Waby for commissioning me to update the bulk of regional Victoria. Was an absolute honour to cover my home state. Totally blown away how much cool stuff there is to visit out here. Thanks to all the tourist visitor centres across the state, who are staffed by a fantastic team of volunteers who are doing a sensational job. Cheers to everyone else for giving me the time of day for a chat, and helping me put together this new edition. As per always lots of love to my family, particularly my partner, Kate, who I had the great fortune of having accompany me around this time round.

ACKNOWLEDGEMENTS

Climate map data adapted from Peel MC, Finlayson BL & McMahon TA (2007) 'Updated World Map of the Köppen-Geiger Climate Classification', Hydrology and Earth System Sciences, 11, 163344.

Cover photograph: Cape Otway National Park, Great Ocean Road, Maurizio Rellini/4Corners ©

THIS BOOK

This 10th edition of Lonely Planet's *Melbourne & Victoria* guidebook was researched and written by Kate Morgan, Kate Armstrong, Cristian Bonetto, Peter Dragicevich and Trent Holden. The previous edition was written by Anthony Ham, Trent Holden and Kate Morgan.

This guidebook was produced by the following:

Destination Editor Tasmin Waby

Product Editor Shona Gray

Senior Cartographer Julie Sheridan

Book Designer Ania Bartoszek

Assisting Editors Janet Austin, Louise McGregor, Vicky Smith

Assisting Cartographer James Leversha

Assisting Book Designer Virginia Moreno

Cover Researcher Campbell McKenzie

Thanks to Kate Chapman, Grace Dobell, Jenna Myers, Kirsten Rawlings, Alison Ridgway, Tracey Whitmey

Index

Map Pages **000**
Photo Pages 000

Map Pages **000**
Photo Pages **000**

Map Pages **000**
Photo Pages 000

N

O

P

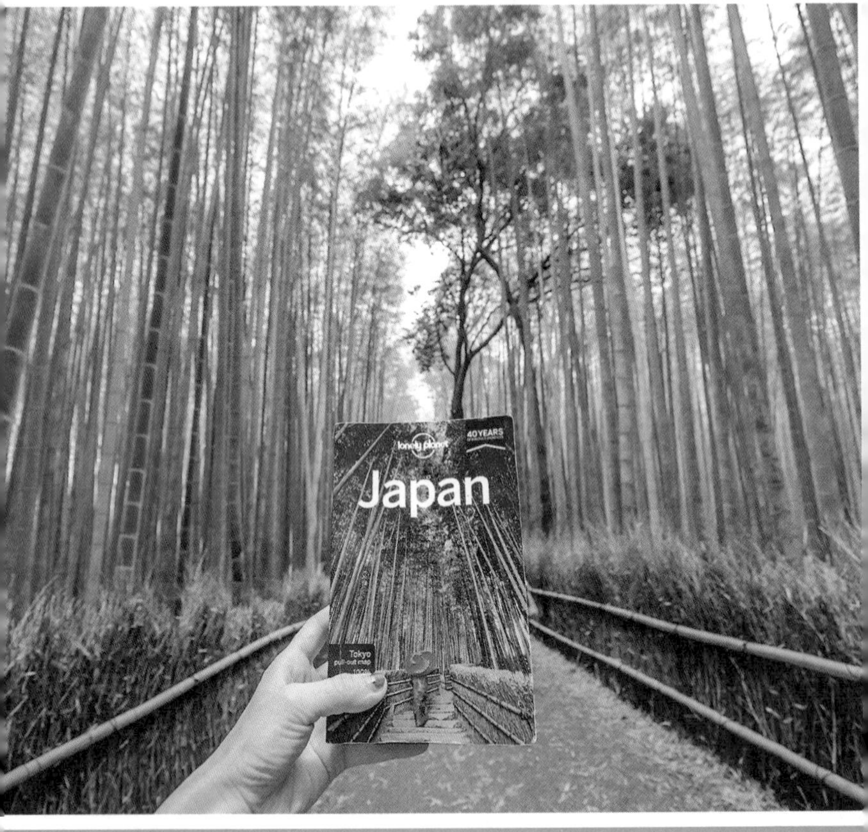
lonely planet
40 YEARS
Japan
Tokyo
pull-out map

Map Legend

Sights
- Beach
- Bird Sanctuary
- Buddhist
- Castle/Palace
- Christian
- Confucian
- Hindu
- Islamic
- Jain
- Jewish
- Monument
- Museum/Gallery/Historic Building
- Ruin
- Shinto
- Sikh
- Taoist
- Winery/Vineyard
- Zoo/Wildlife Sanctuary
- Other Sight

Activities, Courses & Tours
- Bodysurfing
- Diving
- Canoeing/Kayaking
- Course/Tour
- Sento Hot Baths/Onsen
- Skiing
- Snorkelling
- Surfing
- Swimming/Pool
- Walking
- Windsurfing
- Other Activity

Sleeping
- Sleeping
- Camping

Eating
- Eating

Drinking & Nightlife
- Drinking & Nightlife
- Cafe

Entertainment
- Entertainment

Shopping
- Shopping

Information
- Bank
- Embassy/Consulate
- Hospital/Medical
- Internet
- Police
- Post Office
- Telephone
- Toilet
- Tourist Information
- Other Information

Geographic
- Beach
- Gate
- Hut/Shelter
- Lighthouse
- Lookout
- Mountain/Volcano
- Oasis
- Park
- Pass
- Picnic Area
- Waterfall

Population
- Capital (National)
- Capital (State/Province)
- City/Large Town
- Town/Village

Transport
- Airport
- Border crossing
- Bus
- Cable car/Funicular
- Cycling
- Ferry
- Metro station
- Monorail
- Parking
- Petrol station
- Subway station
- Taxi
- Train station/Railway
- Tram
- Underground station
- Other Transport

Note: Not all symbols displayed above appear on the maps in this book

Routes
- Tollway
- Freeway
- Primary
- Secondary
- Tertiary
- Lane
- Unsealed road
- Road under construction
- Plaza/Mall
- Steps
- Tunnel
- Pedestrian overpass
- Walking Tour
- Walking Tour detour
- Path/Walking Trail

Boundaries
- International
- State/Province
- Disputed
- Regional/Suburb
- Marine Park
- Cliff
- Wall

Hydrography
- River, Creek
- Intermittent River
- Canal
- Water
- Dry/Salt/Intermittent Lake
- Reef

Areas
- Airport/Runway
- Beach/Desert
- Cemetery (Christian)
- Cemetery (Other)
- Glacier
- Mudflat
- Park/Forest
- Sight (Building)
- Sportsground
- Swamp/Mangrove

OUR STORY

A beat-up old car, a few dollars in the pocket and a sense of adventure. In 1972 that's all Tony and Maureen Wheeler needed for the trip of a lifetime – across Europe and Asia overland to Australia. It took several months, and at the end – broke but inspired – they sat at their kitchen table writing and stapling together their first travel guide, *Across Asia on the Cheap*. Within a week they'd sold 1500 copies. Lonely Planet was born.

Today, Lonely Planet has offices in Franklin, London, Melbourne, Oakland, Dublin, Beijing and Delhi, with more than 600 staff and writers. We share Tony's belief that 'a great guidebook should do three things: inform, educate and amuse'.

OUR WRITERS

Kate Morgan
Having worked for Lonely Planet for over a decade now, Kate has been fortunate enough to cover plenty of ground working as a travel writer on destinations such as Shanghai, Japan, India, Zimbabwe, the Philippines and Phuket. She has done stints living in London, Paris and Osaka but these days is based in one of her favourite regions in the world – Victoria, Australia.

Kate Armstrong
Kate Armstrong has spent much of her adult life travelling and living around the world. A full-time freelance travel journalist, she has contributed to around 40 Lonely Planet guides and trade publications and is regularly published in Australian and worldwide publications. Kate has worked in Mozambique, picked grapes in France and danced in a Bolivian folkloric troupe. A keen photographer, greedy gourmand and festival goer, she enjoys exploring off-the-beaten track locations.

Cristian Bonetto
Cristian has contributed to over 30 Lonely Planet guides to date, including New York City, Italy, Venice & the Veneto, Naples & the Amalfi Coast, Denmark, Copenhagen, Sweden and Singapore. Lonely Planet work aside, his musings on travel, food, culture and design appear in numerous publications around the world. When not on the road, you'll find the reformed playwright and TV scriptwriter slurping espresso in his beloved hometown, Melbourne.

Peter Dragicevich
After a successful career in niche newspaper and magazine publishing, both in his native New Zealand and in Australia, Peter finally gave into Kiwi wanderlust, giving up staff jobs to chase his diverse roots around much of Europe. Over the last decade he's written literally dozens of guidebooks for Lonely Planet on a disparate collection of countries, all of which he's come to love. He calls Auckland, New Zealand his home – although his nomadic existence means he's often elsewhere.

Trent Holden
A Geelong-based writer, Trent has worked for Lonely Planet since 2005. He's covered 30 plus guidebooks across Asia, Africa and Australia. With a penchant for megacities, Trent's in his element when assigned to cover a nation's capital – the more chaotic the better – to unearth cool bars, art, street food and underground subculture.He also writes books to tropical islands across Asia, in between going on safari to national parks in Africa and the subcontinent.

Published by Lonely Planet Global Limited
CRN 554153
10th edition – Nov 2017
ISBN 978 1786571533

10 9 8 7 6 5 4 3 2 1
Printed in China